THE PREHISTORY OF THE TEHUACAN VALLEY

THE PREHISTORY OF THE TEHUACAN VALLEY

VOLUME THREE

Ceramics

by Richard S. MacNeish, Frederick A. Peterson
and Kent V. Flannery

Published for the
ROBERT S. PEABODY FOUNDATION
Phillips Academy, Andover

UNIVERSITY OF TEXAS PRESS • AUSTIN & LONDON

Published in Great Britain by the
University of Texas Press, Ltd., London

International Standard Book Number 0-292-70068-7
Library of Congress Catalog Card No. 67-17873
Copyright © 1970 by the University of Texas Press
All rights reserved

The preparation and publication of
The Prehistory of the Tehuacan Valley
has been assisted by grants from
the National Science Foundation.

Typesetting by Southwest Typographics, Inc., Dallas, Texas
Printing by The Meriden Gravure Company, Meriden, Connecticut
Binding by Universal Bookbindery, Inc., San Antonio, Texas

PREFACE

This volume is based on nearly a half-million ceramic remains that represent a prehistoric span of almost four thousand years in the Tehuacan Valley of south-central Mexico. At the time of writing, these remains comprise the longest New World ceramic sequence yet described and are one of the largest ceramic assemblages from a single small region ever described. Although, as we shall point out, there are some inadequacies in sampling, we believe we accomplished one of the main purposes of this volume — the establishment of a chronology and the time-space relationships of our region. Whatever the inadequacies of our sequence and its presentation in this book, and whatever debatable issues it raises, the field investigations and the analysis of materials both represent a tremendous amount of work by a large number of people, and I am grateful to each and every one of them.

Our very first task was to obtain the ceramic remains. Frederick Peterson and his helper, Francisco Molina, spent eighteen months literally "beating the bush," collecting almost 200,000 potsherds and other ceramic objects from about four hundred surface sites. They were aided at one time or another by Angel García Cook, James Neely, Jean Brunet, Narciso and Augustín Tejada, and myself, as well as by countless local guides. Even larger ceramic samples were obtained from excavation of stratified sites, and again the prime collector was Fred Peterson, who was in charge of excavations at Ajalpan, Las Canoas, Coatepec, Quachilco, the Coxcatlan ruin, Tr 65, and other sites. He was given a helping hand by Arturo Arbide, Robert Chadwick, Douglas S. Byers and Mrs. Byers, Frederick Johnson, over a hundred local workmen, and myself. Excavation of caves or rock shelters yielded smaller samples of ceramic remains, and we owe thanks to Melvin Fowler, Angel García Cook, Arbide, Chadwick, and the many workmen who excavated them.

Perhaps more important than the collection of ceramic remains were the analysis and description of these materials. Most of this work was done in the field. As a means of thanking the individuals involved I shall indicate who did what as I briefly relate the sequence of analysis. The first endeavor was by Peterson, who in the summer of 1961 studied two Postclassic collections excavated from Tr 62 and Tr 65 and separated them into ceramic classes that had various distinctive attributes. The first actual descriptions and analysis to determine modes, however, did not occur until Kent Flannery studied the sherds from the Canoas site in the summer and fall of 1962. The later part of this study was concomitant with analysis of Ajalpan materials by Peterson and myself and study of the Quachilco materials and further study of the Postclassic remains, both undertaken by Peterson. From these basic studies of five stratified sites of rather different periods we were able to determine the majority of the ceramic modes and trends and to establish some trial types.

In the first part of 1963 I began the attempt to correlate these studies and align the excavated components in chronological order. A mechanism for doing this was study of the stratified remains from the Coatepec site, which extended from roughly Ajalpan through Canoas to Quachilco times. We thus were able to discern ceramic trends and modes for the early part of the sequence, to align components in chronological order, and correlate our earlier trial types. Flannery and I at this time checked the chronological alignment through a study of figurine types. I further checked the sequence by analysis of the Purron Cave ceramics, which cover a long span from before the Ajalpan occupations to seemingly after those of Quachilco. Thus by the summer of 1963, the basic outlines of the ceramic chronology from about 2300 B.C. to after the time of Christ were known. Three unsung heroines aiding this analysis were Nancy Flannery, Mary Hill Gilbert, and Toni Nelken.

Because of differences between the gray wares of

v

the latest levels of Purron Cave and from Quachilco, Peterson next undertook a study and a description of about 10,000 sherds from the surface of Tr 74. In the fall of 1963 I began a study of the ceramics of El Riego Cave. The ceramic occupations seemed to have been laid down from roughly Quachilco times and to have lasted to the end of Venta Salada times — or the time of the materials from Tr 62 and Tr 65. We now seemed to have the final part of our sequence, though the link between late Quachilco materials and early El Riego or late Purron materials — seemingly the time period of Tr 74 — was confusing and not very convincing. For this reason, after Peterson left in October of 1963, Mary Ann Neely, Jean King, and I began a re-analysis and redescription of the Quachilco and Tr 74 materials. Eventually we straightened out the ceramics of this transitional period.

Also in 1963 José Luis Lorenzo asked us to submit to the Laboratory of Anthropology of the Instituto Nacional de Antropología e Historia representative sherds of each of our pottery types for further petrographic and mineralogical analysis. Alfredo Sotomayor, then of the laboratory, undertook these basic and painstaking studies, identifying the nonplastic inclusions in the pastes of ninety-six sherds. He submitted reports of his findings to Lorenzo and myself, and his results were incorporated into our descriptions of the pottery types.

In 1964 we began the final phase of our field analysis. Ann Harvey, Francisco Molina, and Narciso and Augustín Tejada worked with the vast amount of surface-collected material, mainly classifying and counting the collections to furnish a basis for aligning the surface sites in chronological order. While this project was being carried out, I somehow found time to analyze the ceramics from the other caves, classify the spindle whorls, describe the miscellaneous ceramic objects and have preliminary drawings of the ceramic types and features made by Pablo Sanchez and Hector Lopez.

The above pretty much completed our field analysis, but I wish to thank many others who gave us valuable advice and assistance. These include my wife, Diana MacNeish, and Alfonso Caso, Eduardo Noguera, Ignacio Bernal, Román Piña Chan, José García Payón Alfonso Medellín Zenil, John Paddock, Carmen Cook, Bruce Warren, Gareth Lowe, Michael Coe, Robert Squier, James Ford, Gordon Willey, René Millon, Pedro Armillas, and Paul Tolstoy. Also aiding us in many ways, including official permission to dig and to take ceramic samples out of Mexico, were Lorenzo,

Piña Chan, and E. Davalos of the INAH, and we wish to express our gratitude for their help.

The final phase of our work came after we left Mexico and consisted of further analysis and the preparation of this monograph. Perhaps the most significant of these analyses came last — literally at the time of galley proof. The final updating of areal correlations of our Formative ceramic phases or subphases was undertaken by Kent Flannery and based largely upon his excavations and ceramic studies in the Valley of Oaxaca in the spring and summer of 1969. The bulk of his conclusions about the Formative ceramic sequences of Oaxaca, southern Veracruz, and the Valley of Mexico were incorporated in the final chapter (with the exception of Fig. 153). As much of this recent comparative material as possible was fitted into earlier chapters. Although we had set a deadline of 1968 for incorporating new information into the volume, Flannery's additions were just too pertinent to leave out.

Somewhat earlier the correlation of the ceramic survey material and alignment of sites had been accomplished at the University of Calgary, where I was ably assisted by R. Nash, David Sweetman, Carol Crumley, and Charles Eyman. Further assistance in re-analysis, both in Calgary and Andover, was undertaken by Ashley Baker. Mary Hill Gilbert, Irene Dodge, Fred Johnson, Jay James, and Theodora George also helped with various aspects of the report in Andover. Typing and proofing of the manuscript was done by Rachael Penner and Diana Cleveland. The tables were typed by Claire Minty. The final drawings were done by the skilled hand of W. Davis. Photographs were taken by Ashley Baker and Olive Pierce under the supervision of Frederick Johnson. The actual editing of all of the manuscript was done by Chase Duffy, but she also must be credited with real insights in ceramic analysis, an ability to change garbled jargon to prose, and skills in epigraphy of modern texts. And last but not least, I must thank Douglas Byers for his efforts in bringing the publication to fruition. The other authors and myself owe all of the above a never-ending debt. It has been a great cooperative effort. Full credit must go to all of them and I will willingly take the blame for whatever errors are to be found herein.

Now that the ceramic study is completed, I have the nagging feeling that our methods and techniques for studying ceramics were primitive and could have been much improved. On a most basic level, for instance, we never attempted to study the clay sources in the Tehuacan Valley, although we carefully surveyed the valley and had geologists available and an ethnographer studying pottery-making. Studies of the clay and its natural inclusions might have told us much about the origins of our pottery, and it also would have given us clay to experiment with, to discover what we could about prehistoric firing techniques. Studies of the natural inclusions of the clay might have given us the sort of information that microscopic study of the pastes gave us—that is, the amount and size of each kind of nonplastic material tempering the clay. Similar results, of course, could be obtained by various techniques—the use of a petrographic microscope, microchemical analysis, spectrographic analysis, thermal analysis, X-ray microscopy, X-ray refraction, neutron activation, and others. The basic criticism of our microscopic studies of the nonplastic inclusions is that not enough thin sections of sherds could be analyzed in any reasonable amount of time—a limitation more or less true of the other techniques mentioned above. In this day of great scientific advances, cannot the physicists, chemists, or metallurgists develop techniques, such as X-ray microscopy, that will give us these data and record them quickly and cheaply on computer tape or card? Surely X-ray techniques more precise than techniques based on a binocular microscope can be developed to help the archaeologist study the porosity, texture, and consistency of the paste.

The types of studies I have mentioned, together with observation of other physical properties of the sherds and ethnographic studies of the potters in the Tehuacan region, should have told much about the manufacturing techniques of the ancient potters. We should have learned how they prepared their materials and how they shaped and fired the vessels. Our studies failed to do this. Although we tried to record the colors and hardness of a representative sample of each of our pottery types in a consistent manner—using the Munsell system for color and Mohs scale for hardness—we failed to deal with the implications of these attributes in terms of firing techniques. Nor have we utilized the ethnographic data on modern pottery kilns from Altepexi and other areas.

Our study of surface finishes was more systematic, in part because we followed Anna O. Shepard's instructions (1963). However, we lack mineralogical studies of the slips and chemical analysis of the paints covering the surface or used in decoration. In studying decoration we were able to discern and describe the techniques and even the areas of decoration fairly well, but our system of recording and describing design motifs is obviously inadequate. Shepard, Brainerd, and others have made admirable suggestions in this field, but perhaps a mathematical system using x and y coordinates would have more general application and could be codified and recorded to minimize the discrepancies of individual pottery analysis.

We have defined and illustrated our classes of vessel forms and the various ranges of rim profiles. Other pottery reports have used similar techniques, but the range of variation in this type of study is great, the terminology is often overlapping, and the results sometimes, particularly in Mesoamerica, are almost chaotic. Perhaps again a mathematical system, possibly of x and y coordinates, would serve to record uniformly the interior and exterior slope or shape of vessels from lip to base.

Although reports such as this one do describe the pottery according to more or less generally accepted techniques, we should move toward putting the analysis on a more scientific basis, streamlining it so that we will be using precise physical techniques and a set of agreed-upon terms. These suggestions may seem impractical and even impossible, financially and in other respects, for individuals studying a particular group of potsherds. But it should be possible for selected institutions to maintain research staffs and ceramic repositories. These centers could establish specialized or generalized type collections and handbooks of nomenclature and classifications of ceramic types similar to the taxonomic system used in the biological disciplines. It would obviously be cheaper and more efficient in the long run to furnish and maintain a ceramic research center with an adequate staff and all necessary equipment to analyze and record ceramic data, instead of having many small groups of researchers who purchase a little (and inadequate) equipment and maintain a number of technicians to do the same job, rather poorly, in a somewhat uncoordinated manner.

However, is it not only the techniques of studying and recording ceramic information that I feel are inadequate and unsophisticated, but also much of our methodology. Shepard and others have made important contributions to the definition of ceramic attributes, but with more and more archaeological pottery being brought to light, we need a more complete and standardized set of definitions codified in a major handbook to aid in analysis and description. Perhaps the modes, the significant attributes of ceramics in time and space, could be determined more uniformly by statistical formulae programed for computers, and certainly the correlation of modes could be done more thoroughly by intelligently organized computer programs.

Although conclusions arrived at in the present manner do assist in furthering our knowledge of cultural history, should we not devote a portion of our future time and resources to the re-examination and improvement of techniques and methods and concepts used in ceramic studies? And last, but not least, is it not time to attempt to correlate the rapidly accumulating ceramic reports and data into one uniform system?

Thus this report, though it describes a vast amount of pottery, gives us chronology, and may be a basis for further studies, must be considered at best an initial effort. I hope the best is yet to come.

RICHARD S. MACNEISH

Andover, Massachusetts
September 1969

CONTENTS

TABLES

The Prehistory of the Tehuacan Valley

CERAMICS

CHAPTER 1

Introduction

THIS VOLUME is concerned with the classification and description of the ceramic material collected in the Tehuacan Valley in the states of Puebla and Oaxaca by the Tehuacan Archaeological-Botanical Project from 1961 through 1964. The extremely large sample comprises almost 491,000 ceramic remains, which are tabulated below.

we dealt with a total of only ninety-one stratigraphic units.

The methods of excavation of the stratified sites are the subject matter of Volumes IV and V of this series and have been summarized in the first two volumes. Here we shall only comment briefly on the stratified sites relevant to the ceramic analysis. Ts

	Excavated collections	Test trenches	Surface collections	Total
Identified sherds	235,634		63,158	301,792
Trade sherds	1,416		about 1,500	about 2,916
Unidentified sherds	37,570	27,289	120,511	185,370
Whole pots	about 40		about 160	about 200
Figurine heads	178		83	261
Figurine bodies	544		95	639
Spindle whorls	34		12	46
Other objects	1,114		141	1,255

The 235,000 identifiable sherds from excavations served as the basis for analysis of archaeological types. Most of these materials came from fifteen stratified sites, although some are from four single-period occupations. The number of identifiable sherds, the number of excavated zones, and the length of occupations represented in each stratified site varied considerably. The identifiable sherds basic to our analysis came from 101 zones—or subzones—of the multicomponent and single-period sites. Sixteen zones or subzones were combined in the analysis for various reasons (often because of an inadequate sample), so

368e, the deep excavation at the east end of the Coatepec site, which is more or less centrally located on the valley floor east of the Rio Salado, not only had the largest number of strata but each of the eighteen zones was a layer of refuse and aeolian deposits capped by a well-defined occupation. All but Zones D^1 and D^2, which are combined with Zone D for the ceramic analysis, contained sizable samples of identifiable sherds. Ts 368w, a trench along the front of a pyramid west of Ts 368e, had only six occupational zones, but all were clearly defined and had adequate samples of ceramics.

Ts 368e	
Zone	Sherds
A	1,566
B[1]	1,123
B	7,697
C	4,873
C[1]	3,774
C[2]	1,131
D,D[1],D[2]	3,993
E	4,398
F	7,338
G	1,643
H	1,973
I	4,308
J	3,816
K[1]	5,810
K[2]	5,604
K[3]	3,666
	62,713

Ts 368w	
Zone	Sherds
A	3,820
B[1]	3,633
B	3,141
C	3,163
D,E	2,472
	16,229

a huge pit filled with refuse, Zone C[2] was capped by two superimposed occupational layers, Zones C[1] and C. These, in turn, were overlaid by two refuse-filled layers, perhaps alluvial, Zones B and B[1]. In both Test 6 and Test 11 the lower zones, E, F, and G, were occupational zones, but Zones B, C, and D of Test 6 were seemingly alluvial refuse zones. In Test 11 Zone B was alluvial, but Zones C and D were possibly occupational layers.

Tr 218, Test 6		Tr 218, Test 10		Tr 218, Test 11	
Zone	Sherds	Zone	Sherds	Zone	Sherds
A	2,628	A	25,616	A	1,663
B	2,718	B	7,254	B	726
C	1,667	B[1]	9,274	C	823
D	754	C	8,901	D	1,062
E	335	C[1]	6,257	E	1,015
F	940	C[2]	1,766	F	717
G	761			G	900
	9,803		59,068		6,906

The final site on the floor of the valley with good stratigraphy and adequate samples of sherds from some zones is Las Canoas (Ts 367), located just south of the Ajalpan site. Each of the three lowest zones, D[2], D[1], and C, were charcoal floors overlying thin layers of refuse filled with large numbers of sherds. Capping these floors was Zone B of alluvial brown soil with few sherds. At the top was Zone A, a thicker layer of alluvial refuse with abundant sherds.

Ts 367	
Zone	Sherds
A	5,054
B	154
C	5,459
D[1]	4,553
D[2]	1,639
	16,859

Just north of Coatepec, the major excavation in the clay pits near the present town of Ajalpan, Ts 204, had a few well-defined lower zones of refuse capped by floors with adequate samples of sherds, but the upper alluvial layers, Zones A–D, were less easily distinguished and contained few identifiable sherds. Other tests at the Ajalpan site yielding some ceramic materials were Ts 204D and the single-period burial pit designated 204C.

Ts 204		Ts 204D		Ts 204C	
Zone	Sherds	Zone	Sherds	Zone	Sherds
A-B	1,133	A-C	198	pit	1,242
C-E	164	D	474		
F[1]	2,059	super-E	596		
F	2,932	E	1,391		
G[1]	2,386	sub-E	265		
G	3,365				
H	2,239				
	14,278		2,924		

The Quachilco site (Tr 218), also in the center of the valley but on the west side of the Rio Salado, was tested by twelve one-meter-square excavations. Three of these, Tests 6, 10, and 11, yielded adequate samples of sherds from stratified zones. When expanded, these three tests were found to contain large amounts of sherds in slightly different stratigraphy, although Zone A of each test seems to be the same humus-like strata laid down at roughly the same time. In Test 10,

In the thorn-scrub forests along the eastern slopes of the valley is the large rock-shelter we called Coxcatlan Cave, Tc 50. Above twenty preceramic layers were seven clearly defined occupational zones of refuse, ash, and vegetal material. These zones contain limited samples of identifiable sherds. The slope below the cave was also tested (T 51). Two thick alluvial layers, Zones A and B, contained few sherds and for purposes of analysis were treated as a single stratigraphic unit.

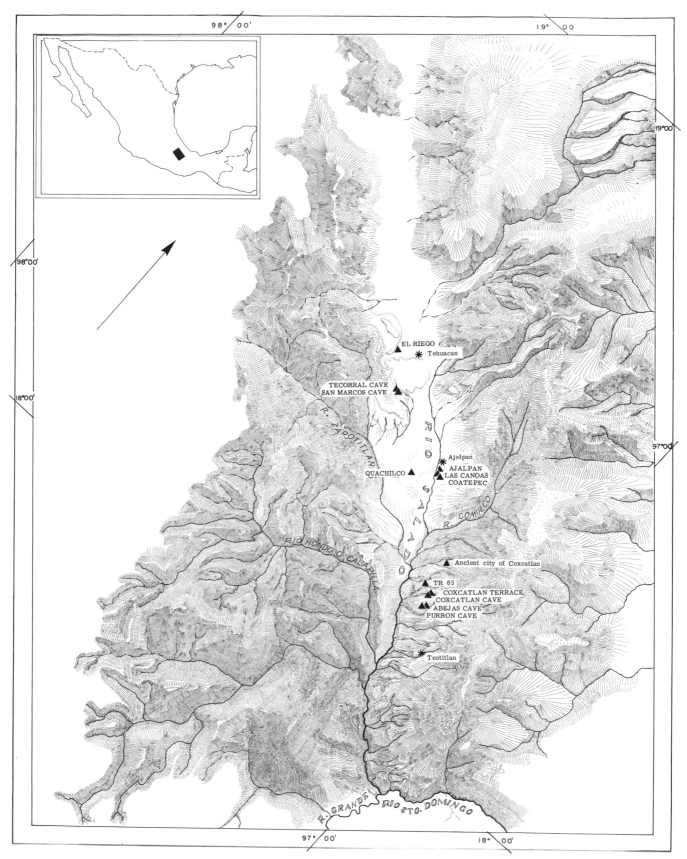

FIG. 1. THE TEHUACAN VALLEY. Pyramids indicate archaeological sites; stars are modern towns.

Tc 50		Ts 51	
Zone	Sherds	Zone	Sherds
I	201	A, B	231
II	267		
III	213		
IV	215		
V	116		
VI	261		
VII	183		
	1,456		

Near Tc 50 and Ts 51 are two large hilltop sites, Tr 65 and Tr 62, the latter being the documented site of the pre-Conquest city of Coxcatlan. Tests of the Coxcatlan ruin yielded 33,308 identifiable sherds from a single occupation. Tr 65, which was dug in arbitrary levels, also provided a huge ceramic sample. Owing to an unfortunate laboratory error, only 652 rim sherds were retained for study, and about 25,000 body sherds were discarded. Even the limited sample remaining had to be treated as though it came from a single stratigraphic unit, although there were indications that this may not have been the case.

South of the Coxcatlan area, in a narrow canyon dissecting the eastern slopes, lie Purron Cave, Tc 272, and Abejas Cave, Tc 307. Twelve of the twenty-five levels of Purron Cave were well-defined ceramic occupations, but contained small to moderately sized samples of sherds. The upper level of Abejas Cave, Zone A, was of limited value to the ceramic analysis, since it contained a total of only seven sherds.

Tc 272	
Zone	Sherds
A	212
B	181
C	259
D,E	351
F	379
G	341
H	344
I	295
J	114
K[1]	60
K	67
	2,603

On the west side of the valley, near the present city of Tehuacan, is El Riego Cave, a rock-shelter with two niches in the face of La Mesa de Tehuacan. The East Niche (Tc 35e) has six well-defined occupations,

Zones A–F, and all but Zone F produced adequate samples of sherds. Because of the similarity of the thirty-three sherds from Zone F to sherds from Zone E, the two levels have been combined for the ceramic analysis. The West Niche of El Riego (Tc 35w) had unclear stratigraphy, except for Level 1, a zone overlying a cement floor, as did Zone A of Tc 35e. Levels 2 and 3 were arbitrary levels dug into dark refuse. All three of these levels had large samples of identifiable sherds. Level 3–4, at the junction of the dark refuse and a gray layer beneath it, contained over a hundred sherds. The excavation of Tc 35w, with its poorly defined upper occupations, was undertaken early in our project and was one of the few times we "sinned" by digging in arbitrary levels.

Tc 35e		Tc 35w	
Zone	Sherds	Zone	Sherds
A	1,338	1	660
B	1,219	2	468
C	1,185	3	662
D	1,085	3–4	154
E,F	632		
	5,459		1,944

Also located on the western side of the valley, in a dry canyon south of Tehuacan, are San Marcos and Tecorral caves, Tc 254 and 255. Each had only two zones with ceramics. Tc 254 yielded 171 sherds in Zones B and C[1], and Tc 255 had a total of 330 sherds in Zones A and B.

We uncovered and used for analysis, therefore, an extensive number of identifiable sherds from the excavated sites. Besides the 235,000 classifiable sherds, we collected over 63,000 sherds from the surface of the various excavated sites; these we counted and cursorily examined to verify that they were no different from the sherds from secure stratigraphic positions. There were additional thousands of sherds excavated that were too fragmentary or too badly eroded to identify; these were counted and the totals are included in Table 6 below.

The other major source of sherds for study was the surface collections from the remaining 437 sites found in the archaeological reconnaissance. Collections from these sites were identified and classified after the basic classification of the excavated materials. Study of these sherds was more difficult for two reasons. First, the eroded and weathered condition of the sherds made identification difficult. Second, some of the sites, particularly those at the peripheries or just beyond our cultural region, contained large amounts of "foreign" sherds or types we had not uncovered in our excavations. For these reasons, there are almost twice as many unidentified sherds from survey sites (120,511) as there are identified sherds (63,158). All in all, however, we identified and studied over 300,000 of the 492,479 sherds found, so that whatever our study may lack in quality is made up for in quantity.

Obviously the 300,000 identifiable sherds, as the material remains of the ancient Tehuacaneros, are part of the archaeological record and as such must be studied and described. Intensive study of these remains gives insight into the ancient cultures of the Tehuacan Valley and elucidates some of the cultural activities of each of the ceramic phases of our archaeological sequence. Besides this intensive use of ceramics to contribute to the reconstruction of cultural concepts, ideas, and activities through time in the Tehuacan region, we found almost at the outset of our research that a superficial use of the pottery helped define the area of our investigations. When we undertook the initial archaeological survey we felt that a correlation of various environmental factors such as rainfall, temperature, topography, and type of vegetation with archaeological material would reveal a cultural subarea or region which could be differentiated from other cultural regions in Mesoamerica, and we assumed that such a region would have cultural continuity through time. Therefore, our gross preliminary definitions of the archaeological regions were based in part upon the spatial distribution of two encompassing sequential classes of sherds: fine gray wares like those from the Formative and Classic periods at Monte Alban and bichrome or polychrome wares like those uncomfortably classified as "Mixteca-Puebla style" of the Postclassic. Thus at the very beginning of our survey the correlation of the spatial distribution of previously ill-defined complexes of sherds were of use in delimiting the region of our investigations.

The analysis of ceramics for the solution of definite chronological problems is, however, much more important than its use for merely descriptive purposes. Pottery, particularly Mexican pottery, has a large number of variable features that reflect concepts in the minds of the makers; for example, kinds of rocks or minerals used to temper the clay, ways of kneading the clay, methods of smoothing and finishing the surfaces, techniques of decoration, decorative motifs, the forms and appendages given the vessels, and so on. These variable features of pottery, based on

cultural compulsives, are particularly susceptible to changes in both time and space. Also, in the late part of our sequence, pottery represents by far the most numerous of the preserved remains of the ancient inhabitants. Therefore, pottery is a medium displaying not only a wide variety of features reflecting cultural concepts varying in time and space, but also a medium represented in late horizons in conspicuous amounts that can give adequate statistical samples. Thus we directed our analysis of the ceramics toward the determination of pottery types, to serve as time markers or humanly devised "index fossils."

These ceramic time markers also served as a mechanism for correlating the various components of the many stratified sites which contained sherds. We found that certain features or complexes of features or types of pottery evolved, flourished for a while, and then died out, thereby composing ceramic trends. The trends were used to plot the chronological alignment of each zone or occupation of each site. Further, a group of ceramic innovations clustering at certain points in time helped us to break the sequences into a series of ceramic periods that could be compared with segmentations in the sequences of subsistence and settlement patterns and of trends of nonceramic artifacts. Thus we were able to divide into further periods or phases of major cultural changes the long sequences uncovered in the excavations within this one region.

Ceramic collections from the surfaces of sites found in our reconnaissance also could be aligned in chronological order by comparisons with the ceramic trends determined from stratigraphic sources. Not only could the survey sites be aligned chronologically and classified as to phase, but the wealth of information they held concerning ecology, demography, and settlement pattern—along with many implications about social organization—could be chronologically arranged. This information not only supplemented our reconstruction of the phases, but provided new insights into changing aspects of the ancient culture.

The analysis of the Tehuacan ceramics is also basic to the task of correlating the local sequence with archaeological sequences from other regions in Mesoamerica. We used three kinds of materials to accomplish this end: those materials that in archaeological jargon we call trade sherds, overlapping types, and horizon styles. Throughout the Tehuacan ceramic sequence, for instance, we can identify certain sherds that were made during definite periods in other regions. In addition to these wares of foreign manufacture, apparently brought into the valley in trade,

7

some of the Tehuacan pottery types are the same as, or are closely related to, types from other regional sequences, thereby indicating relative contemporaneity. Finally, the Tehuacan ceramics reflect certain concepts about pottery that diffused over wide areas of Mesoamerica at roughly the same periods. These horizon styles allow for rough chronological alignment of the Tehuacan periods with ceramic periods in other areas. When such relative chronological alignments are considered in light of associated radiocarbon determinations and calendrical dates, we have a basis for dating our sequence as well as others in "chronometric" (year date) terms (see Volume IV). Thus we have a basis for understanding the extra-areal relationships of the cultures in our southern Puebla valley, and also insight into such cultural phenomena as diffusion, migration, evolution, and so on.

Our use of the pottery from Tehuacan to solve both chronological and cultural problems is based upon a series of assumptions about culture that have been explained more fully in Volumes I and II of this series, as well as in Ford (1962), Krieger (1944), Spaulding (1953), Rouse (1939, 1967), and other works. Our assumptions can be summed up as follows: (1) culture is a continuum of interrelated ideas, concepts, and beliefs through time and space; (2) culture is constantly changing; (3) culture both patterns and gives consistency to customary behavior; (4) pottery, or the concepts involved in the pottery, are reflections of culture. Therefore, the ceramic materials are part of the cultural continuum, are constantly changing, and reflect the internal order of a culture.

Our primary step in analyzing the Tehuacan ceramics in accordance with the above assumptions was to classify the thousands of sherds into units or types that could serve as time markers. To do this we had to survey all the attributes of the sherds—as well as the multiple variations of the interrelated attributes of the sherds. The reconnaissance of ceramic attributes was undertaken in terms of four general categories: paste, surface finish, decoration, and vessel form.

Once we had determined most of the attributes of the sherds, we compared the sherds of one zone with sherds from each of the other zones of the excavated sites to determine which attributes had temporal significance. These attributes, or complexes of attributes, serve as "modes" and form a basis for aligning components in chronological order.

The first set of attributes we considered were those of "surface finish." In Anna O. Shepard's definition of the term, surface finish designates "all surface characteristics that result from the manner in which the vessel was evened and smoothed during the shaping process and subsequently" (Shepard 1965: 186). The phrase usually refers to both inner and outer surfaces, except when applied to vessels with constricted necks or mouths such as ollas or tecomates, which usually have interiors finished differently from the exteriors.

Comparisons of the surfaces of the sherds from each excavated zone revealed that twenty-four kinds of surface finish showed temporal significance. Since the various kinds of surface finish will be discussed in the type descriptions below and since the terminology is of common usage (see Shepard 1965), we shall merely mention the modes by name and number here. Table 1 lists the occurrence of the modes by excavated site and zone and shows the components aligned in chronological order on the basis of trends of surface finish modes. These trends, portrayed graphically in Fig. 2, reveal that the sequence may be divided into five segments in each of which a number of new kinds of surface finish appear. These divisions are a tentative basis for subdividing the sequential components into five phases: Purron, Ajalpan, Santa Maria, Palo Blanco, and Venta Salada. The earliest phase, Purron, has only two components, Zones K and K^1 of Purron Cave (Tc 272). It is characterized by two modes of surface finish: wiped and pocked surfaces (Mode 1) and smoothed surfaces (Mode 2), the latter carrying on into all later phases in diminishing amounts.

The Ajalpan phase, represented by seventeen components, is set off by the addition of four diagnostic modes: specular-red washed surfaces (Mode 3), brushed surfaces (Mode 4), specular-red polished surfaces (Mode 5), and well-smoothed matte surfaces, often stick-polished (Mode 6). Late in Ajalpan times, some sherds display a floated surface (Mode 7), and this technique continued in use throughout the rest of the sequence. The Santa Maria phase was characterized by six new modes of surface finish: a white wash (Mode 8), a plain brown polished surface (Mode 9), a matte black-gray wash (Mode 10), a white slip (Mode 11), a polished mottled black surface (Mode 12), and a fugitive red wash (Mode 13). The occurrence and trends of these modes aligned the forty components of the Santa Maria phase. Also starting in this phase, but more characteristic of the following phase, Palo Blanco, were a poorly polished red slipped surface (Mode 15) and a gray floated or painted surface (Mode 14),

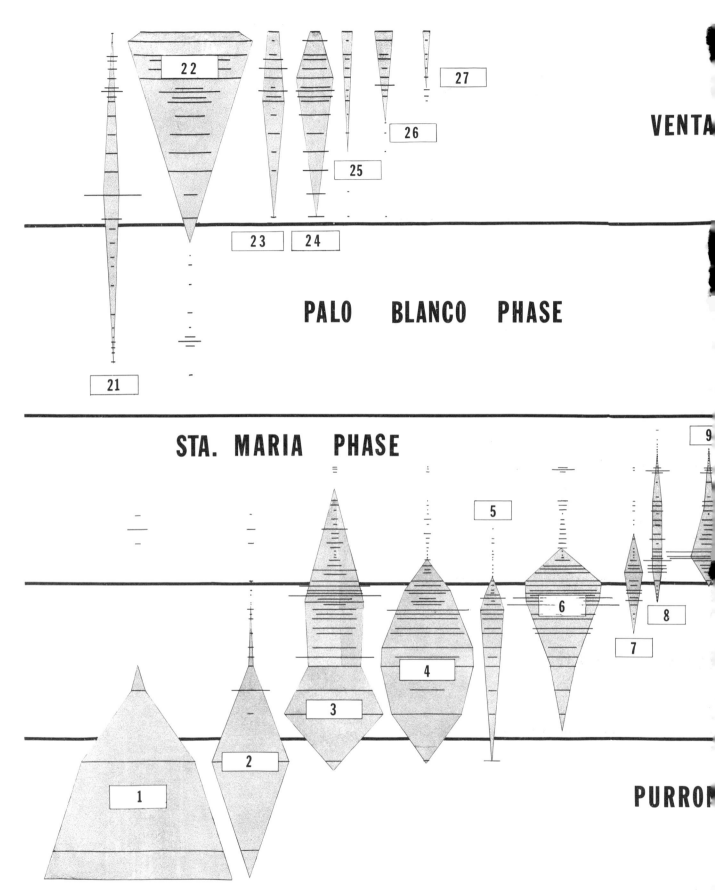

VENTA

PALO BLANCO PHASE

STA. MARIA PHASE

PURRO

Fig. 3. Modes of Paste: percentage distribution in the Tehuac

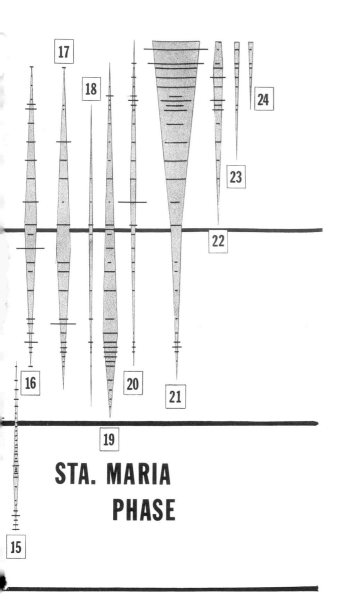

STA. MARIA
PHASE

LPAN   PHASE

ASE

Numbers in squares refer to modes listed in Table 1.

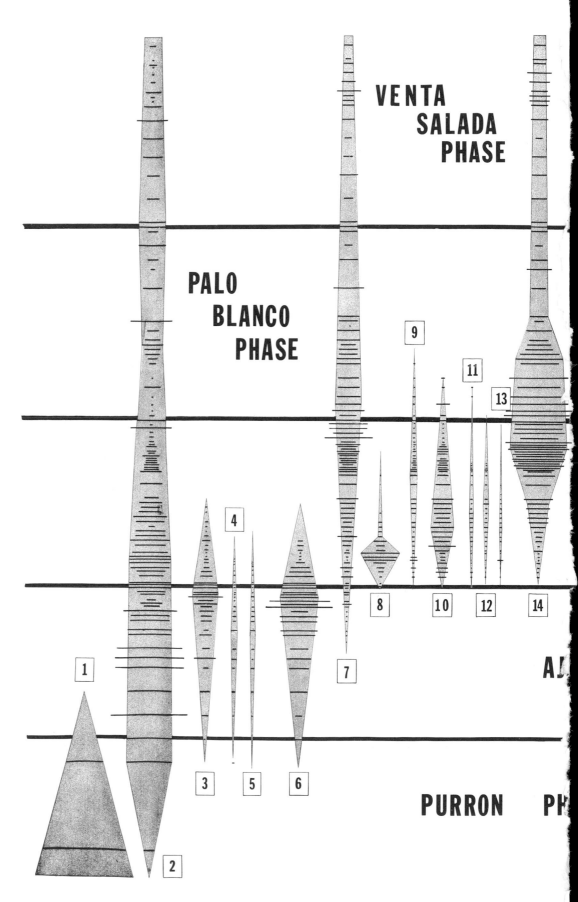

VENTA
SALADA
PHASE

PALO
BLANCO
PHASE

9

11

13

4

8

10

12

14

1

7

3   5   6

AI

PURRON   PH

FIG. 2. MODES OF SURFACE FINISH: percentage distribution in the Tehuacan ceramic sequence.

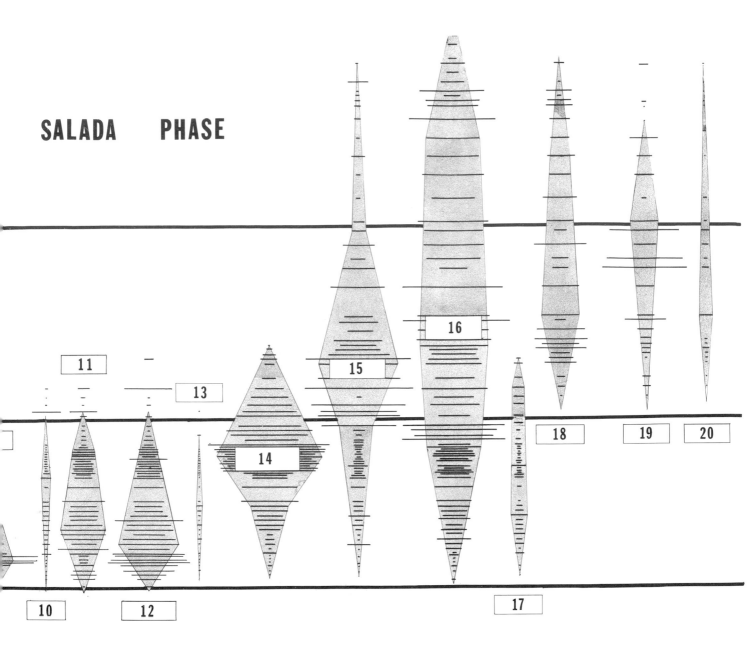

SALADA PHASE

AJALPAN PHASE

PHASE

n ceramic sequence. Numbers in squares refer to modes listed in Table 2.

both of which continued to occur during the rest of the sequence.

Five new kinds of finishes appear in the twenty Palo Blanco components: a "greasy" polished surface (Mode 16), a reddish-orange polished surface (Mode 17), a dull orange slipped surface (Mode 18), a polished black slipped surface (Mode 19), and a finish involving a polished interior surface and a roughened exterior one (Mode 20). Also occurring spasmodically in some Palo Blanco sites was a painted (brown to black) finish that had been brushed or wiped on (Mode 21), but this mode became predominant in many of the sixteen Venta Salada components. Even more characteristic of the Venta Salada phase are sherds with a brushed red slip (Mode 22), a cream to orange wash (Mode 23), and a creamy white slip (Mode 24).

The second set of comparisons involved the paste, or what is referred to by Shepard as the material of which the pots are made and the "preparation of materials" (Shepard 1965: 182). Initially we examined the paste macroscopically. Later, a total of ninety-six sherds, several from each preliminary classification established by macro-inspection, were analyzed microscopically in thin sections. Alfredo Sotomayor carried out the painstaking petrographic and mineralogical studies, which gave us definite identifications of the nonplastic particles appearing in the clay, the size of the particles, and the proportions of the materials of each size that were present, some of which obviously were consciously used to temper the clay. This information allowed us to describe the various pastes in such a manner that the descriptions can be used comparatively with greater exactness to determine the presence of Tehuacan ceramics in other regions. It also supplemented our macroscopic observations, in most cases confirming the preliminary classifications but in others pointing to a need for further analysis.

Obviously, we needed nine hundred sherds or more, not merely the ninety-six sherds that were studied microscopically in thin section, and we needed as well more technical studies of the paste of the sort Shepard has undertaken. In spite of the limitations, however, our crude studies of the paste did yield significant chronological data.

Twenty-seven ceramic modes derived from the gross kinds of paste used to make the pottery substantiated the alignment of components and the delineation of phases based upon the modes of surface finish. The paste modes and the record of occurrence by site and zone are given in Table 2; the trends based on them are shown in Fig. 3. The pottery description

tions will give the details of each type. The paste of Purron sherds was crumbly and composed of pebbles mainly of quartz or mica (Mode 1). A smaller proportion of the sherds had a contorted paste composed of angular fragments of quartz, mica, calcite, and other nonplastic materials, and this type of paste (Mode 2) continued to be used during Ajalpan times.

Paste Modes 3–6 characterized the Ajalpan phase (see Table 2) and continued in limited amounts into early Santa Maria. Paste Mode 7, a sandy paste containing quartz and mica particles of medium size, occurred in late Ajalpan and early Santa Maria levels in about equal proportions. Santa Maria is marked by a large number of new paste types, Modes 8–17. Modes 8–13 are almost entirely confined to the Santa Maria phase, but Mode 14, a very well-knit, laminated paste containing diorite, and Mode 17, a blocky paste with angular, medium-sized particles mainly of andesine, andesite, and labradorite, are common both to Santa Maria and early Palo Blanco. Two pastes that first appeared in Santa Maria continued throughout the rest of the sequence: Mode 15, our most compact paste, with small amounts of very fine calcite, quartz, mica, and limestone particles, and Mode 16, a cruder paste with large amounts of scaly mica. Palo Blanco was characterized by four new types of paste (Modes 18–21), and the final phase, Venta Salada, by Modes 22–27.

As we studied the modes derived from paste, a high correlation of certain kinds of paste with certain kinds of surface finish was readily apparent. These mode clusters, thirty-four in all, were of course better time markers than the individual modes. We regarded them as trial types, some of which might be modified or divided by comparisons with the modes of decoration.

In studying the decoration of our pottery, we did not consider all aspects, but limited analysis to the technique, the location, and only the simplest features of the motifs. Although eighty-seven of the ninety-one excavated components contained at least a few decorated sherds, the number of decorated sherds represents only a small proportion of the total sherds studied (13,139 out of 237,050). In a limited way, trends of decoration did roughly group our components into sequential phases, as shown in Table 3 and Fig. 4.

The Purron phase was distinctive in having no decorated sherds. Ajalpan had only a few decorated sherds, and most of them belong to one decorative mode (Mode 5), which consists of wide lines of specular-red hematite, usually in simple "V" designs.

A few sherds showed a specular-red band at the rim (Mode 1), zoned scratching (Mode 3), unzoned rocker-dentate stamping (Mode 4), and fabric impressions (Mode 6). Santa Maria is distinguished by decorative Modes 6–39, appearing on a small proportion of sherds. Particularly distinctive of the early part of Santa Maria are two to four incised parallel lines, often in "double-line-break" motifs, on the inner rim (Modes 8, 9) or outer rim (Modes 13, 14), sunburst designs incised on interior bottom surfaces (Mode 16), and *raspada* or excised decorations (Mode 18). In late Santa Maria appear parallel wide-line incisions on interior rims (Mode 21), zoned toning (Mode 24), wide-line incisions on exteriors (Mode 25), exterior hachured designs (Mode 23), exterior curvilinear motifs (Mode 35), and exterior engraved or thin-line geometric designs (Mode 26). The geometric motifs continue into Palo Blanco times in some frequency and are contemporaneous with parallel lines and dots (Mode 41) and wide-line *molcajete* incisions on interior surfaces (Mode 40). Decorations characteristic of Venta Salada include stamped interior bottoms, often with glyphic motifs (Mode 42), engraved exterior circles and rectangles (Mode 43), red linear motifs painted on orange or cream grounds (Mode 44), black linear designs painted on orange grounds (Mode 45), polychrome painting of red, orange, and black on whitish grounds (Mode 46), and deep striations or crosshatching on exterior surfaces (Mode 47).

The main value of the study of decoration was not to reveal trends of decoration that would align all components in chronological order, but to allow us to divide further the preliminary types based on the paste and surface finish attributes, and thus make them more accurate time markers (see Table 5). This had little effect on the trial types of the Purron, Santa Maria, or Palo Blanco phases, but it affected one trial type of the Ajalpan phase and a number of wares of the Venta Salada phase. In Ajalpan levels the trial type with a blocky paste containing medium-sized, angular particles of quartz and quartzite (Paste Mode 6) and a matte smoothed or stick-polished surface (Surface Mode 6) had examples with wide, specular-red painted exterior lines (Decoration Mode 5) that occurred only in late Ajalpan levels, while examples without decoration (or rarely with Decoration Modes 2, 3, and 4) occurred throughout the phase. Thus, the trial type could be divided into Coatepec Red-on-buff and Coatepec Plain.

An examination of the trial type Coxcatlan Brushed (Paste Mode 22 and Surface Mode 21) revealed that some of the darker-surfaced examples of the middle of the Venta Salada phase had engraved decorations in rectangular motifs (Decoration Mode 43). These became the Teotitlan Incised type. A Venta Salada type with fine paste (Mode 25) and orange to cream surface finish (Mode 23) had black painted designs during the late part of the phase and red painted designs throughout the phase. These became Coxcatlan Black-on-orange and Coxcatlan Red-on-orange respectively. A similar situation existed in regard to the Venta Salada trial type with a mica temper (Paste Mode 27) and creamy painted surface (Surface Mode 24), for some of these sherds had red designs while others had polychrome designs. They were separated into the trial types Coxcatlan Red-on-cream and Coxcatlan Polychrome. Thus, even with the study of the first three aspects of ceramics—paste, surface finish, and decoration—we found thirty-eight modal clusters that were time markers (see Table 5).

Analysis of the vessel forms was more difficult than analysis of the other kinds of attributes of pottery. In the first place, we had to rely mainly on rim sherds because we dug up few whole pots, making it difficult to determine what kinds of rims went with what kinds of bottoms, bodies, and appendages such as handles, feet, and spouts. The various kinds of appendages were often very sensitive time markers. Second, there were literally thousands of rim profiles discernible from our rim sherds, making it necessary to combine these variations of rims into general classes representing sixty-seven reconstructed vessel forms (see Fig. 5). Obviously, if we had considered the auxiliary features of vessel form the number would have been much larger. Even combining the reconstructed vessel forms based on rim shape with both flat and convex bottoms would have doubled the number of possible vessel forms.

In spite of these difficulties, the sixty-seven reconstructed vessel forms determined from the rim profiles were excellent time markers (see Table 4 and Fig. 6). The Purron phase pottery was dominated by tecomates and ollas over flaring-wall and convex-wall bowls. All but the tecomates continued throughout our sequence, and even the tecomate remained an important vessel form during Ajalpan times. The Ajalpan phase also has other tecomate forms (pumpkin and ellipsoidal) and a few ollas with short angle necks. Bowls with straight outsloping walls become important at this time and last through the rest of the sequence, as do the convex-walled incurved-rim bowls. Also first appearing in late Ajalpan, but becoming more important in Santa Maria are bottles, long-

TABLE 5

Correlation of Paste, Surface Finish, and Decoration Modes in Thirty-eight Trial Types

Trial type	Paste mode	Surface finish mode	Decoration mode
Purron Coarse	1	1	—
Purron Plain	2	2	—
Ajalpan Coarse	3	2 (rarely 4)	—
Ajalpan Coarse Red	3	3	—
Ajalpan Plain	4	2 (rarely 4)	rarely 1
Ajalpan Fine Red	5	5	—
Ajalpan Fine Plain	5	6	—
Coatepec Plain	6	6	rarely 2, 3, 4
Coatepec Red-on-buff	6	6	5
Coatepec Buff	7	7	—
Canoas Heavy Plain	8	2	6
Canoas Orange-brown	9	9	7,8,9,12,13,18,19
Canoas White	9	8	7-18
Coatepec White	10	11	8,9,13,14,18
Coatepec White-rimmed Black	13	12	12,13,18
Rio Salado Gray	11	10	8,9,13,14,18
Rio Salado Coarse	12	2 (rarely 4,13)	—
Quachilco Gray	14	14	13,18,20-39
Quachilco Brown	15	9	8,20-23,25-27,31,37
Quachilco Mica	16	7	—
Quachilco Red	17	15	
El Riego Gray	15	14	20,21,23-30,33,36,37,39
El Riego Black	18	19	23,37,40
El Riego Polished	18	16	—
El Riego Plain	16	2	—
El Riego Orange	19	17	—
Thin Orange	20	18	41
El Riego Marble-tempered	21	20	—
Coxcatlan Brushed	22	21	42
Teotitlan Incised	22	21	43
Coxcatlan Gray	24	14	27,42
Coxcatlan Red	23	22	42
Coxcatlan Coarse	26	7	—
Coxcatlan Red-on-orange	25	23	44
Coxcatlan Black-on-orange	25	23	45
Coxcatlan Red-on-cream	27	24	44
Coxcatlan Polychrome	27	24	46
Coxcatlan Striated Buff	26	2	47

necked beveled-rim ollas, large bowls with externally thickened rims, and funnel-necked ollas, the latter form lasting somewhat longer than the others.

Santa Maria is marked by many new vessel forms, including low flaring-wall dishes with flat bottoms, bowls with flaring walls and internally thickened rims, collared tecomates, convex-wall bowls with internally or externally thickened rims, ollas with straight necks, pot rests, comales, incense burners, and ovate bowls with pinched-in sides. More prevalent in late Santa Maria were composite-silhouette bowls, bowls with thickened incurved rims, collared cylindrical bowls,

cylindrical bowls with a basal bulge, bowls with everted rims either rounded or horizontal or down-slanted, and rolled-rim ollas. First appearing in late Santa Maria and continuing into Palo Blanco, as did some of the previously mentioned forms, are cylindrical bowls with direct rims, ollas with bridged spouts, convex-wall bowls with everted rims, bowls with a basal flange or ridge, small plates or pot covers, bowls with convex bodies and vertical but concave rims, and tripod bowls with mammiform feet.

Tripod vessels increase in early Palo Blanco, the feet being the hollow mammiform, bulbous, cylindri-

11

cal, or rectangular kinds or the solid nubbin type. Other modes of this period include stepped-rim bowls, flower-pot-shaped vessels, thick-lipped ollas, barrel-necked ollas, ollas with long converging or straight necks, short-necked ollas with everted rims, and conoidal bowls with ring bases. Many of these forms continue into late Palo Blanco, albeit in different proportions. New types of this period are vessels with solid slab feet, recurved-rim bowls, long flaring-neck ollas with outangled rims, long cylindrical- or convergent-necked ollas with everted rims, low convex-wall comal-like bowls with direct or incurved rims, short-neck ollas with widely flaring or recurved rims, and deep bowls with rims beveled internally or horizontally everted rims.

Venta Salada vessels, while retaining some earlier shapes, have many new kinds of supports, such as effigy, dumbbell, and plain or stamped stepped feet. Convex-wall bowls with a number of rim variations, pedestal-based or egg-cup shaped vessels, deep bowls with incurved or inangled rims, and deep composite-silhouette vessels are characteristic of the phase.

Perhaps the greatest difficulty in our analysis was that the sixty-seven vessel forms as determined by rim profiles—although they were excellent time markers—did not correlate exactly with trial types based upon clusters of modes of paste, suface finish, and decoration. Nevertheless, a number of vessel forms did correlate roughly and in varying proportions with the previously determined trial types. Thus we could combine the temporally sensitive modes into mode-combinations or types that not only gave trends of types to align our many excavated components, but also marked off this long sequence into a series of phases, each characterized by an influx of new types (see Table 6 and Fig. 7).

The Purron phase, represented by two components, K and K[1] of Tc 272, was dominated by two pottery types—Purron Coarse and Purron Plain. The former represents 67 percent of the total sherds uncovered in this phase, while the latter represents 29 percent. Purron Coarse diminished rapidly in popularity during the Purron phase and died out in earliest Ajalpan times. Purron Plain increased throughout this earliest ceramic phase and then rapidly diminished, representing an insignificant proportion of the pottery in Ajalpan times.

Appearing in insignificant amounts in the later of the two components of the Purron phase are four new pottery types: Ajalpan Fine Red, Ajalpan Fine Plain, Ajalpan Coarse, and Ajalpan Coarse Red. These wares, however, are much more characteristic

of the seventeen components from Ts 204, Ts 204D, Tc 272, and Ts 368e which represent the Ajalpan phase. Ajalpan Fine Red and Fine Plain are minority types in these levels and die out early in Santa Maria times. Ajalpan Coarse, however, is a major type in the earliest Ajalpan components and then in late Ajalpan levels becomes a minority type. It almost completely disappears in early Santa Maria. Ajalpan Coarse Red has a different history, being a persistent minority type in early Ajalpan times, rising in late components of the phase to a majority type, only to die out in early Santa Maria. Ajalpan Plain appears in earliest Ajalpan times, reaches greatest popularity in the middle components of the phase, diminishes in late Ajalpan, and dies out early in Santa Maria.

Dominant forms with these later coarse-pasted types are tecomates and ollas with long flaring necks. The two types with fine paste have bowls with outsloping or convex walls as the dominant vessel forms. The other major type of the Ajalpan phase is Coatepec Plain, in which flaring-necked ollas and convex-wall bowls appear in about the same proportions. Coatepec Plain gradually increased through Ajalpan times, reached its zenith in late Ajalpan, and continued as a diminishing type in early Santa Maria. Late in Ajalpan two minority types appear, Coatepec Buff and Coatepec Red-on-buff. These also die out in early Santa Maria. The trends of these pottery types are the basis for the chronological alignment of the seventeen components mentioned (see Table 6 and Fig. 7).

Santa Maria is represented by forty components from Ts 204, Ts 368e, Ts 368w, Ts 367, Tc 272, Tc 50, as well as the lower levels of Tests 6, 10, and 11 of Tr 218. Trends of twelve new pottery types, plus the dying gasps of some of those previously mentioned, align them in the chronological order shown in Table 6. Canoas White, Canoas Orange-brown, Canoas Heavy Plain, Rio Salado Gray, and Rio Salado Coarse first appear at the very end of Ajalpan times, rise quickly to maximum popularity in early Santa Maria, and diminish in late Santa Maria. Canoas White and Orange-brown and Rio Salado Gray are particularly notable for bowl forms decorated with incising in multiple-line-break motifs, whereas Canoas Heavy Plain and Rio Salado Coarse are utilitarian wares appearing as heavy bowls or ollas. Three minority types, Quachilco Brown, Coatepec White, and Coatepec White-rimmed Black, appear mainly in various bowl forms, reach maximum popularity in the middle of the phase, and except Quachilco Brown, die out by the end of the phase. The latter extends into earliest Palo Blanco levels. Quachilco Red, with predominantly olla forms, is a minority type that continues into early Palo Blanco and is characteristic of that subphase. Quachilco Gray, with a wide variety of vessel forms and incised decorations, is the most characteristic late Santa Maria type. It first appears in early Santa Maria times and continues in diminishing amounts throughout Palo Blanco.

One other late Santa Maria type is, perhaps, really more characteristic of Palo Blanco; this is Quachilco Mica. This undecorated utilitarian ware begins in Santa Maria, reaches its greatest popularity near the end of the phase, and continues throughout the entire sequence, albeit in diminishing amounts and with some changes in vessel form.

The type that is most diagnostic of early Palo Blanco, although it starts in late Santa Maria and ends in Venta Salada, is El Riego Gray, with new bowl forms that often are footed. El Riego Black, decorated by engraving, also reaches its greatest popularity in early Palo Blanco, but lasts into Venta Salada. Beginning in early Palo Blanco, but more popular in late Palo Blanco, are El Riego Orange, El Riego Polished, El Riego Plain, and Thin Orange, if one considers it a resident type. El Riego Marble-tempered, with comal-like forms, is a minority type in both Palo Blanco and Venta Salada times. The alignment of the twenty Palo Blanco components from eight sites is based upon the trends of the previously mentioned types.

The sixteen Venta Salada components from several sites are aligned according to trends of another group of new types (see Table 6). Coxcatlan Brushed, which appeared in a few Palo Blanco components, becomes increasingly dominant throughout the Venta Salada occupations. The related Teotitlan Incised type is a minority ware throughout the phase, as is Coxcatlan Red. Coxcatlan Brushed has a variety of vessel forms, and the two latter types show a predominance of bowl forms. Coxcatlan Gray, with its many stamped-bottom bowls, is an important type that reaches its greatest popularity in the middle of the phase and then diminishes. Coxcatlan Coarse, appearing mainly as braziers, and Coxcatlan Red-on-orange, with delicate painted bowls and pedestal-based vessels, are minority types that increase throughout the phase. Coxcatlan Polychrome, Coxcatlan Red-on-cream, Coxcatlan Black-on-orange, and Coxcatlan Striated are minority types occurring mainly in late Venta Salada times.

Thus, as Fig. 7 shows, our pottery types—composed of clusters of temporally sensitive ceramic attributes—align in chronological order a large number of excavated components. The types, with all their multiple variations, will be fully described in the chapters to follow. In Chapter 11 we shall briefly indicate how this chronology of types allowed us to classify many of the survey sites in chronological order. The classification of the sherds collected from sites discovered in our archaeological survey revealed that we had, in addition to the excavated components, two Ajalpan surface sites, seven early Santa Maria sites, ten late Santa Maria sites, seventy-one early Palo Blanco sites, seventy-seven late Palo Blanco sites, eighty-one early Venta Salada sites, and ninety-three late Venta Salada sites. Thus on the basis of our pottery types, we were not only able to arrange in chronological order and classify as to phase ninety-one excavated components, but also 341 surface sites—for a grand total of 432 components.

One other group of ceramic artifacts could be analyzed in a similar manner to the pot sherds and give similar results. These are the 900 excavated and collected figurine fragments, which we also classified into types that are good time markers. However, figurine fragments did not occur in significant amount in most levels, and a few components had no figurines whatsoever. Even this lack of figurines in the case of the early ceramic levels, such as Zones K and K¹ of Tc 272, was a distinctive feature that indicated that occupation of these floors preceded the occupational zones with figurines.

A cursory survey of the figurine fragments indicated that we could not use exactly the same methods or group of attributes that we had with the vessel sherds. First of all, the paste showed a gradual tendency only from rather crude in the early Ajalpan phases to relatively fine in all later phases, making it difficult to set up modes of paste. Further, although some figurines of the Santa Maria phase had distinctive surface finishes, most fragments were badly worn or the surface finishes were relatively uniform. These circumstances forced us to consider different attributes, such as manufacturing technique, size, and various decorative effects of eyes, nose, mouth, or headdress.

Initially, we classified the figurines according to the way they were made; that is, whether they were formed in molds, were hand-modeled into solid forms, or were hand-modeled into hollow forms. For convenience, we studied the heads separately from the bodies, but the results were roughly the same. Solid hand-modeled heads predominate in Ajalpan and Santa Maria levels, predominate but decrease in importance in Palo Blanco components, and become a minority type in the Venta Salada phase. Hollow figurines are popular in Ajalpan and early Santa Maria levels and then become relatively rare. Mold-made figurines do not appear until the Palo Blanco phase and become dominant in Venta Salada components.

It was apparent that the size of the figurines, particularly the heads, also had some temporal significance. In our preliminary analysis, we divided the heads into two categories: small heads under 30 cm. in height and large heads over 30 cm. in height. Heads tended to become smaller throughout our sequence.

Bodies were classified in terms of matching the large or small heads and showed a similar tendency toward smaller size. A correlation of the three attributes of method of manufacture, size of head, and size of body revealed very neat trends. Large, hand-modeled, solid figurines are most prevalent in the earlier Ajalpan components and die out by the end of the Santa Maria phase. Large, hand-modeled, hollow figurines are most popular late in the Ajalpan phase and early in the Santa Maria phase; they die out in the Palo Blanco phase. Small solid hand-made figurines are popular in all periods, though they increase in popularity steadily from early Ajalpan to late Santa Maria levels and then diminish. Small, solid, mold-made figurines first appear in Palo Blanco levels and are dominant in Venta Salada times. One small, hollow, hand-modeled head occurred in Venta Salada times. The figurine fragments and their occurrence by sites and zones are recorded in Tables 7 and 8.

The body and limb features of the figurines were so varied that we had almost as many preliminary classes as we had specimens. It proved too difficult, even impossible, to correlate the various limb features with the various kinds of heads. Thus we have confined our typology to the heads alone and merely have classified loosely and described the body and limb fragments.

One of the principal decorative features of the heads is the eye. We derived twenty-three modes from different types of eyes. The earliest modes, confined to the Ajalpan phase, consist of conical punched eyes, linear punched eyes, and eyes with rather realistic projecting eyeballs. Almost as early, but lasting into earlier Santa Maria times, were eyes that have well-modeled lids and a rather realistic punched pupil.

First appearing in late Ajalpan levels are heads without eyes or mouth, called the No Face type—thus one mode was lack of eyes. Eyes made by a punch between two parallel appliques of clay occur throughout the Santa Maria phase. Two small heads from an early Santa Maria component have eyes represented by punches inside rectangular appliques of clay; these are the same as the Valley of Mexico Type F. Ploughed eyes occur in early Santa Maria times, as do eyes made by two triangular punches separated by a circular punch. Of the same period are solid Olmec baby-face heads with closed eyes and heads with appliqued eyes resembling coffee beans. The latter we tentatively called the Early Valley of Mexico trial type.

In the middle zones of the Santa Maria phase we noted the following kinds of eyes: eyes formed by two parallel appliques; "outlined eyes" made by a lenticular incision with punctures; eyes shaped by inverted "V" incisions; appliqued doughnut eyes; doughnut eyes with three punches inside; circular punctate eyes; and long oblique incisions for eyes.

The sample of figurines for much of the Palo Blanco phase was very inadequate and almost every figurine eye became a trial mode. These included, besides the oblique incised eye mode mentioned above, eyes of two downpointing triangles, eyes made of a punctate inside an incised circle, and heads with oval ridges for eyes.

In the Postclassic Venta Salada phase a slightly larger sample showed considerably less variation in manufacturing technique, size, and eye type. Only one specimen was modeled by hand; it had eyes painted on a small bulge. The other Postclassic figurines were mold-made with eyes painted on either a bulge or a depression.

The twenty-three modes of eye types when combined with five modes of size and manufacturing technique revealed thirty trial types or mode groups that showed significance in time. After the thirty trial types were established, we compared the figurine material from each component in terms of the various kinds of noses, mouths, headdresses, appendages, and other features. Nine classes of nose show little sequential variation and correlate rather well with the trial types already established, as did such appendages as ear plugs and nose plugs. Twenty-one kinds of mouths showed definite modality and correlated very closely with the trial types previously established, with two possible exceptions. The Negroid trial type showed two lip variations with temporal significance; thus we divided the trial group into two types. The other exception was the small mold-made trial type with bulging eyes. One group of these had very definite snouts and doglike mouths and were separated as the Dog Face type.

The final study was of features of the headdress or hair ornamentation. Here there was great variation, forming thirty-six modes, many of which correlated

TABLE 9
Spindle Whorl Types from Excavated and Surface Components

	Early Venta Salada			Late Venta Salada							
	35e C	35e B	35w 3	35w 1	367 B	367 A	368e A	35e A	368w A	62 A	65 A
Convex, "U" motif											1
Large, stamped motifs								1	2	2	
High cones, plain or tiered						1		1			
Conical, circles in quadrants						1		1	1		
Conical, buns and ridges						2		2	1		
Conical, radiating dashes					1			1			
Conical, appliqued rays				1							
Semiconical, incised			1								
Conical, domed, or bell-shaped	2	1			1	2	1				1
Conical, low to medium high	1				1	3		1			
Total	3	1	1	1	3	9	1	7	4	2	2

	Surface Sites								
	204	73	288	75	329	230	245	342	Total
Convex, "U" motif				1				1	3
Large, stamped motifs	1		2				1		9
High cones, plain or tiered						1			3
Conical, circles in quadrants									3
Conical, buns and ridges									5
Conical, radiating dashes					1				3
Conical, appliqued rays									1
Semiconical, incised									1
Conical, domed, or bell-shaped	1								9
Conical, low to medium high		1	1	1					9
Total	2	1	3	2	1	1	1	1	46

with the trial types. A few did not correlate and seemed to justify separating from the main group twelve more types. The small, solid, parallel-appliqued-eye trial type of Santa Maria times was divided into three types with slightly different temporal distributions. In early Santa Maria helmets occur on heads of this type; in middle levels the heads had incised hair; and in the last part of the phase some of the heads without hair or headdress have large, beaked noses. These figurines became the Helmeted, Valley of Mexico Di, and Big Nose types respectively. The small, solid, double-linear-punched-eye trial type of Santa Maria was divided into the Trapiche Bunned-helmet and Tres Zapotes Chin Strap types. The realistic-eye trial type became an early Santa Maria Crescentic Cap type; a middle Santa Maria Multi-hairknot type; and a late Santa Maria type called Duncecap.

Comparisons of the Valley of Mexico trial types with the types established by George Vaillant helped to divide this material into Types C3a and C3d, on the basis of headdress and other features, and to separate the small, solid, doughnut-eye trial group into the Capped and the Hairlock Doughnut-eye type. The Classic mold-made material became the Tehuacan Portrait, Teotihuacan, and Tlaloc type. The Hollow Old Man head with a heavily wrinkled face was separated from the Ugly Baby Face type. Postclassic molded material was separated into the Appliqued Ear Disk, Toltec, Flat Cap, and Aztec Square Cap types.

Thus we classified 261 figurine heads into forty-eight types that had chronological significance. Although the sample of each type was far too small to allow us to align each component chronologically, the types were sensitive enough to classify various components into phase or subphase, thereby confirming our temporal division and adding to the traits diagnostic of the phases and subphases.

One other group of materials, forty-six spindle whorls, showed great variation and the potential for being excellent time markers for the Venta Salada phase. One basis for classification was the general shape of the spindle whorl, the second set of modes concerns the decoration or lack of it. Combining these two sets of attributes gave us ten attribute-clusters with some temporal significance (see Table 9). However, since our sample is small and our Venta Salada stratigraphy is weak, we have considered the divisions only as preliminary types to be tested by more adequate information.

Besides the ceramic materials which we could at-

tempt to classify, many other objects—stamps, xantiles, whistles, ocarinas, and so on—were uncovered or collected. Owing to inadequate excavated samples, we have not attempted to classify these objects into types but have merely described them in the appropriate chronological position (see Tables 10 and 11 and the appropriate sections of the chapters which follow).

All in all, study of nearly a half-million ceramic specimens from the Tehuacan Valley has provided a sound basis for establishing chronology and tentatively classifying the materials and components into archaeological phases. Many of the significant changes in ceramic types, as we have shown, parallel changes in nonceramic artifacts, subsistence, settlement pattern, and social organization.

TABLE 10

Miscellaneous Objects from Excavated Components

	Early Ajalpan				Late Ajalpan						
	272 S	204 G	204D subE	204 G¹	204 F	204D E	204 F¹	204D D	368e K³	204D C	204C pit
Xantil fragments											
Cylindrical seal or stamp											
Small bell											
Effigy incense burner fragments											
Barrel-shaped spindle whorl(?)											
Small ball											
Disk beads											
Ruffled cone											
Doughnut effigies											
Human hand											
Animal legs											
Incensario horns or prongs											
Serpent head											
Bird heads											
Hollow jaguar											
Beaver-like bird tail											
Seated rodent											
Bird ocarina or whistle											
Other ocarina/whistle fragments											
Stamp, unclassified											
Human effigy whistles											
Table-like animal body										1	
Deer										1	
Dogs or coyotes					1			1			
Animals of unknown species		1									
Whistle mouthpieces		1		1							
Sherd disks, perforated		1			1						
Sherd disks, unperforated	1	2	2	2	1	1	1	2	4	1	1
Total	1	5	2	3	3	1	1	3	6	1	1

(Table continued)

(Table 10, continued)

	Late Ajalpan (cont'd)			Early Santa Maria									
	368e K^2	368e K^1	368e J	368e I	368e H	368e G	368e F	367 D^2	367 D^1	367 C	368e D	368e C^2	368e C^1
Xantil fragments													
Cylindrical seal or stamp													
Small bell													
Effigy incense burner fragments													
Barrel-shaped spindle whorl(?)													
Small ball													
Disk beads													
Ruffled cone													
Doughnut effigies													
Human hand													
Animal legs													
Incensario horns or prongs										1			
Serpent head									1				
Bird heads											1		
Hollow jaguar											1		
Beaver-like bird tail											1		
Seated rodent													1
Bird ocarina or whistle											1		
Other ocarina/whistle fragments				1					1				
Stamp, unclassified			1										
Human effigy whistles			1				1						
Table-like animal body													
Deer													
Dogs or coyotes						1	1						
Animals of unknown species	1		1	1				2	1	1			
Whistle mouthpieces	1		1					1	1	1			
Sherd disks, perforated				1	6	2	1	4	2	2	1	2	3
Sherd disks, unperforated	3	7	2		1		1	3				1	
Total	5	7	6	3	7	3	4	10	6	5	5	3	4

	Late Santa Maria										Palo Blanco		
	368e C	368e B	368w B	204 A-B	218-11 D	218-11 C	218-10 C^1	218-10 C	218-10 B^1	218-10 B	218-10 A	218-6 A	218-11 A
Xantil fragments													
Cylindrical seal or stamp													
Small bell													
Effigy incense burner fragments											1		
Barrel-shaped spindle whorl(?)											1		
Small ball												1	
Disk beads										2			
Ruffled cone		1											
Doughnut effigies	1		1										
Human hand	1												
Animal legs		1						1	1				
Incensario horns or prongs			1										
Serpent head													
Bird heads													
Hollow jaguar													
Beaver-like bird tail													
Seated rodent													
Bird ocarina or whistle													
Other ocarina/whistle fragments	2	1	1	2				1			1		2
Stamp, unclassified													
Human effigy whistles													
Table-like animal body													
Deer													
Dogs or coyotes													
Animals of unknown species													
Whistle mouthpieces	1				1								
Sherd disks, perforated							2				1	1	2
Sherd disks, unperforated					1	1			1	1	9	2	3
Total	5	3	3	2	2	1	2	2	2	3	13	4	7

(Table continued)

	Palo Blanco (cont'd)			Venta Salada										
	272 F	35e E	35e D	35e C	35e B	35w 1	367 B	367 A	368e A	35 A	368w A	62 A	65 A	Total
Xantil fragments				13	16	8	19	17	37	47	39	576	120	892
Cylindrical seal or stamp													1	1
Small bell													1	1
Effigy incense burner fragments			2											3
Barrel-shaped spindle whorl(?)														1
Small ball														1
Disk beads														2
Ruffled cone														1
Doughnut effigies														2
Human hand														1
Animal legs														3
Incensario horns or prongs														2
Serpent head														1
Bird heads							1	4	1					7
Hollow jaguar														1
Beaver-like bird tail														1
Seated rodent														1
Bird ocarina or whistle														1
Other ocarina/whistle fragments			1					2	1		3			19
Stamp, unclassified														1
Human effigy whistles														2
Table-like animal body														1
Deer														1
Dogs or coyotes							1	3	1	1	1	4		15
Animals of unknown species								4	1					13
Whistle mouthpieces														9
Sherd disks, perforated	1		2	1			1	2	3		4	16	4	66
Sherd disks, unperforated		1		2				2	1		1	4		65
Total	1	1	5	16	16	8	22	34	45	48	48	600	126	1114

TABLE 11
Miscellaneous Objects from Surface Sites

	Santa Maria			Early Palo Blanco				Late Palo Blanco				
	67	212	218	243	304	179	189	247	312	344	68	172
Xantil (or brazier) fragments												
side rods												
feet												
hands							1		1			
faces								1				1
head ornaments		1	1	1								
Molds or seals											1	
Ball												
Miniature effigy olla												
Serpent effigy												
Birds			1		1							
Whistle/ocarina fragments						1						
Ocarinas												
Effigy whistles		1										
Dogs				1								
Animals of unknown species												
Whistle mouthpieces												
Figurine/effigy heads	2											
Figurine/effigy bodies		1								1		
Total	2	3	2	2	1	1	1	1	1	1	1	1

	Early Venta Salada											
	210	289	228	293	290	283	123	288	198	233	188	336
Xantil (or brazier) fragments												
side rods		1						1				
feet								1			1	
hands	1								1			
faces		1	2	1	1			1				1
head ornaments		1								1		
Molds or seals												
Ball												
Miniature effigy olla												
Serpent effigy												
Birds												
Whistle/ocarina fragments	1											
Ocarinas									1			
Effigy whistles												
Dogs							1					
Animals of unknown species						1						
Whistle mouthpieces												
Figurine/effigy heads												
Figurine/effigy bodies												
Total	2	3	2	1	1	1	1	3	2	1	1	1

(Table continued)

	Early Venta Salada *(continued)*			Late Venta Salada								
	284	319	213	242	350	285	230	184	245	241	296	294
Xantil (or brazier) fragments												
side rods	3		8					1				
feet			3									
hands			2					1				
faces			2				1			1		
head ornaments			1			1	1					
Molds or seals												
Ball												
Miniature effigy olla												
Serpent effigy												
Birds										1		1
Whistle/ocarina fragments									2			1
Ocarinas												
Effigy whistles								1			1	
Dogs					1							
Animals of unknown species												
Whistle mouthpieces												
Figurine/effigy heads		1							1			
Figurine/effigy bodies				1								
Total	3	1	16	1	1	1	3	2	3	2	1	2

	Late Venta Salada *(continued)*			Unclassified									Total
	75	191	65	204	367	368	360	362	365	40	221	223	
Xantil (or brazier) fragments													
side rods			2	1	1		1						19
feet				2	1				1				9
hands					2							1	10
faces			5	1	4	2					1		26
head ornaments			3		2	1							14
Molds or seals			7										8
Ball					1								1
Miniature effigy olla				1									1
Serpent effigy								1					1
Birds							1			2			7
Whistle/ocarina fragments					3								8
Ocarinas				1	1								3
Effigy whistles	1	1											5
Dogs													3
Animals of unknown species							1						2
Whistle mouthpieces					3								3
Figurine/effigy heads			2		1	4				1			12
Figurine/effigy bodies					2	1	1	1		1			9
Total	1	1	19	6	21	8	4	2	1	4	1	1	141

CHAPTER 2

The Purron Phase

THE ESTABLISHMENT of the Purron phase—or more properly, complex—is based on materials from only two components, Zones K and K¹ of Purron Cave, Tc 272. The 127 sherds found in these two floors are basic to the definition of the phase, for the nonceramic artifacts are much the same as those found in the final preceramic phase of the Tehuacan sequence, Abejas. They also overlap the nonceramic traits of the succeeding Ajalpan phase, except for the presence in Purron of a lipped saucer-shaped metate and a fine blade with a prepared striking platform. Thus, the Purron phase or complex, based only on two distincitive pottery types, Purron Coarse and Purron Plain, is not well defined by transitional artifacts of stone or by changes in perishable materials. We were also unable to find open sites of this phase in our archaeological survey of the Tehuacan region. This early ceramic segment of the Tehuacan sequence obviously should be the subject of further investigation.

Radiocarbon dates of Zone K of Tc 272 fall between 2100 and 1800 B.C. (see Volume IV). Since this component contained no specimens of the later pottery types such as Ajalpan Fine Plain or Ajalpan Fine Red, which were present in small numbers in Zone K¹, it may be considered a pure component, falling well within the span of the Purron phase. It seems logical to assume, therefore, that the beginning of this phase falls between the dates mentioned and about 2600 B.C., the radiocarbon date on the latest preceramic occupation, Zone L of Tc 272. We believe the phase began about 2300 B.C.

The sixty sherds from the second component of the phase, Zone K¹ of Tc 272, were predominantly of the two diagnostic types, Purron Coarse and Purron Plain. However, seven sherds represented four pottery types characteristic of the Ajalpan phase, making it possible to consider the component as the very earliest Ajalpan occupation. Since these sherds were definitely outnumbered by the Purron wares, we chose instead to consider it the second occupation of the Purron phase. Radiocarbon determinations indicate that the phase must have ended shortly after the period of this occupation, or about 1500 B.C.

Pottery Types

PURRON COARSE

165 specimens excavated.

Paste

Microscopic analysis of thin sections shows that the paste contained a large amount of coarse-grained, nonplastic material. The paste consisted of about 70 percent reddish-brown clay; about 10 percent grains 1.0–2.0 mm. in diameter of quartzite, shale, muscovite, biotite, and granite; about 10 percent grains 0.5–1.0 mm. in diameter of the materials mentioned and quartz; about 5 percent grains 0.1–0.5 mm. in diameter of quartz, muscovite, biotite, quartzite, plagioclase, and microline; and about 5 percent grains less than 0.1 mm. in diameter of the same rocks and minerals. The larger granules tend to be rounded like small pebbles, whereas the smaller grains tend to have an angular surface. The heavy temper is one of the diagnostic features of the type.

The paste is grainy, has a very coarse texture, is very poorly knit, and characteristically crumbles into laminar sections. The firing is also quite poorly

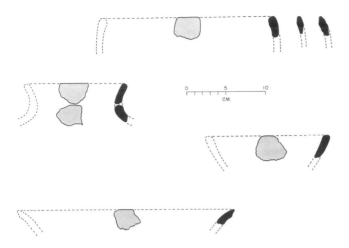

FIG. 8. PURRON COARSE. *From top to bottom*, plain tecomates, olla with short flaring neck, convex-wall bowl, and flaring-wall bowl.

done. In fact, the paste is so weak and crumbly that the first four sherds (including a tecomate rim) disintegrated when we attempted to wash them.

The sherds range in color from black (5.0 Y 2/2) to red (10 R 4/8).[*] In terms of the Mohs scale of hardness, they measure 2.0, or slightly less. One bowl sherd has concentric cracks in it, perhaps an indication that vessels were made by the coil method. The sherds range in thickness from 0.7 to 2.0 cm.

Surface Finish

Both the inner and outer surfaces seem to have been wiped smooth. The exterior surface is usually pock-marked and scales off easily. There is no decoration.

Vessel Forms

Plain tecomates. Six neckless jars with slightly constricted mouths and semiglobular bodies have rim diameters of 18–26 cm. Bottoms presumably were rounded.

Ollas with short flaring necks. Two jars have more or less globular bodies and constricted necks terminating in a slightly flaring rim. Rim diameter, 12–73 cm.

Flaring-wall bowls. Two rim sherds represent widely flaring walls apparently of flat-bottomed bowls. Rim diameter, about 28 cm.; estimated base diameter, about 14 cm.

[*]All designations of color follow the Munsell system of values, hues, and chroma (Munsell Color Company, Baltimore, Maryland).

Convex-wall bowl. One sherd probably represents a fairly small bowl of hemispherical shape. Rim diameter, 16 cm.

Relationships

The Purron Coarse type is obviously ancestral in part to the Purron Plain, Ajalpan Coarse, and Ajalpan Plain types which follow it in the Tehuacan sequence. Exactly what Purron Coarse was derived from or related to on the same time level is difficult to discern. The only ceramics of possibly comparable age in Mesoamerica are the La Mina complex from Queretaro (Cynthia Irwin-Williams, personal communication) and the "Pox pottery" from Charles Brush's excavation at Puerto Marquez on the coast of Guerrero (Brush 1965). Carbon associated with the Pox sherds has been dated between 2590 and 2310 B.C. (H-1258), while the latest preceramic material from Puerto Marquez is dated from 2385 to 2115 B.C. (H–1264), indicating that the Pox pottery is of the same general age as the two Purron pottery types. Further, some of the Puerto Marquez material is made of paste almost identical to Purron Coarse paste, and the few rim sherds from late levels are predominantly in the form of tecomates.

The La Mina materials are also poorly made but represent entirely different vessel forms from those of Tehuacan. Perhaps even at this early date there were different ceramic traditions in the southern and northern parts of Mesoamerica.

PURRON PLAIN

600 specimens excavated.

Paste

Analysis of thin sections indicates that the Purron Plain paste is about 88 percent clay and 12 percent nonplastic material. The latter consists of about 10 percent grains 0.5–1.5 mm. in diameter of quartz, quartzite, andesite, gneiss, shale, biotite, limestone, calcite, marble, and diorite, and about 2 percent grains less than 0.5 mm. in diameter of quartz, feldspar, magnetite, and biotite. Thus Purron Plain has a smaller proportion of temper than Purron Coarse and a temper composed of somewhat different materials. Like that of Purron Coarse, much of the temper has a rounded rather than an angular appearance.

The clay is usually lighter in color, running to more yellowish tones, and tends to adhere to particles of the temper, forming small nodules that do not adhere well one to another. Thus this paste macroscopically

TABLE 12
Purron Coarse Vessel Forms
(sherds by site and zone)

	Purron		Early Ajalpan		Early Santa Maria		Late Santa Maria		Early Palo Blanco	Total
	272 K	272 K1	204 H	272 J	272 I	272 H	272 G	368w C	272 F	
Tecomates, plain	4	2								6
Ollas, short flaring neck	2									2
Bowls										
flaring wall	2									2
convex wall		1								1
Body sherds	53	21	2	8	11	46	10	1	2	154
Total	61	24	2	8	11	46	10	1	2	165

TABLE 13
Purron Plain Vessel Forms
(sherds by site and zone)

	Purron		Early Ajalpan					Late Ajalpan				
	272 K	272 K1	204 H	272 J	204 G	204D subE	204 G1	204 F	204D E	204 F1	204 supE	204 E
Ollas												
long flaring neck		1	4		1		22	17	1	18		2
short flaring neck		1	4		1		1			1		1
Tecomates												
plain	1				9	2	9	7	1	2		
ellipsoidal					2		2	2	1	3		
pumpkin					1		1	1				
Bowl, incurved rim			1									
Body sherds	5	27	49	24	57	6	35	10	7	10	7	4
Total	6	29	58	24	71	8	70	37	10	34	7	7

	Late Ajalpan (continued)						Early Santa Maria			Late Sta. Maria	
	204D D	368e K3	204C pit	368e K2	368e K1	368e J	368e I	272 I	272 H	272 G	Total
Ollas											
long flaring neck		1			1						68
short flaring neck					1						10
Tecomates											
plain											31
ellipsoidal											10
pumpkin											3
Bowl, incurved rim											1
Body sherds	1	31	4	22	43	35	78	9	11	2	477
Total	1	32	4	22	45	35	78	9	11	2	600

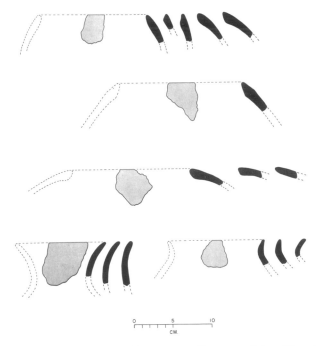

FIG. 9. PURRON PLAIN. *From top to bottom,* plain, ellipsoidal, and pumpkin tecomates; ollas with long and short flaring necks.

has a porous and contorted appearance. The firing is very uneven, with the interior surface ranging from gray (2.5 YR 6/2) to red (10 R 7/8), and the lighter exterior varying from dark brown (10 R 4/4) to yellowish-white (7.5 YR 6/4). Sherds vary in thickness from 0.3 to 1.5 cm. Hardness measures about 2.0 on the Mohs scale.

Surface Finish

Exterior surfaces have been smoothed, probably while the clay was relatively wet, since there are few marks of any smoothing implement. These surfaces are often crazed and occasionally pitted. Interior surfaces are grainier; they have been rather crudely brushed, usually with a horizontal motion, during which process granules of temper were dragged along, scarring the surface. There is no decoration.

Vessel Forms

Ollas with long flaring necks probably had globular to semiglobular bodies terminating in tall necks (over 5 cm.) with flaring rims. Bases presumably were subconoidal or rounded, since we found no sherds indicating flat bottoms. Rim diameter, 10–16 cm.

Ollas with short flaring necks. Bodies and bases

were probably convex in shape. Rim diameter, 10–16 cm.

Plain tecomates have the same general shape as the Purron Coarse neckless jars. Rim diameter, 10–18 cm.

Ellipsoidal tecomates tend to have a "pinched-up" appearance at the rim; they are usually less globular and more elongated in shape than the plain tecomates. Rim diameter, 10–18 cm.

Pumpkin tecomates resemble a squat pumpkin in shape, with very convex walls curving inward to a quite constricted mouth. Rim diameter, 8–15 cm.

Incurved-rim bowl. One incurved-rim sherd seems to represent a bowl rather than a neckless jar. Rim diameter, 12 cm.

Relationships

Although differing in the composition of the paste and the relative popularity of certain vessel forms, Purron Plain was probably derived from Purron Coarse and is in part ancestral to Ajalpan Coarse. In the Tehuacan sequence, this type is proportionally most popular late in the Purron phase, although it evolved in early Purron times and a few sherds appeared in components of the early Santa Maria subphase. The type is possibly related to some of the cruder pottery of the earliest part of the Cotorra phase from Santa Marta Cave in Chiapas (MacNeish and Peterson 1962). It seems to be the same pottery type as some of the finer examples of the Pox pottery found by Brush at Puerto Marquez, Guerrero (Brush 1965).

Ceramic Affiliations

Besides the two wares described above, a few sherds of the following types were present in the later occupation of the Purron phase: Ajalpan Coarse, Ajalpan Fine Plain, Ajalpan Fine Red, and possibly Ajalpan Coarse Red. The first three wares are characteristic of the early Ajalpan subphase and are described in Chapter 3; Ajalpan Coarse Red is representative of the later part of the Ajalpan phase and is described in Chapter 4.

The pottery of the Purron phase is characterized by a series of negative attributes: no figurines, no decoration, and almost no slipped or painted surfaces. In fact, during excavation we often said that this phase had "no chrome" pottery. On the positive side, diagnostic features of the two Purron wares include pastes that are poorly made, crumbly, and coarse-tempered; a predominance of tecomate and long-necked olla forms; and very few bowl forms.

So far few equally early horizons with equally primitive pottery have been uncovered in Mesoamerica. The only two presently known are the La Mina horizon from Queretaro and the complex represented by Brush's early materials from coastal Guerrero. As indicated above, Brush's Puerto Marquez materials appear to be related to the Purron materials not only in terms of the pock-marked surfaces, the crude paste, and the predominant vessel forms, but also in terms of age. The La Mina materials seem less clearly related, particularly in terms of vessel forms and paste, for the paste of some La Mina material resembles that of the later Tehuacan type, Coatepec Plain. If all three horizons are of comparable age, one is tempted to speculate that two different ceramic traditions were beginning even at this early period: one in the northern area represented by the La Mina materials and the other in the southern portion represented by the two Purron pottery types and the earliest ceramics from coastal Guerrero.

In terms of relationships within the Tehuacan Valley, there seems little doubt that the Purron pottery is directly ancestral to that found in the Ajalpan phase. The overlap in nonceramic artifacts confirms this hypothesis. Further, the nonceramic artifacts reveal that Purron in part, if not in sum, developed out of the preceramic Abejas phase. If so, the problem remains as to the source of the Purron pottery.

The source of Purron pottery and, for that matter, of Mesoamerican pottery in general, is one of archaeology's $64,000 questions. Is it not possible that pottery was locally invented, based upon concepts involved in making bowls of stone, together with observations about firing clay derived from burned wattle or clay hearths? Or did Mesoamerican Indians receive the "ideas" about making pottery from earlier pottery-using people in South America? Or did some trans-Pacific migrant or migrants bring pottery or the concept of pottery to Middle America?

Of these three possibilities the South American origin of Mesoamerican pottery presently seems the most reasonable. Radiocarbon determinations associated with pottery from the middle levels of Puerto Hormiga, Colombia, cluster around 3000 B.C. (Reichel-Dolmatoff 1961). If these dates are correct, the Puerto Hormiga pottery is the earliest yet discovered in the New World. Somewhat confirming this hypothesis is the presence below the dated levels of still earlier pottery which is constructed of clay containing coarse fiber temper, which is poorly fired, and which is mainly undecorated. Also, later levels of the site show the development of vessel forms and decoration techniques that appear in materials from other early South American sites such as Valdivia A of Ecuador (Meggers, Evans, and Estrada 1965) and Rancho Peludo of Venezuela (Rouse and Cruxent 1963), as well as in the Monagrillo materials of the Panamanian isthmus (Willey and McGimsey 1954). Is it not possible that the concept of pottery, invented in Colombia and later diffused to Mesoamerica, is indirectly responsible for our earliest Pox-Purron wares?

CHAPTER 3

The Early Part of the Ajalpan Phase

THE AJALPAN PHASE is readily distinguishable from the Purron phase. It is characterized by many new pottery types—Ajalpan Coarse, Ajalpan Plain, Ajalpan Fine Red, Ajalpan Fine Plain, Ajalpan Coarse Red, Coatepec Plain, Coatepec Red-on-buff, and Coatepec Buff—and by the introduction of figurines. It is defined as well by a number of nonceramic artifacts, such as Salado and Zacatenco projectile points, two types of finely made end-scrapers, fine blades with pointed striking platforms, bell-shaped and truncated-cone pestles, basin-shaped and oblong metates, and long manos that are triangular in cross section.

Although the diagnostic nonceramic traits and most of the pottery types remain unchanged throughout the Ajalpan phase, there are minor changes in ceramic types within this period. To highlight these changes and to facilitate correlations with ceramic periods from other regions, we have divided the Ajalpan phase into early and late segments. The early part of the phase is represented by Zones G¹, G, and H of Ts 204, Zone J of Tc 272, and Zone sub-E of Ts 204D. Over 8,000 identifiable ceramic remains (out of a total of 15,600) were uncovered in these occupations, which date from about 1500 to 1100 B.C. The types include the two Purron phase diagnostics described in Chapter 2 and the four new types described below.

Pottery Types

AJALPAN COARSE

4,557 specimens excavated, 75 collected.

Paste

Analysis of thin sections indicates that the proportion of clay (about 88 percent) to nonplastic material (about 12 percent) resembles the paste of Purron Plain. However, the tempering material used in Ajalpan Coarse tends to be angular rather than rounded. About 10 percent of the paste consists of grains 0.5–2.0 mm. in diameter representing a variety of rocks or minerals: quartzite, shale, quartz, gneiss, hematite, diorite, calcite, marble, andesite, plagioclase, aplite, trachite, rhyolite, and occasionally basalt. About 2 percent of the paste consists of grains 0.1–0.5 mm. representing most of the same materials and feldspar and magnetite.

A few cracks near the bases of vessels indicate that they were probably made by the coil method. Sherds range in thickness from 0.3 cm. (a rim) to 1.3 cm., and average about 0.8 cm. The hardness is about 2.0 on the Mohs scale.

The paste is poorly knit, with haphazard cracks all through the core. It is slightly harder and less friable than the Purron wares. In terms of color, cores are darker than either surface, varying from gray (10 YR 2/1) to brown (10 YR 6/8). Interior surfaces usually are slightly darker than exterior surfaces. The latter are frequently orange (7.5 YR 4/4) but range to almost white (2.5 Y 8/2). There is also considerable range in color of the outer surfaces of individual vessels, with the area near the rims tending to be lighter in color as a result of better firing.

Surface Finish

Interior surfaces were wiped with a horizontal motion, apparently while the paste was in a leather-hard condition, since particles of temper dragged across the surface have left quite deep furrows in it. Exterior surfaces were smoothed, and the lack of brushing or other marks seems to indicate that the smoothing was

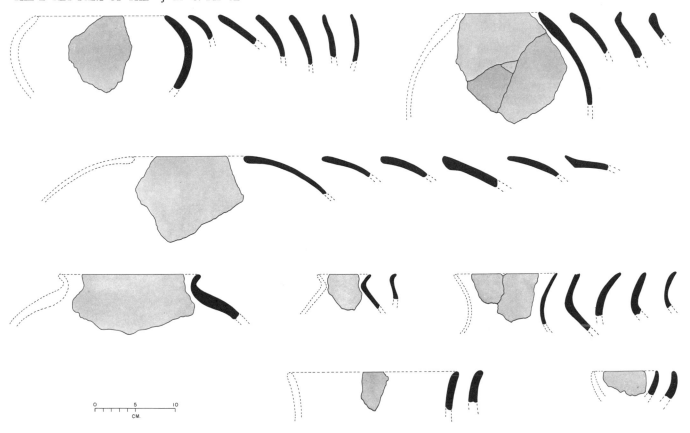

FIG. 10. AJALAPAN COARSE. *Rows 1, 2:* plain, ellipsoidal, and pumpkin tecomates; *row 3:* olla with short flaring neck, miniature ollas, and ollas with long flaring necks; *row 4:* flaring-wall and convex-wall bowls.

done while the clay was wet. External surfaces of a few sherds have a shallow ridged appearance, perhaps the result of stick smoothing. The finish of one sherd almost approaches zoned brushing or stick-polishing. There are no further indications of decoration.

Vessel Forms

Plain Tecomates. The neckless jar with globular body is the predominant vessel form in early Ajalpan levels. Sherds vary greatly in thickness and some rims look quite thin for tecomates. Rim diameter, 16–24 cm.

Ellipsoidal tecomates. This elongated jar form becomes predominant in late Ajalpan levels. Rim diameter, 18–24 cm.

Pumpkin tecomates. These wide jars with very constricted mouths also outnumber plain tecomates in later levels. Rim diameter, 12–20 cm.

Ollas with long flaring necks resemble similar vessels of Purron Plain paste. Rim diameter, 16–22 cm.

Ollas with short flaring necks are present in a range of sizes, from small-scale vessels with rather straight outsloping necks to heavy, globular-bodied jars with more conventional flaring rims. Rim diameter 7–18 cm.

Convex-wall bowls are a minority form. They range from miniature or cup size to bowls with rim diameters of 12–24 cm.

Flaring-wall bowls presumably had flat bottoms. Rim diameter, 18–24 cm.

Outsloping-wall bowls also presumably had flat bottoms. Rim diameter, 10–18 cm.

Relationships

Ajalpan Coarse pottery is diagnostic of the Ajalpan phase in the Tehuacan Valley; it is proportionally most popular in the early part of the phase. The paste and surface finish are obviously derived from Purron Plain. It was often difficult to separate examples of the two types in Zones G and H of Tc 204. However, Ajalpan Coarse is harder, and microscopic analysis revealed that the composition of the temper is different.

TABLE 14
Ajalpan Coarse Vessel Forms
(sherds by site and zone)

	Purron	Early Ajalpan					Late Ajalpan											
	272 K¹	204 H	272 J	204 G	204D subE	204 G¹	204 F	204D E	204 F¹	204D supE	204 E	204D D	368e K³	204D C	204C pit	368e K²	368e K¹	368e J
Tecomates																		
plain		51	1	48	5	43		5			6		2		9	1		
ellipsoidal		23		25	6	19	29	10	13	3					11			1
pumpkin		15		10	3	15	19	2	4	1		1	1		11			
Ollas																		
long flaring neck		2		5	1	4	20	1	13		2		2		2	7	4	1
short flaring neck				4	1	1	2		2			5			1	3	1	
Bowls																		
flaring wall		5				1												
convex wall		1			1				1	1						1		
outsloping wall		1						2							2			
Body sherds	2	942	19	693	87	287	216	221	251	53	9	9	131	3	146	162	161	174
Total	2	1040	20	785	104	370	286	242	283	58	17	10	141	3	182	174	166	176

	Early Santa Maria									Late Santa Maria								
	368e I	368e G	368e F	368e E	367 D¹	367e D	272 I	368e C²	368e C¹	368e C	368w D-E	368e B	368w C	368w B	368e B¹	204 A-B	368w B¹	Total
Tecomates																		
plain		1																172
ellipsoidal																		140
pumpkin																		82
Ollas																		
long flaring neck	2																	66
short flaring neck																		20
Bowls																		
flaring wall																		6
convex wall	1																	6
outsloping wall																		5
Body sherds	98	3	168	73	1	97	5	11	7	4	8	2	2	6	2	5	2	4060
Total	101	3	169	73	1	97	5	11	7	4	8	2	2	6	2	5	2	4557

Also, the various tecomate shapes are the dominant vessel forms instead of long-necked ollas. Both Ajalpan Plain and Coatepec Plain, although they have many different attributes, could be typological descendants.

Outside the Tehuacan region, the closest analogous types are the most crudely finished undecorated tecomate sherds from Santa Marta Cave in Chiapas. The Santa Marta remains seem to represent the early part of Chiapa de Corzo I or the Cotorra phase (MacNeish and Peterson 1962). In terms of vessel forms and general paste type, Ajalpan Coarse displays similarities to the pottery of the Barra and Ocos phases of the Pacific coast of Guatemala (Coe 1961). However, Ajalpan Coarse lacks the red painted rims of the early speci-

mens from Guatemala. It also lacks the long conical appendage–miscalled a tripod foot by Coe (1961: 50)–common to so many early vessels on the Guatemala coast. Some of the Pre–La Venta sherds from Robert Squier's Test C excavation at La Venta in 1964 closely resemble Ajalpan Coarse (personal observation).

In spite of the limited analogous types, it seems reasonable to guess that the tecomate form with a poor paste, no decoration, and a poorly smoothed or a crudely stick-polished surface is a good time marker for the period from 1500 to 1000 B.C. for at least southern Mesoamerica.

It is perhaps significant that the earliest pottery form

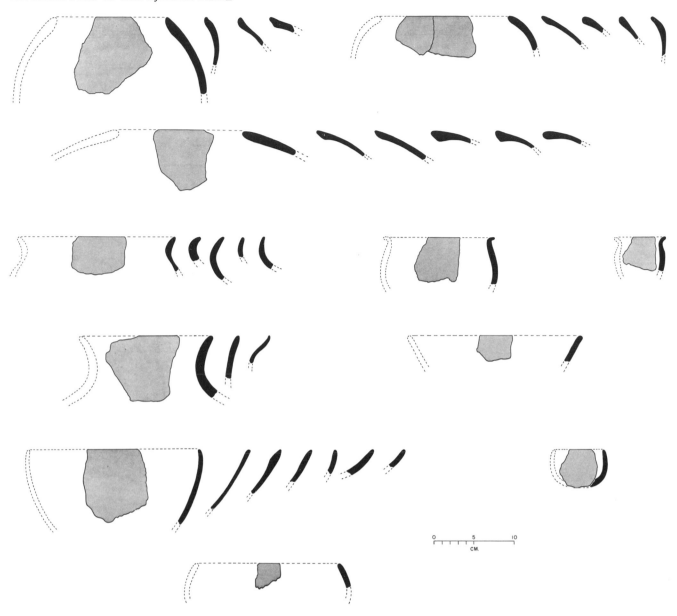

FIG. 11. AJALPAN PLAIN. *Rows 1, 2:* ellipsoidal, plain, and pumpkin tecomates; *rows 3, 4:* ollas with short flaring, long flaring, and funnel necks; *rows 5, 6:* convex-wall bowls, cup, and incurved-rim bowl.

in Colombia, Peru, and Ecuador is also a tecomate. Is this evidence for an early spread of a ceramic concept from south to north, or vice versa?

AJALPAN PLAIN

12,177 specimens excavated, 127 collected.

Paste

Mineralogical analysis of thin sections of sherds of this type show the following composition: about 87 percent clay; about 5 percent grains 0.5–1.0 mm. in diameter consisting of quartz, quartzite, diorite, andesite, marble, limestone, shale, gneiss, rhyolite, and hematite; about 5 percent grains 0.1–0.5 mm. in diameter consisting of most of the materials listed plus biotite, feldspar, calcite, magnetite, and plagioclase; and about 3 percent grains less than 0.1 mm. in diameter consisting of pyroxene, magnetite, biotite, hematite, feldspar, calcite, quartz, and quartzite.

The clay was superficially kneaded with the tem-

T A B L E 15
Ajalpan Plain Vessel Forms
(sherds by site and zone)

	Early Ajalpan					Late Ajalpan							
	204 H	272 J	204 G	204D subE	204 G¹	204 F	204D E	204 F¹	204D supE	204 E	204D D	368e K³	204D C
Tecomates													
plain	40		84	3	27	25	3	18	4	26	2	2	
pumpkin	4		65	1	25	33	9	28	3		2	2	
ellipsoidal	3		21		12	22	10	14	4		2	2	2
Bowls													
convex wall	9		52	2	47	48	14	32	4	9	1	3	
outsloping wall	3		22	3	29	25	4	17				2	
flaring wall	2		8	1	5	2		7				4	
incurved rim			8		2	3		2				1	
Ollas													
short flaring neck	2		14	2	13	20	2	8	1			23	
long flaring neck	6		12	1	21	19	9	4	1	1	1	7	
Flat bases													
Body sherds	770	20	1386	79	989	978	436	528	188	36	63	603	17
Total	839	20	1672	92	1170	1175	487	658	205	72	71	649	19

	Late Ajalpan (continued)				Early Santa Maria								
	204C pit	368e K²	368e K¹	368e J	368e I	368e H	368e G	368e F	368e E	367 D²	367 D¹	367 C	368e D
Tecomates													
plain		2	1										
pumpkin		1			1			2	3				1
ellipsoidal	3												
Bowls													
convex wall		6	1										
outsloping wall				1									
flaring wall													
incurved rim	1	1											
Ollas													
short flaring neck		25	18	4	5								
long flaring neck		17	11	4	7	4							
Flat bases					2								
Body sherds	44	1094	1399	562	742	73	55	381	142	2	1	1	49
Total	48	1146	1430	571	757	77	55	383	145	2	1	1	50

	Early Santa Maria (cont'd)			Late Santa Maria									
	272 I	368e C²	368e C¹	368e C	368w D-E	272 G	368e B	368w C	368w B	368e B¹	204 A-B	368w B¹	Total
Tecomates													
plain													237
pumpkin													180
ellipsoidal													95
Bowls													
convex wall													228
outsloping wall													106
flaring wall													29
incurved rim													18
Ollas													
short flaring neck													137
long flaring neck													125
Flat bases													2
Body sherds	2	24	145	42	86	5	14	16	11	19	11	8	11,021
Total	2	24	145	42	86	5	14	16	11	19	11	8	12,178

per, giving the paste a poorly knit and generally laminated appearance. It seems to be slightly harder than the paste of Ajalpan Coarse and the crude wares of the Purron phase. Although it contains about the same amount of temper as Ajalpan Coarse, the grains are smaller.

The cores are usually a lighter color than the surfaces. The latter show a considerable range in color, from orange to brown and black, perhaps as the result of poorly controlled firing in a crude kiln.

Sherds range in thickness from 0.4 to 1.3 cm., averaging just under 0.7 cm. Hardness measures 2.0–2.5.

Surface Finish

Interior surfaces were crudely brushed while the clay was wet. Exterior surfaces are relatively smooth; on a few sherds the smoothing approaches a dull polish. About 5 percent of the sample have brushed exteriors, some of which are roughly zoned. For instance, a few sherds display a band of horizontal brushings on the outer rim and diagonal brushings on the outer body.

Decoration

Three sherds, all rim fragments of tecomates, have a band about an inch wide of specular red paint encircling the exterior rim just below the lip. There may be objections to classifying these three sherds as Ajalpan Plain, even though paste, surface finish, and vessel form are identical to other examples of the type. It may well be that the decorated specimens—two from Ts 204, Zone G, and one from Zone G^1—are sherds of pots made elsewhere or local imitations of the Mapache Red-rimmed tecomates of the Pacific coast of Guatemala (Coe and Flannery 1967), which also occur in the earliest ceramic phases of Oaxaca, central and southern Veracruz, and Chiapas. The zoned brushing could also be considered a form of decoration, but we feel that it is more correctly considered a surface finish in this instance.

Vessel Forms

Plain tecomates are the dominant vessel and jar form of Ajalpan Plain ware in the early part of the Ajalpan phase. Rim diameter, 14–20 cm.

Pumpkin tecomates are the second most popular jar form. Rim diameter, 14–18 cm.

Ellipsoidal tecomates are less numerous than the preceding types of neckless jars. Rim diameter, 14–20 cm.

Ollas with short flaring necks become the predominant jar shape in late Ajalpan levels. These vessels vary in size from large jars with rim diameters of 12–24 cm. to squat miniature vessels 6.5–14 cm. wide at the rim and 6.0–10 cm. high.

Ollas with long flaring necks resemble in shape the tall-necked jars in earlier pastes. Their popularity increases in later Ajalpan levels. Average rim diameter, 12–18 cm.

Convex-wall bowls are an important vessel form in both early and late Ajalpan levels. They range from truly deep to relatively shallow depth. A miniature bowl of this type is about 5.0 cm. high with a rim diameter of 6.5 cm. Bottoms were probably slightly convex. Rim diameter, 14–22 cm.

Outsloping-wall bowls presumably had flat bottoms. They probably were fairly shallow, though the height is unknown. Rim diameter, 20–26 cm.

Flaring-wall bowls are a minor shape in this ware. Rim diameter, 18–22 cm.

Incurved-rim bowls are usually thinner walled and less constricted at the mouth than tecomates. Rim diameter, 18–20 cm.

Relationships

Ajalpan Plain is a major ware throughout the Ajalpan phase. It reaches its greatest popularity in the middle of the phase. It is probably a descendant of Ajalpan Coarse and contributes to the ancestry of Coatepec Plain.

Of all the Ajalpan pottery types this is the closest to any found in the Ocos phase of Guatemala (Coe 1961) and in Chiapa de Corzo I of lowland Chiapas (Dixon 1959). In fact, some of the zoned-brushed and red-rimmed sherds from Tehuacan, coastal Guatemala, southern and central Veracruz, Oaxaca, and Chiapas are sufficiently close to suggest they are of the same type.

AJALPAN FINE RED

707 specimens excavated.

Paste

There is a large amount of very fine temper in sherds of this type. According to analysis of thin sections, the paste is about 85 percent clay; about 5 percent grains 0.1–0.3 mm. in diameter of microcline, quartz, limestone, quartzite, andesine, calcite, andesite, trachite, diorite, labradorite, hematite, and hornblende; and about 10 percent grains less than 0.1 mm. in diameter composed of roughly the same substances.

The consistency of the paste is well knit but porous. It has a fine sandy character, and sometimes shows a tendency toward lamination. Frequently the

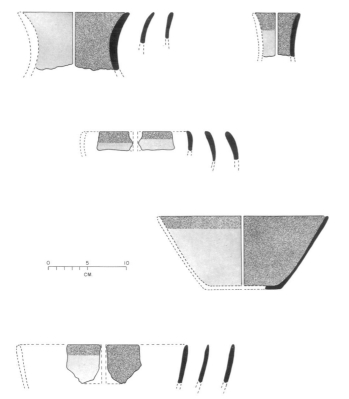

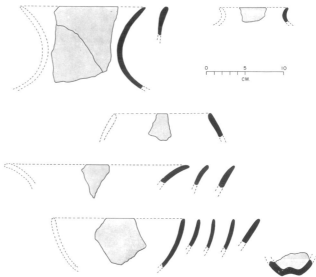

FIG. 13. AJALPAN FINE PLAIN. *From top to bottom*, ollas with long and short flaring necks, incurved-rim bowl or tecomate, flaring-wall bowls, convex-wall bowls, and a dimple-base fragment.

FIG. 12. AJALPAN FINE RED. *From top to bottom*, ollas and bottle with long flaring necks, incurved-rim bowls, outsloping-wall bowl, and convex-wall bowls.

surfaces and the core differ in color owing to conditions of firing. The core ranges from dark gray (7.5 YR 3/0) to light brown (7.5 YR 6/4). Hardness is about 2.7. Sherds range in thickness from 0.3 to 0.9 cm., with the average about 0.5 cm.

Surface Finish

The outer surface is usually completely covered by a slightly streaky wash ranging from red (5.0 R 4/6) to dusky red (10 R 3/4). The red wash—of the type known as specular or hematite red—seems to have been applied by brushing. It generally extends over the lip of the vessel and down the interior wall a centimeter or more in a fairly even band. Occasionally no red at all shows on the inner surface, or, in the case of rim fragments of two convex-walled bowls, the entire inner surface is red and the outer surface is left plain. The exterior surfaces have a slightly waxy luster which is dulled by wide, shallow depressions left by a rounded polishing tool such as a hard stick or a pebble. The polishing marks are both horizontal and vertical. Interiors are also well polished, but only

horizontal markings are seen. There is no decoration besides the red washed surface.

Vessel Forms

Deep outsloping-wall bowls are the most numerous vessels in this paste. Bottoms of this and other bowl forms were flat or slightly concave, according to the basal fragments found. Rim diameter, 16–22 cm.

Flaring-wall bowls had flat bases. Rim diameter, 16–20 cm.

Convex-wall bowls were of medium depth to quite deep. The few "dimple" bases (bottoms with a pronounced exterior concavity at the center) probably belong to this shape. Rim diameter, 16–28 cm.

Incurved-rim bowls are a minor form. Rim diameter, 12–26 cm.

Bottles with tall flaring or converging necks presumably had globular bodies. Rim diameter, 6.0–7.0 cm.

Ollas with long flaring necks are evident only in later levels. Rim diameter, 14–16 cm.

A pumpkin tecomate is the only neckless jar represented in Ajalpan Fine Red paste. Rim diameter, 8.0 cm.

Relationships

Ajalpan Fine Red is confined mainly to the early and late parts of the Ajalpan phase and always ap-

TABLE 16
Ajalpan Fine Red Vessel Forms
(sherds by site and zone)

	Purron	Early Ajalpan					Late Ajalpan								
	272 K¹	204 H	272 J	204 G	204D subE	204 G¹	204 F	204D E	204 F¹	204D E	204 E	204D D	368e K³	204D C	204C pit
Bowls															
outsloping wall, deep				19	2	18	23	4	9	5	3	3		1	4
flaring wall		1		10		3	4	2	3	2	3			1	
convex wall		1		6		3	4	4	4					1	1
incurved rim						1	1		3	2				1	
Bottles				11		2	1		1						
Ollas, long flaring neck															2
Tecomate, pumpkin				1											
Body sherds	2	23	3	59		72	99	24	72	9	9	6	15	1	24
Total	2	25	3	106	2	99	132	34	92	18	15	9	15	5	31

	Late Ajalpan (continued)			Early Santa Maria											Total
	368e K²	368e K¹	368e J	368e I	368e H	368e G	368e F	368e E	367 D²	367 D¹	367 C	272 I	368e C²	272 H	
Bowls															
outsloping wall, deep															91
flaring wall			1	1											31
convex wall	1		3												28
incurved rim															8
Bottles															15
Ollas, long flaring neck		1													3
Tecomate, pumpkin															1
Body sherds	18	11	8	15	5	4	25	6	3	2	8	3	3	1	530
Total	19	12	12	16	5	4	25	6	3	2	8	3	3	1	707

pears as a minority ware. The application of specular red is one of the earliest kinds of surface finish or decoration of pottery from La Victoria, Guatemala (Coe 1961), Chiapa de Corzo (Dixon 1959), Oaxaca, and Veracruz. A few of the earliest small red bowls from James Ford's 1964 excavation at Chalahuites, Veracruz, seem to be either the same or a quite similar pottery type. Sherds of Ajalpan Fine Red occur in levels of the tentatively named Matadamas complex of the Valley of Oaxaca.

AJALPAN FINE PLAIN

1,074 specimens excavated.

Paste

The paste appears to be finely tempered like Ajalpan Fine Red paste, but microscopic examination of thin sections reveals that much of the temper of Ajalpan Fine Plain is actually of larger size. About 3 percent of the paste consists of grains 0.5–0.9 mm. in diameter composed of oligoclase, trachite, quartz, quartzite, limestone, andesite, and hematite; about 5 percent is grains 0.1–0.5 mm. in diameter composed of most of the same materials and andesine, pyroxenes, and calcite; 3 to 8 percent is grains less than 0.1 mm. in diameter made up of quartz, calcite, hematite, magnetite, pyroxenes, biotite, plagioclase, labradorite, and andesine.

The paste is well knit and rather porous, with either a blocky or a sandy character. The outer surface is extremely thin and resembles a slip, but the resemblance has actually resulted from polishing the paste. Minute, glittering specks of pyroxenes can be seen on the surfaces and often in the core.

TABLE 17
Ajalpan Fine Plain Vessel Forms
(sherds by site and zone)

	Purron	Early Ajalpan					Late Ajalpan						
	272 K1	204 H	272 J	204 G	204D subE	204 G1	204 F	204D E	204 F1	204D supE	204 E	204D D	368e K3
Bowls													
convex wall		6		8	1	2	1		1	1	1		1
outsloping wall, deep		4		8		3	3	5	1		2		
flaring wall		1		2		1	2		1		1	1	2
incurved rim				1		1	1						1
Ollas													
long flaring neck		1		4			3		1				
short flaring neck							1			1			
angle neck				1									
Tecomates													
ellipsoidal				1		1			1				
pumpkin		1		1		1							
Body sherds	2	38	3	115	9	126	165	84	124	44	3	30	36
Total	2	51	3	141	10	135	176	89	129	46	7	31	40

	Late Ajalpan (continued)					Early Santa Maria							
	204D C	204C pit	368e K2	368e K1	368e J	368e I	368e F	368e E	367 D2	367 D1	367 C	368e C2	Total
Bowls													
convex wall		4	2										28
outsloping wall, deep	1		1										28
flaring wall	1	1	2		1								16
incurved rim													4
Ollas													
long flaring neck													9
short flaring neck						1	1						5
angle neck													1
Tecomates													
ellipsoidal													3
pumpkin													3
Body sherds	19	60	14	19	17	9	4	1	4	35	13	4	978
Total	21	65	19	19	18	10	5	1	4	35	13	4	1074

Surface color varies from tan (7.5 YR 6/4, 6/6) to brown (5.0 YR 4/3). The core is generally dark brown to very dark gray (7.5 YR 3/0 to 10 YR 3/1). The hardness measures over 3.0. Sherds range from 0.3 to 0.7 cm. in thickness.

Surface Finish

The exterior surface is well polished generally to a matte luster, but a few pieces are somewhat shinier. Wide but extremely shallow horizontal smoothing marks show on some sherds. There is no decoration.

Vessel Forms

Convex-wall bowls are the most numerous form. They were usually flat-bottomed, according to the basal fragments found. Four sherds representing small convex-wall bowls with a prominent centrally located basal dimple occurred in late Ajalpan components. Rim diameter, usually 14–22 cm., with some miniature bowls of 6–8 cm.

Outsloping-wall bowls are deep bowls except for two definitely shallow examples from late Ajalpan components. Bottoms presumably were flat. Rim diameter, 12–18 cm.

Flaring-wall bowls presumably were flat-bottomed. Rim diameter, 16–20 cm.

Incurved-rim bowls are not a popular shape in Ajalpan Fine Plain. Rim diameter, 8–12 cm.

Ollas with long flaring necks have rim diameters of 12–16 cm.

Ollas with short flaring necks have rim diameters of about 9 cm.

Olla with angle neck. One sherd represents an olla with a short neck slanting outward at an acute angle to the shoulder. The rim diameter is only 8.0 cm. The shape somewhat resembles ollas of the Pavon complex of the Panuco region of northern Veracruz (MacNeish 1954: fig. 12, no. 11).

Pumpkin and *ellipsoidal tecomates* are quite minor forms. Rim diameter, 8–12 cm.

Relationships

In the Tehuacan sequence this minority type is a diagnostic trait of the Ajalpan phase. It reached its greatest popularity in middle Ajalpan times. It is difficult to find early analogies that are convincing. Although fine paste and two vessel forms, angle-neck ollas and convex-wall bowls, are characteristics common to both Ajalpan Fine Plain and the earliest type in the Panuco region, Progreso Metallic (MacNeish 1954), other features of the two types are very different. Sherds of Ajalpan Fine Plain bowls appear in the tentatively named Matadamas complex of Oaxaca.

Miscellaneous Objects

Aberrant sherds were found in early Ajalpan levels of Ts 204; two in Zone G and two in Zone G¹. We are fairly certain that the record shows their actual chronological position. Two sherds with highly polished surfaces and traces of specular-red paint appear to represent vessels with incurved rims (see Fig. 26). Decoration on these sherds consists of quite deep, short, parallel, vertical grooves around the exterior rims. The third sherd, with a highly polished black exterior and a rather rough gray interior, resembles Ajalpan Fine Plain (Fig. 26). It is such a small fragment that little can be said about it, except that it is decorated by two deep parallel grooves which appear to be deliberate attempts at gadrooning. These sherds are all very like Coton Grooved Red from the Barra phase of coastal Chiapas (Green and Lowe 1967: 99).

FIG. 14. SPHERICAL PUNCHED-FEATURE HEADS AND *(bottom row)* MOUSE EFFIGY.

The fourth sherd, from Zone G¹, is from a flat-bottomed cylindrical-walled vessel (Fig. 26). The sides of the vessel are decorated by shallow vertical grooves or gadroons about the width of a thumb which create a ridged effect. Both interior and exterior surfaces are very well polished and are a pinkish tan color. There is a heavy interior thickening or reinforcing at the junction of wall and base. The cross section from outer edge to inner angle is 1.7 cm. thick, whereas the wall thins to 0.6 cm. as it extends upward and the base is about 0.8 cm. thick.

Worked sherds (8 specimens excavated) were found in all levels of Ts 204 but Zone H. Some of these sherds are worked into the crudest disks that we have noted in Mesoamerica. The disk-makers did not bother to rub off the jagged edges, often leaving the sherd more rectangular than circular in shape. One sherd was perforated with a conical hand drill used on both surfaces. Most of the sherds are of Ajalpan Coarse or Ajalpan Plain.

Animal effigy. This specimen has a small conical snout, now broken, with two punctations above it for eyes (Fig. 14). The top of the head is split by a deep groove. A disk of clay is attached at right angles to one side of the head and another disk is attached parallel to the other side of the head, making asymmetrical ears. The head may have been attached to a globular whistle.

35

FIG. 15. FLAT PUNCHED-FEATURE HEADS.

Mouthpieces of whistles. Two short rounded mouthpieces with horizontal slits through them must have broken off large hollow spherical whistles.

Figurines

SPHERICAL, PUNCHED-FEATURE HEADS

7 specimens excavated.
Dimensions in cm.: height (5 specimens), 2.8–4.3, average, 3.4; length (5 specimens), 2.0–3.6, average, 2.6; width (4 specimens), 2.2, 2.9, 3.1, 3.2.
Paste: resembles Ajalpan Coarse Red.
Surface finish: specular red wash (5 specimens).

These small, crude, spherical heads were modeled from slightly flattened balls of poorly knit clay. Two small ellipsoidal globs formed on opposite sides represent ears. The ears are incised with three to five parallel horizontal lines on the facial side. The hairline is indicated by a series of short radiating lines or punches, which continue down the back of the head of one figure. A third, more elongated lump represents a rather large beak-like nose, beneath which two squarish or conical punches side by side make a crude mouth. On either side of the nose double punches form eyes, with a slight gouge or depression in each case connecting the two deeper punctures. Prominent horizontal ridges formed in this way along the eyes of two specimens superficially resemble the applied fillets of the coffee-bean type of eye. Although no heads were found attached to bodies, the appearance of the heads in some of the same zones as the primitive, sexless gingerbread torsos and limbs makes one suspect that they belong together.

These heads are the earliest type of figurine found in the Tehuacan Valley and, at the time of writing, in Mexico. So far no similar heads have been reported from sites in Central or South America. Our samples are mainly confined to the earlier components of the Ajalpan phase, although two heads and a few sexless bodies were uncovered in later Ajalpan levels.

36

FLAT, PUNCHED-FEATURE HEADS

3 specimens excavated.
Dimensions in cm. of 2 complete heads: height, 2.3, 3.3; width, 2.7, 3.2.
Paste: very close texture; tight fine-grained temper.

These small, crude, flattened heads are fragments of apparently complete figures made from elongated slabs of clay. A groove serves as a neck to divide the head from the broken torso. Ears are applied semicircles and are decorated with one to several punch marks on the facial side. The prominent nose of one specimen, made of an applied strip of clay, is without nostrils. A second has a less prominent applied nose with two punched nostrils. Eyes and mouth are formed by double punched depressions. To make each feature, a flat, pointed object, like the tooth of a comb, was pushed into the clay in opposite directions at an oblique angle to the surface. The deep points of the punctures are the corners of the eye or mouth, and the shallow, wider ends almost meet to form the center of the feature. One of the two complete heads has a row of three holes punched through it above the hairline, and the other has two curved lines on either side of the forehead looping down behind the ears.

Just below the head, two cylinders of clay were added to the flattened slab at either side to form shoulders and arms. Two small cones applied to the upper torso make breasts. Legs were made of conical pieces applied to the bottom of the original slab. This type of punch-featured head seems, then, to go with the Trackwoman body type described below.

The three specimens appear in the two earliest zones of the Ajalpan phase. Analogous types have not been reported from other regions.

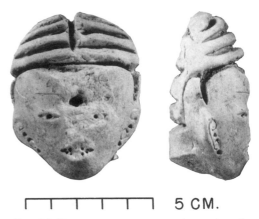

FIG. 16. PROJECTING-EYE HEAD (two views).

PROJECTING-EYE HEADS

4 specimens excavated.
Dimensions in cm.: height (2 specimens), 5.2, 6.2; length (3 specimens), 2.7, 2.8, 4.0; width (3 specimens), 3.8, 4.7, 4.6.
Paste: resembles Ajalpan Coarse.
Surface finish: thin wash.

Only one of four heads is complete. The other fragments are from generally large heads and are ellipsoidal in outline. The delicately formed facial features seem to have been modeled from the initial mass of clay. The nose is short and pointed, the chin is dimpled, and the facial contours are realistic. The eyes of the complete specimen were made on slightly bulging portions of the face by pressing a flat pointed object into the clay in opposite directions. The more deeply impressed points become the corners of the eyes; the less deeply impressed and wider bases barely overlap to form the center. This central portion of the eye has been pierced by a sharp-pointed object to depict the pupil. The nostrils were made by similar fine punctures, and the interior of the mouth also contains small holes. The mouths of two specimens have well-modeled lips which are parted. The ears of the complete specimen are rather realistically modeled. The auditory meatus is indicated in an interesting manner by a fine scrolled incision with two punches. This motif appears again in a slight variation on the Hollow Dwarf type of the late Ajalpan phase. Two specimens wear high crescentic headdresses. That of the complete specimen is marked by a series of deep, parallel, horizontal grooves and is split by a single medial groove at the top. The complete head retains traces of red or pinkish paint, and a second specimen was painted with specular-red hematite.

In the Tehuacan sequence these heads are confined to the Ajalpan phase, and represent middle levels, overlapping the early and late segments of the phase. Although details of the mouth and ears are not the same, the general cast of the features, the diagnostic eye type, and the crescentic cap are common to the Realistic Projecting-eyeball type of the Ponce phase at Panuco, Veracruz (MacNeish 1954: 589-591), to heads from Trapiche I of central Veracruz (García Payón 1966: pl. LII), and to at least one specimen from Chiapa de Corzo II of Chiapas. A similar depiction of the folds of the ear occurs on a large hollow figurine from a San Lorenzo zone (215–285 cm.) of Test C at La Venta (Squier, personal communication).

FIG. 17. SEATED AND STANDING GINGERBREAD BODIES.

GINGERBREAD TORSOS AND LIMBS

28 specimens excavated: 10 standing bodies, 3 seated bodies, 10 legs, 5 arms; collected from surface, 1 seated figure.
Dimensions in cm.: length of bodies, 4.0–10.0; of legs, 1.0–4.5; of arms, 0.5–2.5; width of torso, 1.5–6.0.
Paste: resembles Ajalpan Coarse Red.

These fragments are extremely simple unpainted models; they vary greatly in size. They are made in a distinctive way from two elongated cones of clay pressed together at the bases and then inverted, so that the two points become legs that are slightly

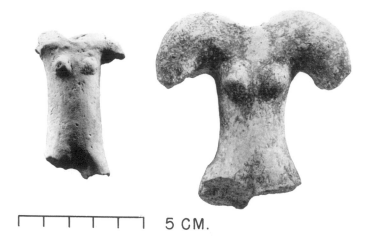

5 CM.

FIG. 18. STANDING TRACKWOMAN BODIES.

spread. The torsos are thick and somewhat rounded, with crudely formed shoulders and little indication of hips or breasts. Short, stubby arms apparently extended parallel to the body. Legs of both seated and standing figures are footless. Legs of seated figures extend at right angles to the trunk of the body and at an acute angle to each other. The buttocks of the seated torsos are absolutely flat. Unlike the crude spherical heads, on which various features are represented by punctures, incised lines, or modeled projections, these bodies and limbs are unadorned by marks of any kind.

In the Tehuacan Valley these crude models appear in the Ajalpan phase, in association with the crude spherical heads, with the greater number occurring early in the phase. It is interesting to note that these bodies are formed in the same manner as the Valdivia type described and illustrated by Meggers, Evans, and Estrada (1965: 96–97).

TRACKWOMAN BODIES

22 specimens excavated: 1 torso attached to head, 11 standing figures, 10 seated figures; collected from surface: 1 standing figure, 1 seated figure.
Dimensions in cm.: body length, 3.0–7.0; width, 1.5–4.0; thickness, 0.9–2.0; shoulder width, 3.0–7.0.
Paste: resembles Coatepec Plain.

These figures are formed from flattened slabs of clay. The bodies are long and narrow. Hips seem very narrow, although the legs may have been fairly bulbous. Shoulders are extremely wide and athletic-looking, owing to the manner in which conical pieces of clay were applied to make short, downward-pointing arms. Breasts are quite small. The standing figures probably had slightly parted legs; the seated figures (see Fig. 31) also had spread legs.

Judging from the No Face and Flat, Punched-feature heads with attached body fragments, we suspect that Trackwoman bodies belong with both types of head.

Seated and standing Trackwoman figures appear through most of the Ajalpan phase; the standing ones are slightly more prevalent in the last part of the phase. A very few fragments from early Santa Maria levels actually may not belong in this classification. These seated and standing figures are unlike figurine bodies known from other parts of Mexico.

ARM AND LEG FRAGMENTS

Cylindrical skinny arms (12 specimens: 8 excavated, 4 collected). Dimensions in cm.: length, 3.0–4.0; diameter, about 1.0. Paste: resembles Coatepec Plain. These arms are longer, thinner, and more consistently cylindrical than the conical arms described below. A knot of clay at the distal end represents a hand or fist. The arms may have been attached to Trackwoman bodies. They appear mainly in the Ajalpan phase and are most prevalent early in the phase.

Conical arms (12 specimens excavated). Dimensions in cm.: length, 2.5–3.5; thickness at shoulder, 1.0–2.5. Paste: resembles Ajalpan Coarse and Coatepec Plain. These arms are relatively short, slightly curved, and very definitely taper to a point or small knob from the thick shoulder end. They could have been attached to standing Trackwoman bodies, but they more likely belong to the Seated Mother figures described in Chapter 5. The arms appear throughout the Ajalpan phase and are too general for comparisons with limbs from other regions of Mexico.

Heavy, solid, unpolished limbs (17 specimens: 16 excavated, 1 collected). Dimensions in cm.: length of arms, 6.0–8.0; of legs, 6.0–10.0; diameter of arms, about 3.0; of legs, 2.5–6.0. Paste: resembles Ajalpan Coarse. These limbs, though they vary in size, are all large and heavy. For some reason, we found no large body fragments, perhaps because some of the large pieces called "wattle and daub" are actually bodies of this type.

Arms are long, thick, and fairly conical. They evidently extended down the sides of the bodies. The figures were probably standing, with feet slightly apart. Legs are long and tapering, and one small foot from Zone F[1] of Ts 204 had incisions marking rather pointed toes. None of the surfaces are polished, but a

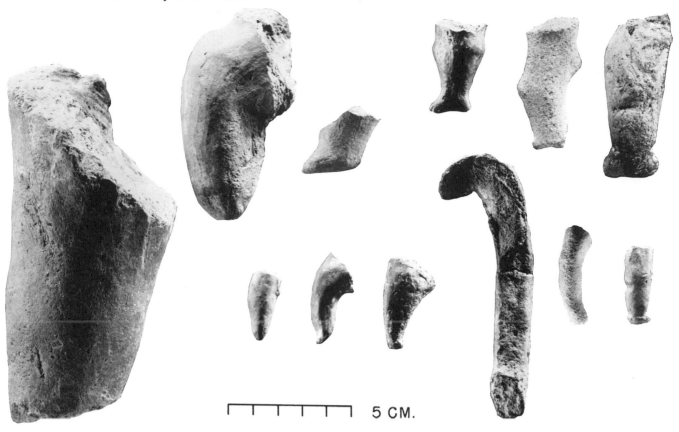

5 CM.

FIG. 19. MISCELLANEOUS LIMB FRAGMENTS. *Row 1:* heavy solid and squat legs; *row 2:* three conical arms, leg from a seated Trackwoman body, and two cylindrical arms.

few show small specks of red paint indicating that they may once have been decorated.

The limbs occur in the earliest part of the Ajalpan phase and the earlier zones of the Santa Maria phase. They somewhat resemble body fragments found in early parts of the Panuco sequence of northern Veracruz.

Ceramic Affiliations

Although the early Ajalpan pottery has distinctive characteristics that should allow one to make convincing linkages with pottery from other areas, thus far little pottery from horizons of comparable age has been uncovered in Mesoamerica. Very strong similarities can be seen between early Ajalpan and the Matadamas complex and subsequent Tierras Largas phase in the Valley of Oaxaca. Further secure evidence of extraregional connections are the sherds in early Ajalpan levels that seem to be of the Coton Grooved Red type (Green and Lowe 1967) from the Barra phase of coastal Chiapas.

Another cultural assemblage that early Ajalpan might be related to is that part of Chiapa de Corzo I represented in Santa Marta Cave in the Grijalva depression of Chiapas. Evidence of cultural links on this early time level between this part of Chiapas and southern Puebla lies in the dominance of tecomate vessel forms over small convex-wall bowls or flat-bottomed, flaring-wall bowls; the occurrence of tecomates with zoned brushed and zoned stick-polished surfaces; the painting of specular red bands around the rims of tecomates; and the monochrome use of specular red hematite on tecomate and other forms.

There are hints of other extraterritorial relationships of early Ajalpan, but they are based on traits that are too generalized and insufficient in number. For instance, angle-necked ollas made of fine paste suggest a connection between early Ajalpan and the Pavon period at Panuco. The tecomate form and use of zoned brushing and specular red paint suggest a relationship between early Ajalpan and the phases known as La Barra and Ocos of the Guatemalan Pacific coast. However, as will be shown in the following sections, the Ocos phase seems more securely connected with middle Ajalpan than with early Ajalpan. The same may be said of Trapiche I of central Veracruz (García Payón 1966).

The 1964 sounding by Squier at La Venta, Tabasco, has yielded in Test C deposits underneath the La Venta levels (100–210 cm.) and San Lorenzo-like levels (215–285 cm.). The lower levels (285–365 cm.) may be called Pre–La Venta. In these Pre–La Venta levels Squier has uncovered red-rimmed sherds like Mapache Red-rimmed, sherds like Ajalpan Coarse and perhaps Ajalpan Plain pottery, as well as fragments of large hollow and solid figurines with the scroll-incised ear similar to that of our Projecting-eye type. As yet analysis of these materials is unpublished, but they seem to contain good evidence of a connection between earliest Pre–La Venta and early Ajalpan. It may

also be significant that one of the differences between the two ceramic assemblages is the presence in the Pre–La Venta material of a white and a black pottery that is closely related to Progreso White and Ponce Black of Panuco (MacNeish 1954).

At San Lorenzo, Veracruz, Michael Coe has uncovered materials related to early Ajalpan. He has established two early phases, called Ojochi and Bajio, that seem equivalent to Pre-La Venta.

Some of the sherds from Levels 28 to 22 of Puerto Marquez, Guerrero, resemble Ajalpan Coarse Red, Ajalpan Coarse, Ajalpan Plain, and the large, solid body fragments. Again there are hints of a relationship to Ajalpan.

All in all, cultural relationships between early Ajalpan and other ceramic complexes are not very satisfactory and point to a zone of ignorance in Mesoamerican archaeology.

CHAPTER 4

The Late Part of the Ajalpan Phase

Late Ajalpan materials occurred in eleven components of four stratified sites and in one burial pit. In chronological order they are: Zone F of Ts 204, Zone E of Ts 204D, Zone F¹ of Ts 204, Zone super-E of Ts 204D, Zone E of Ts 204, Zone D of Ts 204D, Zone K³ of Ts 368e, Zone C of Ts 204D, the burial pit of Ts 204C, Zones K², K¹, and J of Ts 368e. Although late Ajalpan components are more numerous than early Ajalpan ones, they represent a shorter interval of time. The late Ajalpan subphase extends roughly from 1100 to 850 B.C. The larger number of late Ajalpan components means, of course, that our sample of sherds is larger also. Most of the same pottery and artifact types occur in both early and late parts of the phase. However, Purron Coarse, a minority type, did not last into late Ajalpan times, and two new minority types, Coatepec Buff and Coatepec Red-on-buff, first appear in late Ajalpan levels. There are also changes in the popularity of some of the diagnostic Ajalpan ceramic types such as Ajalpan Plain and Ajalpan Coarse, Ajalpan Coarse Red, and Coatepec Plain, as well as the addition in late Ajalpan of new decorative elements such as incising and rocker-dentate stamping.

Appearing in the latest component of the last part of the Ajalpan phase (Ts 368e, Zone J) were a few sherds of Canoas White, Coatepec White, Rio Salado Gray, and Rio Salado Coarse, which represent the beginning of a new ceramic tradition and become typical of the early part of the Santa Maria phase.

Pottery Types

Ajalpan Coarse Red

10,018 specimens excavated, 120 collected.

Paste

Studies of thin sections show that about 5 percent of the paste is large grains (0.5–1.5 mm. in diameter) of mica, andesite, diorite, granite, limestone, graywacke, and sandstone. Another 5 percent or so consists of grains 0.1–0.5 mm. in diameter and includes most of the materials mentioned as well as hematite, quartz, oligioclase, plagioclase, andesine, calcite, and pyroxenes. About 2 percent is composed of grains less than 0.1 mm. in diameter, consisting of calcite, muscovite, hematite, magnetite, biotite, microcline, and quartz. Macroscopically, this paste resembles both the earlier Ajalpan Coarse paste and the Rio Salado Coarse paste that appears later.

The poorly knit paste has a laminated to blocky character. A distinctive characteristic is a sharp firing break between periphery and core. The outer layers are an orangish-pink color (5.0 YR 7/4–7/6), while the interior is dark to medium gray (10 YR 5/1–6/1).

Sherds vary in thickness from 0.5 to 1.6 cm., with the average about 0.9 cm. Hardness is about 2.5.

Surface Finish

Exterior surfaces were wiped, usually leaving fine horizontal striations. Traces of a red wash (approach-

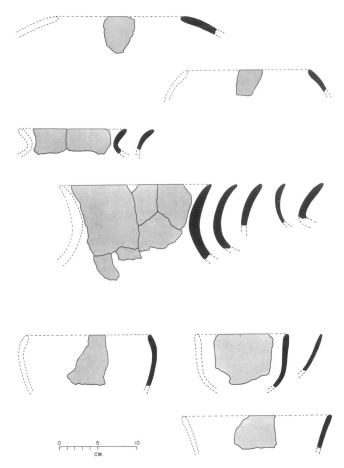

FIG. 20. AJALPAN COARSE RED. *From top to bottom,* pumpkin and plain tecomates; ollas with short and long flaring necks; incurved-rim, convex-wall, and flaring-wall bowls.

ing 10 R 6/8) remain on some exterior surfaces. The wash may extend over the lip onto the uppermost part of the inner rim. The interior surface shows crude horizontal brushing marks that are less rough than those found on the other Ajalpan and Purron types. Apart from the red wash, there is no decoration.

Vessel Forms

Ollas with long flaring necks, wide mouths, and relatively rounded lips are the most common vessel form. The necks merge gradually into the bodies, which presumably were elongated with rounded or flattened bases. In the later levels in which Ajalpan Coarse Red appears, the long-necked ollas tend to become more like those of the Rio Salado Coarse

type, with flattened or beveled lips and, usually, a funnel neck rising at an angle to the shoulders. Rim diameter, 14–24 cm.

Ollas with short flaring necks are the second most common vessel form. They also tend to become more like their counterparts in the Rio Salado Coarse paste. The mouths become less flaring, and the necks, which in early examples blended gradually into the bodies, show an angular break where they begin to slope outward from the body. Rim diameter, 10–19 cm.

Funnel-neck ollas are represented only at the Coatepec site. These fragments of long- to medium-necked ollas show a sharp angle at the point where the neck joins the body.

Beveled-lip ollas. These long-necked ollas are present only in the latest Ajalpan levels. The lips instead of being rounded and tapering are sharply beveled on the interior surface.

Convex-wall bowls are a minority form, as are all bowl forms in this paste. These vessels are usually fairly deep. Rims range from slightly incurved to nearly upright to definitely divergent. Rim diameter, 16–22 cm.

Flaring-wall and *outsloping-wall bowls* had flat bottoms and rim diameters of 18 to 20 cm. Three *incurved-rim fragments* seem to represent bowls rather than tecomates; rim diameter, 16 cm.

Tecomates are few in number. *Pumpkin tecomates* have diameters at the mouth of about 16 cm. *Plain tecomates* have rim diameters of 8–16 cm. One rim sherd of an *ellipsoidal tecomate* was found in a late Ajalpan level.

Bottle. This form is represented by one sherd indicating a rim diameter of 8 cm.

Relationships

This basically late Ajalpan ware first appeared in early Ajalpan times and lasted into the early Santa Maria subphase. Ajalpan Coarse Red definitely contributed to the ancestry of Rio Salado Coarse; some of the early Santa Maria examples are difficult to classify into one or the other type. It seems to have been derived from the Ajalpan Coarse and Purron Plain types, plus the introduction of the concept of a red wash. It vaguely resembles some of the early red-washed varieties of Heavy Plain from Panuco and pottery of the earliest phases of the central and southern Veracruz coast. There are similarities as well to some of the materials from the lowest levels of Puerto Marquez of coastal Guerrero (Brush 1965).

TABLE 15

Ajalpan Coarse Red Vessel Forms
(sherds by site and zone)

	Purron	Early Ajalpan					Late Ajalpan											
	272 K¹	204 H	272 J	204 G	204D subE	204 G¹	204 F	204D E	204 F¹	204D supE	204 E	204D D	368e K³	204D C	204C pit	368e K²	368e K¹	368e J
Ollas																		
long flaring neck		10	2	7	1	10	5		13	1	10	1	41		12	43	45	63
short flaring neck		1		7		6	8	1	5	1	2		46	1		30	16	16
funnel neck													1		1	21	13	1
beveled lip													4			7	5	
Bowls																		
convex wall		6		1					6	1	6		1				1	
flaring wall									2					2			3	
incurved rim								1				2						
outsloping wall																	1	
Tecomates																		
pumpkin															1			
plain							1											
ellipsoidal																		1
Bottle									1									
Body sherds	1	132	24	135	6	171	271	74	184	60	5	46	950	31	429	1448	1493	1188
Total	1	149	26	150	7	187	285	76	211	63	23	49	1043	34	443	1549	1577	1269

	Early Santa Maria												Late Santa Maria								
	368e I	368e H	368e G	368e F	368e E	367 D²	367 D¹	367 C	368e D	272 I	368e C²	368e C¹	368e C	368w D-E	368e B	368w C	368w B	368e B¹	204 A-B	368w B¹	Total
Ollas																					
long flaring neck	44	16	18	43	18	3	8	5	8	1	6	6									440
short flaring neck	8	4	3	4	5																164
funnel neck																					37
beveled lip																					16
Bowls																					
convex wall	3		3																		28
flaring wall																					7
incurved rim																					3
outsloping wall																					1
Tecomates																					
pumpkin	2	1		2																	6
plain				1					2												4
ellipsoidal																					1
Bottle																					1
Body sherds	872	226	167	383	143	13	50	38	93	6	21	142	78	63	51	122	76	19	24	75	9310
Total	929	247	191	433	166	16	58	43	103	7	27	148	78	63	51	122	76	19	24	75	10,018

COATEPEC PLAIN

15,829 specimens excavated, 94 collected.

Paste

About 5 percent of the paste consists of grains 0.5–1.0 mm. in diameter composed of quartz, quartzite, limestone, hematite, sandstone, and pyroxenes. Another 5 percent is grains 0.1–0.5 mm. in diameter composed of the materials mentioned and biotite, andesite, hornblende, oligoclase, magnetite, and feldspar. About 2 percent of the paste is grains less than 0.1 mm. in diameter.

The paste has a blocky and laminated structure. The core tends to be a darker shade (5.0 Y 3/2, 10 R 3/1) than the brown or tan outer surfaces (10 YR 4/2–7/6). In thickness sherds range from 0.4 to 1.3 cm., averaging about 0.6 cm. The hardness is about 3.0.

Surface Finish

Exterior surfaces, like those of the Ajalpan Plain type, are well smoothed, and many sherds have sections that look as though they have been stick-polished. The polishing runs in wide horizontal bands.

Decoration

Decoration is usually lacking, but fourteen sherds exhibit three different kinds of decoration. Five sherds from Ts 204D (three from Zone E and two from Zone super-E), all representing the globular bodies of jars, display fine rocker-dentate stamping. Three of these are shown in Fig. 21.

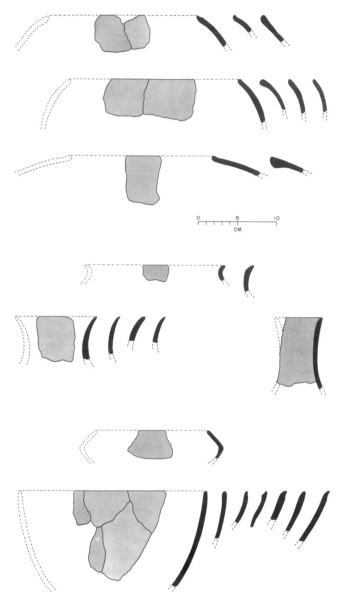

FIG. 22. COATEPEC PLAIN. *From top to bottom, ellipsoidal, plain, and pumpkin tecomates; ollas with short and long flaring necks; bottle; incurved-rim bowl; deep convex-wall bowls.*

Six sherds display rocker-dentate stamping in zones outlined by wide-lined incising (one sherd each from Ts 204, Zone F; Ts 204D, Zones E and super-E; and Ts 368e, Zone K^2; and two sherds from the burial pit, Ts 204C). This decoration appears on body fragments of bowls or ollas. See Fig. 21, top right.

The remaining three sherds (from Ts 204D, Zones E and C, and Ts 368e, Zone K^3) are decorated with parallel or crosshatched lines inside zones outlined

5 CM.

FIG. 21. COATEPEC PLAIN. Sherds decorated with zoned incising and zoned and unzoned rocker-dentate stamping.

TABLE 19
Coatepec Plain Vessel Forms
(sherds by site and zone)

	Early Ajalpan											Late Ajalpan						Early Santa Maria		
	204 H	272 J	204 G	204D subE	204 G^1	204 F	204D E	204 F^1	204D supE	204 E	204D D	368e K^3	204D C	204C pit	368e K^2	368e K^1	368e J	368e I	368e H	368e G
Bowls																				
convex wall	2		52		16	36	13	34	13		8	24	3	18	48	53	34	25	6	5
flaring wall			8	1		5	6		2			8	1	1	13	2	13	8		3
outsloping wall	1		23		8		1	11	2		3	8	1	4	1	3	4	10	1	
incurved rim			8	2	1	1	2	1			1	2		2	1	1	2	10	2	
Ollas																				
short flaring neck			2		1	2	1	2			2	17	2		41	58	20	24	13	7
long flaring neck			3				2	3	2		1	18	1		29	25	29	29	8	
funnel neck												7				1	1			
Tecomates																				
pumpkin			5			6	10		5		4	1	3	2	1		2	2	2	
plain			3	1		1	3		4		2	1		1	2	1	2			
ellipsoidal					1	1	3		3		2	1					1	2		2
Bottles			2		2															
Body sherds	72	10	334	38	326	779	409	590	154	20	252	1265	83	386	1996	1858	1320	1475	470	356
Total	75	10	440	42	355	831	450	642	185	20	275	1352	94	414	2132	2002	1428	1583	502	373

	Early Santa Maria (continued)										Late Santa Maria								
	368e F	368e E	367 D^2	367 D^1	367 C	368e D	272 I	368e C^2	368e C^1	272 H	368e C	368w D-E	368e B	368w C	368w B^1	368e B	204 A-B	368w B^1	Total
Bowls																			
convex wall	11	3				4		4											412
flaring wall	7					4													82
outsloping wall																			81
incurved rim																			36
Ollas																			
short flaring neck		5				4		4											205
long flaring neck	41	4							3										198
funnel neck																			9
Tecomates																			
pumpkin	7	4						1	3										58
plain	1	1				4													28
ellipsoidal																			13
Bottles																			4
Body sherds	1201	236	8	21	13	122	8	19	50	9	87	35	256	86	111	21	93	134	14,703
Total	1267	253	8	21	13	138	8	28	56	9	87	35	256	86	111	21	93	134	15,829

by incising. One sherd is illustrated in Fig. 21, top left.

Vessel Forms

Convex-wall bowls range from deep to medium deep. These bowls total over four hundred and are the dominant vessel form. Rim diameter, 16–24 cm.

Flaring-wall and *outsloping-wall bowls* are much less numerous. They apparently had flat bottoms. Rim diameter, 22–30 cm.

Incurved-rim bowls had rim diameters of 10–22 cm.

Ollas with short flaring necks number over two hundred. They have rim diameters of 14–20 cm.

Ollas with long flaring necks are almost as common. They have rim diameters of 16–20 cm.

Funnel-neck ollas are a minor long-necked form.

Pumpkin tecomates are the dominant neckless jar form. They have an average rim diameter of 12 cm.

Plain tecomates have rim diameters of 8–16 cm.

Ellipsoidal tecomates have an average rim diameter of 14 cm.

Bottles are confined to early Ajalpan levels. Rim diameter, 6–8 cm.

Relationships

The Coatepec Plain type occurs throughout most of the Ajalpan and Santa Maria phases, but reaches maximum popularity in late Ajalpan levels. It is probably derived from the Ajalpan Plain type, and is in part ancestral to Coatepec Buff. Coatepec Plain ollas and convex-wall bowls are common in the Tierras Largas phase of the Valley of Oaxaca.

Because it is a plain ware with relatively simple forms, it is difficult to relate specifically to other types from more distant regions. Some of the russetware bowls from El Arbolillo I and II are similar (Vaillant 1935: 222–223) as are some of the brown wares from Trapiche (García Payón 1966: 81–83, 101–108). However, whether these two types are actually related to Coatepec Plain is difficult to say. The zoned and unzoned rocker-dentate stamping and the zoned hatching or crosshatching do suggest that Coatepec Plain is related to a similar paste type from Trapiche I (García Payón 1966: pls. XV, XLIII).

The occurrence of these three decorative techniques together in the Ocos phase of Guatemala (Coe 1961: 53) and in late Ajalpan, suggests that perhaps these two phases were roughly contemporaneous and were somehow connected. As will be pointed out later, there is further evidence in the form of possible trade sherds for connecting Ocos and the late Ajalpan phase of Tehuacan.

Coatepec Red-on-buff

1,368 specimens excavated, 20 collected.

Paste

Macroscopically the paste appears much like that of Coatepec Plain. Microscopically, it is slightly different: about 3 percent of the paste consists of grains 0.5–1.0 mm. in diameter of quartz, quartzite, limestone, shale, and chlorite; about 10 percent is grains of the same materials measuring 0.1–0.5 mm. in diameter; and 5 percent is grains under 0.1 mm. in diameter including the materials mentioned and calcite, microline, biotite, magnetite, hematite, plagioclase, and muscovite.

In thickness, texture, consistency, and hardness the paste is very similar to Coatepec Plain.

Surface Finish

Surfaces are also similar to Coatepec Plain examples, being well smoothed and in some cases having a dull luster.

Decoration

The main difference from Coatepec Plain is that Coatepec Red-on-buff is decorated with specular-red hematite paint. Over half the body sherds and all the rim sherds display horizontal, vertical, or diagonal red stripes 1.0–5.0 cm. wide. Many bowls have one completely red surface and bands or stripes of red on the opposite surface. Still other vessels have a single red band around the lip that extends over both interior and exterior surfaces. Stripes around the interior rim are more popular on late Ajalpan examples; on Santa Maria specimens bands encircling the exterior rim are more common. A less common form of decoration consists of parallel stripes extending down from the lip or "V's" or inverted "V's" of red paint. A few aberrant specimens display incised decoration (Fig. 24).

Vessel Forms

Convex-wall bowls are the dominant shape in Coatepec Red-on-buff paste. These bowls are usually somewhat smaller and squatter than the Coatepec Plain convex-wall bowls. Rim diameter, 12–22 cm.

Flaring-wall bowls are a rather minor, flat-bottomed form with rim diameters of 16–28 cm. Other minor bowl forms are *incurved-rim bowls* (rim diameter, 12–20 cm.) and *outsloping-wall bowls* (rim diameter, 19 cm.).

Ollas with long flaring necks are usually larger

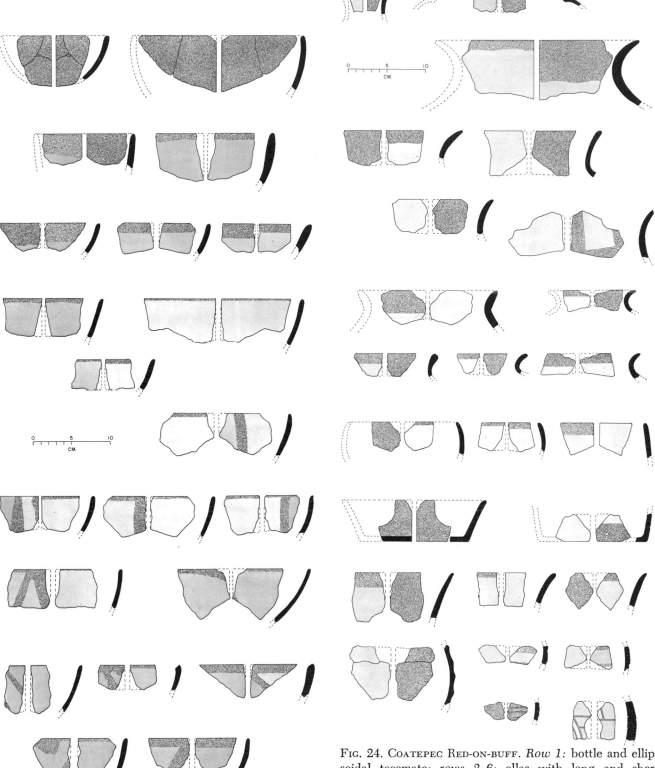

FIG. 23. COATEPEC RED-ON-BUFF. Convex-wall bowls, showing (left) interior and (right) exterior decoration.

FIG. 24. COATEPEC RED-ON-BUFF. Row 1: bottle and ellipsoidal tecomate; rows 2–6: ollas with long and short flaring necks; rows 7, 8 (right): incurved-rim bowls and rim and basal sherds of cylindrical jar; rows 8 (left), 9: outsloping- and flaring-wall bowls; rows 10, 11: ridged and incised body sherds.

T A B L E 20

Coatepec Red-on-buff Vessel Forms
(sherds by site and zone)

	Late Ajalpan											Early Santa Maria						
	204F	204D E	204 F1	204D supE	204 E	204D D	368e K3	204D C	204C pit	368e K2	368e K1	368e J	368e I	368e H	368e G	368e F	368e E	367 D2
Bowls																		
convex wall							20	1		27	14	34	25	14	5	16	13	
flaring wall							3					9	4			4		
outsloping wall							1			2		2	1			3		
incurved rim												5	4					
Ollas																		
long flaring neck	1																	
short flaring neck								1			3		1		2	1	5	
angle neck											3						2	
Bottles												1		4		3	1	
Tecomate, pumpkin											1							
Body sherds	4	3	7	12	3	7	42	11	7	60	65	78	98	50	19	182	89	2
Total	5	3	7	12	3	7	66	13	7	89	86	129	133	68	26	209	110	2

	Early Santa Maria (continued)								Late Santa Maria								Total
	367 D1	367 C	368e D	272 I	368e C2	368e C1	272 H	368e C	368w D-E	272 G	368e B	368w C	368w B	368w B1	204 A-B	368w B1	
Bowls																	
convex wall			10		1	5											185
flaring wall																	22
outsloping wall						2											9
incurved rim																	9
Ollas																	
long flaring neck																	13
short flaring neck																	5
angle neck																	2
Bottles																	9
Tecomate, pumpkin																	1
Body sherds	3	3	45	6	16	46	3	34	20	1	65	24	30	9	35	36	1113
Total	3	3	55	6	16	53	3	34	20	1	65	24	30	9	35	36	1368

and heavier than the short-necked jars. Rim diameter, 16–29 cm.

Ollas with short flaring or *angle necks* have rim diameters of 11–22 cm.

Bottles have rim diameters of 6–8 cm.

One *pumpkin tecomate* has a rim diameter of 16 cm.

Ridged sherds. Two fragments from late Ajalpan levels may be pieces of decorated rounded bodies of ollas or of figurines.

Relationships

A few red-on-buff sherds were uncovered in Trapiche I and II of central Veracruz (García Payón 1966: 195–199) and are probably contemporaneous with the late Ajalpan and early Santa Maria specimens of the Tehuacan Valley. Obviously, our Tehuacan type evolved in part from the earlier Coatepec Plain type. A few of the Ocos specular-red bowl sherds that do not have the red outlined by incising are quite similar (Coe 1961: fig. 18), although the pastes of the Tehuacan and Guatemala wares are different. Coatepec Red-on-buff is one of the dominant types of the Tierras Largas phase in the Valley of Oaxaca.

COATEPEC BUFF

2,701 specimens excavated, 19 collected.

Paste

This type is a transition from the earlier grit-tempered Coatepec wares to the more heavily mica-tempered Rio Salado wares. The paste contains about 18 percent nonplastic materials. Less than 2 percent is grains 0.5–1.0 mm. in diameter of quartz, quartzite, plagioclase, biotite, and rhyolite. About 10 percent consists of grains 0.1–0.5 mm. in diameter of the materials mentioned and pyroxenes, labradorite, trachyte, and volcanic glass. About 6 percent is grains under 0.1 mm. in diameter of quartz, labradorite, biotite, pyroxenes, magnetite, hematite, and plagioclase.

The paste has a sandy feeling. It is evenly knit but porous. The color of the surfaces is brown (5.0 YR 3/2 to 7/4), and the exterior is lighter than the interior. The hardness is about 3.0.

Surface Finish

The vessels were initially roughly smoothed. The fact that the interior is much darker than the exterior surface suggests that a thin wash of clay, almost a slip or float, was brushed over the outer surface when the pots were still wet. A few of the later tecomate forms have horizontal brushing on the exterior surface.

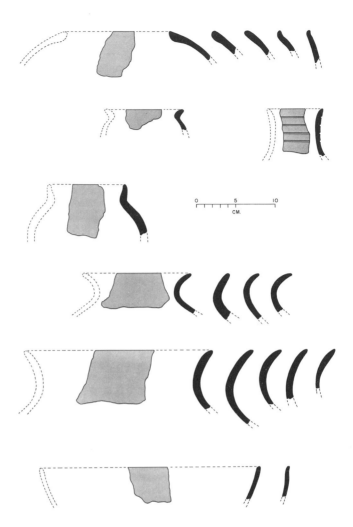

FIG. 25. COATEPEC BUFF. *From top to bottom,* plain and ellipsoidal tecomates, miniature olla, bottle, ollas with short and long flaring necks, and convex-wall bowls.

With one exception—a fragmentary bottle neck with a series of encircling grooves—decoration is absent.

Vessel Forms

Ollas with short flaring necks are the most common vessel shape. These and the other ollas described below may have had flat bottoms, according to a few basal fragments attached to rather globular body sherds. Rim diameter, 12–20 cm.

Ollas with long flaring necks are somewhat larger than the short-necked form. Rim diameter, 14–24 cm.

Angle-neck ollas are short-necked jars with straight outsloping to almost vertical rims joining the body abruptly. Rim diameter, 14–20 cm.

49

TABLE 21
Coatepec Buff Vessel Forms
(sherds by site and zone)

	Late Ajalpan										Early Santa Maria				
	204 F	204 F¹	204D supE	204D D	368e K³	204D C	204C pit	368e K²	368e K¹	368e J	368e I	368e H	368e G	368e F	368e E
Ollas															
short flaring neck					4	1		15	26	28	36	2	8	2	4
long flaring neck					2		3	11	10	11	19	4	5	12	3
angle neck					6			3	4		1			1	
Bowls															
convex wall					3			4	8	4	16	4	2	8	
flaring wall					1			2	2		4	2		2	
outsloping wall					4			1	3		2			2	
incurved rim							1	1			4	1			
Tecomates, plain									3	4	6	2		6	
Bottles										1					1
Body sherds	6	2	2	20	305	8	44	417	415	68	73	171	84	413	122
Total	6	2	2	20	325	9	48	454	471	116	161	186	99	446	130

	Early Santa Maria (continued)						Late Santa Maria								
	367 D²	367 D¹	367 C	368e D	368e C²	368e C¹	368e C	368e D-E	368e B	368w C	368w B	368e B¹	204 A-B	368-w B¹	Total
Ollas															
short flaring neck				1	3	1									131
long flaring neck				3	2	2									87
angle neck															15
Bowls															
convex wall				1		1									51
flaring wall															13
outsloping wall															12
incurved rim															7
Tecomates, plain				1		1									23
Bottles															2
Body sherds	2	6	2	13	5	12	12	20	45	27	31	3	9	23	2360
Total	2	6	2	19	10	17	12	20	45	27	31	3	9	23	2701

Convex-wall bowls were medium deep to deep vessels, perhaps with flat bottoms. Rim diameter, 24–28 cm.

Flaring-wall bowls and *outsloping-wall bowls* presumably were flat-bottomed vessels, but no rim-to-base sherds of these shapes were found.

Incurved-rim bowls were distinguished from tecomates on the basis of thinner walls.

Plain tecomates. Most of the plain, collarless teco-mates from Santa Maria levels are made of the Coatepec Buff paste.

Bottles. An early Santa Maria example has a slightly flaring neck decorated with four parallel encircling grooves. Rim diameter, 8 cm.

Relationships

Although Coatepec Buff seems to be transitional from the Ajalpan wares to the later mica-tempered

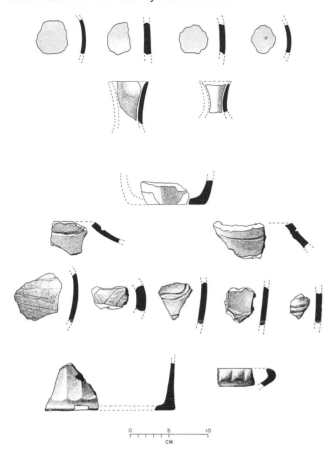

FIG. 26. SHERD DISKS AND ABERRANT SHERDS FROM THE AJALPAN PHASE. Row 1: disks; rows 2, 3: mottled (differentially fired) bottles; row 4: incised shoulder fragments; row 5: incised exterior wall or interior bottom sherds; row 6: grooved or gadrooned sherds from early Ajalpan components; the smaller two resemble Coton Grooved Red or coastal Chiapas; the flat-bottomed sherd resembles specimens recently recovered from the Ojochi phase of southern Veracruz.

types of the Santa Maria phase in the Tehuacan Valley, it is difficult to relate to types outside the valley.

Aberrant Wares

Among the sherds found in late Ajalpan levels that possess features not typical of wares made in the Tehuacan Valley are a few examples decorated with broad-line incising on a paste resembling Ajalpan Plain or Ajalpan Coarse. Two sherds are fragments of ollas with a line encircling the shoulder. Others represent vessel bottoms with incisions on the inner surface or body fragments with curvilinear incisions on the exterior.

Besides these probable trade sherds, a number of sherds show definite similarities to pottery of other regions.

One small polished brown sherd has hatching inside a zone outlined by incising. It is apparently of the same type as specimens from Trapiche I described by García Payón (1966: 55–61), which we shall call Trapiche Zoned Incised.

Fragments of polished pottery (black or orange) have rocker-dentate stamping inside zones outlined by broad incised lines. One of these represents a short, squat, cylindrical jar and looks like zoned rocker-dentate examples from Trapiche I (García Payón 1966: pl. XLV–17). A smaller, sandy-pasted sherd with longer dentate stampings resembles Ocos Buff (Coe 1961: fig. 47).

Three sherds are of hard paste and have deep curvilinear incisions outlining alternate specular-red-painted zones and unpainted polished zones. These specimens are very similar to variants of Victoria Coarse or Mapache Red-rimmed from the Ocos phase of Guatemala (Coe 1961: figs. 16–17; Coe and Flannery 1967: 26).

TABLE 22
Late Ajalpan Trade Sherds
(by site and zone)

	204 F	204D E	204 F[1]	204D D	368e K[3]	204C pit	368e K[2]	368e K[1]	368e J	Total
Tlatilco Mottled					1	1	16	8	6	32
Tilapa Red-on-white							1			1
Ponce Black			1				3		2	6
Mapache Red-rimmed	1		1		1					3
Trapiche Dentate-stamped	2	1	1	1		4				9
Trapiche Zoned Incised						1				1
Total	3	1	3	1	2	6	20	8	8	52

5 CM.

FIG. 27. LATE AJALPAN TRADE SHERDS. *Row 1:* Tilapa Red-on-white zoned rocker-stamped sherd and two Mapache Red-rimmed tecomate fragments; *row 2:* Trapiche Zoned Incised and Zoned Rocker-dentate-stamped sherds; *rows 3, 4:* Trapiche Zoned Rocker-dentate-stamped sherds, except center sherd in *row 3*, which is Ocos Buff.

Six polished black sherds had scattered white (limestone) specks in the paste. In cross section the sherds are black from surface to surface and thus must have been fired in a reducing atmosphere. One has a ridged surface. These are probably Ponce Black sherds from Panuco or some other region of Veracruz (MacNeish 1954: 570).

A dark gray sherd of gray sandy-tempered paste is like no other we uncovered. It is a fragment of a deep bowl with straight, outsloping sides. Just below the rim on the outside is an encircling shallow groove or incision, under which are a series of short, plain, horizontal rocker-stampings, filled with red paint. The character of the rocker-stamping and the sherd's other features are very like Tilapa Red-on-white of the Cuadros phase of Guatemala (Coe and Flannery 1967: fig. 18*h*), a type that also occurs in the Cotorra phase of Chiapas.

Fragments of bottles unlike other Ajalpan ceramics occurred in the lower levels of Ts 368e and the burial pit of Ts 204C. The bottles were made of white chalky paste with a polished surface. The white or yellowish surfaces are marked by black streaks or firing clouds that look like an attempt at negative painting. The black markings tend to radiate down the bodies from the necks. This same type of mottled bottle occurs in Trapiche I, Chicharras and early San Lorenzo in Veracruz, Tierras Largas and San Jose in Oaxaca, and early levels at Tlatilco.

Miscellaneous Objects

Worked sherds (24 specimens). Sherd disks 4–10 cm. in diameter were made from all the known Ajalpan pottery types. About two-thirds of the sample have unsmoothed edges, and the remainder have smoothed or ground edges. One with rough edges has a hole in it.

Animal effigies include a small dog, a deer head, a large hollow head, several body fragments, and an ocarina in the form of a dog.

Whistles. Two large hollow globular pieces are obviously from the bodies of whistles. One apparent whistle fragment is a human head wearing a "dunce cap" (Fig. 28, bottom row).

Pottery stamp. A piece of gray clay with deep grooves cut in it may have served as a stamp.

Skull. A human death's head was modeled with mouth askew and bulging globular eyes. The back had originally been applied to a flat surface.

Figurines

Types of figurines discovered in early Ajalpan levels and described in Chapter 3 continued to appear in late Ajalpan levels. These types include Spherical and Projecting-eye heads, Gingerbread bodies and limbs, Trackwoman bodies, and conical or cylindrical arms and large, crude, solid limbs. Other figurine types that occur in the last part of the Ajalpan phase but are described with early Santa Maria types in Chapter 5 are Venus and Seated Mother bodies, various kinds of arms, and one foot.

Hollow Dwarf Figures

74 specimens; 1 complete figure, 25 head fragments, 26
  body fragments, 14 arm fragments, 8 leg fragments.
Dimensions in cm.: Whole figure, height, 50.0; width at
  shoulder, 22.0; width at waist, 9.0. 3 heads, height, 7.8,
  13.0, 16.4; length, 4.0, 6.0, 9.1; width, 6.8, 10.6, 13.8.
  Length of body fragments, 15.0–25.0; of arm fragments,
  5.0–8.0; of leg fragments, 8.0–15.0.
Paste: resembles Ajalpan Plain or Ajalpan Coarse Red.
Surface finish: thin clay wash, some areas covered with
  specular red paint.

These large, hollow figures (as represented by one
almost complete specimen from the burial pit of Ts
204C and many small fragments) have large heads,
elongated torsos, and truncated, stubby limbs. Tiny
breasts indicate that they are feminine. They might
well represent achondroplastic dwarfs. Although the
heads are unnaturally flat in back, the facial features
are realistically formed. There is a resemblance to ancient Egyptian figures in the combination of large, almond-shaped, black-outlined eyes and a high headdress or hair style that is wide at the top.

Five specimens with the lower face intact have
well-defined chins, heavy lips, and a wide mouth indicated by a narrow horizontal slit, which in three specimens is cut through to the hollow interior. The three
intact noses are long and narrow with upturned tips
and conical punctures for nostrils. Four specimens
have eyes still intact; these features are almond-shaped
and slant slightly toward the center of the face. They
are outlined by narrow ridges for lids. On two of the
specimens, both the eyelids and the eyes themselves
are painted black, perhaps with asphalt ("chapopote")
paint. The eyes were shaped by a flat, pointed object
that was pushed downward toward the outer and inner corners, leaving a raised portion in the center that
was pierced by a large conical punch. The punches go
through to the interior of two specimens. The eyebrows are slightly raised, and on three specimens are
painted black.

Three heads have ears intact; these are elongated
ellipsoidal projections. The upper or lower portions,
or both, are pierced, and one head fragment wears a
"napkin-ring" earplug. The complete figure has a naturalistic, projecting ear with a variation of the scroll-
like incision seen on the Projecting-eye head described
above in Chapter 3. The incision is "S"-shaped on the
left ear and a reverse "S" on the right. Each ear has
two holes punched one above the other in the curves
of the "S."

The figures wear high, backward slanting head-

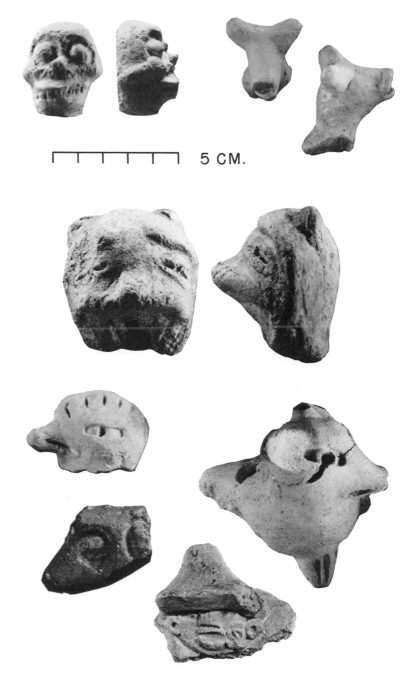

FIG. 28. MISCELLANEOUS OBJECTS. *From top to bottom,*
human skull, deer, hollow dog, bird, dog ocarina, seal or
stamp, and head from an effigy pot or whistle.

dresses (or hair styles) that are wide across the top.
These are uniformly depicted in the earlier examples
but vary on some of the later heads. The earlier headdresses, represented by nine fragments and the complete figure, are depicted by wide lines incised low

53

Fig. 29. Hollow Dwarf figurine (two views).

across the forehead, along the temples, over the ears, and down and across the back of the neck. Each head-piece has a wide vertical band running from center front to mid-back. Two outlined crescentic portions sweep back from the temples and down behind the ears. Two circles or ovals, also outlined by incision, are placed at the top on either side of the medial band. The band, the crescents, and the circular sections are painted black, except for a late fragment with deep crosshatching in place of paint. Another late fragment has a disk of clay on one side instead of an incised circle and a braid-like applique instead of the medial band. Two other late specimens have plainer headdresses. One has a series of parallel incised lines radiating from the forehead, and the other has "snowshoe" rocker-stamping covering the back of the head, which may have been fired black.

All torso and leg fragments seem to represent standing figures with legs slightly apart, like the stance of the complete specimen. The figures have extremely wide shoulders, long narrow-waisted torsos, round holes for navels, and small protruding buttocks. Short vestigial arms extend downward from the exaggerated shoulders. The legs are also disproportionately short, with bulbous thighs. Toes and fingers are indicated on small hands and feet by short, incised lines. It is interesting to note that the right hand of the complete figure has six incisions and the other limbs have five. All bodies are painted red and apparently were unclothed.

The complete figure has sets of holes about half a centimeter in diameter in the front and back of the headdress, behind the ears, and under the arms, probably so that the figure could be manipulated by strings.

Hollow Dwarf figurines are represented by only one fragment in very early Ajalpan components, but they extend through the rest of the Ajalpan phase and into early Santa Maria times. One ear portion of a large hollow figurine from a San Lorenzo level of Squier's Test C at La Venta has an identical incised pattern depicting the fold of the ear. There is little doubt that the Ajalpan and Pre–La Venta figurines are related. Similar figurines have also been uncovered in the Barra phase of Chiapas, in San Jose Mogote, Oaxaca, and in Trapiche I of central Veracruz (García Payón 1966: pl. LXIV–12).

The Ajalpan figurines have some characteristics in common with stylistically different specimens from Tlatilco and with other Olmec manifestations. In terms of our dating, the Ajalpan Hollow Dwarfs may well be contemporaneous.

FIG. 30. HOLLOW DWARF HEAD FRAGMENTS.

No Face Heads

10 specimens excavated.

Dimensions in cm.: height (7 heads), 2.9–5.0, average 3.8; length (8 heads), 1.7–2.0, average 1.8; width at ears (7 heads), 3.1–4.0, average, 3.5.

Paste: resembles Coatepec Plain.

These small heads were modeled from flat rectangular pieces of clay, one end of which was pinched up to form a headdress. Two small ellipsoidal lumps of clay were applied to represent ears. A portion of clay was pinched up on one surface to form a narrow pointed nose. No other facial features are indicated. Five examples have a wide strip of clay wrapped around the top of the head. Three examples have two large holes punched through the flattened top of the head, and one example has three smaller holes at the top.

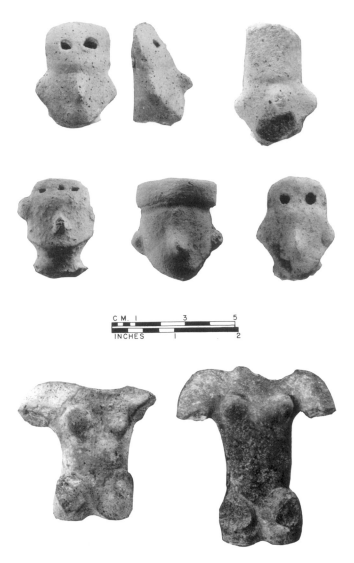

FIG. 31. NO FACE HEADS; SEATED TRACKWOMAN BODIES.

Four heads show faint traces of red paint, and one seems to have been painted yellow. The paint seems to have been applied mainly to the back of the head and neck (and perhaps the body).

The neck is usually at an acute angle to the head, suggesting, perhaps, that this type of head goes with the seated Trackwoman type of body shown in Fig. 31.

No Face heads were found mainly in late Ajalpan levels, although a few survive into the early Santa Maria phase. The type has not been recorded in other regions.

LEG FRAGMENTS

Long cylindrical legs (5 specimens excavated). Di-

mensions in cm.: diameter, 1.5–2.0; length, 6.0–8.0. Paste: ranges from Ajalpan Coarse to Coatepec Plain. These long cylindrical fragments are obviously legs that were attached to seated figurines, perhaps the Trackwoman type. One has marked toes. No hips, knees, or calf areas are indicated, nor were seat portions found attached to legs like these.

The legs occur mainly in the last part of the Ajalpan phase and are too general and fragmentary to use for comparative purposes.

Squat "booted" legs (16 specimens: 14 excavated, 2 collected). Dimensions in cm.: length, 3.5–6.5; diameter at hip, 2.0–3.0. Paste: resembles Coatepec Plain. These short, slightly bent legs have thick thighs (Fig. 19, upper right). The knee is indicated by a slight bend in the clay. The calf is slightly tapering, and the ankle is well rounded and set off by a groove. The foot looks almost as though it has a short boot on it. It is hard to know whether the legs were attached to the seated Trackwoman type or the Seated Mother type, but they look as though they should be attached to a seated figure.

These legs occur in late Ajalpan and early Santa Maria levels in the Tehuacan Valley. They are not specifically like any other types reported from Mesoamerica.

Ceramic Affiliations

Unlike the early part of the Ajalpan phase, late Ajalpan offers good evidence of extraterritorial cultural connections. This is rather surprising, since most of the resident pottery types characteristic of the late Ajalpan phase either began in early Ajalpan or were derived from early Ajalpan wares. A few innovations did occur, such as the Coatepec Buff and Coatepec Red-on-buff wares, the No Face heads, and new figurine body and limb types, but the main differences between early and late Ajalpan really lie in the percentage decreases or increases in the basic pottery and figurine types and in shifts in popularity of various vessel forms.

The most obvious and reliable means of establishing cultural relationships between Tehuacan's late Ajalpan materials and assemblages of artifacts from other regions is on the basis of trade—that is, on the appearance of pottery types made in other regions in late Ajalpan components, and conversely, on the presence of Ajalpan wares in sites beyond the Tehuacan region. The rocker-dentate sherds, Ajalpan Fine Red, Coatepec Plain, and Coatepec Red-on-buff bowls that occur in late Ajalpan are also common to Trapiche I of the central Veracruz coast. Mapache Red-rimmed tecomates and Tlatilco mottled bottles also occur as foreign or trade sherds in both areas. Supporting this connection in late Ajalpan are four trade sherds of Ponce Black ware from Trapiche or the Panuco-Tampico area and sherds of Trapiche zoned rocker-dentate and zoned crosshatched wares. Also common to all three manifestations—late Ajalpan, Trapiche I, and Ponce of Panuco—is the Projecting-eye figurine type. Finally, connection among the Ponce, Trapiche I, and San Lorenzo phases is indicated by the presence in all three of the hub-and-spoke variant of Progreso White of Panuco.

On a more general level, the occurrence of bowls with externally thickened rims and of large hollow figurines in Trapiche I and late Ajalpan hint of other connections. Thus, there is concrete evidence of cultural interchange to the east and north along the Gulf Coast among late Ajalpan, Trapiche I, and Ponce.

Evidence of cultural relationships to the south lies in the presence of trade sherds of Mapache Red-rimmed and Ocos Buff from the Pacific coast of Guatemala or Chiapas in late Ajalpan, San Lorenzo of southern Veracruz, San Jose of Oaxaca, and late Cotorra of Chiapas. Tilapa Red-on-white rocker-stamped sherds from the Cuadros phase of Guatemala occur in Cotorra, San Jose, and Ajalpan. Sherds similar to Ponce Black are also common to all three areas.

Ajalpan Fine Red, rocker-stamped Ocos Buff, white bottles with mottled fire-cloud patterns, Trapiche zoned and unzoned rocker dentate, and Hollow Dwarf figurines suggest connections between late Ajalpan and the Olmec area during the San Lorenzo phase (Coe 1967). Hints of connections between late Ajalpan and San Lorenzo are indicated by the presence of hollow figurines; the predominance of plain tecomates, often with zoned brushing; Ponce Black sherds; bowls with externally thickened rims; and bowls with a white wash and an interior sunburst design.

Other than such overlapping types of trade wares as Ocos Buff, Mapache Red-rimmed, Tilapa Red-on-white, wide plain rocker-stamping, and sherds similar to Ponce Black, evidence of connections between late Ajalpan and Chiapa de Corzo I is not extensive. It is only in the more nebulous horizon styles that one discerns further connection between the two areas.

Moreover, the predominance of tecomates and the existence of flat-bottomed bowls with flaring walls, convex-wall bowls, figurines with pin-hole eyes or mouths, zoned brushing, shallow grooving around the rims of tecomates, rocker-stamping, and specular-red bands around the rims of convex-wall bowls or tecomates, all hint of links between late Ajalpan, Chiapa de Corzo I, and Ocos in Guatemala, as does the presence in all three of bowls made of stone. Coe (1961) has indicated still other evidence for linking Ocos with Chiapa de Corzo I: for instance, flat-bottomed dishes with thickened specular-red rims, zoned rocker-stamping, oval lobes on tecomates, and bowls with incised thickened rims.

Other traits such as cylindrical punctates link Pavon of Panuco and Chiapa I, while outsloping-wall bowls made of white paste connect Pre–La Venta, Chiapa I, Pavon, and Ponce. Hub-and-spoke decoration on flat-bottomed bowls may link Ponce, Pre–La Venta, and Trapiche I.

Finally, late Ajalpan is linked to Tolstoy's new Ayotla and Justo phases in the Valley of Mexico, as well as to early Tlatilco, by Ponce Black, hub-and-spoke grater bowls, red-rimmed tecomates, wide plain rocker stamping, dentate stamping, large hollow dwarf figurines, and Tlatilco mottled bottles.

CHAPTER 5

The Early Part of the Santa Maria Phase

EARLY SANTA MARIA materials were uncovered in Zones I–D, C², and C¹ of the east end of the Coatepec site (Ts 368e) and in Zones I and H of Purron Cave (Tc 272). Supplementing the remains from these stratigraphic levels, were materials from the relatively "pure" components, Zones D², D¹, and C of the Canoas site (Ts 367).

There is some overlapping of artifact types from Ajalpan to Santa Maria, including the Coatepec Red, Coatepec Buff, and Coatepec Red-on-buff wares; fine blades with pointed striking platforms; Zacatenco and Salado projectile points; ovoid, lipped oblong, saucer-shaped, and basin-shaped metates; long manos; bell-shaped pestles; spherical beads; and paint palettes. There are also a host of new traits appearing in the Santa Maria components to distinguish this phase from Ajalpan. Among the nonceramic innovations are Matamoros points, fine snapped blades, flat-iron pestles, cylindrical manos, and plain-weave cotton cloth. The new ceramic traits are Canoas White, Canoas Heavy Plain, Canoas Orange-brown, Rio Salado Coarse, Rio Salado Gray, Coatepec White, Coatepec White-rimmed Black, Quachilco Brown, Quachilco Gray, and Quachilco Mica. The Coatepec and Quachilco wares first appear in early Santa Maria components but are more popular in late Santa Maria levels. They will be described in Chapter 6.

Among the architectural features characteristic of early Santa Maria are villages with pyramids, sometimes built around plazas, and the first structures built for purposes of irrigation. The subsistence by this period is firmly based on agriculture, with about 60 percent of the food derived from farming.

The sample of over 41,000 identifiable sherds from

the thirteen excavated components of the early Santa Maria subphase is unusually large. Analysis was initially restricted to the representative sample of about 12,000 sherds from the early Santa Maria zones of Las Canoas (Ts 367), but eventually included the remaining sherds from the other early Santa Maria components. Most of the early Santa Maria pottery suffers from what Coe, describing the pottery of La Victoria (1961: 47), has called "the family effect": an effort, through "varying firing conditions on a few varieties of slips, to manufacture several kinds of ceramics with the minimum of cost or effort." The result is that the lines of demarcation between related types are sometimes hard to draw. The family effect is strong at Las Canoas, in Chiapa de Corzo II, in the Conchas phase at La Victoria, and probably at most Middle Formative sites in Mesoamerica. Most authors dealing with pottery of this period note two or three "wares" made on the same paste (Vaillant 1930, Drucker 1952).

If such a blending of distinguishing features hindered the Canoas pottery analysis, the task was considerably lightened in turn by the great similarity of Canoas ceramics to those of contemporary Middle Formative sites. Such striking resemblances were noted with wares of Chiapa de Corzo II, Conchas 2, and La Venta that much of the early Santa Maria terminology relating to shape has been borrowed directly from reports on those sites. Subsequently, ties to Oaxaca have appeared in the new Guadalupe phase. Ties with the Panuco area (Ponce and Aguilar phases), Trapiche II, El Arbolillo, early Zacatenco, and Tlatilco from the Valley of Mexico are also strong. These relationships are discussed below and documented in detail in the pottery type descriptions themselves.

58

Basically, the locally made pottery can be separated into two groups on the basis of tempering materials. One group of types is tempered with carefully selected quartz or quartzite sand containing crystals of amphiboles and pyroxenes; the other is tempered with quartzite sand and mica. Sherds of the former group have surfaces characteristically flecked by tiny elongate crystals visible to the unaided eye. The wares of this "amphibole-pyroxene" group are Canoas White and the subtype White-rimmed Orange, Canoas Orange-brown, and Canoas Heavy Plain. Sherds of the mica group—whether Rio Salado Gray or Rio Salado Coarse—in some cases appear to have a fairly carefully selected temper with a small range of reasonably fine particles, while in other cases the nonplastic material is almost certainly unselected mica-bearing quartzite sand. None of the amphibole-pyroxene wares appear to have such coarse or unselected tempers.

The distribution of the Canoas types versus the Rio Salado types has interesting implications for the temporal and spatial significance of Middle Formative ceramics in the Tehuacan Valley—implications that become still clearer when one takes into consideration the vessel shapes and decoration within each type. It is the Rio Salado mica-tempered wares which continue through two or more cultural phases in Tehuacan prehistory and constitute local traditions; the wares of the Canoas amphibole-pyroxene group, restricted to the Santa Maria phase only, are the ones which resemble wares in other regions of Mesoamerica. Through the amphibole-pyroxene group flow the style currents which characterize the Middle Formative in its widest inter-regional aspects.

We thus have two ceramic axes for the early Santa Maria phase: one vertically distributed through time along the banks of the Rio Salado, the other horizontally distributed from the Huasteca to the Pacific coast of Guatemala.

Of the amphibole-pyroxene-tempered pottery types, the one with the most far-reaching relationships is Canoas White, and it is on this ware that the bulk of our interareal correlations can be made. Canoas White makes up about 15 percent of the early Santa Maria sherds. The principal shape in which it appears is a flat-bottomed dish with flaring sides, decorated with incised interrupted parallel lines in a style Coe has called "the double-line break" (1961: 61). White-washed incised dishes of precisely this shape and decoration link the Conchas phase of the Pacific coast of Guatemala; Chiapa de Corzo II in the Grijalva Basin of Chiapas; the Guadalupe phase of Oaxaca; Aguilar in the Panuco region of Veracruz; Trapiche II in cen-

tral Veracruz; the sites of La Venta in Tabasco and Tlatilco, El Arbolillo, and early Tecaxic-Calixtlahuaca in the central highlands of Mexico; the middle levels of Puerto Marquez in Guerrero; and a number of contemporary settlements. Other forms of Canoas White which have wide distribution are "pseudo-grater" bowls with incised interior bottoms, ollas with slightly outsloping necks, double-line incisions on convex-wall bowls, and dishes with widely spaced tabs on the rim.

Early Santa Maria pottery, like that of La Venta, is monochrome with decoration usually restricted to incising and polishing. Only a few fragments of handles appeared; there are no supports, no spouts, no lugs, no flanges, and only a few examples of wide everted rims. The composite silhouette is rare and such modes as dimple bases and fluting are almost absent. Tecomates and flaring-neck ollas last into Santa Maria times but are little changed from Early Formative examples. Altogether the pottery so closely resembles wares of La Venta, Guadalupe, Conchas 1 and Chiapa de Corzo II–III that its placement in the period between 900 and 400 B.C. is hard to dispute.

Earlier types, described in preceding chapters, continue to appear in early Santa Maria components. These include Purron Plain, Ajalpan Coarse, Ajalpan Plain, Ajalpan Fine Red, Ajalpan Fine Plain, Ajalpan Coarse Red, Coatepec Plain, Coatepec Red-on-buff, and Coatepec Buff. Types appearing in small numbers in early Santa Maria components and becoming diagnostic of the later part of the phase include Coatepec White, Coatepec White-rimmed Black, and Quachilco Gray. These are described in Chapter 6.

Amphibole-Pyroxene Group

CANOAS WHITE

6,706 specimens excavated, 46 collected.

This pottery type is the hallmark of the Middle Formative in the Tehuacan basin and central Oaxaca. Its general color range, temper, vessel shape and size, and systems of decoration make it the Tehuacan equivalent of several other Middle Formative wares, among them the white wares from Trapiche II (García Payón 1966), La Venta Coarse Buff (Drucker 1952: 81) Conchas White-to-buff at La Victoria (Coe 1961: 64), the Grijalva Valley wares, Guerrero Cream (Sanders 1961: 18), Chiapa de Corzo II White Monochrome (Dixon 1959: 23), and Mirador II Smudged White (Peterson 1962). In form and decoration Canoas White has more distant relations with Progreso White from the Panuco region (MacNeish 1954: 569) and some of the white wares from Tlatilco (Piña Chan

1958) and El Arbolillo (Tolstoy and Guenette 1965).

The term "white" was selected after much soul-searching, for many sherds could as accurately be called "cream" or "buff." Similar problems existed in the case of the related pottery types listed above; Coe named his ware "White-to-buff," and Drucker explains that "Coarse Buff" at La Venta varied from ivory yellow to vinaceous buff. Canoas White varies from yellow-white to gray-white, and like its aforementioned relatives, was probably a purer and more attractive monochrome white before its 2500- to 3000-year deterioration in the ground.

Paste

Thin-section and mineralogical analysis were made on five sherds from five different locations. Only two sherds had grains 0.5–1.0 mm. in diameter, probably representing about 4 percent of the paste. Only granite was common to both sherds, although basalt, andesite, gneiss, limestone, quartzite, and plagioclase occur in one or the other. All five sherds had as 10 or 11 percent of their total matter grains 0.1–0.5 mm. in diameter. Occurring in four of the samples were grains of andesite, basalt, labradorite, andesine, and amphibole; pyroxenes and limestone occurred in three samples; in one or two samples were quartz, biotite, augite, hematite, and oligoclase. Grains less than 0.1 mm. in diameter compose 3 to 5 percent of the sherds. All five examples had grains of hematite, magnetite, amphibole, and pyroxenes; a lesser number had quartz, calcite, biotite, plagioclase, andesine, and labradorite. Thus, the sherds are composed of about 20 percent nonplastic materials that most commonly range between 0.1 and 0.5 mm. in diameter and usually include amphibole, pyroxenes, andesine, and hematite.

The characteristic appearance of the paste in cross section is that of a gray core sandwiched between orange or pink layers. Firing, however, is variable enough so that some sherds are pink clear through or gray clear through, and different sections of the same vessel may exhibit these variations. The gray core may vary from a brownish gray (5.0 YR 4/1) to dark gray (2.5 YR 1/3). The layers sandwiching or sometimes replacing it run from salmon (2.5 YR 6/6) to yellowish pink (5.0 YR 6/4).

The paste is quite hard (Mohs scale: 3.0–3.5) with a rough and irregular texture.

Surface Finish

This ware is finished with a soft- to medium-hard coating of clay, which in some cases is no more than a wash, but reaches the thickness of a true slip on oth-

er specimens. Its color is determined by a number of variables, but normally runs from a yellowish-white (2.5 Y 8/2) to light gray-white (10 YR 7/1). The yellower sherds frequently exhibit the "rust-colored streaks" described by Coe (1961: 64) as perhaps intentional on some examples of Conchas White-to-buff. As a rule, it is the yellower examples of Canoas White which seem to have the thicker surface coating.

Sanders (1961: 19), in his description of Burrero Cream, notes a tendency for slip color to vary with the color of the paste over which it is laid; the same is true of Canoas White. A thin wash over the sherds whose paste is fired gray clear through appears gray-white almost exclusively, while that resting above pinkish-fired paste is invariably cream or yellow-white. Thus, both colors can exist on the same vessel, and the situation is further complicated by an occasional gray firing cloud. Normally the slip or wash covers the whole vessel, but it may be extremely thin or even absent or simply worn away on the underside of the base. Frequently the inside of a dish shows extensive destruction of the wash through scrubbing, and in these cases the streaky appearance suggests that washing may have been done with a handful of fiber.

The texture of the surface is smooth to silky and in about 80 percent of all sherds has a matte appearance. The remaining sherds are from vessels polished on either one or both sides. In no case was an extremely high polish noted.

Decoration

The most common surface decoration applied to this

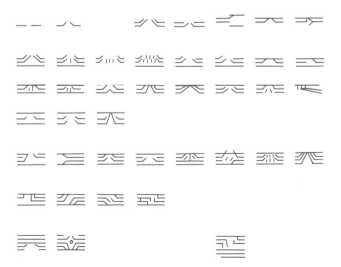

FIG. 32. CANOAS WHITE. Decoration motifs.

ware is the incising of parallel lines after the paste had dried but before the vessel was fired. The lines cut through the wash or slip and expose the color of the paste below. Frequently, two, three, four, or even five parallel lines encircle the vessel just below the rim, either internally or externally. Also, one or two lines may be incised around the outer wall just above the base. The encircling lines are usually interrupted at intervals, with one or more of the lines turning up or down to meet the others or separating to expose small areas of stab marks. This is precisely the decorative effect which Coe (1961: 61), in describing the double-parallel-line variants on Conchas White-to-buff vessels, christened "double-line break." For Las Canoas (and also La Venta), this terminology will have to be expanded to include triple- and quadruple-line breaks. Identical parallel-line-break motifs occur in the

Grijalva Basin of Chiapas, the Gulf Coast, the Guatemalan highlands, coastal Guerrero, the Valley of Mexico, Oaxaca, and the Maya lowlands in the Middle Formative, and will be discussed below. At most of these sites, the association of these motifs with flat-based, white monochrome bowls and dishes gives every indication of constituting a horizon marker.

Large fragments of one flat-bottomed, flaring-rim bowl exhibit on the outer wall an elaborate design combining broken quadruple parallel lines, incised circles, and wide excised or "raspada" areas. These elements form borders of quadruple-line-break motifs around a continuous frieze of upside-down and right-side-up "faces" consisting of large circles for eyes, an inverted "V" for a nose, a wide raspada band for a mouth, and in some instances two pairs of triple- or quadruple-line curves for a goatee (see Fig. 33). The

TABLE 23
Canoas White Decorated Sherds
(by site and zone)

	Early Santa Maria										
	368e I	368e H	308e G	368e F	368e E	367 D²	367 D¹	367 C	368e D	272 I	368e C²
Incised motifs											
1 line around rims of											
flaring/outsloping-wall bowls, ext.			1		1			2			
2 lines around rims of											
flaring/outsloping-wall bowls, ext.			2			2	4	6			
flaring/outsloping-wall bowls, int.	2	1	3	8	9	13	33	37	2		1
everted-rim bowls, int.			1				1	1			
incurved-rim bowls, ext.									2		
2-4 lines around rims of											
convex-wall bowls, ext.			3	15		1	9	14	7	1	15
cylindrical, direct-rim jars, ext.						1	9	11			
cylindrical, collared-rim jars, ext.							6	5			
composite-silhouette bowls, int.							7	7	1		
short-neck ollas, ext.						2	4				
collared tecomates, ext.							4	4			
3 lines around rims of											
flaring/outsloping-wall bowls, ext.			1		2	5	21	31			
flaring/outsloping-wall bowls, int.	1			21	15	39	129	181	4		6
4 lines around rims of											
flaring/outsloping-wall bowls, ext.				3	2	13	18	17			
flaring/outsloping-wall bowls, int.				6	11	17	48	36	1		1
5 lines around rims of											
flaring/outsloping-wall bowls, ext.				6		2	4	4			
hatching on rims of											
flaring/outsloping-wall bowls, ext.							1	2			
other motifs on flaring-wall bowls, ext.				1	1	6	14	20			
sunburst motif on bottom, int.			4	8	1	4	28	22			
Raspada designs on exterior walls	1	10	10					2			1
Total	4	11	25	68	42	105	340	402	17	1	24

(Table continued)

(Table 23 continued)

	Early Santa Maria (cont'd)		Late Santa Maria							
	368e C¹	272 H	368w D-E	368e B	368w B	218-11 G	218-11 F	368w B¹	218-10 C²	Total
Incised motifs										
1 line around rims of										
flaring/outsloping-wall bowls, ext.										4
2 lines around rims of										
flaring/outsloping-wall bowls, ext.										14
flaring/outsloping-wall bowls, int.										109
everted-rim bowls, int.										3
incurved-rim bowls, ext.										2
2-4 lines around rims of										
convex-wall bowls, ext.	5	1	23	8	2	1	3	2	2	112
cylindrical, direct-rim jars, ext.										21
cylindrical, collared-rim jars, ext.										11
composite-silhouette bowls, int.										15
short-neck ollas, ext.										6
collared tecomates, ext.										8
3 lines around rims of										
flaring/outsloping-wall bowls, ext.										60
flaring/outsloping-wall bowls, int.	7									403
4 lines around rims of										
flaring/outsloping-wall bowls, ext.										53
flaring/outsloping-wall bowls, int.										120
5 lines around rims of										
flaring/outsloping-wall bowls, ext.										16
hatching on rims of										
flaring/outsloping-wall bowls, ext.										3
other motifs on flaring-wall bowls, ext.										42
sunburst motif on bottom, int.										67
Raspada designs on exterior walls										24
Total	12	1	23	8	2	1	3	2	2	1,093

aspect of the faces is glyphic, and the design is obviously Olmecoid. The same motif appears at the rim of a Conchas Red-on-buff bowl from La Victoria, Guatemala (Coe 1961: fig. 33*j*).

Another motif apparently of Olmec derivation (see Coe 1965: fig. 43*g*) incised on a Canoas White sherd is a cross formed by four curving lines with a circle in the middle. This design is similar to an incised pattern on a wall sherd from La Victoria (Coe 1961: fig. 25*d*, upper left), which has four smaller circles in the outer corners formed by the cross.

An unusual sherd, apparently from the body of a Canoas White olla, displays an incised design resembling a loosely tied square knot. The incised knot is flanked by wide lines cutting through to the paste. So far as we know, no similar design has been reported from other Middle Formative sites in Mesoamerica.

Pseudo-grater bases occur in Canoas White ware. These are flat bowl or dish bases, incised inside with sunburst designs. They resemble specimens from Panuco (MacNeish 1954: fig. 12), La Victoria (Coe 1961) El Trapiche (García Payón 1966: pl. XLIX), La Venta (Drucker 1952: fig. 33), Tlatilco (Piña Chan 1958: figs. 10*p* and 34), and El Arbolillo (Vaillant 1935: fig. 19, no. 5). It is interesting that the Las Canoas specimens, like those from Panuco (MacNeish 1954: 569), are too shallowly incised to have served as true "grater" bowls or *molcajetes* but are strictly ornamental. Those from La Victoria, on the other hand, were clearly functional graters (Coe 1961: 68).

Still another type of decoration observed on Canoas White is "smothering," the purposeful production of

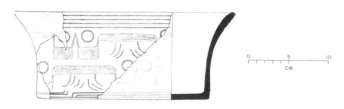

FIG. 33. CANOAS WHITE. Bowl with Olmec motif.

unoxidized gray or black surfaces, often combined with or imitated by smudging with carbon. We found, as did Dixon in studying some of his Chiapa II White Monochromes (Dixon 1959: 7), that one or both surfaces of some sherds might have "a medium to dark gray or even a deep black" color. Deep bowls in particular appear to have been fired in an inverted position which maintained a reducing atmosphere inside the vessel while allowing the exterior to assume its normal oxidized dull-white color. Such firing tricks were almost never attempted with open dishes, or some of the other wide-mouthed shapes. Tecomates were invariably smothered or smudged in this manner, although it often appeared that the effect had been produced by rubbing charcoal over the sun-dried white slip before firing. Because intentional smudging seemed to be more closely associated with the interior of deep bowl or jar shapes than with other forms, it may even represent a subtype of Canoas White. We are here regarding it, however, as simply one of the more common decorative techniques within the ware, accounting for about 25 percent of the decorated sherds. It is interesting to note that a peculiarly shaped body fragment of smudged Canoas White has a tiny triangular attachment in its polished white side which may be interpreted as an *incensario* horn.

Intentional smothering or smudging recalls Warren's comment (1961: 77) that during the contemporary Dili (Chiapa de Corzo II) period, inexpert tries at producing white-rimmed black ware were being made in the Grijalva Valley. A few such attempts are represented among smudged examples of Canoas White, but all resulted in a "unifacial" white-rimmed effect rather than true white-rimmed black ware.

Twenty-five sherds of Canoas White, many the smudged variety, show traces of once-heavy coatings of red powder (possibly cinnabar). This pigment was rubbed into the decorative incisions. In at least one case the red powder may even have been ground or stored in a Canoas White bowl.

Vessel Forms

Flat-bottomed bowls or dishes with flaring or outsloping walls total nearly 1,200 examples. The range of variation within this category is impressive and forms a continuum which does not lend itself to division at any point. The point between "bowl" and "dish" is particularly hard to draw. Extremes of the continuum, however, run from true bowls with the sides inclined outward at an angle of 100° (measured from the plane of the base) to true dishes with sides curving outward at 140°. The majority of these vessels have sides that

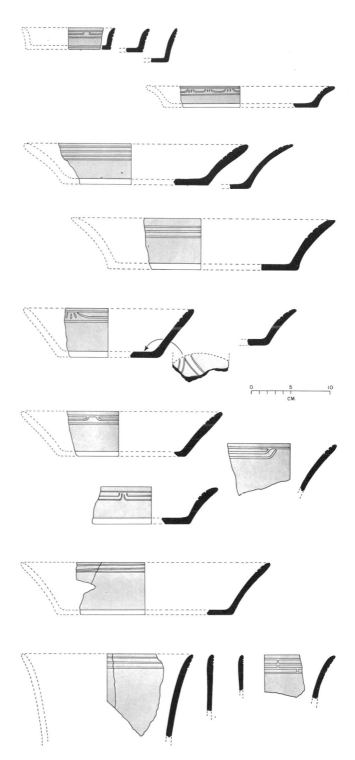

FIG. 34. CANOAS WHITE. Flaring-wall dishes and bowls.

flare or slope outward between 125° and 130°. Vessels of this kind range from 4–9 cm. high, have a base diameter of 10–30 cm., and a rim diameter of 14–42 cm. Wall thickness ranges from 0.5 to 1.1 cm. The most common vessels have rim diameters of 23–30 cm. One small-scale model, decorated with external parallel-line incising, from Ts 367, Zone D, has a smear of red paint on the interior.

According to Drucker (1952: 110) flat-bottomed dishes with flaring walls were "one of the most frequent" shapes in all wares at La Venta, just as they are in early Santa Maria at Tehuacan. Fig. 38a of his report is indistinguishable from Canoas White flaring-wall specimens and probably lies near the middle of the continuum for this shape at La Venta. At the latter site, Drucker noted an "unbroken range of diameters," similar to ours, from vessels so low and wide they "might be considered trays" to others which were narrower and taller; wall angles varied from 110° to 130° (*ibid.*, 109).

At both La Venta and Tehuacan, these vessels are incised with parallel lines in double- and triple-line-break motifs. Rim forms at both sites are direct or occasionally beveled. One example of the wide everted rim occurred at Las Canoas, a mode which is also rare at La Venta. Rim tabs, or widely spaced scallops, occur on dishes at both La Venta and Las Canoas.

Statistics on the parallel-line incising give a rough idea of which wall-inclination angles were most common. According to the sixty-three rim sherds from Canoas which preserved a part of the base also, the incising generally appears on the outside of vessels whose walls flare at an angle of less than 120°; examples whose walls flare in the range of 120°–140° are incised on the inside. Of the incised direct rims observed, less than a fifth were externally incised. These were probably from vessels with walls in the 100°–120° spread; the remaining vessels, with internal incisions, very likely had more widely flaring walls. Drucker (*ibid.*, 110) also found at La Venta that "on pieces in which sides and rim curve outward, the lines are usually on the interior of the rim; on straight-sided pieces, about the exterior."

Comparative material from other Middle Formative sites is abundant. This type of vessel in white monochrome, complete with incised double-line-break designs, is one of "the markers of the Conchas phase" at La Victoria, Guatemala (Coe 1961: 66). Other examples are found at El Trapiche and in late San Jose and Guadalupe of Oaxaca. It is common in white monochrome in Chiapa de Corzo II, where Dixon divided the continuum into its taller versus its shallower variants (Dixon 1959: figs. 23a, 28b-i). At Las Canoas, rims of these flat-based dishes and bowls represent 88 percent of all Canoas White rim sherds.

Of the bases of this type of vessel from Las Canoas,

18 percent display the pseudo-*molcajete* hub-and-spoke or sunburst incising mentioned as typical of La Venta, La Victoria, Tlatilco, El Arbolillo, and Aguilar-Ponce in the Panuco area.

Convex-wall, flat-bottomed bowls are much less common than the preceding shape. The continuum of this shape lends itself to division more readily than does that of the flaring-to-outsloping-wall bowls or dishes. All these vessels, whether shallow, medium deep, or deep, have a rounded transition from convex wall to flat base, rather than a sharp break. Shallower specimens are internally incised with multiple-line-break motifs. The deeper bowls have parallel-line incising on the outside and are often internally "smothered" or smudged with gray.

The deep convex-wall bowls are similar to those shown by Coe from La Victoria in Conchas White-to-buff (1961: fig. 27c). Convex-wall, medium-height bowls appear at La Venta (Drucker 1952: fig. 38d). One of the Canoas specimens has the externally incised design resembling a circle in a cross which we described above. Bowls of similar shape occur also at Zacatenco (Vaillant 1930: pl. IVc). Shallow convex-wall bowls with thickened rims are illustrated by Dixon (1959: fig. 29) in Chiapa de Corzo II White Monochrome, and Coe (1961: fig. 29f) shows examples with a somewhat different thickened rim in Ocos Black ware.

Dimensions in cm. of shallow bowls: rim diameter, 18–23; height, 5–7; base diameter, 60 percent of rim diameter; wall thickness, 0.7–1.0. Medium-height bowls: rim diameter, 20–24; height, 8–12; base diameter, 50–70 percent of rim diameter; wall thickness, 0.5–1.0. Deep bowls: rim diameter, 22–28, but one stray reaching 38; height, 16–20, average, 18; base diameter, 30 percent of rim diameter; wall thickness, 0.5–1.0.

Convex-wall bowls with externally thickened rims. The majority of these vessels are roughly hemispherical in shape and seem to have had rounded bases that were flattened at contact points. Five examples were much deeper than the others and at least one vessel had a constricted mouth. The rims are bolstered externally by a rounded projecting band, which may be either plain or incised on top in multiple-line-break patterns. Interiors may be smudged. Similar rim profiles occur at Chiapa de Corzo on large vertical-wall bowls and on flaring-wall bowls (Dixon 1959: figs. 25, 39a), at El Trapiche (García Payón 1966: pl. XIX), and at Panuco in the Aguilar phase (MacNeish 1954: fig. 15, nos. 7–9; fig. 17, no. 43). Dimensions in cm.: rim diameter, 24–32, average about 28; base di-

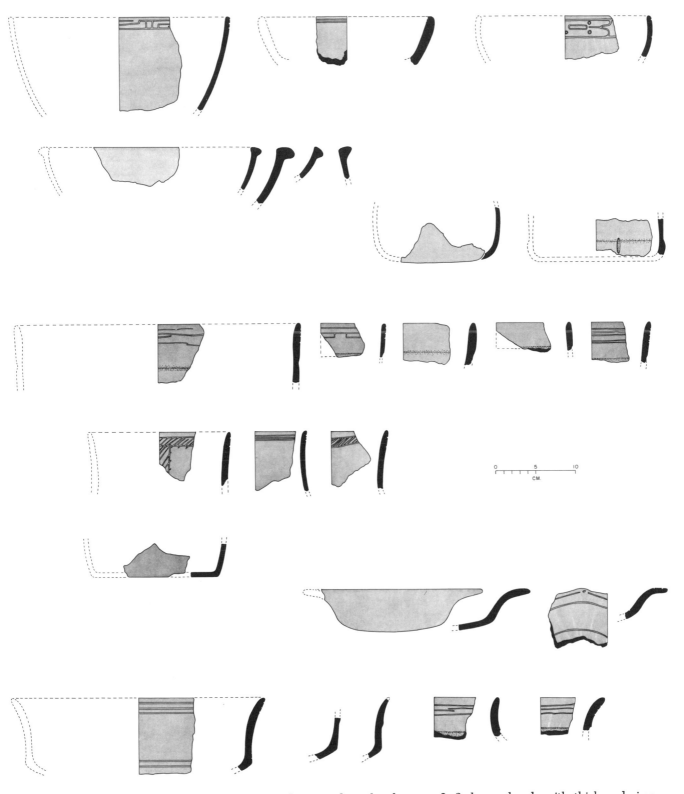

FIG. 35. CANOAS WHITE. *Row 1:* convex-wall and incurved-rim bowls; *rows 2, 3:* heavy bowls with thickened rims and two basal fragments; *row 4:* cylindrical vessels with collared rims; *rows 5, 6:* cylindrical vessels with slightly concave rims and a basal fragment; *row 7:* semi-everted-rim bowls; *row 8:* composite-silhouette bowls with and without collared rims.

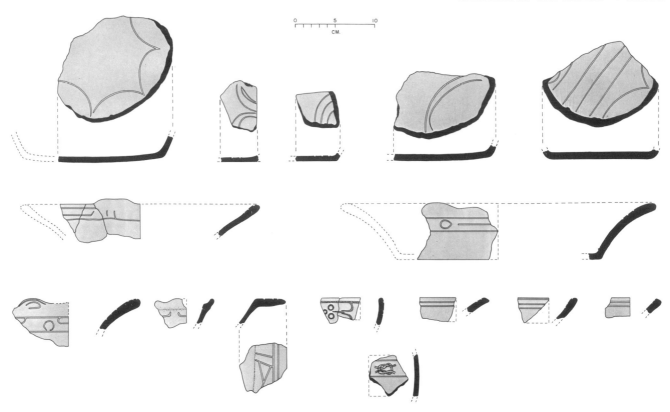

FIG. 36. CANOAS WHITE. *Top to bottom,* incised interior bottom sherds; bowls with tabbed or horizontally everted rims; miscellaneous decorated sherds.

ameter, usually 40–50 percent of rim diameter; height, 10–14; wall thickness, 0.5–1.0, average 0.7.

Bases, probably of deep bowls. Four specimens of slightly rounded bowl bases occurred in Canoas White. As no rims were found with them, the form of the vessel they represent is difficult to conjecture. Dimensions in cm.: base diameter, 9.4–10; wall thickness, 0.5–0.7; height, unknown but apparently greater than 8.0.

Cylindrical bowls. These bowls are of two varieties. One has a simple direct rim and a wall profile which is vertical or slightly flaring. The other has a vertical wall and a rim that resembles a flattened collar. Both varieties seem to have had flat bottoms. Cylindrical vessels are widespread in the Middle Formative, occurring in the Conchas phase at La Victoria (Coe 1961: fig. 27c), at La Venta (Drucker 1952: 115), at Tlatilco (Piña Chan 1958: fig. 35o), and in Trapiche II (García Payón 1966).

Decoration consists of external incising in parallel-line-break motifs or occasionally of bands of hachure. The collar of the collared variety bears the incising.

Lines are often incised on the lower wall just above the base also. The walls are at a 90° angle to the plane of the base, with a sharply pronounced basal break, very like the Chiapa de Corzo II specimens illustrated by Dixon (1959: fig. 34) and that shown from La Victoria (Coe 1961: fig. 29g). Dimensions in cm. of both rim types: rim diameter, 14–36, average, 22–24; base diameter, identical to or slightly less than rim diameter; wall thickness, 0.6–0.8; height, unknown.

Composite-silhouette bowls. Vessels with convex bases and concave walls, whose profiles present a "curved, then recurved" appearance, are rare in Canoas White and do not appear in the six earliest Santa Maria components. Three types were noted. One is a flaring-wall bowl similar, except as regards the shape of its base, to specimens from the flat-based dish group; some of the rims flare widely, but most tend to be nearly vertical. The bowls are frequently parallel-line incised. Another type of composite silhouette has a "flattened bolster rim" very similar to some of the grater-bowl profiles in Conchas White-to-buff at La Victoria (Coe 1961: fig. 26f-h). A third type has a plain or an incised everted rim with widely spaced "tabs" or scallops.

Composite silhouettes commence in the Middle Formative, and are more abundant in Late Formative times, where they branch out into forms like the cuspidor and the Z-angle bowl, which are not seen among Canoas wares. Of the eighteen Canoas White examples, the direct-rimmed specimens resemble bowls from Early and Middle Zacatenco (Vaillant 1930: pls. I*c, m*; IV*d, o*), La Venta (Drucker 1952: fig. 38*f*), and the Conchas phase at La Victoria (Coe 1961: fig. 27*l*). The scalloped-rim specimen finds its closest parallel at Zacatenco (Vaillant 1930: pl. IV*h*). Resemblances of the "flattened bolster rim" bowls to Conchas specimens have already been mentioned.

Dimensions in cm.: Direct-rim composite silhouettes: rim diameter, 28–34; base diameter, 24–32; height, 3–12; wall thickness, 0.8. Composite silhouettes with flattened bolster rims: rim diameter, usually 24–28, one aberrant, 43; base diameter, usually 21–23, one aberrant, 35; height, usually 8–9, one aberrant, 10; wall thickness 0.7–0.9. Composite silhouette with scalloped everted rim: rim diameter, 24; base diameter, 14; height, 3; wall thickness, 0.8.

Semi-everted- and everted-rim bowls. Seven semi-everted-rim sherds were found in Zone E of Ts 368e and one in Ts 367, Zone D[1]. These rims present almost an "S"-curve in profile, with the upper portion of the curve being much more pronounced internally than externally. They are similar to specimens illustrated by Vaillant from Early and Middle Zacatenco (1930: pls. II*d*, V*c-e*).

A single wide everted and incised rim came from Zone C of Ts 367. Incised everted rims are somewhat more frequent in Chiapa de Corzo II White Monochrome (Dixon 1959: fig. 27), but did not occur at La Victoria in the Conchas phase and were infrequent at La Venta.

Incurved-rim bowls. Two vessels had convex walls that curved inward at the mouth.

Miniature barrel-shaped vessels. Small, flat-based almost cylindrical vessels whose greatest diameter occurs in the middle may represent a shape that was present also in larger sizes, but fragments of which were not recognizable as such. Larger "barrel-shaped jars" were found in the Conchas phase at La Victoria (Coe 1961: 65). Dimensions in cm. of the Canoas White examples: rim diameter, 6–8; base diameter, same as rim diameter; height of one intact example, 6; wall thickness, 0.5.

Bowl with basal bulge. This term is borrowed from

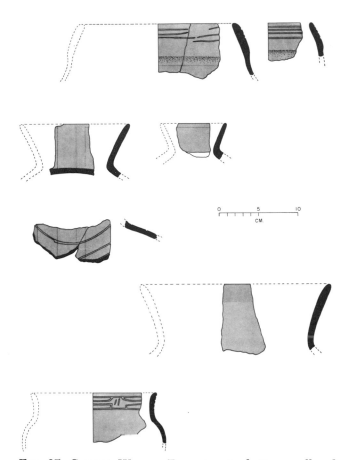

Fig. 37. Canoas White. *From top to bottom*, collared tecomates, funnel-neck ollas, incised shoulder fragment, and flaring-neck ollas.

Drucker (1952: 114) to describe a single sherd from Zone C of Ts 367. The vessel seems to have been a cylindrical bowl with a slight "spare-tire" bulge at the joint between base and wall, vaguely similar to specimens from La Venta (*ibid.*: fig. 38*g, h*). The bulge has a shallow vertical groove in it that may be part of a repeated decoration. Dimensions in cm.: base diameter, 16; wall thickness, 0.8.

Incensario horn. A sherd of Canoas White, smudged variety, from Zone C, Ts 367, has what appears to be a pinched, triangular, nubbin-sized incensario horn attached to the unsmudged surface. This seems to be the only instance of a possible incensario made from Canoas White.

Pumpkin-shaped or collared-rim tecomates. The globular or subglobular neckless jar with restricted mouth is one of the Early Formative's most popular shapes. Varieties of these jars—pumpkin-shaped, plain or direct-rim, or collared-rim—last well into the Middle Formative in most areas and continue even later in some regions. Las Canoas examples fall into two categories: pumpkin-shaped vessels with plain rims and other, usually less squat jars with a wide raised band or "collar" around the rim. Most examples have parallel-line incising around the mouth, and all are smudged and polished. The pumpkin-shaped tecomate is a continuation of a form popular in the Ajalpan phase, which throughout Santa Maria times has a tendency to become less insloping at the rim and therefore wider mouthed, thus approaching the plain direct-rim form. It becomes increasingly difficult to distinguish between fragments of tecomates and of incurved-rim bowls in later levels at Tehuacan.

Dimensions in cm.: rim diameter, 14–30, average, 18; wall thickness, 0.5–1.0; estimated height, slightly greater than rim diameter. Bases are rounded, with flattened contact points which are often very worn.

Tecomates occur at almost all Middle Formative sites, but were not always recognized at the time the sites were excavated. The vessels were given their Mesoamerican name by workers in the Grijalva Basin (MacNeish and Peterson 1962: 30; Sanders 1961: 17), who adapted the term from a gourd container of identical shape.

The pumpkin-shaped and collared-rim varieties occur in a similar monochrome white ware in the Conchas phase at La Victoria (Coe 1961: pumpkin in figs. 25a, 27a; collared form, fig. 27d) and in period II at Chiapa de Corzo (Dixon 1959: pumpkin, fig. 30b). The Coarse Buff ware of La Venta, which is often white with amphibole temper, also displays these tecomate forms (Drucker 1952: collared form, figs. 25b, c; pumpkin form, figs. 28f, 39a), as does some of the "cafe o bayo" ware from El Trapiche (García Payón 1966: collared form, pl. XL–28; pumpkin form, pl. XLI–35–37). The tecomate form is less prevalent in white ware in the Valley of Mexico, but some pumpkin-shaped tecomates are recorded for Tlatilco (Piña Chan 1958: p. 93 and fig. 38) and collared examples occur in early Zacatenco (Vaillant 1930: pl. In).

Ollas with long flaring or funnel necks are large, globular jars whose necks are fairly tall with simple direct rims slightly flaring away from the vertical. Similar jars with more vertical necks from Chiapa de Corzo II, also in white monochrome, are illustrated by Dixon (1959: fig. 33b, e). The ollas are also present at La Venta (Drucker 1952: fig. 39c), La Victoria (Coe 1961: fig. 27p), and in the Panuco area (MacNeish 1954: fig. 17, no. 49). One example from Canoas has incised parallel lines on the shoulder just below the

neck, but most are undecorated. Dimensions in cm.: rim diameter, 10–24, average, 16; neck height, 3.0–7.5, average, 5.0; wall thickness, 0.5–1.0.

Ollas with short flaring necks are smaller jars similar in shape to La Venta specimens (Drucker 1952: fig. 38k), having globular bodies and vague outward curving necks. Parallel lines with "break" motifs encircle the necks of all Santa Maria specimens. Dimensions in cm.: rim diameter, 14–16; neck height, 3.0; wall thickness, 0.6.

SUBTYPE: CANOAS WHITE-RIMMED ORANGE

This subtype, whose paste and hardness are similar to those of Canoas White, is distinguished from the latter in that it is only partially slipped or washed with white, is almost never decorated, and for the most part occurs in different forms (see above, Table 24). There is not much variety in shape, all but four sherds being from convex-wall bowls. The whole of the interior is coated, but on the exterior only a band extending down from the lip 2.0 to 4.0 cm. has a white wash; below this, the surface is bare orange paste with metallic sparkles from the inclusions of amphiboles and pyroxenes and has an over-all appearance of having been wiped smooth with a handful of grass. In the case of the convex-wall bowls, it is clear that the area below the band was not visible and hence did not need a slip or wash. Thus the ancients did not really observe the "White-rimmed Orange" effect; our terminology is for convenience in classifying the rim sherds of this subtype.

White-rimmed Orange pottery seems to be known so far only from two other Formative sites outside the Tehuacan Valley, both in central Veracruz, the mound of Chalahuites and Trapiche II. Sherds of this type from the latter site are from convex-wall bowls identical to those from Las Canoas. The hardness is identical to Canoas White.

Surface Finish

The grass-wiped exterior of the vessel, before slipping, is usually buff-orange (7.5 YR 6/4), with a few sherds appearing rusty (5.0 YR 6/4), or brownish (7.5 YR 5/2). Over this base color is applied a thin slip or wash whose color varies from a cream-white to a gray-white, through the same range as the Canoas White surface coatings. As stated above, this coating is complete only on the interior of the vessel, where it is always polished and occasionally streaked with cinnabar. The partially slipped ("white-rimmed") outside is always matte.

Decoration

Only two examples are incised on the exterior of the rim; no other types of decoration were observed.

Vessel Forms

Bowls with thin, convex walls. This is the typical form in which White-rimmed Orange appears—wide, shallow open bowls whose base attributes are unknown because sherds from that part of the vessel are lacking. Bowls of this shape are always polished on the inside, but show no incising or other form of decoration. A variation on this form, however, has a rim with a very slightly raised collar and incised decoration.

Dimensions in cm.: rim diameter, 24–32, average, 29; height and base diameter, unknown; wall thickness, 0.4–0.7.

Bowls with flaring or outsloping walls. Two sherds may be from medium-sized, flat-bottomed flaring-wall bowls like those of Canoas White. Dimensions in cm.: rim diameter, 20–24; wall thickness, 0.6–0.8. A single rim-to-base section is thick and fairly coarse and bears only a vague resemblance to Canoas White or Rio Salado Gray bowls of similar outline. The low walls (4.0 cm.) are slightly concave and nearly vertical. The rim diameter is 20 cm. and the wall thickness ranges from 0.8 to 1.0 cm.

Bowls with thick convex walls are vessels with walls 1.0 cm. thick and a rim diameter of 32 cm.

CANOAS ORANGE-BROWN

2,317 specimens excavated, 305 collected.

During the initial definition of trial types, this pottery actually began as two wares: one orange and one brown. On the third day of analysis, two sherds from the same dish were found and fitted together. One was a clear example of our "trial orange" ware, the other was typical "trial brown." The fairly impressive color difference took place right at the break, indicating that the lighter sherd had been subjected to refiring since the destruction of the vessel. Re-examination of the shapes and other criteria used in definition of the trial types indicated that the oranges and browns were simply firing variants of a single pottery type, and so Canoas Orange-brown came into existence.

This is an unslipped but usually well-polished member of the amphibole-pyroxene group made with a paste and temper similar to that of Canoas White and having several shapes in common with the latter type. It constitutes a much smaller percentage of the sherds

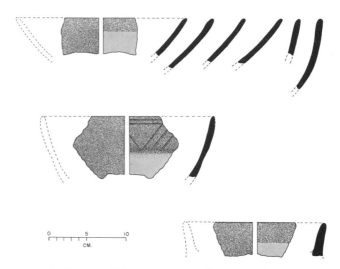

FIG. 38. CANOAS WHITE-RIMMED ORANGE. *From top to bottom,* convex-wall bowls, bowl with collared rim, and flaring-wall dish.

than does Canoas White, however, and has a somewhat different set of double-line-break motifs.

Paste

The paste is fairly compact, breaking with a rough and irregular fracture. It is almost always fired one color clear through and does not display the "sandwich" effect typical of Canoas White. The sole exceptions to this rule are a few sherds of large, heavy, thickened-rim vessels which (presumably because of the thickness of their walls) have not been oxidized in the very center.

Thin sections of four sherds reveal that less than 1 percent of the volume is grains over 1.0 mm. in diameter, and these are of limestone. About 3 percent of the volume is grains 0.5–1.0 mm. in diameter of quartz, quartzite, sandstone, limestone, basalt, and calcite. About 9 percent of the paste, while containing the above rocks and minerals, has a slightly larger proportion of augite, labradorite, pyroxenes, and andesine in grains 0.1–0.5 mm. in diameter. From 4 to 5 percent of the volume is grains less than 0.1 mm. in diameter, including most of the materials mentioned above and hematite, magnetite, and diorite. Thus the temper comprises about 17 percent of the paste, over half of it is grains 0.1–0.5 mm. in diameter, and it commonly includes quartz, quartzite, basalt, limestone, calcite, augite, and andesine.

The usual color of the paste ranges from cinnamon orange (5.0 YR 5/4) to cinnamon brown (5.0 YR

5/2). Extremes were as light as orange-buff. (5.0 YR 6/4–6/6) or as dark as drab reddish-brown (5.0 YR 4/3). The hardness measures about 2.5–3.0.

Surface Finish

Surfaces are unslipped. Virtually all vessel interiors are polished, and usually the exteriors also. Bases are normally worn enough to retain little or no polish, and frequently the potter seems to have lost interest in polishing by the time the lower part of the exterior wall was reached. Surface color is usually orangish to brown (5.0 YR 5/6–5/3); darker specimens reach dirty brown (5.0 YR 4/1) and lighter specimens reach orange-buff (5.0 YR 5/6–6/6).

Decoration

Decoration consists of incised parallel-line motifs as seen in Canoas White, but with a more limited range of variation. Two- and three-line examples with breaks are most common. A few one-line specimens occur, but there are no four- or five-line motifs. Some of the double-line-break designs are identical to Chiapa de Corzo II examples (Dixon 1959: fig. 28). Several flat-based dishes have incised pseudo-grater bases. The decorative lines are incised through the polished surface of the vessel, exposing a paste whose color is virtually no different from the exterior.

One sherd exhibited plain, long-line, rocker stamping and a small fragment displayed raspada decoration.

Vessel Forms

Flat-bottomed bowls or dishes with flaring walls comprise the bulk of the Canoas Orange-brown vessels. Dishes with a rim diameter of 28–30 cm. and a base diameter of 18–20 cm. are most common, as they were in Canoas White, but the taller and narrower bowls with rim diameters of 10–22 cm. are not represented in Canoas Orange-brown, perhaps because of a much smaller sample. A majority of the examples have plain rims. The rest are incised in one-to-three-line patterns on the interior of the rim. Two examples are fragments of incised pseudo-molcajete bases. The absence of external parallel-line incising is probably explained by the lack of appropriately tall and narrow vessels. Dimensions in cm.: rim diameter, 24–34; base diameter, 16–22; height, 3.0–6.0, usually 5.0; wall thickness, 0.6–0.9, usually 0.7–0.8.

A variation of this form (13 specimens) has straight outsloping instead of flaring walls. Rim diameters are about 30 cm. and the base diameters about 20 cm.

Convex-wall bowls were probably of medium or shallow depth. They apparently had flat bottoms. Decoration consists of external two-line or three-line incising. Dimensions in cm.: rim diameter, about 30; estimated base diameter, about 18; wall thickness, 0.7.

Large bowls with externally thickened rims. These heavy bowls have thickened rims similar to Rio Salado Gray examples, but the walls of Canoas Orange-

TABLE 25
Canoas Orange-Brown Decorated Sherds
(by site and zone)

	Early Santa Maria											
	368e I	368e H	368e G	368e F	368e E	367 D²	367 D¹	367 C	368e D	368e C²	368e C¹	Total
Incised motifs												
1 line around rims of flaring/outsloping-wall bowls, int.	1					1	1				1	4
2 lines around rims of flaring/outsloping-wall bowls, int.					2	14	8	4	1		1	30
2-3 lines around rims of convex-wall bowls, ext.		4	2	9	4	1	1		3	1		25
3 lines around rims of flaring/outsloping bowls, int.					1	3	7	10	2			23
Molcajete-like motifs on bottoms, int.				1								1
Raspada motif on ext. walls				1								1
Plain rocker-stamping on ext. walls	1			4			1	1				7
Total	2	4	2	15	7	19	18	15	6	1	2	91

TABLE 26
Canoas Orange-Brown Vessel Forms
(sherds by site and zone)

	Early Santa Maria												
	368e I	368e H	368e G	368e F	368e E	367 D²	367 D¹	367 C	368e D	272 I	368e C²	368e C¹	272 H
Bowls													
flaring wall	2			3	3	20	22	16	8	2		3	
convex wall													
direct rim		4	2	9	4	1	1		3		1		
thick rim		1			2		1		3			1	
large, ext. thick rim		5		2	3	1	3	4	1				
outsloping wall	1			3	4				1			4	
composite silhouette				1									
Ollas, long flaring neck							4	2					1
Tecomate, direct rim							1						
Bases													
flat	3			18	4	1	9	3					
convex				2		1	2	1					
Body sherds	87	55	25	124	60	94	254	202	109	10	24	114	11
Total	93	65	27	162	80	118	297	228	125	12	25	122	12

	Late Santa Maria												
	368e C	368w D-E	368e D	368w C	368w B	218-11 G	218-11 F	368e B¹	204 A B	368w B¹	218-11 E	218-6 E	Total
Bowls													
flaring wall													79
convex wall													
direct rim													25
thick rim													8
large, ext. thick rim													19
outsloping wall													13
composite silhouette													1
Ollas, long flaring neck													7
Tecomate, direct rim													1
Bases													
flat													38
convex													6
Body sherds	115	107	272	110	139	4	3	41	47	106	4	3	2120
Total	115	107	272	110	139	4	3	41	47	106	4	3	2317

brown specimens range from outflaring to nearly vertical to insloping. The rims are similar to specimens from Chiapa de Corzo II (Dixon 1959: 25) and Trapiche II (García Payón 1966: pl. VIII and p. 72). Dimensions in cm.: mouth diameter, 32–40; wall thickness, 0.9–1.2. The thickened rim may add another 6.0–7.0 cm. to the diameter at the mouth.

Convex-wall bowls with thickened rims resemble Canoas White specimens. Dimensions in cm.: mouth diameter, about 30; wall thickness, 0.7.

Composite-silhouette bowl. One sherd represents a vessel with convex base and concave sides.

Ollas with long flaring necks are a minor shape. They had globular bodies, and a few sherds suggest that bases may have been round with flattened contact points. Dimensions in cm.: rim diameter, 12; neck height, 6.5; wall thickness, 0.7.

Tecomates. The only sherd of this form has a plain rim. Dimensions in cm.: rim diameter, 20; wall thickness, 0.6.

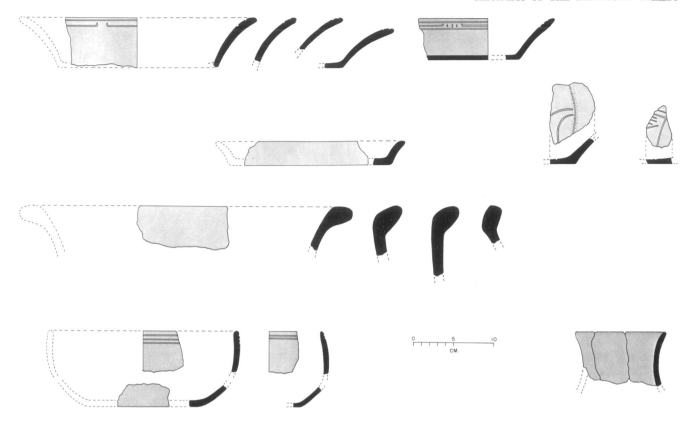

Fig. 39. Canoas Orange-brown. *From top to bottom,* flaring-wall bowls, dish and incised bases, heavy bowls with thickened rims, incurved-rim bowls and olla with long flaring neck.

Relationships

Polished monochrome brown wares are common at highland Middle Formative sites such as El Arbolillo and Zacatenco. Strong similarities in paste, decoration, and vessel form occur at La Venta (Drucker 1952: 92–93), Trapiche II (García Payón 1966: pl. XXXVIII and p. 101) and in the Guadalupe phase of Oaxaca.

Canoas Heavy Plain

4,433 specimens excavated, 357 collected.

Paste

This utility ware is the coarsest member of the amphibole-pyroxene group and was used principally for making flat-based pot rests or supported pot stands. The paste is coarse, crumbly, and poorly knit. It breaks with a rough and irregular fracture bristling with quartz or basalt grains. Although the clay of which this paste is made somewhat resembles that of Canoas White, the paste is far more poorly fired. The temper appears in larger amounts than in Canoas White, ranging from 18 to 28 percent of the total volume of the sherd and averaging about 22 percent. No amphibole crystals exist in the sherds tested, but pyroxenes are present. Grains over 1.0 mm. in diameter of either basalt or limestone comprise only 2 percent or so of the paste. About 7 percent of the volume is grains 0.5–1.0 mm. in diameter consisting of the former materials and small amounts of andesite, quartz, plagioclase, and labradorite. Almost 9 percent is grains 0.1–0.5 mm. in diameter; these include the materials mentioned and calcite, andesine, and pyroxenes. Grains less than 0.1 mm. in diameter make up about 4 percent of the total volume and are predominantly of pyroxenes, magnetite, calcite, labradorite, and hematite.

The paste usually presents a gray core sandwiched between pink or salmon-colored layers, but individual sherds may be either gray or pink clear through. The drab gray core centers around 2.5 YR 4/2, with the pink peripheries ranging about 5.0 YR 6/6–6/7. The hardness measures 2.5–3.0.

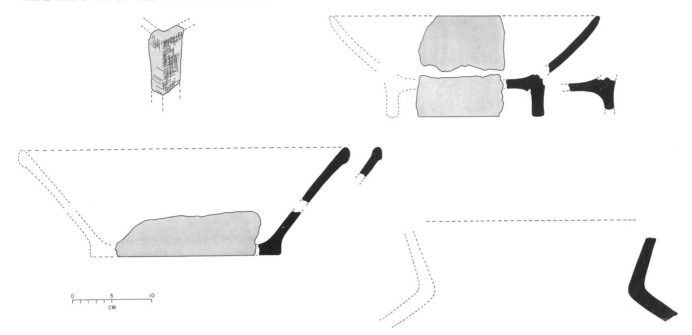

Fig. 40. Canoas Heavy Plain. *From top to bottom,* fragment of rectangular vessel, supported pot stand, flat-based pot rest, and olla neck fragment.

Surface Finish

Surfaces are unslipped and often totally un-smoothed, with numerous pockmarks and a very rough texture. At most the surface may have been wiped with a handful of grass. The exception to this rule is the occasional imprint of plain-weave fabric on a surface which was smoothed before the impression was made—some examples constituting early evidence of loom-weaving in the Tehuacan Valley. Owing to erratic firing, the surface color varies greatly, depending on whether the sherd is fired gray clear through or has a pink layer near the surface. The lightest specimens are a pinkish buff (5.0 YR 7/6) sparkling with pyroxene crystals and blotched with gray firing clouds; the darkest are a drab gray (5 YR 6/1).

Decoration

The only decoration observed was the impressing of coarse, plain-weave cloth into the smoothed wet clay of pot stands or pot rests.

Vessel Forms

Supported pot rests are vessels with the shape of a flat plate suspended between slightly concave surrounding walls. The wall below the plate is vertical; the wall above the plate is outsloping. The inner junction of wall and plate is gently curving, as if shaped to receive an olla with rounded base and flattened contact points. Since the plates of these vessels are never burned, we are sure they did not serve as incense burners. The walls seem to have been too high to allow them to have been pottery stools. The supporting bases, while circular, are not true "ring bases" because they are actually just a continuation downward of the vessel wall. The upper surfaces of some of the plates are fabric-impressed in the same manner as the under side of the pot rests mentioned below. Dimensions in cm.: rim diameter, 34–44, average, 40; base diameter, 22–24; wall thickness, 1.0–1.6, average 1.5. The plates are suspended about 3 cm. above the ground.

Convex-wall vessels, probably pot rests. The vessels from which these rim sherds come had wide mouths and sides curved in such a manner that they could have held large round-based ollas. No rim-to-base fragments were found. Dimensions in cm.: rim diameter, 30–38, average, 35; wall thickness, 1.0–1.6.

Flaring or outsloping-wall bowls are medium-sized vessels with direct rims. Dimensions in cm.: rim diameter, 20–24; wall thickness, 0.6–0.8.

Flat bases, probably of pot rests, resemble thick,

TABLE 27
Canoas Heavy Plain Vessel Forms
(sherds by site and zone)

	Late Ajalpan					Early Santa Maria								
	204D D	368e K³	368e K²	368e K¹	368e J	368e I	368e H	368e G	368e F	368e E	367 D²	367 D¹	367 C	368e D
Pot rests, rims														
outsloping wall, direct/thick rim							5		18	11	12	10	16	3
convex wall, direct rim									16	11	4	4	3	6
Pot rests, basal sections														
supported											4	10	10	8
flat based										7	4	3	4	
Ollas														
long flaring neck						1	11		30					
short flaring neck														
straight neck														
angled neck fragments												3		
Tecomates														
Bowls														
flaring/outsloping wall						3				3	5	7	10	
stepped rim														
Braziers														
Handles, loop										2				1
Rectangular vessel													1	
Bases														
Body sherds	1	3	1	2	11	70	186	165	671	620	80	209	220	196
Total	1	3	1	2	11	74	202	165	735	654	109	246	264	214

	Early Santa Maria (continued)			Late Santa Maria									
	272 I	368e C²	368e C¹	368e C	368w D-E	272 G	368e B	368w C	368w B	218-11 G	218-11 F	368e B¹	204 A-B
Pot rests, rims													
outsloping wall, direct/thick rim		1											
convex wall, direct rim	1	5	5										
Pot rests, basal sections													
supported		7											
flat based													
Ollas													
long flaring neck			4										
short flaring neck										1			
straight neck													
angled neck fragments													
Tecomates										1			
Bowls													
flaring/outsloping wall													
stepped rim													
Braziers										1			
Handles, loop													
Rectangular vessel													
Bases													
Body sherds	1	72	143	106	121	2	469	157	150	2	3	65	139
Total	2	85	152	106	121	2	469	157	150	5	3	65	139

(Table continued)

(Table 27, continued)

	368w B1	218-11 E	218-6 G	218-10 C2	218-6 F	218-11 D	218-11 C	218-10 C1	218-10 C	218-10 B1	218-10 B	218-6 E	50 VII	Total
						Late Santa Maria (continued)								
Pot rests, rims														
outsloping wall, direct/thick rim														76
convex wall, direct rim														55
Pot rests, basal sections														
supported														39
flat based														18
Ollas														
long flaring neck														46
short flaring neck				1		2		7	12	7	8			38
straight neck				2				5	2	5	2			16
angled neck fragments														3
Tecomates		2	6	1	1	2	1	8	19	15	18			74
Bowls														
flaring/outsloping wall														28
stepped rim								1		3	2			6
Braziers					1			1						3
Handles, loop														3
Rectangular vessel														1
Bases	1			1				2	1	1				6
Body sherds	142	7	2	2						1		1	1	4021
Total	143	9	8	7	2	4	1	24	35	31	30	1	1	4433

heavy, flat-based bowls, but some unusual features of their outline lead us to believe that they are probably rests for large ollas with rounded bases and flattened contact points. First, they bulge noticeably at the base, the juncture of wall and floor being reinforced as if the vessel were expected to support an exceptional weight. Second, the inner junction between base and wall, instead of being sharp as in most Las Canoas bowls, curves gently, as if to receive a rounded olla bottom. The under side of the base of all these vessels is impressed with coarse fabric woven in a one-over-one pattern. Dimensions in cm.: rim diameter, 34–44, average 40; base diameter, 20–30, average, 25; height, over 12; wall thickness, 1.0–1.6.

Ollas with long flaring necks had globular bodies and divergent necks. Three fragments from Canoas show a sharp angle between neck and body. Dimensions in cm: rim diameter, 25–30; neck diameter, 18–22; wall thickness, 1.0–1.5.

Small rectangular vessel. A single specimen seems to be the corner of a rectangular box. The corner makes a true right angle, as does the rim with the wall. This "box" most closely resembles the "small rectangular vessel" from La Venta illustrated by Drucker (1952: pl. 17, lower left). The box was over 10 cm. high. The walls are 1.0–1.5 cm. thick.

Loop handles. Three fragments of thick handles, rounded in cross section, undoubtedly were attached to the ollas described above.

Later forms. In late Santa Maria levels of the Coatepec and Quachilco sites, Canoas Heavy Plain was a minority ware. However, this paste did appear in vessel shapes not found earlier: plain tecomates, ollas with short flaring or straight necks and direct rims, stepped-rim bowls, and braziers.

Relationships

Canoas Heavy Plain is confined to Early and Middle Formative levels in the Tehuacan Valley. Some examples of La Venta Coarse Brown ware described by Drucker (1952: pp. 92, 94; pl. 24 d, e) have a similar coarse paste and fabric impressions. His sherds may contain, in fact, amphibole-pyroxene temper, since he describes "shiny black plaques" among the inclusions in the temper (p. 93). Ekholm (1944: 346) mentions "textile-marked" wares in the El Prisco period at Panuco. A similar ware from Trapiche II is mentioned by García Payón (1966: 103) as being "cord"-impressed.

Lupita Heavy Plain in the Guadalupe phase of Oaxaca is similar.

Mica Group

RIO SALADO COARSE

22,818 specimens excavated, 289 collected.

This coarsest, most poorly made ware of the early Santa Maria phase occurs principally in the form of large, thick-walled storage jars, or ollas, with a limited set of variations on the same neck pattern. *Incensarios* constitute the second most common shape.

Paste

The paste is crumbly and breaks with a very jagged fracture. Temper is abundant; thin-section studies of eight sherds reveal that it often composes 25 percent of the volume of the sherd. About 6 percent of the paste is large grains 1.0–2.0 mm. in diameter, usually quartz or quartzite, although muscovite appears in fair amounts, along with some plagioclase, gneiss, microcline, and biotite. About 7 percent of the paste is grains 0.5–1.0 mm. in diameter made up of the same substances. About 8 percent is composed of grains 0.1–0.5 mm. in diameter, including the same materials and small amounts of feldspar, pyroxenes, and amphibole. About 4 percent is grains under 0.1 mm. in diameter, including all the previously mentioned materials and hematite, magnetite, sericite, chlorite, and diorite.

The mixture of clay and temper is uneven, and very irregular firing is characteristic. The paste varies in color from brick red (10 R 5/6) through dark reddish-gray (10 R 4/1) to a very dark gray (7.5 YR 1/3). Any one or two of these shades may occur in the same vessel. The hardness measures 2.5–3.0.

Surface Finish

Surfaces are rough, unslipped, and sandpapery. Some olla necks have a rippled outer surface, as if finger-wiped as a finishing touch, but many were simply brushed. Sometimes the surface sparkles with tiny or medium-sized mica flecks, but more often it is exceedingly dull. The normal background color range is from brick red (10 R 5/4) to either purplish-red, reddish-brown, or purplish-gray (10 R 4/2–3/1). Against this background, gray, gray-brown, or almost black firing clouds are common and extensive. In general the vessels have a rude, poorly finished appearance.

Decoration

Only a few sherds representing small, thin-walled ollas show decoration. One type of decoration consists of very faint finger-wiped stripes of lusterless orange paint, applied to the body. A second type is produced by vertical stripes scratched onto the body by means of a thin slat of wood (probably the local river-bottom cane).

Vessel Forms

Ollas with tall to medium-high flaring or funnel necks. These are large globular, or subglobular, jars with wide mouths and necks whose flaring rims terminate in one of four possible lip profiles. In early Santa Maria levels, the most common lip is beveled (200 sherds), which in some cases appears to have been done with a slat or cane. Fifty rims exhibit a groove on top, perhaps caused by inaccurate or careless beveling. The second largest group of rims are direct (166 sherds). Another group of 89 sherds display a flat top associated with external thickening. In the latter case, the shape of the neck is somewhat funnel-like, resembling Vaillant's Bay Ware funnel-neck ollas from El Arbolillo (1935: fig. 18). Body diameters are largely unknown, but in all cases must have been over 30 cm., with most examples over 40 cm. Rim diameters fall mostly between 24–28 cm. but range from 15 to 36 cm. Necks are usually 5.0–7.0 cm. high, but some are as low as 3.0 cm. Walls range from 0.6 to 1.0 cm. thick, with 0.7–0.9 cm. the usual thickness.

In late Santa Maria and early Palo Blanco levels the ollas with tall flaring or funnel necks tend to have direct rather than modified rims (late Santa Maria, 244; early Palo Blanco, 86). The beveled-lip variety numbered 108 in late Santa Maria and the grooved-lip variety 26. No flat-lipped ollas were found in late Santa Maria or Palo Blanco components.

Ollas with short, flaring necks are smaller vessels than the longer necked ollas and have noticeably thinner body walls. Most of the rims are direct, but a few are everted. Dimensions in cm.: rim diameter, 10–14; neck height, 2.0–2.5; wall thickness, 0.2–0.5.

Ollas with short, straight necks usually have direct rims, but some rims are everted. A few neck and body sherds show the stripes of pale orange paint described above, and two sherds have vertical cane-scratched stripes. Dimensions are approximately the same as those of the ollas with short flaring necks.

Rolled-rim ollas have short necks and the rolled-over or beaded rim which is a characteristic trait of the late Santa Maria phase.

Incense burners or pot rests have the shape of very wide, low egg cups. They consist of a shallow dish suspended between surrounding concave walls. In over

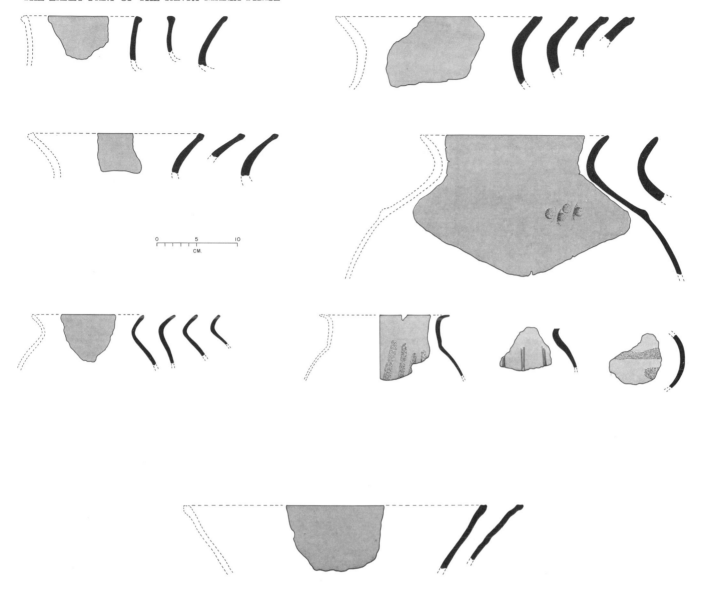

FIG. 41. RIO SALADO COARSE. *Rows 1, 2:* long-necked ollas with flat, grooved, beveled, and rounded lips; *row 3:* ollas with short flaring necks, olla with straight neck and everted rim, decorated neck and body sherds; *row 4:* outsloping-wall bowls with beveled rims.

70 percent of the sample, the inside of the dish, where presumably incense was burned, is charred black. There is no decoration. Much taller incensarios, though constructed along the same lines, were recovered at Mirador, Chiapas, by Peterson (1963: figs. 97, 98), but from a later Formative phase. Dimensions in cm.: diameter of suspended dish, about 15–20; vessel height, over 12–15; dish usually suspended 3.0–5.0 cm. above bottom; wall thickness, 0.5–1.0.

Pumpkin tecomates and *plain tecomates.* These crude jars lack decoration. One of the early Santa Ma-

ria specimens is so poorly smoothed inside that traces of coiling can be seen. Dimensions in cm.: rim diameter, 12–16; body diameter (one specimen), 20; wall thickness, 0.5–0.7.

Minor forms include a few crudely shaped bowls with outsloping walls, beveled lips, and rim diameters of 34–38 cm. Comales and convex-wall bowls with direct rims and with externally thickened rims also were made.

Handles or *incensario horns.* A few curved, cylindrical objects appear to be incensario horns or prongs, for they extend upward from the very rim of the attached vessel. They also could be remains of handles. One flattened strap-like handle is 2.7 cm. wide; six specimens with more oval-shaped cross sections have diameters of 1.5 by 2.5 cm.

Relationships

Although crumbly, undistinguished utilitarian wares are widespread in Mesoamerica, Rio Salado Coarse seems to be of local manufacture. It is locally derived from Ajalpan Coarse Red and is probably ancestral to the later Quachilco Mica type. The funnel-neck ollas are a good Middle Formative time marker and are common in El Arbolillo and Zacatenco and at Guadalupe in Oaxaca. Fidencio Coarse of the Valley of Oaxaca is a similar ware, also featuring finger-wiped stripes of lusterless paint.

RIO SALADO GRAY

13,914 specimens excavated, 201 collected.

This type begins the long gray-ware tradition in the Tehuacan Valley, but is itself mainly confined to the two segments of the Santa Maria phase. It undoubtedly contributes to the ancestry of the later, harder gray wares of Late Formative and Classic times—Quachilco Gray and El Riego Gray. Outside the valley, it may be related to Socorro Fine Gray in the Guadalupe phase of the Valley of Oaxaca.

The type was established initially in Flannery's study of the early Santa Maria pottery from the Canoas site. Somewhat later Peterson undertook analysis of the materials from the Quachilco site and set up a trial type called Granular Gray. He noted that vessel form and decoration of the trial type seemed identical to those of Rio Salado Gray, but believed the paste to be coarser. Meanwhile MacNeish began to analyze the sherds from the Coatepec site, which overlaps with both Las Canoas and Quachilco. He found he could not readily distinguish among the various gray-ware sherds, although later examples often show in cross section a dark core neatly sandwiched between uncharacteristically light surface layers. The later sherds also show occasional light and dark surface contrasts from firing clouds.

When thin-section studies of the petrographic composition of the various pastes were completed, they showed that in reality the Granular Gray trial type was neither more granular nor more abundantly tempered than the Rio Salado Gray type and that the tempering materials were the same. There was, in fact, only one early gray paste. Apparently the contrast between dark core and lighter peripheries and the clouded surfaces noted on later examples were the results of changing firing techniques.

Paste

A study of thin sections of six sherds from three different sites revealed that about 20 percent of the paste is nonplastic material. The paste looks as though the tempering matter were even more abundant, perhaps because of holes left by leached limestone particles. From 1 to 3 percent of the paste consists of grains over 1.0 mm. in diameter, mostly limestone, although a few grains of basalt and plagioclase are of this size. From 3 to 5 percent of the volume is grains 0.5–1.0 mm. in diameter—also mainly limestone, although basalt and plagioclase are present. About 11 percent is grains 0.1–0.5 mm. in diameter, composed about equally of basalt, plagioclase, limestone, quartz, quartzite, and biotite. About one percent is fine grains under 0.1 mm., mainly quartz, plagioclase, calcite, magnetite, and biotite, along with a few grains of hematite, labradorite, andesine, microcline, and pyroxenes.

The paste of the early Santa Maria examples is fired one color clear through, usually a medium ashy gray (5.0 YR 1/5); extremes range from dark brownish-gray (5.0 YR 3/1) to very light gray (10 YR 7/1). The late Santa Maria sherds often have a darker gray core surrounded by a lighter outer layer about 2 mm. thick.

Surface Finish

Surfaces are unslipped. The simpler vessel shapes have a matte surface, while the more sophisticated shapes such as dimple-based and pinched-walled bowls may have a polished or "stick-burnished" appearance. The color of the surface is usually an even gray, somewhere in the range between a very dark blue-black tone and a fairly light neutral gray. Later specimens are sometimes mottled with firing clouds. Yellowish sparkles from mica (biotite) platelets are a prominent feature on some sherds; on others they are detectable only after careful inspection.

Decoration

Vessels are externally or internally incised with parallel-line-break motifs as on Canoas White. The lines do not cut through a slip, however, but simply penetrate the smoothed surface. The technique called "zoned toning" appears on several late Santa Maria examples and on a few earlier sherds. Three specimens collected from Tr 218 had isosceles triangles incised along the rim; the areas inside the triangles are highly polished and contrast with duller surrounding

TABLE 29
Rio Salado Gray Decorated Sherds
(by site and zone)

	Early Santa Maria												
	368e I	368e H	368e G	368e F	368e E	367 D²	367 D¹	367 C	368e D	272 I	368e C²	368e C¹	272 H
Incised motifs													
1 line around rims of flaring/outsloping-wall bowls, int.													
2 lines around rims of													
flaring/outsloping-wall bowls, int.				2				1	1	3			2
convex-wall, direct-rim bowls, ext.													
convex-wall, wedge-rim bowls, int.					2		1	2		1		2	
2-4 lines around rims of													
convex-wall, direct-rim bowls, ext.													
convex-wall, int. thick-rim bowls	1		3	5	5	1	2	3	1			16	
convex-wall, ext. thick-rim bowls			1	3	3	1	1	3	1			6	
3 lines around rims of													
flaring/outsloping-wall bowls, int.		12	3	18	3	2	4	7	4	2	3	2	1
flaring/outsloping-wall bowls, ext.		12	4	8	3		4	5	3	1		2	
convex-wall, direct-rim bowls, int.			1	6	1		2	3	6		2	2	
convex-wall, direct-rim bowls, ext.			1				2	2	2		1	1	
convex-wall, deep bowls, ext.						1	1		1				
triangle on cylindrical vessels, ext.													
multiple lines on bodies of bowls, ext.						2	1	2		2			
molcajete-like motifs on bottoms, int.						2	1	2	1				1
Grooved/incised motifs, pinched-wall bowls, ext.				2		2	1	4	1			2	
Raspada motifs on bowls/jars, ext.									4			6	
Zoned-toning on bowls/jars, ext.													
Total	1	24	13	44	17	9	21	33	26	10	6	39	4

	Late Santa Maria											
	368e C	368w D-E	368e B	368w C	368w B	218-11 G	218-11 F	368e B¹	204 A-B	368w B¹	218-11 E	218-6 G
Incised motifs												
1 line around rims of flaring/outsloping-wall bowls, int.												
2 lines around rims of												
flaring/outsloping-wall bowls, int.	16	5	11		2	1	1	1	1	2	1	1
convex-wall, direct-rim bowls, ext.	10	1	6			1	1					
convex-wall, wedge-rim bowls, int.	27		3	10	6							
2-4 lines around rims of												
convex-wall, direct-rim bowls, ext.	7	2	2									
convex-wall, int. thick-rim bowls	1		16	10	10	10		1				
convex-wall, ext. thick-rim bowls	10	3		8								
3 lines around rims of												
flaring/outsloping-wall bowls, int.	6	5	9		3				3	3		
flaring/outsloping-wall bowls, ext.												
convex-wall, direct-rim bowls, int.	2	2	8		2							
convex-wall, direct-rim bowls, ext.												
convex-wall, deep bowls, ext.												
triangle on cylindrical vessels, ext.												
multiple lines on bodies of bowls, ext.												
molcajete-like motifs on bottoms, int.												
Grooved/incised motifs, pinched-wall bowls, ext.								1				
Raspada motifs on bowls/jars, ext.	2		4	4								
Zoned-toning on bowls/jars, ext.	1		2									
Total	82	18	61	28	27	12	2	3	4	5	1	1

(table continued)

(Table 29, continued)

	Late Santa Maria (continued)										Early Palo Blanco		
	218-10 C²	218-6 F	218-11 D	218-11 C	218-10 C¹	218-10 C	218-10 B¹	218-10 B	218-11 B	218-6 B	218-10 A	218-6 A	Total
Incised motifs													
1 line around rims of													
flaring/outsloping-wall bowls, int.								2					2
2 lines around rims of													
flaring/outsloping-wall bowls, int.	1	1			2	2	1				5	1	64
convex-wall, direct-rim bowls, ext.					1	2			1				23
convex-wall, wedge-rim bowls, int.	1		1	3	3	4	5		1				72
2-4 lines around rims of													
convex-wall, direct-rim bowls, ext.					1		1	1					14
convex-wall, int. thick-rim bowls	2	4		6	2	5	5	2	1				112
convex-wall, ext. thick-rim bowls	2		1										43
3 lines around rims of													
flaring/outsloping-wall bowls, int.					1			1					92
flaring/outsloping-wall bowls, ext.													42
convex-wall, direct-rim bowls, int.	1												38
convex-wall, direct-rim bowls, ext.													9
convex-wall, deep bowls, ext.													3
triangle on cylindrical vessels, ext.											4		4
multiple lines on bodies of bowls, ext.													7
molcajete-like motifs on bottoms, int.													7
Grooved/incised motifs, pinched-wall bowls, ext.													13
Raspada motifs on bowls/jars, ext.						6							26
Zoned-toning on bowls/jars, ext.	1				1	2	2	1					10
Total	8	5	2	9	11	21	14	7	2	1	9	1	581

areas which were merely smoothed. A fourth sherd shows highly burnished areas contrasting with dull unburnished zones. Similar decoration occurs in the Conchas phase at La Victoria (Coe 1961: 49). Zoned-toned decoration also occurs on Quachilco Gray sherds and on sherds from Yagul (Chadwick 1966: figs. 5–7).

Body sherds from vessels of unknown shape exhibit two kinds of decoration: the incising of narrow lines and the application of wide, shallow grooves. In both cases the pattern seems to involve long, curvilinear strokes. The latter technique appears on an ovate bowl with pinched-in sides which will be described under vessel forms below.

Vessel Forms

Flat-bottomed bowls or dishes with flaring or outsloping walls are the most prevalent vessels and are similar to Canoas White specimens. Like their white-finished counterparts, they may be externally incised (if relatively tall) with three or four parallel lines or internally incised (if relatively low and wide) with two to four parallel lines. The few examples of incised pseudo-grater bases probably belong to this form. Dimensions in cm.: rim diameter, 20–32, average, 26, aberrant, 40; base diameter (6 sherds only), 16–24, aberrant, 38; height, 4.0–10, average, 5.0; wall thickness, 0.6–0.8.

Convex-wall bowls, direct rims. A pair of bases which seem to go with this form are convex with flattened contact points. Over a dozen basal sections of convex-wall bowls have an appliqued flange almost at the very bottom. Most of the convex-wall bowls range from shallow to medium deep; in the former case they are internally incised and in the latter case externally incised. The few clearly deep variants are a minority. A few examples of this form show "stick-burnishing" streaks inside the vessel. Dimensions in cm.: rim diameter, 24–34, average, 28; wall thickness, 0.5–0.9, average, 0.7.

Convex-wall bowls, internally thickened rims. The rims form a thickened and sometimes slightly everted platform on which parallel lines or parallel-line-break

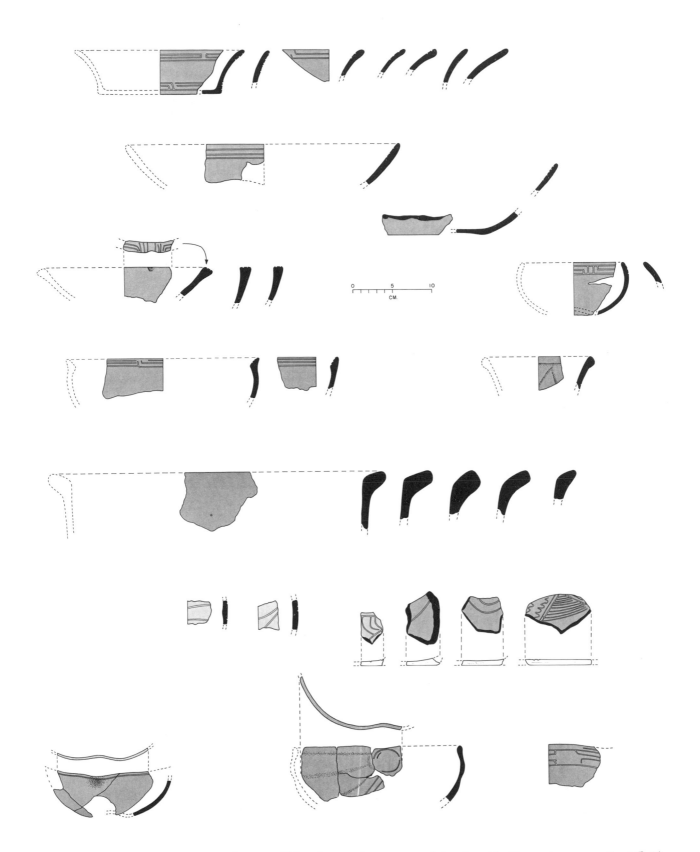

FIG. 42. RIO SALADO GRAY. *Row 1:* flaring-wall bowls; *row 2:* convex-wall bowls with direct rims, *rows 3, 4 (left):* convex-wall bowls with wedge rims, incurved rims, and internally thickened rims; *rows 4 (right),* 5: bowls with externally thickened rims; *row 6:* incised body and basal sherds; *row 7:* ovate bowls with pinched-in sides.

ternally until they arrive at the rim with a wedge-shaped outline, flattened on top. The flat surface is incised with two parallel lines. Although wedge-rim sherds are more numerous in the late part of the Santa Maria phase, in terms of percentages, the sample is about the same for both parts of the phase because of the much larger late Santa Maria total sample. Dimensions in cm.: rim diameter, 32; wall thickness, 0.7, thickening to 1.0 at rim.

Convex-wall bowls, externally thickened rims are slightly smaller versions of the shape already described under Canoas White. Dimensions in cm.: rim diameter, 16–18; height (one specimen), 4.5; wall thickness, 0.5. Base diameter seems to average about 6.0 cm. less than the rim diameter.

Large vessels with externally thickened rims. Most of these heavy vessels have nearly vertical walls and unusually bulky rims, bolstered externally to give a slightly everted effect. They are similar to Chiapa de Corzo II White Monochrome vessels (Dixon 1959: 25) and similar rims are found at Trapiche and Chalahuites (García Payón, 1966: pl. XXXII, 1–6). Dimensions in cm.: rim diameter, 20–42, average, about 35; wall thickness, 0.9–1.2.

Incurved-rim bowls with dimple bases are small vessels that rest on the edges of a shallow circular depression, or dimple, in the bottom. They have convex walls and constricted mouths. Most of the rims are externally three-line incised. One has the deeply incised "break" motif shown in Fig. 42 (row 3, right). These bowls are stick-burnished inside and out. Dimensions in cm. of illustrated bowl: rim diameter, 13; dimple diameter, 4.5; height, 6.5; wall thickness, 0.5.

Dimple bases are a mode appearing in the Middle Formative and continuing in the Late Formative period. They are present in the Conchas phase at La Victoria (Coe 1961: fig. 6g).

Ovate bowls with pinched-in sides. We have borrowed Vaillant's term (1935: 223) for this strange and possibly ceremonial vessel form. The shape appears in Chiapa de Corzo II and during late El Arbolillo I. It was used on at least one occasion as a grave offering (Vaillant, *loc. cit.*). The two most complete of the thirteen Rio Salado Gray examples will be described individually. Both are illustrated in Fig. 42 (bottom row).

One bowl, from Zone D of Ts 367, resembles a small gravy boat with a dimple base and two additional depressions, probably centered on each side, near the rim. The latter give the vessel a pinched-in appearance. It has a single line incised around the outer wall just below the rim. Its maximum height of about

5 CM.

FIG. 43. RIO SALADO GRAY. Effigy sherds and late variants.

motifs are customarily incised. The bowls are virtually identical to examples from the earliest period at Zacatenco (Vaillant 1930: pl. IIf). Dimensions in cm.: rim diameter, 26–30, average, 28; wall thickness, 0.5–0.6; thickened rims, about 0.8–1.2.

Convex-wall bowls, wedge-shaped rims. Sherds from these vessels expand gradually externally and in-

FIG. 44. EARLY SANTA MARIA TRADE SHERDS. *Upper left:* Zacatenco Red-on-white, Black with Red-filled incisions, White-slip Red-paste (La Mina White); *center:* La Venta Black Raspada; *upper right:* Zacatenco Brown Incised; *lower left:* La Venta Zoned Rocker-stamped and Dili Punctate; *lower center:* Ocos Buff with shell-edge rocker-stamping; *lower right:* La Venta Zoned and Unzoned Rocker-stamped.

7.0 cm. is reached at each end of the long axis, which measures about 14 cm. The width must have been about 8.0 cm. The diameter of the dimple base is 3.5 cm. Wall thickness ranges from 0.5 to 0.7 cm.

The second pinched-sided bowl, from Zone C of Ts 367, is somewhat larger, with an estimated long axis of over 20 cm. and a width of about 16 cm. Its maximum height must have been about 10 cm. The wall thickness averages 0.5 cm. This example is decorated with wide, shallow grooves which radiate out from the point of maximum "pinching" and curve downward around the sides of the bowl. The extant depression or "pinch" in the wall is outlined by fine incising.

Comales or plates. Over a dozen sherds represent flat, platelike vessels with long upturned rims.

Pumpkin tecomate. The single rim shows some flattening at the edge on the outer surface. Rim diameter, 14 cm. Wall thickness, 0.7 cm.

Bottle. One sherd of a flaring-rim bottle was found.

Later forms. Early Palo Blanco shapes not found in Rio Salado Gray in the Santa Maria phase include incense burners, effigy fragments, cylindrical vessels with direct rims and with wide everted rims, and ollas

with funnel necks, short straight necks, and long or short flaring necks.

Aberrant or Trade Wares

After the majority of the sherds from early Santa Maria had been classified, over 2,500 sherds remained that were not readily classifiable into major or resident types. Over 2,200 of these were too badly worn to attempt to classify, but 312 sherds in good condition failed to fit our resident types. About one hundred of these appeared to be wares common in other regions and were identified by the Tehuacan Project staff. Others were identified by such distinguished visitors to Tehuacan as Ignacio Bernal, Michael Coe, James Ford, Gareth Lowe, Alfonso Medellín Zenil, John Paddock, Román Piña Chan, Robert Squier, Paul Tolstoy, and Bruce Warren. For their assistance we are very grateful.

Unfortunately, many of these trade wares have not been described in print, nor have they been identified under the binomial system. For convenience we have taken the liberty of so naming them, somewhat in the hope that we stimulate or provoke others to name and describe them fully. In the following descriptions we have listed them when possible according to the region in which we believe they were made.

VALLEY OF MEXICO WARES

Tlatilco Negative-painted. Fourteen bowl fragments of gray paste have a white-slipped surface and black designs, probably firing clouds, on them. These sherds were identified by Piña Chan as similar to bowls occurring at Tlatilco. One similarly fire-clouded sherd from a bottle was also found in Zone I of Ts 368e (see Piña Chan 1958: fig. 38).

Zacatenco Brown Incised. Seventeen sherds of incurved-rim bowls have a reddish-brown surface and a single groove around the lip. Parallel lines extend down the body from the groove. This type goes back to earliest El Arbolillo times in the Valley of Mexico (Tolstoy and Guénette 1965).

Zacatenco Brown ollas. Polished brown body sherds of what seem to be ollas number a dozen; one funnel-neck fragment occurred in Zone D of Ts 368e. Piña Chan identified these sherds as coming from Zacatenco. Tolstoy notes that such ollas occur mainly in early and middle Zacatenco times (Tolstoy and Guénette 1965).

Zacatenco Red-on-white. Two sherds have a red slip over white paste. One has lines cut through the red surface revealing the white paste. Similar sherds are found in Gualupita, Morelos (Vaillant and Vaillant 1934: 81). The second sherd is undecorated except for the red slip and resembles sherds from middle Zacatenco and Ticoman (Vaillant 1930: 88; 1931).

Morelos and *Zacatenco Orange Lacquer.* Two sherds have an all-over orange lacquer surface. Piña Chan identified one as characteristic of Morelos in Middle Formative times (cf. Piña Chan 1958: fig. 42 *k*, *l*). The other sherd resembles the matte orange specimens from middle Zacatenco (Tolstoy and Guénette 1965: fig. 4).

Cerro de Tepalcate Punctate. Four bowl sherds have a polished brown surface and fingernail punctates inside zones outlined by incising. According to Piña Chan, similar sherds were found in abundance at Cerro de Tepalcate of Middle to Late Formative times in the Valley of Mexico (Piña Chan 1958: 119).

Ticoman Red and *Ticoman Orange.* In two of the latest Santa Maria components a red sherd of a flaring-wall bowl and an orange body sherd were identified by Piña Chan as Ticoman Red and Ticoman Orange respectively (see Vaillant 1931: 284, 286).

VALLEY OF MEXICO OR OLMEC WARES

Hard Buff. A number of hard buff-colored sherds with large flecks of amphibole-pyroxene temper occurred in the earlier levels of Santa Maria. They have a superficial similarity to Coatepec White and according to García Payón may have affiliations with the Gulf coast. One has a painted red rim. Piña Chan commented that similar sherds occur in some abundance at Tlatilco. We are unable, however, to find illustrations or descriptions of this type for either the Valley of Mexico or the Veracruz coast.

Kaolin White. Forty-four sherds of a distinctive thin, fine-tempered paste are snow-white from surface to surface and have a kaolin-like feel. This paste is hard and brittle. Three rim sherds are from small tecomates, three are from small bowls with flaring rims, and one is from a bottle. According to Piña Chan these examples are identical to specimens found in Morelos and in burials from the middle levels of Tlatilco (Iglesia subphase) in the Valley of Mexico. They also occur in Trapiche I and II and the San Lorenzo and La Venta phases of the central Gulf Coast, the Jocotal phase of the west coast of Guatemala (Coe and Flannery 1967: 69), and in the San Jose and Guadalupe manifestations in Oaxaca. On the basis of geological studies, Michael Coe is of the opinion that this type is made from clay in the Olmec region. In fact, Kaolin White must be the same type as Coe's Xochiltepec White of San Lorenzo, Veracruz.

White-slip Red-paste. Thirty-one sherds of glossy white-slipped pottery made on a hard, finely tempered, brick-red paste occur throughout early Santa Maria levels. They show similar vessel forms and a similar geographical range to those of Kaolin White. Coe is of the opinion that these sherds were also manufactured in the Olmec region. At San Lorenzo, he calls this ware La Mina White.

(La Venta) Black Raspada. Five sherds with polished gray to black surfaces show post-firing excised areas, the kind of "raspada" technique common at Tlatilco (Piña Chan 1958: 36), La Venta, Tres Zapotes (Weiant 1943: 73), San Jose in Oaxaca, Aguilar of Panuco (MacNeish 1954: fig. 15), Conchas of the Guatemala Pacific coast (Coe 1961: fig. 28), and Trapiche II of central Veracruz (García Payón 1966). Most of the sherds are too small to allow tracing of the design, but one gray-ware sherd from Zone D¹ of Ts 367 has an abstract "S"-shaped motif scraped out of the hard paste. Another sherd shows raspada areas set apart from smooth areas by deeply carved lines which

84

were made while the paste was still soft. According to Squier, this type is very abundant at La Venta, where polished black reduced wares have a long history. Thus, we would guess that this type was manufactured in the La Venta region. However, it is also abundant in the Valley of Oaxaca.

(La Venta) White Raspada. Four sherds have a paste like the finer examples of Canoas White and a white slip like Coatepec White. They have designs made by cutting through the white slip. Geographically, they have a distribution similar to the black raspada sherds and may have originated in the same region.

(La Venta) Zoned and Unzoned Rocker-stamped. Eight sherds, each made of a different kind of paste, were decorated with plain rocker-stamping. On four sherds the stamping was unzoned. Two bowl sherds had fine plain rocker-stamping inside zones outlined by incising; two tecomate sherds had crude rocker-stamping inside zones below collared rims. This is the kind of long, narrow, rocker-stamping that occurs at Trapiche II (García Payón 1966), Tlatilco (Piña Chan 1958), La Venta (Drucker 1952), and San Lorenzo (Coe, personal communication).

Trapiche Black-rimmed Orange. Three orange sherds with rims fired black resemble those found in Trapiche II and III (García Payón 1966).

Trapiche Orange. A single rim from a flaring-wall bowl resembles orange sherds which occur in Trapiche II (García Payón 1966). The sherd has a buff paste tempered with grayish grit particles and is coated with a soft orange slip.

CHIAPAS OR GUATEMALA PACIFIC COAST WARES

Dili Resist. One sherd of an orangish convex-wall bowl has wide vertical reddish stripes extending from the lip, made by the negative paint or resist technique. Gareth Lowe expressed the opinion that it resembled bowls found at Chiapa de Corzo in Dili (Chiapa II) deposits.

Dili Fingernail Punctate. Five rims of small tecomates resemble more than anything else specimens from Chiapa de Corzo (see Dixon 1959: fig. 52d). The paste is gray, with a coarse, sparkling, grit-and-mica temper. The decoration consists of rows of fingernail punctations set off from the lip by a wide incised line. Tecomates with mouths encircled by concentric rings of punctations are decidedly foreign to the Tehuacan Valley, but occur in the Grijalva Basin during the Dili or Chiapa II phase. A design of this general type from La Venta is illustrated by Drucker (1952: fig. 28f);

García Payón illustrates a similar one from Trapiche II (1966: pl. XLIV–10).

Escalera Orange. Five sherds, all probably from the same flaring-wall flat-bottomed bowl, had a paste and reddish-orange color like Mars Orange of Mamom of the Peten (R. E. Smith 1955). Gareth Lowe, after examining them, ventured the opinion that they were not Mars Orange, but a variant thereof, found in the Escalera phase of Chiapas.

Conchas Orange. Five polished orange sherds with a distinctive paste and incised designs, one a double-line-break motif, resemble closely Conchas Orange of Conchas 1 and 2 from the Guatemala Pacific coast (Coe 1961: 76–79).

Ocos Buff. Six sherds of a polished brown ware have shell-edge rocker-dentate-stamping set off by incised lines. Sherds with similar stamping occur in Ocos levels at La Victoria in Guatemala (Coe 1961: 57).

Suchiate Brushed. A single tecomate rim sherd has horizontal polishing on the rim and oblique brushing on the shoulder below it. This resembles Suchiate Brushed of the Cuadros to Conchas 1 phases of Guatemala (Coe and Flannery 1967: p. 30 and fig. 8).

MISCELLANEOUS WARES

Patterned burnished. A sherd resembling Quachilco Gray has an area polished lightly in one direction at right angles to a heavily burnished area that turned almost black. Although the sherd resembles zoned-toned variants of Quachilco Gray, the lack of incising to set off the differently polished zones and the black color make it aberrant in our collections.

White slip rubbed with red. These sherds have a paste and slip like Coatepec White, but a reddish to purplish pigment—probably hematite—has been rubbed into the surface until a fine polish has been attained. The finish is obviously foreign to our area. Medellín Zenil thought these sherds came from undescribed horizons on the Veracruz coast.

Black ware with red-filled incisions. Two dozen polished black sherds are decorated with wide incised lines filled with red paint. The practice of rubbing dry red pigment into incisions or excisions is extremely common in the Middle Formative, occurring at El Arbolillo (Vaillant 1935: 255), La Victoria (Coe 1961: 71), and other sites.

Sherd with criss-cross grooving. One gray sherd with a paste not typical of the Canoas complex shows wide, shallow grooving in the form of criss-crossed lines set into the unslipped surface of the paste before firing.

FIG. 45. MISCELLANEOUS OBJECTS. *From top to bottom,*
bird whistles, snake head, beaver-like bird tail, seated
rodent, and jaguar and coyote (two views each).

Double cup. One large fragment of brown ware resembles a double cup, or two cups joined along one side, similar to a double cup from Middle Formative times in the Valley of Mexico (Vaillant 1930).

Ring base. A single ring base from Zone C, Ts 367, was made of a drab brown paste. Circular bases have occurred in Middle and Late Formative sites elsewhere in Mesoamerica, but are extremely rare in the Middle Formative at Tehuacan.

Single sherds of foreign wares were found in various components. They are listed with other trade sherds in Table 31.

Miscellaneous Objects

Sherd disks. The thirty disks found in early Santa Maria levels were usually made of Rio Salado Coarse or Canoas White paste. Many are pierced. One unpierced disk was ground from an aberrant red sherd with a white line painted on it.

Bird effigies (whistles?). Five bird heads of amphibole-pyroxene-tembered paste coated with a drab brick-red slip seem to have been attached to rounded hollow bodies. They vaguely resemble bird effigy whistles from La Victoria (Coe 1961: fig. 58, no. 9). Animal effigy whistles are common at Middle Formative sites from Zacatenco (Vaillant 1930: pl. XXXVIII), La Venta (Drucker 1952: 139) and Tres Zapotes (Weiant 1943: pls. 48–52) to the Pacific coast of Guatemala.

Effigy ocarina or whistle body fragments. One of three fragments found appears to have been a hollow fat man holding his stomach; the mouthpiece is flattened and the blow-hole lenticular. A specimen from Tres Zapotes (Weiant 1943: pl. 47, no. 15) somewhat resembles ours, except that the Tres Zapotes ocarina has a large mouth opening at the navel.

Mouthpieces. Three mouthpieces of whistles were made of paste similar to the body fragments.

Coyote effigy. One sherd, with a white slip and red paint on red paste, is part of a hollow, realistically modeled coyote's head.

Other animal effigies include a seated mouse or rat, an object with birdlike feet (ocarina?), a beaver-like bird's tail, a hollow facial fragment of a jaguar, and a fragmentary hollow snake's head that resembles vessel supports from later phases.

Pestle. A small, well-formed, bell-shaped pottery pestle was found at Las Canoas.

Figurines

Fragments of late Ajalpan figurine types continued to be found in early Santa Maria levels: Hollow Dwarf

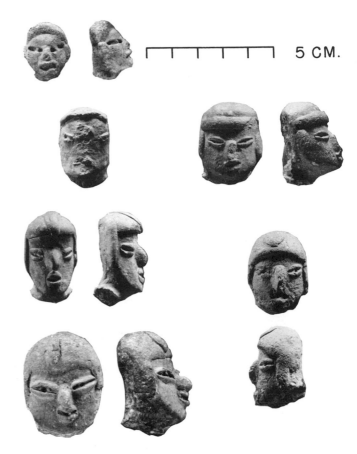

FIG. 46. HELMETED HEADS.

heads, bodies, and limbs; No Face heads; Trackwoman seated body fragments; and large solid limbs.

HELMETED HEADS

11 specimens: 8 excavated, 3 collected.

Dimensions in cm.: height (9 specimens), 2.6–3.3, average, 3.1; length (10 specimens), 1.7–2.3, average, 2.0; width (10 specimens), 1.9–2.6, average, 2.4.

Paste: somewhat like Rio Salado Coarse with large angular pieces of temper.

The heads are small, relatively long in outline, and plano-convex in cross section. Chins jut forward and appear pugnacious. Mouths are an oval applique of clay with a horizontal slip in the middle; two examples have a pinpoint punctuation in the center of the slit. Noses, which are appliqued, are large and aquiline. Very prominent eyes are made by a narrow applique with a wide slit in it and have a central punctation for a pupil. The top of the head is covered by a crescentic helmet with sides that extend down over the ears. Four helmets have a medial ridge applied over

FIG. 47. BABY FACE HEADS.

the top; two helmets have a medial disk, one helmet has a horizontal strip like a brim across the front, and three have no appliques at all. The headdresses of the remaining specimens were not extant.

In the Tehuacan Valley these heads were uncovered in early Santa Maria levels. One figurine head from Trapiche II seems to be of this type and, what is more, it even looks as if it were made of the same paste as those from Tehuacan (personal observation). One of the Type E heads from middle Tres Zapotes (Drucker 1943a: pl. 27h), some of the Type Di heads from the Valley of Mexico (Vaillant 1930: pl. XIX, 6, 7), and the Type Dii heads from Morelos (Vaillant and Vaillant 1934: fig. 6, no. 6) seem related.

BABY FACE HEADS

6 specimens: 4 excavated, 2 collected.
Dimensions in cm.: height (4 specimens); 2.8–4.6, average, 3.6; length (5 specimens), 1.5–3.6, average, 2.5; width (5 specimens), 1.8–3.2, average, 2.2.
Paste: fairly fine-tempered clay with slip; resembles Canoas White.

In outline these small to medium solid heads are oval, but in cross section they are plano- or concave-convex. The usual effect is of a round-faced individual, with a rounded chin and full cheeks. However, one example has flat cheeks and a square jaw. Mouths are downturned, crescentic appliques with a down-

FIG. 48. HOLLOW LOWLAND HEADS AND LIMBS.

pointing crescentic gash in them. Three examples have shallow punctations in each corner of the mouth, further emphasizing their downcast character. One also has vertical punctations depicting teeth. Noses are small, wide, and triangular in outline. Nostrils on the unbattered specimens are marked by tiny punctations. Eyes are represented by elongated appliques of clay with shallow horizontal grooves in them and in some cases conical punctation for pupils. These figurines wear crescentic caps or helmets. Elongated appliques below the cap represent ears. Five of the specimens were painted or slipped white and two had red paint in the mouths.

This type occurred in early Santa Maria times in the Tehuacan Valley. It is similar to, or the same type as, other Baby Face heads of the general triangular area encompassed by Guerrero on the south, Tampico on the north, and Tabasco on the east.

HOLLOW LOWLAND HEADS

17 specimens: 13 excavated, 4 collected.
Dimensions in cm. of one complete head: height, 6.3; length, about 4.0; width, 5.5.
Paste: ranges from Canoas White to Coatepec Plain.
See also: Hollow White Bodies and Limbs (below).

The heads are large and hollow, with oval faces. They are almost as thick as they are wide. The chins (four specimens) are round with the suggestion of a dimple; the cheeks are full. The lower lips (five specimens) are thinner than the thicker applied upper lips, giving a pouting countenance. Mouths are parted and made by two triangular plough marks pushed outward. Two examples show incisions depicting incisors. Noses are relatively wide and flat. Ten preserved eyes were made on a bulging surface by pushing a triangular object toward each corner and then piercing the raised portion in the center with a large conical punch. Six heads wear crescentic caps, and four of these also have appliqued buns, three of which are incised. The three incised buns are medially located; the one without decoration is placed to one side.

These heads occur in early Santa Maria times in the Tehuacan Valley and in Trapiche II of Veracruz. They also resemble figurines from Tlatilco, San Jose Mogote, San Lorenzo, middle Tres Zapotes (Drucker 1943a: pl. 28x), and Conchas 1 (Coe 1961: fig. 54).

TRAPICHE BUNNED-HELMET HEADS

4 specimens: 3 excavated, 1 collected.
Dimensions in cm.: height, 4.0–4.7, average, 4.5; length, 1.9–3.0, average, 2.4; width, 2.6–2.8.
Paste: resembles Canoas White (2 specimens); fine temperless clay (2 specimens).

The heads in outline are long and elliptical. They have straight to concave backs and more or less convex faces, with the most raised part of the face being a jutting chin. Three of these prominent chins have small appliques on them, perhaps representing beards. A lenticular applique of clay, split by two horizontal

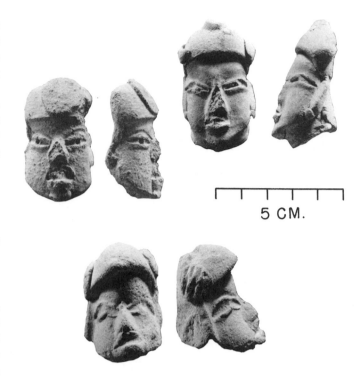

FIG. 49. TRAPICHE BUNNED-HELMET HEADS.

gouges, represents the lips. Noses were triangular appliques of clay, but all save one are battered and fragmentary. Eyes are large and crescentic, with downcurving or down-pointed appliqued lids and eyeballs formed by two down-pointing plough marks. One specimen has a punctation at the center of the eye to indicate the pupil. Headdresses are basically crescentshaped and project outward over the forehead. Two headdresses have a single medial disk appliqued over the forehead; one example has a medial disk in the position of a topknot and disks on either side. The remaining specimen has disks over each ear and none in the center. Ears are represented by elongated appliques of clay. The heads were probably painted red, for the medial-bunned head still has traces of paint on headdress and mouth.

Although this is the dominant figurine type in Trapiche II in central Veracruz, only four specimens of this type were found in the Tehuacan Valley. The three excavated examples are from early Santa Maria levels. The type also appears at La Venta (Drucker 1952: pls. 30a, 37d), at Tres Zapotes (Drucker 1943a: pl. 29p), and at Cerro de las Mesas (Drucker 1943b: pl. 52p). In a vague way they resemble the "Coarse Flat Rectangular-eyed" type of the Aguilar and Chila phases at Panuco (MacNeish 1954: 593). They also

5 CM.   5 CM.

FIG. 50. VALLEY OF MEXICO TYPE DI HEADS.   FIG. 51. CRESCENTIC CAP HEADS.

show similarities in eye form and other features to some Type A figurines of middle Zacatenco times in the Valley of Mexico (Vaillant 1930: pl. XXI, nos. 2, 4, 7, and 10).

VALLEY OF MEXICO TYPE DI HEADS

34 specimens: 10 excavated, 24 collected.
Dimensions in cm.: height, 2.2–4.4, average, 3.3; length, 1.5–2.6, average, 1.8; width, 1.3–3.3, average, 2.1.
Paste: resembles Rio Salado Coarse.

These heads are elliptical, with slightly convex backs and roughly convex to straight facial planes. They have prominent chins and aquiline noses. Eighteen of the twenty-one more complete specimens have lips made by an oval applique of clay. Four of these have mouths made by a wide horizontal incision across the applique; eight have two overlapping linear punches in the applique; and five have overlapping punches with a small, round hole at the junction for the mouth. The four specimens without appliqued lips

have only two overlapping linear punches to serve as a mouth. Noses are elliptical to conical appliques which are sometimes pinched along the ridge. Eyes are made on lenticular or long ovoid appliques that slant downward toward the nose. An incision down the long axis of the applique has a small hole in the center to complete the eye. Five heads have incised eyebrows just above and paralleling the eye.

All have a head- or hairdress marked by vertical or radiating lines, but the style of coiffure varies. Five have radiating lines from the edge of the forehead to make what looks like a crew cut; twelve have a central hairknot decorated with vertical incisions; eleven have incised hairknots on either side of the top of the head; one has three hairknots; and two have a single medial braid on top of a crescentic cap. Ears are usually indicated by elongated strips of clay.

In Tehuacan this type appears in middle Santa Maria times. If the Type Di head with hairknots from the Valley of Mexico is not the same type, it is very closely related (Vaillant 1930: pls. XVIII, nos. 1, 5, 6, 9). It was also unearthed in Trapiche II (García Payón 1966: pl. LII, no. 8) of central Veracruz. Figurines from La Venta (Drucker 1952: pl. 39) and Tres Zapotes (Drucker 1943a: pl. 27i; Weiant 1943: pl. 21, no. 13; pl. 27, nos. 5, 8) are also closely related. In fact, this type may be a good link for many Middle Formative sites in central Mexico.

CRESCENTIC CAP HEADS

13 specimens: 10 excavated, 3 collected.
Dimensions of 3–5 specimens in cm.: height, 5.2, 5.5, 8.6; length, 3.0, 3.0, 3.2, 3.3, 3.5; width, 3.5, 3.6, 4.5, 5.5., 6.0.
Paste: ranges from Canoas White to Rio Salado Gray.
Surface finish: white wash.

The heads are oval in outline and plano-convex or concave-convex in cross section. Chins are fairly well marked and rounded. Cheeks are also rounded. The lips are parted. The upper lip is definitely projecting, but is not made by an applique; instead it seems to have been pushed up and out by the formation of the open mouth. The lower lip is less pronounced. The mouth was formed by two deep conical punctations at the corners connected by a wide incision. As Coe (1961: p. 95, fig. 54e) notes, the open mouth gives some of these figures an expression of "intelligent" surprise. Nostrils are relatively large and are formed by conical punctations. One specimen may be wearing a nose plug. Ears are long appliques and have discoidal or doughnut-shaped earplugs that slant toward the back of the head. Eyes were made on a bulging surface by horizontal overlapping triangular punches pushed toward opposite corners. Pupils are indicated by conical punctations in the center of the eye. Two examples have eyebrows made of long, curved ridges of clay. The forehead is relatively constricted. A small crescent cap is perched on top of the head. One cap is decorated with two conical punches. Another specimen has a fringe or roll of hair, indicated by multiple punch marks, across the back of the neck. Most of the specimens were covered with a white wash, traces of which remain. Remains of red paint are found in the mouths and along the hairline of all specimens.

This is an early lowland type that for some unknown reason has not often been found in excavation in the highlands. Some of the large examples of the Crescentic Cap type of Panuco (MacNeish 1954: fig. 33, no. 26) and some of the heads from Trapiche I and II (García Payón 1966: pl. LII, nos. 6, 7, 11–14), from Tres Zapotes (Weiant 1943: pl. 12, nos. 4, 6, 17, 22), from La Venta (Drucker 1952: pl. 30o), from

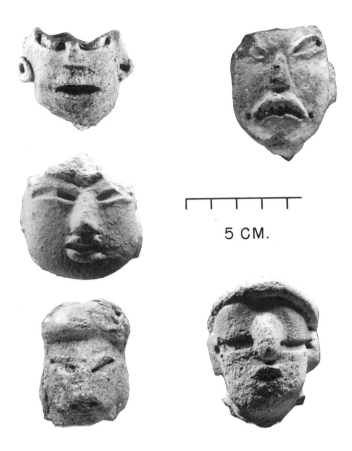

FIG. 52. PLOUGHED-EYE HEADS.

Chiapa de Corzo II–IV (Lowe and Mason 1965: fig. 9), and from the Conchas phase in Guatemala (Coe 1961: fig. 54 e, nos. 1, 6) seem to be closely related.

PLOUGHED-EYE HEADS

11 specimens: 7 excavated, 4 collected.
Dimensions of 3–8 specimens in cm.: height, 4.2, 4.6, 5.7; length, 2.6–3.4, average, 2.9; width, 2.8–4.7, average, 3.9.
Paste: excavated specimens resemble Canoas White; surface specimens, Rio Salado Gray.
Surface finish: thin, fine slip.

The heads are oblong in outline, and more or less plano-convex in cross section. Chins are wide but well defined, and cheeks are wide and full. Lips are made by two crescentic fillets of clay, and mouths are made by a wide incision, which in six examples is pointed downward at the corners and gives the faces a sad or pouting expression. Noses are long with a prominent ridge; nostrils are not depicted. Eyes are made on a raised portion of the face (though one is made in fillet) by two long, wide, overlapping plough marks that usually point slightly downward at the corners. Long fillets at the sides of the head indicate ears or braids of hair. One example has doughunt-shaped earplugs. Caps are intact on only three specimens, they are fairly high and are crescent shaped. One has the remains of two disks on either side at the top.

In Tehuacan these heads occur in the late part of the early Santa Maria period. They are a common type in Trapiche II (García Payón 1966: pl. LIX, nos. 1–3). Some specimens from La Venta (Drucker 1952: pl. 30a) and Tres Zapotes (Weiant 1943: pl. 21, nos. 1, 5, 18) are similar, as is one from El Arbolillo II (Vaillant 1935: fig. 10, no. 1).

LA VENTA HAIRKNOT HEADS

3 specimens collected.*
Dimensions of 1–2 specimens in cm.: height, about 3.0; length, 2.7, 3.0; width, 2.5, 3.4.
Paste: abundantly tempered fine gray.

The heads are made of gray paste unlike any resident pastes of the Tehuacan Valley. Only one specimen is nearly complete and most of our description will be based upon this head, found at the edge of the profile in Ts 367. This small head, like the other specimens, is spherical in form. It has a well-defined jutting jaw and puffed cheeks, each of which has a conical punch in it (rather like a dimple). The mouth is wide open with creases at either side, giving a laughing appearance. The lips are made by two crescent-shaped appliques of clay. A wedge-shaped linear punch has been pushed in between the lips to hollow out the mouth. Above the upper lip two small appliques of clay represent a nose plug. The nose is short and aquiline. The large eyes are outlined by an oval incision. The pupils are a single large conical punch. In the middle of the forehead on all three specimens, a single hemispherical applique seems to represent a hairknot. The hairknot is mottled by a number of small fine punctations. Across the top of the head and extending down the back is another applique covered with fine linear punches, representing hair. The ears are also appliqued, as are two round earplugs which stick almost straight out from the sides of the head.

Although evidence is rather slim in the Tehuacan Valley, this type seems to come from about the middle of the Santa Maria phase. It has great similarity to a head found at La Venta in the 1943 excavations (Drucker 1952: pl. 43a) and seems to provide an extremely good link between middle Santa Maria and at

*One of two heads from Ts 367 was from the edge of the profile, at a depth roughly equivalent to Zones C, D¹, and D², and must represent the early to middle Santa Maria period.

5 CM.

FIG. 53. TRES ZAPOTES CHIN-STRAP AND LA VENTA HAIRKNOT HEADS.

least part of the La Venta occupations. Also, one figurine from a Chiapa de Corzo II level is of this type (G. Lowe, personal communication).

TRES ZAPOTES CHIN-STRAP HEAD

1 specimen excavated.
Dimensions in cm.: height, over 4.0; length, 2.2; width, 3.2.
Paste: resembles Canoas White, but more heavily tempered.

The head is plano-convex in profile and roughly rectangular in outline. Below the chin is a large wide strap with punctate decoration. This strap or collar terminates at either side, just below large discoidal earplugs. The mouth is formed by two horizontal linear punctates that barely overlap. The nose has broken off, but it obviously was relatively long and narrow. The eyes are also made by two horizontal overlapping linear punches. Most of the headdress is missing, but it probably was a rectangular or crescentic helmet. A side piece extends down to overlap the chin-strap.

The only example from Tehuacan comes from Ts 367, Zone D, an early Santa Maria level. It seems to be the same type as two heads Weiant illustrates from Tres Zapotes (1943: pl. 20, nos. 2, 4). Also, one of the bun-helmeted type of Trapiche II has a chin strap and might be related (García Payón 1966: pl. LXIII, no. 3).

VALLEY OF MEXICO TYPE F HEADS

3 specimens: 2 excavated, 1 collected.
Dimensions in cm.: height (2 specimens), 3.0, 3.4; length, 1.5, 1.7, 2.2; width, 3.0, 3.5, 3.7.
Paste: resembles Coatepec Plain, but with less temper.

The three specimens are crudely made and are badly eroded as well. The heads are relatively flat

FIG. 54. VALLEY OF MEXICO FIGURINE TYPES. *Row 1*, Early F; *row 2*, Types C3a and C3d.

and wide. They have fairly sharp chins. Mouths are two rectangular punctates placed side by side. Noses are not well defined. Each eye is two elongated punches. Two of the heads have slightly raised eyelids surrounding the punches. Whether the lids are the result of a thin applique or of the punching is hard to discern. In either case, the eyes are transitional between the Type C and Type F eyes. All three heads have or had simple elongate topknots—more like Type F than the more elaborate forms of Type C. One specimen has two holes side by side just beneath the place where its topknot broke off.

In the Tehuacan Valley, the two excavated heads come from an early Santa Maria zone. In the Valley of Mexico this type of figurine dates from early Zacatenco and El Arbolillo I (Vaillant 1935: fig. 12).

VALLEY OF MEXICO TYPE C3A HEAD

1 specimen excavated.
Dimensions in cm.: height, 3.1; length, 1.8; width, 2.6.
Paste: finely knit, lightly tempered; unlike any resident paste.
Surface finish: fine dark reddish-brown slip.

The specimen is almost an equilateral triangle in outline and is plano-convex in profile with the tip of

the nose being the top of the convexity. The jaw is wide. The upper lip is a fillet of clay, but the lower lip (or chin?) was pushed out by the formation of the open mouth. The beak-like nose is a wide triangular applique with nostrils indicated by extremely prominent slits that slant widely outward and downward, similar to specimens in Vaillant (1935: fig. 17, no. 5). The eyes are formed by crudely applied fillets that appear to be slit horizontally. The slits, however, are actually two punctures toward either corner of each eye.

The top of the head has been shaped into a conical cap or turban. A large wide medial strip is plastered to the front of the cone and over the top. Long crude appliques represent ears; backsweeping doughnut-shaped fillets at the bottom represent earplugs. Both earplugs originally rested on small spheres of clay, probably the beads of a necklace, but only one bead remains.

The form of this head, the way it is made, and even the paste are so similar to Vaillant's Type C3a of early El Arbolillo I (1935: fig. 14, no. 1) that there is little doubt they are the same type. Our Tehuacan specimen might have come from the Valley of Mexico.

VALLEY OF MEXICO TYPE C3D HEAD

1 specimen excavated.
Dimensions in cm.: height, 4.7; length, 1.9; width, about 4.7.
Paste: fine grayish-brown clay with little temper; unlike any resident paste type.

The head is quite flat and for the most part is solid, but two small slots in the neck portion indicate that the head may have been attached to a hollow body or a rattle. Our specimen is squarish or oblong in outline and is relatively large. The chin is jutting and may represent a small beard (see Vaillant 1935: fig. 14, no. 7). Two elongated appliques (one now missing) formed the lips and small fine punctations between them represent the mouth or teeth. The nose on the Tehuacan specimen is worn off, but it probably originally was a wide triangular fillet. The eyelids are two oblong appliques of clay. Each eye has a vertical slot at each corner. Doughnut earplugs (only one remains) were appliqued to globs of clay representing the ears. The headdress is missing, but may have had wide horizontal strips of clay to represent the wrappings of a turban.

This head from the early Santa Maria phase seems to be Type C3d of late El Arbolillo I of the Valley of Mexico (Vaillant 1935: fig. 14, nos. 11–12; fig. 13, no. 9).

FIG. 55. NEGROID HEADS WITH HAIRKNOT.

NEGROID HEADS WITH HAIRKNOT

10 specimens: 5 excavated, 5 collected.
Dimensions of 4–6 specimens in cm.: height, 3.8–5.2, average, 4.6; length, 2.4–3.2, average, 2.7; width, 3.6–4.2, average, 4.0.
Paste: Rio Salado Coarse.

The heads are more or less conical with the top being the blunted apex of the cone. The chins are wide, round, and blend into round full cheeks. The lips originally were thick, long appliques of clay, with mouths usually indicated by two horizontal linear punctations. Noses originally were short, wide, and triangular. Ears are elongated and terminate in doughnut-shaped earplugs, which form the widest part of the head. Eyes were made by three punch marks; the pupil is a single conical perforation, while the two corners of the eyes are punctations made with a blunt flat object. Some heads have evidence of a small crescentic cap; all have or had on top of the head large roundish hairknots decorated by a series of short vertical jabs. Like similar specimens from the Conchas phase of Guatemala (Coe 1961: fig. 54*f*), many of the heads show evidence of having been battered about the mouth and nose. One head, with most of the body attached, has a hollow body of a type that is found in the lowland Maya Mamom phase.

This type was found in levels representing the middle of the Santa Maria phase. It has widespread lowland affiliations: similar specimens have been found at Panuco in the Aquilar phase (MacNeish 1954: fig. 23, nos. 19–21), in Trapiche II (García Payón 1966: pl. LII, no. 10), at Tres Zapotes (Weiant 1943: pl. 2, no. 15), at La Venta (Drucker 1952: pl. 26*e*), in Chiapa de Corzo II–IV (photographs supplied by Gareth Lowe), in the Conchas phase of the Guatemalan Pacific coast (Coe 1961: fig. 54*f*), and in the Mamom phase of the Peten (Peabody Museum, Cambridge). A few Type A specimens (Vaillant 1931: pl. XXI) from the Valley of Mexico show vague similarities.

MULTI-HAIRKNOT HEADS

9 specimens: 5 excavated, 4 collected.
Dimensions in cm.: height (5 specimens), 3.9–6.1, average, 5.1; length (7 specimens), 2.4–2.9, average, 2.7; width (8 specimens), 3.6–5.1, average, 4.3.
Paste: ranges from Rio Salado Gray to Canoas White.
Surface finish: thin orange slip.

The heads are oval and in cross section are mainly concave-convex, although one is plano-convex. The faces have a realistic cast. Jaws are wide and fairly

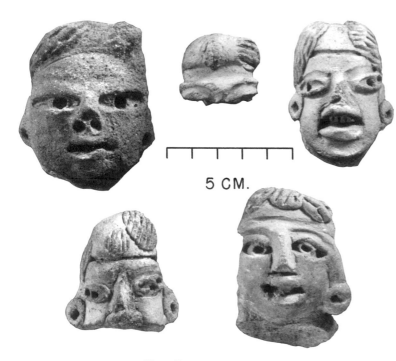

FIG. 56. MULTI-HAIRKNOT HEADS.

well defined; the jowls and cheeks are rounded. Lips are two crescentic appliques placed fairly well apart. A deep wide jab between the lips gives the face a pleased expression. Two heads have incisions indicating the upper teeth. Noses are long and aquiline. Only two specimens have nostrils, which are indicated by conical punctures. Eyes are shaped by three jabs, one toward each corner made with a flat pointed object and a third centrally located and made with a fairly large conical punch. Most of the heads have eyebrows raised by a wide crescentic incision. Short fillets at the side of the head indicate ears, and doughnut-shaped appliques represent earplugs.

A cap or hair line is marked off by a groove above the forehead. Several appliques of varying shapes, covered with incised lines, have been plastered on the cap. Some resemble shells and others look like hair or feathers. Four caps have appliques at opposite corners at the top of the head; one cap has an applique at the corner and another in the middle; and two caps have three appliques each, one at either side and one in the middle.

In Tehuacan these heads occur only in the middle of the Santa Maria period. The type is also found in the Conchas phase in Guatemala (Coe 1961: fig. 55) and in Chiapa de Corzo III–IV (photographs supplied by Gareth Lowe). The Tehuacan heads have some resemblance to heads from the Mamom phase at Uaxactun (Peabody Museum, Cambridge) and from La Venta (Drucker 1952: pl. 30), Tres Zapotes (Weiant 1943: pl. 10, 14) and El Trapiche.

HIGH-TURBAN SLIT-EYE HEADS

4 specimens excavated.
Dimensions in cm.: height (2 specimens), 3.3–3.5; length (3 specimens), 2.1, 1.2, 1.6; width (3 specimens), 3.0, 2.7, 2.7.
Paste: two similar to Rio Salado Coarse; two untempered fine silty clay.
Surface finish: slipped.

The heads are roughly rectangular in outline and although they are relatively flat, the features cause the face to be more convex than the back of the head. Two specimens have rather broad chins still intact. One chin is poorly defined while the other is well marked. On each of these specimens the mouth and lips are indicated by two long, narrow appliques of clay. Noses are narrow, long, and aquiline. Oversized eyes are indicated by two long narrow appliques of clay. Narrow foreheads are topped by high rectangular caps with

FIG. 57. HIGH-TURBAN SLIT-EYE HEADS.

punched or gouged appliques. Disk-shaped or doughnut-style earplugs have been appliqued at the sides of the heads.

One head is attached to a wide neck and narrow shoulders and has one undersized undulating arm still extant.

This type appears in the middle of the Santa Maria phase and is vaguely similar to figurines found in Monte Alban I in Oaxaca (Caso and Bernal 1952: fig. 479). It also has a vague resemblance to Type G of Lower II of Cerro de las Mesas in Veracruz (Drucker 1943b: pl. 52).

SEATED MOTHER BODIES

40 specimens: 36 excavated, 4 collected.
Dimensions in cm.: body length, 3.5–7.0; width, 3.0–5.0; thickness, 1.5–3.0.
Paste: resembles Rio Salado Coarse.

Some of these fragmentary seated bodies have portions of the leg attached. The legs were apparently either crossed or spread apart. There is a sharp break between legs and body. The torsos are relatively short, fairly thick, and have small, bulbous bellies. They are probably meant to represent pregnant women. The breasts are crudely formed and are sometimes pendulous. Shoulders are relatively narrow. Arms are bent and either rest on the chest or extend forward in a receptive position. A number of different kinds of head types may have been attached to this body type.

Although three specimens were found in very late Ajalpan levels, this type of body is mainly confined to the Santa Maria phase and is slightly more popular in early Santa Maria levels than in later components. In terms of wider geographical distribution, this type is particularly common at La Venta and in middle and early levels at Tres Zapotes. It also occurs in Middle

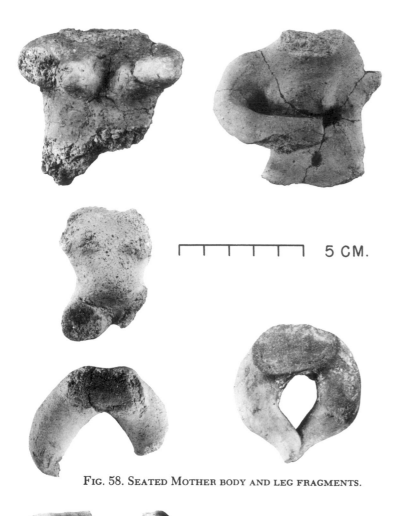

FIG. 58. SEATED MOTHER BODY AND LEG FRAGMENTS.

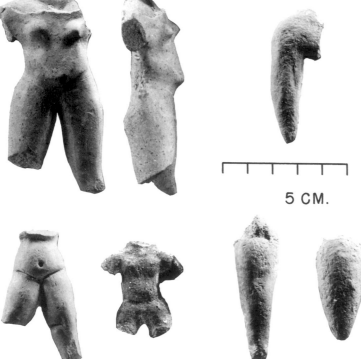

FIG. 59. VENUS BODY AND LIMB FRAGMENTS.

Formative times in other highland regions, particularly the Valley of Mexico and Morelos.

VENUS BODIES

33 specimens: 31 excavated, 2 collected.
Dimensions in cm.: length, 3.0–5.0; width at hips, 2.5–3.5.
Paste: resembles Canoas White.
Surface finish: thin white slip on half the sample.

The bodies are well-formed with plump thighs. They are rather highwaisted, with the narrowest part of the body (1.5–2.5 cm.) somewhat above the navel indication. They have small pointed breasts and sloping shoulders. Arms are usually missing. The junction of legs and hips and the crotch area are usually indicated by incised lines.

Exactly what type of head was attached to these bodies is difficult to determine; some of the Helmeted heads, the smaller Baby Face specimens, or the Trapiche Bunned-helmet type might have appeared on these bodies.

In the Tehuacan region Venus bodies occur from late Ajalpan through late Santa Maria times and are most popular in early Santa Maria levels. They have general similarities to many of the Tres Zapotes and La Venta figurine bodies from the Gulf Coast.

HOLLOW POLISHED WHITE BODIES AND LIMBS

35 specimens: 10 body fragments, 13 feet or legs, 4 arms or hands excavated; 2 body fragments, 6 feet or legs collected.
Dimensions in cm.: length of legs, 5.0–8.0; diameter of legs at hip, 3.0–5.0; diameter of arms at shoulder, about 3.0.
Paste: similar to Canoas White or Coatepec White.
Surface finish: polished white slip or wash.

The body fragments are extremely small. All figures are females with small breasts and rather large stomachs. Some seem to have been seated.

Legs are extremely short and are thick in the hip area. Toes are marked by incisions. The arms, of which we have a very poor sample, seem to be quite long (one specimen is 11 cm.) and usually are bent. These fragments may be parts of seated figures that go with our Olmecoid Hollow Lowland heads (see Fig. 48).

The body fragments appear in the early Santa Maria phase and have almost the same extra-areal distribution as the Hollow Lowland heads. Similar hollow, polished, white bodies and limbs occur in Middle Formative times in the Valley of Mexico, particularly at Tlatilco, in Morelos at Gualupita, and on the Gulf Coast in middle Tres Zapotes and at La Venta.

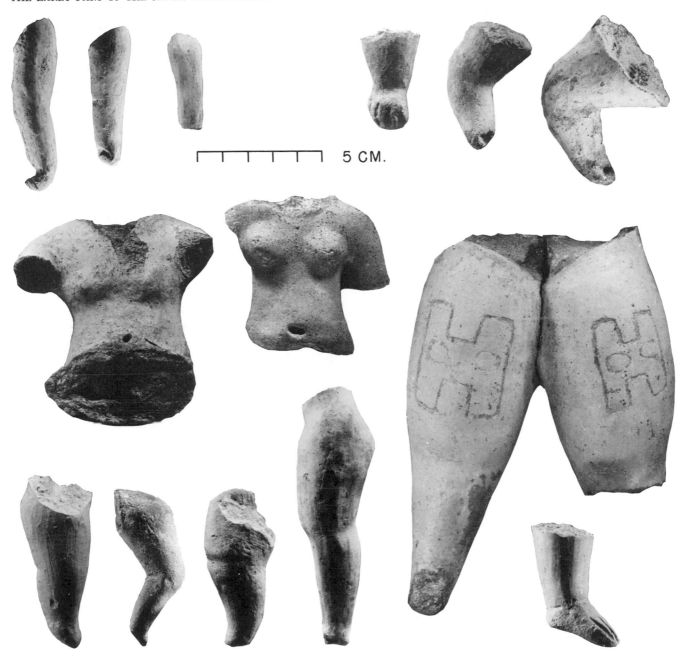

5 CM.

FIG. 60. SOLID POLISHED BODY AND LIMB FRAGMENTS.

SOLID POLISHED WHITE BODIES AND LIMBS

Paste: resembles Canoas White.
Surface finish: polished white wash or slip.

Seated bodies (8 excavated). Dimensions in cm.: length, 6–10; diameter at waist, 4.0–6.0. These large seated figures have wide sloping shoulders, rounded breasts, high narrow waists, round stomachs with large navels, and narrow hips. The bodies were probably attached to legs with huge bulging thighs. These figures are representative of the so-called Olmec complex of Middle Formative times. In the Tehuacan Valley they appear in early Santa Maria components and may well be associated with the Crescentic Cap or Ploughed-

97

eye heads, as well as with a number of solid white polished arm and leg forms.

Straight arms (19 excavated, 4 collected). Dimensions in cm.: length, over 5.0; diameter, 1.5–2.5. These fairly large straight arm fragments appear in the Tehuacan region near the middle of the Santa Maria phase. They may have been attached to polished white seated bodies.

Bent arms (14 excavated, 2 collected). Dimensions in cm.: length, 7.0–9.0; diameter at shoulder, 2.0–4.0. These arms are short, stocky, and bent nearly at right angles. The maximum width is next to the shoulder. The hands are closed into a fist. One would guess that some of these arms fit the solid polished white seated bodies and probably were bent in front of the chest or back from the body. The arms occur in the middle of the Santa Maria phase. Some Olmec figurines have this kind of arm.

Arms with fists (8 excavated, 3 collected). Dimensions in cm.: diameter of fist, 1.5–2.5; length, unknown. Our specimens are fragmentary remains of tapering arms. The distal end has been flattened and doubled over to indicate a closed hand or fist. On some examples small marks indicate the fingers. In the Tehuacan Valley the arms appear mainly in the early part of the Santa Maria phase and are probably associated with the solid white polished body type.

Bulbous legs (35 excavated, 7 collected). Dimensions in cm.: diameter of thigh, 2.0–8.0. Surface finish: polished white paint or simply polished. These legs are large and generally straight and must have been parted. The thighs are quite bulbous. The legs taper sharply at the foot. The intact examples have no break at the ankle and lack any indication of toes. One large pair of legs has an incised design (glyph?) repeated on each thigh; it looks like a large hollow "H" containing circles at either end of the crossbar. The legs occur throughout the Santa Maria phase. They seem to be most popular in the middle part of the phase, but were found in fairly large numbers in the later part of the Santa Maria phase.

Legs with incised toes (17 specimens excavated). Surface finish: polished white paint or simply polished. These leg fragments taper at the ankle. The rather pointed foot is separated from the leg by a groove. Toes are indicated by four incisions at the end of the foot. The legs occur in middle Santa Maria times in the Tehuacan Valley.

Other Limb Fragments

Bent arms (31 excavated, 6 collected). Dimensions in cm.: length, 3.0–6.0; maximum diameter, 1.0–2.5.

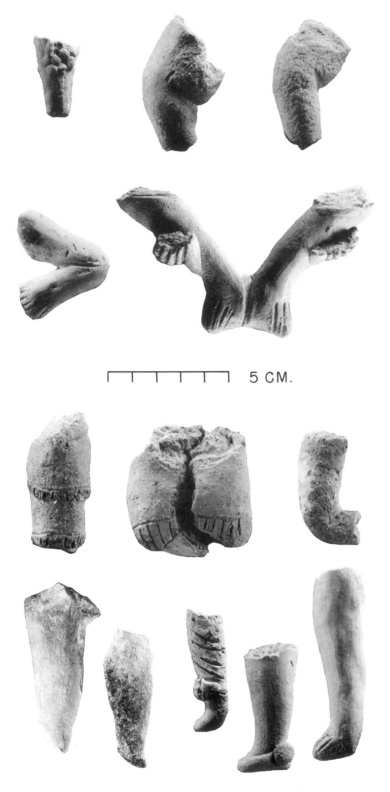

Fig. 61. Figurine limb fragments. *From top to bottom,* decorated arm and arms with bent elbow, hands on legs, decorated hips and knees, conical legs, foot with "legging," foot with sandal, foot with marked toes.

5 CM.

Surface finish: unpolished. These short conical arms are bent at the elbow. The upper arm is muscular, and the forearm is quite tapering. A few examples have hands, most of which are indicated with a slight flattening at the end of the arm. These arms probably were attached to Seated Mother figures, although they could have occurred with other body types. In the Tehuacan Valley they have a distribution similar to that of the Mother figures, with a few appearing in late Ajalpan levels, the majority appearing in early Santa Maria components, and some appearing in late Santa Maria levels. Wider comparisons are not worthwhile because of the general character of this kind of arm.

Long tapered arms (29 excavated, 3 collected). Dimensions in cm.: length, 4.0–6.0; diameter at shoulder, 1.0–2.0. Paste: ranges from Rio Salado Coarse to Coatepec Plain. Surface finish: unpolished. The arms taper from the shoulder almost to a point at the distal end. They may have belonged to Venus bodies, Trackwoman bodies, or even Seated Mother figures. Although a few arms appear in late Ajalpan, most occur in the Santa Maria period. It is a common arm type which is duplicated in many places in Mesoamerica.

Hands-on-legs fragments (6 specimens excavated). Dimensions in cm.: length of leg, 10; probable length of arm, 8.0. These legs, joined at the feet and with hands attached below the knees, must have come from seated figures. The bent hands have incised fingers and are probably from arms with bent elbows. This type is found at La Venta and in middle Tres Zapotes. In the Tehuacan Valley it occurs in early Santa Maria times.

Decorated legs (9 specimens excavated). Dimensions in cm.: length below knee, 5.0; diameter, 1.5. The legs seem to have come from seated figurines. All have the same paste. Two examples seem to have indications of a sandal, three have decorated anklets, and one has an indication of a garter or band at the knee. There are also three examples with some sort of covering over the thighs. These legs occur with seated figurines throughout Middle Formative times in Mesoamerica, as they do in the Tehuacan Valley in the early part of the Santa Maria phase.

Conical legs with curved tapered feet (9 excavated, 5 collected). Dimensions in cm.: length, 6.0–10; diameter at hips, 2.0–3.0. Paste: resembles Coatepec Plain. Surface finish: unpolished. The plump legs are often slightly bent at the knee. The ends of the legs terminate in a slightly curved gentle point for a foot. The legs seem to have been attached to seated figurines. In the Tehuacan Valley they occur throughout the Santa Maria phase. They have a similar distribution in Middle and Late Formative times in much of the rest of Mesoamerica.

Ceramic Affiliations

Although early Santa Maria is not represented by a much larger ceramic sample than is late Ajalpan and has a smaller sample than late Santa Maria, the sample of sherds provides evidence of much wider interareal relationships than existed earlier. One reason for this is because early Santa Maria pottery shows a wide range of decorative elements, vessel forms, and figurine features that allow one to make concrete comparisons. Another reason is that a large number of identifiable sherds brought or traded into the Tehuacan Valley from other regions were found in early Santa Maria components, along with specimens of overlapping types that are present in a number of other sequences. That we were able to identify a number of the aberrant sherds as definite types from other Middle American sites reflects the fact that for this time period more well-documented and widespread archaeological materials have been reported than for earlier periods. However, one cannot help but wonder if it is not also because a wide network of cultural exchanges —interactions and diffusions—was evolving during Middle Formative times, perhaps along with actual movements of peoples. This is within the period of the spread of the "Olmec" complex, but we have shown in the type descriptions that more than just Olmec elements were on the move.

Santa Maria has its most intimate set of relationships with central Veracruz, especially with such complexes as Trapiche II (García Payón 1966) and the Middle Formative remains dug by Ford, Medellín Zenil, and Wallrath at such sites as Chalahuites and ones near Cempoala. Contact between the two areas is evidenced by a number of overlapping types, such as Canoas White and the subtype White-rimmed Orange, Rio Salado Gray, and such figurine types as Helmeted, Ploughed-eye, Hollow Lowland, Baby Face, Trapiche Bunned-helmet, Crescentic Cap, Negroid with Hairknot, and Tres Zapotes Chin-strap. Early Santa Maria deposits also contained a number of sherds apparently not of local manufacture of wares common in Trapiche II, such as Hard Buff, Kaolin White, White-slip Red-paste, Trapiche Orange, Trapiche Black-rimmed Orange, Dili Puncate, La Venta Rocker-stamped, and La Venta White Raspada and Black Raspada.

Besides these very concrete evidences of contacts, early Santa Maria and Trapiche II have a number of ceramic modes or horizon styles in common. These include rocker-dentate stamping, zoned plain rocker-stamping, raspada decoration, bowls with externally thickened rims, flat-bottomed flaring-rim bowls or dishes with multiple-line-break motifs, pseudo-grater bowls with hub-and-spoke or sunburst designs, pinched-in bowls, convex-wall bowls with double-line incisions, funnel-necked ollas, bowls with internally thickened rims, bowls with wide everted rims and with decorated rim tabs, and the firing technique resulting in smothering, which can give the rim a contrasting color.

Trapiche II has many types overlapping with the Aguilar phase in the Tampico region such as Aguilar Red, Progreso White, and various figurine types. As might be suspected since they are geographically farther apart, early Santa Maria and Aguilar are less closely related, having in common only a few figurine types, such as Baby Face, Crescentic Cap, and Negroid with Hairknot, which also occur in Trapiche II. Common vessel forms and decorative motifs include basal-bulge bowls, multiple-line-break motifs, hub-and spoke designs, raspada decoration, and white-rimmed black ware. Thus it appears that early Santa Maria, Trapiche II, and Aguilar are related and roughly contemporaneous.

Both Trapiche II and early Santa Maria show relationships to La Venta and perhaps middle and early Tres Zapotes. Here we will confine ourselves to resemblances among early Santa Maria, La Venta, and Tres Zapotes. A white-finished ware—Canoas White in Tehuacan—is common to all three phases, as are Helmeted, Baby Face, and Negroid with Hairknot figurines. Design and vessel form elements in common are multiple-line-break motifs, hub-and-spoke designs on pseudo-grater bases, raspada decorations, composite-silhouette vessels, thickened lip tabs, and white-rimmed black ware. Tres Zapotes also has a white-slipped ware very much like Coatepec White, which occurs sparingly in early Santa Maria but is a diagnostic trait of late Santa Maria.

La Venta, however, has a number of elements and types of early Santa Maria that do not seem to occur in early or middle Tres Zapotes. The types include, besides the ones listed above, Multi-hairknot, Ploughed-eye, Hollow Lowland, Trapiche Bunned-helmet, Crescentic Cap, and La Venta Hairknot figurines. Early Santa Maria and La Venta also share sherds traded from one to the other or from still other regions: La Venta Rocker-stamped, Canoas White-rimmed Orange, Hard Buff, Black Raspada and White Raspada, Morelos Lacquer, Dili Resist, Tlatilco Mottled bottles, Kaolin White, and White-slip Red-paste. Modes common to early Santa Maria and La Venta, but lacking in Tres Zapotes, include bird effigy whistles, rectangular vessels, low cylindrical vessels, convex-wall bowls with thickened rims incised with double-line-break motifs, and incisions filled with red paint. These similarities indicate that La Venta was related to and contemporaneous with all of early Santa Maria, whereas early and middle Tres Zapotes overlap only with the latter part of early Santa Maria.

As Warren (1961) and Sanders (1961) of the New World Archaeological Foundation have indicated, La Venta materials occur in Chiapa de Corzo II and III and vice versa. Thus, one would expect connections between Chiapa de Corzo II and III and early Santa Maria. Both have white-finished pottery as a dominant ware, effigy bird whistles, bowls with externally thickened rims, dimple-base bowls, convex-wall bowls with double-line incisions at the rim and with thickened incised rims, pinched-in bowls, white-rimmed black ware, bowls with wide everted rims, composite-silhouette vessels, double-line-break and hub-and-spoke decorations. The only overlapping figurine types seem to be Hollow Lowland, Baby Face, Crescentic Cap, and Negroid with Hairknot. The aberrant early Santa Maria tecomates with zoned punctate or fingernail-impressed decoration—here called Dili Punctate—may have originated in Chiapas. The Dili Resist and Escalera Orange sherds may also have been brought from Chiapa II or III.

The Conchas 1 and Jocotal materials from the Pacific coast of Guatemala, which Coe (1961) has demonstrated to be very like those of Chiapa de Corzo II (Dili), also have a significant number of resemblances to early Santa Maria. These include the Hollow Lowland, Crescentic Cap, and Negroid with Hairknot figurines, and white wares, bird effigy whistles, low cylindrical bowls, externally thickened-rim bowls, double-line incisions on convex-wall bowls, incisions filled with red paint, double-line-break and hub-and-spoke motifs, rocker stamping, and a few composite-silhouette bowls. A majority of flat-bottomed bowls with flaring walls is characteristic of the ceramic complexes of both regions. Both complexes also have in common such trade materials as Kaolin White, White-slipped Red, Black Raspada, Dili Punctate, and tecomates with fingernail or crescentic punctations. Also early Santa Maria has sherds of Conchas Orange, Suchiate Brushed, and Ocos Buff from this region.

Nearer to Tehuacan than any of the lowland areas

we have discussed is the Valley of Oaxaca. The cultural manifestations found there up to the time we were working in Tehuacan did not share many similarities with our Tehuacan materials. Monte Alban I did have in common with middle Santa Maria pseudo-grater bowls, raspada and zoned-toned decorations and the High-turban Slit-eye figurine type. However, on the basis of ceramics collected near Etla, we felt that eventually manifestations resembling early Santa Maria would be uncovered. Recent excavations throughout the Valley of Oaxaca (Flannery *et al.* 1967) have uncovered remains now classified as the Guadalupe phase with some of the same materials characteristic of Las Canoas in Tehuacan, a typical early Santa Maria manifestation. Both complexes have trade sherds of Kaolin White, White-slip Red-paste, Dili Punctate, Dili Resist, and other types that are widespread at this period.

Another nearby archaeological zone is the region around Cholula, just north of Tehuacan. This region logically should have remains comparable to both those from Tehuacan and those from the Valley of Mexico, and as mentioned in Chapter 12, the German expedition there has recovered materials related to late Ajalpan and early Santa Maria, descriptions of which are not yet published.

As indicated in the previous discussions, the materials from early (Iglesia subphase) and middle (Totolica subphase) Tlatilco, early and middle El Arbolillo, and early and middle Zacatenco display similarities to early Santa Maria remains. The Tlatilco similarities include Helmeted, Hollow Lowland, Baby Face, Type Di, early Type F, Type C3d, and Type C3a figurines; Tlatilco mottled or negative-painted bottles; Morelos lacquer sherds; Zacatenco Brown and Red-on-white sherds; Kaolin White sherds; and White-slip Red-paste sherds. Besides these very specific resemblances, early Santa Maria and Tlatilco share bird effigy whistles, zoned or unzoned rocker-stamping, double-line-break and hub-and-spoke motifs, raspada decoration, low cylindrical bowls, pinched-in bowls, flat-bottomed flaring-wall bowls, and white-rimmed black ware.

Other early manifestations in the Valley of Mexico do not have so great an assemblage of similarities to early Santa Maria, but they have enough to indicate some overlapping in time. Early El Arbolillo and early Santa Maria share Types C3a, C3d, and Di figurines and dimple-base bowls, convex-wall bowls with double-line incisions, bowls with externally thickened rims, double-line-break and hub-and-spoke motifs, and red-filled incisions on black ware. Although both phases have composite-silhouette bowls and flat-bottomed flaring-wall bowls, early El Arbolillo has more of the former than the latter shape, while the reverse is true of early Santa Maria.

From early Zacatenco Santa Maria received in trade the following Zacatenco wares: Brown, Orange, and Red-on-white. Early Zacatenco has in common with Santa Maria bird effigy whistles, funnel-neck ollas, convex-wall bowls with double-line incisions, bowls with internally thickened rims, bowls with wide everted rims, double-line-break motifs, decorated lip tabs, and early Type F and Type C3d figurines. Middle Zacatenco and middle El Arbolillo also show similarities to early Santa Maria, and in addition to some of the features already mentioned, have Hollow Lowland and Type Di figurines, pinched-in bowls, and bowls with a basal bulge. Thus both the early and middle periods of El Arbolillo, Tlatilco, and Zacatenco appear to have relationships with early Santa Maria. Even allowing for some cultural lag between the two areas (though trade sherds hint that there may have been little, if any), they all apparently overlapped in time to some extent.

The time period of early Santa Maria is a rather remarkable one in Mesoamerican ancient history, for there are a series of cultural similarities that appear to extend from Honduras to Tampico. It was these kinds of materials of this time period that were the basis for Spinden's remarkably astute hypothetical "Archaic" horizon, which he considered to be the base for the development of Middle American civilizations (Spinden 1917).

CHAPTER 6

The Late Part of the Santa Maria Phase

I N TERMS of new artifact types there are few differences between the early and late parts of the Santa Maria phase. However, there is a decided shift in emphasis and popularity of the ceramic types previously known. Rio Salado Gray, Rio Salado Coarse, Canoas White, Canoas Orange-brown, and Canoas Heavy Plain, which were the principal types of early Santa Maria, now become minority types. Coatepec White replaces Canoas White, and Quachilco Mica and Quachilco Gray, which were minority types in early Santa Maria, become the two most popular wares in late Santa Maria times. Because of these shifts in popularity, and because pyramid-building greatly increased in late Santa Maria, we often debated whether the phase should be made into two separate phases. However, since the total artifact complex of both the early and late segments were almost the same and the settlement and subsistence patterns remained unchanged in major aspects, we decided that a single phase was more effective in terms of our total sequence.

On the basis of numbers of sherds and numbers of excavated components from a variety of sites, late Santa Maria is one of the best documented segments in the Tehuacan sequence. Our analysis is based on over 74,000 sherds from twenty-six components: Ts 368w, Zones B, B¹, C, and D; Ts 368e, Zones B, B¹, and C; Ts 204, Zones A and B; Tc 50, Zone VII; Tc 272, Zone G; and Tr 218, Test 10, Zones B, C, C¹, D; Test 6, Zones B–G; and Test 11, Zones B–G. These occupations represent a span of about 400 years, extending from about 550 to 150 B.C. The majority of the components represent the last half of this span.

A few sherds of our earliest pottery types, Purron

Coarse and Purron Plain were uncovered in late Santa Maria components of Purron Cave, Tc 272. These probably are the result of prehistoric excavations, as are also sherds of Ajalpan Coarse Red, Ajalpan Plain, Coatepec Plain, and Coatepec Buff and Red-on-buff. The Canoas wares—White, Orange-brown, and Heavy Plain—continued to be made in diminishing amounts through the earlier part of late Santa Maria, but died out completely during the final segment of the phase.

Rio Salado Gray ware continued in use throughout the span of late Santa Maria. As mentioned previously, the paste is about the same for both the early and late subphases, but in late Santa Maria there is a tendency for the surface finish to be a slightly lighter gray, ranging to buff-white, and the surface often shows differential firing effects. Decoration is slightly less frequent than it was in early Santa Maria; it usually consists of two parallel lines around the rim, often with double-line breaks. A few sherds have triple-line breaks, some have "raspada" decoration, and a few now show "zoned-toning" effects.

In terms of vessel form, late Santa Maria examples of Rio Salado Gray are the same. Flaring-wall bowls and convex-wall bowls with and without thickened rims predominate. The deep convex-wall, almost cylindrical bowls, which were rare in early Santa Maria, become a form of some importance in late Santa Maria times. Flat-lipped, flaring-necked ollas, bowls with a basal ridge, and convex-wall bowls with stepped lips are also represented among the late Santa Maria vessels.

The Rio Salado Coarse type, described in the previous chapter, continues into late Santa Maria relatively unchanged. The dominant vessel forms are ollas

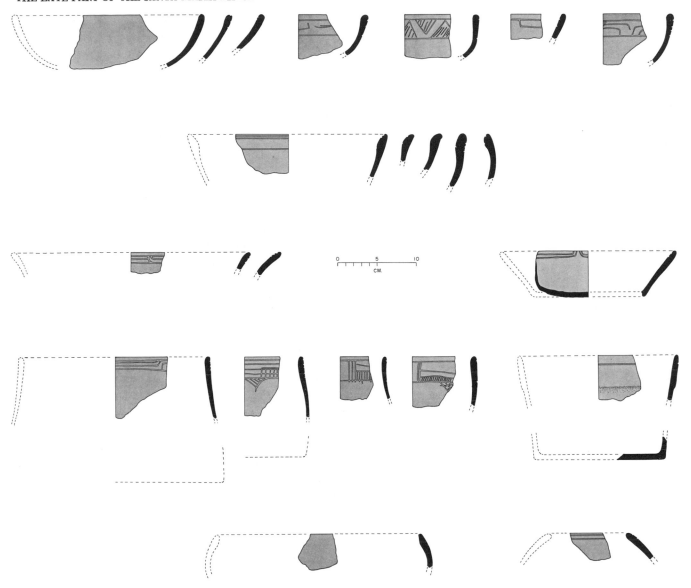

FIG. 62. COATEPEC WHITE. *Rows 1, 2:* convex-wall bowls with direct and internally thickened rims; *row 3:* flaring-and outsloping-wall bowls; *row 4:* cylindrical vessels, *(far right)* with collared rim; *row 5:* incurved-rim bowl and tecomate.

with long or short flaring necks, ollas with funnel necks, and convex-wall bowls. Rolled-rim ollas and straight-necked ollas occur in late Santa Maria and only rarely in early Santa Maria. There are also a few examples of incense burners and new types of comales in late Santa Maria. This diagnostic type of the Santa Maria phase extends as a minority type into Palo Blanco times.

Sherds of El Riego Gray and Quachilco Red were found in some late Santa Maria levels. These types, however, are more characteristic of the early Palo Blanco subphase and will, therefore, be described in the following chapter.

Pottery Types

COATEPEC WHITE

1,778 excavated specimens, 110 collected.

Paste

The paste is fairly heavily tempered, with nonplastic material accounting for about 20 percent of the volume. About 10 percent of the paste consists of grains

FIG. 63. COATEPEC WHITE. Decorated sherds.

5 CM.

color varies from off-white (2.5 Y 8/0, 10 YR 8/0) to light reddish-gray (5.0 YR 7/1, 10 R 6/1) to dark gray or almost black (7.5 YR 3/0). Sometimes the slip appears to be charred. The slip is easily seen on the cross section of a sherd. Its hardness is about 3.0 on Mohs scale. The slip does not always cover both surfaces. It may, for instance, cover the entire interior and only 1 or 2 cm. of the exterior edge, or vice versa.

The slip was applied before firing, and changes in the firing conditions made the slip turn different tones. This slip has good covering qualities. Examination under a microscope shows that the sherds were decorated with an instrument such as a small stick, which penetrated the slip with a dragging effect that left the edges of the incised area irregularly plastered down. The darker clay underneath the slip generally glistens through where the slip was removed and contrasts sharply with the white slip, further defining the decoration.

Decoration

The commonest form of decoration is by relatively wide incising. There are only three late Santa Maria examples of raspada decoration. Over a third of the rim sherds and a much smaller proportion of the body sherds are decorated. Usually the decoration is on the outer rather than the inner rim. The commonest motifs are two, three, and sometimes four parallel lines around the rim. When compared with Canoas White, there are far fewer examples of breaks in these lines. Some double-line-break motifs do occur, mainly on the earlier examples. Some decorated sherds show the horizontal lines of the rim combined with two, three, or more parallel vertical lines or with hachured triangles, semicircles, or rectangles. Double-line hook motifs also occur.

Vessel Forms

Convex-wall bowls of low to medium depth are the predominant vessel form. These bowls had flat or flattened bases and direct rims with rounded lips. The more numerous later examples are deeper than the generally shallow specimens from early Santa Maria levels, but four of the earlier bowls could be classed as "deep." About half the sample are decorated, usually with two parallel lines around the outer rim. Dimensions in cm.: rim diameter, 18–28; estimated wall height, 4.0–7.0; wall thickness, 0.5–0.9.

Flaring-wall bowls These flat-bottomed bowls were very popular in early Santa Maria times but were gradually replaced later in the phase by the relatively

0.1–0.5 mm. in diameter of quartz, quartzite, andesite, andesine, amphiboles, pyroxenes, basalt, plagioclase, biotite, and occasionally labradorite and muscovite. About 5 percent of the paste is grains less than 0.1 mm. in diameter of the same items plus magnetite and hematite. About 4 percent is grains 0.5–1.0 mm. in diameter and grains over 1.0 mm. in diameter are even rarer —1 percent. These larger grains are most often quartz, quartzite, and basalt, and very occasionally limestone or andesite.

The paste has a coarse, granular appearance. The core is dark, varying in color from brown to gray to black, and stands out in contrast to the white surface.

Surface Finish

Surfaces are finished with a thick, polished slip. The

TABLE 32

Coatepec White Decorated Sherds
(by site and zone)

Incised motifs	Early Santa Maria										Late Santa Maria					
	368e G	368e F	368e E	367 D2	367 D1	367 C	368e D	368e C2	368 C1	272 H	368e C	368w D-E	272 G	368e B	368w C	368w B
1 line around rims of																
convex-wall, direct-rim bowls, ext.																
flaring/outsloping-wall bowls, ext.														2		
cylindrical, direct-rim jars, ext.		1					1				1					
2 lines around rims of																
convex-wall, direct-rim bowls, ext.	1	1		1	1	2	3	2		1	1	4	2	4	4	
convex-wall, direct-rim bowls, int.											2	2		2		2
flaring/outsloping-wall bowls, ext.											5	3		2	4	2
cylindrical, direct-rim jars, ext.		1				2					2	1	4			
convex/outsloping-wall bowl, int. thick-rim bowl, int.							2		2		2	1				
convex-wall, wedge-rim bowls, int.											1					
2-4 lines around rims of																
incurved-rim bowls, ext.											1					
short str.-neck ollas, ext.											1			8		
hatching on rims or walls of convex-wall bowls, ext.												1				
cylindrical vessels, ext.											1					
Raspada motifs on ext. walls											2			1		
Total	1	2	3	2	1	2	6	2	2	1	18	11	6	19	8	6

Incised motifs	Late Santa Maria *(continued)*													Early Palo Blanco		
	218-11 G	218-11 F	368e B1	368w B1	218-11 E	218-6 G	218-10 C2	218-6 F	218-11 C	218-10 C1	218-10 C	218-10 B1	218-10 B	218-10 A	218-11 A	Total
1 line around rims of																
convex-wall, direct-rim bowls, ext.														3		3
flaring/outsloping-wall bowls, ext.														1		1
cylindrical, direct-rim jars, ext.									1							1
2 lines around rims of																
convex-wall, direct-rim bowls, ext.	5	2	2	2	3		2	2		6	4	6	1	2	1	64
convex-wall, direct-rim bowls, int.	2		2		1						1					2
flaring/outsloping-wall bowls, ext.	1	2					1			1	1	2		1	1	15
cylindrical, direct-rim jars, ext.	2				1	2	1			1	1	2		2		28
convex/outsloping-wall bowl, int. thick-rim bowl, int.							1									11
convex-wall, wedge-rim bowls, int.											2					7
2-4 lines around rims of																
incurved-rim bowls, ext.										1	1	1				10
short str.-neck ollas, ext.								2	1	1	1					5
hatching on rims or walls of convex-wall bowls, ext.	1										1		1			3
cylindrical vessels, ext.	1			1			1		1	1		2				9
Raspada motifs on ext. walls										1					2	3
Total	10	4	3	2	5	4	4	2	2	10	11	11	4	7	2	162

TABLE 33
Coatepec White Vessel Forms
(sherds by site and zone)

	Late Ajalpan	Early Santa Maria																Late Santa Maria					
	368e J	368e I	368e H	368e G	368e F	368e E	367 D²	367 D¹	367 C	368e D	272 I	368e C²	368e C¹	272 H	368e C	368w D-E	272 G	368e B	368w C	368w B	218-11 G	218-11 F	368e B¹
Bowls																							
convex wall																							
direct rim			1	5	2			2	4	8		4	1	1	15	10	2	25	6	5	6	3	14
int. thick rim					1					2					2	1		4					
wedge rim															2	1							
flat bases													5										
flaring wall		2		1	9	1	1	6	5	9			1		11	4		8					
incurved rim															1			8		3		2	
outsloping wall															3			5					
incurved rim/tecomate															2								
stepped rim																2							
Cylindrical vessels					1			3	3			1	1		7	3		2	4	2	3		1
Ollas, short str. neck															1								
Bottles						1									2								
Tecomates, collared										1													
Flat bases					6	2						3	3		18	1		4					8
Body sherds	11	9	9	4	21	42				97	4	38	76	9	144	61	10	232	71	92	15	5	26
Total	11	11	10	10	41	46	1	11	12	117	4	46	87	10	208	83	12	288	81	102	25	10	49

	Late Santa Maria (continued)															Early Palo Blanco							
	204 A-B	368w B¹	218-6 G	218-11 E	218-10 C²	218-6 F	218-11 D	218-11 C¹	218-11 C	218-10 C	218-10 B	218-11 B	218-10 B¹	218-6 E	218-6 B	218-10 A	307 A	218-6 A A	218-11 A A	272 F	272 E	272 D	Total
Bowls																							
convex wall																							
direct rim		4	3	4	3	3	1	1	16	12	2	8				3	1						178
int. thick rim					2		1	1	2	7	4	4							2				32
wedge rim										2	1	1											7
flat bases																							5
flaring wall			1	2	1	1				1	1												73
incurved rim									1	1													10
outsloping wall																							8
incurved rim/tecomate										1	2												5
stepped rim																							2
Cylindrical vessels			2	2					1	2	2					4							47
Ollas, short str. neck					2				1	1													5
Bottles																							4
Tecomates, collared									1														2
Flat bases																							45
Body sherds	3	115	2	4	33	1	5	4	49	42	28	66				13		4	2	1	1	1	1355
Total	3	119	8	12	41	5	6	6	71	69	40	82				20	1	4	4	1	1	1	1778

cylindrical vessels described below. Decoration usually consists of two incised lines on the interior rim. Dimensions in cm.: rim diameter, 18–32; base diameter, 14–22; wall height, 5.0–6.0; wall thickness, 0.5–0.8.

Cylindrical vessels have walls that are relatively vertical, but which often show slight concavity near the rim. A collared specimen of this form had straight, slightly outsloping walls and has a single line incised a centimeter below the rim. Parallel-line incisions, often in combination with geometric motifs, are more usual decorative designs. Dimensions in cm.: rim diameter, 14–24; base diameter, nearly the same as the rim diameter; wall thickness, 0.4–0.7.

Bowls with internally thickened rims seem to have had flat bases. The walls are usually convex and outsloping; occasionally the rims appear slightly incurved or somewhat everted, owing to the manner of thickening, which leaves a raised convex internal surface. Decoration is usually incised parallel lines on the rounded inner portion of the rim. Dimensions in cm.: rim diameter, 20–30; height, 5.0–12; wall thickness, 0.5–1.5.

Minor forms in this paste include tecomates or incurved-rim bowls, collared tecomates, outsloping-wall bowls, wedge-rim and stepped-rim bowls, ollas with short straight necks, and bottles.

Relationships

Coatepec White is a minority type in the Tehuacan Valley and is slightly more popular in late Santa Maria than in early Santa Maria. However, pottery with the same characteristics as Coatepec White is commonly found in central Veracruz in Trapiche II and in middle levels of Chalahuites (García Payón 1966: 66–69). On the Pacific coast of Guatemala, Conchas Fine White-to-buff of Conchas 2, as well as some of the white wares of Chiapa de Corzo IV–VI of Chiapas, is analogous to Coatepec White (Coe and Flannery 1967: 44). In all these regions, as in the Tehuacan Valley, the Coatepec White type of paste with a white slip is at first less popular than the Canoas White types, but gradually becomes more popular and eventually outlives the earlier type. This pattern is exhibited also in Panuco in northern Veracruz, where Progreso White pottery with a white wash is finally replaced by Chila White with a white slip. A few sherds personally observed from Tres Zapotes are more similar to Coatepec White than to Canoas White, suggesting a slightly later placement of early and middle Tres Zapotes, making these periods roughly contemporaneous with late Santa Maria.

Some early Monte Alban White-on-buff or Type C. 5 sherds are very similar to Coatepec White (Caso, Bernal, and Acosta 1967: p. 46, pl. IId, e) and sherds from Guadalupe are definitely related. A few examples of Tlatilco and El Arbolillo *blanco pulido* wares—particularly the convex-wall bowls with double-line decoration on the thickened or unthickened rims—are similar and may be distantly related to Coatepec White. Even more distantly related are some of the Las Charcas white wares of highland Guatemala (Shook 1951).

TABLE 34
Coatepec White-rimmed Black Decorated Sherds
(by site and zone)

	Early Santa Maria							Late Santa Maria					
	368e H	368e F	368e E	368e D	368e C²	368e C¹	272 H	368e C	368w D-E	368e B	368w B	218-10 C	Total
Incised motifs													
1 line around rims of convex-wall, direct/thick rim bowls, ext.	4	2		3		1				2			12
2 lines around rims of													
convex-wall bowls, ext.	1	1				1							3
flaring/outsloping-wall bowls, int.		2											2
incurved-rim bowls, ext.		1											1
cylindrical, direct-rim vessels, ext.			2	2	2	2	1						9
3 lines around rims of													
convex-wall bowls, int./ext.												1	1
Raspada motifs on walls of													
convex-wall, ex.-thick-rim, ext.										1		3	4
flaring/outsloping-wall bowls, ext.								1	1		2		4
Total	5	6	2	5	2	4	1	1	1	3	2	4	36

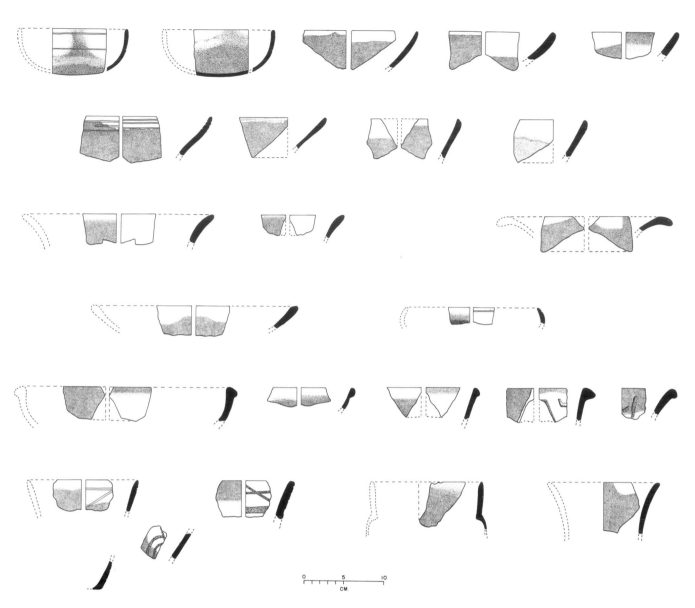

FIG. 64. COATEPEC WHITE-RIMMED BLACK. *Row 1, 2:* convex-wall bowls; *row 3:* flaring-wall bowls; *row 4:* wedge-rim and incurved-rim bowls; *row 5:* bowls with externally thickened rims; *row 6:* vase-shaped "cylindrical" jars and ollas with straight and with long flaring necks.

COATEPEC WHITE-RIMMED BLACK

790 specimens excavated, 26 collected.

Paste

About 11 percent of the paste is composed of particles 0.1–0.5 mm. in diameter of quartz, plagioclase, and quartzite, with occasional fragments of biotite, muscovite, rhyolite, andesite, and volcanic glass. The rest of the nonplastic material makes up less than 5 percent of the paste, is under 0.1 mm. in diameter, and includes the substances mentioned above plus magnetite and hematite. The sherds are hard (about 3.0 on the Mohs scale), are very compact, and the cores have a fine, sandy appearance.

The sherds were fired for the most part (except for the white rims) in a "reducing" atmosphere and are dark or medium gray from surface to surface (10 R 2/1–5/1).

Surface Finish

The surfaces have a fine slip that has been polished almost black on the bodies and white to buff on the rims. Occasionally the bodies show gray or even white firing clouds. The area fired white along the rim is usu-

Coatepec White-rimmed Black Vessel Forms
(sherds by site and zone)

	Early Santa Maria												Late Santa Maria				
	368e I	368e H	368e G	368e F	368e E	367 D²	367 D¹	357 C	368e D	368e C²	368e C¹	272 H	368e C	368w D-E	368e B	368w C	368w B
Bowls																	
convex wall																	
direct rim	2	12	4	10	4				9		6		14	13	19	15	22
wedge rim				1													
flaring wall																	
direct rim	1	1	1	6	2	1	1	1		1		2	6	2	5	2	7
everted rim													1	1		1	
outsloping wall				7									2	1		3	13
ext. thick rim															2	4	1
incurved rim		2	2		2				1								
Cylindrical vessels								2	2	2							1
Bottles		1						1		3	1	1					
Ollas																	
long flaring neck											4						
short str. neck													1				
Flat bases			1	1			1		1		3		1	2	1	2	
Body sherds		10	11	44	17	5	9	6	35	7	42		34	38	53	42	46
Total	3	26	19	69	25	6	11	10	48	13	58	3	59	57	80	69	90

Late Santa Maria (*continued*)

	218-11 G	218-11 F	368e B¹	204 A-B	368w B¹	218-11 E	218-6 G	218-10 C²	218-6 F	218-11 D	218-11 C	218-11 C¹	218-10 C	218-10 B¹	218-10 B	50 VII	Early Palo Blanco 218-10 A	Total
Bowls																		
convex wall																		
direct rim	1	1	3		7	1			1	1	2	2	8	1	3	1	2	168
wedge rim																		1
flaring wall																		
direct rim					4			4				2						47
everted rim					1													4
outsloping wall					2			1										28
ext. thick rim					1										1			9
incurved rim	1																	8
Cylindrical vessels																		9
Bottles																		7
Ollas																		
long flaring neck																		4
short str. neck																		1
Flat bases																		12
Body sherds	8	2	2	3	22	2	1	6	4	5	1	4	19	1	4	2	7	492
Total	10	3	5	3	37	3	1	11	5	6	3	8	27	2	8	3	9	790

ally irregular, but becomes an almost even band in late specimens. This border is narrow on one surface and wide on the other, with the wider side sometimes on the outside and sometimes on the inside. A few of the latest rim sherds from Ts 368w, and a few early ones from Tr 218, have borders fired a brownish color instead of white and are closely related to a diagnostic type from Trapiche III.

Decoration

Other than the white rims, decoration is rare. Bowls sometimes have one or two horizontal lines incised on the exterior rim. A few thickened-rim and deep out-sloping-wall bowls display raspada decoration, usually crude, and two flaring-wall bowls have parallel lines incised on the inner rim.

Vessel Forms

Low to medium-deep convex-wall bowls had flat bottoms. Some examples show convexity only in the upper wall, the lower portion being more outsloping. Dimensions in cm.: rim diameter, 14–30; wall height, 5.0–10; wall thickness, 0.4–1.0.

Flaring-wall bowls had flat bottoms. Dimensions in cm: rim diameter, 18–24; estimated wall height, 5.0–7.0; wall thickness, 0.4–1.0.

Minor forms include flat-bottomed bowls with out-sloping walls, convex-to-vertical-wall bowls with heavy externally thickened rims, cylindrical vessels, incurved-rim bowls, flaring-wall bowls with everted rims, one wedge-rim bowl, ollas with long flaring necks, one olla with short straight neck, and bottles.

Relationships

The concept of contrasting tones achicvcd through firing probably was imported from the Gulf Coast (Peterson 1963). As far as the Tehuacan Valley is concerned, differential firing is a fairly good time marker for middle Santa Maria times. The technique of white-rimming, however, shows considerable variation and perhaps its use in Mesoamerica extended over a thousand years during the Formative. For instance, pots fired black with whitish firing clouds through use of a reducing atmosphere, such as some examples of Huastec Ponce Black (MacNeish 1954), appear to be an early variation on this theme. The practice of firing pots white on one surface and black on the other seems to range slightly later in time, and since it occurs on Canoas White, at least seems to be contemporaneous with Coatepec White-rimmed Black in the Tehuacan Valley. Well-defined wide white rims, such as those which occur in late Trapiche and Chiapa de

Corzo IV–VI (García Payón 1966: 87-92; Peterson 1963), appear on some of our Coatepec White-rimmed Black pots just before the technique disappears entirely. Also in middle and late Santa Maria levels there were sherds from central Veracruz of Chalahuites Orange-rimmed Black ware and Trapiche Black-rimmed Orange ware (García Payón 1966: 87–92) that may represent later variants of the technique, as do a few of the Quachilco Gray sherds with rims that are a lighter gray than the bodies. Thus, from many standpoints the variations of the differential firing technique are better time markers than the inclusive Coatepec White-rimmed Black type itself.

QUACHILCO MICA

23,900 specimens excavated; 2,080 collected.

Paste

The paste contains 20 to 30 percent nonplastic material. Ten to 15 percent of the temper is grains over 0.5 mm. in diameter and a small proportion is as large as 1.0–2.0 mm. As the name of this type would lead one to expect, the larger fragments are of muscovite, biotite, quartz, quartzite, and oligoclase, with some occurrence of hematite and andesite. Another 10 to 12 percent consists of particles of the same minerals 0.1–0.5 mm. in diameter. The remaining 3 percent of temper consists of fine grains under 0.1 mm. in diameter, including magnetite and plagioclase in addition to the other materials listed.

Unlike the tempering material of Rio Salado Coarse, the particles of temper are flat rather than angular. The general consistency of the paste is laminated, but it is evenly kneaded and quite compact considering the large amount of temper it contains. The firing varies considerably from uneven to even. There is usually little difference in color between core and periphery, though the core tends to be a bit darker. The sherds break in fairly straight lines with slightly crumbly edges—not as irregularly or crumbly as the Rio Salado ware. The coil method of making this pottery can often be discerned at the termination of the lip and at the junction of the neck and body of ollas.

The color of the surface often varies because of shallow surface firing clouds. The range is as follows: reddish-brown (2.5 YR 4/4–5/4, 5.0 YR 6/3–5/3), reddish-gray or pink (5.0 YR 4/2–5/2, 7/4), brown to pinkish-gray (7.5 YR 5/4, 6/2). The inner surface is generally somewhat darker than the exterior.

Surface Finish

The surface is usually smoothed, but occasionally

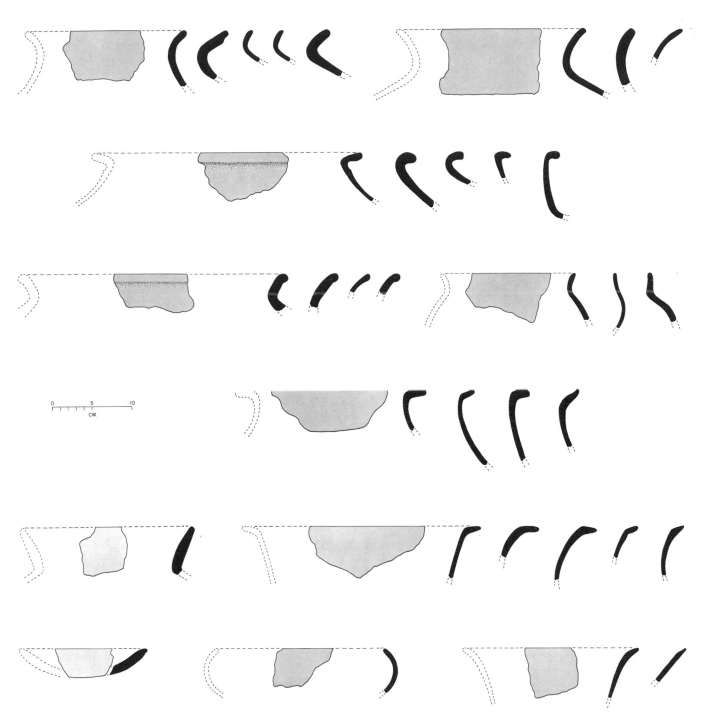

FIG. 65. QUACHILCO MICA. *Row 1:* ollas with short to medium-high flaring necks; *row 2:* rolled-rim ollas; *row 3:* beaded-rim ollas, small ollas with short flaring and straight necks; *row 4:* convergent-neck ollas with outangled or everted rims; *row 5:* angle-neck and funnel-neck ollas; *row 6:* low convex-wall bowl, incurved-rim bowl, and flaring- and outsloping-wall bowls.

shallow horizontal striations are visible. An even float coating covers both surfaces, which gleam from numerous mica flecks. The texture of the surface is sandy to slightly granular, with rather irregular surface planes. Some sherds show traces of a fugitive red wash.

Decoration

Punctate decoration is fairly common on fragments of comales or platelike vessels and on loop handles presumably from incense burners. It will be described below.

Vessel Forms

Ollas make up the vast majority of Quachilco Mica vessels. Bowl shapes account for only a small portion of the vessels, as do comales, incensarios, and bottles. A few miniature ollas of various forms were present.

Ollas with short-to-medium-high flaring necks make up by far the largest category of rim sherds. Lips vary from rounded to flattish to tapered. Dimensions in cm.: rim diameter, 20–30; neck height, 2.8–5.0; wall thickness, 0.5–1.4.

Rolled- or beaded-rim ollas are more characteristic of the Palo Blanco phase in this paste. This category includes nineteen specimens from early Santa Maria levels which have short flaring necks and thickened beaded rims rather than the turned-over rolled rim of the majority of our sample. Dimensions in cm.: rim diameter, 13–34, with 30–32 most common; wall thickness, 1.0–1.5.

Ollas with long flaring necks have lips that vary from beveled or thickened and tapering to rounded. Dimensions in cm.: rim diameter, 24–32; neck height, 5.0–6.5; wall thickness, 0.6–1.3.

Funnel- or angle-neck ollas vary in neck height from medium high to tall. Some rims are direct, but everted rims are more common. Dimensions in cm.: rim diameter, 18–30; neck height, 5.0–over 7.5; wall thickness, 1.0–1.4.

Straight-neck ollas are smaller vessels than the other kinds of ollas. Their necks are short and upright; the rims are direct. Dimensions in cm.: rim diameter, 8.0–18; neck height, 1.5–3.0; wall thickness, 0.4–1.0.

Convergent-neck, everted-rim ollas were found only in Postclassic levels. The bodies gradually merged into vague necks that are more constricted at the mouth than at the shoulder. They have almost horizontal everted rims. Dimensions in cm.: rim diameter, 22–26; wall thickness, 0.5–1.0.

Shallow platelike vessels are of two varieties. One

kind, with the upper or lower surface roughened by all-over punctate decoration, is almost completely flat with a very short vertical or slightly outsloping rim, sometimes also covered with punctate decoration. These vessels could have been *comales,* the flat round or oblong griddles on which tortillas are baked. The rim diameters seem to range between 30 and 40 cm., but measurements are hard to estimate from broken pieces of such crudely made pottery. Also, a few of these flat, punctate-decorated fragments are obviously from vessels of irregular shape. Rims are 1.0–2.0 cm. high. The punctate decoration consists of deep pre-firing jabs in the form of wedges, short lines, or circles, applied crudely to an entire surface and sometimes to the exterior of the rim. Several broken loop or strap handles, some of which are also punctate-decorated, may have been attached to the rims of these vessels.

The other kind of flat platelike vessel has no punctations and seems to have had a slightly higher rim in relation to the vessel's diameter. The diameter is difficult to determine, however, since at least some examples were elliptical or oblong in shape, instead of evenly round. Nevertheless the indications are that these vessels are too small to be very useful as comales. Rims range from 1.0 to 4.5 cm. high. The bottoms are quite flat. On the exterior, the rim is vertical to slightly outsloping, but inside, the surface curves smoothly upward to the rounded lip. One rim fragment retained a thick elliptical lug about 6.5 cm. long and 3.0 cm. deep. The lip of another specimen had a wide groove pressed into it.

These vessels may have been used as incense burners, but no evidence remains of anything having been burned in them. It is possible that the long, heavy, rectangular handles to be described below were attached to these vessels in the manner of a modern metal handle to a modern metal frying pan.

Convex-wall bowls usually have direct rims, but some are thickened and slightly everted. Some of these vessels may be fragments of the "frying pan" type of incense burner described below. Others may have served as pot rests. Dimensions in cm.: rim diameter, 16–26; wall height, 3.0–over 5.0; wall thickness, 0.6–1.0.

Incense burners. Several broken fragments represent the wall and a fragment of midsection of vessels divided horizontally in the manner of eggcups; that is, the walls slant or curve inward from the rim to the midsection of the vessel, then slant outward again to the edge of the hollow pedestal base. No complete rim-to-base sherds were found, so that no indication of

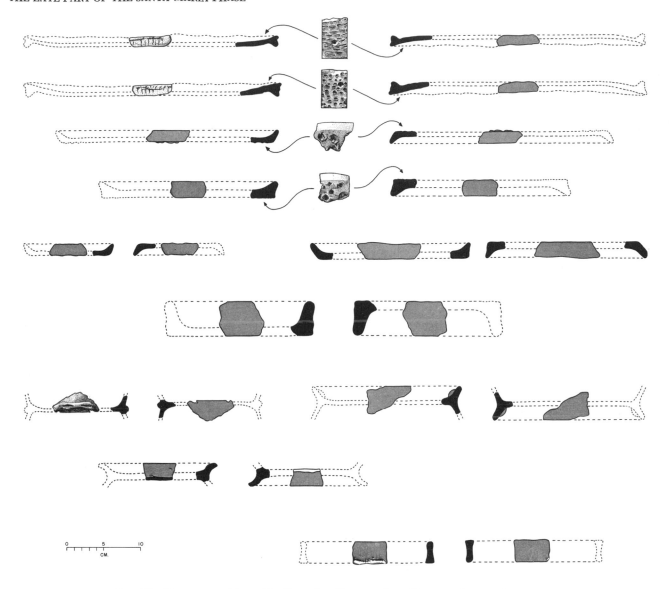

FIG. 66. QUACHILCO MICA. Shallow platelike vessels and incense-burner fragments.

over-all height can be given, but one sherd is complete enough from rim to midsection to give a wall height of 2.0 cm., a rim diameter of 20 cm., and a diameter at the midsection of about 18 cm. Another sherd indicates that the "waist" of one vessel was girdled by a punctate-decorated fillet. Still another sherd indicates that a thickened applique (handle? lug?) has broken off the inner edge of the rim.

The fragments of the eggcup-shaped and platelike vessels may indicate the presence in the Tehuacan Valley in late Santa Maria times of multiple-compo-

nent "assemble-it-yourself" incense burners similar to those described by Borhegyi (1959) in connection with Lowland Maya forms.

Elongated handles, apparently of frying-pan or ladle-shaped incense burners, were found in several late Santa Maria components. These handles are rectangular in cross section and measure about 2.5 cm. thick by 3.0 cm. wide. The longest fragment is 7.0 cm. long, but complete handles were undoubtedly longer. Some examples have a wide groove on one surface that terminates in a large round perforation at the distal end.

113

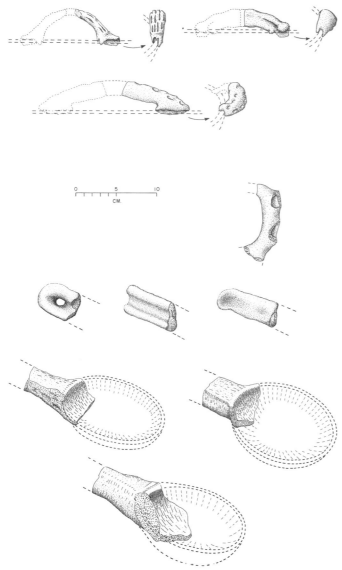

FIG. 67. QUACHILCO MICA. Fragments from incense burners.

Four examples show fragments of these handles joined to fragmentary convex-wall bowls or dishes. The point of attachment is only slightly wider than the handle itself, and both handle and bowl rim are smoothed into an unbroken, single unit which is flat across the top. Surprisingly, two of these specimens have the wide grooves mentioned above running down the underside of the handle. A second example seems rather unusual in that the narrower face of a handle oval in cross section forms the upper surface.

In addition to the long extended handles, fragmentary loop or strap handles were also found. Usually oval in cross section, these handles are 1.0–2.0 cm.

114

thick and 2.0–3.0 cm. wide. The most complete fragment measures 9.0 cm. long; others were obviously longer when complete. One example displays two broken attachment points on top for hollow circular objects. Other handles have punctate decoration similar to that used on the platelike vessels. The attachment points on two examples show that the handles were placed horizontally along the rim of the parent vessel.

Minor bowl forms include small incurved-rim bowls, flaring-wall bowls, and cylindrical bowls. One fragmentary ring base and three lugs were among the other features uncovered. The lugs are merely short rectangular horizontal protuberances. Each is decorated differently: one has a slash which runs the length of the lug, another has a series of deep vertical slashes, and the third has a central perforation. A luglike projection was found on the rim of a small, low, concave-necked olla and consists of a short, elliptical, down-curved protuberance arising directly from the lip of the vessel.

Relationships

The Quachilco Mica type began in early Santa Maria times and probably derived from Rio Salado Coarse. By the end of the Santa Maria phase, it is one of the dominant wares of the Tehuacan Valley. In fact, it continues throughout the rest of the sequence as the basic utilitarian ware, undergoing minor changes in vessel form and minor shifts in popularity. Although it may show a few changes that parallel changes in utilitarian wares from other regions, it is basically a Tehuacan type without external relationships.

QUACHILCO BROWN

1,967 specimens excavated, 51 collected.

Paste

Of the various Formative wares made in the valley, this type has the finest paste. The nonplastic particles in the paste account for about 10 percent of its composition. The larger amount, or about 7 percent, consists of grains under 0.1 mm. in diameter, including quartz, biotite, calcite, muscovite, hematite, magnetite, quartzite, and occasionally plagioclase, andesine, oligoclase, and hornblende. About 3 percent of the paste is particles 0.1–0.3 mm. in diameter of the rocks and minerals mentioned except for hornblende, magnetite, and hematite. One sherd contained particles of diorite of this size. Particles over 0.3 mm. are rare and usually are quartz. The paste is extremely well knit and well fired. Rarely is there any difference in

TABLE 37
Quachilco Brown Grooved or Incised Sherds
(by site and zone)

	Early Santa Maria				Late Santa Maria								
	368e G	368e D	368e C²	368e C¹	368e C	368w D-E	368e B	218-11 G	218-11 F	368w B¹	218-11 E	218-6 G	218-10 C²
1 line around rims of convex-wall, ext. thick-rim bowls					1								1
2 lines around rims of bowls													
flaring wall, direct rim, ext.		1	1		1		3						1
flaring wall, round everted rim, int.					2		2			2		2	1
flaring wall, sharp everted rim, int.							1	2					1
convex wall		1											
basal flange, ext.											1		1
2-4 lines around rims of flaring wall bowls, ext.	1	1	1	2	1		2		1				
str.-neck olla, ext.													
Hatching on cylindrical vessels, ext.					1	1							
Steps on basal-flange bowl, ext.									1				
Zigzags on cylindrical vessels, ext.													
Semicircles on rims of flaring-wall, everted-rim bowls, int.									1				
Parallel lines on bottom, int.													
Total	1	3	2	2	6	1	8	2	3	2	1	2	5

	Late Santa Maria (continued)									Palo Blanco		
	218-6 F	218-11 D	218-10 C¹	218-10 C	218-10 B¹	218-10 B	218-11 B	218-6 C	218-6 B	218-10 A	35e E	Total
1 line around rims of convex-wall, ext. thick-rim bowls			1		1		1					5
2 lines around rims of bowls												
flaring wall, direct rim, ext.						1						8
flaring wall, round everted rim, int.	2	3	2	2	12	6		1		5		42
flaring wall, sharp everted rim, int.					1	1						6
convex wall												1
basal flange, ext.				2	3					6		13
2-4 lines around rims of flaring wall bowls, ext.				1		2			1			13
str.-neck olla, ext.			1									1
Hatching on cylindrical vessels, ext.		2	1	1	2	1		1		3		13
Steps on basal-flange bowl, ext.												1
Zigzags on cylindrical vessels, ext.		1	1									2
Semicircles on rims of flaring-wall, everted-rim bowls, int.				1					1			3
Parallel lines on bottom, int.											1	1
Total	2	6	6	7	19	11	1	2	2	14	1	109

float coat which resembles a slip. The surface texture is smooth to waxy, and the luster is slightly waxy.

Decoration

Two main kinds of decoration occur: the incising of fairly wide lines around the inner or outer rims and occasionally on the bodies, and the engraving of fine lines on the exterior of the vessels. The most popular form was wide-line incising on the upper surface of everted rims. Two, three, or four parallel lines were most popular, but parallel-line-break motifs, opposed triangles, wavy lines, and open semicircles occur. Except for a few parallel-line incisions, exterior decorations are usually fine lines cut with a sharp implement into the polished surface of the dried clay. The motifs include crosshatched triangles, zigzag lines, a stepped motif, three or four parallel lines, and opposed triangles. The designs are usually applied in horizontal bands around the vessel. There are also occasional examples of raspada decoration and zoned-toned designs.

Decoration on base or body sherds of unidentifiable vessel form consisted of the following: an interior bottom surface incised with multiple parallel lines combined with wavy lines; an exterior bottom surface scored with short punctate strokes in a circular pattern; an exterior wall with fillets applied in rectilinear motifs.

Vessel Forms

Flaring-wall bowls with direct rims had either flat or convex bottoms. A small number of sherds were decorated on the inner surface of the rim. Dimensions in cm.: rim diameter, 20–32; estimated base diameter, 14–22; estimated height, 4.0–8.0.

Flaring-wall bowls with rounded everted rims had flat or convex bottoms. Almost half the rims are incised on the upper surface. The rims range from wide rolled-over eversions to narrower forms. Dimensions in cm.: rim diameter, 30–44; estimated base diameter, 20–34; estimated height, 5.0–10.

Flaring-wall bowls with sharply everted rims had flat bottoms only, with an abrupt angle at the junction of wall and base. The lower wall slants outward gradually, but as the wall begins to curve, it flares widely. The divergency is accentuated by the everted rim, which turns downward at a sharp angle. Nine sherds are decorated on the upper surface of the rim with incised semicircles, parallel horizontal lines, double-line-break motifs, or wavy lines. The semicircular motifs appear on a scalloped rim. Dimensions in cm.: rim diameter, 32–34; estimated height, over 3.0.

5 CM.

FIG. 68. QUACHILCO BROWN. Sherds decorated by wide-line incising *(rows 1 and 2)*, zoned toning *(row 3)*, fine-line incising *(row 4, left and right)*, and raspada *(row 4, center)*.

color between the core and the surfaces, although occasional firing clouds appear on the surface. The hardness is over 3.5.

Surface Finish

The surface color is in the brown range, generally from reddish brown (5.0 YR 5/4, 5/3) to orange (5.0 YR 6/6, 6/4) to gray (7.5 YR 6/4, 6/2). Some vessels were a lighter tone on the outside or inside.

This pottery is invariably well smoothed and usually is highly polished, often on both surfaces. The preliminary smoothing was done with a very smooth hard object, such as a polishing pebble. Visible traces remain in the form of very shallow horizontal striations. The smoothing and polishing process produced a thin

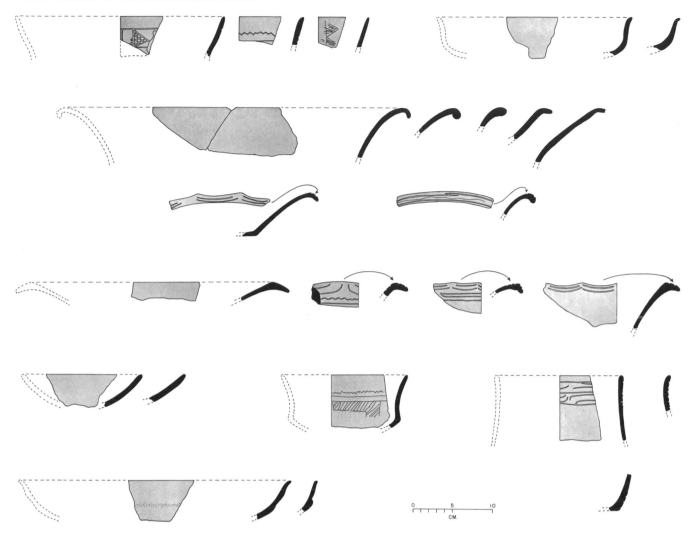

FIG. 69. QUACHILCO BROWN. *Row 1:* convex-wall bowls with direct or thickened and rounded rims; *rows 2–4:* flaring-wall bowls with rounded everted rims and with sharply everted rims; *row 5:* low convex-wall bowl, composite-silhouette vessel, and cylindrical jar with basal bulge; *row 6:* bowls with basal flanges.

Convex-wall bowls have low walls, rounded lips, and flattened or convex bottoms. They are usually undecorated, but a few sherds have parallel lines incised around the outer rim. Dimensions in cm.: rim diameter, 14–22; height, 4.0–8.0.

A closely related minor form are *convex-wall bowls with thickened rims.* Some of these have one line encircling the lip. The diameter at the rim ranges from 20 to 24 cm. and the height seems to have been about the same as the range for the convex-wall bowls with direct rims.

Convex- or outsloping-wall bowls with basal flanges apparently had rounded bottoms, though no wall-to-base sherds were found. Rims are direct. The walls slope outward and usually are slightly convex. Encircling the lower portion of the side is a sharp ridge or rounded fillet, not so pronounced or protruding as those on similar vessels of Quachilco Gray to be described below. One sherd, apparently of this shape, has an incised stepped motif. Seven sherds have a groove around the body along the upper side of the ridge, emphasizing the ridge in profile. Dimensions in cm.: rim diameter, 24–34; wall thickness, 0.6–0.8; estimated height, 5.0–6.0.

Outsloping-wall bowls had flat or convex bottoms. Only a few sherds were decorated, all on the exterior. Rim diameter, 22–30 cm.

Cylindrical vessels had either vertical, slightly con-

117

TABLE 38
Quachilco Brown Vessel Forms
(sherds by site and zone)

	Early Santa Maria									Late Santa Maria						
	368e H	368e G	368e F	368e E	367 D1	367 C	368e D	368e C2	368e C1	368e C	368w D-E	368e B	368w C	368w B	218-11 G	218-1 F
Bowls																
flaring wall																
direct rim		1					2	2	2	8	2	8	2	2	1	2
round everted rim										5	2	5	1			1
sharp everted rim										1		9			2	
convex wall																
direct rim				4				1	3	8	4		2	2	1	8
thick rim							1		2	1						
basal flange																
outsloping wall							4	2				1				
ovate, pinched wall											1	4	2	3		
basal flange																2
incurved rim							2		1							
composite silhouette																
Cylindrical vessels										3	2	2				
Ollas																
short str. neck												1				
short flaring neck																
Bottles															1	1
Incense burners												1				
Bases																
flat							4					1				
convex												2				
Strap handle																
Spout							1									
Body sherds	3	3	8	8	1	3	29	4	12	34	39	145	41	34	37	28
Total	3	4	8	12	1	3	43	7	22	60	50	179	48	41	42	42

	Late Santa Maria (continued)															
	368e B1	204 A-B	368w B1	218-11 E	218-6 G	218-10 C2	218-6 F	218-11 D	218-11 C	218-10 C1	218-10 C	218-10 B1	218-10 B	218-11 B	218-6 E	218 D
Bowls																
flaring wall																
direct rim	4	4	2	2		3		2			8	3	6			3
round everted rim		1	4	1	4	3	4	7	2	5	3	15	10			1
sharp everted rim						1						1	1			
convex wall																
direct rim			1				1	1		1	9		3			2
thick rim						1				1		1		1		
basal flange																
outsloping wall			1			1				1	11	3	8			1
ovate, pinched wall	6		5	3	4	2	3	1								
basal flange			1			2		2			4	4		1		
incurved rim												1				
composite silhouette											1					
Cylindrical vessels						4	1	3		2	5	4	3			1
Ollas																
short str. neck						1		1				2	1		1	
short flaring neck										1			1			
Bottles												1				
Incense burners										1					•	
Bases																
flat											2		1			
convex											4		2			
Strap handle																
Spout																
Body sherds	38	32	52	26	19	64	16	18	12	46	126	52	72	9	3	11
Total	48	37	65	35	27	82	25	35	14	58	173	87	108	11	4	19

(Table continued)

(Table 38, continued)

	Late Santa Maria (continued)			Early Palo Blanco						Late Palo Blanco				
	50 VII	218-6 C	218-6 B	218-10 A	218-6 A	218-11 A	272 F	51 A-B	50 VI	272 C	254 B	35e E	35e D	Total
Bowls														
flaring wall														
direct rim		5	10	16	2	3	1	1		1		4	2	114
round everted rim		1	1	14		1		1						92
sharp everted rim														15
convex wall														
direct rim		5	1	31		1							1	90
thick rim														8
basal flange				11										11
outsloping wall			2	39	4	1								79
ovate, pinched wall														34
basal flange														16
incurved rim														4
composite silhouette							1							2
Cylindrical vessels		1		15	1	1								48
Ollas														
short str. neck														7
short flaring neck														2
Bottles														3
Incense burners														2
Bases														
flat												1		10
convex				7										16
Strap handle									1					1
Spout														1
Body sherds	4	19	44	231	33	39	3	2	3	1	1	2	5	1412
Total	4	31	58	364	40	47	4	4	4	2	1	8	7	1967

vex, or slightly concave walls. Some walls bulge at the bottom and are slightly concave toward the top. The vessels ranged from squat to tall and had flat or slightly convex bottoms. No supports were noted. The rims are usually direct with flattish or tapering lips, but a few examples have a short everted lip with a groove on the outside to facilitate the everting process. About a third of these bowls are decorated, all on the exterior, the majority by incising. One sherd displays an excised or raspada design. The incised motifs are hachured triangles; zigzag, discontinuous, or hooked lines; a stepped motif; and up to four horizontal parallel lines. The decoration is generally applied in horizontal bands around the rim and just above the base, although several sherds seem to show an over-all pattern. Dimensions in cm.: rim diameter, 10–18; base diameter, 12–16; wall thickness, 0.5–0.9; estimated height, 3.0–10.

Ovate bowls with pinched-in sides have at least one wall that is constricted or "dimpled" in the center section. Individual sherds of this form have irregular pro-

files and appear warped. Only two of thirty-four sherds are decorated. The exterior of one is incised with a horizontal line near the rim and two half-circles underneath. The other sherd has three parallel horizontal lines incised on the interior rim zone, with several comma-shaped punctate marks underneath. Because of the irregular shape of these bowls, measurements could not be taken.

Incurved-rim bowls or tecomates are very minor shapes. One sherd is decorated on the exterior surface with parallel lines incised in a seemingly all-over horizontal pattern. Other sherds have a single groove just below the lip on the outer surface.

Composite-silhouette bowls are represented by only two excavated examples and others from the surface. They were fairly deep vessels with convex bottoms and upright but concave walls. The excavated specimens are undecorated. One sherd from the surface is incised with zigzag and straight horizontal lines combined with a hachured stepped motif. Rim diameters range from 12 to 16 cm.

119

Ollas. Few vessels with necks were made in Quachilco Brown. Nine rim or neck sherds, all from late Santa Maria components, represent two olla shapes. All are undecorated. One wide-mouthed jar with a short flaring neck appears almost miniature (rim diameter, 12 cm.). The other sherds represent larger vessels (rim diameter, about 16 cm.) with short to medium-high flaring, vertical, or insloping necks and direct or everted rims. The fragments give no indication of the shapes of body or base.

Minor forms and appendages include three rim sherds of bottles, two ring bases about 8 cm. in diameter and one cm. high, two quite thick fragments possibly representing incense burners, one fragmentary spout, and one fragment of a strap handle.

Relationships

The Quachilco Brown type is closely related to Quachilco Gray in the Tehuacan Valley. External relations are more difficult to discern. However, Type K. 6 of Monte Alban I and II is quite similar and may well be the same type as Quachilco Brown. Caso, Bernal, and Acosta (1967: 52–53) believe examples of K. 6, which make up a very small percentage of their sample, are intrusive in the Oaxaca Valley.

QUACHILCO GRAY

38,256 specimens excavated; 2,034 collected.

Paste

The tempering matter is small in size and comprises about 12 percent of the paste. Less than 1 percent is grains 0.5–1.0 mm. in diameter, made up of feldspar, quartz, and quartzite. About 7 percent is grains 0.1–0.5 mm. in diameter consisting of a large range of rocks or minerals, most commonly quartz, quartzite, and calcite, and less frequently, pyroxenes, diorite, limestone, and oligoclase. Still less common are muscovite, biotite, marble, microclines, feldspar, and andesine. About 5 percent of the paste is composed of grains less than 0.1 mm. in diameter, and these include most of the above materials plus magnetite and hematite. Occasional holes in the sherds indicate that particles of limestone may have leached out. The hardness of the sherds is about 4.0.

The color indicates even firing and ranges widely from bluish-gray to dark gray and from various brownish hues to black. The general consistency is fine and compact, although occasional sherds have a more granular appearance. The sherds fracture with a regular to sharp break in straight lines. Occasional coil marks are visible on imperfectly smoothed olla interiors.

This paste seems very similar to that analyzed by Shepard (Caso, Bernal, and Acosta 1967: 477–484) from Monte Alban I. In terms of pottery types established for Monte Alban (*ibid.*: 18–20), Types G. 5, G. 7, G. 12–18, G. 24, G. 26, G. 32, and G. 33 appear to have the same or a very similar paste and the same range of surface colors described below for Quachilco Gray. These Monte Alban gray-ware types originate and are dominant in period I, but carry on as minor types in period II.

Surface Finish

The surface coloration varies greatly, but generally can be divided into grays and dark browns. Exterior and generally the interior surfaces of the gray variety range from light gray (5.0 YR 7/2) through pinkish-gray (7.5 YR 7/2) to dark gray or grayish-brown (10 YR 4/1–4/2), with some bluish overtones. The brownish variety has the following coloration on both exterior and interior surfaces: reddish-brown (2.5 YR 5/4), dark gray (2.5 Y 4/0), brown (7.5 YR 5/4–6/4), and gray to grayish-brown (10 YR 5/1–5/2).

Both inner and outer surfaces are well polished, with the exception of interiors of narrow-necked ollas and the exteriors of bowls with flaring sides and everted rims. The latter bowls show deep and wide horizontal striations over the entire exterior surface. Even the well-polished surfaces generally show horizontal striations with smooth edges, as though a rounded polishing stone had been used for the smoothing process. Occasionally straight-sided bowls, as well as some exterior bottoms, show striations that are parallel, criss-cross, or V-shaped. A thin float coat or wash covers exterior surfaces and is slightly darker than the paste beneath. Where the vessel is only lightly smoothed, the surface is of the same color as the paste. Quachilco Gray wares usually have a matte to dull luster, but occasional pieces are polished to a silky luster.

Decoration

Fine-line incising is the most common technique used to decorate Quachilco Gray vessels. The incising was done with a sharp tool such as an obsidian blade, usually while the clay was leather-hard, for the sharp ridges raised by the blade have been polished smooth. Some examples retain the sharp edges along the incisions, indicating that the clay was polished before being incised.

FIG. 70. QUACHILCO GRAY. Decoration motifs on everted-rim flaring-wall bowls. Center sherd in bottom row is from a stepped-rim bowl.

5 CM.

FIG. 71. QUACHILCO GRAY. *Rows 1–5*, incised or grooved motifs on various bowl forms; *bottom row*, zoned-toned sherds.

Far less common as a technique of decoration is fine-line engraving made after the vessel was fired, resulting in narrow lines with broken edges. Rarer still are examples of raspada decoration, a technique which involves wide excised areas and sometimes a raised main motif.

Many of the engraved lines and excised areas retain traces of red powder. Evidently ground cinnabar or hematite or other pigment was rubbed into the grooves to emphasize the design. The red powder was also applied in fairly wide bands around the exterior rims of hemispherical bowls or over the entire outer surface of ollas and basal ridge vessels.

Other minor techniques of decoration used on Quachilco Gray are grooving and gadrooning. Punctate decoration is found only on early examples, usually ollas. Stick-polishing or pattern-polishing occurs on occasional sherds, generally in fairly wide but shallow parallel grooves forming a hachured or crosshachured or horizontal pattern. Zoned-toning is occasionally seen on late Santa Maria examples of Quachilco Gray. The tonal differences given the exterior of vessels by this technique were made after an initial over-all polishing. Certain areas, often triangular or rectangular, were then drawn on the vessel surface; some smudging material was applied to the outlined areas, which were further polished, while the remaining areas were left untouched or were polished at right angles.

A small number of convex-wall bowls of Quachilco Gray have light-colored rims on much darker bodies or large, evenly distributed, but irregular areas of two tones. These effects may have been deliberate and are perhaps related to the earlier differential firing technique that produced white rims on dark bodies. If so, this is surely the dying gasp of that particular technique.

The relief technique of applied decoration is rarely seen on Quachilco Gray ware, except in the placing of dots, bars, and fillets of clay along the necks of ollas or on bowls.

About fifty sherds had been perforated by conical hand drills from two surfaces. The majority of the holes thus produced were located along broken edges and may have been designed to hold cracked pottery together in what has been called the "crack-lacing technique." Many holes were in the center of sherd disks. Other holes were on the bottom of vessels, and some are so large as to make "crack-lacing" out of the question.

The style of decoration on Quachilco Gray ware is, generally speaking, geometric, with curvilinear motifs in the minority. What at first glance seems a tremendously complicated array of decorative motifs is actually only an interplay, by seemingly endless combinations, of a few simple design elements: parallel lines, either straight, zigzag, or wavy; crosshatching; punctation; and steps. The designs are usually combined in horizontal bands encircling the rims or bodies, depending on the vessel form.

Triangles are a popular motif. The triangles generally are long and narrow but sometimes are equilateral. They most frequently appear in horizontal panels, alone or combined with other elements, near the rim of the vessel or at both rim and base. The triangles are generally filled with hatching or crosshatching at approximately a 45-degree angle to the base, and, very rarely, at a 90-degree angle. The triangles may be tilted and several of them joined to form a zigzag or stepped effect. They are often combined with parallel wavy, vertical, or horizontal lines. Two to five horizontal lines at times appear under the triangle base. Triangles may also be combined with zigzag elements, stepped motifs, and rectangular elements. Sometimes they are placed in alternating fashion—that is, point up, point down, point up—with considerable space between the elements. Four triangles may touch at the corners to enclose a diamond-shaped motif. Occasionally triangles are combined to form short vertical rows on the walls of fairly deep vessels.

Many of the incised triangular designs of Quachilco Gray occur on Monte Alban I Types G. 15–18 and G. 24 (Caso, Bernal, and Acosta 1967: figs. 4–12).

A variation on the classic triangle is the concave-sided triangle with a straight base. The motif occurs only occasionally. The point may be facing up, down, or sideways. When the point is sideways, four or five triangles are usually connected and placed between vertical parallel lines. Often a series of concave-sided triangles are placed vertically point to point to form ellipses. They may be filled with hatching, but are rarely crosshatched. They generally are combined with two to twelve (usually two or three) delimiting horizontal and/or vertical lines with a wavy line at the bottom of the series. Concave-sided triangles appear on gray ware from Oaxaca exhibited at the Frissell Museum in Mitla.

Discontinuous parallel lines, usually horizontal and arranged in a series of two to ten, form a small portion of the total motifs. They are probably the last gasp of the "double-line-break" motif characteristic of Middle Formative white wares. In fact, only a few sherds display a formal double-line-break pattern, and these are generally the dark brown variety of Quachilco Gray. The lines usually terminate in an upward or down-

FIG. 72. QUACHILCO GRAY. *Row 1 and row 2, right:* interior decoration on low vessels; *rows 2–5:* exterior decorations; *row 6:* bowl with perforated ring base, ornamental fragments from incense burners, and hollow mammiform foot.

ward hook, and sometimes one hook will point up and the other down. Often the lines are not straight but have a rough freehand quality. They run in a concentric pattern near the rim of the vessel but sometimes are found in an over-all design. They form a fairly popular motif on Types G. 15 and G. 17 of Monte Alban (*ibid.*: figs. 8–10, 12).

Wavy or undulating lines make up approximately a fifth of the total motifs. They may be continuous or interrupted, and may run either in horizontal and concentric or in vertical and zoned patterns. They also occur as short, isolated motifs in combination with short, multiple parallel lines. One to four wavy lines may appear together, or a wavy line may be used both above and below two or three straight parallel lines. Wavy lines are also combined with hooked lines, triangles, rectangles, stepped elements, and semicircles. Wavy or undulating lines occur on Monte Alban Types G. 12 and G. 15 (*ibid.*: figs. 4, 8).

Semicircular motifs occur on a small fraction of Quachilco Gray ware. Some are placed so closely together and have been made in such a loose, free-hand manner that it is difficult to tell where the semicircular motif leaves off and wavy lines begin, as is the case when this motif is used on Types G. 15–17 of Monte Alban I (*ibid.*: figs. 8, 12).

Parallel lines, used alone or in combination with other motifs, make up the majority of the decorative elements. Practically all of the other elements so far listed are combined with parallel lines. Parallel lines may be horizontal, slanting, or vertical and sometimes occur in a series which would ultimately come together in a "V"-shape. Parallel lines are used as bases for triangles and usually form delimiting rim and base lines for other motifs. Other motifs use parallel lines in forming steps, "U"-shaped elements, and sharp corners. Parallel-line motifs occur on Monte Alban Types G. 12, G. 13, and G. 15 (*ibid.*: figs. 4, 7, 9).

A subvariety of the parallel-line motif is made up of two undulating parallel lines, free-hand in character and of varying lengths. Most were incised before firing; however, a few were made afterward. These lines are found in many positions and combinations. They are often accompanied by short straight lines and one or two lines on the rim. Occasionally lines of punctations are found between the parallel lines.

Zigzag lines are very rare. They occur both as isolated motifs and as an over-all pattern, generally in a horizontal direction, and are often delimited by a horizontal straight line on the rim and the base of the vessel.

Hachure, or the use of short parallel lines in various directions either inside or outside decorative motifs, is frequently displayed on both the interior and exterior of vessels. A step motif with hachure inside is sometimes found on exterior surfaces fairly close to the rim, but also appears either as an isolated motif or in over-all fashion. Crosshatching is used to delimit zones around or within elliptical, triangular, or other geometric elements. Generally the crosshatching is at an acute angle to the base of the vessel. It may be combined with certain free-hand elements, particularly with two parallel undulating lines. Both hatching and crosshatching are common on Monte Alban I gray wares (*ibid.*: fig. 11).

"Free-hand" elements are found in the form of undulating lines, spirals, or short curving lines with hooked ends. These make up a small part of the total decorative motifs. They appear on Monte Alban Type G. 17 (*ibid.*: fig. 12).

Zoned toning is made up of triangular and diamond-shaped elements, as well as narrow, converging bands of alternating light and dark tones which have been further delimited by incised lines at the junction of the two tones. Typical examples of zoned-toned decoration appear on sherds from the Yagul tombs said to be of Monte Alban I style (Paddock 1966: p. 250, fig. 6, extreme left, and second row, far right; p. 252, fig. 7, right).

Other incised motifs, which occur in quite small numbers or as unique examples, are circles with short radiating lines, short strokes placed one above the other to give a raindrop effect, a series of "V"-shaped or chevron elements, double parallel lines forming arches, a variation of a step motif, various short undulating lines which combine with semicircles, and semicircular lines placed one above another to form an "eye" motif.

Vessel Forms

Convex-wall bowls with direct rims are the most numerous form, totaling over one thousand examples from late Santa Maria components alone. They have rounded or flat bases and low convex walls, sometimes slightly incurving at the rims. No supports were found. The proportion of decorated to undecorated bowls is small. Incising was used for the following motifs: crosshatching on the exterior only; hachured triangles, generally on the interior, but occasionally on the exterior; wavy lines, sometimes combined with straight lines, generally on the exterior but occasionally on the interior; crosshatched step motif, more often on the interior than the exterior; two-to-four horizontal parallel lines on the interior or exterior; and free-hand dis-

5 CM.

Fig. 73. Quachilco Gray. Decorated olla sherds and, *lower left,* fragments of a bridged spout and notched handle.

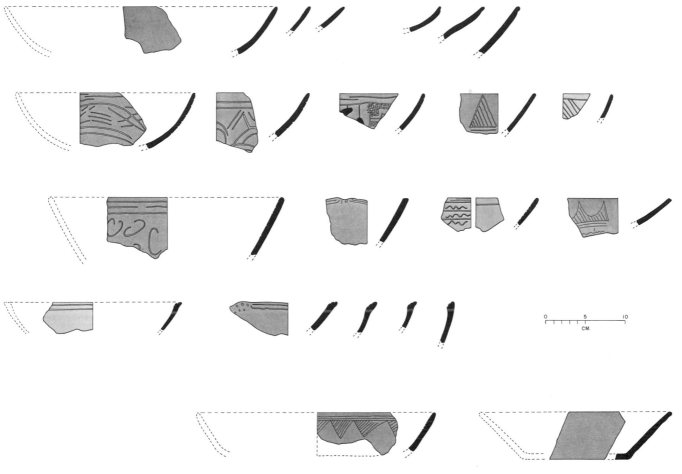

FIG. 74. QUACHILCO GRAY. Convex-wall bowls with direct, grooved, or internally thickened rims. *Bottom row*, out-sloping-wall bowls.

continuous lines. Numerous specimens have a single line incised just below the lip on either the interior or exterior. A shallow groove just below the rim on the exterior often is used in combination with a single-line incision encircling the inner rim. Some bowls display large irregular whitish or lightened areas brought about by differential firing. Several sherds show that both surfaces had once been covered with powdered red pigment. Dimensions in cm.: rim diameter, 8.0–38; estimated height, 3.0–8.0; wall thickness, 0.4–0.6.

Flaring-wall bowls with direct rims are also numerous. They have flat or convex bottoms, with a sharp angle at the junction of base and wall. The walls slant gently then flare rather widely outward, ending usually with a rounded lip. Several base sherds from early Palo Blanco components had attachments for supports. No indications were found of the type of support, except for one miniature bowl which had three solid conical supports.

Most of these bowls are undecorated. When present, decoration consisted of the following motifs: crosshatching on the exterior only; concave-sided triangles on either the exterior or the interior; hachured triangles on the exterior only; wavy lines, on interior or exterior; hooked or discontinuous lines on either surface; parallel lines, more often on the exterior than the interior; zigzag and parallel undulating lines on the exterior; and free-hand designs on either surface. Red coloration was noted on a dozen of these sherds and probably a closer examination would have disclosed more. Zoned toning appears on one interior rim zone. Several sherds display raspada designs. One bowl has a notched rim. Dimensions in cm.: rim diameter, 14–38; estimated base diameter, 6.0–22; estimated height, 3.0–10; wall thickness, 0.7–1.1

Flaring-wall bowls with rounded everted rims are another very common vessel form. They have flat or slightly convex bottoms. The walls and base meet at

127

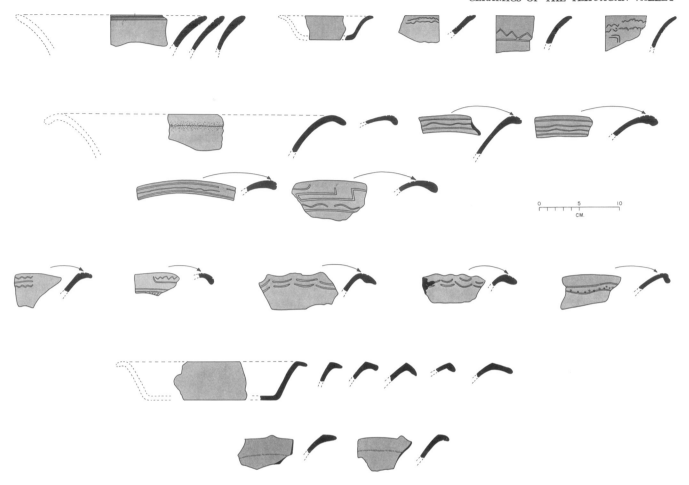

FIG. 75. QUACHILCO GRAY. Flaring-wall bowls with direct, rounded everted, and sharply everted rims.

an angle. The walls flare upward, and the rims, which are usually somewhat thickened, then curve outward and sometimes downward. Lips are rounded, flattish, or beveled on the interior.

Decoration on these bowls is common in the early zones of Quachilco but diminishes on examples from the upper layers. The rims are often modeled into lugs, scallops, notches, and buttons. Incising is the major technique of decoration and appears mainly on the upper surface of the rim. Motifs include a majority of parallel wavy, straight, and discontinuous lines. Hachured triangles are fairly common; crosshatched stepped motifs are rare. The zoned-toning technique occasionally was used in combination with rim lugs or an undulating rim. A number of rims are encircled with a series of punctate dots inside parallel sinuous lines. One raspada-decorated sherd and numerous rims with semicircular designs were found. Semicircular motifs generally occur on notched or scalloped rims. Dimen-

sions in cm.: rim diameter, 12–38; estimated base diameter, 6.0–24; estimated height, 3.0–8.5; wall thickness, 0.4–0.9.

Flaring- or outsloping-wall bowls with sharply everted rims are closely related to the preceding shape and in the very earliest zones at Quachilco rival it in popularity. These bowls have flat or slightly convex bottoms, with base and wall meeting at an angle. The walls either curve or slope outward; they vary in profile from flaring to straight to slightly convex. Their divergence is accentuated by a sharply everted rim which either slants downward or, less commonly, extends horizontally. No supports have been found on this shape.

Over three-quarters of the rim sherds displayed decoration, making this shape the most decorated of all the forms. This heavy proportion of decoration, however, appears in the lower zones at Quachilco and tends to fade and even disappear in the top zones. The

128

most common design consists of parallel-line motifs, which are usually applied as wide and shallow incising, or more accurately, grooving. Wavy parallel lines are frequent, as are discontinuous lines. Also common are triangular or rectangular motifs in thin, fine incising. Zoned toning was used less frequently. A few sherds display punctate decoration between semicircular, discontinuous, or undulating lines. Some sherds have half-circle patterns on the rims. At times the upper surface of the rim is grooved to give the effect of a labial ridge at the junction of rim and body. Many of the incised motifs are combined with modeled rims in the form of lugs, notches, and flanges. Small dots or button-like decorations are occasionally applied to the top of the rim. Dimensions in cm.: rim diameter, 22–34, estimated base diameter, 13-22; estimated height, 5.0–8.0; wall thickness, 0.5–0.8.

Outsloping-wall bowls have fairly straight walls that slant outward at an angle of 40–80 degrees from the plane of the base. The walls terminate in direct rims with flat or rounded lips. The bowls usually have flat bottoms, but a few basal fragments were slightly convex. Supports are lacking on this shape in early levels, but a hollow mammiform leg is found in later levels and may have been used, persumably in tripod fashion, with it.

Only a small proportion of these bowls are decorated, although apparently much use was made of a powdered red pigment on both exterior and interior surfaces. About a dozen sherds show the effects of differential firing, with contrasting whitish areas in the manner of white-rimmed black wares. Incision, however, is the preferred technique of decoration, used most often on the interior surface. Motifs include straight or wavy parallel lines, hooks or discontinuous lines, concave-sided and hachured triangles, and crosshatching. Dimensions in cm.: rim diameter, 16–34, usually 22–30; estimated base diameter, 10–26; estimated height, 4.0–10; wall thickness, 0.4–0.9.

Bowls with basal flanges have walls that are outsloping and either definitely convex or nearly straight or walls that are flaring and usually fairly upright. Most of the bowls have convex bottoms, probably flattened to rest evenly. The junction of base and wall is emphasized by a fillet or modeled protuberance in the form of a basal flange or ridge. Lips vary from flat, thinned, or beveled, to grooved. The position of the flange varies considerably in relation to the convexity of the base and when placed high on a low-walled bowl gives a flanged-rim effect. The thickness of the flange or the degree to which it projects from the wall also varies. Some of the ridges turn downward, others extend horizontally; some are grooved at the bottom, but the majority are slightly grooved on the upper side at the junction to the vessel wall.

Decoration appears on exterior surfaces only, on the walls or the upper surface of the flange. In the latter location it usually consists of incised triangles or motifs with wavy lines, and more rarely, of notches, finger impressions, and circular punctate designs. On the body of the vessel concave-sided and hachured triangles appear most frequently, but multiple parallel vertical or horizontal straight or wavy lines are fairly common. Hachured stepped motifs are rare. One unusual design consists of opposed hachured triangles placed sidewise to enclose diamond-shaped areas in which hollow circles are incised. Several sherds show the remains of powdered red pigment.

Dimensions in cm.: rim diameter, 16–41; estimated height, 3.0–8.0; thickness at flange, 0.9–1.1; wall thickness, 0.5–0.7.

Convex-wall bowls with wedge-shaped, internally, or externally thickened rims have outsloping walls which terminate in a rim that gradually becomes thicker either on the interior or exterior or bilaterally. When thickened on the interior, the rims have a slightly everted appearance, as do identical rims on convex-wall bowls of Rio Salado Gray and Coatepec White. The rims thickened bilaterally usually have a flattened effect across the top, giving a wedge-shaped appearance, also a characteristic of certain bowls of Rio Salado Gray. A few sherds have a deep groove on top of the thickened lip, giving it a stepped effect. No bases or supports were found.

Decoration occurs on most of the sample in the form of parallel lines incised around the interior of the rim or directly on the lip. Occasional examples display discontinuous lines and hooks and multiple diagonal or vertical shallow punctations or lines. Small elliptical luglike projections are fairly common in conjunction with the incised rims.

Thickened-rim bowls do not carry over into early Palo Blanco times, although two examples with externally thickened rims represent levels of the early part of the phase. The bowls seem to have derived from the early Santa Maria subphase, during which time convex-wall bowls with thickened rims are fairly common in Rio Salado Gray. Dimensions in cm.: rim diameter, 16–22; wall thickness, 0.4–0.6; thickness at rim, 0.8–1.2; base diameter and wall height, unknown.

Cylindrical vessels have generally upright walls that are slightly concave, sometimes flaring markedly at the rim and sometimes concave at the top but slightly bulging or barrel-shaped at the base. Bottoms are flat,

129

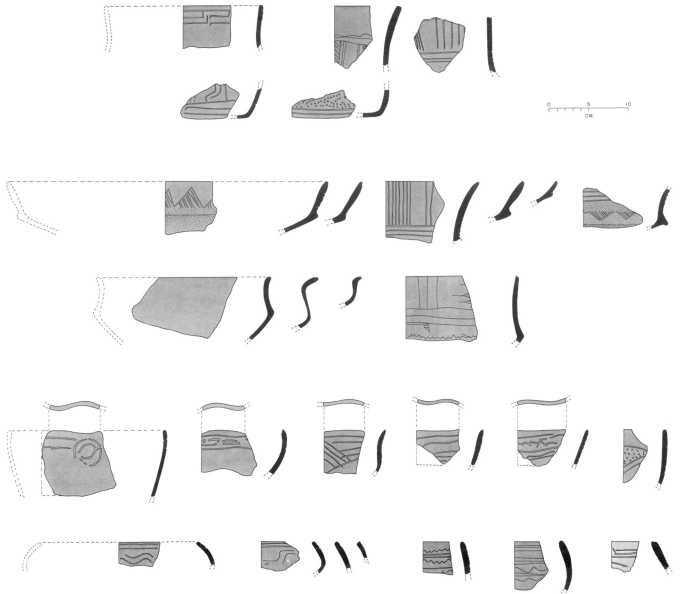

FIG. 76. QUACHILCO GRAY. *From top to bottom,* cylindrical vessels, bowls with basal flanges, composite-silhouette vessels, bowls with pinched-in sides, and incurved-rim bowls.

although two slightly convex bases may belong to this form. No supports were noted.

Almost half of these vessels are decorated, almost always on the outer surface. A number of specimens were smeared with red pigment. Incising is the most common technique of decoration. Motifs are hachured or plain triangles, hachured stepped motifs, horizontal wavy lines, multiple parallel lines, and zigzag lines. The motifs are usually combined in horizontal bands or panels outlined by incised lines. One sherd has a large irregular panel of punctations on the exterior

wall near the bottom. Dimensions in cm.: rim diameter, 10–24; base diameter, slightly smaller than rim diameter; wall thickness; 4.0–9.0; height, unknown, probably over half the rim diameter.

Incurved-rim bowls or tecomates. Well over a hundred sherds represent rather squat vessels which range from plain tecomate shapes to low bowls with incurved (or inslanted) rims. Most have convex walls, but a few examples show an angle at the junction of convex base and insloping walls, rather like the carinated bowls seen in some of the Venta Salada wares.

Most lips are rounded, but one sherd has a lip pinched up into a brief vertical rim.

Decoration is applied in the form of wide-line or fine-line incising and consists of parallel lines around the mouth, or of discontinuous lines, wavy lines, undulating lines, and stepped motifs. Four sherds were decorated by the zoned-toning process. Several sherds show traces of powdered red pigment on the outer surface. Dimensions in cm.: rim diameter, 6.0–22; height, about 10–12.

Composite-silhouette bowls are vessels with fairly deep convex bottoms topped by walls that slant or curve sharply inward and then flare outward at the rim. The flaring rim is much more pronounced on some examples than others. Lips are usually rounded or bilaterally tapering. No supports have been found on this form.

Many of these vessels are decorated on the outer surface. Incised motifs include hachured triangles, vertical or horizontal parallel lines, and semicircular designs. Punctation appears on one sherd and zoned-toning on another.

Rim diameters generally fall into a range of 14–22 cm. Dimensions in cm. of one complete specimen: diameter at rim, 19.0, at junction of wall and base, 19.5, at basal point of contact, 8.0–9.0; over-all height, 13.0; height of wall, 7.5.

Ovate bowls with pinched-in sides have rounded or elliptical bottoms, although a few seem to have been flat. Viewed from the top the form is generally oval, but the pinched-in sides would give it the outline of a figure eight; or if only one side is pinched, it would be kidney-shaped. Lips are either rounded or beveled on the interior. Individual sherds of this form have irregular profiles and appear warped. No supports were found.

The majority of the bowls are decorated. Incising or shallow grooving are the usual techniques. Parallel lines, generally horizontal, form the most common motif and appear on both surfaces. The outer surface, however, is more often decorated, with the decoration usually appearing near the rim. Other motifs include discontinuous lines, hachured triangles, and wavy lines. One vessel has a grooved "eye" motif filling the pinched-in section of the wall. Several sherds show traces of powdered red pigment.

Zone C[1] of Ts 367 produced a Quachilco Gray sherd with a tiny handle, apparently from an ovate bowl with pinched-in sides.

Because of the irregular shape of these bowls, rim sherds rarely give any indication of the diameter along the longer axis or the width across the center.

FIG. 77. QUACHILCO GRAY. Composite-silhouette bowl.

The bowls were probably about 7 or 8 cm. high, and may have been about 20 cm. long by 8–12 cm. wide.

Ollas with medium-high to tall flaring necks are most prominent among olla shapes of Quachilco Gray from all levels, but ollas are never a majority form in this paste. The ollas described here have only slightly flaring necks emerging from the body in a very gradual manner. Bodies must have been globular or sub-globular in shape, perhaps with rounded bottoms. Lips are flattish or rounded. One sherd displays zoned-toned decoration and two were incised. Dimensions in cm.: rim diameter, 10–25; neck height, 4.8–8.0; wall thickness, 0.5–0.8.

Ollas with short flaring necks tend to be smaller and thinner-walled than the category described above. Some are miniature in size. The rims are generally more flaring than rims of the longer-necked variety, and mouths are sometimes quite wide. Bodies must have been globular, or somewhat squatter than globular, resting on rounded bases. Some examples are decorated on the outer surface of rim and neck with wide-line incising in patterns using discontinuous lines, hooked lines, and bands of parallel lines. A few show a single-line groove or appliqued fillet at the junction of neck and shoulder. Several sherds display a sort of scalloped border on the upper portion of the body, consisting of a series of parallel semicircular motifs outlining a row of punctations. Dimensions in cm.: rim diameter, 4.0–20; neck height, 2.7–3.5; wall thickness, 0.5–0.7.

131

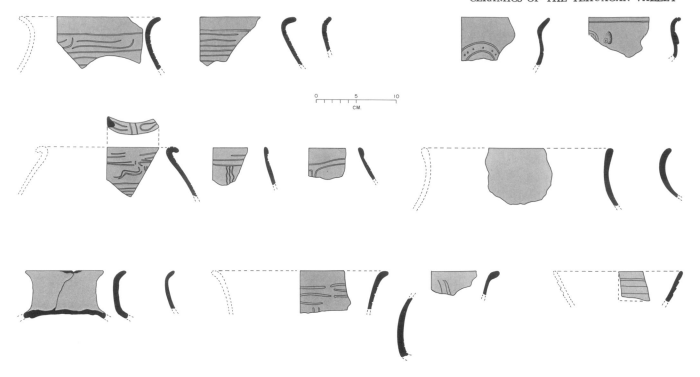

FIG. 78. QUACHILCO GRAY. *Row 1:* ollas with medium-high to tall flaring necks and with wide mouths and short flaring necks; *row 2:* ollas with rolled rims and with long flaring necks; *row 3:* straight- or convergent-neck ollas with everted rims and funnel-neck ollas with and without everted rims.

Rolled-rim ollas have relatively small mouths and globular bodies. The brief necks are formed by the rolling out of the rims, which range from a solid bead-like projection to a rolled flange. Most of the sample were decorated with incised parallel straight or wavy lines, discontinuous lines, and presumably hooks and semicircles. Rim diameter, 12–26 cm.

Funnel-neck ollas have a longish neck emerging like a funnel from the body. Rims are usually short and horizontally everted. A few sherds are decorated with wide-line incising in linear motifs around the necks either beneath the rim or just above the junction of neck and body. One sherd had a vertical design of wavy lines in fine-line incising. Rim diameter, 10–26 cm.

Straight-neck ollas usually have long necks, the walls of which are either vertical or slightly convergent. Some examples have direct rims; others have short outslanted, outcurved, or horizontally everted rims. Incised decoration consists of crosshatching, parallel encircling lines, punctate dots, and semicircular motifs. Rim diameter, 10–18 cm.

Miscellaneous olla fragments. Four neck sherds are of the "corrugated" variety—that is, they are encircled with a series of wide, shallow grooves, placed at even intervals around flaring or funnel-shaped necks. A number of fragments show that ollas were elaborately decorated, usually with incised designs, over most of the body surface. Motifs include crosshatched rectilinear or curvilinear zones, hachured zones, parallel straight lines (sometimes combined with punctate dots), curved and zigzag lines, curvilinear patterns, and raspada or scraped-away areas combined with curvilinear patterns. Some of the decorations are shown in Fig. 73. An unusual small flaring-neck olla had an appliqued object resembling a tiny ear on the body (Fig. 78, upper right).

Miscellaneous features. Six stepped-rim sherds, apparently from flaring-wall bowls, and six fragments of plates or comales failed to give an accurate indication of the size or true shape of the vessels. The inner surface of a sherd from a flat vessel is decorated with vertical parallel lines combined with an inverted hachured triangle in an arrow-like design (Fig. 72, row 1, center). This pattern resembles designs incised on a number of vessel bottoms. Some of the latter combine wavy and straight parallel lines, hachured triangles, and scalloped zones. One design includes a small glyphlike motif.

Other fragments include a few strap handles, some of which are neatly notched down the center; miscellaneous pieces of what must have been incense burners; fragments of hollow bulbous or mammiform feet; the remains of bridged spouts; and perforated ring bases.

Relationships

Locally, the Quachilco Gray type was undoubtedly derived from Rio Salado Gray or a similar ware from a neighboring region. It gradually fades into the El Riego gray type of the Classic period. Quachilco Gray is an excellent time marker for the Late Formative period in the Tehuacan Valley.

In terms of paste, Quachilco Gray is very similar to gray wares of Monte Alban I and II. The combination of tempering materials in Quachilco Gray indicates a connection with the Oaxaca Valley (Shepard in Caso, Bernal, and Acosta 1967: 478). There are as well overwhelming similarities in vessel form and decoration between Quachilco Gray and the contemporaneous gray pottery of Monte Alban I and some of the gray pottery of Monte Alban II. The dominant vessel forms of both Quachilco and Monte Alban wares include flaring-wall bowls with direct rims or with rounded or sharply everted rims, convex-wall bowls, bowls with composite silhouettes, bridge-spouted ollas, and funnel-necked ollas.

The decorations on the various vessel forms are almost identical for the two regions, such as incised parallel lines on the inner or upper surface of rims, poorly executed double-line-break motifs, parallel zigzag lines, parallel semicircular motifs, triangles, rectangular designs, outlined areas filled with hatching and crosshatching, and many others. Ignacio Bernal, upon seeing examples of Quachilco Gray during the field season at Tehuacan, concluded that this ware was identical to Monte Alban Types G. 12–18 and G. 21 (personal communication; Bernal 1949). Since then the monumental report on Monte Alban pottery has been published (Caso, Bernal, and Acosta 1967), and it appears that Types G. 5, 7, 24, 26, 32, and 33 are also very close or identical to Quachilco Gray. From our own observations of the ceramics of Monte Alban I and II, Quachilco Gray is obviously not identical to all the fine gray pottery of early Monte Alban, but rather shares about 80 percent of its features with the period I and II gray wares.

The presence of this same gray pottery as trade ware in Chiapa de Corzo III burials and refuse as well as in burials of Chiapa de Corzo IV and VI (Lowe and Mason 1965: 215) tends to temporally align Chiapa III–VI, Monte Alban I–II, and late Santa Maria. Some of the gray ware from early and middle Tres Zapotes, particularly at Ranchito (Weiant 1943: 09–84), has similar vessel forms decorated with some of the same motifs as does Quachilco Gray. The paste of the Tres Zapotes gray pottery seems slightly different, but this may be more apparent than real, for the lowland sherds are badly eroded.

Ocos Gray, a dominant type in Conchas 2 of the

TABLE 41
Late Santa Maria Trade Sherds
(by site and zone)

	368e C	368w D	368e B	368w C	368e B	218-11 G	218-11 F	368e B¹	368w B¹
Usulutan Negative-painted								1	
Mars Orange	1		1						
Ticoman Red-on-buff							1		
Zacatenco Black-on-red	1						2		
Zacatenco Orange Lacquer	1	1	2			1			
Ticoman Orange	1		2	1					
Ticoman Red	1		1		2				1
Tres Zapotes Black Incised							1	1	
Chalahuites Orange-rimmed Black	2		1	1	2	4	3		2
(La Venta) Rocker-stamped	1								
Total	8	1	7	2	4	5	7	2	3

(Table continued)

(Table 41, continued)

	218-6 G	218-10 C²	218-11 D	218-10 C¹	218-10 B¹	218-11 B	218-6 B	Total
Usulutan Negative-painted		1						2
Mars Orange								2
Ticoman Red-on-buff								1
Zacatenco Black-on-red								3
Zacatenco Orange Lacquer								5
Ticoman Orange			2			1		7
Ticoman Red				2	1	2	3	13
Tres Zapotes Black Incised								2
Chalahuites Orange-rimmed Black	6				2			23
(La Venta) Rocker-stamped								1
Total	6	1	2	2	3	3	3	59

Pacific coast of Guatemala, also seems distantly related to Quachilco Gray (Coe and Flannery 1967: 47).

All in all, Quachilco Gray is a good time marker in the Tehuacan Valley and a good link to the Oaxaca Valley, Chiapas, and south-central Veracruz.

Aberrant or Trade Wares

A large number of sherds from late Santa Maria components were not immediately classifiable. Some of the sherds were too badly worn ever to be identified, some are variations upon our resident types, and a very few are definitely sherds that were brought in from other regions. A plain rocker-stamped sherd probably came from southern Veracruz. Other trade sherds are more assuredly identified. James Ford and Robert Squier recognized a number of black-ware sherds with rims fired brown to red as examples of resident types from southern Veracruz. These are Tres Zapotes Black Incised (Weiant 1943: 17–31) and Chalahuites Orange-rimmed Black of Trapiche III times. Román Piña Chan also identified a number of sherds as examples of Ticoman Red, Ticoman Orange, Ticoman Red-on-buff, Zacatenco Orange Lacquer (Vaillant 1931), and Zacatenco Black-on-red wares (Piña Chan 1958: fig. 46e). Two gray sherds displaying black negative-painted lines resemble Usulutan ware from the southern Mesoamerica highlands (Lothrop 1933). Two sherds of Mars Orange, a type diagnostic of the Mamom phase of the Peten (Smith 1955), were identified by Robert E. Smith.

Miscellaneous Objects

Sherd disks. Six disks from 2.5 to 15 cm. in diameter were found in late Santa Maria levels. Two were pierced. Most were made of Quachilco Mica paste.

Disk beads. Two small pierced disks measured 1.0 and 1.7 cm. in diameter.

Whistle or ocarina fragments. Three mouthpieces of whistles and seven fragments of hollow globular objects — either figurines, whistles, or ocarinas — were recovered from late Santa Maria components. One human face with doughnut-like eyes and mouth applied to a flat fragment of clay could have been part of a whistle or ocarina, but more likely came from an effigy bowl.

Ruffled cone. A small cone with rounded tip and three horizontal ridges encircling the wide end like starched ruffles could have been an ornament, figurine leg or headdress, or vessel support. It is 3.5 cm. long and has a maximum diameter of 2.7 cm.

Polished cone. A fragment split in half longitudinally and broken off at the wide end measures 7.0 cm. long by 2.7 cm. wide. The nearly black surface is well polished and along one broken edge is a small area of light tannish color resulting from differential firing. This could have been a vessel support or the prong of an incense burner.

Figurines

The late Santa Maria phase is represented by a large sample of figurines. The earlier levels contained a number of figurine types that have already been described, including Baby Face, Multi-hairknot, Trapiche Bunned-helmet, Crescentic Cap, Negroid with Hairknot, and High-turban Slit-eye heads; Hollow Dwarf body and limb fragments and Venus and Seated Mother bodies; and several of the polished and unpolished limb types found in earlier levels (see Table 8). A Remojadas head, which resembles some Classic heads from Veracruz, will be described with early

5 CM.

FIG. 79. BIG NOSE HEADS.

Palo Blanco figurines in Chapter 7. The figurine examples most typical of late Santa Maria are described by type below.

BIG NOSE HEADS

6 specimens: 4 excavated, 2 collected.
Dimensions in cm. (5 heads): height, 2.2–3.8, average, 2.8, width, 1.8–3.2, average, 2.7; thickness, 1.2–2.5, average, 2.0.
Paste: resembles Rio Salado Coarse.
Surface finish: reddish slip.

The main trait of these crudely modeled heads is a flat face that slopes outward from forehead to chin. The eyes consist of horizontal incisions with conical punctates for pupils. Noses are applied, are beaklike in shape, and are large in proportion to the rest of the face. Mouths are usually represented by punched lines. The backs of the heads are flat or slightly concave.

The excavated heads are all from early levels of the late Santa Maria subphase, making them representative roughly of the middle of the Santa Maria phase. They are so crude that it is difficult to make valid comparisons with figurines from other regions.

MATAMOROS HEAD

1 head excavated.
Dimensions in cm.: height, 4.5; width, 3.0; thickness, 1.6.
Paste: very well knit, fine white temper, apparently foreign.

This head has been carefully modeled and decorated. Viewed from the front, it is rectangular in outline. The face is relatively flat except for the prominent appliqued nose and mouth. Each eye is formed by two ploughed incisions. The long eyebrows, which almost meet above the nose, are slightly curved incisions.

Below the one intact pinched-out ear a large doughnut-shaped earplug is appliqued. The figurine has almost no neck, so that the earplug rests on the shoulder. The small remaining portion of shoulder re-

sembles shoulders on figurine bodies from Ticoman. Perhaps this head was attached to a similar body.

The rounded turban with its three-part design resembles the headdress of the Hollow Dwarfs. On this figurine the design elements are a central appliqued "braid" and two lateral areas of oblique linear incisions.

The single Matamoros example from the Tehuacan Valley comes from a zone representing roughly the middle of the Santa Maria phase. Although the eyes and headdress resemble those of figurines found in Veracruz (see Panuco Type C in Ekholm 1944: p. 442 and fig. 35), the only heads exactly like the Tehuacan example come from the Formative site at Matamoros near the Pan American highway in the state of Puebla. A similar head also was found in Chiapa de Corzo VI (Lowe, personal communication).

DUNCECAP HEAD

1 head excavated.
Dimensions in cm.: height, 5.2; width, 3.4; thickness, 2.8.
Paste: resembles Rio Salado Gray.
Surface finish: thin crude gray slip.

This head and cap are oval in outline. The crown of the cap has been pinched up from the top of the head. The brim is a long piece of clay applied across the forehead. Below the brim three oval appliques may represent decorations hanging from the brim. The nose is a cylindrical applique extending from the central decorative oval to a spool-shaped nose plug just above the mouth, which is a doughnut-shaped applique with a a deep cylindrical punch in the center. The eyes are distinctive and resemble those often seen on figurines from the southern coast of Mexico and Guatemala. Each eye is shaped by two triangular

5 CM.

FIG. 80. MATAMOROS, DUNCECAP, AND MONTE ALBAN OUTLINED-EYE HEADS.

135

marks whose tips form the corners and between which a deep conical punch forms the pupil. The ears are cylindrical appliques of clay.

This head dates from an early level of the late Santa Maria subphase. Although many of the early figurines of the Panuco area have conical caps, no figurines from other parts of Mexico seem to resemble this Tehuacan specimen.

MONTE ALBAN OUTLINED-EYE HEADS

2 heads: 1 excavated, 1 collected.
Dimensions in cm.: height 6.6; width 4.9; thickness, 3.5.
Paste and surface finish: resemble Rio Salado Gray.

Since the excavated specimen is fragmentary, the following description is based on a complete head from the surface of the Canoas site (Ts 367).

The most striking features are the deeply incised eyes, shaped like two tadpoles swimming toward the nose. Each pupil is a centered hole. Although the nose and mouth of the figurine from the surface are badly eroded, the nose appears to have been long and narrow, with two punctations for nostrils. The corners of the mouth are formed by two quite deep plough marks, between which is a row of small incised holes. The chin is prominent and probably was even more so originally. The one extant ear is applied and has a hole representing an earplug. An incised line extending across the forehead marks the lower edge of a plain tight-fitting cap.

The two examples of this figurine type date from roughly the middle of the Santa Maria phase. They are similar to a figurine said to be characteristic of Monte Alban I and II shown in the Frissell Museum at Mitla, Oaxaca.

CAPPED DOUGHNUT-EYE HEADS

3 heads: 2 excavated, 1 collected.
Dimensions in cm.: height (1 complete head), about 6.0; width (2 heads), 4.5 and 6.1; thickness (2 heads), 2.1 and 2.4.
Paste: resembles Canoas Orange-brown but with sandier temper.
Surface finish: smoothed while wet; traces of red paint.

The wide-jawed heads rest directly on disproportionately small bodies. The top of the head has been elongated to form a high cap, across the front of which is applied a thick band decorated with incised crosshatching. The eyes look like goggles. This effect is derived from large flattened oval appliques, punched in the middle with an implement leaving an oval impres-

sion. The two more complete heads have incised eyebrows that almost meet on the nose.

The applied nose is quite broad. Between it and the mouth are two incised lines, representing either a nose plug or a moustache. The mouth is also appliqued. The most complete head has a protruding upper lip (with plug?) and a linear incision across the middle. Ears and earplugs are also appliques.

These heads appear to be characteristic of the late Santa Maria phase. No similar heads have been reported from other regions of Mesoamerica. The eyes alone resemble eyes of Type Gi figurines from Ticoman (Vaillant 1931: pl. XXVII) and eyes of a few Teotihuacan I figurines. The caps and the general flatness of the Tehuacan specimens, however, are entirely different from Valley of Mexico figurines. The eye type and the headdress are perhaps most like

5 CM.

FIG. 81. DOUGHNUT-EYE HEADS: Capped and Hairlock types.

those of figurines from Monte Alban I and II and Chiapa de Corzo VII.

HAIRLOCK DOUGHNUT-EYE HEADS

3 heads excavated.

Dimensions in cm.: height, 3.2–7.0; width, 2.7–5.1; thickness, 2.0–2.8.

Paste and surface finish: resemble Rio Salado Coarse; traces of red paint on some surfaces.

The faces are quite wide through cheek and jaw. The mouth is an oblong applique marked with an "H" to define the lips and corners. The nose is a large round glob. Doughnut-shaped eyes are made by two round appliques punched in the center and pressed down at the sides. All the heads have high foreheads; two have a sideswept forelock applied obliquely across the forehead, and the third has a hairdress divided by a central part and an applied disk in the center of the forehead.

Two heads are from components of the late Santa Maria subphase. One was found in Zone A of Test 10 of Tr 218, indicating that the type may have lasted into the early Palo Blanco phase. As previously mentioned, the doughnut-eye feature is present in the Valley of Mexico at Ticoman and in Teotihuacan I. However, other aspects of this Tehuacan Valley type are unlike Valley of Mexico figurines.

LATE SANTA MARIA ABERRANT TYPE 1

1 head excavated.

Dimensions in cm.: height from waist, 5.1; width, 3.7; thickness, 2.1.

Paste and surface finish: resembles Canoas White paste; traces of white on surface.

This figurine is broken at the waist and its arms are missing. It has crudely applied breasts, almost no neck, a small protruding chin, wide squared jaws, a huge rounded nose, and eyes crudely indicated by two flattish punch marks each. A smaller appliqued blob beneath the nose may be the mouth or a lip or nose plug. The headdress gives the effect of a slightly projecting helmet or bonnet with appliqued disks on either side of the top. Smaller oval appliques on each side at eye level may be decorations or even the ears.

This figurine comes from Ts 368, Zone B[1], in the Tehuacan Valley.

VALLEY OF MEXICO TYPE Gi FIGURES

3 figures excavated.

Dimensions in cm.: height (2 heads), 2.5–4.5; width, 3.3–4.0; thickness, 1.4–2.4.

FIG. 82. VALLEY OF MEXICO FIGURINES. *Row 1,* Type Gi; *row 2,* Type Eiii; *row 3,* Type Eii.

Paste and surface finish: resemble Rio Salado Coarse; remains of red paint.

The most complete specimen has wide cheeks, a thick-lipped mouth showing the lower gum or teeth, and a long nose. Eyes are very prominent. Each eye is an applique bearing three punch marks, the deepest at the center. At the side of the head are long ears and doughnut-shaped earplugs. The headdress on all three figurines has a medial ridge or hairknot.

One figure is broken at the hips and the arms are missing. The chin rests on a large disk centered on the chest. A punch mark indicates the navel. A second figure, definitely seated, retains one bent arm but no other limbs. Three punches represent nipples and navel.

This figurine type of the late Santa Maria subphase is similar or identical to Vaillant's Type Gi, found most commonly in the Ticoman period (Vaillant 1931: pl. LVII).

137

VALLEY OF MEXICO TYPE EII

4 heads: 2 excavated, 2 collected.

Dimensions in cm.: height (2 heads), 3.8, 3.9; width (3 heads), 2.5–3.3.

Paste and surface finish: fine, hard orange to brown paste; polished.

These heads are made of paste unlike any found among the Tehuacan pottery. The backs of the heads are flat to concave; projecting nose and mouth areas make the facial surfaces very nearly conical.

Both excavated heads sit on relatively flat oval necks, with small chins sticking sharply out at right angles to the neck. Just above the chin, and very close to it, a sharp-edged lenticular punctation forms an open mouth. One of the excavated heads has a large curved parrot-like beak for a nose, pinched up from the facial surface itself and extending from forehead to upper lip. An eye has been cut into one side of the beak and has a punctate pupil. The other side lacks an eye. Each cheek is hollowed out by a wide oval punctation, similar to the mouth. The top and sides of this head are bordered by a narrow fillet, which is surmounted by a complex high headdress with a broken cylindrical projection at the top. A circular ornament dangles over the forehead, and two round earplugs decorate the ears.

The second excavated head has a delicately modeled, wide, flat, triangular-shaped face with a small narrow nose and crescent-shaped eyes with pinpoint punctates for pupils. The eyes appear to be shaped by thin appliques, but are really punctates like the mouth. Elongated strips are applied at the side of the face as ears or part of a headdress. The top of the head has broken off.

This type of figurine is characteristic of the Late Formative period in both Tehuacan and the Valley of Mexico. In Tehuacan it appears in late Santa Maria levels and in the Valley of Mexico it occurs with Ticoman materials (Vaillant 1931: pl. LVI, bottom row).

VALLEY OF MEXICO TYPE EIII

1 head excavated.

Dimensions in cm.: height, 3.0; width, 3.8; thickness (excluding nose), 0.8. Nose is almost 1.0 cm. long.

Paste: fine orange clay with little temper.

The head is a thin disk with a sharply protruding nose and a pair of eyes on one surface. The eyes are two circular incisions placed just below the level of the nose. The face is broken off about where the mouth or chin should be. Encircling the face is a band set off by an incised line and divided into sections by a series of short incisions radiating out from the hairline.

In the Tehuacan Valley the single example of this type appears late in the Santa Maria phase—that is, at the end of the Formative period. The head is similar to one illustrated by Vaillant (1931: pl. LV, bottom row, no. 5) as representing the Ticoman period in the Valley of Mexico. The strange form and foreign paste of the Tehuacan specimen suggest that it was brought to the region from the Valley of Mexico during Late Formative times.

TICOMAN HEADS

5 heads: 4 excavated, 1 collected.

Dimensions in cm.: height (2 heads), 3.2, 3.3; width, 3.2–3.4.

Paste: 3 heads resemble Rio Salado Gray, 2 Tepei Thin Orange.

The heads tend to be flat and quite wide. Faces are square in outline and in some cases rest directly on the chest with only a slight groove to denote the chin line. However, one head has a square jutting jaw and a girlish long neck bordered by two flowing locks of hair. The mouths are eroded or broken, but one was made of an oval applique, apparently split by a gash across it. The noses are rarely intact but seem to have been triangular appliques. Eyes are made by two horizontal punches to shape the corners and a round central punch for a pupil. The examples with part of the headdress intact have a raised crescentic band across the hairline, marked with a series of vertical incisions or punctures. Two headdresses have a central circu-

5 CM.

FIG. 83. TICOMAN HEADS.

FIG. 84. SLOT-FEATURE HEADS.

lar ornament and circular objects applied above the ears. Three of the heads have doughnut earplugs intact.

These heads show general similarities to Vaillant's Valley of Mexico Types A and Hii. They were found in late Santa Maria components in the Tehuacan Valley and occur in Late Formative sites in the Valley of Mexico.

SLOT-FEATURE HEADS

11 heads excavated.
Dimensions in cm.: height (5 heads), 4.3–8.1, average 6.7; width (4 heads), 6.0–7.1, average 6.5; thickness (9 heads), 1.4–3.0, average 2.2.
Paste: resembles Quachilco Gray and Quachilco Mica.
Note: at least four of these figurines are large and hollow and may have come from small effigy vessels.

The heads are all fragmentary. As a rule, the chins and cheeks are not well defined and blend into the neck or body. The lips are usually appliqued in one or two pieces. A straight incision across the middle produces a slightly open mouth. The nose is applied and realistically shaped. On each figurine the eyes are made in the same way the mouth has been made, usually by long appliques with a wide incision in the middle. On one head a punctation in the center of the eye forms the pupil. Usually the eyes are horizontal, although on two specimens the eyes slant toward the

nose. Some heads have appliqued ears. None of the heads is intact across the top.

In the Tehuacan Valley Slot-feature heads occur in late Santa Maria and early Palo Blanco components and are a good link between the Formative and Classic periods. They are similar to figurines and effigy bowls found in the Oaxaca Valley near Monte Alban, dating to periods I, II, and III (Caso and Bernal 1952: pls. 495, 519). They also occur in the Mixteca at Yatachio in period I (Paddock 1953: fig. 35).

HOLLOW OLD MAN HEAD

1 head excavated.
Dimensions in cm.: height, 7.1; projected width, 5.5.
Paste: Quachilco Red.

The features of this large hollow figurine all appear to point downward. The elongated eyes slant toward the nose. Above and below them incised lines run in the same direction as the eyes, giving the face a seamed or heavily wrinkled appearance. The lines on the cheeks extend down across the sides of the nose. The nose itself is large and realistically conceived, though the end is now broken. The mouth is oddly shaped, the smaller upper lip overlapping the outsized protruding lower lip. The chin has been modeled to jut forward above the neck. Traces of red paint are visible along the side of the face.

FIG. 85. LATE SANTA MARIA ABERRANT TYPES 1 AND 2 AND HOLLOW OLD MAN.

The Old Man head comes from a late Santa Maria component in the Tehuacan Valley. It resembles faces on urns from Monte Alban II and III (Caso and Bernal 1952: 225-228) and the face of a Monte Alban urn pictured in Paddock (1966: 172). In fact, the Santa Maria specimen could well be a fragment from an urn.

LATE SANTA MARIA ABERRANT TYPE 2

1 figure collected.
Dimensions in cm.: total height, 5.4; maximum width, 2.9.
Paste: fine silty yellow clay.

This small seated figurine is almost complete. The head makes up almost half the length of the entire figurine. The ears and prominent nose are pinched out of the flattened clay from which the head is modeled. The mouth is applied and punched to form open lips. The crown of the hat or headdress is part of the original mass of clay, but a rounded strip laid across the brow forms a brim. The eyes each consist of two triangular impressions and a centered conical punch. The one remaining arm is an applied cylindrical strip. It is bent at the elbow and has three incisions at the end to indicate fingers. The body is more rounded than the head, but lacks realistic contours. A punched navel is the only indicated feature. The intact leg is conical in shape, has no differentiations, and is only half as long as the arm.

The figurine was collected from the Coatepec site and probably represents the latter part of the Santa Maria phase.

FIGURES WITH MEDALLIONS

14 bodies: 10 excavated, 4 collected.
Dimensions in cm.: height, approx. 3.0–8.0; width, approx. 2.0–5.0.
Paste: resembles Rio Salado Coarse.

Nine figures are seated, four are standing with legs spread, and the posture of one torso fragment cannot be determined. Bodies of the seated figurines are heavy and squat, usually with full bellies, a large punched navel, and small breasts. Between or slightly above the breasts is a medallion in the form of a disk or a small horizontal applique with a disk under it.

Legs of the standing figures are disproportionately short; they taper and turn outward at the toe. Between the legs of one a small incised applique represents pubic hair or a covering. This specimen and one seated figurine are broken off above a wide, drooping chin or collar that extends across the top of the chest.

140

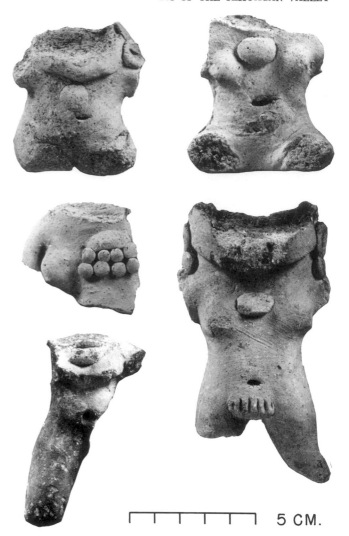

5 CM.

FIG. 86. FIGURES WITH MEDALLIONS.

Only part of one arm, one breast, and the medallion remain on the torso fragment. The medallion differs from the others on figurines of this type in that it is composed of an oblong applique above two rows of circular appliques.

These body fragments occur in late Santa Maria levels in the Tehuacan Valley.

FIGURES WITH HANDS ON BREASTS

6 bodies excavated.
Dimensions in cm.: height, 2.0–5.0; width, 1.0–3.0.
Paste: probably Quachilco Red.

Six fragments are of figures seated with legs spread. Bellies are prominent and have a large punched navel. Some figures have one hand on the opposite breast and the other hand at the side of the body. On other figures both hands rest on or below the breasts. An appliqued and incised armband (or broken-off hairbraid) lies across the upper arm of one fragment.

These figurines were uncovered in late Santa Maria components in the Tehuacan Valley. A few similar figurines occur at Tres Zapotes (Weiant 1943: pl. 34, no. 4).

FIGURE WITH HAIRBRAID

1 body excavated.
Dimensions in cm.: height, 4.3; width at waist, 2.3.
Paste: resembles Rio Salado Coarse.

This figurine has a prominent belly with a large navel. Two applied globs on the upper chest are breasts. The shoulders are wide, and the arms, now broken, were probably extended. An applied hairbraid extends in front of the left shoulder and down the arm.

The fragment occurred in a late Santa Maria component in the Tehuacan Valley.

FIGURES WITH JAGUAR SKINS

5 specimens: 1 body and 1 arm excavated, 3 bodies collected.
Dimensions in cm.: body length, 4.0–6.0; body width, 2.0–3.5.
Paste: resembles Quachilco Red.

These figures seem to have been standing with legs slightly spread and arms extending forward or down the sides. The torsos are completely or partially covered with small punctations that seem to represent spots on a jaguar-skin cloak. On three figures the jaguar skin fits the body like a jacket. The excavated body fragment wears a spotted skin down one side only; this figure has an erect penis and a testicle. The arm fragment is tapered.

The figures are from late Santa Maria components in the Tehuacan Valley. Figures wearing jaguar skins are widespread in Mexico and are probably representative of the jaguar cult.

TICOMAN WASP-WAIST BODIES AND LEGS

25 specimens: 6 bodies and 9 legs excavated, 10 bodies collected.
Dimensions in cm.: leg length, 2.0–3.0; shoulder width, 2.0–3.0; waist width, 1.0–2.5; estimated figurine height, 5.0–6.0.
Paste: some resemble Quachilco Brown.
Surface finish: sometimes polished.

Four of the figures seem to have been seated. The rest are standing with legs set apart. The shoulders and chest are wide, and some of the figures have small

FIG. 87. FIGURES WITH HANDS ON BREASTS AND WITH HAIRBRAID.

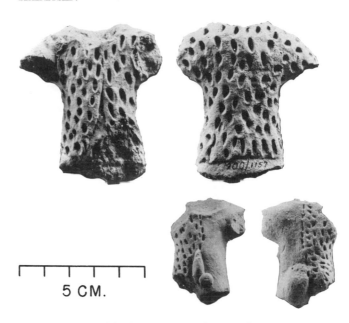

FIG. 88. FIGURES WITH JAGUAR SKINS.

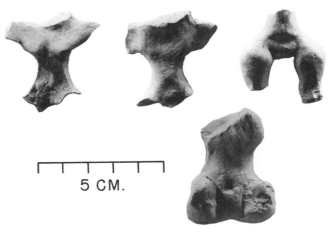

FIG. 89. TICOMAN BODIES.

breasts. The body narrows at the waist and then spreads again to form wide hips and bulging thighs. The legs are more or less conical, with thick thighs and pointed or squared-off feet. Two of the legs were decorated. Arms usually hang at the side of the body. They are short and conical with no hands indicated. Two of the figures have necklaces.

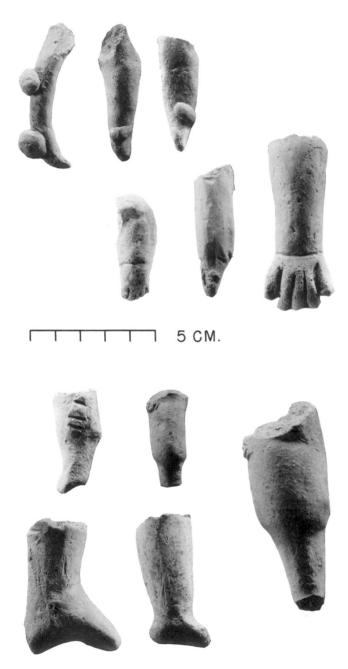

5 CM.

FIG. 90. FIGURINE LIMB FRAGMENTS. *Row 1*, decorated arms or legs; *row 2*, arms with realistic hands; *row 3*, bottle legs; *row 4*, legs with arched feet.

142

These figurines occur in components of the late Santa Maria phase in the Tehuacan Valley. They are identical to those found with Ticoman and Teotihuacan I remains in the Valley of Mexico (Vaillant 1931: pl. LXII).

MISCELLANEOUS LIMB FRAGMENTS

Decorated arms or legs (5 excavated) are of pastes resembling Quachilco Red and Quachilco Brown. Three limbs are more or less conical in shape, tapering to a point at the distal end. It is difficult to tell from the broken fragment whether the limb is an arm or a leg. About a centimeter from the tip is an appliqued bracelet or anklet. One long skinny arm has two appliqued balls along the side instead of a bracelet. Three specimens are from late Santa Maria components and one is from an early Santa Maria level. Dimensions in cm.: length, 4.6–5.5; maximum diameter, 1.9.

Arms with realistic hands (13 excavated, 2 collected) are usually of a paste resembling Quachilco Red. The hands are attached to fragments of conical arms, which range in maximum diameter from 1.0 to 3.0 cm. Length of the arms remains unknown. In some cases, a narrowing of the arm indicates the wrist and incisions mark off the fingers. The two specimens illustrated (Fig. 90) have grooves marking the wrist. The smaller one is of whitish paste with a light gray core. These hands were recovered from late Santa Maria and early Palo Blanco components.

Arched feet (4 excavated) extend forward at right angles from heavy legs. They are stubby and slightly to highly arched. One specimen differs from the others in having a white slip; it is the only arched foot with incisions marking off the toes. The four specimens are of differing pastes. All were found in late Santa Maria zones. Dimensions in cm.: maximum leg diameter, 2.0; foot length, 2.0–3.8.

Stubby legs (7 excavated) are of pastes resembling Quachilco Red. The short round lower leg is not as thick as the short cylindrical thigh. The legs terminate in short wide feet arched at the bottom. A ridged applique decorates the thigh of one leg. The leg of the more complete Figure with Medallion (Fig. 86) is of this type. This type of stubby, fat leg occurs in late Santa Maria components in the Tehuacan valley and is found at Formative sites throughout Mexico. Dimensions in cm.: length 4.9–5.0; maximum thickness, 2.0–3.0.

Bottle legs (2 excavated) are of paste resembling Canoas White. The thigh is large and cylindrical and narrows abruptly at the knee. The calf is smaller and more conical in shape. On the upper part of each leg are remains of a decoration that originally must have covered the pubic area. The foot of the larger specimen, though now broken, extended forward at right angles to the leg. This type of leg and the stubby legs described above probably blend into each other. The two bottle legs were recovered from late Santa Maria components. Diminsions in cm.: length, 3.8, 8.0; maximum diameter, 1.7, 3.0.

Tapering legs or arms (12 excavated, 8 collected) are of pastes resembling Rio Salado Coarse and Quachilco Red. Most of the sample are leg fragments, and all may be so, but it is difficult to tell arms from legs in some cases. The limbs are not realistically formed; viewed from the side, they are roughly triangular in shape, the pointed foot or hand being the vertex of the triangle. Most of the legs are bent slightly at knee and ankle. Feet or hands are set off by horizontal grooves at ankle or wrist; vertical incisions mark off toes or fingers. The limbs are from late Santa Maria components. Dimensions in cm.: length, 5.0–7.0; maximum thickness, 2.0–4.0.

Ceramic Affiliations

As is perhaps readily apparent, late Santa Maria and Monte Alban I–II are very closely related, although not quite closely enough to classify them as the same phase. Characteristic of both are gray wares that not only share a preponderant number of similar or identical vessel forms and decorations but that also have pastes in which diorite or altered diorite is a consistent tempering material. Further, sherds seen at Mitla in a collection called Monte Alban I–II resemble two other Tehuacan types, Coatepec White and Quachilco Brown. Three figurine types of late Santa Maria—the Capped Doughnut-eye, Slot-feature, and Outlined-eye heads—also are present in the Monte Alban I–II figurine complexes.

Although the late Santa Maria phase does not reveal nearly as many basic resemblances to cultural phases of the Valley of Mexico as it does to Monte Alban, a number of objects imported from the valley were present in our excavations, and there are overlapping figurine types, such as the Valley of Mexico Types Gi, Eii, Eiii, and Ticoman and Hairlock Doughnut-eye heads.

Trade sherds include specimens of Ticoman Orange, Ticoman Red, Ticoman Red-on-buff, Zacatenco Orange Lacquer, and Zacatenco Black-on-red wares. Usulutan negative-painted ware, which occurs in late Santa Maria, is also present in Tezoyuca (Millon 1966).

Thus there has been a shift from the early Santa Maria subphase, when there were many contacts with the Gulf coastal region and only a few with the highlands. Nevertheless, there are still some lowland contacts in late Santa Maria. The gray ware from Tres Zapotes, particularly that from Ranchito, resembles Santa Maria's Quachilco Gray. Other evidence of contact are the presence in late Santa Maria of sherds of Chalahuites Orange-rimmed Black and Tres Zapotes Black Incised, and the presence in both regions of a white-rimmed black ware and Coatepec White. Usulutan ware is reported from Lower Remojadas (Medellín Zenil 1960: pl. 40) and from Tres Zapotes (Drucker 1943a: 75), and this trade ware and Remojadas figurines are present in late Santa Maria. All these links are present in the later levels at Trapiche in central Veracruz. Relationships of late Santa Maria to the Panuco region of northern Veracruz consist only of the general resemblance of Chila White to Coatepec White.

Contacts to the south are indicated by a few similarities between late Santa Maria and several phases at Chiapa de Corzo. White-rimmed black ware is prominent in Chiapa de Corzo IV, V, and VI, and one of the negative-painted Usulutan sherds from late Santa Maria looks like examples from Chiapa VI. A figurine very much like the Santa Maria Matamoros type comes from Chiapa VI, and a Capped Doughnut-eye figurine occurred in Chiapa VII. Pots resembling Quachilco Gray were found in tombs of Chiapa de Corzo III, IV, and VI, and a Tres Zapotes gray-ware pot was found in a Chiapa IV context. Some of the white-slipped sherds of Chiapa IV–VI, as well as the Conchas Fine White-to-buff type of the Pacific coast of Guatemala have a general resemblance to Coatepec White of late Santa Maria. Also, Usulutan sherds are present in both Guanacaste of Chiapas (Lowe and Mason 1965: 218) and late Santa Maria.

Two sherds of Mars Orange found in late Santa Maria components are trade sherds from the Mamom period of the Peten of Guatemala. This type also occurs as trade sherds in Chiapa de Corzo III and IV, as well as in the earliest phases of the Yucatan Peninsula. The Usulutan sherds present in late Santa Maria, and which appear in Late Formative manifestations throughout Mesoamerica, occur in Miraflores and Balam of the Guatemalan highlands (Rands and Smith 1965: 101), in Crucero of coastal Guatemala (Coe 1961: 85), in Tihosuco of Yucatan (Smith and Gifford 1965: 507), and in the proto-Classic phases of the Peten of Guatemala (Willey 1966).

Beside these rather specific links to other regions,

Santa Maria has a series of traits or horizon styles that were widespread over much of Mesoamerica in Late Formative times. These traits are tripod (or tetrapod) vessels with mammiform feet, vessels with bridged and unbridged spouts, bowls with basal flanges or ridges, bowls with wide everted rims which are often grooved, rolled-rim ollas, cylindrical vessels with a basal bulge, crosshatched triangles or rectangles or stepped designs incised on black or gray wares, and three types of figurine eyes: downward-slanting slot eyes, doughnut eyes, and ploughed eyes like those on a Matamoros head.

Late Santa Maria seems to be the period when Tehuacaneros severed ties with the older coastal tradition that had prevailed in Ajalpan and early Santa Maria and embarked on a new tradition that is common to southern Puebla and the Oaxaca Valley during the Late Formative and Classic periods. Exactly why this shift took place is uncertain, but the new orientation of late Santa Maria—and perhaps other contemporaneous highland cultures—to irrigation agriculture may have been a factor of considerable importance. The dying out of the Olmec cults may have been another factor. At this period it would be extremely difficult to consider both the highland and lowland cultures as belonging to the same culture area. Perhaps future research can more adequately explain the great divergence between the two regions.

CHAPTER 7

The Early Part of the Palo Blanco Phase

THE EARLY PART of the Palo Blanco phase is represented by about 31,000 sherds from nine excavated components: Tr 218, Test 10, Zone A; Tc 307, Zone A; Tr 218, Test 6, Zone A; Tr 218, Test 11, Zone A; Tc 272, Zone F; Ts 51, Zone A–B; Tc 50, Zone VI; Tc 272, Zones E and D. Although 31,000 sherds would appear to be a satisfactory sample recovered from a sufficient number of components, there are deficiencies we feel we must point out. Five of the components, three from Tr 218 and one each from Tc 307 and Ts 51, represent zones next to the surface, where materials from earlier and later times are more likely to be mixed into the sample than is likely with materials from more deeply buried components. What is worse, almost 30,000 of the 31,000 sherds come from the top zones of tests of Tr 218, leaving the sample of sherds from other components quite unbalanced.

While still in the field, we were aware that our sample from this period was not perfect, but unfortunately, instead of digging some of the stratified Classic remains that appear in the clay pits of Ajalpan, we made a large collection from an important hilltop site, Tr 73, which we thought at the time to be "pure" Palo Blanco. Later we discovered that this so-called pure site had many sherds representative of the Venta Salada phase and that many of the sherds (particularly the non-gray ones) were so badly eroded that they defied classification. Although the collection from Tr 73 did nothing to relieve our sampling error, it did provide us with a huge sample of the Palo Blanco diagnostic pottery, El Riego Gray. Besides the 9,844 identifiable sherds from Tr 73, an additional 10,131 sherds were collected from seventy-one other surface sites attributable to this subphase.

In spite of the inadequacies of the early Palo Blanco excavated sample, we had enough information to differentiate this subphase from the subphase that precedes it, late Santa Maria, and the one that comes after it, late Palo Blanco. Most of the distinctive Santa Maria types—the Canoas wares, Coatepec White Coatepec White-rimmed Black, Rio Salado Gray, Rio Salado Coarse, Quachilco Brown, and certain figurine types—appeared in such small proportions that it seemed safe to assume that they had died out by early Palo Blanco times. Quachilco Gray, which had been the dominant type in late Santa Maria, decreased significantly during early Palo Blanco. El Riego Gray and Quachilco Red, which were of little importance in late Santa Maria levels, became dominant types during early Palo Blanco times. El Riego Black, El Riego Polished, and El Riego Plain appeared for the first time in early Palo Blanco components, along with new figurine types and many sherds of Thin Orange. Only Quachilco Mica maintained about the same proportions through the two periods.

Perhaps as diagnostic of early Palo Blanco as the differences in types were the changes in decoration and vessel form. Decoration per se is much less common in Palo Blanco than in Santa Maria and motifs are restricted to triangular or rectilinear designs usually made by cutting through the outer surface. Decoration is rare on vessel interiors. Significantly, footed vessels became much more prevalent and include new types of supports, such as slab feet. Ring bases also occur in significant amounts. Wide-everted-rim bowls and cylindrical vessels with or without feet become important forms. All in all, Palo Blanco was readily distinguishable from Santa Maria, even in our unsatisfactory ceramic sample. Future investigations will surely add to the number of ceramic differences between the two phases.

Coatepec White, Rio Salado Gray, Coatepec White-rimmed Black, Quachilco Brown, Rio Salado Coarse, and Quachilco Gray continue as minority types in the earliest levels of the Palo Blanco phase. They have been previously described. Quachilco Mica, also previously described, occurs in slightly smaller proportions and shows some changes in vessel form. The ollas with funnel necks and long straight necks now comprise only a very small proportion of all shapes. Rolled-rim ollas, which were a minority shape in late Santa Maria, become a major form in early Palo Blanco.

El Riego Orange, El Riego Plain, and El Riego Polished are Classic wares that are present in small proportions in early Palo Blanco components, as are sherds of Thin Orange. These types are more popular in the later part of the Palo Blanco phase and will be described in Chapter 8.

Pottery Types

EL RIEGO GRAY

16,635 specimens excavated; 19,442 collected.

Paste

El Riego Gray, along with Quachilco Brown, is one of the finest of the Tehuacan pastes. It is very similar to Quachilo Gray, but besides being finer, is more brittle and porous. Thin sections of five sherds from three different sites indicate that only 3 percent of the paste consists of nonplastic particles as large as 0.1–0.5 mm. in diameter. These are mainly quartz and plagioclase, but some grains of biotite and calcite appear. Quartzite, sericite, feldspar, and diorite were identified in only one sherd. The majority of the temper (about 8 percent) is less than 0.1 mm. in diameter and usually consists of quartz, plagioclase, magnetite, biotite, and hematite, although quartzite, basalt, muscovite, calcite, and pyroxenes are present.

Visible to the naked eye are white particles varying from a fraction of a millimeter to about a millimeter in diameter and holes of the same size left by the leaching during firing of limy material. These holes and particles represent less than one percent of the total volume, but they are one of the notable differences between the El Riego Gray paste and the Quachilco Gray paste.

The paste is very finely knit. Firing is fairly even, with little color difference between core and periphery. A darker periphery seems to be correlated with the finishing process, in which polishing compacts the clay and probably causes it to fire darker. Some incompletely fired pieces have a light-brown hue. The color range is the following: reddish-brown (2.5 YR 5/4), reddish-gray (5.0 YR 5/2), grayish-brown (2.5 Y 5/2), gray (2.5 Y 6/0–5/0), light gray to gray (10 YR 7/1–6/1) to very dark gray (7.5 YR 4/0–3/0). The sherds are extremely hard, measuring 3.5–4.0.

Surface Finish

The majority of the sherds, which were collected from the surface, show little difference in color between exterior and interior surfaces. Other examples, with a highly polished surface, are darker. Generally speaking, the surface color is a mousy gray, but some of the polished surfaces are almost black. The surface shows occasional tiny holes owing to the disappearance during firing of the calcareous temper and a few white "specks" of this temper which survived the firing process, as well as smaller particles of shiny quartz and biotite.

Some surfaces have been smoothed but not polished. The finishing process left wide uneven striations, pits, finger marks, and irregular surface planes. Such surfaces are dull in appearance and feel slightly sandpapery. Other surfaces have been polished with a stick or stone, leaving narrow, rather even striations, with alternating bands of light and darker tones. The direction of the strokes is usually horizontal, though this depends primarily on the form of the vessel. The polished streaks are quite lustrous, almost waxy, and rather slick feeling. Another difference between El Riego Gray and Quachilco Gray is that Quachilco Gray is lustrous and waxy all over, and El Riego Gray has lustrous and waxy streaks.

Decoration

Decoration is generally by incision. It is rare—particularly when compared with Quachilco Gray—and will be described with the vessel forms on which it occurs.

Vessel Forms

Flaring-wall bowls are the most common El Riego Gray vessel. They definitely had flat bottoms and some examples had supports. Walls are usually quite flaring, but occasionally the flare is so slight the walls could almost be classified as straight and outsloping. Lips range from rounded to beveled to flat; some of the lips are grooved on top or on the exterior surfaces. There are a few flaring-wall sherds with thickened rolled rims.

Decoration is generally made by incision before the

vessel was fired, but some examples of engraving after firing were noted. There are 189 decorated sherds out of a total of 942 sherds representing this shape. All are incised or engraved with simple linear motifs; the largest portion, 176 sherds with flat, grooved lips, had a single line encircling the interior surface beneath the rim, above which opposing groups of short slanted parallel lines are placed so as to form "V"'s if they were extended. Four other rims were decorated on the inner surface with zigzag, wavy, and straight lines; parallel stepped lines; and triangles.

Nine sherds are decorated on the exterior with hachured triangles pointing upward. Two sherds from surface sites also showed decoration on the exterior

TABLE 42
El Riego Gray Decorated Sherds
(by site and zone)

	Late Santa Maria								Early Palo Blanco			
	368e C	368e B	368w B1	218-10 C1	218-10 C	218-10 B	218-6 D	218-6 B	218-10 A	218-6 A	218-11 A	51 A-B
Incised motifs												
1-3 lines around rims of												
flaring wall, direct-rim bowls, int.									2			
convex-wall, direct-rim bowls, ext.									2	1		
outsloping-wall, direct-rim bowls, int.									4	2		
cylindrical jars, ext.									1	1		
basal-flange bowl, ext.									1			
flanged-rim bowl, ext.									8	2		
outsloping-wall, everted-rim bowl, int.			2	2								
on bodies of vessels									2	9	4	
Horizontal line(s) with "V"'s around rims of												
flaring-wall, direct rim bowls, int.									173	3		
outsloping-wall, direct-rim bowls, int.									1	1		
on bodies of vessels, ext.									2	1	1	
Zigzag or wavy lines around rims of												
flaring-wall, direct-rim bowls, int.									2			
outsloping-wall, direct-rim bowls, int.									1	1		1
basal-flange bowls, ext.									1			
on bodies of vessels, ext.									4	1	1	1
Semicircular motifs on rim of												
composite-silhouette bowl, ext.									1			
Triangles on rims or walls of												
flaring-wall, direct-rim bowls, ext.									9			
convex-wall, direct-rim bowls, ext.									3			
cylindrical jars, ext.									4			
basal-flange bowls, ext.									2			
flange-rim bowls, ext.									6			
on bodies of vessels, ext.									31	7	6	1
Rectangles on rims or walls of												
cylindrical jar, ext.									6			
cylindrical jar w. basal bulge		1				3						
on bodies of vessels									3	1		
Hatching on rims or walls of												
flanged-rim bowls, ext.									1			
outsloping-wall, everted-rim bowl, ext.				1	2	2	3	1				
cylindrical jar, ext.	1	1				1						
cylindrical jar w. basal bulge, ext.		1										
on bodies of vessels, ext.						1	1	1	56	10	9	1
Lines in quadrants on												
bottoms of bowls, int.									11			
Punctates inside lines on ollas												
Zoned-toned motif on body									1			
Total	1	3	2	3	2	7	4	2	338	40	21	4

(Table continued)

	Early Palo Blanco (continued)			Late Palo Blanco						Early Venta Salada	Late Venta Salada	
	50 VI	272 E	272 D	272 C	272 B	254 B	50 IV	35e E-F	35e D	35e C	368e A	Total
Incised motifs												
1-3 lines around rims of												
flaring wall, direct-rim bowls, int.												2
convex-wall, direct-rim bowls, ext.					1							4
outsloping-wall, direct-rim bowls, int.												6
cylindrical jars, ext.						1	1					4
basal-flange bowl, ext.				1								2
flanged-rim bowl, ext.												10
outsloping-wall, everted-rim bowl, int.												4
on bodies of vessels				1	1			1	2	1	1	22
Horizontal line(s) with "V"'s around rims of												
flaring-wall, direct-rim bowls, int.												176
outsloping-wall, direct-rim bowls, int.												2
on bodies of vessels, ext.									2			6
Zigzag or wavy lines around rims of												
flaring-wall, direct-rim bowls, int.												2
outsloping-wall, direct-rim bowls, int.												3
basal-flange bowls, ext.												1
on bodies of vessels, ext.												7
Semicircular motifs on rim of												
composite-silhouette bowl, ext.												1
Triangles on rims or walls of												
flaring-wall, direct-rim bowls, ext.												9
convex-wall, direct-rim bowls, ext.							1					4
cylindrical jars, ext.			1				1		3			9
basal-flange bowls, ext.												2
flange-rim bowls, ext.												6
on bodies of vessels, ext.				1	2			2	6			56
Rectangles on rims or walls of												
cylindrical jar, ext.												6
cylindrical jar w. basal bulge												4
on bodies of vessels												4
Hatching on rims or walls of												
flanged-rim bowls, ext.												1
outsloping-wall, everted-rim bowl, ext.												9
cylindrical jar, ext.												3
cylindrical jar w. basal bulge, ext.												1
on bodies of vessels, ext.					1				1	1		82
Lines in quadrants on												
bottoms of bowls, int.							1	1	1			14
Punctates inside lines on ollas	1	1										2
Zoned-toned motif on body												1
Total	1	1	1	3	5	1	4	4	15	2	1	465

rim. One has three vertical incised lines and the other had at least two encircling lines, on the uppermost of which rest two groups of three concentric semicircles. The pattern must have continued around the rim.

Over seventy rim-to-base sherds from late Santa Maria, early and late Palo Blanco, and Venta Salada excavated zones show that the flaring-wall bowls were flat-based. Only a few of the excavated sherds have sufficient fragments of the bottom remaining to show that these bowls rested on supports, but the surface collections yielded a number of fragments with supports, including the types of feet we have called "nubbin," solid conical, and hollow cylindrical. It is possi-

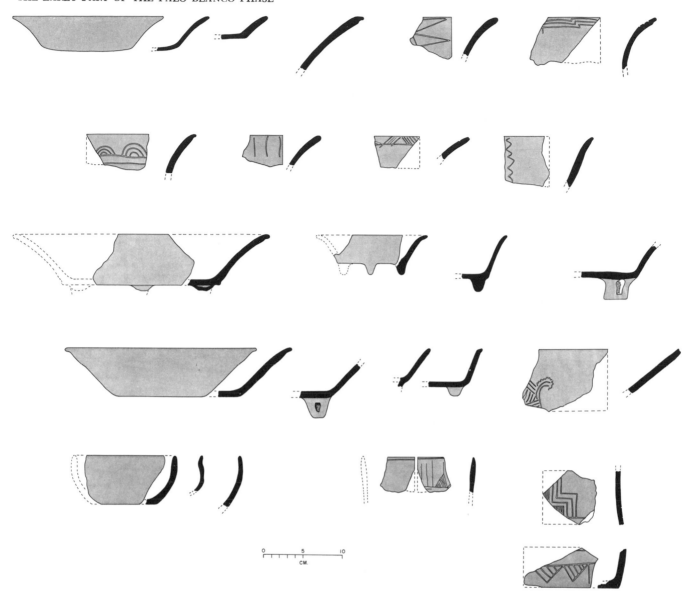

FIG. 91. EL RIEGO GRAY. *Rows 1–4:* flaring-wall bowls, some with nubbin, conical, and hollow cylindrical feet; *row 5:* convex-wall bowls and cylindrical jars.

ble that hollow slab feet appeared on these bowls too. The supports on the excavated specimens were hollow and either cylindrical or bulbous; they were round where attached and were about 3 cm. in diameter. Dimensions in cm.: rim diameter, 12–40; base diameter, 8–28; wall height, 2.8–12.5; thickness, 0.6–1.2.

Convex-wall bowls with direct rims are of medium to shallow depth. They have flat bottoms, usually with a gentle groove at the junction of base and side. Lips vary as follows: flat, rounded, tapered bilaterally, flat-ish with an irregular groove, and beveled on the interior.

Decoration is rare and usually consists of shallow grooves around the outer rim. Three of four sherds with triangular motifs have engraved triangles extending down from the lip. No supports were found with this form.

Dimensions in cm.: rim diameter, 10–28; base diameter, 6.0–18; height, 4.0–9.5; thickness, 0.5–0.8.

Outsloping-wall bowls have straight sides that slant

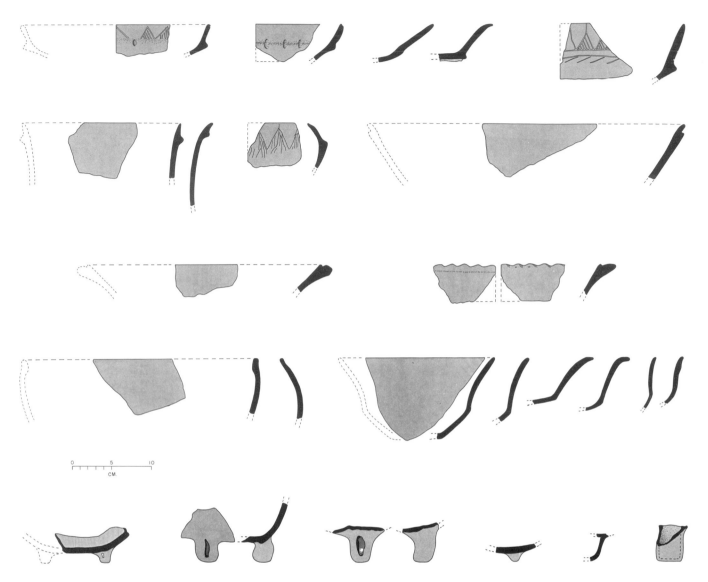

FIG. 92. EL RIEGO GRAY. *Row 1:* bowls with basal flanges; *rows 2, 3:* bowls with flanged and stepped rims and externally thickened grooved rims; *row 4:* incurved-rim bowls and composite-silhouette vessels; *row 5:* hollow bulb, solid nubbin, and hollow cylindrical supports.

outward. Two sherds have hollow bulbous supports, and one fragment retains a small solid conical foot. Over half the lips on this form are flat, many are rounded or beveled, and a few are grooved or out-angled.

Decoration is by incising and is rare. The paucity of decoration, in fact, is one of the larger points of difference from Quachilco Gray pottery. There were only eleven decorated sherds among over five hundred El Riego Gray sherds representing this vessel form. Five have a glyphlike half-circle with radiating or zigzag lines high on the interior rim. Two of six grooved-lip

sherds have incised lines on the interior of the rim. One has a line encircling the rim that serves as a base for short parallel lines inclined at about 80 degrees from the horizontal. The other has an intricate motif incised in the midsection. Occasional differential polishing effects seem to be accidental.

Dimensions in cm.: rim diameter, 10–32; base diameter, 7.0–20; height, 3.5–8.5; thickness, 0.4–0.9.

Cylindrical to vasiform vessels have varying types of bottoms: flat with an abrupt angle to the vertical side, convex merging into a vertical side, and a very reduced flat base followed by a short convex section with a sharp angle connecting the vertical side. The sides themselves may be short and vertical, tall and slightly concave, tall and slightly divergent, tall and vertical, or tall and vertical but with an outcurved rim. Lips are either flat, rounded, or slightly tapering. No supports were noted.

Some sherds have incised decorations in various positions on the outer surface. The motifs are combinations of horizontal parallel lines possibly forming rectangles, stepped lines, and triangles with hachure. One sherd has a vaguely "U"-shaped motif, and another has part of the design scraped away in the raspada technique. One complete vessel has a narrow horizontal groove on the exterior near the base. Dimensions in cm.: rim diameter, 14–22; base diameter, 11–16; height, 7.5–10; thickness, 0.6–0.8.

Basal-flange bowls have slightly flaring or slightly convex outsloping sides. The lips are usually rounded or tapering. The bowls generally seem to have had convex bottoms, though a variation of this shape has a flat bottom of which the flange or ridge is merely an extension. A few fragments of bottoms indicate that some bowls had supports, though no supports were intact. The places of attachment are easily visible and indicate that the supports were hollow and circular at the top and from 3 to 6 cm. in diameter.

These bowls have a pronounced ridge or flange usually applied a centimeter or two above the junction of base and side. Some of the flanges are deeply notched at more or less regular intervals. Instead of a flange, a few examples show a very abrupt angle at the junction of wall and flat base: the junction has a thickened cross section and thereby protrudes slightly. On specimens with low sides, the ridge may occur quite high on the vessel, making it difficult to determine whether it is a basal flange or a flanged rim.

Five examples are decorated by incision on the exterior surface. Two of the sherds have hatched triangles combined with parallel lines, the third has a hatched stepped or zigzag motif, and the other two have linear motifs. Dimensions in cm.: rim diameter, 20–30; wall thickness, 1.5.

Stepped-rim vessels. Rims of these bowls are thickened or slightly offset, making a very narrow horizontal shelf on the exterior. There are several variations on this theme, depending on the position of the shelf on the exterior wall, its width, the angle of the offset, and the form of vessel on which it is found.

(*a*) On vessels with outsloping or flaring walls, the rim is thinned on the exterior 0.7 to 1.5 cm. from the lip. The lip is rounded. No decoration or bottoms were found on this type of vessel. Dimensions in cm.: rim diameter, 22–40; rim thickness, 0.7–0.9; wall thickness, 1.0–1.4.

(*b*) On vessels with convex walls the rims take three slightly different forms: vertical, incurved, or inangled. Six sherds had flat bottoms attached but no indications of supports. Lips of the incurved rims are bilaterally beveled or rounded and two have a groove, one on the interior and the other on the exterior; dimensions in cm.: rim diameter, 22–24; maximum diameter, 28–29; rim width 3.0–3.4; wall thickness, 0.6–0.9. Lips of the vertical rims are generally rounded, but some are bilaterally beveled and several are outcurved; dimensions in cm.: rim diameter, 12–18, maximum diameter, 12–20; rim width, 1.4–3.1; wall thickness, 0.5–0.7. Inangled-rim lips are often thickened and rounded but may be beveled; dimensions in cm.: rim diameter, 16–22; maximum diameter, 16.5–23.5; rim width, 2.1–3.0; wall thickness, 0.5–0.7. No decoration other than the simple groove mentioned on the incurved-lip type was noted.

(*c*) Some stepped-rim sherds do not fit into the preceding types. Some have two grooves on the exterior in addition to the stepped or offset effect. Other sherds represent a convex wall with an outcurved rim, an outsloping wall with an incurved rim, and a tecomate shape. No decoration other than the grooves was found. Dimensions in cm.: rim diameter, 14–22; maximum diameter, 16–24; rim width, 1.5–5.2; wall thickness, 0.6–1.2.

Bowls with externally thickened grooved rims are usually large vessels with walls that slope outward. The thickened rim is deeply grooved on the upper surface, giving a stepped, flanged, or slightly everted effect. Dimensions in cm.: rim diameter, 30–34; rim width, 1.4–1.5; wall thickness, 0.5–1.1

Flanged-rim bowls have an applied fillet on the exterior rim one or two centimeters below the lip. The flange is usually carefully blended into the wall and slopes slightly downward. The vessel profile is also distinctive. The wall near the base may be nearly vertical or slightly divergent, while the upper portion always curves outward from about the midsection, and sometimes the rim also flares. An aberrant flanged sherd has an incurved rim with a crude unsmoothed fillet on the exterior. These vessels probably had flat bottoms and may have had supports, but no complete examples were found. The lips are generally rounded or slightly tapered bilaterally. The distance which the flange protrudes from the vessel varies from 0.3 to 1.0 cm.

Seventeen sherds are decorated on the exterior surface. Six motifs are incised triangles, one of which has hachure inside. All the triangles point upward and are

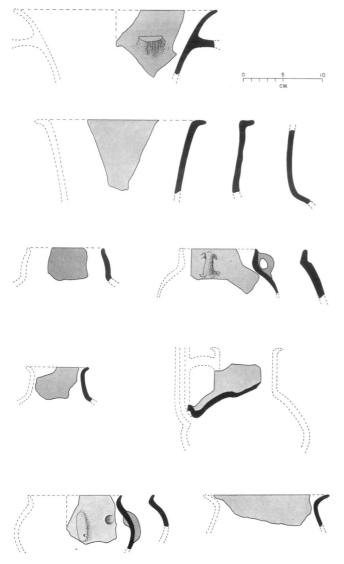

FIG. 93. EL RIEGO GRAY. *From top to bottom:* funnel-neck olla with strap handle; ollas with long straight necks and everted rims; barrel-neck olla and olla with short straight neck and loop handle; straight-neck olla with everted rim and a spouted fragment; everted-rim effigy olla and convergent-neck olla with everted rim.

arranged in a horizontal series, usually with the bases resting on a horizontal line. Ten sherds have a groove on the lip. One displays zoned toning. Dimensions in cm.: rim diameter, 18–34; wall thickness, 0.5–0.9; thickness with flange, 0.9–1.9 cm.

Incurved-rim bowls have convex sides with the curve of the wall continuing inward to make a constricted mouth. The amount of constriction seems to vary in proportion to the height, the deeper vessels

having the smaller mouths. Some of the sherds seem to be from vessels tall enough to be called tecomates. No bottoms were found. Lips are tapered, rounded, or beveled. Decoration is absent. Dimensions in cm.: rim diameter, 14–18; maximum diameter, 17–24; wall thickness, 0.4–0.9.

Composite-silhouette bowls have a medium-deep to shallow convex base with a small flattened center portion, concave walls that range from nearly vertical to widely diverging, and direct or flaring rims. Lips are rounded or tapering. The variety of this form with a sharp break at junction of wall and base is related to the flanged-based bowls described above. Dimensions in cm.: rim diameter, 14.5–28.0; wall thickness, 0.6–0.8. Measurements of one nearly complete specimen: diameter at rim, 19.8, at junction of wall and base, 13.6, at flat center of base, 6.5; height of wall, 6.5, of vessel, 10.0.

Funnel-neck ollas have tall necks that angle outward; rims are usually slightly outcurved. Lips are tapered or rounded. No body fragments were attached. The exterior of one sherd has a thick horizontal fillet with slashes cut into it, making a ropelike effect at the junction of neck and shoulder. This is the only example of decoration. One sherd shows that this form was provided with strap handles (Fig. 93). Dimensions in cm.: rim diameter, 10–28; wall thickness, 0.3–0.8.

Ollas with short flaring necks have small, globular bodies. Lips are rounded or bilaterally thinned. No bottoms were found, but presumably they were convex with a reduced flat area. One strap handle was found. No decoration was noted. These ollas are well smoothed on the interior. Dimensions in cm.: rim diameter, 14–20; wall thickness, 0.5–1.1.

Ollas with long flaring necks. Judged from the tallness of the necks and two attached body pieces, these ollas were quite large with somewhat globular bodies. No decoration was noted. Dimensions in cm.: rim diameter, 12–20; wall thickness, 0.5–1.0.

Everted-rim ollas are small vessels with squat globular bodies and fairly wide mouths. They have no neck proper, merely a short rim which has been turned outward. No bottoms or handles were found. Lips are rounded or bilaterally tapered. Often there is a small groove around the exterior at junction of body and rim. One sherd was a fragment of an effigy vessel with the remains of a face on the body (Fig. 93, bottom row, left). The ear is a long vertical lug, pierced at the bottom. The eye is a deep circular depression. Nose and mouth are broken off. Dimensions in cm.: rim diameter, 14–26; rim width, 1.5–2.0; wall thickness, 0.5–0.9.

FIG. 94. EL RIEGO GRAY. Decorated sherds and fragments of ollas.

Ollas with long straight necks have horizontally everted or outcurved rims on tall, nearly vertical neck portions. The longest neck fragment measures 10 cm. No decoration was noted. Dimensions in cm.: rim diameter, 10–22; wall thickness, 0.6–0.9.

Barrel-neck ollas have a fairly tall convex or barrel-shaped neck, usually with a very short outcurved rim. One fragment of a human effigy vessel of this type, collected at Tr 73, has a large incised circle for an eye, a thin modeled nose, and a wide horizontal incision for a mouth (Fig. 94, middle of second row). This fragment resembles a complete animal effigy olla from Oaxaca illustrated in Caso, Bernal, and Acosta (1967: fig. 90).

Convergent-neck ollas have tall vague necks that narrow at the mouth. Rims are outangled.

Ollas with short, straight necks are small vessels characterized by a smooth transition from the rounded body to the very short, nearly vertical neck. Rims are usually direct. Dimensions in cm.: rim diameter, 6.0–16; wall thickness, 0.4–1.0.

Pot covers are represented by several fragments of small shallow platelike vessels.

Appendages. A characteristic of Classic pottery is the variety of spouts, handles, lugs, and supports accompanying the vessel shapes. El Riego Gray ollas had both strap and loop handles and bridged and perhaps unbridged spouts, as well as solid "spout" handles. Many El Riego Gray bowls rested on three supports. These feet are of different shapes, some solid and some hollow, and will be described below. Some vessels had ring bases.

Strap handles were most numerous among El Riego Gray handle fragments. They are flat strips of clay bent in semicircular fashion and generally applied vertically to ollas, with one end attached to the neck wall and the other end to the body. The range of dimensions in cm. is 3.0–7.0 long, 1.2–4.4 wide, and 0.6–1.2 thick.

Loop handles are formed from rounded strips of clay. One fragment shows that it was attached vertically at the neck of an olla. Usually the opening form-

153

ed by the loop of the handle and vessel wall is smaller than openings formed by strap handles. Our fragments range in length from 2.5 to 4.3 cm. Two much longer cylindrical fragments were found, measuring 4.5 and 8.5 cm. long by 1.1 and 1.4 cm. in diameter. Whether these are pieces of handles is open to question.

Perforated lug handles are made by applying a lump of clay to a vessel, squeezing it to flatten the sides, then punching a hole in it along the vessel wall. One such handle, applied vertically on the vessel wall, belongs to a fragmentary small effigy olla and apparently represents a human ear.

Bridged spouts and solid spout handles are represented by only nine excavated fragments. Although the excavated sample is small, fragments of El Riego Gray spouts are numerous in the surface collections. The spouts usually are made of two parts. First there is the nearly vertical pouring spout, which is curved and thickened where it connects with the lower portion of the vessel. Second, there is a horizontal brace or crosspiece which extends from the upper end of the spout to the vessel. Holes in the spouts vary greatly in diameter, ranging from wire-thin to about a centimeter in diameter. The diameter through the whole spout ranges from 1.3 to 2.4 cm. Some spouts, however, had only decorative or symbolic significance, and were not hollow at all, or were hollow at one end and not at the other. One aberrant example was applied directly to the vessel wall.

We found no complete examples of bridged or unbridged spouts, either attached to a parent vessel or just a spout complete in itself. Noguera, however, earlier found a number of bridged-spout vessels in Tehuacan tombs; he illustrates funnel-neck ollas (Noguera 1940: fig. 25) with bridged spouts on one or two sides.

The hollow and solid spouts, or spout handles, seem to appear mainly on two kinds of vessels, either singly or in pairs. Both kinds appear on large funnel-neck ollas. Smaller, solid spout handles seem to be used most often on bottle-like forms with or without ring bases, like those illustrated by Paddock (1966: figs. 190–193). The ring-based fragment we show in Fig. 94, with a small globular body and fragments of two solid spout handles, must have been a vessel of this general type. The tiny funnel-neck vessel also illustrated was probably similar but lacks a ring base.

Ring bases are a diagnostic feature of the Classic period. They usually appear on conoidal or hemispherical bowls, but examples also appear on bottles and ollas. The ninety-five El Riego Gray specimens range from 5.0 to 8.2 cm. in diameter and from 1.0 to 3.0 cm. in height.

One of the significant differences between Quachilco Gray and El Riego Gray is the prevalence of various kinds of vessel feet used with the latter, apparently in tripod fashion. The kinds of supports made of El Riego Gray seem to change throughout the long span of this pottery and parallel changes in kinds of vessel supports in other Mesoamerican regions.

The earliest foot—and one that continues throughout the Tehuacan sequence—in the hollow bulbous shape. This and the majority of hollow supports are pierced or slashed to allow for the expansion of air during firing. The hollow bulbous feet of El Riego Gray vessels range in diameter at the point of attachment from 2.0 to 4.7 cm. and are 1.8 to 3.6 cm. high.

Hollow mammiform feet, which are larger than bulbous feet and have a nipple-like extension at the lower end, appear only with early Palo Blanco vessels in El Riego Gray, but the form itself is known from late Santa Maria wares. The Late Formative and early Classic time range is typical of mammiform feet elsewhere in Mesoamerica. The El Riego Gray feet range from 3.0 to 6.0 cm. in diameter and 3.0 to 8.0 cm. high.

Large hollow slab or rectangular feet, which are diagnostic of early Classic pottery elsewhere in Mesoamerica, occur in El Riego Gray vessels only in early Palo Blanco components.

Small solid conical feet appear with early Palo Blanco examples of El Riego Gray bowls.

Small solid nubbin feet occur throughout the Palo Blanco phase and elsewhere in Mesoamerica during the Classic period. They range from 1.0 to 2.5 cm. in diameter and from 1.0 to 2.0 cm. in height.

Hollow cylindrical feet occur on bowls throughout the Palo Blanco phase and are common in some other regions of Mesoamerica in late Classic times. El Riego Gray examples range in diameter from 1.8 to 3.5 cm. and in height from 1.7 to 4.2 cm.

Solid slab or rectangular feet are roughly the same size as the hollow slab variety. They have the same temporal and spatial range as the hollow cylindrical supports.

Relationships

Although a few sherds of El Riego Gray occurred in both late Santa Maria and early Venta Salada components, El Riego Gray is predominantly diagnostic of the Palo Blanco phase. It is only slightly more popular in the early part of the phase than in the late part. This gray ware is obviously derived from Quachilco Gray and contributes to the origin of Coxcatlan Gray; it is a key link in the gray-ware tradition in the Tehuacan Valley.

In terms of external relationships, this type is vaguely similar to gray wares of Monte Alban II and III, but without the close relationships in paste and decorative elements existing between Quachilco Gray and earlier Monte Alban wares. El Riego Gray shares with Monte Alban II and III gray ceramics such elements as bridged spouts, nubbin and mammiform supports, solid and hollow slab feet, ring bases, narrow basal flanges, cylindrical vessels, barrel-neck ollas, stepped-rim bowls, composite-silhouette bowls, flat-bottomed flaring-wall bowls with and without supports, and pot covers.

Other extra-areal relationships are more difficult to discern. Some of the gray wares from Upper Tres Zapotes are vaguely like El Riego Gray. Although some El Riego Gray decoration and vessel form attributes are like those of some of the vessels of Teotihuacan II and III, the pastes and surface finishes are very different.

Like Rio Salado Gray, El Riego Gray is more of a local ware, with only general affiliations with other manifestations of the early Classic period in Mesoamerica.

QUACHILCO RED

3,483 specimens excavated, 79 collected.

Paste

The paste contains a large amount of medium coarse tempering material. About 1 percent is composed of white limestone grains about 1.0 mm. in diameter. About 6 percent is grains 0.5–1.0 mm. in diameter, mostly of labradorite, andesite, and andesine. About 10 percent of the paste is grains 0.1–0.5 mm. in diameter, with labradorite, andesite, and andesine most common, and fewer grains of hornblende, hematite, calcite, and diorite. About 3 percent is grains under 0.1 mm. in diameter of the above-mentioned materials and augite, pyroxene, and magnetite.

The paste is poorly knit and is porous and blocky in appearance. However, it is relatively hard, measuring about 3.3 on the Mohs scale, probably owing to the method of firing. Cross sections of sherds reveal black or gray cores that lighten very noticeably to orange or red near both surfaces.

Surface Finish

The sherds have both a thin reddish slip and a coat of red paint. They have been polished or very well smoothed. The reddish-orange paint is not specular hematite. Exterior surface ranges in color from light red (10 R 6.8) to reddish yellow (5.0 YR 7/8) to red (10 R 4.6). The polishing is horizontal and is often streaky. There is no decoration other than the red paint covering the surface.

Vessel Forms

Like other utilitarian wares, such as Canoas Heavy

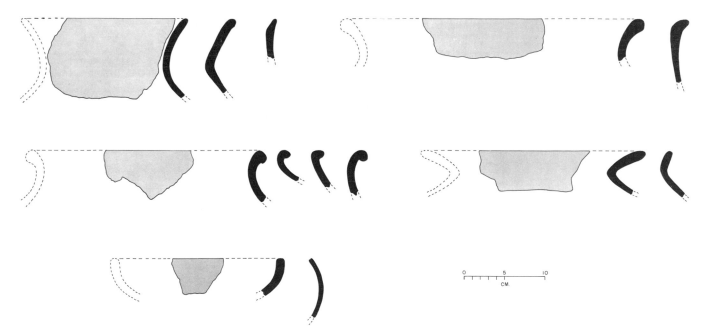

FIG. 95. QUACHILCO RED. *From top to bottom:* ollas with long flaring necks with and without thickened lips; ollas with rolled and beaded rims and with short flaring necks; convex-wall bowls with direct and incurved rims.

TABLE 44
Quachilco Red Vessel Forms
(sherds by site and zone)

	Early Santa Maria							Late Santa Maria						
	368e F	368e E	368e D	272 I	368e C²	368e C¹	272 H	368e C	368e D-E	272 G	368e B	368w C	368w B	218-11 G
Ollas														
rolled/beaded rim								21	7			14	27	
long flaring neck														
direct rim								9	19		21	7	22	
thick lip														
short flaring neck												4	8	
Bowls, convex wall								12	3		5	3	3	
Flat bases														
Body sherds	2	1	141	2	59	108	26	177	87	15	690	107		11
Total	2	1	141	2	59	108	26	219	116	15	716	135	60	11

	Late Santa Maria (continued)													
	218-11 F	368e B¹	204 A-B	368w B¹	218-11 E	218-6 G	218-10 C²	218-6 F	218-11 D	218-11 C	218-10 C¹	218-10 C	218-10 B¹	218-10 B
Ollas														
rolled/beaded rim	1	4		16			28		2	2	6	21	2	8
long flaring neck														
direct rim		3	6	14			2		2	1	2	8	1	8
thick lip														
short flaring neck							2				3	5		10
Bowls, convex wall							1					6		4
Flat bases												1		1
Body sherds	17	49	52	72	16	11	102	18	29	15	66	184	83	219
Total	18	56	58	102	16	11	135	18	33	18	77	225	86	250

	Late Santa Maria (continued)						Early Palo Blanco							
	218-11 B	218-6 E	218-6 D	50 VII	218-6 C	218-6 B	218-10 A	218-6 A	218-11 A	272 F	51 A-B	50 VI	272 E	Total
Ollas														
rolled/beaded rim					1	7								167
long flaring neck														
direct rim						7	2	8	2		1		1	146
thick lip							17		4					21
short flaring neck						6								38
Bowls, convex wall											1	1		39
Flat bases														2
Body sherds	15	13	19	4	18	50	364	125	72	14	8	6	3	3070
Total	15	13	19	4	19	70	383	133	78	14	10	7	4	3483

Plain and Quachilco Mica, the vessels in this paste are mainly ollas. Only one bowl form was noted.

Rolled- or beaded-rim ollas are short necked and wide mouthed with the characteristic rounded roll or bead at the rim. They must have had huge globular bodies. Rim diameter, 18–40 cm.

Ollas with long flaring necks and simple rims have rounded or thinned lips and rim diameters of 14–28 cm.

Ollas with flaring necks and thickened lips are the dominant early Palo Blanco olla shape in Quachilco Red but do not appear in other subphases. Necks are

TABLE 45
El Riego Black Decorated Sherds
(by site and zone)

	Early Palo Blanco			Late Palo Blanco						Early Venta Salada		Late Venta Salada	
	218-10 A	50 VI	272 D¹	272 C	272 B	272 A	50 V	50 IV	35e D	35e B	50 II	50 I	Total
Incised motifs													
1-3 lines (or grooves) around rims of													
flaring-wall, direct-rim bowls, int.							1		2				3
ext.					12	1							13
convex-wall, direct-rim bowls, int.				1									1
ext.				1									1
tall composite-silhouette jar, ext.	1		1		6			1	3				12
1-3 lines on bodies, ext.			1	1						3	1	2	8
triangles on rims or walls of													
tall composite-silhouette jars, ext.	2		2		6			1	3				14
indeterminate forms, ext.					12	1							13
hatching on rims or walls of													
tall composite-silhouette jars, ext.	1		1	1	4			1	2				10
wavy lines on rims or walls of													
tall composite-silhouette jars, ext.					4			1	3				8
molcajete lines in quadrants on bottoms, int.				2	4	1	1						8
Grooves and punctates on olla body, ext.		1					1						2
Total	4	1	5	6	48	3	3	4	13	3	1	2	93

generally of medium height with a rounded thickened lip on the usually flaring but sometimes almost vertical and concave rim. Rim diameter, 14–38 cm.; thickness at lip, 0.8–2.0 cm.

Ollas with short flaring necks usually flare widely from shoulder to lip, but a few rims are almost vertical. Rim diameter, 12–29 cm.

Convex-wall bowls with direct or incurved rims range from true hemispherical shapes to bowls with definitely incurving rims and constricted mouths. Rim diameter, 12–22 cm.

Relationships

Quachilco Red occurs only in late Santa Maria and early Palo Blanco levels, with minor shifts in popularity of olla forms from Late Formative to Classic times.

EL RIEGO BLACK

517 specimens excavated, 445 collected.

Paste

Thin-section analysis was done on only two sherds, and both were almost identical in composition. About 5 percent of the paste is grains 0.1–0.5 mm. in diameter consisting of calcite, quartz, quartzite, microline, plagioclase, and occasionally biotite and diorite. About 15 percent of the paste is grains under 0.1 mm. in diameter, including the materials mentioned and magnetite, hematite, sericite, and hornblende.

The pottery is relatively hard (about 3.5) and well knit. However, the paste has visible laminations, and the surface has a tendency to scale off. The core usually ranges from gray (10 YR 3/1) to light brownish-gray (10 YR 6/2).

Surface Finish

A thin dark slip was applied to the surface and then polished. Although there are occasional brownish-gray (2.5 Y 6/6) firing clouds, the surface usually ranges from a shiny near-black (2.5 Y 2/0) to a very shiny dark gray (2.5 Y 4/0 or 5.0 Y 4/1).

Decoration

The most common decoration consists of relatively fine incisions made through the polished surface when the vessel was dry but still unfired. Such decoration usually appears on exterior surfaces. Deep wide incisions forming quadrants of parallel lines appear on the interior bottoms of flat-based molcajetes. The fine-line motifs are usually crosshatched or hachured triangles or steps inside a wide band outlined by two or three parallel lines, sometimes with crude concave-sided tri-

TABLE 46
El Riego Black Vessel Forms
(sherds by site and zone)

Form	Early Palo Blanco									Late Palo Blanco						
	218-10 A	218-6 A	218-11 A	272 F	51 A-B	50 VI	272 E	272 D	272 C	272 B	272 A	50 V	254 B	50 IV	35w 3-4	35e E
Bowls																
convex wall																
everted rim									10		2		2			
direct rim									2			3	3	1		
flaring wall												1				2
composite silhouette, deep	2					1		2		18	1			1		
basal ridge																
incurved rim																
Ollas, short flaring neck		2				3	1		1	1						
Bottle						3										3
Flat Bases			2								2					
Strap handles									2	4	1	2		2		
Spouts													1			
Supports																
stepped																
hollow bulb									1							
Body sherds	12	17	14	8	9	27	28	13	20	7	23	13	9	21	5	8
Total	14	17	16	8	9	31	29	15	36	30	29	19	15	25	5	13

Form	Late Palo Blanco (cont'd)			Early Venta Salada							Late Venta Salada					Total
	255 B	35e D	35e C	255 A	50 III	35w 3	35e B	50 II	35w 2	35w 1	367 B	50 I	367 A	35e A	368w A	
Bowls																
convex wall																
everted rim	1		5		5		1		1	3		2				32
direct rim		8	5				1									23
flaring wall	1	13	5		4	1	1	3	1	3			2			36
composite silhouette, deep		3														27
basal ridge		1														2
incurved rim								1								1
Ollas, short flaring neck		2														10
Bottle								1								1
Flat Bases		1	1				1									18
Strap handles																2
Spouts								1								2
Supports																
stepped			1													2
hollow bulb			1													1
Body sherds	5	18	12	1	8	2	15	6	5	11	2	15	14	9	2	360
Total	7	47	30	1	17	3	19	12	7	17	2	17	16	9	2	517

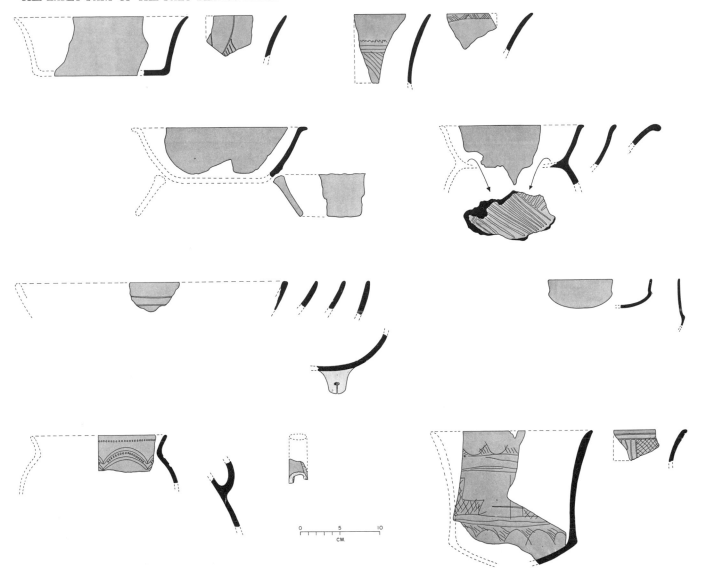

FIG. 96. EL RIEGO BLACK. *Row 1:* flaring-wall bowls; *row 2:* convex-wall bowl with everted rim and stepped foot, and footed bowl with outangled or flaring rim and incised bottom; *row 3:* convex-wall, direct-rim bowl with bulb-footed fragment, and miniature composite-silhouette bowl; *row 4:* olla with short flaring neck, strap handle and spout fragments, and tall composite-silhouette vessel.

angles at the outer edges of the band. One olla has around the shoulder a series of grooved semicircles outlining rows of hemiconical punctations.

Vessel Forms

Flaring-wall bowls are the most numerous bowl shape, but are not represented in the early Palo Blanco sample. The bowls had flat bottoms. Interior surfaces are usually better polished than exterior surfaces. Some sherds display an incised border on the inner or outer surface of the rim or an incised design lower on the exterior wall. Dimensions in cm.: rim diameter, 18–32; height, 5.0–8.0.

Convex-wall bowls with flaring or everted rims are almost as common as the flaring-wall bowls. They are also restricted to late Classic or Postclassic levels. The bowls have flat bottoms and narrow outcurved or everted rims. One large fragment has a flat, solid piece of foot attached and wide molcajete incisions on the interior surface of the bottom. Probably all or most of

159

TABLE 47
Early Palo Blanco Trade Sherds
(by site and zone)

	218-10 A	218-6 A	218-11 A	272 F	51 A-B	50 VI	272 E	272 D	Total
Thin Orange: bodies		1		1		1			3
ring-based convex-wall bowls							2	2	4
hollow slab foot					1				1
Texcoco Fabric-impressed: bodies	23	6							29
flower-pot-shaped jars	7	2	2						11
rolled-rim ollas						2			2
convex-wall bowls						1			1
Total	30	9	2	1	1	4	2	2	51

these bowls had similar supports (probably stepped) and incisions. Dimensions in cm. of two specimens: rim diameter, 18, 28; diameter of bottom, 14, 15; wall height, 4.5, 6.5; height of supports, over 2.5 and unknown. One unattached stepped foot of a size that seems consistent with the proportions of the larger bowl measured 5.5 cm. high by 5.5 and 4.5 cm. wide at its upper and lower ends.

Convex-wall bowls with direct rims are vessels of greater rim diameter than the shape described immediately above. Walls range from distinctly convex to some Venta Salada examples that are almost straight and outsloping. Two of the latter are simply decorated; one with two shallow grooves encircling the outer surface and one with a single thin line incised around the inner lip. A fragmentary flat bottom that is quite convex where bottom and walls merge has a hollow bulbous foot attached. This type of base and support may belong to this bowl shape. Rim diameter, 20–40 cm.

Tall composite-silhouette vessels have flaring or concave walls and shallow convex bases, with a sharp edge where wall and base join. The outer walls are usually decorated with fine-line designs which include a central panel bordered by horizontal parallel wavy or straight lines or by hachured triangles. The panel may contain crosshatched steps, large hachured triangles, or an area set off by a widely undulating line. Dimensions in cm.: rim diameter, 18–26; wall height (4 specimens), 10–16; depth of base (2 specimens), 2.0–4.0; diameter at junction of wall and base, 2.0–4.0 less than rim diameter.

Basal-ridge bowls are a minor form with a sharp ridge (modeled, not applied) on the exterior where the convex base joins the nearly vertical concave wall. One tiny bowl is almost complete; its dimensions in

cm. are: rim diameter, 8.0; over-all height, 3.5; wall height, 1.5. The only other bowl excavated has a diameter at the rim of 18 cm., and the wall above the ridge is 4.5 cm. high.

Short-neck ollas have flaring rims, wide mouths, and globular bodies. One example has a decorated shoulder and rim (Fig. 96). Rim diameter, 14–18 cm.

Other features. Fragments of spouts and wide strap handles were probably attached to ollas. One bottle fragment and a piece of incurved rim were also found.

Relationships

El Riego Black is related to San Martin Incised of Teotihuacan III–IV (Tolstoy 1958: fig. 8) and the black incised ware of the Classic period of Cholula (Noguera 1954). The calcite temper of the Tehuacan examples suggests the possibility that this type may have been imported from an unknown area.

It is interesting that although Type C. 35 of Monte Alban III has a black finish on a gray paste and shares some vessel shapes with El Riego Black, the decoration is almost entirely different and the majority of the vessel forms and particularly the supports are different also (Caso, Bernal, and Acosta 1967: 80–82).

Trade Wares

Two types of trade sherds were present in early Palo Blanco components: Thin Orange, which will be described in Chapter 8, and Texcoco Fabric-impressed, which is discussed below with other ceramic affiliations.

Miscellaneous Objects

Human effigy incense burner. A hand fragment about 5.2 cm. long and 2 cm. wide occurred in Zone A of Tr 218, Text 10. Badly eroded and barely distinguishable fragments from surface sites, particularly Tr 73, indicate that large human effigy burners, which resemble those of Monte Alban II, were common in the Tehuacan Valley in this period. Undoubtedly, we would have uncovered more fragments if our excavations had included tombs and temples.

Barrel-shaped spindle whorl or bead. This small object, about 2.5 cm. in diameter and 2.2 cm. high, has a central hole through it about 5 mm. in diameter. Paste and surface finish resemble Quachilco Gray. If this object is a spindle whorl, its appearance in the first part of the Palo Blanco phase is early compared to the appearance of spindle whorls in other regions.

Sherd disks. Five pierced and fourteen unpierced disks are made from sherds of Quachilco Mica.

Human effigy whistles or ocarinas. Two fragments with hands adhering to hollow globular bodies and a third sherd may have been parts of whistles or ocarinas.

Small ball. A polished gray ball is 1.5 cm. in diameter.

Figurines

The Hairlock Doughnut-eye and Slot-feature heads recovered from an early Palo Blanco level are carryover types from the Formative period and have been described in Chapter 6. New types of figurines characteristic of the early Classic period are described below.

REMOJADAS HEADS

2 heads excavated.
Dimensions of more complete head in cm.: height, 5.0; width, 5.6; thickness, 2.1.
Paste: resembles Quachilco Brown.
Surface finish: thin slip, smoothed.

Both heads are so badly broken that their original outline cannot be determined. Both are thin and flat. The larger fragment has a prominent, realistically shaped nose and small nostrils. The eyes are deep, downward-slanting incisions, and the mouth is a straight incised line. The eyes of the smaller fragment are applied below the bridge of the nose and extend horizontally from nose to temple. Deep horizontal slashes through the appliques raised sharp ridges to represent upper and lower eyelids. Nostrils are indicated by punch marks and the eyebrows are broad incised lines slanting upward from the top of the nose. No indications remain of ears, earplugs, or headdress.

In the Tehuacan Valley one head was recovered from a late Santa Maria component, and the second head from an early Palo Blanco component. The heads are very similar to Classic figurines from the Remo-

5 CM.

FIG. 97. REMOJADAS, PUFFED CHEEK, AND PORTRAIT HEADS.

jadas site in central Veracruz (Medellín Zenil 1960: fig. 4, p. 69).

HOLLOW PUFFED CHEEK HEAD

1 head excavated.
Dimensions in cm.: height, 3.7; width, 4.6; thickness, 1.7.
Paste: resembles El Riego Orange.

The head is hollow. The face is round in shape and has rounded features, except for a straight nose flattened at the end. The cheeks are puffed, and the lips are thick and protruding. Deep grooves at the corners of the mouth accentuate the rounded cheeks. Each crescent-shaped eye is made by two punches.

The single head dates from early Palo Blanco or early Classic times in the Tehuacan Valley. Similar heads apparently have not been found or reported from other parts of Mexico.

TEHUACAN PORTRAIT HEADS

1 head excavated.
Dimensions in cm.: height, 3.9; width, 3.3 thickness, 2.6.
Paste: resembles Thin Orange.
Surface finish: slipped.

The face is roughly oval in shape and slants gradually forward from cap to chin. The nose is wide and slightly hooked. Eyes and mouth have been made in the same way; each feature is a raised oval of clay marked at each end with shallow impressions. Above the eyes are ridges for eyebrows. A line across the

161

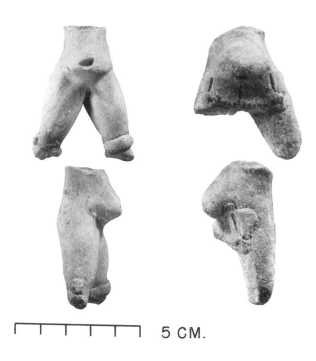

5 CM.

FIG. 98. PREGNANT STANDING FIGURES.

forehead marks the edge of cap or hairline. Small globs of clay form the ears.

The single specimen from the Tehuacan Valley dates from the Palo Blanco phase or early to middle Classic times. It is very much like some of the portrait figurines found in Teotihuacan III in the Valley of Mexico.

PREGNANT STANDING FIGURES

5 bodies; 2 excavated, 3 collected.
Dimensions in cm.: height, approx. 6.0–9.0; width at waist, 1.6–3.0.
Paste: resembles El Riego Orange.
Surface finish: smoothed.

These figurines are standing with legs apart. The legs usually taper to a rounded end and are without features. One example, however, has small feet and an appliqued band or anklet. The bellies are very protruding and were apparently made to look pregnant. Below the belly of all figurines except the one with an ankle decoration there is an applied loin cloth decorated with incised dots and lines. Chests are narrow and the breasts small. The arms must have hung at the sides of the body. No heads were found with these bodies.

In the Tehuacan Valley these figurines appear at the beginning of the Classic period.

Ceramic Affiliations

The continuation from late Santa Maria into early Palo Blanco of the four pottery types, Quachilco Gray, El Riego Gray, Quachilco Mica, and Quachilco Red, together with other classes of artifact types, clearly indicates that the former is the ancestor of the latter. There are, however, many diagnostic early Classic traits in early Palo Blanco, including a portrait-head figurine, fine-line decoration, flanged and stepped rims, basal flanges, ring bases, bridged or unbridged spouts, pot covers, vessels with solid or hollow rectangular feet, and bowls with nubbin or bulbous feet. These attributes also occur in Teotihuacan I, II, and sometimes III; Istmo VII and Jiquipilas VIII from lowland Chiapas; Monte Alban II and sometimes III; Classic Remojadas; Tajin I and II; Pithaya (Panuco III); Upper Tres Zapotes; and Lower II of Cerro de las Mesas. They are also present in many early Classic and proto-Classic manifestations in the Maya region. In fact, these attributes are considered horizon styles for the period from roughly 200 B.C. to about A.D. 200 (Willey and Phillips 1958: 182–188).

Actual trade sherds or types that occur in two or more regions were much rarer in our early Palo Blanco ceramic sample than in the Santa Maria material. This lack is probably not because relationships between regions were less flourishing, but rather because of the limitations of our sample. Among the specimens we can consider trade sherds are a few Thin Orange sherds, mainly from the later of the early Palo Blanco components. Forty-three fabric-impressed sherds of coarse paste, definitely the same type as the Postclassic Texcoco Fabric-impressed ware of the Valley of Mexico (see below), are obviously imports, but whether from the Valley of Mexico at this period is open to question.

Like late Santa Maria, early Palo Blanco exhibits more connections to cultures of the Oaxaca Valley than to those of any other region. Quachilco Gray, which continues into early Palo Blanco, extends its similarities to some of the gray wares of Monte Alban III. The slab, mammiform, and nubbin feet; bridged spouts, cylindrical vessels with or without basal bulges; bowls with sharply everted rims; and basal-flanged bowls are late Santa Maria and early Palo Blanco features of Quachilco Gray which are shared by gray wares of Monte Alban II; while cylindrical jars with covers, ring bases, hollow cylindrical feet, hollow or solid slab feet, and flanged-rim bowls made in both El Riego Gray and Quachilco Gray are shared with gray wares of Monte Alban III. The Remojadas figurines of early Palo Blanco resemble some of the flat slant-eyed types of Monte Alban II; the Palo Blanco Portrait Head is similar to examples from Monte Alban III.

Quachilco Red ollas of early Palo Blanco are also similar to some of the ollas from early Monte Alban III. Also, Thin Orange vessels with slab feet were traded into both Monte Alban III and early Palo Blanco.

The Thin Orange sherds, the Portrait Head figurine, and the resemblance of El Riego Black to San Martin Incised indicate connections between early Palo Blanco and Teotihuacan in the Valley of Mexico, as well as between early Palo Blanco and Cholula II of northern Puebla (Noguera 1954). The figurine type, the vessel form of and lack of incising on the Thin Orange pottery, the nubbin feet of other wares, and the cylindrical vessels generally hint that early Palo Blanco connects most closely with Teotihuacan I and II, and possibly with the earliest part of period III. As we shall see, late Palo Blanco is related to Teotihuacan III and IV on somewhat stronger evidence.

One other similarity shared by Tehuacan and the Valley of Mexico is the flower-pot-shaped Texcoco Fabric-impressed salt jars. On the basis of present temporal evidence the presence of such vessels in early Classic Tehuacan is difficult to explain. Texcoco Fabric-impressed pottery is not definitely present in the Valley of Mexico until Postclassic times (Tolstoy 1958: 51-53), whereas at Tehuacan fabric-impressed jars begin in the early Classic period. Their appearance in Tehuacan at this time perhaps confirms Mayer-Oakes tentative identification of questionable sherds from Classic levels of El Risco as Texcoco Fabric-impressed (Mayer-Oakes 1959: 341). Although salt-making was established in Tehuacan in early Classic times, the small number of early Palo Blanco salt-making sites and the relatively small number of salt pans or jars found in our stratigraphic excavations caution one not to conclude that there was a diffusion of fabric-impressed salt jars from Tehuacan to the Valley of Mexico. Such jars probably evolved in still another area (Cuernavaca, according to Tolstoy 1958, p. 53), diffusing first to Tehuacan and later to the Valley of Mexico.

In contrast to the Santa Maria phase, connections between Tehuacan and the lowland cultures during early Palo Blanco are not numerous. What connections do exist are mainly in terms of horizon styles and in the presence of early kinds of Thin Orange wares in both areas. The distinctive flat Remojadas figurines in late Santa Maria and early Palo Blanco, however, show connection with central Veracruz in the general time period from 200 B.C. to A.D. 250. Some of the pottery in Upper Tres Zapotes (Drucker 1943a) and Lower II of Cerro de las Mesas (Drucker 1943b) share certain features with wares from early Palo Blanco. Although the polychrome wares (some of them gray slipped) with little or no temper of Upper Tres Zapotes differ in paste from El Riego Gray, such features as flanged and stepped rims, cylindrical vessels, spouted ollas or bottles, flat-bottomed bowls with flaring walls, and mammiform, nubbin, and slab feet (1943a: fig. 71) are similar.

More striking relationships between Upper Tres Zapotes and early Palo Blanco are to be seen in the black wares of the two cultures. El Riego Black and Tres Zapotes Black have similar cylindrical vessel forms and a number of common incised motifs such as hachured concave-sided triangles (Drucker 1943a: pl. 20d); crosshatched steps (ibid: fig. 36a); parallel straight or wavy lines; and herringbone type borders. Also, perforated ring bases like the incensarios of Upper Tres Zapotes (ibid.: fig. 40k-l) occur in El Riego Gray. El Riego Black and El Riego Gray of early Palo Blanco are apparently even more similar to the polished brown and black wares of Lower II of Cerro de Las Mesas. The wares of both areas have besides a black or gray surface finish, similar engraved or incised geometric motifs (Drucker 1943b: pls. 19, 20; figs. 82–99), cylindrical vessels, hollow cylindrical supports, nubbin and slab feet, and hollow rectangular feet (ibid.: fig. 12). Perhaps future investigation of Palo Blanco sites and the Papaloapan drainage in lowland coastal Veracruz will reveal more evidence of highland and lowland connections in early Classic times.

Regardless of whether we find more ceramic connections between the highlands and lowlands of Mesoamerica, it is in this Classic period that the differences between the two zones become further emphasized. Much of the agriculture of the highlands was based upon irrigation, while lowland farming employed slash-and-burn techniques. The highland ceremonial centers during this period seem to have had a relatively dense population and a rather secular orientation, while the lowland centers developed the opposite characteristics. The fundamental differences between highland and lowland cultures are also reflected in ceramics. Although there may have been a good deal of trade between lowland and highland cultures and, of course some interactions in terms of styles and beliefs, this was the period in which many regions developed vigorous local florescent styles and ceased to be dominated by a panregional set of horizon styles.

CHAPTER 8

The Late Part of the Palo Blanco Phase

A TOTAL OF 3,152 sherds were excavated from eleven late Palo Blanco components. Although not a large number, these sherds constitute a better sample than the early Palo Blanco sherds. Only one of the eleven components is a top zone, and eight of them yielded over 150 sherds each. However, only two components have samples of over 600 sherds, and all the excavated components are cave occupations and thus probably are not truly representative of the more typical open village sites. Unfortunately, analysis of the late Palo Blanco materials came so late in our program that neither time nor funds remained for digging one of the large open sites of the period. Another shortcoming of the late Palo Blanco ceramics is that this subphase covers a span of some 500 years—roughly from A.D. 200 to 700—a span which eleven components with limited numbers of sherds cannot adequately represent. We can, however, supplement the excavated sample with the 10,902 sherds collected from surface sites, and we do have the record supplied by Noguera (1940: 306–319) of the many vessels excavated from Tehuacan tombs of this subphase.

The ceramic materials are numerous enough to make it possible to align the excavated components in rough chronological order on the basis of ceramic trends. Zone C of Tc 272 is the earliest in this series; it is followed by Zones B and A of Tc 272, Zone V of Tc 50, Zones C¹ and B of Tc 254, Zone IV of Tc 50, Level 3–4 of Tc 35w, Zone E–F of Tc 35e, Zone B of Tc 255, and Zone D of Tc 35e.

Of the pottery types previously described which are still found in late Palo Blanco components Quachilco Gray, Quachilco Red, and Quachilco Brown appear in very insignificant amounts. El Riego Gray continues to be an important type, but is diminishing in popularity. Quachilco Mica, although diminishing somewhat in popularity, continues into the Venta Salada phase with some strength. There are minor changes in some of the olla forms in this paste and a slight tendency for the size of the mica temper to increase. El Riego Black actually becomes more important in late Palo Blanco levels than it was in early Palo Blanco components.

El Riego Marble-tempered sherds were found in late Palo Blanco levels but since this is mainly an early Venta Salada type, it will be described in the following chapter.

Pottery Types

EL RIEGO ORANGE

1,331 specimens excavated, 980 collected.

Paste

The paste is not well knit and has a slightly porous and contorted appearance. The tempering ingredients in the brownish clay are very noticeable gray or black specks. About 1 percent of the paste consists of basalt grains 1.0–2.0 mm. in diameter, and about 4 percent is basalt grains 0.5–1.0 mm. in diameter, together with occasional grains of andesite. Nearly 15 percent is composed of grains 0.1–0.5 mm. in diameter of basalt, andesite, andesine, labradorite, augite, hornblende, magnetite, and hematite. Three percent is grains under 0.1 mm. in diameter, including all the materials mentioned except basalt and andesite.

Hardness ranges from 3.0 to 4.0 in the Mohs scale. The sherds tend to be well fired with both core and

FIG. 99. EL RIEGO ORANGE. *From top to bottom,* low convex-wall bowls with flat bottoms, rim and base sherds of cylindrical vessels, incurved- and carinated-rim bowls, flaring-rim fragments, ring base, and hollow bulb support.

periphery colored brown or dark brown. The necks and bodies of ollas of this paste seems to have been made separately and then welded together.

Surface Finish

Surfaces have been painted and then polished. They range in color from red (10 YR 4/6) to orange (2.5 YR 5/8) to almost yellow (2.5 YR 6/8). Ollas are paint-ed and polished only on the exterior and the upper-most part of the inner rim; interiors are roughly brushed horizontally. The polishing on the exterior tends to be vertical on the bodies and has a streaky appearance. Bowls are polished horizontally on both surfaces. Interiors are usually better preserved than exteriors. The bowl surfaces also appear streaky, with occasional black streaks on the orange surface where

165

TABLE 48
El Riego Orange Vessel Forms
(sherds by site and zone)

	Early Palo Blanco					Late Palo Blanco							
	272 F	51 A-B	50 VI	272 E	272 D	272 C	272 B	272 A	50 V	254 C¹	254 B	50 IV	35w 3-4
Bowls													
convex wall, low										1			40
incurved rim													20
carinated rim												5	
flaring wall		2											
Cylindrical vessels													
Ollas													
funnel neck								1					
short flaring neck													
long flaring neck	1	3											
barrel neck												1	
Pot covers/comales						2							
Bases													
flat						5						3	
conoidal													
Ring bases													
Supports													
slab													
nubbin													
bulb													1
Body sherds	11	5	1	2	6	10	10	11	10	3	16	11	8
Total	12	10	1	2	6	17	10	12	10	4	16	20	69

	Late Palo Blanco (cont'd)			Early Venta Salada							Late Venta Salada		
	35e E	255 B	35e D	35e C	255 A	50 III	35e B	35w 3	50 II	35w 2	35w 1	35e A	Total
Bowls													
convex wall, low	43	2	26	12		2	1	1			1	3	132
incurved rim	10		24	2			3	3					62
carinated rim													5
flared wall								2					4
Cylindrical vessels	6		2					9					17
Ollas													
funnel neck	27		28	25		1	2	1				3	88
short flaring neck	2		3		1			1			2		9
long flaring neck						1		1					6
barrel neck													1
Pot covers/comales				4									6
Bases													
flat	19		14	3		3	1	1			3	6	58
conoidal	3			1								2	6
Ring bases			2										2
Supports													
slab	2						1						3
nubbin			2										2
bulb				1									2
Body sherds	146	17	283	122	4	15	106	86	1	1	10	33	928
Total	258	19	381	173	5	22	123	96	1	1	16	47	1331

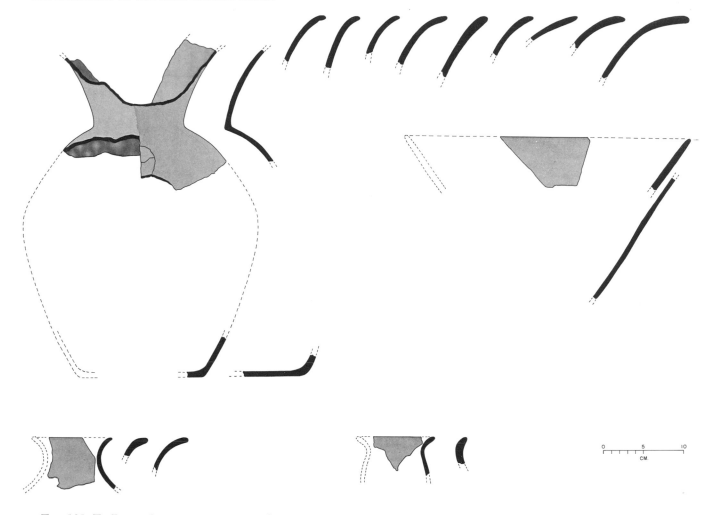

F<small>IG</small>. 100. E<small>L</small> R<small>IEGO</small> O<small>RANGE</small>. *From top to bottom,* ollas with tall flaring or outsloping funnel necks and smaller flaring-neck ollas.

the polishing has been particularly heavy. There is no decoration other than the paint.

Vessel Forms

Low, convex-wall bowls. These flat-bottomed bowls are the dominant vessel form. Dimensions in cm.: rim diameter, 16–30; wall height, 4.9–8.0.

Incurved-rim bowls are somewhat deeper than the low convex-wall bowls and show a greater range of sizes. Bottoms were probably rounded. Dimensions in cm.: rim diameter, 8–30; wall height, 5–14.

Cylindrical vessels. Some of these tall vessels have slightly bowed walls or slightly flaring rims. Dimensions in cm.: rim diameter: 22–36; base diameter, 8.4–25.5.

Shallow vessels. These examples could be fragments of either comales or pot covers. The rims are very

slightly convex. Dimensions in cm.: rim diameter, 24–32; depth, less than 6.0.

Flaring-wall vessels. A few flaring-rim fragments might have come from bowls with mouth diameters of 18–36 cm. Since none of the sherds were attached to basal fragments, wall height and type of vessel cannot be determined. The fragments may be rims of ollas with the exterior surface finish carried over to the interior of the rim.

Carinated-rim bowls have a deep convex bottom and a short inward-sloping concave rim. There is a horizontal lug at the sharply marked junction of rim and base. Dimensions in cm.: rim diameter, 30; maximum diameter, 36; height, about 14.

Funnel-neck ollas are the most common jar shape. They have very tall, usually flaring necks which form a sharp angle on the interior where the neck joins the

167

body. The body blends into a small flat base. Dimensions in cm.: rim diameter, 20–40; height of neck, 10–20.

Ollas with short flaring necks are not numerous. They have outcurved rims and squat globular bodies. Dimensions in cm.: rim diameter, 8–22; height of neck, under 10.

Other ollas. A few sherds seem to be from ollas with long flaring necks and from a barrel-neck olla. Some of the ollas may have had spout handles.

Vessel appendages in El Riego Orange from late Classic components include bulb, slab, and nubbin feet, and two ring bases. The more complete ring base has a diameter of about 5.0 cm. and is 0.7 cm. high.

Relationships

The tempering materials in the paste suggest that El Riego Orange is of local origin. It is a good time marker for the late Classic, although specimens occur in early Palo Blanco and the earliest part of Venta Salada. Two of the ollas Noguera found in Tombs 1 and 2 near the Calvario in Tehuacan are of this type (1940: fig. 25a). Relationships to other areas are difficult to discern. Coarse orange ollas with funnel necks and flaring rims, flat bottoms, and spout handles occur in Monte Alban III (Caso, Bernal, and Acosta 1967: 335) and may be related to our El Riego Orange. In the Valley of Mexico, San Martin Orange Plain, which is an important type in Teotihuacan IIa (Tlamimilolpa) and III (Xolalpan), but begins in period I (Tzacualli), has ollas with flat bottoms and flaring rims as the dominant vessel form (Tolstoy 1958: 32–33). These bear a general resemblance to El Riego ollas.

El Riego Plain

2,360 specimens excavated, 3,499 collected.

Paste

This paste is heavily tempered with coarse-grained mica material. Two sherds analyzed in thin section reveal that about 10 percent of the paste is grains 0.5–2.0 mm. in diameter, and another 10 percent is grains 0.1–0.5 mm. in diameter. The particles in these two groups are mainly quartzite, muscovite, biotite, basalt, sericite, quartz, and quartziferite, and infrequently, plagioclase, granite, and microcline. About 7 or 8 percent of the paste is grains under 0.1 mm. in diameter, consisting of most of the materials mentioned, plus hematite, chlorite, magnetite, and olivine. The sherds are fairly soft, ranging from 2.5 to 3.0. The paste is well knit but coarse and shows evidence of coil breaks.

168

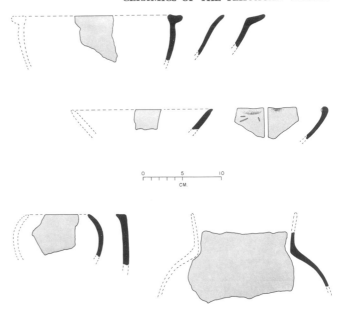

FIG. 101. EL RIEGO PLAIN. *From top to bottom,* convex-wall bowls with thickened, flaring, and everted rims, low convex-wall bowls with direct rim and dimpled rim, incurved-rim bowls, and straight-neck olla.

Surface Finish

Interiors and exteriors are usually reddish-brown (5.0 YR 3/1 to 5/8), but the interior is generally a shade lighter than the exterior. The inner surfaces are brushed, and exteriors are crudely smoothed or wiped. There is no decoration.

Vessel Forms

This paste is used for utilitarian vessels, mainly ollas.

Ollas with long flaring necks are the most common shape. They had globular bodies and small flat bases. Rim diameter, 14–28 cm.

Ollas with short flaring necks have wide mouths and presumably had flat bottoms. Rim diameter, 22–36 cm.

Angle-neck ollas are a variation on the preceding form, with the neck slanting outward at a definite angle to the shoulder.

Straight-necked ollas had globular bodies and vertical necks ranging from short to medium high. Rim diameter, 13–15 cm.

Funnel-neck ollas, found only in the Venta Salada phase, have necks that range from outsloping to flaring.

Low convex-wall bowls with direct rims have walls that range from quite convex to almost straight and

TABLE 49
El Riego Plain Vessel Forms
(sherds by site and zone)

	Early Palo Blanco			Late Palo Blanco											Early Venta Salada	
	50 VI	272 E	272 D	272 C	272 B	272 A	50 V	254 C1	254 B	50 IV	35w 3-4	35e E	255 B	35e D	35e C	255 A
Ollas																
long flaring neck					1	1				5		5		4	3	
short flaring neck						1	1		1							1
funnel neck																
angle neck	2												1	3	2	1
straight neck														1		
Bowls																
convex wall																
direct rim	1					7	1					1		2		
everted rim																
incurved rim																
outsloping wall																
composite silhouette																
basal ridge	1															
Comal																
Flat bases															1	
Ring bases						3	1									
Strap handle										1		4				
Loop handle																
Spout			1													
Body sherds	13	13	18	40	38	20	11	8	31	39	7	65	36	136	334	25
Total	17	13	19	40	39	32	14	8	32	45	7	75	37	146	340	27

	Early Venta Salada *(cont'd)*					Late Venta Salada									
	50 III	35e B	35w 3	50 II	35w 2	35w 1	367 B	50 I	367 A	368e A	35e A	368w A	62 A	65 A	Total
Ollas															
long flaring neck			2		2	1			6		2	3	7		42
short flaring neck	1	4	2		8	2		1		2	3	2	2		31
funnel neck						2	2				2	2	9		17
angle neck		1		1	1										12
straight neck		1				1									3
Bowls															
convex wall															
direct rim				1	2										15
everted rim		1				2							4		7
incurved rim					2										2
outsloping wall						1									1
composite silhouette						1									1
basal ridge															1
Comal				1											1
Flat bases			15		4	5					2				27
Ring Bases															4
Strap handle	2			2					3						12
Loop Handle		1													1
Spout															1
Body sherds	24	244	128	87	63	118	4	33	199	9	87	27	321	4	2182
Total	27	252	148	91	82	133	6	34	208	11	96	34	343	4	2360

outsloping. One rim was so shallow that the vessel could be considered a plate. Another sherd has an aberrant rim that is slightly thickened and dimpled or scalloped at the lip. Rim diameter, 18–26 cm.

Convex-wall bowls with flaring or everted rims are of about the same size range as the direct-rim bowls. They have short to relatively wide rims that turn outward at a gradual or sharp angle.

Incurved-rim bowls. The sherds represent small deep vessels. One specimen has convex walls and a truly constricted mouth; the other has nearly vertical walls and a lip flattened on top and extending inward. Rim diameter, 8.5 and about 10 cm.

Other forms represented by one example each include an outsloping-rim fragment, a composite-silhouette vessel, a platelike fragment and a body sherd of a bowl with basal ridge. Most of the bottom fragments are flat. There are four ring bases, which may have been attached to bowl or olla forms. The strap and loop handles obviously are appendages of the ollas.

Relationships

This utilitarian ware is similar to and perhaps derives from Rio Salado Coarse and Quachilco Mica. However, the greater amounts of quartz in the paste, the flat-bottomed olla form, and the smooth surface finish are features not shared by the ancestral types. Further, El Riego Plain, unlike the two earlier types, occurs over a brief and very well-defined period of time. Since all three types are local products with few distinctive attributes and were made to serve local utilitarian needs, extra-territorial relationships are difficult to discern.

EL RIEGO POLISHED

889 specimens excavated, 807 collected.

Paste

About 7 percent of the tempering material is grains 0.5–1.0 mm. in diameter, 10 percent is grains 0.1–0.5 mm. in diameter, and about 5 percent is under 0.1 mm. in diameter. Even as we sorted the sherds, we noted some difference of tempering materials within the type, but there was no temporal significance among sherds of slightly different appearance. Mineralogical analysis of three sherds in thin section revealed that some of the paste contained calcite and sericite but not basalt and labradorite, and some contained the latter two materials but not calcite and sericite. All sherds contained small amounts of quartz, quartzite, biotite, hematite, magnetite, and horn-

blende. Most of the paste is porous and poorly knit and has a sandy appearance.

Surface Finish

Interior surfaces were wiped horizontally while the paste was still wet. Outer surfaces were polished—usually with a stick used in circular fashion—when the pot was dry. The exteriors have a greasy feel and range in color from light brown to brown (10 R 4/2 to 10 YR 7/6).

There were no decorated sherds.

Vessel Forms

Rolled- or beaded-rim ollas had globular bodies and quite short necks with beaded lips. Rim diameter, 20–26 cm.

Long-necked ollas with flaring rims may have had loop or strap handles and flat or ring bases. Rim diameter, 26–34 cm.

Ollas with tall convergent necks and everted rims and with *medium-tall straight necks and direct rims* had rim diameters of 24–30 cm. Two *funnel-neck olla* fragments were found.

Convex-wall bowls are low vessels with flat bases. Rim diameter, 20–36 cm.

Incurved-rim bowls have rim diameters of about 30 cm.

Other forms include a flat vessel, probably a comal, and two flaring rims, probably of bowls. Vessel appendages include ring bases, strap handles, and one loop handle, all from Venta Salada components.

Relationships

El Riego Polished, despite the limited size of our sample, is a good time marker for late Palo Blanco and early Venta Salada in the Tehuacan Valley. We were unable to find any significant similarities between this Tehuacan type and pottery from other areas. A larger sample and further study of this type is needed.

Trade Wares

THIN ORANGE

117 specimens excavated, 430 collected.

Paste

Mineralogical analysis of three thin sections reveal that about 5 percent of the paste is composed of grains 0.5–1.0 mm. in diameter of quartz, quartzite, calcite, and sericite. About 10 percent consists of grains 0.1–0.5 mm. in diameter of the same materials. About 5 percent of the paste is grains under 0.1 mm. in diam-

TABLE 50
El Riego Polished Vessel Forms
(sherds by site and zone)

	Early Palo Blanco			Late Palo Blanco										
	50 VI	272 E	272 D	272 C	272 B	272 A	50 V	254 C¹	254 B	50 IV	35w 3-4	35e E	255 B	35e D
Ollas														
rolled/beaded rim														
long flaring neck														
convergent neck, everted rim				1	2	2	1							1
funnel neck														
straight neck, direct rim														
Bowls														
convex wall everted rim				1					2	1				2
direct rim	1													
flaring wall	1	1												
incurved rim				1								1		
Comal														
Flat bases														1
Ring bases														
Strap handles														
Loop handle														
Body sherds	14	2	4	6	4	30	10	1	14	16	7	43	34	49
Total	16	3	4	9	6	32	11	1	16	17	7	44	34	53

	Early Venta Salada							Late Venta Salada					Total
	35e C	255 A	50 III	35e B	35w 3	50 II	35w 2	35w 1	367 B	50 I	367 A	35e A	
Ollas													
Rolled/beaded rim	6			8				1				6	21
long flaring neck	3		1	1						4		2	11
convergent neck, everted rim													6
funnel neck								1					2
straight neck, direct rim	1						1						2
Bowls													
convex wall everted rim													6
direct rim			2	2									5
flaring wall													2
incurved rim													2
Comal							1						1
Flat bases					2		4	2					9
Ring bases				2									2
Strap handles				3							2		5
Loop handle				1									1
Body sherds	135	36	5	157	64	18	51	59	1	3	10	41	814
Total	145	36	8	174	66	18	57	63	1	9	10	49	889

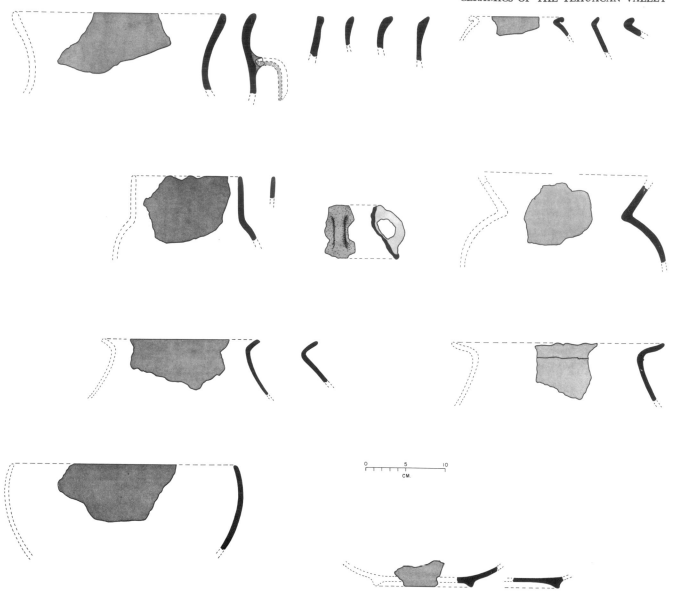

FIG. 102. EL RIEGO POLISHED. *Row 1:* ollas with long flaring necks and rolled-rim ollas; *row 2:* straight-neck ollas, fragment with loop handle, funnel-neck olla; *row 3:* convergent-neck ollas with everted rims; *row 4:* incurved-rim bowl and ring-base fragments.

eter, including magnetite, hematite, quartzite, quartz, calcite, and rarely pyroxenes and feldspar. Macroscopically, the orange paste is speckled with white, shows a laminated tendency, and reveals in cross section a few lines of porosity that could be coil breaks. The ring bases were obviously applied to the bodies as separate units. Generally speaking, the paste is well knit and compact. Hardness averages about 4.0.

Surface Finish

Most sherds have a well-defined slip that has been smoothed or lightly polished. Surface color ranges from orange to reddish-yellow (5 YR 6/6–8/4).

Decoration

Decoration is usually applied by means of shallow

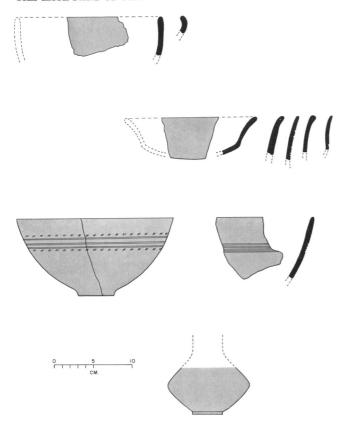

FIG. 103. THIN ORANGE. *From top to bottom,* convex-wall bowls with direct and incurved rims, composite-silhouette bowl, deep convex-wall bowl with ring base, bottle with ring base.

incisions. Less than half the sherds are decorated, always on the outer surface well below the rim. The most common decoration consists of two to five encircling lines. Sometimes dots occur above and below the lines. In a few cases a row of dots is used instead of encircling lines. The decorated examples are all from late Palo Blanco levels.

Vessel Forms

Fairly deep convex-wall bowls with ring bases predominate among the excavated sample; they have rim diameters of 18–24 cm. and were 8–16 cm. high. Sometimes the rims become incurved. There is one flaring-rim sherd from excavation, but more were collected, as well as sherds representing vessels with a composite silhouette. A few small bottles with squat bodies and ring bases also were collected. Two early Palo Blanco excavated examples are cylindrical vessels and probably had slab feet.

A Thin Orange vessel Noguera found in Tomb 2 at Tehuacan had nubbin feet on a cylindrical body (1940: pl. XII*b*). Evidently a variety of cylindrical vessels occurred in Tombs 1 and 2, with cylindrical, rectangular, and stepped supports. Noguera found as well pot covers and effigy vessels.

Relationships

Recent mineralogical studies of Thin Orange by Alfredo Sotomayor (Sotomayor and Castillo 1963) reveal that all examples of this type were not manufac-

TABLE 51
Late Palo Blanco Trade Sherds
(by site and zone)

	272 C	272 B	272 A	50 V	254 B	50 IV	35w 3-4	35e E	255 B	35e D	Total
San Martin Fresco-decorated: bodies			1								1
San Martin Incised: bodies					3		1				4
San Martin Stamped: bodies		1					1			1	3
Thin Orange: bodies	2	1			8	1	3	8	4	22	49
convex-wall bowls	4	1	2		2			2		12	23
flaring-wall bowls								1			1
cylindrical jar								2			2
ring bases							2	1		9	12
Texcoco Fabric-impressed: bodies				1			2		2		5
Total	6	3	3	1	13	1	9	14	6	44	100

tured at a single location. However, subgroups 1 and 2 of the Group A subtype seem to have been made in the general area of southern Puebla. The Tehuacan Thin Orange examples belong to these two subgroups. Sotomayor's thin-section studies reveal that during the Classic period these two subgroups were sent to Teotihuacan, Tepexpan, San Lorenzo, and Chalco in the Valley of Mexico; San Marcos and Calpulalpan in Tlaxcala; Culhuacan, Muacatlan, Morelos, Tulancingo, Hidalgo, and Nanahuatipan in Puebla; Napatecuhtlan and Remojadas in Veracruz; Monte Alban in Oaxaca; and Kaminaljuyu in Guatemala. Thus we have an excellent trait linking these various archaeological manifestations.

Other Trade Wares

Sherds of San Martin Stamped of Teotihuacan II to IV (Miccaotli to Metepec) were found in three different late Palo Blanco components. One San Martin Fresco-decorated sherd indicates ties with Teotihuacan IIa to III (Tlamimilolpa to Xolalpan) (see Tolstoy 1958: graph 3). Other Valley of Mexico types in late Palo Blanco components are San Martin Incised and Texcoco Fabric-impressed.

Miscellaneous Objects

One unperforated disk of Quachilco Mica is 5 cm. in diameter. Two perforated disks measure about 4 cm. in diameter. A whistle with an interior pellet and the form of a long-snouted rodent (Fig. 105) came from Tc 35e, zone D. Two well-polished fragments of feet from a large seated figure probably came from an incense burner.

Figurines

UGLY BABY FACE HEAD

1 head excavated.
Dimensions of head in cm.: height, 3.6; width, 3.6; maximum thickness, 2.4.
Paste: resembles El Riego Orange.
Surface finish: slipped and polished.

The face is wide and flat; the flatness is partly due to the fact that the nose has been broken or has worn off. The lips are raised slightly above the level of the face and the mouth is incised. At the corners of the mouth are two small punctations filled with red paint. Above the upper lip an incised line curves downward at each end. The whites of the eyes are shallow impressions and the pupil is a deep punctation. One eye is outlined by incising. Eyebrows are curved incised lines. A sim-

FIG. 104. UGLY BABY FACE, TEOTIHUACAN, AND TLALOC HEADS.

ple headdress comes down over the ears. There is a deep punctation on each side of the head where the face and ear meet.

This head from the Tehuacan Valley occurs in a late Palo Blanco context. No similar heads have been reported from other parts of Mexico.

TEOTIHUACAN HEADS

3 heads: 1 fragment excavated, 2 collected.
Dimensions in cm. of one head: height, 3.9; width, 3.5; thickness, 0.8.
Paste: Thin Orange.

These mold-made figurines are quite small. The faces are complex and carefully composed. The most complete head has an open mouth emphasized by an oval ridge of clay and beaklike nose which is part of the mouth. Curved ridges outline upper and lower eyelids. Above each eye a pair of crescent-shaped ridges form the brows. Above the face, two bands filled with radiating lines probably represent a headdress. At the sides of the head are flat round earplugs and along the chin is a row of raised balls. The other describable head has the same kind of eyes and headdress, but the lower part of the face is missing.

This figurine type appears in late Palo Blanco components in the Tehuacan Valley and is typical of the Teotihuacan IV or Metepec period in the Valley of Mexico (Vaillant 1966: fig. 14). Similar figurines occur in Monte Alban III (Caso and Bernal 1965: fig. 18) and at Cerro de las Mesas (Drucker 1943b: pl. 49c).

Teotihuacan Tlaloc Head

1 head collected.
Dimensions in cm.: height, 4.5; width, 4.0; thickness, 1.8.
Paste: El Riego Orange.

This mold-made head is round in outline. The back is concave and the front convex. It has a large mouth filled with teeth and fangs at the corners. The nose is broken off. The eyes are like goggles and are encircled by curved lines. There are faint radiating impressions on the forehead.

The head was collected from a surface site attributable to the late Classic period. It resembles figurines from Teotihuacan III (Xolalpan) in the Valley of Mexico.

Classic Plain-frock Figures

6 bodies: 1 excavated, 5 collected.
Dimensions in cm.: length, 6.0–10.0; maximum width, 3.0–6.0; thickness, 1.0–2.0.
Paste: resembles crude orange or El Riego Gray.

These body fragments are flat like gingerbread men. Some are mold made. Because they are straight-sided and almost devoid of body contours, they appear to be wearing long plain frocks. Arms either continue more or less straight to the hips or are bent and rest against the front of the body about at waist level. One specimen has fingers indicated by incised lines. Another figurine has flat rectangular feet which extend at right angles from the body and were obviously designed to make the figurine stand up. The two bodies with bent arms have small nubbin breasts and a hole punched through the body under each arm.

These body fragments occur in the Classic period in the Tehuacan Valley and bear resemblances to figurines found in Teotihuacan II–III and in Monte Alban III (Caso and Bernal 1965: fig. 18). They seem to be ancestral to the Postclassic Plain and Decorated Frock figures.

Ceramic Affiliations

Many traits of late Palo Blanco are carried over from the early part of the phase. Quachilco Mica, El Riego Gray, and El Riego Black continue relatively unchanged through both parts of the phase. El Riego Orange, El Riego Plain, and El Riego Polished, all of which originated in early Palo Blanco, reach their greatest popularity in late Palo Blanco.

As the following chapter will show, the ceramics indicate that Palo Blanco developed into Venta Salada, even though something happened to Venta Salada ceramics to make them significantly different from the Palo Blanco wares.

The indications of external relationships of the Palo Blanco pottery are more important than the relationships within the valley. The first report of scientific archaeological endeavors in Tehuacan, ironically enough, yielded evidence of external relationships characteristic of the late part of our Palo Blanco phase.

FIG. 105. CLASSIC PLAIN-FROCK FIGURES and an effigy whistle.

Noguera (1940) uncovered two late Classic tombs near the Calvario in the west side of the town of Tehuacan. He found a large number of pots, most of which he considered to be either Zapotec or Teotihuacan types. Examples of these "Teotihuacan" wares are all Thin Orange of several varieties. Noguera reported (pp. 309–310):

Vessels of thin orange ware predominate, with incised and carved designs. There are also bowls of the same ware with cylindrical legs and vases of artistic value having smooth sides and crenellated legs and the base surrounded with tiny little heads, a detail typical of Teotihuacan. Two of these boast a sculpture in the round, one of a tiger, another of a monkey. Common also are small vases, with flat bottoms and conical or cylindrical legs, equipped with covers, as well as cups of brown ware, bowls of cream ware with a finely polished cerise slip, and others of less archaeological signficance and inferior artistic value.

Some of the vessels of "inferior artistic value" are Thin Orange convex-wall bowls with ring bases like specimens from most of our late Palo Blanco components.

Other indications of connections with Teotihuacan from our investigations were three San Martin Stamped sherds diagnostic of Teotihuacan II–IV (Tolstoy 1958: 16–35). These sherds came from three separate components. A San Martin Fresco-decorated sherd, diagnostic of Teotihuacan IIa–III, was found in a fourth component.

Besides the actual trade sherds from Teotihuacan, we have in late Palo Blanco a resident type, El Riego Black, which is closely related to the Teotihuacan type, San Martin Incised. El Riego Orange of late Palo Blanco shows similarities to San Martin Orange Plain of Teotihuacan. Two mold-made figurine head types of late Palo Blanco are Teotihuacan III–IV types.

Besides these specific links between the Valley of Mexico and Tehuacan in late Classic times, a number of horizon styles are common to both, including cylindrical vessels; cylindrical vessels with slab, hollow rectangular, bulb, or nubbin feet and pot covers; bridged spouts; mold-made figurines; hemiconical vessels with ring bases; and flat-based funnel-neck ollas.

As is perhaps obvious, the so-called Teotihuacan horizon at Cholula is also related to late Palo Blanco. The Classic incised black sherds collected at Cholula in 1962 by members of the Tehuacan Project (as well as the ones described by Noguera 1954: 183-196) are related to, if not the same type as, El Riego Black.

Late Palo Blanco also shares relationships with Monte Alban III. Associated with the Teotihuacan vessels in the tombs in Tehuacan excavated by Noguera(1940: 308, 309) were, "vessels of the purest Zapotec style of black or grey ware ... including ollas with two vertical spouts, simple ollas, small vases with the God Tlaloc in relief, and bowls with incised and painted decoration." Some of the gray ware Noguera uncovered from the tombs was El Riego Gray, typical of both parts of the Palo Blanco phase. The resemblance of El Riego Gray to some of the gray ware of Monte Alban III, as well as the similarity of El Riego Black to Type G. 35 of Monte Alban and the presence of feathered-headdress figurines in both late Palo Blanco and Monte Alban III, leave little doubt that the two manifestations are closely related.

In the late Classic period the presence in many regions of two types, Thin Orange and San Martin Stamped, allow one temporally to equate a whole series of cultural manifestations. Thin Orange in late Palo Blanco, Teotihuacan I–IV (Sotomayor and Castillo 1963), Cholula II(Noguera 1954), Remojadas II, Tajin II–III, the Cerro de las Mesas and Cerro de las Conchas phases of southern Veracruz, Monte Alban III, Chiapa de Corzo VIII–X (Lowe and Mason 1965), Tzakol at Uaxactun, Manik at Tikal in Guatemala, phase 1 of the Early Period in Yucatan (Smith and Gifford 1965), Barton Ramie in British Honduras, Copan in Honduras, Esperanza in Guatemala City, and the San Francisco phase (Thompson 1948: fig. 27e) of the Pacific coast of Guatemala indicate that they all overlap in time. San Martin Stamped also serves to link late Palo Blanco and Teotihuacan II–IV, Zaquil of the Huasteca (Ekholm 1944), Eslabones of the Sierra de Tamaulipas (MacNeish 1958), Tajin II–III of Veracruz (Du Solier 1945, Medellín Zenil 1960), Monte Alban III of Oaxaca, Cerro de las Mesas, Manik of Tikal, San Francisco of coastal Guatemala (Parsons 1967: 140), and Esperanza of Guatemala City (Kidder, Jennings, and Shook 1946).

The San Martin Fresco-decorated type appears in Teotihuacan IIa–IV, Monte Alban III, and Esperanza, as well as in late Palo Blanco. Thus Palo Blanco is linked with a number of cultural manifestations throughout Mesoamerica during the general period A.D. 200–700.

176

CHAPTER 9

The Early Part of the Venta Salada Phase

THE EARLY PART of the Venta Salada phase is represented by 4,222 sherds recovered from seven components: Zone C of Tc 35e, Zone A of Tc 255, Zone III of Tc 50, Zone B of Tc 35e, Level 3 of Tc 35w, Zone II of Tc 50, and Level 2 of Tc 35w. Although this is a better sample of sherds than was available from the late part of the Palo Blanco phase, it is unbalanced because all seven components are cave occupations. We did, however, examine 11,218 sherds from about ninety surface sites.

Most of the Palo Blanco ceramic types—El Riego Gray, El Riego Plain, El Riego Polished, Quachilco Mica, and El Riego Black—persist in this period as minority wares. However, they are all on the wane. More important in early Venta Salada are the new types: Coxcatlan Gray, Coxcatlan Brushed, Teotitlan Incised, El Riego Marble-tempered, Coxcatlan Red, and Coxcatlan Red-on-orange. In addition, spindle whorls, new types of figurines, and *xantiles* or effigy ollas are added to the artifact, settlement pattern, and subsistence traits that compose the Venta Salada cultural phase.

Perhaps as significant as the new types themselves, however, is the addition of a complex of new ceramic attributes. These new attributes include mold-made vessels, stamped and incised tripod molcajetes, red-on-orange (or buff) bichrome pottery; polychrome decoration; dumbbell, stamped stepped, and effigy feet; xantiles; Mixtec-type ladles and censers; pedestal-based vessels; and spindle whorls. These horizon styles appear suddenly in many regions of Mesoamerica about this time (roughly A.D. 700–1100). Whether these ceramic elements can be correlated with, or are part of, the Mixteca-Puebla religious and ceremonial (and political?) complex, which diffused over a wide area from Honduras to Sinaloa at this period, remains to be seen.

Certainly the Venta Salada ceramic complex is not just the result of internal developments and a few ceramic attributes that spread into the Tehuacan Valley. One cannot help but feel that the new ceramic features are material reflections of a great social—that is, economic, political, and perhaps religious—upheaval that occurred not only in southeast Puebla but throughout Mesoamerica. The whole area became unified for the first time into a true culture area. Obviously, the exact nature of this social upheaval cannot be determined by a study of the ceramics, but it poses a problem worthy of intensive investigation.

Of the pottery types occurring earlier and previously described, El Riego Gray becomes less popular in early Venta Salada and begins to fade into a new type, Coxcatlan Gray. Other El Riego wares—Black, Orange, Plain, and Polished—are dying out as new types replace them. Quachilco Mica continues into the Venta Salada phase and undergoes a number of changes consistent with Postclassic horizon styles. In the middle of the phase it gradually gives rise to and is replaced by Coxcatlan Coarse.

A few sherds of large painted Xantiles, Coxcatlan Polychrome, Coxcatlan Red-on-cream, and Coxcatlan Coarse were found in early Venta Salada components, but since these wares are more numerous in late Venta Salada, they will be described in Chapter 10.

Pottery Types

EL RIEGO MARBLE-TEMPERED

1,354 specimens excavated, 1,618 collected.

Paste

The major tempering materials, according to three sherds analyzed in thin section, are marble, quartz, chlorite, basalt, and sericite. About 5 percent of the paste is grains 1.0–2.0 mm. in diameter. About 10 percent is grains 0.5–1.0 mm. in diameter. Another 10 percent is grains 0.1–0.5 mm. in diameter of the aforementioned materials plus small amounts of hornblende and biotite. About 5 percent of the paste is grains under 0.1 mm. in diameter of the same materials and traces of magnetite, calcite, and labradorite.

The paste is not well knit, is porous, and has a blocky appearance. A couple of long rim sherds are broken parallel to the lip, perhaps along coil marks. The sherds have a soapy feel that may be the result of the marble and chlorite temper. The sherds seem to have been evenly fired, with cores only slightly darker in color than the surfaces. Hardness ranges between 2.5 and 3.0.

Surface Finish

Surface color ranges from mahogany brown (10 R 4/2) to pale cream (2.5 YR 6/6). Ollas are polished on the outside, but not inside. Flaring-wall bowls are polished on both surfaces. Convex-wall bowls or plates are usually polished on the interior and the uppermost portion of the outer rim, with the rest of the exterior horizontally brushed or roughened. A few fragments of these bowls had no polishing on the exterior at all. Some of the roughening seems to be the result of setting the outer surface against some sort of irregular surface. The polished surface seems to have been

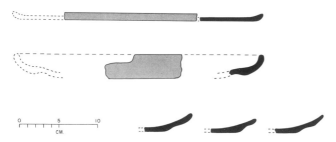

FIG. 106. EL RIEGO MARBLE-TEMPERED. Comales and low convex-wall bowls.

uniformly rubbed with a stick or polishing pebble in a circular motion. Since few polishing strokes show, vessels must have been polished when the clay was thoroughly dry. There is no decoration.

Vessel Forms

Low convex-wall bowls or comales comprise the bulk of marble-tempered vessels. They have flat bottoms that are smaller in diameter than the rim diameter. A few of the vessels have rims that curve slightly inward. Dimensions in cm.: rim diameter, 19–38; depth, probably not over 5.0.

Comales or plates are flatter versions of the previous shape, with very short outsloping rims that appear to be continuations of the large flat bottoms. Dimensions in cm.: rim diameter, 22–34, perhaps even larger; depth, about 2.0.

Flaring-wall bowls have flat bottoms and are not very deep. Dimensions in cm.: rim diameter, 19–26; depth, about 7.0.

Straight-neck ollas have relatively short necks and rim diameters of about 20 cm. One *angle-neck olla* has a short outsloping rim rising at an angle from the shoulder and a rim diameter of 18 cm.

Relationships

Although El Riego Marble-tempered first occurred in Palo Blanco, it is mainly an early Venta Salada diagnostic type that lasts into late Venta Salada times. The most important attribute of the type is the *comal* form. The rise of this type in the Postclassic period reflects the resurgence of plates or comales, which have not been very popular since late Santa Maria times. This trend toward a resurgence of comales also occurs in the Valley of Mexico (Tolstoy 1958) and Oaxaca (Paddock 1966). In fact, one could well consider the prevalence of comales with brushed exterior surfaces a Postclassic horizon style in central Mexico.

The El Riego Marble-tempered type in terms of vessel form, lack of decoration, and kinds of interior and exterior surface finish, is very similar to the Postclassic Texcoco Brown and Dark Brown comales of the Valley of Mexico Burnished Ware (Tolstoy 1958: 38).

COXCATLAN BRUSHED

28,699 specimens excavated; 15,428 collected.

Coxcatlan Brushed is one of our largest and most inclusive types. It should be restudied to refine the classification into two or more types that will be more sensitive temporally. In spite of the considerable range

TABLE 52
El Riego Marble-tempered Vessel Forms
(sherds by site and zone)

	Early Palo Blanco		Late Palo Blanco										Early Venta Salada		
	50 VI	272 D	272 C	272 B	272 A	50 V	254 B	50 IV	35w 3-4	35e E	255 B	35e D	35e C	255 A	50 III
Bowls															
low convex/comales	2		6	1	1			2				5	18	9	6
flaring wall													1	2	1
basal flange															
Comales															
Ollas															
short str. neck														1	
angle neck													1		
Flat bases															
Body sherds	1	1				1	3		1	13	3	28	68	49	5
Total	3	1	6	1	1	1	3	2	1	13	3	33	88	61	12

	Early Venta Salada (*cont'd*)				Late Venta Salada									Total
	35e B	35w 3	50 II	35w 2	35w 1	367 B	50 I	367 A	368e A	35e A	368w A	62 A	65 A	
Bowls														
low convex/comales	21	6	10	6	14	2	11	46	2	13	78	63	5	327
flaring wall	1				1			2		2	1			11
basal flange											1			1
Comales					1						12		1	14
Ollas														
short str. neck	2													3
angle neck														1
Flat bases		2		2	1							30		35
Body sherds	43	10	2	10	13	15	4	138	83	33	131	307		962
Total	67	18	12	18	30	17	15	186	85	48	223	400	6	1354

in the color of the brushed surface of this ware and despite the variety of decorative and vessel form attributes, we assumed during our macroscopic examination that the paste and temper were uniform. When the petrographic analysis of sherds in thin section was finally completed and showed differences in the composition of the paste, it was too late to re-analyze the type to see if it could be subdivided. Although our present classification accurately describes the sherds uncovered and groups them into a dominant type that is diagnostic of the entire Venta Salada phase, it is unfortunately of little use in delineating ceramic changes within that phase.

Paste

The tempering matter seems to fall into three or four similar groups, all of which contain quartzite, biotite, and plagioclase. One sherd studied in thin section included as well muscovite, hornblende, quartz, magnetite, and hematite; 10 percent of this sherd was grains 0.1–0.5 mm. in diameter, 8 percent was grains under 0.1 mm. in diameter, and only 3 percent was grains over 0.5 mm. in size. A second sherd analyzed lacked the hornblende of the previous sherd; 10 percent of this sherd was grains under 0.1 mm. in diameter, 5 percent was grains 0.1–0.5 mm. in diameter, while only 1 percent was grains over 0.5 mm. in diameter. A third sherd contained the three materials common to all sherds plus calcite; 10 percent of the grains in this paste were over 0.1 mm. in diameter. Further thin-section analysis might reveal still other kinds of tempering matter, as a few sherds display small specks of limestone and sherd temper.

Although a small proportion of the sherds are poor-

TABLE 53
Coxcatlan Brushed Decorated Sherds
(by site and zone)

	Early Venta Salada					Late Venta Salada		
	35e C	50 III	35e B	35w 3	50 II	35w 1	367 B	50 1
Crosshatched, interior walls and bottoms								
convex-wall, everted-rim bowls				1				
incurved-rim bowls			1		1	1		
carinated or inangled-rim bowls	1		1					1
indeterminate bowl forms	2		1	2				
Stamped interior bottoms								
convex wall, direct rim bowls	2		10	6	2	8	3	1
convex wall, out-angled rim bowls		20	20		1			
convex wall, everted rim bowls								
indeterminate bowl forms		1	5	3	1	1	2	1
Total	5	21	38	12	5	10	5	3

	Late Venta Salada (continued)						
	367 A	368e A	35e A	368w A	62 A	65 A	Total
Crosshatched, interior walls and bottoms							
convex-wall, everted-rim bowls	1				5	1	8
incurved-rim bowls	3	1	1	6	19	1	34
carinated or inangled-rim bowls	1	2		2	16	2	26
indeterminate bowl forms	3				449		457
Stamped interior bottoms							
convex wall, direct rim bowls	88	9	80	249	1625	51	2134
convex wall, out-angled rim bowls	5		2		600		648
convex wall, everted rim bowls	1			6	17	2	26
indeterminate bowl forms	44	7	15	45	570	37	732
Total	146	19	98	308	3301	94	4065

ly knit and masses of the tempering material tend to cling together, most of the clay is well kneaded but remains porous.

Many of the convex-wall bowls with modified rims were made on convex pottery molds. These include both the stamped-bottomed *molcajetes* and many, if not all, of the more delicate bowls without stamped bottoms. The convex molds (often of the Coxcatlan Striated type) not only had intaglio molcajete designs on the flat outer bottom surface but also had deeply incised sides, obviously to keep them from sticking to the overlying paste. The molds did not have the central handle or "stem" of the "mushroom" molds described by Foster (1948, 1955), nor is there evidence that any pots were molded in vertical halves.

After a round layer of Coxcatlan Brushed paste was shaped over the mold, the lips of the bowl being formed must have been everted so that the dried bowl could be pried loose. When the newly shaped bowl was removed, the markings left by the striations of the mold were wiped smooth, and the surface was painted. On some of the wiped inner walls, however, faint ridges remain reflecting the mold's crisscross or cobweb-like incisions. Also, a few fragments of Coxcatlan Brushed show similar impressions on exterior surfaces, indicating that some vessels must have been formed in concave molds rather than over convex ones.

The firing of this ware was even, with little difference in color between core and periphery. The usual color is light brown to tan, but occasionally is reddish- to yellow-brown. The sherds are quite hard, about 4.0 in the Mohs scale.

Surface Finish

Surfaces were smoothed and painted. Coloration varies within a blackish-brown to brown to red range.

The firing considerably changed the color of the paint as is shown by a nearly complete range of hues and tones on a single large sherd: light red, reddish-gray (2.5 YR 6/4–4/2), red and brownish-red (10 R 4/6–6/8), dark reddish-gray (10 R 4/1–4/2). The light brown paste usually shows through, making it difficult to determine the exact surface tone.

The finish varies according to vessel form. Bowls are usually painted on both surfaces, generally in the same color. Ollas are painted on the exterior and on the interior of the rim only. There are occasional firing clouds of red to dark reddish-gray or light brown, especially when the surface has a reddish hue. On both surfaces the body color often shows through in horizontal streaks with swirled ends, showing that the paint was probably applied with a fiber brush or a coarse cloth that left multiple parallel striations on the surface.

In general, two tones appear on this pottery, a brown and a red. This led at first to a tentative classification as two trial types. However, there turned out to be no significant temporal difference between the two categories. Often both tones are present on the same sherd, so the two trial types merged into one.

Decoration

The major form of decoration is molcajete stampings and incisions. These will be described below and

TABLE 54
Coxcatlan Brushed Vessel Forms
(sherds by site and zone)

	Early Palo Blanco	Late Palo Blanco								Early Venta Salada			
	51 A-B	272 C	272 B	272 A	50 V	254 B	50 IV	35w 3-4	35e E	35e C	255 A	50 III	35c B
Bowls													
convex wall													
direct rim										2			10
flaring/outangled rim											5	9	31
with stamped bottoms												20	20
large, everted rim													4
incurved rim												1	2
carinated rim										6		1	9
outsloping wall												1	3
flaring wall										23		1	
composite silhouette													2
recurved rim													
Ollas													
long str. neck, everted rim													2
short flaring neck			1								1		2
angle neck											1		
miscellaneous													
long flaring neck													
Cylindrical vessels													
Plates/comales													
Strainer/censer													
Flat bases										2		1	25
Strap handles				1						3			2
Supports													
serpent													
stepped													1
dumbbell													
conical													
old man													
Body sherds	4	14	19	10	1	3	3	1	2	65	7	12	135
Total	4	14	20	11	1	3	3	1	2	101	14	46	248

(Table continued)

(Table 54, continued)

	Early Venta Salada (continued)			Late Venta Salada									Total
	35w 3	50 II	35w 2	35w 1	367 B	50 I	367 A	368e A	35e A	368w A	62 A	65 A	
Bowls													
convex wall													
direct rim	6	2	2	8	3	1	99	9	80	291	1636	42	2,191
flaring/outangled rim	10	4	9	4	4	3	61	8	2	151	126	16	443
with stamped bottoms		1					5		2		600		648
large, everted rim	1	1			1		50		6	210	665	19	957
incurved rim	1	1	3	8			32	7	2	61	489	8	615
carinated rim		1	3			2	33	7		18	278	49	407
outsloping wall			1				4			11	117	4	141
flaring wall	1		1	3			23	1			8	2	63
composite silhouette							2			1	5	1	11
recurved rim			1				3				1		5
Ollas													
long str. neck, everted rim	1			2			25		3	8	491	12	544
short flaring neck			6				1			17	1	1	30
angle neck							1			9	9	1	21
miscellaneous				2			5			2	3	2	14
long flaring neck											9		9
Cylindrical vessels	1		4				1				5	1	12
Plates/comales							1			1	5		7
Strainer/censer											2		2
Flat bases	13	1	14	1	10	1	202	97	19	277	1792	51	2,506
Strap handles		2			2		144	2	2	18	794	9	979
Supports													
serpent						1	2	1	1	9	98	23	135
stepped					1	2	6	3	1	2	59	24	99
dumbbell							4			22	33	2	61
conical					2		3		1	3	2	5	16
old man							2				8		10
Body sherds	56	25	52	80	23	17	1401	509	431	1025	14857	21	18,773
Total	90	38	96	108	46	27	2110	644	550	2136	22093	293	28.699

are illustrated in Figs. 112 and 113. Bowl-shaped molds are decorated over the interior or on both surfaces with linear incisions in a crisscross pattern.

Vessel Forms

The forms, at first glance, appear to be numerous, but upon analysis are reduced to a few basic forms with variations in rim and lip shapes. The great majority are shallow to medium deep bowls, many of which are molcajetes with decorative roughened interiors against which chili peppers or other substances could be ground. A few early Venta Salada bowls and many late Venta Salada ones were footed. Some bowls have horizontal lugs about midway down the wall.

Convex-wall bowls with direct rims number over 2,100 examples. These bowls have flat bottoms. Most lips are rounded, but a few are flat or internally beveled and have a narrow horizontal groove on the lip or exterior surface of the rim. Some of these vessels have incised interior surfaces. A large proportion have a stamped design covering the interior bottom. No supports were found attached to this kind of vessel. Dimensions in cm.: rim diameter, 10–24; height, 2.7–6.5.

Convex-wall bowls with flaring or outangled rims are represented by over 1,000 examples. They have flat bottoms. The rims are slightly outangled or outcurved. Over 600 of the interior bottoms are stamped. None were incised. A number of sherds show remains of attached supports. In the early part of the Venta Salada phase this was the most popular vessel form in

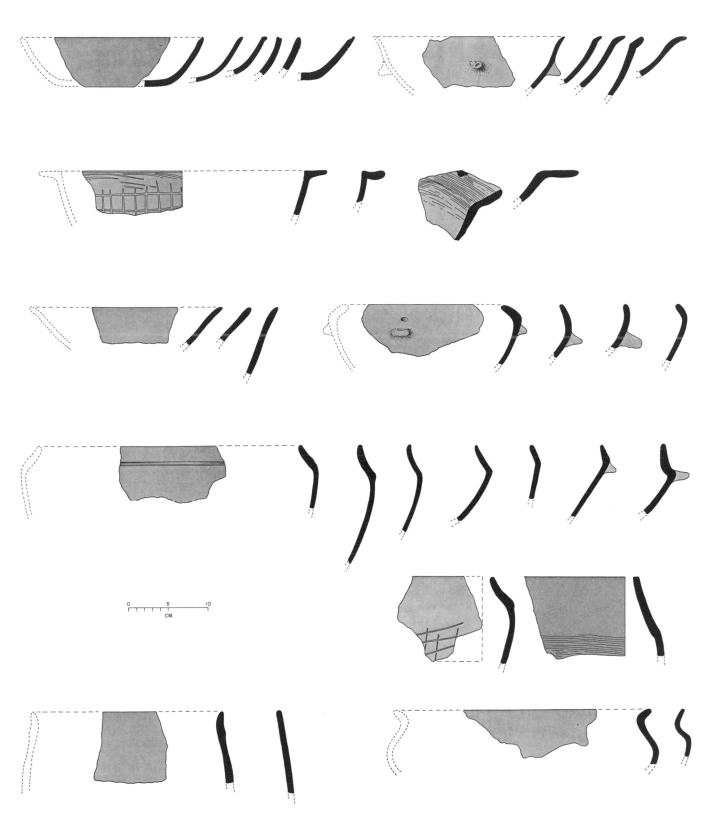

Fig. 107. Coxcatlan Brushed. *Row 1:* convex-wall bowls with direct or grooved rims and with flaring or outangled rims: *row 2:* bowls with wide everted rims; *row 3:* flaring-wall and incurved-rim bowls; *rows 4, 5:* carinated-rim bowls; *row 6:* cylindrical vessels and bowls with recurved rims.

5 cm.

FIG. 108. COXCATLAN BRUSHED. Olla and bowls.

this paste. Dimensions in cm.: rim diameter, usually 12–32, with some 40–48; wall height, over 5.0–over 8.0.

Large convex-wall bowls with everted rims are common in late Venta Salada components, but are rare in earlier ones. They were fairly deep and had small flat bottoms. Rims are horizontally everted, with tapered or rounded lips. Most of the examples have rims between 2.0 and 4.0 cm. wide, but seven quite large bowls have rims that range in width from 4.8 to 8.5 cm. Exterior surfaces and the upper surface of the rim are covered with streaky paint, but interior surfaces are unpainted. Most of the interiors are smooth, but some examples are deeply incised with crisscross lines. A few have stamped bottoms. Dimensions in cm.: rim diameter, 24–40; height, 7.5–10.0; width of rim, 2.2–3.2; rim thickness, 0.8–1.3; body thickness, 0.5–0.9.

Deep incurved rim bowls probably had flat bottoms. The incurved portion of the rim is fairly short, compared with the over-all wall height. Flat, horizontal, elliptical lugs are placed on the exterior, below the point where the wall begins to curve inward. The junction between rim and body is rounded on the exterior and tends to be grooved on the interior, but these bowls blend into the carinated shape described below. A few sherds have deeply incised crosshatching on the interior. The rim is often thicker than the body. Dimensions in cm.: rim diameter, 8–32; body diameter, 10–37; rim height, 1.0–3.3; wall thickness, 0.4–1.1.

Carinated-rim bowls have flat or elliptical bottoms. The sides are convex, and the rim slants sharply inward and is often concave. A pronounced horizontal ridge or keel marks the junction between rim and body on the exterior; on the interior there is a horizon-

5 CM.

FIG. 109. COXCATLAN BRUSHED. Molcajete sherds and fragments of a strainer vessel and a large pipe.

tal groove. Some bowls have lugs at the junction of rim and body. The interior of the vessel is either smooth or scored by deep prefiring incisions in cross-hatched motifs covering the entire interior up to the junction of the body with the rim. The bodies appear to have been quite deep, but the exact proportions are unknown, as no complete profile was found. Dimensions in cm.: rim diameter, 14–34; rim height, 2.5–4.3; body diameter, 16–38; wall thickness, 0.3–1.0. One rare specimen had the following dimensions: rim diameter, 8.0; rim height, 1.6; body diameter, 9.5; wall thickness, 0.4–0.6.

Outsloping-wall bowls have direct rims with beveled or rounded lips. Bottoms were flat. No decoration was noted. Rim diameter, 16–32 cm.

Flaring-rim bowls have a faintly convex lower wall. Lips are flattish to rounded. Rim diameter, 24–32 cm.

Cylindrical vessels have either vertical or slightly convergent walls. Lips are rounded, flat, beveled, or thickened. No bottoms were found. Rim diameter, 10–28 cm.

Composite-silhouette vessels have a squat convex base, an inslanted wall, and a concave or vertical rim. Rim diameter, 8–30 cm.

Bowls with recurved rims have rather squat convex bodies and rims that turn inward then curve outward. Some examples have a ridge on the outer surface where the rim joins the body. Rim diameter, 26–32 cm.

Ollas with straight necks and everted rims are a typical Postclassic olla shape. Unfortunately, no body fragments were attached to the neck sherds, so that the complete olla profile is unknown. The necks are usually quite tall and vertical with fairly wide horizontally everted rims and rounded lips. Some of these ollas may have had supports, probably of the dumb-

185

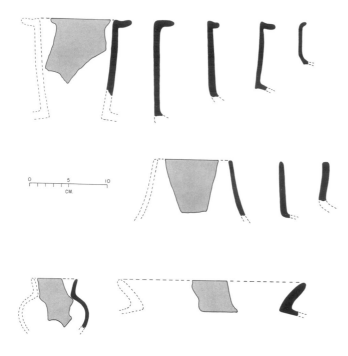

FIG. 110. COXCATLAN BRUSHED. *From top to bottom,* ollas with tall straight necks and everted rims, ollas with convergent or straight necks and direct rims, miniature and angle-neck ollas.

bell variety. Dimensions in cm.: rim diameter, 6.0–16; neck height, 5.0–13.5; rim width, 0.7–3.1

Ollas with short flaring necks usually range in rim diameter between 12 and 14 cm.

Angle-neck ollas have short necks slanting outward at an angle to the shoulder. Rim diameter, 20–24 cm.

Miscellaneous ollas or bottles have rim diameters of 10–12 cm. Several of these are straight-necked fragments with direct rims; others have convergent rims or undulating lips and may be fragments of pouring spouts. Several sherds represent ollas with long flaring necks. A miniature olla of this shape has a rim diameter of 6.0 cm. and a neck height of 2.0 cm.

Small plates or pot covers are miniature shapes with a slightly upcurved rim. Rim diameter, 9.1–12 cm.

Strainer vessels have perforations in the body. Although only two examples were excavated, a number of fragments were collected from surface sites. These probably are the typical Mixtec *incensarios* found throughout Postclassic Mexico. One fragment suggests that the vessels rested on two feet and a long cylindrical handle.

Serpent effigy supports are conical and hollow except for the head at the lower end. An irregular hole

jabbed through the upper portion, usually in the back but sometimes on the sides or front, allowed steam to escape during firing. Some supports also contained a rattling pellet. They most often appear on flat-bottomed bowls with convex walls and direct or short outangled rims. The face tends to be anthropomorphic. The large lidded eyes are the most prominent feature; some are hollow pits and others have a round ball for a pupil. Sometimes a very regular row of teeth is depicted in the open mouth, but no fangs are shown. The configuration of the nose is more mammalian than ophidian; in fact, some of the heads look more like parrots, turtles, seals, barracudas, or otters than serpents. These supports, although similar to other serpent shapes in Postclassic pottery, tend to rest on the tip of the chin rather than on the flat underside of the head (cf. Caso, Bernal, and Acosta 1967: pl. XIX). Dimensions in cm.: height, 5.9–6.5; maximum diameter, 3.1–4.2.

Stepped supports are flat, solid slabs shaped into two or more superimposed truncated triangles, giving the sides a stepped effect. This effect has been achieved either by squeezing the sides into shape or by cutting well-defined edges. Some of the supports are mold made, including fifty-two from late Venta Salada with stamped decorations. Stepped supports are generally placed at the extreme edge of the vessel and are more upright than the dumbbell type described below. They are used on flat-bottomed convex-wall bowls. A third of the supports show that the parent vessel had a plain interior; the rest were attached to bowls with stamped bottoms. Dimensions in cm.: height, 5.0–6.1; width at base, 3.2–5.4; width at top, 3.6–4.1.

Dumbbell or bulb-end supports have a conical or cylindrical body with a spherical or bulb-shaped lower end. They are found on convex-wall bowls with both stamped and plain bottoms, but were more often used on stamped-bottom vessels. They seem to have been attached as much to the side of the vessel as to the base and slant out at a wide angle from the base. Most of the supports are hollow or have hollow stems and solid bulb ends. The completely hollow ones have been perforated or slit on the side or back, generally in the midsection, but sometimes at the base of the bulb. The hole, of course, allowed steam from the firing process to escape. Dimensions in cm.: height of support, 5.2–7.2; stem diameter, 1.8–2.5; bulb diameter, 2.2–3.0.

Conical supports are hollow and have a conical profile and a round cross section. They were used on flat-

5 CM.

FIG. 111. COXCATLAN BRUSHED. *From top to bottom,* notched and pierced lugs; strap handle; stepped, dumbbell, conical, serpent-head, animal effigy, and old-man vessel supports.

bottomed bowls. Dimensions in cm.: height, 5.1–6.2; diameter at top, 3.0–3.5; base diameter, 1.4–1.6.

Old-man effigy supports have a roughly circular cross section with slightly flattened sides. The point of attachment is quite large. The stem of the support is long and terminates in an effigy head. The upper section or stem is hollow and has a small irregularly shaped perforation. Two of the supports contained rattle-pellets.

The face is that of a shrunken old man with large eye pits without pupils; shrunken, deeply grooved cheeks; a shriveled mouth, and a tiny chin or beard which is flattened at the tip to serve as the basal end of the support. Some of the heads appear to be fleshless representations of a death god, but it is more likely that this type of support represents Huehueteotl, the "Old, Old God," on an especially bad day. Dimensions in cm.: height, 6.8–7.5; diameter at top, 2.8–3.3; diameter at chin, 1.2–1.5.

Luglike support. One solid support has a conical profile and flattened sides. Dimensions in cm.: height, 2.1; length, 2.7.

Lugs are fairly common on Coxcatlan Brushed vessels and are of two main types. (1) Horizontal, long,

187

FIG. 112. Coxcatlan Brushed and Coxcatlan Gray. Stamped bottoms of molcajetes. Sherds to the left and right of stamped fragment at top are deeply incised molds.

and flat lugs are the major type and are commonly found on grater bowls. Their dimensions in cm. are: length, 4.5–9.7; width, 1.5–2.3; thickness, 0.5–2.6. A variation is vertically grooved in the middle; its dimensions are the same. (2) Vertical, elliptical lugs have a round perforation at the junction of the lug with the vessel and look like small loop handles. The perforation was made after the lug was placed on the vessel.

Strap handles made of wide flat strips, were undoubtedly used on ollas. They form an arch along the side of the vessel, but usually with one end arched higher than the other, extending from 1.5 to over 3.0 cm. from the vessel wall. Sometimes a wide but shallow groove runs the length of the outside of the handle. Dimensions in cm.: length, 3.5–8.7; width, 2.4–4.3; thickness, 0.6–1.2. One long and narrow strap handle was attached to a rim at one end; the other end was broken off. Dimensions in cm.: width, 2.6; thickness, 1.4; length, over 9.0.

Stamped bottoms. Many of the convex-wall bowls with various types of rims had flat bottoms with simple or complex designs impressed on the inner surface. The excavated sample of stamped fragments totals 732. The designs consist of raised lines in geometric patterns contained within the circular outline of the bowl. The designs are usually symmetrical, and most are divided into quadrants. The simplest design consists of quadrants of raised "V"'s within "V"'s, sometimes with an outer border of "U" motifs, which may represent plumes. More complex, probably glyphic, motifs seem to represent various kinds of facial features, birds, serpents, butterflies, trees, and other natural forms. These devices are extremely stylized, which makes their interpretation from worn fragments difficult.

The stamped bottoms vary from 10 to 14 cm. in diameter. Some show attachments for feet, but a smaller proportion of these Coxcatlan Brushed molcajetes than Coxcatlan Gray ones seem to have had supports. The raised design served as a rough surface against which chili peppers and other foods were ground.

Some of the bottoms of bowls or convex molds had designs deeply incised on the exterior surface to make the positive come out in low relief. Interior surfaces are either brushed smooth or, oddly enough, have worn stamped designs on them. Several fragmentary molds for the grater bottoms show portions of some of the very same designs that appear on our stamped fragments.

Large pipes, or fragmentary hollow cylinders, of Coxcatlan Brushed were collected from surface sites. They were evidently used to conduct water, for many have thick lime deposits on the interior. One intact end of a pipe is modified slightly so that it would fit inside another segment. None of the sample was intact in length. The diameter through the cylinder ranged from 5.7 to 7.5 cm. and the wall thickness from 0.6 to 1.8 cm.

Relationships

The Coxcatlan Brushed type appears to be new to the Tehuacan ceramic complex in Venta Salada times. The paste is not radically different from that of El Riego Plain, but surface finish, vessel forms, and decoration are entirely different. In terms of external relationships, Coxcatlan Brushed has few exact counterparts, although some Cholulteca I sherds are vaguely similar. The distinctive stamped molcajete designs are, of course, similar to stamped designs from Cholula, the Mixteca Alta, Cempoala, Isla de Sacrificios, and sites in southern Veracruz such as Cerro de las Mesas. Unfortunately the reports on these sites do not include detailed reproductions of the various stamped-bottom motifs, so comparisons are difficult to make.

During the span of Coxcatlan Brushed there are some internal changes that reflect external changes throughout the Postclassic period in many parts of Mesoamerica. Vessels without supports and the few vessels with stepped feet in the early Venta Salada sample are replaced in the latter part of the phase by vessels with effigy supports. Stamped bottoms in bowls become dominant over plain or incised bottoms. Handles and perforated censers (or strainers), absent from early levels, appear in the last part of the Venta Salada phase.

COXCATLAN GRAY

7,270 specimens excavated; 7,233 collected.

Paste

The temper is extremely fine and used in small quantity. Only 3 percent of the paste is particles 0.1–0.5 mm. in diameter, consisting of biotite, quartz, and plagioclase. The rest of the temper, accounting for about 10 percent of the paste, is under 0.1 mm. in diameter and includes the above-mentioned materials plus pyroxenes, magnetite, and hematite. Microscopic examination of some of the fine holes in the paste reveal fine fiber-like impressions which indicate that

189

FIG. 113. STAMPED BOTTOM SHERDS. The sherds at the beginning of the first three rows are molds.

fiber (perhaps cattail fluff; see Foster 1955: 8) may have been still another tempering material.

Coxcatlan Gray has a well-knit texture, but it is not so brittle or tightly knit as the earlier gray types. The paste has a chalky feel and is finely porous. There appear to be a few coil breaks in olla fragments, but many bowls were made on convex molds, as were some olla bodies.

The pottery was well fired and shows little difference in color between surface and core. Hardness of sherds averages 3.5, but ranges up to 4.0.

Surface Finish

Both inner and outer surfaces are slipped, except for ollas. There is little difference in color between interior and exterior surfaces. Some sherds display light-

190

er firing clouds. The color of the slip ranges from black through dark gray and grayish-brown to waxy pearl gray (2.5 YR 2/1, 5 YR 7/1–7/2, 10 YR 5/2–6/2). The slipped surface is polished to a waxy luster; wide stick-polishing striations are visible. Most of the smoothing marks were removed by the slipping process. The slip is quite thin and brittle and easily flakes off, like thickly applied paint. It was spread in an even opaque coating and is slightly darker than the paste.

Decoration

Decoration is displayed on the stamped bottoms of molcajetes (described below) and on stamped vessel supports. Thirty-one body sherds from Tr 62 were incised prior to firing. The curvature of the sherds indicates that all are probably fragments of ollas. The primary motif consists of a series of undulating or zigzag lines radiating from the neck of the vessel. There are also a step design, one *xicalcoliuhqui* or stepped fret, rectangular and triangular shapes boxed one within another, and a circular design. Three incised molcajete bottoms were uncovered in early Venta Salada components.

Vessel Forms

The forms are fairly simple. The great majority of the vessels are convex-wall bowls, differentiated mainly by rim and lip variations.

Convex-wall bowls with slightly outangled rims are the most numerous shape. They generally have lips beveled on the interior. Many sherds show that stepped supports had been attached. A great many bowls had stamped bottoms. Dimensions in cm.: rim diameter, 18–20; height, 4.5–5.3.

Convex-wall bowls with direct rims have flat bottoms and lips that range from rounded to externally beveled to flat. Many of the flat rims are grooved. Most of these bowls were tripod vessels with stamped bottoms. A fragment of a small bowl has a bird head on the rim. Dimensions in cm.: rim diameter, 6–20; wall height, 1.5–6.0.

Convex-wall bowls with flaring rims have either smooth or stamped flat bottoms and appear both with and without stepped supports. Dimensions in cm.: rim diameter, 16–24; wall height, 2.5–4.1.

Convex-wall bowls with everted rims have either smooth or stamped flat bottoms. The majority have stepped supports. The lip is rounded or beveled. A subvariety are larger, heavier vessels with convex bottoms and wider, slightly thickened everted rims. Dimensions in cm.: rim diameter, 16–30; rim width, 1.5–3.0; wall height, 4.0–8.5.

FIG. 114. COXCATLAN GRAY. Bowls with stamped and plain stepped feet.

191

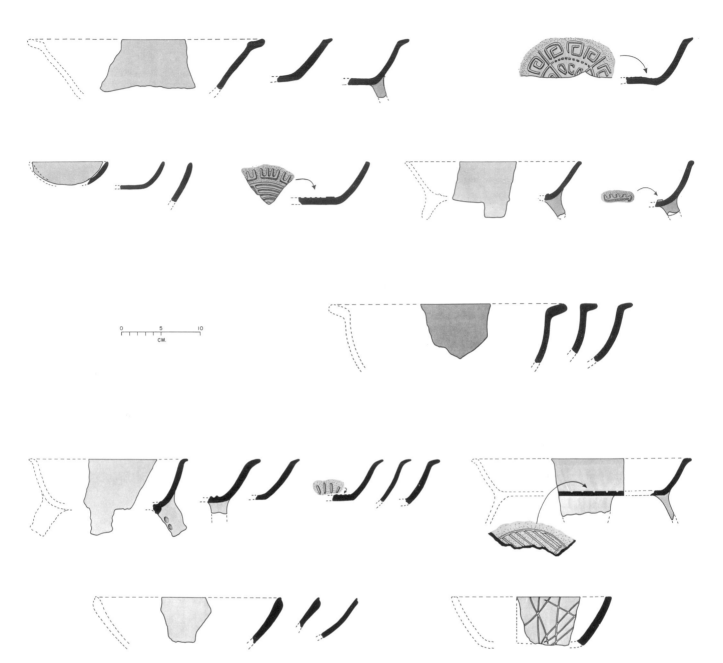

FIG. 115. COXCATLAN GRAY. Convex-wall bowls with everted, outangled, direct, flaring, or grooved rims. Many bowls have stamped or incised bottoms and stepped supports. *Lower right,* flat-lipped convex mold with incised exterior.

Composite-silhouette bowls with vertical, concave, or incurved rims have shallow to deep convex bodies. The base is flattened to rounded. The junction between body and rim is generally a pronounced ridge; several sherds have a horizontal lug, sometimes notched or bifurcated, along the ridge. Some of the rims are vertical and concave, and some of these have a horizontal groove from 1.5 to 2.8 cm. below the lip. Other rims are incurved and slightly convex with a shallow groove just above the ridge between body and rim. Lips are flattish, rounded, or slightly beveled. There are numerous minature vessels in this group, with rim diameters from 5.0–10 cm. and a height of about 4.0 cm. Dimensions in cm. generally: rim diameter, 12–26; approximate height, 4.0–16.

Flaring-wall bowls have flat bottoms, rounded or beveled lips, and a rim diameter of 16–28 cm.

Cylindrical to beaker-shaped bowls. This category

TABLE 55
Coxcatlan Gray Decorated Sherds
(by site and zone)

	Early Venta Salada						Late Venta Salada							Total
	35e C	50 III	35e B	35w 3	50 II	35w 2	35w 1	50 I	367 A	35e A	368w A	62 A	65 A	
Incised motifs on olla bodies														
zig-zag lines												31		31
boxed triangles												3		3
boxed rectangles												2		2
stepped frets												2		2
steps												1		1
circles												1		1
Incised crosshatching on bowl rims														
convex wall, direct rim	2	1			1							16		20
convex wall, everted rim							1			1	1	18		21
convex wall, flaring rim	2	1	1	4	1		1		18	3	1	25		57
indeterminate forms	1		1		1									3
Stamped motifs on bowl bottoms		1	1	2	2	2	4	2	20	9	8	314	2	367
Total	5	3	3	6	5	2	6	2	38	13	10	413	2	508

includes vessels with both direct and "bulged" rims, the latter being a convex rim on a vertical or outsloping wall. No bottoms were found: presumably they were flattened or slightly rounded and had no supports. Lips are flat, rounded, and bilaterally beveled. Rim diameter, 12–20 cm.

Deep incurved-rim bowls have a convex body with an incurved rim and rounded lip. They may have had a small flat base. One example is of miniature size (rim diameter, 8.0; height, 3.5 cm.) and may have been an incensario. Dimensions in cm.: rim diameter, 14–18; approxmate height, 8–10.

Carinated bowls have deep convex bodies and a horizontal ridge setting off the short concave inangled rims. Dimensions in cm.: rim diameter, 8–12; approximate height, 4.5.

Outsloping-wall bowls have flat bottoms and divergent straight sides. The lips are beveled, rounded, or slightly everted. One example with a striated bottom showed that a wide stepped support had been attached. Dimensions in cm.: rim diameter, 20–22; wall height, 4.4–6.5.

Ollas with straight necks and everted rims. Necks are fairly tall with vertical or slightly convergent walls and short everted rims. One example has an unusually wide upward-sloping everted rim, and a second unusual example has a very wide upward-curving "cupped" rim. Dimensions in cm.: external rim diameter, 10–18; rim width, 1.2–3.5; neck height, 6.0–11; wall thickness, 0.5–0.9.

Ollas with straight necks and direct rims have short necks and fairly wide mouths. One rim has a horizontal groove or dent half way between lip and shoulder. Rim diameter, 16–18 cm.

Ollas with short flaring necks are represented by two specimens with rim diameters of 14 and 16 cm. Necks are quite short, 0.9 and 2.4 cm. There is one *olla with long flaring neck*, which has a rim diameter of 11 cm. The neck wall is 7.0 cm. high.

Miscellaneous forms. Two comales or plates, collected from the surface, have flat bottoms and short, slightly upturned rims. Interior surfaces are smoothed and exteriors roughened. The outer surfaces of one example is blackened by smoke. The rim diameters of both examples are about 26 cm.

A number of small shallow round vessels were found, with flat bottoms and either short upturned rims or thickened edges that make a rim. Both surfaces of some examples are polished; other specimens have polished interiors and fairly rough exteriors. These vessels may be miniature plates or pot covers. Dimensions in cm.: rim diameter, 8.0–12; height, 0.8–1.5; thickness, 0.3–0.8.

One sherd from the body of a vessel of undetermined shape has a steplike opening cut through it. This fragment could be from an incense burner of the Mix-

193

TABLE 56
Coxcatlan Gray Vessel Forms
(sherds by site and zone)

| | Early Venta Salada | | | | | | | | | | Late Venta Salada | | | | | | |
	35e C	255 A	50 III	35e B	35w 3	50 II	35w 2	35w 1	367 B	50 I	367 A	368e A	35e A	368w A	62 A	65 A	Total
Bowls																	
convex wall																	
outangled rim	7			1	6	2	1	7		2	67	6	44	17	757	6	914
direct rim		2	4	7	12	1	3	14		5	53	5	34	11	671	3	833
flaring rim				3		1	2	1			12	1			136		156
everted rim	8		2	25	1	6	3	8		1	2	2	8	6	58		130
composite silhouette											2				166		168
flaring wall	10		1	10			2	2	1		60			1	15	1	103
cylindrical/beaker				1			3	1			17			3	71		96
incurved rim	1			1							16			3	6		28
carinated					20			3			1			1	1	1	27
outsloping wall				14	1					1	1				5		22
Ollas																	
str. neck, everted rim					1					1	4		1	3	44	1	55
str. neck, direct rim											1		2	2	10	2	17
short flaring neck															2		2
long flaring neck															1		1
Flat bases			1	19	3	5	4	12		2	98		9	18	590		764
Supports																	
stepped			3	8	3	2		3			7	4	8	1	366		406
dumbbell											1		11	2	4		18
animal effigy											1		2		5		8
conical				1	1									2			4
pedestal				2													2
cylindrical															1		1
Strap handles								4							54		58
Body sherds	55	18	16	81	7	27	54	73	31	20	665	189	44	450	1725	2	3457
Total	84	20	27	173	55	43	72	128	32	32	1008	207	163	520	4688	18	7270

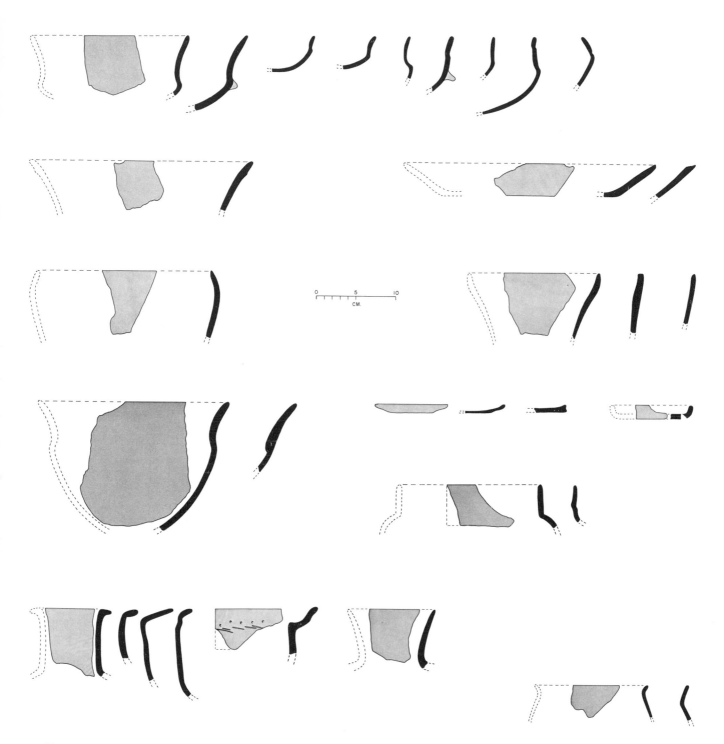

FIG. 116. COXCATLAN GRAY. *Row 1:* composite-silhouette bowls with concave or incurved rims; *row 2:* flaring and outsloping-wall bowls; *row 3:* deep incurved-rim bowl and beaker-shaped or cylindrical bowls; *row 4:* composite-silhouette vessels with deep convex body, small plates or comales, and ollas with short straight necks; *row 5:* ollas with long straight or convergent necks and everted rims (including an aberrant cupped rim) and ollas with long and short flaring necks.

tec type illustrated by Caso and Bernal (1965: fig. 24) and by Caso, Bernal, and Acosta (1967: pl. XXXI).

Two pedestal bases were excavated from early Venta Salada components; four more examples are from surface collections representing the latter part of the phase. These bases are hollow and flaring at the lower edge and roughly bell-shaped. They probably supported vessels of larger size than they are themselves. Dimensions in cm.: diameter at junction with vessel, 4.0–12; diameter at lower edge, 6.0 to over 16; height, 2.5 to over 9.0.

Strap handles, undoubtedly from ollas, measure 2.4–6.2 cm. wide, and the broken lengths ranged from 3.8 to 6.6 cm. One long, flat, slightly curved fragment may have been part of a stirrup handle; it is 8.2 cm. long, 3.6 cm. wide, and 1.0 cm. thick.

Of the seven lugs found on sherds of Coxcatlan Gray, three were divided by a notch or groove into two sections and one was perforated. All were small and elliptical in outline and extended horizontally from the vessel wall.

Supports, most of them from late Venta Salada components, include over four hundred plain or stamped stepped feet, eighteen bulb-end or dumbbell feet, eight slotted "bird-beak" feet, four conical or wedge-shaped feet, and one hollow cylindrical foot. The "bird-beak" variety is a solid support, round at the top but tapering to a curved beaklike end. The sides are somewhat flattened, adding to the general resemblance to a bird's head. The supports are slashed vertically along opposite sides, sometimes making a long slot clear through the support, but sometimes not penetrating the solid center. The slot or slash suggests an open beak. Small blobs of clay applied above the slot serve as eyes on some specimens. A variant of this type of support is less representational and has wider, unslotted, more flattened sides and a tip that is more curved than tapering.

One support is shaped like an animal's paw, with small notches making five toes. It is interesting to note that there are no old-man or serpent effigy supports in Coxcatlan Gray and that their place is taken by the "bird-beak" support.

Stamped bottoms with raised designs are from molcajete or grater bowls. Some of the designs are worn nearly smooth. They cover the entire interior bottom, which ranges from about 12 to 14 cm. in diameter. Designs consist of both rectilinear and curvilinear patterns. Generally one or two delimiting circles around the periphery enclose panels containing highly stylized motifs similar to those appearing on Coxcatlan Brushed molcajete bottoms. A border of "U"-shaped

units is common. The most popular central motifs are chevrons or multiple "V" elements arranged in quadrants. A circle with a dot in the middle appears often in central panels, probably the eye of an animal or deity. Other motifs seem to represent stylized serpents, birds, and butterflies. In early Venta Salada undecorated bottoms far outnumbered stamped ones, but in late Venta Salada stamped bottoms become almost as numerous as plain ones.

Several deeply incised molds for making stamped bottoms were found.

Examples of Coxcatlan Gray stamped bottoms are illustrated above (Fig. 112) with similar specimens of Coxcatlan Brushed.

Relationships

The Coxcatlan Gray type is obviously a continuation of the gray-ware tradition that began in the Tehuacan Valley some 1500 years earlier with Rio Salado Gray in the early Santa Maria phase. Coxcatlan Gray, however, has a different paste and surface finish from previous gray wares and, of course, has many Postclassic attributes such as stamped bottoms and stepped, effigy, and dumbbell feet. Neither it nor even a related type has been reported from Cholula. This type is present at the Quauhtochco site near Huatusco, Veracruz (Medellín Zenil 1960) and it, or a related type, may occur in Upper Cerro de las Mesas (Drucker 1943a). The Monte Alban tripod convex-wall bowls of gray paste with long serpent-shaped feet are apparently related to this type (Caso, Bernal, and Acosta 1967: fig. 376). It is interesting to note that on page 7, bottom row, of the Codex Borgia a blue-gray tripod convex-wall bowl with stepped (possibly stamped) feet may be an aboriginal depiction of this type.

COXCATLAN RED

1,408 specimens excavated; 1,102 collected.

Paste

About 10 percent of the paste is composed of nonplastic particles 0.1–0.5 mm. in diameter made up of limestone, quartz, sandstone, plagioclase, and schist. Only 2 percent or so comprises grains 0.5–1.0 mm. in diameter of quartz, plagioclase, calcite, biotite, muscovite, magnetite, hornblende, and hematite.

The clay, though relatively well knit, is quite porous and has a sandy character.

There are a number of fragments of stamped bottoms, indicating that some vessels were mold made, but others seem to have been manufactured by the coil method.

196

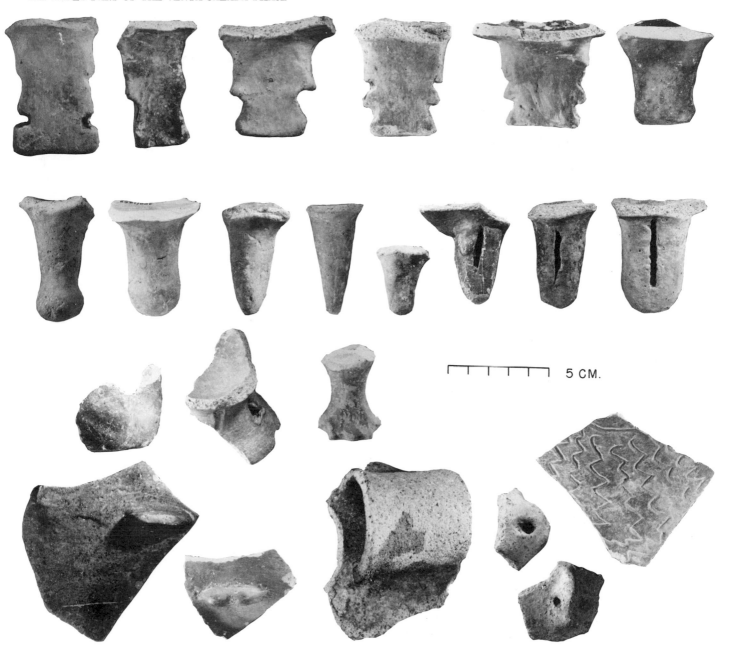

FIG. 117. COXCATLAN GRAY. *Row 1:* stepped feet; *row 2:* dumbbell, conical, and slotted feet; *row 3:* hollow cylindrical foot, perforated ring base, and animal effigy support; *row 4:* lugs, handle, and incised sherd.

Firing was even, with cores ranging from light tan to dark gray (usually the latter). The slip or outer surfaces are reddish to light tan. Hardness ranges from 3.0 to nearly 4.0 in the Mohs scale.

Surface Finish

The surface coloration is about the same on both surfaces, ranging from red (10 R 4/8) to weak red (10 R 4/4). The surfaces were covered with an orange slip 0.5 to 1.0 mm. thick that contrasts with the gray core. The slip was polished with a smooth instrument, and a streaky red paint was applied. This painted surface was then rubbed and marks of the polishing stone can be seen. It has a dull luster.

197

FIG. 118. COXCATLAN RED. Convex-wall bowl.

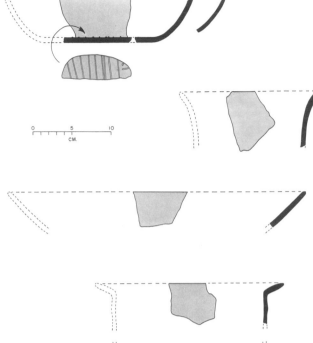

FIG. 119. COXCATLAN RED. *From top to bottom,* convex-wall bowl with direct rim and stamped bottom, flaring-wall vessel, outsloping-wall bowl, and olla with straight neck and everted rim.

Decoration

At first glance Coxcatlan Red pottery appears to have been undecorated, but under a strong light some sherds show a slight discoloration where a fugitive white paint was applied. Not enough paint remains to show any designs.

Vessel Forms

Convex-wall bowls with direct rims are the most common bowl form. They probably had flat bottoms and/or three supports. Some of the bottoms have stamped designs. Dimensions in cm.: rim diameter, 14–26; wall thickness, 0.4–0.6; wall height, about 6.0.

Convex-wall bowls with outangled rims range from 20 to 26 cm. in rim diameter and are about the same thickness and height as the preceding form.

Flaring-wall bowls apparently had flat or footed bottoms. Rim diameter: 14–22 cm.

Outsloping-wall bowls have straight, widely divergent walls. They may have had stepped feet. Rim diameter: 20–36 cm.

Cylindrical Vessels have direct rims about 20 cm. in diameter.

Miscellaneous bowl forms. Incurved-rim bowls and inangled- or carinated-rim bowls had rim diameters of 12 to 18 cm. and wall heights of 4 to 6 cm. Three sherds of bowls with undulating rims were too fragmentary to indicate complete forms or even the rim diameters. The rims show undulations or indentations similar to those on bowls found in Aztec times in the Valley of Mexico.

Ollas with straight-necks and everted rims and *ollas*

FIG. 120. COXCATLAN RED. Slab, stepped, and serpent-head supports.

198

TABLE 57
Coxcatlan Red Vessel Forms
(sherds by site and zone)

| | Early Venta Salada | | | | | | Late Venta Salada | | | | | | | | | |
	35e C	50 III	35e B	35w 3	50 II	35w 2	35w 1	367 B	50 I	367 A	368e A	35e A	368w A	62 A	65 A	Total
Bowls																
convex wall																
direct rim			1			2	2			10	2	14	24	4	9	68
outangled rim			1			2	4	1		17		2	13	3	2	45
flaring wall			1					1		10	1	3	6	5	2	29
outsloping wall		1										2	1	23		27
incurved rim							2			1		2		2	3	10
carinated rim										1		2			3	6
Ollas																
long str. neck, everted rim				4			1			8				1	2	16
short flaring neck							1			2			2	1		6
Cylindrical vessels			3				1			3			3		2	12
Flat bases			8			11	5			55	30	2	42	20	5	178
Supports																
serpent										6					2	8
stepped						1								3	3	7
Strap handles										1		2	2	2	2	9
Body sherds	4	3	24	21	8	41	39	23	5	319	208	118	68	102	4	987
Total	4	4	24	39	8	57	55	25	5	433	241	147	161	166	39	1408

with short flaring necks had rim diameters between 12 and 20 cm.

Stamped bottoms are outnumbered by flat, undecorated fragments (164).

Appendages. Supports for tripod vessels include stepped feet with and without stamped designs and effigy or serpent-head feet. Five flat elliptical lugs, about 4 cm. long, were applied horizontally. Nine strap handles were 8.0–10 cm. long, 2.0–3.0 cm. wide at the distal end and 3.0–4.0 cm. wide at the proximal end, and 1.8–2.5 cm. thick.

One large sherd disk about 38 cm. in diameter might be considered a plate or comal.

Relationships

The Coxcatlan Red type could have been derived from concepts involved in Quachilco Red, but its paste and vessel form attributes are very different. Examples apparently of this same type occur in small amounts throughout the Cholulteca sequence (Noguera 1954). The stepped feet and stamped bottoms, however, are features that seem to be unique to the Tehuacan Valley. Plate 57 of Codex Borgia shows a red bowl with stepped feet that may be a depiction of this type.

COXCATLAN RED-ON-ORANGE

580 specimens excavated, 922 collected.

Paste

The temper is fine textured and comprises about 15 percent of the paste. About 10 percent is grains 0.1–0.5 mm. in diameter, identified as shale, quartzite, muscovite, plagioclase, biotite, and quartz. Less than 5 percent is grains less than 0.1 mm. in diameter, including the same materials plus hematite and magnetite.

The paste is well knit, but has some porosity usually in the form of very short fine laminations. It has a chalky to sandy quality.

Further analysis might well divide this type into two or three types, since the amount of mica temper increases through time and the surface finish shifts from orange to creamy white from early to late. There are also a wide variety of painted motifs which seem to change with time.

Four body sherds of ollas are definitely mold-made, as are the few stamped-bottom bowls. The pedestal-based or eggcup-shaped vessels and cylindrical-necked ollas are made in parts and cemented together.

Most sherds show little difference in firing colora-

Fig. 121. Coxcatlan Red-on-orange. *Rows 1–3:* rim sherds of convex-wall bowls with direct rims; *rows 4, 5:* sherds of convex-wall bowls with outangled rims; *row 6:* pedestal bases.

tion between periphery and core, both ranging from orangish to light brown, but a few sherds have slightly darker cores. Sherds are over 3.5 in the Mohs hardness scale.

Surface Finish

The surfaces are covered by a thin film or wash in the following range of colors: pinkish or tannish orange (2.5 YR 6/6, 5.0 YR 7/4–7/6, 7.5 YR 8/2) to very pale buff or cream (10 YR 8/4–8/2, 2.5 Y 8/4). The pale tones tend to occur late in the sequence. The earliest sherds of this type seem to have uncoated smoothed orange surfaces.

Decoration

Painted on the orange or buffy background are designs in deep red (5.0 R 4/6, 7.5 R 4/8, 10 R 4/6). During late Venta Salada, however, a few black designs or panels appear together with the red decorations. The commonest element in the painted designs are horizontal lines of varying thinness or thickness that usually divide the exterior wall of the vessel into horizontal bands. Some of these borders are in turn divided into rectangular panels by vertical lines. Within the panels making up a border are a series of two or more motifs. One distinctive combination that appears on sherd after sherd consists of a solid stepped element attached to either a spiral or a concentric rectilinear element, or sometimes to a straight vertical line. A small hollow triangle is frequently left between the stepped element and the element it is attached to. This motif is used with diagonal zigzag or wavy lines and sometimes with comma-like hooks, "V" 's, solid triangles, two or more short vertical or horizontal lines, chevrons or sidewise "U" 's, and hollow outlined "S" 's.

Another frequently repeated design consists of a series of thick hollow circles placed between thin bordering lines and underscored by a third quite thick horizontal line. The larger decorated fragments show that different panel or border combinations were placed one above another, sometimes repeating vertically one element in the design while varying others. The unit made up of horizontal lines and circles often appears beneath two or more borders made up of stepped and other motifs. The designs and motifs vary slightly with different vessel forms, as we shall note in the following section.

Vessel Forms

Convex-wall bowls with direct rims are the most numerous vessels. They usually have rounded or

FIG. 122. COXCATLAN RED-ON-ORANGE. *Row 1:* small bowl sherds; *rows 2, 3:* olla neck and body sherds; *row 4:* dumbbell foot and a ladle fragment.

slightly beveled lips and flat bottoms, although it is likely that some of the rim sherds are from pedestal-based bowls. There are no indications that the bowls rested on feet.

Over 95 percent of the designs are on the exteriors, but six sherds show radiating vertical lines inside and three sherds have spirals on the interiors. The dominant element appearing on the exterior is one or more horizontal encircling lines. One line is always used to encircle the lip, and others divide the exterior surface into two or more horizontal bands. The most common combination of elements is a band of horizontal lines next to a band enclosing stepped combinations and diagonals. Also common are bands containing steps and "V" 's next to bands with hooks and verticals. Bands of steps and "V" 's occasionally occur next to bands with spirals and inverted "U" 's. Another motif includes a band containing circles beneath bands with either steps and hooks, verticals and hooks, inverted

201

TABLE 58
Coxcatlan Red-on-orange Vessel Forms
(sherds by site and zone)

	Early Venta Salada						Late Venta Salada							
	35e C	255 A	35e B	35w 3	50 II	35w 2	35w 1	367 A	368e A	35e A	368w A	62 A	65 A	Total
Bowls														
convex wall														
direct rim							11				36	63		110
outangled rim			2	2			2			14	25	30	1	76
flaring wall				1			7			2		2		12
incurved rim		3				1	1				6			11
Ollas														
str. neck, everted rim											3	10		13
Flat bases				1				2		3	7	5		18
Pedestal bases	2							12			9	21		44
Cylindrical/dumbbell feet								2		1	2			5
Body sherds	2		2		1	2	3	64	27	7	63	89	31	291
Total	4	3	4	4	1	3	3	99	29	27	151	220	32	580

"U"'s and rectangular elements, steps and verticals or steps and spirals. Single panels of diagonals, steps, rectangles, or verticals and hooks are rare. Dimensions in cm.: rim diameter, 6.0–18; height, 2.0–7.0; thickness, 0.4–0.8.

Convex-wall bowls with outangled or everted rims have flat bottoms. Some examples have stamped bottoms and dumbbell-shaped supports. Lips are rounded or very slightly beveled on the interiors. Decorations on this shape show the complete range of motifs described above. Dimensions in cm.: rim diameter, 16–28; height (unsupported) 4.0–7.0; wall thickness, 0.5–1.0.

Pedestal-based or eggcup-shaped vessels are divided at the midsection, and are not so common as the previously mentioned form. The convex-wall bowl that makes up the top unit rests on an open pedestal with flaring sides and rounded edges. Some of the convex-wall rim sherds may belong to this shape. Designs on the hollow flaring bases are sometimes limited to thick and thin horizontal lines and sometimes include a border of more complex motifs, undoubtedly repeating designs used on the bowl portion. Popular elements within this band are stepped lines, inverted "U"'s or "V"'s, vertical lines, circles, and spirals. Dimensions in cm.: base diameter, 14–19; height, 4.0–7.0; wall thickness, 0.4–1.0; diameter at midsection, 7.0–12.

Flaring-wall bowls have rounded lips and flat bottoms. All twelve rim sherds display horizontal lines as decoration, but few other elements could be dis-

cerned. Some sherds have stepped designs, and a few show spirals and/or hooks. Dimensions in cm.: rim diameter, 14–20; wall thickness, 0.5–1.0; height, unknown.

Incurved-rim bowls have convex walls, constricted mouths, and flattened bases. They are small vessels, some being of miniature proportions. Horizontal bands around the lip and on the exterior are the common form of decoration. Two sherds show stepped or wavy lines; another has thick diagonal lines within horizontal bands; and one has parallel vertical lines extending from lip to base. Dimensions in cm.: rim diameter, 6.0–16; height, 2.5–6.0.

Ollas with straight necks and everted rims. Four of the thirteen rim or neck fragments actually may represent bottles rather than ollas. The ollas apparently had elaborately decorated bodies and a pair of loop or strap handles. Decoration on the neck consists mainly of horizontal bands. Mouth diameters are between 8 and 12 cm.

Miscellaneous fragments include two sherds with stamped bottoms, five dumbbell feet, one fragmentary ladle handle, one strap handle, and one sherd from a small bowl with an undulating rim or the pouring lip of a pitcher.

Relationships

Coxcatlan Red-on-orange is a new diagnostic type for the Venta Salada phase in the Tehuacan Valley. It is closely related to a red-on-orange ware that occurs throughout the Cholulteca sequence (Noguera 1954).

The Tehuacan examples, however, display a greater range of decorative motifs and lack the distinctive "S" element of examples from Cholula. The two wares are obviously not the same type. Superficially Coxcatlan Red-on-orange resembles both Tula Red-on-buff and Mazapan Red-on-buff (Tolstoy 1958), but the resemblances are not striking. It seems closer to the Coyotlatelco pottery with its hollow "S" motifs, spirals, steps, and concentric rectangles (Rattray 1966: figs. 7c, 24f, 25), but the vessel forms of the two types are different. Some of the pedestal-based pots in Codex Borgia (pls. 2, 4, 5, 7), the convex-wall bowl on bulb feet decorated with red "V"'s on a white or yellow ground (pl. 7), and cylindrical vessels with red "V"'s (pls. 6, 11, 15, 18, 63) might be aboriginal depictions of this pottery type. The deep flaring-wall bowl in the center of pl. 44, with red steps connected to a Greek fret, horizontal bands, and triangles is almost exactly like some of our Coxcatlan Red-on-orange pottery.

TEOTITLAN INCISED

551 specimens excavated, 2,515 collected.

Paste

About 10 percent of the paste is composed of nonplastic materials under 0.1 mm. in diameter, including quartzite, quartz, biotite, muscovite, plagioclase, mag-netite, and hematite. Only 5 percent is grains 0.1–0.5 mm. in diameter, and occasional grains of quartzite measure 0.5–1.0 mm. in diameter.

The paste is well knit but porous. Occasional sherds show coil breaks; olla fragments show that these vessels were mold made. Hardness is 3.5 to 4.0. Firing is fairly even: the core ranges from gray to light brown to reddish-brown, but regardless of its color, it is not well differentiated from the clay near the surfaces. The paste resembles the finer specimens of Coxcatlan Brushed.

Surface Finish

The light brown, reddish, or more often, gray paste is covered by a thin slip or wash ranging in color from tan or medium gray to dark reddish-gray (5 YR 6/1–6/4) to reddish-brown (2.5 YR 4/8) and charcoal black (10 YR 3/1). Sometimes fine horizontal striations or brushings mark the surface.

Decoration

Decoration usually occurs as engraving on exterior surfaces, made by means of a sharp narrow implement after the vessel was slipped and fired. The instrument, probably an obsidian blade, cut through the outer surface leaving a clean, thin line.

Most common motifs are straight lines, used either as parallel lines or to form a horizontal band. Often a

TABLE 59
Teotitlan Incised Decorated Sherds
(by site and zone)

	Early Venta Salada					Late Venta Salada		
	50 III	35e B	35w 3	50 II	35w 2	35w 1	367 B	50 I
Engraved motifs								
1-4 lines around rims of								
incurved-rim bowls, ext.	1	6	20		2	1	2	
convex-wall, flaring-rim bowl, ext.								
on bodies, ext.	3		6	2	8	2	1	2
Wavy line(s) around rims of								
incurved-rim bowls, ext.		2		2				
Circular motifs inside panels on								
convex-wall, direct-rim bowls, ext.			2					
incurved-rim bowls, ext.		11	9					
convex-wall, flaring-rim bowls, ext.		1	7					
carinated-rim bowls, ext.								
cylindrical bowl, ext.								
bodies of angle-neck ollas								
Hatching on direct rims of convex-wall								
bowls, ext.								
Stamped motifs on bowl bottoms, int.								
Total	4	20	44	4	10	3	3	2

(Table continued)

203

(*Table 59, continued*)

| | Late Venta Salada (*continued*) | | | | | | |
	367 A	368e A	35e A	368w A	62 A	65 A	Total
Engraved motifs							
1-4 lines around rims of							
incurved-rim bowls, ext.	38	2	3	48	47	10	180
convex-wall, flaring-rim bowl, ext.	5			4	2		11
on bodies, ext.	41	18	16	72	22	2	195
Wavy line(s) around rims of							
incurved-rim bowls, ext.		1	6	18	3		32
Circular motifs inside panels on							
convex-wall, direct-rim bowls, ext.							2
incurved-rim bowls, ext.	4	2	11	6	2		45
convex-wall, flaring-rim bowls, ext.	12			10	2		32
carinated-rim bowls, ext.	2			3			5
cylindrical bowl, ext.	1						1
bodies of angle-neck ollas				5			5
Hatching on direct rims of convex-wall							
bowls, ext.					4	1	5
Stamped motifs on bowl bottoms, int.						1	1
Total	103	23	36	170	80	12	514

horizontal band defined by two sets of parallel lines is divided into rectangular panels by two or more vertical lines. Less commonly, diagonal lines divide the bands into a series of diamonds and triangles. No matter what the shape of the panels, about half of them contain one or more circles, ovals, or spirals; less common are wavy lines, crosshatched steps or other areas, and hooks. Two bowl sherds display beneath the rim different versions of the day sign "Flint Knife," both versions of which are found only in Codex Borgia (see Volume I, pp. 115–117, of this series, and Fig. 124 below).

Vessel Forms

Convex-wall bowls with incurved rims are vessels of medium depth. The convex walls round off to a flat bottom. Some of the bowls may have rested on stepped feet. Lips are rounded or possibly beveled on the interior. Decoration occurs only on the upper part of the exterior body. The rim zone is delineated by horizontal lines, two above and one or two below. Inside this border the following motifs appear: two or three parallel vertical or diagonal lines, which separate the border into rectangular or diamond-shaped panels, inside which are circles, "eye" elements, triangles with vertical hachure, linked scrolls or hooks, and wavy lines. Dimensions in cm.: rim diameter, 10–18; height, 3.5–9.0; wall thickness, 0.3–0.7. One large fragment measured 18 cm. at the rim, 20 cm. across the widest part of the vessel, and about 14 cm. across the bottom.

Convex-wall bowls with flaring rims have flat bottoms and probably rested on stepped feet. Lips are rounded or internally beveled. Decoration is on the outside only. Just below the flaring rim is a horizontal border set off by two sets of single or parallel lines. The borders contain various motifs: "eye" elements, triangular and rectangular units, "U" or plumelike elements, and the two examples of Flint Knife glyphs mentioned above. Dimensions in cm.: rim diameter, 10–18; height, 3.0–5.5; wall thickness, 0.3–0.6.

Convex-wall bowls with direct rims have rounded lips. Bottoms were probably flat, and one rim-to-base fragment shows that the bottom interior bore a stamped design, although all the base but the raised line around the edge of the inner surface and a small fragment of attached support have broken away. All specimens have incised designs around the exterior surface. Rim diameters range from about 18 to 24 cm. The rim-to-base sherd indicates a rim diameter of 23 cm. and a wall height of 4.5 cm.

Carinated-rim bowls are much like the bowls with incurving rims, but the rim is straight and insloping instead of curved. Bottoms may have been flat. The

FIG. 123. TEOTITLAN INCISED. Incurved-rim bowl.

5 CM.

FIG. 124. TEOTITLAN INCISED. *Row 1:* incurved-rim bowls; *row 2:* convex-wall bowls with flaring rims (note two sherds with Flint-knife glyph); *row 3:* sherds with cross-hatched decoration; *row 4:* olla body fragment, cylindrical bowl, convex-wall bowl sherds with rounded rims, and body sherd with glyphic device.

TABLE 60
Teotitlan Incised Vessel Forms
(sherds by site and zone)

	Early Venta Salada					Late Venta Salada									
	50 III	35e B	35w 3	50 II	35w 2	35w 1	367 B	50 I	367 A	368e A	35e A	368w A	62 A	65 A	Total
Bowls															
incurved rim	1	19	29	2	2	1	2		42	5	20	72	52	10	257
convex wall															
flaring rim		1	7						17			14	10		49
direct rim			2		1							4	1		8
carinated									2			3			5
cylindrical									1						1
Ollas, angle neck												5			5
Flat bases			5									19	1		25
Stepped feet			1	1	2							2			6
Body sherds	3		6	2	8	2	1	2	41	18	16	72	22	2	195
Total	4	20	50	4	12	5	3	2	103	23	36	191	86	12	551

only decoration noted consists of parallel lines. Dimensions in cm.: rim diameter, 12–16; wall thickness, 0.5; height, unknown.

Low cylindrical bowl. The single excavated example had a flat bottom; whether it was footed or not cannot be determined. Sherds of this bowl form from the surface collection show horizontal bands, sometimes divided into diamonds. Dimensions in cm.: rim diameter, 14–18; wall thickness, 0.4–0.9; height, unknown.

Angle-neck ollas have parallel lines decorating the necks or outer rims. One shoulder fragment has a horizontal border set off by parallel lines. The border is divided by diagonal parallel lines into triangles and hexagons with small diamonds or triangles inside the panels. Rim diameter, 10–12 cm.

Relationships

Teotitlan Incised is a new type in the Venta Salada phase. It is closely related to the Coxcatlan Brushed type in paste and surface finish. Sherds similar to this type occur at Cholula in Cholula Incised, characterized by wide-line incising and more curvilinear designs (Noguera 1954: 111). A few sherds of the Teotitlan type occur at Quauhtochco near Huatusco, Veracruz (Medellín Zenil 1960), and Drucker (1943b) reported some examples apparently of this type from Upper Cerro de las Mesas.

The designs engraved on Teotitlan bowls are major decorative elements throughout Codex Borgia (see Volume I, Chapter 7, of this series). More significant-

ly, they appear in depictions of vessels of the same shapes and color as Teotitlan Incised (Volume I: fig. 72). Such vessels appear frequently in the codex and show the same design motifs as those engraved on Teotitlan pots, including circles and rectangles (Codex Borgia 1961: pls. 1–7, among many others), cross-hatched steps (pls. 6, 69); diagonal lines only (pls. 14, 24, 47), and diamond-shaped zones with circles in the center (pls. 4, 70). Also, the two variations of the Flint Knife glyph found on Teotitlan sherds are versions of the glyph diagnostic of Codex Borgia.

Trade Wares

Dr. Román Piña Chan and Robert E. Smith identified many of the trade sherds from early Venta Salada levels. These sherds include examples of Thin Orange, X Fine Orange, Y Fine Orange, Tohil Plumbate, Tula Red-on-buff, Cholula Polychrome Lacquer, Cholula Incised, and Texcoco Fabric-impressed wares. Some of these specimens are shown in Fig. 137 in Chapter 10. One sherd of San Juan Plumbate was collected from Tr 210.

Miscellaneous Objects

Three sherd disks about 5 cm. in diameter were found in Zone C of Tc 35e. One was pierced.

Spindle Whorls

The early Venta Salada spindle whorls (see Table 9 above and Fig. 140 below) are small circular plano-

TABLE 61
Early Venta Salada Trade Sherds
(by site and zone)

	35e C	255 A	50 III	35e B	35w 3	50 II	35w 2	Total
Cholula Polychrome Lacquer—body							1	1
X Fine Orange: bodies	1							1
flaring-wall jar	6			3	1			10
cylindrical jar	2	2	1	3	1	2	2	13
Y Fine Orange: bodies	8							8
cylindrical jar	8			1				9
Tohil Plumbate: body						1		1
Tula (Mazapan) Red-on-buff: bodies	2			2				4
Thin Orange: bodies	4	3		2			1	10
convex-wall bowls	2	1		2				5
ring bases	4			1				5
Texcoco Fabric-impressed: body		1						1
Total	37	7	1	14	2	3	4	68

convex objects with a hole through the center. They were mold-made with fine-grained, sometimes sandy-tempered paste. The lower surfaces of the spindle whorls are flat, but upper surfaces are raised, giving the spindle whorls distinctive shapes, ranging from wafer-like forms to truncated or high cones and true bell shapes with steep convex walls terminating in flaring rims.

Except for one example with an incised circle-and-dash design on the upper surface, the early Venta Salada spindle whorls are undecorated save for the remains of black and white paint. The black paint, probably asphalt, is well preserved on several examples. It was often used to cover both surfaces, but in at least two cases was applied in a pattern—once in a wide circle around the central hole of a high conical spindle whorl, the rest of which was painted white, and once in a band around the flat under surface and the nearly vertical lower wall of another high-topped specimen.

We have classified the early Venta Salada spindle whorls by both shape and design, as set forth below.

Low to medium-high cones (6 excavated, 3 collected) generally are larger in diameter than the high domed or conical variety. They range from a disk with a slightly convex upper surface to truncated cones that are low to medium high. The flattened tops of the truncated cones range from 0.7 to 1.9 cm. in diameter. A late Venta Salada example shows a lightly incised scalloped design around a flattened edge. Another spindle whorl, a medium-high cone, shows remains of

black paint. Spindle whorls that share general resemblances to this generally plain and inclusive type occur over a wide area. The specimens from one early Venta Salada and five late Venta Salada components of the Tehuacan Valley specifically resemble spindle whorls from the Flores and Panuco phases of Tampico, Veracruz (Ekholm 1944: fig. 46, *d'*, *f'*), from Cholula (Noguera 1954: p. 150, no. 12) and in the Soncautla complex at Tres Zapotes (Drucker 1943a: pl. 65a, e). Dimensions in cm.: diameter, 2.2–3.6; height, 0.3–0.8; diameter of hole, 0.3–0.5.

High cones, domes, or bell shapes (8 excavated, 1 collected) include a variety of shapes, but generally all are quite tall in relation to their diameter. Besides the truly conical and bell shapes, there are combinations of cylindrical lower portions topped by domes or truncated cones and one purely convex or domed spindle whorl. Most of these examples are painted black, and one is black and white, as described above. Similar spindle whorls occur in the Soncautla complex at Tres Zapotes (Drucker 1943a: pl. 65b, d, f, g) and in Cholulteca I (Noguera 1954: p. 150, nos. 15, 16). Dimensions in cm.: diameter, 0.8–2.6; height, 0.8–1.4; diameter of hole, 0.3–0.5.

Semiconical, with incised circle-and-dash design (1 excavated). This spindle whorl is fairly large in diameter. The sides slope gently upward to a steeper central portion which is now broken. Around the gently sloping portion two sets of four short lines radiated out toward the rim, which is set off with an encircling

FIG. 125. TOLTEC HEADS.

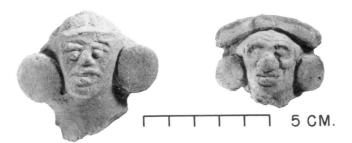

FIG. 126. HEADS WITH APPLIQUED EAR DISKS.

FIG. 127. POSTCLASSIC PLAIN-FROCK FIGURES.

line. The lines occur between what must have been two series of two longer incised lines with circles at the ends placed slightly in from a midline through the circle. Both surfaces were painted black. Spindle whorls with similar designs have not been reported from other areas. Dimensions in cm.: diameter, 3.0; height, 1.0; diameter of hole, 0.5.

Figurines

TOLTEC HEADS

3 specimens: 2 excavated, 1 collected.
Dimensions in cm. of 2 heads: height, about 4.5; width, 5.2 and 5.0; thickness, 1.4 and 1.8.
Paste: resembles Thin Orange.

These mold-made figurines have very lightly impressed features. The features of one head were made bolder by incising along the impressions left by the mold. All three heads have large square headdresses; one is bifurcated and the others are decorated with braids or buns.

The figurine with the bifurcated headdress comes from a late Venta Salada component and resembles Vaillant's Mazapan type (1938: fig. 2m) and figurines from Cholulteca I (Noguera 1954: 154c, 155a). The other two figurines, one from the surface of Ts 367 and the other from the earliest Venta Salada level, are like Vaillant's Coyotlatelco type (1938: fig. 2q, r).

HEADS WITH APPLIQUED EAR DISKS

4 specimens collected.
Dimensions in cm. of 2 heads: height, 3.1 and 4.3; width, 4.1 and 5.3; thickness, 2.2 and 2.3.
Paste and surface finish: resembles Coxcatlan Brushed; thin wash.

These mold-made heads have well-defined eyebrows, eyes, noses, and mouths. Large discoidal earplugs applied at the sides of the face make the head wider than it is high. The heads once had headdresses, but only one incomplete example remains in the form of a long strip applied across the top of the head. It has an applied disk in the center and was painted red; a broken edge at the back indicates that there was once more to it. There are traces of red paint on the forehead of another figurine.

In the Tehuacan Valley these figurines come from sites which date from the early Venta Salada phase. Similar figurines appear in early Postclassic times at Coyotlatelco (Rattray 1966: pl. XIj-l) and at Cholula (Noguera 1954: 160a).

POSTCLASSIC PLAIN-FROCK FIGURES

6 bodies excavated.

Dimensions in cm.: height (3 specimens), about 4.0-8.5; width (5 specimens), 2.5–6.2; thickness (6 specimens), 0.8–1.5.

Paste: resembles Coxcatlan Brushed.

These flat mold-made figurines resemble the Plain-frock Bodies of the late Palo Blanco subphase. They appear to be wearing long gowns, the hems of which can be seen against the figurines' legs. Arms are marked off by a groove; sometimes they rest at the side of the body and sometimes they lie across the body beneath a "V"-shaped *quechquemitl* or capelet. Some of the figurines have a groove at the waist indicating the top of the skirt; others are thinned at the waist. Some have nubbin breasts and all have holes running through the body under the arms. Flat feet extend at right angles to the body and are large enough for the figurine to stand on. All the bodies bear traces of white paint, and one has remains of red lines.

These figurines resemble some of the Valley of Mexico and Cholulteca bodies of Postclassic times.

Ceramic Affiliations

The continuation in diminishing amounts of Quachilco Mica, El Riego Gray, El Riego Polished, El Riego Plain, and El Riego Marble-tempered from late Palo Blanco into early Venta Salada certainly indicates that in large part the latter developed from the former. The development of Coxcatlan Gray from El Riego Gray, the presence of a few sherds of Coxcatlan Brushed in late Palo Blanco, and the continuation of the mold-made Plain-frock figurine type further confirm such an evolution.

However, a number of new pottery types emerge, giving the Venta Salada phase a distinctive ceramic congery: Coxcatlan Red, Coxcatlan Red-on-orange, Teotitlan Incised, two types of mold-made figurines, and mold-made spindle whorls. The new types, as well as such continuing wares as Coxcatlan Brushed and Coxcatlan Gray, are characterized by such new attributes as stamped bottoms; effigy, stepped, and stamped stepped supports; red paint on orange paste; different design motifs; and a variety of vessel forms. Many of these traits are distinctive of the so-called "Mixteca-Puebla" ceramic style and have no predecessors in our valley. They must have rather rapidly intruded from a currently unknown source, perhaps from the Mixteca-Alta or perhaps even from Cholula (if Cholulteca I or its predecessors turn out to be earlier than Venta Sal-

ada). Certainly it seems safe to speculate that profoundly different influences with significant social and political implications had entered the Tehuacan Valley. Whether actual Mixtec or Nahuatl dynasties were part of this intrusion or invasion is difficult to determine, but certainly Tehuacan had come under the influence or sway of these incipient imperialists. The similarity of the Venta Salada pottery to much of the pottery depicted in Codex Borgia, as well as the cultural continuity within Venta Salada leading up to historic times when many towns in the valley were definitely ruled by Mixtec caciques, tends to confirm the hypothesis of a Mixtec cultural and political invasion.

As might be expected if the Tehuacan Valley was part of an imperialistic unit, there are many evidences of contacts with other regions. Tula or Mazapan Red-on-buff sherds in early Venta Salada components link Venta Salada to the Tula-Mazapan horizon of the Valley of Mexico, as do the Texcoco Fabric-impressed sherds. Tula or Mazapan Red-on-buff also occurs in Isla de Sacrificios and Tajin III of central Veracruz, Las Flores of Panuco in northern Veracruz, and Cholulteca I. Coxcatlan Red-on-orange resembles Coyotlatelco Red-on-brown, and El Riego Marble-tempered and Burnished ware comales are similar; both sets of similarities are indicative of a relationship between Tehuacan and the Valley of Mexico, as are many similar figurine types.

Contacts between Tehuacan and Cholula are attested to by the presence in early Venta Salada components of spindle whorl, figurine, and pottery types characteristic of Cholulteca I, including Cholula Incised, Cholula Red-on-orange, and Cholula Polychrome Lacquer pottery and Cholula Types 1 and 2 figurines.

The Y Fine Orange sherds of early Venta Salada components indicate connections to and contemporaniety with Tepeu II of the Peten of Guatemala, Cehpech of Yucatan, Pokom and Pamplona of highland Guatemala, Paredon of Chiapas, Tajin III and Isla de Sacrificios I of central Veracruz, where they also occur. The X Fine Orange traded into the Tehuacan Valley in early Venta Salada is also found over a wide area, in such cultural manifestations as Las Flores, Cempoala, and Isla de Sacrificios I of Veracruz, Ayampuc of highland Guatemala, Tohil of the Pacific coast of Guatemala, Ruiz of lowland Chiapas, Jimba in the Peten, Sotuta of Chichen Itza, Monte Alban V, Cholulteca I, and Tula-Mazapan of the Valley of Mexico. Sherds of San Juan Plumbate (identified by Robert E. Smith) collected from Tr 210 connect earliest Venta Salada

209

with the San Juan phase of the Pacific coast of Guatemala, the Amatle phase of central highland Guatemala, the Maravillas phase of lowland Chiapas, and Coyotlatelco of the Valley of Mexico. Tohil Plumbate, traded from Guatemala to the latest part of early Venta Salada has similar and even wider contacts from Cempoala I of Central Veracruz to Tohil of Guatemala and El Salvador.

Cholula Polychrome Lacquer is also widespread at this time. It is abundant in early Venta Salada and occurs in early Cempoala, Coyotlatelco in the Valley of Mexico, Monte Alban IV, Upper Cerro de las Mesas, Paredon in Chiapas, and in late manifestations of the Guatemala Pacific coast.

The Venta Salada spindle whorls resembling those of the Soncautla complex of Tres Zapotes in central Veracruz indicate that the latter manifestation must be of this time period. Stamped-bottom decorative styles and techniques and engraved designs involved in similar spindle whorl types also seem to indicate that early Venta Salada is related to various late manifestations on the Veracruz coast.

The early Postclassic period, then, of which early Venta Salada is part, was a crucial one in Mesoamerica. It is the period of the "fall of the Maya Empire" to the south and of the rise of militarism and dynastic empire in highland Mexico. Until careful cross-cultural studies and exact chronologies are determined, we can truly understand neither these phenomena nor the tribal movements of historic peoples.

CHAPTER 10

The Late Part of the Venta Salada Phase

ABOUT 48,000 SHERDS and clay artifacts were uncovered in nine late Venta Salada components: Zone 1 of Tc 35w, Zone B of Ts 367, Zone I of Tc 50, Zone A of Ts 367, Zone A of Ts 368e, Zone A of Tc 35e, Zone A of Ts 368w, and tests in the large ruins of Coxcatlan (Tr 62) and Pueblo Nuevo (Tr 65). Three of the components were cave occupations, four were tests on large open sites, and two were tests on extensive ruins. However, over 33,000 of the 48,000 specimens came from a single component, Tr 62, thus making our sample somewhat unbalanced. Tr 62 is the historically documented town of Coxcatlan, which was occupied when the Spanish arrived in the valley. Tr 65 is probably of the same period. In addition to the excavated material, about 22,000 sherds were collected from over ninety surface sites, including almost all of the documented ancient villages of the valley.

Trends in ceramics from the stratified levels are, of course, the basis for the alignment of our components in sequential order, as well as for separating late Venta Salada from early Venta Salada. The Palo Blanco types, El Riego Gray, El Riego Orange, El Riego Plain, El Riego Polished, and El Riego Black, which were diminishing in popularity throughout early Venta Salada, almost disappear in late Venta Salada times. Quachilco Mica, which has been present since early Santa Maria, also continues to diminish in this final period. El Riego Marble-tempered, Coxcatlan Red, and Coxcatlan Gray, all of which increased very slight-

ly through early Venta Salada, diminish gradually in the later part of the phase. Coxcatlan Brushed and Coxcatlan Coarse, which increased throughout the early segment of the phase, continue this trend in popularity up to the Spanish conquest. Four types that were just beginning to emerge in early Venta Salada increase in the later part of the phase: Coxcatlan Red-on-cream, Coxcatlan Polychrome, Coxcatlan Black-on-orange, and Coxcatlan Striated.

Besides these pottery types, there also are new spindle whorl and figurine types. In fact, we debated dividing the Venta Salada phase into two cultural phases on the basis of the new ceramic types. However, the new types are of minority status in terms of the total ceramic complex, and the nonceramic artifact types and the subsistence and settlement patterns are not radially different in the early and late Venta Salada subphases. Thus, the total trait complex remains relatively uniform, though new ceramic types indicate some change within the phase.

The final significant and distinctive aspect of late Venta Salada ceramics is the presence of a large number of trade sherds. Moreover, most of these can be identified not only with an archaeological culture, but also with an ethnic or even a political group. Thus our ceramic relationships hint at various kinds of social relationships. As Volume I of the Tehuacan series has pointed out, several of the pottery types of this phase can be identified among vessels depicted in Codex Borgia, an indication that the Borgia was probably the

FIG. 128. COXCATLAN COARSE. Sherds of braziers.

5 CM.

product of a late Venta Salada material culture and was drawn by people living in or near the Tehuacan Valley.

Pottery Types

COXCATLAN COARSE

2,412 specimens excavated; 1,443 collected.

Paste

Coxcatlan Coarse gradually develops out of Quachilco Mica during Venta Salada times. The paste has a coarser texture and is more poorly knit than Quachilco Mica paste. Although the temper is of larger size and is used in greater quantity, one type blends into the other, making the separation of coarse examples of Quachilco Mica and fine examples of Coxcatlan Coarse rather arbitrary.

Three sherds that we considered fairly typical of the type were studied in thin section. Analysis showed that about 8 percent of the paste is grains 1.0 mm. or more in diameter of quartz, quartzite, muscovite, biotite, shale, and hornblende. About 7 percent is grains 0.5–1.0 mm. in diameter of the same materials and plagioclase. Another 8 percent is grains 0.1–0.5 mm. in diameter. Fine grains under 0.1 mm. compose about 5 percent of the sherds and are of the same materials plus hematite and magnetite.

Occasional vegetable fibers (cattail fluff?) were noted in some brazier fragments. The mixture has a medium-coarse look and is sometimes sandy, though it is fairly compact. The firing varies from uneven to even. Some sherds show no difference in color between periphery and core, but others have quite thin surface layers in the reddish-brown range and thick cores in the gray range. The paste is not very hard, measuring about 2.5 in the Mohs scale.

Surface Finish

The surface coloration is generally in the reddish-brown to brownish-gray range with some firing clouds. We noted the following variations: black to red to reddish-brown to light red (2.5 YR 1/2, 5/4–4/4, 5/6–6/8), Reddish-gray to dark gray (5.0 YR 5/2, 4/1), and gray (10 YR 5/1).

The surface generally was well smoothed, probably with a polishing stone or stick, leaving wide but shallow striations. A wash appears to have been applied to the vessel; it is of uneven thickness and distribution and wears off easily. The surface texture is rough to sandpapery on the exterior, and the interior is slightly rougher with many fingermarks and pits visible. The

5 CM.

FIG. 129. COXCATLAN COARSE. Handles and sherds with painted and appliqued decoration.

213

TABLE 62
Coxcatlan Coarse Vessel Forms
(sherds by site and zone)

| | Early Venta Salada | | | Late Venta Salada | | | | | | | | | |
	35e C	35e B	35w 3	35w 1	367 B	50 I	367 A	368e A	35e A	368w A	62 A	65 A	Total
Braziers		2		4	1		15			3	501	2	528
Ollas													
straight neck						2	18			2	144	3	169
long flaring neck							15		7	3	101	2	128
short flaring neck				1						1	1	12	15
rolled/beaded rim											4	1	5
miniature											38	2	40
Bowls													
convex wall													
everted rim											8	1	9
direct rim											4	2	6
cylindrical, everted rim								1			8		9
incurved rim										2	1	1	4
Handles													
strap							4			1	91	7	103
lug											11	3	14
loop											1	1	2
Body sherds	2	3	2	15	2	20	221	43	63	101	902	6	1380
Total	2	5	2	19	6	20	274	43	70	113	1815	43	2412

inner rim is generally well smoothed on ollas, but the rest of the interior is just barely smoothed.

Decoration

Decoration usually consists of bands of red paint on a white background, fingernail impressions, and appliqued bands, balls, cones, and stamped motifs. Traces of black and yellow paint also remain. The decoration will be described in detail with the vessel forms.

Vessel Forms

Braziers are the most commonly represented vessel form. No complete example was found, nor even a single complete profile from rim to base. It is thus difficult to reconstruct these vessels, some of which were undoubtedly representations of deities. It is obvious, however, that they resemble the braziers found by Acosta at Tula (*Rev. Mex. de Estudios Antro.* 1940 and 1945) and the fragments uncovered by Noguera at Cholula (1954: 118–119). They are large, thick-walled, nearly cylindrical vessels, usually with slightly concave sides. They may have flat lips or horizontally everted rims. Some examples have widely scal-loped pedestal bases, but others had flat bottoms and slablike legs. A raised horizontal band 5 to 10 cm. wide often encircles the outside of the rim like a flat collar. Some of the bands are further decorated by finger-tip or thumbnail impressions. Occasionally the rim is topped by a tall crest in the form of a triangle, semicircle, or oval, probably representing a headdress typical of a certain deity. The remains of large vertical slabs or rectangular lugs on some body sherds may represent the deity's ears.

The walls are often decorated by large conical appliques of the same paste as the vessel; these project outward like spikes. One or two thick bands, 1.5 to 2.0 cm. wide are sometimes applied around the base or midsection; these are decorated with finger-impressions. Another applied decoration consists of a row of thick round balls pressed tightly against one another along the top of everted rims. Appliqued balls also appear on the sides of vessels, enclosed between two thick horizontal fillets or arranged in a circle. Other decoration consists of applique stamped ornamentation in symbolic or glyphic form. Rosettes were applied to the walls and to the slab legs of some vessels. Many pieces are covered on the exterior by a thick

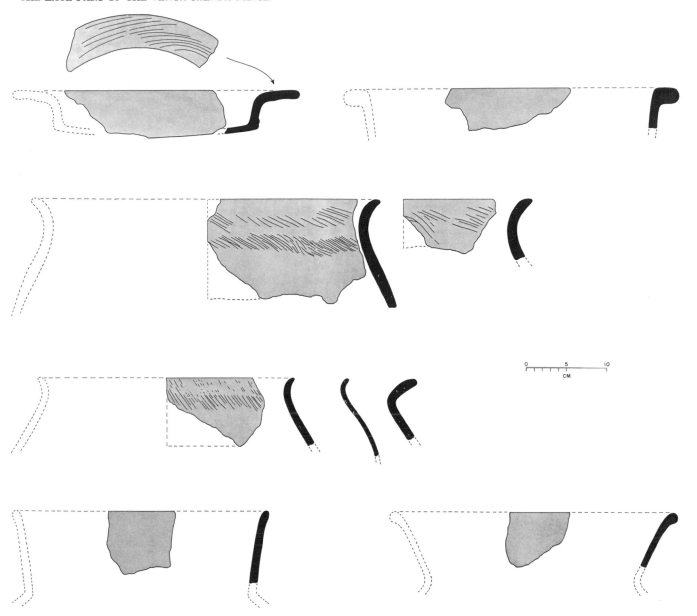

FIG. 130. COXCATLAN COARSE. *Row 1:* shallow bowl with wide everted rim and everted-rim cylindrical vessel; *rows 2, 3:* ollas with long and short flaring necks; *row 4:* straight neck and rolled-rim ollas. Diagonal markings represent striations left by the polishing tool.

white paint. Some sherds show bands of red paint against the white surface. Others have traces of complex designs in black, red, and deep yellow.

Several body sherds of braziers have a flat horizontal lug protruding within the vessel. These lugs probably served to hold a comal-like dish for burning incense inside the brazier. Dimensions in cm.: rim diam-eter, 28–40; thickness of body wall, 0.9–1.2; rims, 0.5 cm. thicker than the walls.

A second type of brazier is represented by fifty-two sherds from the Coxcatlan site, Tr 62. This type of brazier resembles in many respects the Mayan "as-semble-it-yourself" composite brazier described and illustrated by Borhegyi (1959). The fragments from

215

Tr 62 are from fairly large pedestal bases (vessels?), closed around the sides and across the top, except for round holes in the top about 2 cm. in diameter. The holes must have held prongs, which would in turn support shallow incense dishes. The pedestal portions have rim diameters of 22–28 cm.

Still other sherds representing vessels of unique shape were found. They too probably are fragments of braziers.

Ollas with long or short flaring necks have a very smooth transition from rim to large spherical body. Traces of white limy paint occasionally show on the exterior. Outer surfaces were first brushed diagonally and then the lower neck and body were smoothed horizontally, leaving a band of diagonal striations at rim and neck. Rim diameter, 28–44 cm.

Straight-neck ollas. The neck walls are sometimes slightly divergent. The same sort of brushed but un-smoothed band appears on the necks of these ollas as on the preceding form. One incomplete neck sherd was 9 cm. long. Rim diameter, 24–34 cm.

Ollas with rolled rims have longish necks with beaded lips. Rim diameter, 32–36 cm.

Miniature ollas have the same shapes and surface finish as the larger olla forms. Rim diameter, 10–18 cm.

Convex-wall bowls with wide everted rims have slightly convex bottoms, low walls, and very wide rims with flattish lips. One sherd has traces of white limy paint on the interior, another has traces of red powder over the entire exterior, and some rims have diagonal brushing striations on the upper surface. Dimensions in cm.: rim diameter, 32–36; rim width, 4.0–8.6; height, 5.0–7.0.

Cylindrical vessels with everted rims must have been large, tall vessels. They resemble the braziers, but the walls are not concave. Dimensions in cm.: rim diameter, about 40; rim width, 3.2; height, unknown.

Incurved-rim bowls have convex walls and a rim diameter of about 18–20 cm.

Convex-wall bowls with direct rims have generally straight to slightly convex sides. The lips are rounded or flattish. Some may be the comal-like vessel of composite or "assemble-it-yourself" braziers. Some have white limy paint on the interior. Rim diameter, 6.0–28 cm.

Handles. Numerous flat strap handles are probably from ollas: width, 2.9–5.3; thickness, 1.1–2.1 cm. Solid handles that are rounded in cross section are probably from incense burners, since some sherds of shallow bowls show signs of attachment of this type of handle. The complete length is unknown, but the

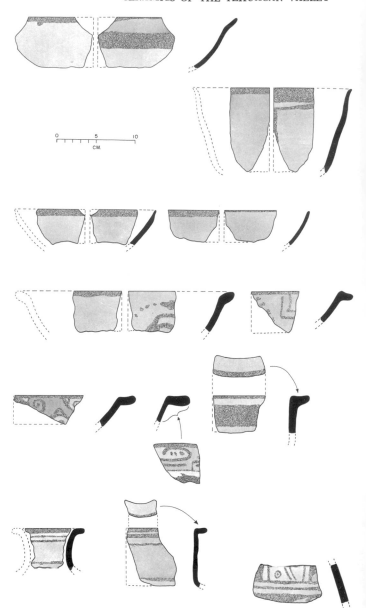

FIG. 131. COXCATLAN RED-ON-CREAM. *From top to bottom, shallow and deep convex-wall bowls with flaring rims, convex-wall bowls with direct and with everted rims, straight-neck ollas with everted rims and a decorated body sherd.*

largest fragment is 12 cm. long, and the handles are 2.0–3.5 cm. thick. Hollow, tubular handles with one end rounded may have been attached at the other end to incensarios or ladles. They range in diameter from 2.5 to 3.4 cm. Luglike handles are shortish flat horizontal handles with or without a round perforation in the center. They may have been attached to incense dishes and have supported them inside the braziers.

TABLE 63
Coxcatlan Red-on-cream Vessel Forms
(sherds by site and zone)

| | Early Venta Salada | Late Venta Salada | | | | | | | | | |
	35w 2	35w 1	367 B	50 I	367 A	368e A	35e A	368w A	62 A	65 A	Total
Bowls											
convex wall											
flaring rim					5			3	37		45
direct rim								1	5		6
everted rim								3	2		5
flaring wall		3			8				34		45
Ollas											
str. neck, everted rim								2	15	2	19
Body sherds	1	4	5	1	17	7	2	21	59	2	119
Total	1	7	5	1	30	7	2	30	152	4	239

Relationships

The Coxcatlan Coarse type obviously derives locally from concepts involved in Quachilco Mica. It is similar to, or may even be the same type as, the coarse ware found in the late zones of Cholula and in Monte Alban IV (Caso, Bernal, and Acosta 1967: 85–86). It is mainly a late Venta Salada type in the Tehuacan Valley, but outside the region seems to be as early as Cholulteca I. If this type dates as early as Cholulteca I and Monte Alban IV and is mainly of late Venta Salada times in Tehuacan, then many of the concepts concerning decoration and function may have been imported from Cholula or Oaxaca.

COXCATLAN RED-ON-CREAM

329 specimens excavated, 273 collected.

Paste

The paste is fairly heavily tempered and contains a large proportion of coarse material. About 5 percent of the paste is composed of grains 1.0–1.5 mm. in diameter identified as shale, quartz, quartzite, muscovite, biotite, plagioclase, and hornblende. About 10 percent is grains 0.5–1.0 mm. in diameter of the same materials. Smaller particles, 0.1–0.5 mm. or less in diameter, comprise only about 5 percent of the paste and consist of the same materials plus magnetite, hematite, and occasionally calcite.

The mixture is fair; the paste has a coarse, laminated consistency. The firing was even and resulted in little difference in color between the periphery and the core. The sherds break in an even fracture. Hardness ranges about 2.5 in the Mohs scale.

Sherds of Coxcatlan Red-on-cream are similar in surface characteristics to the cream surfaced sherds of Coxcatlan Red-on-orange. The Red-on-cream paste, however, is thicker, coarser, and more heavily tempered.

Surface Finish

Both surfaces are covered with a thick coat of paint ranging from creamy white (about 2.5 YR 8/1 or 10 YR 8/1) to a pale buff (10 YR. 8/2).

Decoration

The vessels are decorated with a thick red or orangish paint ranging from weak red (10 R 4/4 or 4/6) to reddish-brown (2/5 YR 4/4, 4/6). The designs vary with the vessel forms and will be described in the following section.

Vessel Forms

Flaring-wall bowls had flat unsupported, tripod, or pedestal-based bottoms. Decoration usually consists of a single red band encircling the inner and outer edges of the rim. Dimensions in cm.: rim diameter, 22–30; wall height, 5.0–8.0.

Convex-wall bowls with flaring rims had flat bottoms with or without supports. Decoration usually consists of a red band encircling the lip and a wider red band beneath the rim on the exterior surface. Dimensions in cm.: rim diameter, 20–26; wall height, 5.0–11.

Convex-wall bowls with direct rims presumably had flat unsupported or tripod bases. Decoration usually consists of a red band painted around the inner and outer lip. Dimensions in cm.: rim diameter, 16–30; wall height, 5.0–8.0.

Convex-wall bowls with everted rims presumably had flat unsupported or footed bottoms. They are more elaborately decorated than the preceding shapes with merely horizontal bands. A narrow band of red encircles the lip; beneath this on the outer surface is painted a combination of motifs, making a wide border or perhaps an all-over pattern. The motifs are very like the elements decorating vessels of Coxcatlan Red-on-orange, but the Red-on-cream designs are looser and more freely painted. Among the motifs are spirals attached to step elements, hooks, "V" 's or triangular elements, rectilinear and linear designs, circles with a dot or smaller circle in the middle, and a series of dots. Dimensions in cm.: rim dameter, 20–32; wall height, 5.0–over 7.0; wall thickness, 0.5–0.8.

Straight-neck ollas with everted rims presumably had globular bodies and flat bottoms. Designs include a small horizontal band around the lip and pairs of bands around the top of the neck and at the junction of neck and body. The bodies seem to have been more elaborately decorated. Dimensions in cm.: rim diameter, 9.0–12; wall thickness, 0.6–1.0.

Supports. The only supports found besides pedestal-

base fragments are of the dumbbell or bulb-end variety.

Relationships

This late Venta Salada type is closely related to Coxcatlan Red-on-orange in the Tehuacan Valley. It is similar to pottery at Cholula, and since some of the latter are earlier in Cholulteca I, it may be that the Tehuacan type is derived from that region.

COXCATLAN POLYCHROME

173 specimens excavated, 400 collected.

Paste

The paste is coarse and very similar to Coxcatlan Red-on-cream. About 10 percent of the volume is grains 0.5 to 1.0 mm. in diameter, including quartz, biotite, muscovite, quartzite, and hornblende. About 5 percent is grains 0.1–0.5 mm. in diameter of the same materials and plagioclase, and 3 percent is grains less than 0.1 mm. in diameter of magnetite, hematite, and calcite.

Surface Finish

Surfaces are finished in the same manner as Coxcatlan Red-on-cream.

Decoration

Decoration on Coxcatlan Polychrome vessels differs according to vessel form and sometimes according to

TABLE 64
Coxcatlan Polychrome Vessel Forms
(sherds by site and zone)

| | Early Venta Salada | Late Venta Salada | | | | | | | |
	35w 2	35w 1	367 A	368e A	35e A	368w A	62 A	65 A	Total
Bowls									
convex wall									
flaring rim						3	37		40
everted rim						5	17		22
direct rim			3				8		11
flaring wall	2	1				5	2		10
Ollas									
str. neck, everted rim							3		3
Body sherds		3	16	3	2	11	31	21	87
Total	2	4	19	3	2	24	98	21	173

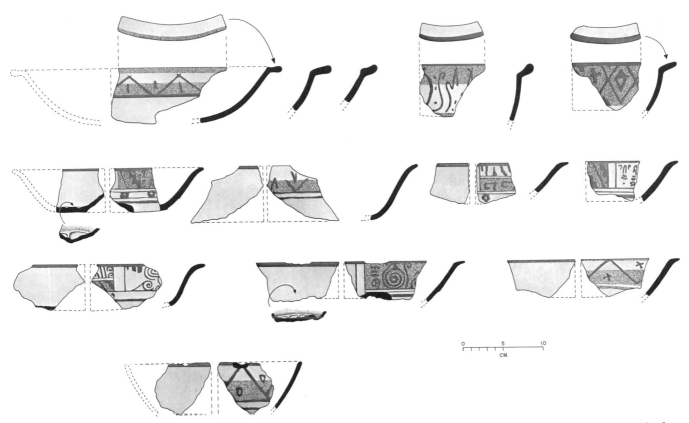

FIG. 132. COXCATLAN POLYCHROME. Convex-wall bowls with everted, flaring, and direct rims. Some bowls had stamped bottoms.

colors used. Patterns tend to cover more of the surface, are more varied, and of course use more colors than Coxcatlan Red-on-cream, with which it has many motifs in common. Colors used on the white or cream background include red, black, and orange.

Vessel Forms

Convex-wall bowls with flaring rims. These vessels have flat bottoms, convex walls, short flaring rims, and rounded or beveled lips. The interior surface of the lip is encircled by a red or orangish band. The exterior of the body displays a variety of decoration. Some vessels are decorated in red and black and sometimes orange in some of the same motifs as appear on Coxcatlan Red-on-orange. The motifs are also similarly arranged in horizontal bands or panels. Borders are made up of panels of zigzag diagonals, stepped elements, spirals, hooks, rectangles, and inverted or opposing "V"'s, for example, and sometimes appear above the characteristic row of hollow circles between two narrow lines which is underscored by a wider band. Another frequently used design is a wide orange band over which narrow red lines make wide inverted "V"'s resting on a narrow red horizontal line. The triangular sections contain a centered red "X." Sometimes the "V"'s are drawn with wavy or zigzag lines and contain small hollow triangles. Three fragments retained the edges of stamped bottoms and two of these sherds had attachments for supports. Dimensions in cm.: rim diameter, 18–30; wall height, 5.0–7.0.

Convex-wall bowls with everted rims. The bottoms are presumed to have been flat. Decoration consists of a painted red band on the lips and usually a wide horizontal band of black or light orange beneath the outer rim with superimposed red connected "V"'s, resting on a narrow band of red. Short vertical lines appear within the "V"'s. One sherd has a wide orange band extending from under the rim well down the body. This band is overlaid with a diamond pattern in red, with a sloppy "X" or small diamond inside each diagonal panel. Another sherd has a wide border of red, orange, and black in a poorly preserved design using curves

219

and dots. Dimensions in cm.: rim diameter, 26–36; rim width, 1.8–2.9; wall height, 7.0–9.0.

Convex-wall bowls with direct rims. The lips are beveled on the interior or exterior or may be rounded. A dark red band overlaps both surfaces of the lip. On the exterior a wide orange band is divided into triangular panels by overlaid dark red lines. Within the panels are hollow circles or triangles. Rim diameter, 16–22 cm.

Flaring-wall bowls. Decoration resembles that on convex-wall bowls with flaring rims. Rim diameter, 26 cm.

Straight-neck ollas with everted rims seem to have had elaborately decorated globular bodies. The upper surface of the horizontal rim is broken into panels by red lines. The panels contain hooks or circles or other elements. The lip is painted red and the underside of the rim is white. The neck is set off at top and bottom with horizontal red and white stripes. The space between is orange overlaid by red lines, which on one fragment divide the neck diagonally into diamond-shaped zones, each of which contains two small red "x"'s. A second fragment is divided into vertical panels by groups of straight and wavy lines and sidewise "u"'s placed one above the other. The bodies seem to have been painted orange, red, and white in all-over patterns. One body fragment with a small strap handle is divided into rectangular panels, and the rectangles in turn are filled with various motifs, including a circle within a circle and a circle surrounded by dots. Another body fragment, with remains of a loop handle, is decorated with concentric circles and radiating lines in a cobweb pattern. Dimensions in cm.: rim diameter, 10–12; height of neck, 6.9–8.5; wall thickness, 0.5–0.7; width of rim, about 1.5.

Miscellaneous features. One sherd of a bowl with an undulating lip, two small strap handles, a loop handle, and a perforated luglike handle were found in Venta Salada excavated or surface sites.

Relationships

This type could be considered a variant of Coxcatlan Red-on-cream, and perhaps like it, could have been derived from Cholula or the earlier Coxcatlan Red-on-orange. In reality the closest analogies to this type are with the finer dull buff polychrome of Upper Cerro de las Mesas (Drucker 1943a) and Isla de Sacrificios (Medellín Zenil 1960). Until these sites are better dated it is difficult to tell which is derived from which.

COXCATLAN BLACK-ON-ORANGE

107 specimens excavated, 249 collected.

Paste

This paste is fairly finely tempered, with about 16 percent of the volume composed of nonplastic materials. Only 3 percent is grains 0.5–1.0 mm. in diameter, identified as shale, quartzite, and muscovite. About 10 percent is grains 0.1–0.5 mm. in diameter of the same materials and quartz, biotite, plagioclase, and limestone. About 3 percent of the paste is grains under 0.1 mm. in diameter, including the materials mentioned and calcite, hematite, and magnetite.

The paste is well knit, though somewhat porous. Firing was usually quite even, for cores and peripheries are about the same orangish color. Hardness is about 4.0 in the Mohs scale.

Surface Finish

Exterior surfaces are covered by a thin, smoothed slip. The surface color ranges from reddish-yellow (5.0

TABLE 65
Coxcatlan Black-on-orange Vessel Forms
(sherds by site and zone)

| | Late Venta Salada | | | | | | | |
	367 B	367 A	368e A	35e A	368w A	62 A	65 A	Total
Bowls								
pedestal based convex wall		2	4		2	25		33
direct rim		2			1	14		17
outangled rim					3	1		4
Body sherds	1	7	1	3	4	35	2	53
Total	1	11	5	3	10	75	2	107

YR 7/6) to very pale brown (10 YR 7/4). The painted decoration is dark brown (7.5 YR 4/2) to dark gray (5.0 YR 4/1–3/1). Horizontal shallow, narrow, brushing striations are occasionally visible on the interior surface.

A second variety of Black-on-orange has a core fired dark gray and one or both surfaces covered by a thin orange slip.

Decoration

Decoration will be discussed under the individual vessel forms.

Vessel Forms

Pedestal-based vessels are the most prominent vessel form. They consist of a convex-wall bowl resting on a medium-high to tall hollow base with flaring sides. The decoration consists of black linear designs painted on the exterior only. A common motif is a series of hollow "S"-shaped elements used with dots, horizontal lines, or small circles. "U"-shaped motifs, rectangular elements, and solid triangles also appear. Dimensions in cm.: rim diameter, 10–14; height of base, 5.0–7.0; diameter of base, 10–12; wall thickness, 0.4–0.7.

Convex-wall bowls with direct rims. Some rim shreds are attached to flat or flattened bottoms, but others could have come from bowls with pedestal bases. Decoration consists of a painted reddish-black line inside the lip and sometimes on the exterior surface of the lip, and a border of narrow horizontal lines enclosing hollow "S"-shaped motifs, wavy lines, circles, heavy step-

5 cm.

FIG. 133. COXCATLAN BLACK-ON-ORANGE. Convex-wall bowl.

5 CM.

FIG. 134. COXCATLAN BLACK-ON-ORANGE. Convex-wall and pedestal-base sherds.

ped designs, spirals, and "U" elements. The stepped motifs and spirals occur on the slipped variety of Black-on-orange. Dimensions in cm.: rim diameter, 6–18; height, 2.5–7.0; wall thickness, 0.4–0.6.

Convex-wall bowls with outangled rims are rare. They may have had flat bottoms. Decorations are horizontal bands, sometimes enclosing hollow "S" motifs. Rim diameters are about 18 cm.

Relationships

The closest similarities of Coxcatlan Black-on-orange are to the black on orange or yellow ware of Cholulteca I (Noguera 1954: 99–100). However, the Tehuacan type has fewer and simpler decorative motifs, sharing only steps, circles, and spirals with the Cholulteca ware. If the two types are related, the Cholula specimens, which are earlier, could be ancestral to Coxcatlan Black-on-orange.

COXCATLAN STRIATED BUFF

1,434 specimens excavated, 348 collected.

Paste

The paste is heavily tempered. About 15 percent is grains of nonplastic matter between 0.5 and 1.0 mm. in diameter, about 5 percent is grains 0.1–0.5 mm. in diameter, and another 5 percent is grains less than 0.1 mm. in diameter. The temper is composed of quartz, quartzite, plagioclase, muscovite, biotite, and schist; some of the finer particles are hematite and magnitite.

The clay is well knit, porous, and evenly fired, with a hardness of about 3.5. Some sherds show that some vessels were definitely mold-made, but others give no evidence of the technique of manufacture.

Surface Finish

The surface color ranges from pale brown (10 YR 7/3, 7/4), which represents the majority coloration of this type, to reddish-yellow (7.5 YR 7/6, 7/5) to light gray (10 YR 7/2). The latter represents the badly fired specimens, has a black core, and is rare.

Most of the surfaces were wiped horizontally while the clay remained plastic. The finish varies in smoothness from specimen to specimen and will be described further below.

Vessel Forms

All examples of Coxcatlan Striated Buff seem to be fragments of convex molds (rim sherds, 591). Wall fragments are roughened on the exterior by deep horizontal brushing marks or by incisions, usually in the form of irregular crosshatching, but sometimes as crudely parallel vertical or horizontal lines. The striations rarely continue on the exterior bottom. We believe they served as air vents to keep the superimposed pot from sticking to the mold.

On the exterior surface of the bottoms of some molds (represented by over twenty sherds) are deeply incised designs for making the stamped bottoms of grater bowls. Some of these are shown in Fig. 135. A few bottom sherds had both incised molds on the exterior surface and stamped designs on the interior, showing that the molds were made in molds and may also have served as graters themselves. A dozen fragments showed pits, bubbles, and warping obviously caused by reheating in kilns.

The similarity of the incised bottom designs to the stamped bottoms of Coxcatlan Gray, Coxcatlan Red, and Coxcatlan Brushed show that Coxcatlan Striated Buff molds probably were used to make molcajetes in all these pastes. Further, the inner walls of some of these stamped-bottom bowls plainly show smoothed-over traces of the crosshatched striations, as do some of the molds made in molds. See Fig. 135.

The molds have fairly thick and uniform convex

TABLE 66
Coxcatlan Striated Buff Vessel Forms
(sherds by site and zone)

| | Late Venta Salada | | | | | | |
	367 A	368e A	35e A	368w A	62 A	65 A	Total
Convex molds or bowls	2			4	569	16	591
Flat bases					72	35	107
Body sherds	1	2	6	24	641	62	736
Total	3	2	6	28	1282	113	1434

5 CM.

FIG. 135. COXCATLAN STRIATED BUFF. *Above and to the right of scale,* molds and impressions left by molds; note faint unobliterated impressions of striations on inner wall of large bowl, especially at junction of wall with bottom. *Below scale,* mold fragments showing different kinds of striated surfaces.

walls ranging from 3.6 to 12 cm. high and terminating in lips that are perfectly flat across the top. Most of the attached bottom fragments are flat, but at least one is rounded. The larger, deeper molds may have formed the lower (or upper) halves of ollas. Rim diameters range from 10 to 36 cm.

Relationships

Pottery molds similar to the convex molds of Cox-

catlan Striated Buff have not yet been reported from other regions, but mold-made stamped-bottom pottery was widespread in Postclassic Mesoamerica.

Today in the Tehuacan Valley the small town of Altepexi is a center for the production of mold-made stamped-bottom vessels, commonly used as ashtrays. Other modern mold-made Mexican pottery is described by Foster (1948, 1955).

While most of our latest Venta Salada sites yield-

223

FIG. 136. XANTIL OR BRAZIER FRAGMENTS.

5 CM.

ed fragments of molds for pottery, the earlier sites show a spotty distribution, perhaps indicating only a few centers of production by specialists.

TEHUACAN XANTILES

892 specimens excavated, 78 collected.

Xantiles are large hollow figurines made in the Postclassic period and exist in abundance throughout the Tehuacan Valley. They represent many deities, including Xipe Totec, Xochiquetzal, Macuilxochitl, Tlaloc, and others. They were used ceremonially and examples are to be found at hilltop shrines, in caves, and in tombs throughout the valley—or, rather, one finds the pitiful fragments that remain after searchers for loot have finished with the offertory caches. Many of these ceremonial objects were found near Classic buildings and sometimes are found buried within them. It is doubtful, however, that xantiles were made in Classic times, but rather were a type of dedicatory offering from Postclassic peoples.

Paste

The fragments are of different pastes. The examples analyzed in thin section were heavily tempered. From 10 to 15 percent of the volume of the sherds analyzed is made up of quartz, quartzite, and shale in particles 0.5–1.0 mm. in diameter. Only about 3 percent of the nonplastic particles were over 1.0 mm., and about 5 percent were under 0.5 mm. The quartz is a white crystalline translucent type, occurring with shale and quartzite as big grains; and with muscovite, biotite, magnetite, and hematite among the small grains. The clay does not adhere very well to the quartz particles. The mixture is poor to fair, and the consistency is coarse. The fracture is irregular.

The periphery is usually in the reddish-brown range, but varies according to the paste. Generally there is a well-defined core in the reddish-gray to light gray range. Surface coloration varies according to paste, ranging from light brown (7.5 YR 6/4) to reddish-brown to reddish-gray (5.0 YR 5/2, 6/3, 7/6).

Decoration

The outer surface is generally covered with remains of a thick white paint, and occasional traces are seen of red, dark yellow, light green, turquoise blue, and black paint. There is no doubt that the features were once painted. Other decoration includes stamped and incised appliques.

Vessel Form

The base of the xantil figurine is cylindrical and open; the body is shaped somewhat like a large milk bottle to which undersized limbs are attached. The large head is made in a separate mold, as are earplugs, headdress, ornamentation, and other apparel. Some heads have openings through the eyes or mouths, or the top of the head was left open. The figures usually have a complex headdress characteristic of the god being portrayed. The ears are generally rectangular slabs placed at right angles to the head, and many have round earplugs attached. The mouth is often open and perforated. The eyes were shaped and then painted. Noses are quite naturalistic and sometimes have nose-plugs.

The limbs are sometimes realistically shaped and sometimes are barely representational. A number of xantil fragments are shown in Fig. 136.

The figures are almost always in a seated position, with the knees drawn up at the sides against the body, although a few figures are cross-legged.

Relationships

The Tehuacan Valley is noted as the main source of xantiles. Similar large figures, called "Monumental Ware idols," are known from Upper Cerro de las Mesas (Drucker 1943a: pls. 47–48). Seler, on the basis of mask decorations on xantiles from Teotitlan del Camino and similar ones in Codex Borgia concluded that the codex was painted in the Tehuacan Valley.

Trade Wares

The latest components in our sequence abound in trade sherds. A total of 868 identifiable sherds were uncovered in excavation, and many more were collected from surface sites attributable to the late Venta Salada subphase.

One tiny sherd with an eroded blue-gray glaze was identified by Robert E. Smith as Tohil Plumbate. There is some reason to question whether this sherd, from Zone A of Ts 367, is actually a late Venta Salada trade sherd. A similar larger sherd occurred in an early Venta Salada level of Tc 50, and it is possible that the sherd from Ts 367 could have been exhumed by the ancient inhabitants from an earlier level. The same is true of the seven sherds of X Fine Orange, also identified by Smith, from the top levels of El Riego Cave. Sherds of the same type are very numerous in the earlier levels of the cave.

Fig. 137. Venta Salada trade sherds. *Rows 1, 2:* Cholula Incised and Polychrome Lacquer; *row 3:* Cholula Polychrome Firme (four sherds) and Polychrome Matte (one sherd); *rows 4, 5:* Tenayuca Black-on-orange (two sherds),
Texcoco Fabric-impressed (one sherd), Texcoco Black-on-red (three sherds) and Black-and-white-on-red (one
sherd, *far right*); *rows 6, 7:* X Fine Orange (five sherds, all incised), Isla de Sacrificios Polychrome (one sherd),
Cerro de las Mesas Polychrome (three sherds), Tancol Polychrome (one sherd, *far right*).

TABLE 67
Late Venta Salada Trade Sherds
(by site and zone)

	35w 1	367 B	367 A	368e A	35e A	368w A	62 A	65 A	Total
Tancol Polychrome							1		1
Mixteca Polychrome							1		1
Cerro de las Mesas Dull Buff Polychrome			2	6		4	4		16
Isla de Sacrificios Polychrome	2		3	1			22		28
Texcoco White-and-black-on-red			3	1	5	1	31	1	42
Tenayuca Black-on-orange			5		2	3	17	2	29
Texcoco Black-on-red	7		19	1	12	2	143	2	186
Cholula Coarse Decorated							62	9	71
Cholula Polychrome Firme						11	59	3	73
Cholula Polychrome Matte				1	2	4	9		16
Cholula Incised		2	3	7	1	4	7	2	26
Cholula Polychrome Lacquer	9		17	4	23	47	19	1	120
X Fine Orange: body	1								1
cylindrical jar	4				2				6
Tohil Plumbate			1						1
Thin Orange: body					1				1
ring base	1								1
Texcoco Fabric-impressed: bodies		4	3	5		34	89		135
Flower-pot-shaped jars				1		7	18	90	116
Total	24	6	56	27	48	117	482	110	870

The other identifiable trade sherds, however, are stratigraphically more secure. The largest number of identified trade wares from excavated levels comes from the Valley of Mexico. They are, in order of popularity, Texcoco Fabric-impressed, Texcoco Black-on-red, Texcoco Black-and-white-on-red, and Tenayuca Black-on-orange (Tolstoy 1958, Noguera 1945). The proportions found of these Aztec types indicate that they were probably traded into late Venta Salada during Aztec II–IV times. Dr. Piña Chan identified these sherds.

Wares from Cholula were almost as popular in the Tehuacan excavations as those from the Valley of Mexico and are actually more popular in the surface collections. The proportions of the Cholula wares uncovered suggest that they are of Cholulteca II–III times (Noguera 1954). In order of popularity, the types are: Cholula Polychrome Lacquer, Cholula Polychrome Firme, Cholula Decorated Coarse, Cholula Incised, and Cholula Polychrome Matte. Drs. Ignacio Bernal and John Paddock identified these sherds, as well as a single sherd of Mixteca Polychrome of the Monte Alban V period, which is often associated with the Cholula types we have listed.

In late Venta Salada excavated levels were twenty-eight sherds of Isla de Sacrificios Polychrome from the latest phase of central Veracruz, identified by José García Payón and Alfonso Medellín Zenil (Medellín Zenil 1960). Sixteen sherds of Cerro de las Mesas Dull Buff Polychrome came from the Upper Cerro de las Mesas phase of southern Veracruz (Drucker 1943a). MacNeish identified a single sherd from Tr 65 as Tancol Polychrome from the Panuco period (VI) of northern Veracruz (Ekholm 1944).

Another 200 or so sherds were obviously foreign to the Tehuacan region, but neither we nor the archaeologists we solicited were able to identify them.

Miscellaneous Objects

Birds are most common among the late Venta Salada animal effigies in clay; some of these were parts of whistles or ocarinas but others are not. A few retain traces of white or red paint. Dogs are also popular; we found both crudely made body fragments and heads that were more carefully made. The heads are usually painted white with the features defined in red and black. Most specimens have the flat muzzles typical of Mexican hairless dogs. The heads may have been attached to the crude bodies or they could have broken off pots or whistles. There is one serpent head among the animal effigies and some crudely formed heads of various mammals.

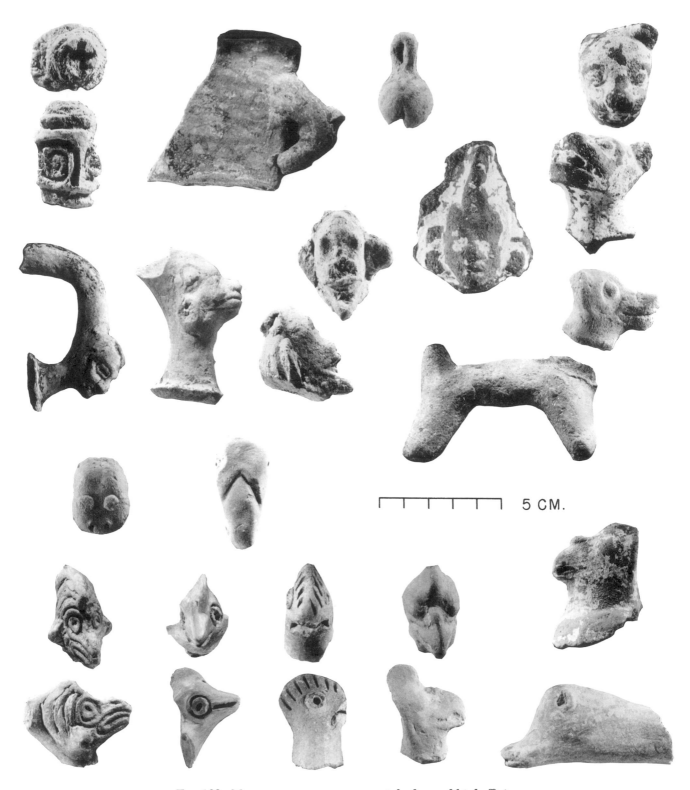

Fig. 138. Miscellaneous objects: mainly dog and bird effigies.

5 CM.

FIG. 139. MISCELLANEOUS OBJECTS FROM SURFACE SITES: toy olla, whistles, ball.

Other ceramic objects include a cylindrical seal or stamp with a spiral motif repeated four times around its sides, a small bell or tinkler bearing a curvilinear design in red and turquoise paint, and whistles or ocarinas or fragments thereof.

Most of the late Venta Salada ceramic miscellany were recovered from levels lying just below the surface, making their chronological placement somewhat insecure. These items and others collected from the surface include the unclassified figurine fragments il-lustrated in Fig. 146 and the toy olla, small ball, whistles, and other objects shown in Fig. 139.

Spindle Whorls

All late Venta Salada spindle whorls were formed in molds. They are perforated circular objects with a flat lower surface and a raised upper surface, rang-ing from only slightly convex to a high conical or domed shape. Generally, the higher the upper surface

229

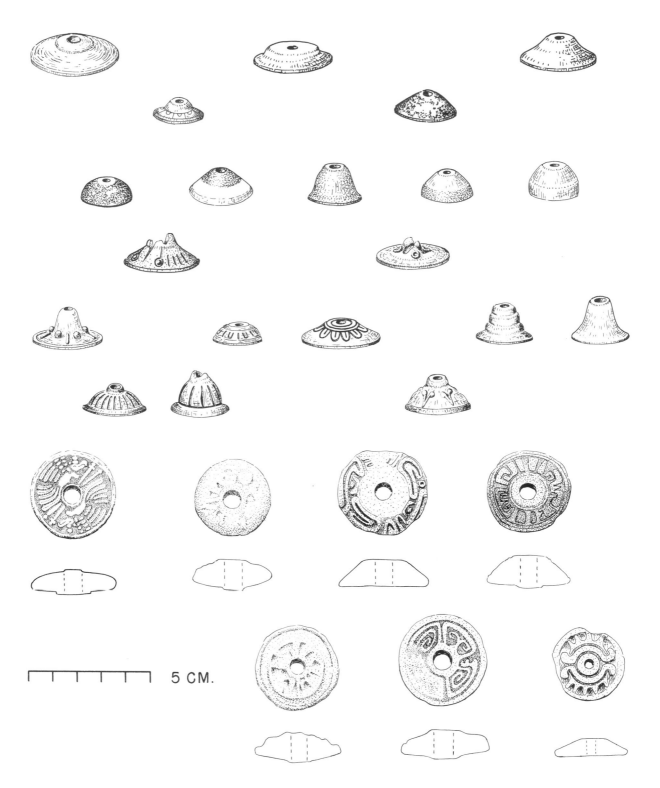

FIG. 140. SPINDLE WHORLS FROM EARLY AND LATE VENTA SALADA COMPONENTS. *Rows 1, 2:* low to medium-high conical specimens; *row 3:* conical, domed, or bell-shaped examples; *row 4:* semiconical with circle-and-dash design and conical with circles in quadrants; *row 5:* conical with buns and ridges, convex with "U" motifs, plain or tiered high conical; *row 6:* conical with dashes and with appliqued rays; *rows 7, 8:* large spindle whorls with stamped glyphs or geometric designs.

is, the smaller the diameter of the spindle whorl and of the central hole. Unlike most early Venta Salada specimens, the upper side is usually decorated with molded or incised designs. The more complex motifs usually appear on the larger, more disklike spindle whorls.

We have classified the late Venta Salada spindle whorls according to decoration, or to shape where decoration is absent. They are described below according to both shape and decoration.

Slightly conical, with circles in quadrants (3 excavated). The slightly raised surfaces of these spindle whorls are divided into quadrants by alternating ridges and depressions. Each quadrant contains a circle, the outline of which is raised in the example illustrated in Fig. 140, and depressed on the other specimens. The illustrated specimen was painted white all over; another was painted black, but no paint shows on the third. This late Postclassic type of spindle whorl is also present in Upper Cerro de las Mesas (Drucker 1943*b*: fig. 177) and in the Soncautla complex at Tres Zapotes (Drucker 1943*a*: pl. 65*t*). Dimensions in cm.: diameter, 2.5–3.1; height, 0.6–1.1; diameter of hole, 0.4.

Conical, with alternating buns and ridges (5 excavated). The upper surface of four specimens rise directly from the outer edge to a high cone; the fifth, shown in Fig. 140, has a tall conical center surrounded by a flattish rim on which the alternating raised buns and short radial ridges appear. There would be six of each element if the specimen were complete. Both surfaces are covered with shiny black paint, probably asphalt. This specimen partially resembles a spindle whorl from Upper Cerro de las Mesas illustrated by Drucker (1943*b*: fig. 176). Dimensions in cm.: diameter, 1.7–3.3; height, 1.0–2.2; diameter of hole, 0.3.

Convex, with band of "U" devices (1 excavated, 2 collected). The convex surface is decorated with concentric circles around the hole and a border of "U" elements. Designs that are somewhat similar appear on a spindle whorl from Cholula (Noguera 1954: p. 150, no. 6) and on spindle whorls from Las Flores in the Tampico-Panuco region of Veracruz (Ekholm 1944: fig. 46*d, p*). Dimensions in cm.: diameter, 2.0–3.2; height, 0.6; diameter of hole, 0.3–0.5.

High cone, plain or tiered (2 excavated, 1 collected). These spindle whorls are small in diameter and rise to a high conical center. One example, shown in Fig. 140, appears to have been made by superimposing four rings of clay, each smaller than the one below it. It is similar to a spindle whorl illustrated by Druck-

er from Upper Cerro de las Mesas (1943*b*: fig. 171). One of the plain cones from Tehuacan resembles another specimen from Cerro de las Mesas (*ibid.*: fig. 175). Dimensions in cm.: diameter, 1.3–2.4; height, 1.6; diameter of hole, 0.4–0.5.

Conical, with radiating dashes (2 excavated, 1 collected). The low to high conical or domed surface is decorated with nine to fourteen stamped or incised lines radiating from the center. Similar spindle whorls have been found in Upper Cerro de las Mesas (Drucker 1943*b*: figs. 178–180). Dimensions in cm.: diameter, 2.1–2.6; height, 0.9–1.8; diameter of hole, 0.2–0.5.

Conical, with "ray" devices (1 excavated). The paste of this spindle whorl resembles Coxcatlan red-on-orange. Four raised "rays" pointing outward are evenly spaced around the steeply slanting sides of the upper surface. Traces of black paint remain between the design elements, which are shaped somewhat like "V"'s with thick curled ends. They are a common device on Postclassic ceramic and nonceramic artifacts. The idea of four rays or compass points appears in decoration on spindle whorls from the Tampico-Panuco region of Veracruz (Ekholm 1944: fig. 45*f, j*) and from Cholula (Noguera 1954: p. 150, nos. 3, 8). Dimensions in cm.: diameter, 2.8; height, 1.2; diameter of hole, 0.4.

Large, with complex designs (5 excavated, 4 collected). These spindle whorls generally have a coarser paste, larger diameter, and larger hole than the types previously described. The upper surface varies from slightly convex to a more nearly conical shape and includes a truncated cone with fairly steep sides and a wide flat top. Three specimens are decorated with stamped or carved stylized birds, serpents, or other animals; unfortunately, the decorated surfaces are too worn to interpret clearly. The zoomorphic decorations resemble design elements on spindle whorls from the Tampico-Panuco region (Ekholm 1955: fig. 44). Other specimens have geometric designs similar to decoration on spindle whorls from Tenayuca in the Valley of Mexico (Noguera 1935: pls. 11 and 6) and on an example from Cholula (Noguera 1954: p. 150, no. 1). Most of the Venta Salada specimens retain traces of shiny black paint, and a few show touches of white or red paint. Dimensions in cm.: diameter, 3.0–3.8; height, 0.5–2.0; diameter of hole, 0.6–0.9.

Figurines

DOG FACE HEADS

7 heads: 5 excavated, 2 collected.

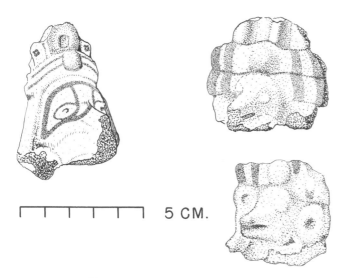

FIG. 141. DOG FACE HEADS.

Dimensions in cm. of 3 heads: height, 3.5–5.9; width, about 4.5; thickness, 3.0–4.1.
Paste: resembles Coxcatlan Brushed.

These mold-made heads are plano-convex or concave-convex. The most prominent feature is a large protruding snout. The eyes and mouth are indicated by depressions left by the mold and originally were painted. Around the face is a headdress composed of a raised band and a disk over the forehead. The band is surmounted by a thinner section which is partly broken.

All of the figurines were painted white. One has black outlines defining the eyes, hairline, and different parts of the headdress. The other heads show traces of red (7.5 R 4/6) and turquoise (5.0 BG 7/4) paint. One torso fragment indicates that these heads were attached to bodies having a human rather than an animal form.

These figurines seem to be a late Venta Salada type. Similar heads have been found at Cholula and in Aztec sites in the Valley of Mexico and are widespread in Postclassic Mesoamerica.

AZTEC SQUARE CAP HEADS

11 heads: 7 excavated, 4 collected.
Paste: resembles Coxcatlan Coarse but contains no mica.

The heads are mold-made and tend to be flat front and back. The face and squared cap are roughly triangular in outline. Eyes, mouth, and the lower edge of the cap are indicated by impressions. The raised nose is long and narrow.

The heads were painted white. Some have red paint on various parts of the face: at the corners of the eyes,

in the mouth, and on the cheeks. The head illustrated has a touch of turquoise paint under the chin.

These figurines represent the late Venta Salada phase in the Tehuacan Valley. At Cholula similar heads, classified by Noguera as Type 3, are diagnostic of Cholulteca II (Noguera 1954: p. 156, a-f). These heads occur at about the same time in other parts of Mexico and seem to be associated with the expansion of the Aztec empire.

FLAT CAP HEADS

2 heads: 1 excavated, 1 collected.
Dimensions in cm.: height, 4.4 and 3.2; width, 3.5 and about 4.5; thickness, 1.5 and 2.2.
Paste: resembles Coxcatlan Brushed.

The heads are mold-made, with eyes, eyebrows, and open mouth in low relief. The nose is large. A flat cap squares off the top of the head and has narrow sides that come down to the ears. The ears, or ears and earplugs, are large and are squared off at the bottom.

The Tehuacan specimens resemble Type 2 heads from Cholula, which are considered diagnostic of Cholulteca I (Noguera 1954: p. 155, b-d). Similar heads occur with Aztec remains (Noguera 1935: pl. XLV). The Tehuacan heads also resemble Type II-A figurines from Upper Cerro de las Mesas (Drucker 1943b: pl. 29, bottom, left).

TRAPEZOIDAL HEADS

2 heads excavated.
Dimensions in cm. of each fragment: height, 5.3 and 6.4; width, 6.1 and 4.9; thickness, 1.6 and 1.9.
Paste: fine sandy orange paste.

These head and shoulder portions of mold-made figurines are generally flat except for slightly protruding oval faces. Eyes, mouth, hair, and earplugs are indicated by shallow impressions. The hair lies flat across the top of the head and flows down to or over the shoulders.

The figurines were once covered with white paint, and the features were outlined in black. One figurine has red traces in the mouth and in one eye. Red and turquoise once filled in sections of a collar or necklace. One body was pierced beneath the arms.

Figurines similar to this late Venta Salada type are known from Cholulteca III (Type 6, Noguera 1954: p. 159, a-d).

PROGNATHIC OLD MAN

1 head excavated.
Dimensions in cm.: height, 3.8; width, 3.3; thickness, 2.9.
Paste: fine sandy orange paste.

This head is thicker and more realistically formed than the preceding types. It appears to be hand modeled rather than mold made. The back of the head is flat, but the face slopes outward from forehead to chin. The mouth is indicated by a single horizontal groove, around which two sets of concentric lines represent wrinkles. The white of each eye is made by two shallow punctations and the pupil by a deep conical punch. The nose is long and flat and has two punched nostrils. A series of short vertical lines around the hairline indicate either hair or a headdress. Below this extend ears with a deep conical punch to indicate ear ornaments. Traces of red paint are visible in most of the lines or depressions.

Although found in a late Postclassic context in the Tehuacan Valley, this specimen may have been dug up from an earlier horizon. Similar figurines have not been reported from other parts of Mexico.

HOLLOW POSTCLASSIC PAINTED HEAD

1 head excavated.
Dimensions in cm.: height, 5.1; width, 5.8; thickness, 2.9
Paste: resembles Coxcatlan Brushed.

This hand-modeled hollow head is flat across the back and convex across the front. The only facial feature in relief is the now eroded nose. Other features were painted in black and red over a surface of white paint. Traces of turquoise and yellow remain on the cheeks. The eyes are half-moon shaped with the straight side on top. Two concentric semicircles depict eyeball and pupil. The headdress is crescentic, with three sets of vertical bands, one in the center and one on each side.

No figurines of this type have been reported from other regions.

FIGURES WITH LOIN CLOTHS

4 bodies: 2 excavated, 2 collected.
Dimensions in cm.: length, about 6.0–12; width, about 2.0–3.0
Paste: resembles Coxcatlan Brushed.

These mold-made figurines are flat across the back and tend to be somewhat long and narrow. One of the specimens shown in Fig. 145 has feet that extend forward at right angles so that it can stand erect. This figure wears a V-shaped loin cloth and has a protruding pregnant-looking abdomen with arms and hands alongside it; holes are punched through the body beneath the arms.

The other specimen illustrated, a waist-to-foot fragment, looks as though it might have come from an

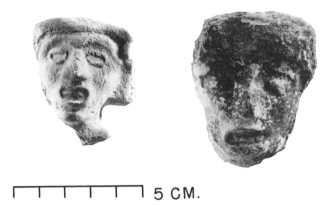

FIG. 142. AZTEC SQUARE CAP AND FLAT CAP HEADS.

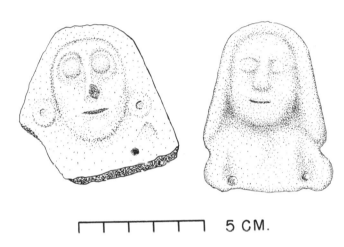

FIG. 143. TRAPEZOIDAL HEADS.

FIG. 144. PROGNATHIC OLD MAN AND HOLLOW PAINTED HEADS.

5 CM.

Fig. 145. Figurine bodies. *Rows 1, 2:* front and side views of figures with Loin Cloths, with Pierced Bellies, and with Tripod support; *row 3:* Seated (kneeling) figure and Cholula Decorated bodies.

Egyptian tomb. A loin cloth crosses the abdomen and extends in a narrow flap to the slightly flexed knees. The feet point downward, as though the body were in a lying position. Toes are indicated by impressions.

The excavated bodies come from a late Venta Salada context. They are similar to figurines from the Tula-Mazapan horizon in the Valley of Mexico and from Cholulteca III (Noguera 1954: p. 159, *f–h*).

Cholula Decorated Figures

6 bodies: 4 excavated, 2 collected.
Dimensions in cm.: length, about 3.0–9.0; thickness, about 1.0–2.0; width, about 3.0–6.0.
Paste: resembles Coxcatlan Brushed and Coxcatlan Gray.

The flattish, mold-made figurines are roughly rectangular in shape when viewed from the front. They are a late manifestation of flat plain-frocked bodies. They wear a short skirt and a decorated collar or necklace. Arms are bent at the elbow so that the hands rest against the abdomen. A hole under each arm could have been used for lines to suspend the figurine. The feet are broken but originally extended forward at right angles from the body. The larger figurine illustrated was once covered with white paint. Traces of black and red decoration remain.

These figures occur in Postclassic horizons in the Tehuacan Valley and are quite similar to figurines found with Aztec remains in the Valley of Mexico and with Postclassic remains in the southern Oaxaca–Monte Alban region. They are the same type as Noguera's Type 5 from Cholulteca III (Noguera 1954: p. 158, e–h).

SEATED FIGURES

6 bodies: 5 excavated, 1 collected.
Dimensions in cm.: height, about 6.0; width, about 5.0; thickness at chest, about 1.0.
Paste: resembles Coxcatlan Brushed.

These figures are mold made. They are flat across the back and most of the front. They appear to be kneeling but actually are seated in a typical Indian position with buttocks on the ground and legs bent to the back of the body. The feet splay out to the back and sides. Arms are at the sides of the body, and the hands rest on the thighs. There are holes on either side beneath the arms. The figurines were apparently painted white with details of the clothing added in black lines.

No similar figures are known from other regions.

PIERCED-BELLY FIGURES

10 bodies excavated.
Dimensions in cm.: height, 5.3–9.7; maximum width, 2.8–4.6; maximum thickness at base of skirt, 1.7–4.2.
Paste: resembles Coxcatlan Brushed.

These thick standing figurines are crudely hand modeled. The figurines appear to be wearing a smock which stands away from the front of the body because of a large hole punched upward in front of the legs. Buttocks are indicated on some of the bodies. A hole

FIG. 146. UNCLASSIFIED FIGURINES FROM SURFACE COLLECTIONS.

235

in the position of the navel runs completely through the body. The figurines are covered with white paint and features of the dress are added in black, red, and turquoise.

This late Venta Salada type resembles some figurines from Cholula.

TRIPOD SQUARE-SKIRT FIGURES

4 specimens: 2 excavated, 2 collected.
Dimensions in cm. of one figure: length, over 6.0; width, over 5.0; thickness, 1.0–1.5.

The most complete specimen is a standing figure with feet and head missing. The back is slightly concave and the front slightly convex. The figure wears a long skirt, a waist-length *quechquemitl*, and an elaborate necklace. The hands, with wrists and fingers indicated, extend from beneath the quechquemitl. Although the figure was formed in a mold, details of the necklace and hands are emphasized by incising. A round prop or handle extends from the back downward. Other specimens of this type are fragments displaying only the square skirt.

The nearly complete figure resembles a figurine illustrated by Paddock (1966: fig. 126) and is similar to drawings in Codex Borgia (e.g., pl. 9).

CRUDELY MODELED STANDING FIGURES

2 bodies excavated.
Dimensions in cm.: height, 4.3, 4.6; width, 3.8, 4.9; thickness, 1.4, 1.9
Paste: sandy orange clay.

The bodies are rectangular when viewed from the front; they have square shoulders and no waist. Arms probably hung at the sides of the body. Legs are missing, but seem to have extended in a standing position.

The specimens are too fragmentary for comparison.

Ceramic Affiliations

The late Venta Salada period lasts into historic times. One of its major components, Teotitlan del Camino, is recorded in early historic documents as a trade center, so it is not surprising to find considerable evidence of widespread ceramic relationships and contacts. The most obvious evidence of such contacts are the many sherds (868 from excavation and many more from surface collections) of wares that were brought into Tehuacan from as far north as Tampico and as far south as Honduras.

Primary consideration is naturally given the nearby Cholula region. Many late Venta Salada components contained sherds of Cholula Polychrome Lacquer, Cholula Polychrome Firme, Cholula Polychrome Matte, Cholula Incised, and Cholula Decorated Coarse. Common to both late Cholula and late Venta Salada seem to be red-on-orange and black-on-orange bichrome types, brushed types, and red ware including a red ware with cream decoration.

Most of the mold-made figurine and spindle whorl types of late Venta Salada occur at Cholula. In fact, when we were surveying the area north of Tehuacan, it was often difficult if not impossible to tell whether a site was late Venta Salada or Cholulteca II–III. However, the presence of Coxcatlan Gray and Coxcatlan Polychrome in lieu of the Cholula polychrome types would establish it as belonging to our subregion.

Monte Alban V of Oaxaca bears a somewhat similar relationship to late Venta Salada. Both have trade sherds of the Cholula polychrome types—Lacquer, Matte, and Firme—as well as such Aztec types as Tenayuca Black-on-orange and Texcoco Black-and-white-on-red. One sherd of the red-based Mixteca polychrome typical of Monte Alban V occurred in the excavated component, Tr 62, while others occurred in surface collections of this subphase. Some of the sherds of Coxcatlan Brushed are like brushed crude brown ollas (Types K. 10M and K. 1M) from Monte Alban. Some of the figurine types and most of the spindle whorl types of the two regions are extremely similar if not the same. However, the gray wares of Monte Alban V and late Venta Salada, while bearing some similarity in vessel form, serpent-like feet, and a few other features, are for the most part very different in paste and type of surface finish. Although gray bowls from the Valley of Oaxaca lack stamped bottoms, stamped-bottom gray (or black) tripod bowls do exist from Coixtlahuaca, usually classified as Monte Alban V. However, the designs appear, from the published material, to be far less complex than the stamped designs of Tehuacan bowls. Again it was difficult to draw sharp boundaries between the ceramic zone of late Venta Salada and that of Monte Alban V of the Valley of Oaxaca and the Mixteca Alta. However, differences in interior bottom stamping, the variations in gray wares and in polychromes, and the lack of Teotitlan Incised in Oaxaca were all distinguishing features.

Thus, the immediate neighbors to the north and to the south, and west of the Tehuacan Valley are not only linked to it by trade sherds, overlapping types, and period styles, but all four regions are so closely related ceramically that they could well be considered local variations of a single, more encompassing ceramic complex, Mixteca-Puebla, which occupies a single large cultural subarea of central Mesoamerica.

236

Still another area which influences the Tehuacan Valley, and much of Mesoamerica as well, is the Valley of Mexico. Many of the late Venta Salada trade sherds are obviously connected with the spread of the Aztec Empire. In both excavated components and surface sites we found sherds of such Valley of Mexico types as Tenayuca Black-on-orange, Texcoco Fabric-impressed, Texcoco Black-on-red, and Texcoco Black-and-white-on-red, indicating connections between late Venta Salada and several ceramic phases of the Valley of Mexico: Mazapan, Zocango (Aztec II), Chimalpa (Aztec III), and Teacalco. The same types of Cholula polychromes are found as trade wares both in the Valley of Mexico phases and in late Venta Salada. Some figurine types of late Venta Salada and Aztec II–IV are the same, and some of the spindle whorls are very similar. Needless to say, the general horizon markers—such as molcajetes, bowls with effigy feet, Mixtec censers, and pedestal-based vessels, as well as the use of convex molds, the increased use of polychrome decoration, and so forth—are common to both the Tehuacan Valley and the Valley of Mexico in the latest period. Thus, in the late Postclassic period there seems to have been steady contact between the two regions.

Another region which had many contacts with Tehuacan is coastal Veracruz. Trade sherds of X Fine Orange and Isla de Sacrificios Polychrome in middle Venta Salada levels and sherds of Cerro de las Mesas Dull Buff Polychrome in late Venta Salada components attest to connections between late Isla de Sacrificios and Upper Cerro de las Mesas phases of the southern Veracruz–Tabasco region and late Venta Salada of southern Puebla. Trade sherds of Teotitlan Incised in Upper Cerro de las Mesas deposits are further evidence of connections with late Venta Salada (Medellín Zenil 1960). Like late Venta Salada, Upper Cerro de las Mesas has many trade sherds from Cholula, as well as Texcoco Black-on-red sherds from the Valley of Mexico. Similarities are found in interior stamped-bottom motifs, vessels with stepped and animal effigy feet, spindle whorls, Aztec and Toltec figurine types, and various xantil-like vessels (Drucker 1943b: pls. 29–39, 45–46, 53; figs. 170–199). In fact, the numerous

similarities to the Mixteca suggested to Drucker that Upper Cerro de las Mesas represented a Mixtec invasion of the coast in late Postclassic times and was still another subdivision of the Mixteca-Puebla complex (ibid.: 81–87).

Relationships between late Venta Salada and phases of central Veracruz are of a slightly different nature. They lie in the presence in the two regions of similar trade types, such as Isla de Sacrificios Polychrome, Cerro de las Mesas Polychrome, Tenayuca Black-on-orange, Texcoco Black-on-red, Tancol Polychrome, and Cholula Polychrome. However, trade pots of the Venta Salada type Teotitlan Incised do occur at Quauhtochco, which is roughly of Cempoala III–IV times (Medellín Zenil 1960: 130–137). Further evidence of contacts lies in the similarities of spindle whorls with incised or stamped designs, square-headdressed types of figurines, stamped-bottom motifs, vessels with serpent-like feet, and ladles or censers.

Ties between late Venta Salada and northern Veracruz are very tenuous. However, we do have a Tancol Polychrome sherd in a late Venta Salada component, and Tenayuca Black-on-orange sherds from the Valley of Mexico are common to both areas. Some spindle whorl types of both regions are the same and general mold-made figurine types are similar.

Connections to Tehuacan from regions south of the ones we have discussed are vague and unsatisfactory. In the earlier Venta Salada subphase, X Fine Orange and Tohil and San Juan Plumbate gave evidence of connections to Maya areas. In late Venta Salada the only direct evidence for connection is a single badly eroded sherd of Tohil Plumbate from the alluvial surface deposits of Ts 367, and even Zone A of Ts 367 is early in the late Venta Salada subphase. There are indirect connections, which we discuss in Chapter 12 below.

Thus, the final subphase of the Tehuacan ceramic sequence, late Venta Salada, can be tied chronologically to the cultures of the Valley of Mexico, Veracruz, and Oaxaca with considerable precision, but little indication exists of connections with Guatemala, Chiapas, Yucatan, and other regions to the south.

CHAPTER 11

Ceramics from Surface Sites

A COMPLETE SUMMARY of the ceramics from the Tehuacan Valley must include examples collected in the archaeological survey of the region, as well as a description of the remains from the excavated sites. Certain periods, such as Palo Blanco and Venta Salada, have limited numbers of occupational floors and limited numbers of components with ceramics. The archaeological survey of the valley, however, yielded large amounts of ceramics from surface sites of these two periods, providing more data in terms of time and space.

Most of the surface collections of ceramics were undertaken by Frederick Peterson while locating and surveying sites during our first two seasons in the field. The collections generally consist of random samples, though we tended to pick up rim sherds and sherds that were not too badly eroded. In round numbers, 185,000 sherds were collected from the surface. Ideally these sherds should have been classified and analyzed at the outset of our field work, as a basis for selection of sites to be excavated. Owing to the overwhelming number of sherds collected, however, this procedure proved impossible. It took our two cataloguers almost three years to wash and number them all, and it was not until 1964, when excavations had been completed, that we were able to classify and analyze them. Be that as it may, we did establish ceramic types initially from the excavated materials, and we were able to check the surface collections against them which allowed us to align the surface collections in chronological order on the basis of the excavated ceramic trends. This was done by transposing the counts of sherds by types into percentages of types, which were compared with the trends of ceramic types from the excavated sequence.

With this data on hand, we shall briefly review the sequence of ceramic phases and subphases. It will become obvious that the survey data significantly supplement the excavated materials previously described, for they indicate not only the relative proportions of components of each subphase, but also the cultural boundaries of each period and the direction of strongest cultural relationships.

Purron Phase

Only two components of the Purron phase are known from excavation, Zones K^1 and K of Tc 272, or Purron Cave, and none were discovered in the survey. From many standpoints, Purron might be considered a tentative phase, but then all phases are tentative.

The phase is represented by only two ceramic wares: Purron Coarse and Purron Plain. The surface of Purron Coarse was crudely wiped while the pot was wet, whereas the surface of Purron Plain was wiped and smoothed after the pot was dry. Characteristic of both pottery types is the lack of any kind of decoration. Another characteristic is the limited kinds of vessel forms, which include simple tecomates without thickened lips, flaring-wall bowls that presumably were flat-bottomed, convex-wall bowls, and ollas with flaring necks. No figurines or other ceramic types are known at this period.

Among the chipped and ground stone artifacts that can be considered diagnostic of the Purron phase are fine blades with both prepared and unprepared striking platforms, various types of crude blades, end-of-blade scrapers, and a fragmentary saucer-shaped metate.

Another characteristic of this phase is the derivation of the subsistence, which we published in Volume I. About 35 percent of the food consumed during the Purron phase was estimated as coming from agriculture, 34 percent from the collection of wild plants, and 31 percent from animals (these figures are actually projections, rather than estimates). Although the excavated plant remains are limited to a few cobs of early tripsacoid maize and a few wild-plant species, a number of cultivated plants probably were known at this time. In the previous period, the preceramic Abejas phase, remains of a number of agricultural foods were uncovered and identified, including corn, squash, tepary beans, black and white sapotes, and chili peppers.

These artifact and plant remains then, are the characteristics of Purron, and they are meager at best. What is worse, they come from only two components at one spot in the whole valley, Purron Cave, making the spatial distribution of the Purron culture even more obscure than its temporal sequence.

Early Ajalpan Subphase

Early Ajalpan remains also come only from excavation; we found none in survey. However, the sample of sherds and other artifacts is considerably better than the sample from Purron, and we do have a brief sequence of components. On the basis of ceramic trends, the earliest component is Zone H of Ts 204, which seems to be followed respectively by Zone J of Tc 272, Zone G of Ts 204, Zone sub-E of Ts 204D, and finally Zone G^1 of Ts 204. Although the spatial data is extremely poor, we know that at least in two spots in the Tehuacan Valley we have early Ajalpan components: at Purron Cave (Tc 272) in the south end of the valley and at the Ajalpan site (Ts 204), more or less in the flat central or north-central area of the valley.

Although the two older Purron pottery types still occur, six new types emerge to characterize this period. The type that is more prevalent in the early levels is Ajalpan Coarse; it decreases throughout the sequence of components. This ware with a smoothed or brushed surface is dominated by the tecomate form, though olla and bowl forms are present. The other five types all increase slightly throughout this early Ajal-

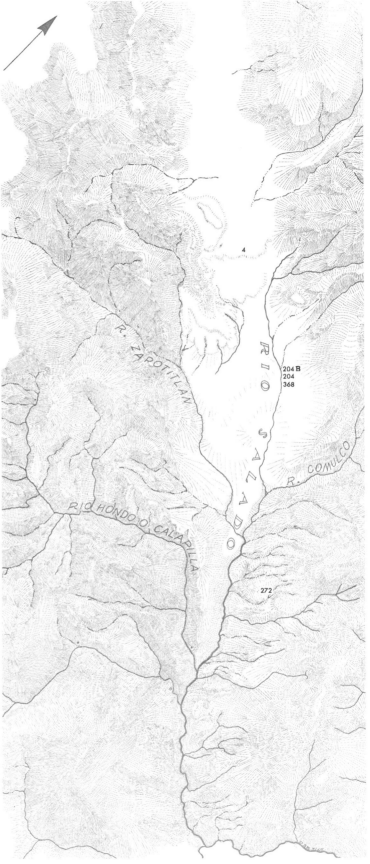

FIG. 147. SITES OF THE AJALPAN PHASE.

pan period. An important one is Ajalpan Plain. Again tecomates are the dominant vessel form, but small convex-wall bowls are almost as popular. Ollas and other bowl forms also occur. Two other wares are minority types, Ajalpan Fine Red and Ajalpan Fine Plain. Both types have a finely knit paste, with a polished red surface on Ajalpan Fine Red. Flat-bottom, flaring-wall bowls are more popular in Ajalpan Fine Red, and convex-wall bowls are slightly more popular in Ajalpan Fine Plain.

Related to Ajalpan Fine Red, but much coarser in paste, is Ajalpan Coarse Red. A few sherds of this ware were uncovered in the later Purron level; it remains a minority ware in early Ajalpan but steadily increases in popularity. The thin red hematite film covering this type is nowhere near as effective as the wash on Ajalpan Fine Red. In fact, Ajalpan Coarse Red seems to be mainly a utilitarian ware; large olla forms predominate, and tecomates are rare.

Beside the pottery types, some early figurine types may be considered diagnostic of the early Ajalpan subphase, though they carry on into late Ajalpan times. The earliest figurine type is a small crudely formed spherical head with punched features; it is associated with gingerbread bodies. Almost as early, is a small flat head, also crudely modeled, with punched features and a squared, flat headdress. It too probably went with gingerbread bodies. Rather late in this early Ajalpan period, a larger finely modeled head appeared; it has rather realistic eyes and other features. There are also a few fragments apparently from large, well-modeled, hollow figurines. Both of the latter types, but particularly the hollow figurines, are more characteristic of the late Ajalpan subphase.

The nonceramic artifacts that distinguish the Ajalpan phase from other phases include Shumla, Garyito, Salado, and Zacatenco projectile points, fine endscrapers, crude blades, fine blades with pointed and with prepared striking platforms, bell-shaped and truncated-cone pestles, oblong and basin-shaped metates, and long manos that are triangular in cross-section. The subsistence data that may be considered diagnostic of early Ajalpan unfortunately are limited, coming only from Zone J of Tc 272. On the basis of projected figures, we assume that about 40 percent of the food eaten was derived from agricultural plants, 31 percent from wild plants, and 29 percent from animal sources. Agricultural produce included both early cultivated and early tripsacoid maize. According to the date for Abejas and early Santa Maria, we suspect that several other domesticated plants were used at this time.

Late Ajalpan Subphase

Late Ajalpan components are more numerous and contained many more artifacts than were present in the earlier part of the phase. The eleven components found in excavation were aligned according to ceramic trends in the chronological order shown in the distribution tables in Chapter 4. Both plants and tools indicate that the lower part of Zone C of San Marcos Cave (Tc 254) probably also belongs to this general time period. Only one site found in survey can be considered definitely of the Ajalpan phase, and it is of the very latest part of the phase at that. This was Tr 4, part of a small ruin on the southeast edge of the town of Tehuacan. However, the northern end of Ts 204, the Ajalpan area, was in terms of pottery distribution completely separate from the southern end. This site, designated Ts 204B, also may be considered a surface site. Thus we have a total of six sites of late Ajalpan, Ts 204, Ts 204B, Ts 368e, Tc 272, Tr 4, and probably Tc 254.

Most of the same pottery types occur in both early and late Ajalpan, as Tables 14–21 in Chapters 3 and 4 show. However, there are minor differences in ceramic attributes and some shifts in popularity of various wares. Coatepec Plain, a relatively minor but constantly increasing type in early Ajalpan, becomes a dominant ware in late Ajalpan times. Convex-wall bowls are more important than olla and other forms. Ajalpan Coarse Red, still basically an olla paste, is also one of the more popular wares. Ajalpan Plain, Ajalpan Fine Plain, Ajalpan Fine Red, and Ajalpan Coarse, and even a few sherds of Purron Plain appear in diminishing amounts and with few changes within the types.

There are only two pottery types completely new to late Ajalpan, and both of them are minority types, representing only a very small percentage of the total Ajalpan ceramic complex.

The figurine types of early Ajalpan, except for the flat punched-feature heads, extend into late Ajalpan, but as minority types. The Hollow Dwarf figures now become dominant. The one completely new type in late Ajalpan is the No Face figurine. Among the few minor ceramic traits, effigy whistles and a fragment of a stamp are distinctive.

The subsistence of late Ajalpan is not well known and was probably little different from that of early Ajalpan. Perishable materials were obtained only from Zone Lower C of Tc 254. The corn cobs include many of the early Tripsacoid and early cultivated varieties, as well as a few examples of the early Nal-tel and

Chapalote races. The total agricultural complex probably includes a number of other plants that were cultivated from Abejas times onward.

The nonceramic artifacts, like the pottery, for the most part are the same types as those of early Ajalpan, some of which show very minor shifts in popularity. The only nonceramic traits represented in late Ajalpan components and not earlier are fine ovoid plano-convex and flat-topped end-scrapers, flat-iron pestles or smoothers, square-polled celts and adzes, distal-end metapodial awls, rib-bone tools, tubular earplugs, twilled petates, and perhaps plain-weave cotton cloth. None of these artifact types, we might add, are very prevalent in late Ajalpan times, and they may be absent from early Ajalpan only because of the poorer sampling. Although we do seem to have a distinctive set of percentages in popularity of types and several minor new types in the late Ajalpan phase, they are not sufficient justification for dividing early and late Ajalpan into two separate phases. The majority of di-

agnostic traits are the same from the beginning to the end of the phase.

Early Santa Maria Subphase

The Santa Maria phase is characterized by many new nonceramic and ceramic types and is extremely well represented by a large number of components containing a great amount of material. In the early Santa Maria subphase, we have a good sample from thirteen excavated components, which, on the basis of ceramic trends, can be aligned in the chronological order shown in the distribution tables in Chapter 5. Seven sites discovered in the survey also can be classified as early Santa Maria components. These too may be aligned in chronological order on the basis of ceramic trends, as shown in Table 68. With these twenty components, thirteen from excavation and seven from the surface, we can vaguely plot the distribution of sites during the early part of the Santa Maria phase as shown below in Fig. 148. All sites appear in bottom

TABLE 68

Pottery Types from Ajalpan and Santa Maria Surface Sites

	Ajalpan		Early Santa Maria						
	204B	4	278	363	369	449	376	435	15
Coxcatlan Red-on-orange									1
Coxcatlan Gray									2
El Riego Marble-tempered									
Thin Orange									
El Riego Orange									
El Riego Plain									
El Riego Polished									
El Riego Black									
El Riego Gray					1				2
Quachilco Red					2				
Quachilco Mica			2		1				2
Quachilco Brown					1				
Quachilco Gray			7	1	5	2	1		3
Rio Salado Coarse			2	3	3			8	12
Rio Salado Gray			6	8	3	9		15	16
Coatepec White-rimmed Black			2		2		1		
Coatepec White				1	29	8	1	1	
Canoas White			2	2	8	2		2	5
Canoas Orange-brown			54	88	3			2	3
Canoas Heavy Plain	1		7	7	8			4	9
Coatepec Buff	9		9						
Coatepec Red-on-buff	11	9							
Coatepec Plain	90	4							
Ajalpan Plain	125	2							
Ajalpan Coarse Red	120								
Ajalpan Coarse	75								
Total	431	15	91	110	66	21	3	32	55

(Table continued)

241

(*Table 68, continued*)

| | \| Late Santa Maria | | | | | | | | | | |
	25	450	67	366	452	260	235	212	243A	355	Total
Coxcatlan Red-on-orange	2		2								5
Coxcatlan Gray	15		7	10				40		3	77
El Riego Marble-tempered										4	4
Thin Orange								2	1	14	17
El Riego Orange								2	5	4	11
El Riego Plain			1					11	2	6	20
El Riego Polished									2		2
El Riego Black									11		11
El Riego Gray	13		12	8	1			40	99	10	186
Quachilco Red				4				2	1		9
Quachilco Mica	2	1	92	8		1		13	26		148
Quachilco Brown	4		1			1		19	9		35
Quachilco Gray	55	4	92	77	13	8	2	233	109	13	625
Rio Salado Coarse	38	13	45	39				15	8		186
Rio Salado Gray	19	15	17	9	4		1	14	8		144
Coatepec White-rimmed Black	7			3		1					16
Coatepec White	1	3	12	12	7			6	6	2	89
Canoas White	9	1	4	5	2						42
Canoas Orange-brown	123	2	16	7	1	1		5			305
Canoas Heavy Plain	313	2	2	3		1					357
Coatepec Buff											18
Coatepec Red-on-buff											20
Coatepec Plain											94
Ajalpan Plain											127
Ajalpan Coarse Red											120
Ajalpan Coarse											75
Total	601	41	302	186	28	13	3	402	287	56	2743

lands and only to the north at Santa Maria de la Alta do they have a definite boundary.

Most of the older pottery types—Purron Plain, Purron Coarse, Ajalpan Fine Red, Ajalpan Fine Plain, Ajalpan Plain, Ajalpan Coarse Red, Coatepec Plain, Coatepec Red-on-buff, and Coatepec Buff—last into and die out in early Santa Maria times. More distinctive of early Santa Maria are five new pottery types: Canoas White, Canoas Orange-brown, Canoas Heavy Plain, Rio Salado Gray, and Rio Salado Coarse. These are the diagnostic pottery types of the early part of the phase, but Coatepec White, Coatepec White-rimmed Black, Quachilco Gray, Quachilco Brown, Quachilco Mica, and Quachilco Red occur as minority types.

The five types that are most popular in early Santa Maria times display a number of attributes that are distinctive of the period 850–550 B.C. Of the three Canoas wares with amphibole-pyroxene temper—White, Orange-brown, and Heavy Plain—Canoas White is the most characteristic type of early Santa Maria times. It appears in larger numbers and also has many characteristics popular only at this general period. These include not only the white surface finish, but the bowl forms incised with multiple parallel lines around the inner or outer rim. Some of the lines turn up or down at intervals in what Coe has termed the double-line-break effect. Further, hub-and-spoke or sunburst designs are incised on the interior surface of some of the flat-bottomed bowls. Although such Canoas White vessel shapes as the flaring-wall dish and convex-wall bowls are common to all phases, other forms appear that are distinctive of early to middle Santa Maria times. These include large bowls with heavy thickened rims, thinner convex-wall bowls with thickened rims, convex-based deep bowls, cylindrical bowls with a basal bulge, collared tecomates, composite-silhouette bowls, and everted-rim bowls with rim tabs.

The Canoas Orange-brown type, with polished surfaces, utilizes mainly the relatively common Formative vessel form, flat-based bowls or dishes with flaring walls. Other vessel forms and characteristics distinctive of early Santa Maria are convex-wall and heavy bowls with externally thickened rims and the incised parallel-line-break motifs on bowl rims and sunburst motifs on bottom interiors.

Canoas Heavy Plain is the utilitarian ware among the amphibole-pyroxene-tempered pastes. It is in the main undecorated, although some vessels had fabric impressions roughening the underside of the base. Canoas Heavy Plain vessel forms are somewhat unclear but seem to represent mainly flat-based pot rests and supported pot stands. The one rectangular vessel is unique for Tehuacan.

The other two types distinctive of early Santa Maria are the mica-tempered wares, Rio Salado Gray and Rio Salado Coarse. These have fewer distinctively Middle Formative characteristics than Canoas White does, but they do have some ceramic features that occur mainly in early Santa Maria times. Rio Salado Coarse, which is a utilitarian ware having many olla forms common to all periods, does have funnel-necked ollas with beveled or flattened lips, a form that seems unique to Santa Maria. There are also pedestal-based *incensarios* and beveled-rim bowls in this ware which do not occur in earlier or later periods.

Rio Salado Gray has many Middle Formative characteristics and also features that are more distinctive of later Formative times. Many of its decorations are similar to those of Canoas White, consisting of parallel-line-break motifs and incised interior bottoms. Many of the vessel forms are similar too: the large bowls with externally thickened rims, convex-wall bowls with thickened or wedge-shaped rims, ovate bowls with pinched-in sides, and dimple-based bowls, are all forms that occur with some frequency only in early to middle Santa Maria times. Thus the five pottery types that are most popular in the early part of the Santa Maria phase have many secondary features that set off this ceramic subphase.

The No Face and Hollow Dwarf figurine types continue from the Ajalpan phase. Confined to early Santa Maria are several new types: Helmeted, Valley of Mexico Type F, Ploughed-eye, and Hollow Lowland. Extending from early Santa Maria to late Santa Maria are the Valley of Mexico Type Di, Baby Face, Trapiche Bunned-helmet, Crescentic Cap, Tres Zapotes Chin-strap, Valley of Mexico Types C3a and C3d, and Negroid with Hairknot figurines.

Supplementing these ceramic characteristics and defining the phase are a series of nonceramic artifacts. Continuing from the Ajalpan phase are Zacatenco and Salado points, lipped oblong and saucer-shaped metates, ovoid plano-convex and basin-shaped metates, bell-shaped pestles, two-handed manos, fine blades with pointed striking platforms, and one-over-one woven cloth. Traits distinctive to Santa Maria, or that start in Santa Maria, include Palmillas, Matamoros, and Tehuacan points, fine snapped blades, fine bifacial knives, cylindrical manos, pointed-poll celts, flattened spool-shaped earplugs, lip plugs, and various kinds of rope such as four-ply cotton cord, coarse braid, three-ply cord, and cornleaf cord, and probably a round-toed sandal.

In the early part of the Santa Maria period there are major innovations in the subsistence. We have our first direct evidence of irrigation in the form of a masonry dam. In this subphase we estimate that about 58 percent of the people's food came from agricultural plants, only 17 percent came from wild plants, and 25 percent was meat. Our knowledge of what agricultural plants were used is limited, as foodstuffs were preserved in only three zones of Tc 272. These levels contained remains of cotton, squash (*Cucurbita moschata*), such fruits as avocado, cosahuico (*Sideroxylon* sp.), coyol (*Acrocomia mexicana*), ciruela (*Spondias mombim*), and a number of kinds of corn, including Nal-tel and Chapalote and early tripsacoid. We suspect that chili peppers, amaranth, *Cucurbita mixta* and *C. pepo*, gourds, and tepary and common beans—all of which appeared in earlier phases—probably also were utilized at this time, but did not occur in the very limited deposits of preserved vegetable remains. Thus there is good evidence not only for a shift in ceramic and nonceramic types, but also for a shift in subsistence activities and domesticated plants between the Ajalpan phase and the Santa Maria phase. There is no doubt that we are dealing with a different cultural entity. Volume V will point out a shift in architectural features and other aspects of the settlement pattern.

Late Santa Maria Subphase

The best ceramic sample of our entire sequence in terms of numbers of sherds and numbers of components comes from late Santa Maria times. For the first time we have a fair number of survey sites representing a subphase of our sequence. From the trends of ceramic types, we were able to arrange the twenty-nine excavated components in the sequential order shown in the distribution tables in Chapter 6. All of the excavated components yielded large numbers of ceramics.

The excavated sites also give us information concerning the spatial distribution of late Santa Maria. The five excavated open sites—the east and west parts of the Coatepec site (Ts 368e and 368w), the Ajalpan site (Ts 204), and the Quachilco site (Tr 218)—are

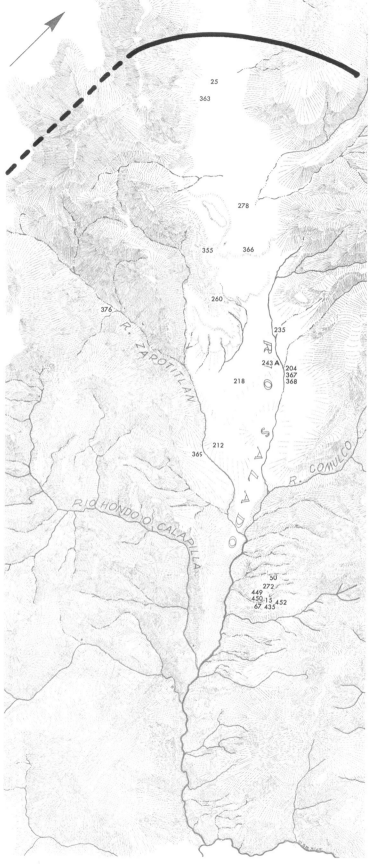

located on the alluvial plains in the north-central part of the valley. Coxcatlan and Purron caves (Ts 50 and Tc 272) are located on the southeastern slopes. Supplementing the distribution of the excavated sites, are ten sites from survey. The distribution of these fifteen sites indicates for the late Santa Maria period some fairly well-defined boundaries. The eastern boundary is the state of Veracruz, or the peaks of the Sierra Madre, for beyond that limit an Orizaba site has Remojadas ceramic types. At the north end of the valley, Tr 25 near Tlacotepec has diminishing middle Santa Maria remains mixed with remains that seem related to the Valley of Mexico. On the west, the Matamoros site in Puebla seems to be definitely out of our area. However, remains from near Huajuapan de Leon, to the southwest, and much of the material to the south from the Oaxaca Valley of the Monte Alban I and II periods (Paddock 1953) are very closely related to late Santa Maria materials. Thus we have good northern and eastern boundaries for late Santa Maria, but boundaries to the west and south are poorly defined and hint that late Santa Maria is a more northern extension of that cultural region.

The ceramic types of early Santa Maria times continue, of course, into late Santa Maria. However, Rio Salado Gray and Rio Salado Coarse, Canoas White, Canoas Orange-brown, and Canoas Heavy Plain appear in diminishing numbers. The Coatepec White and Coatepec White-rimmed Black wares, which became fairly prominent near the end of early Santa Maria times, continue in fair prominence in the earlier levels of late Santa Maria, and then they too begin to diminish. Most typical of this period is the heavy predominance of Quachilco Gray, which appears along with smaller but still sizable quantities of Quachilco Mica and Quachilco Brown.

Each of the five pottery types that are most popular in late Santa Maria times—Quachilco Gray, Quachilco Mica, Quachilco Brown, Coatepec White, and Coatepec White-rimmed Black—exhibit ceramic modes that mark off this period from all other periods. Coatepec White has a very hard white slip, which seems to be a characteristic of this period. It also has the "raspada" type of decoration involving large excised areas. This technique of decoration is characteristic of middle Santa Maria times, carries on to late Santa Maria times, and apparently dies out during the Palo Blanco phase. Much of the decoration of Coatepec White,

FIG. 148. SITES OF THE SANTA MARIA PHASE, with northern boundary suggested by the archaeological survey.

however, is of the double-line-break variety, a continuation from early Santa Maria times. These parallel-line decorations are often associated with crosshatching and with rectangles or triangles filled with hatching or crosshatching. Such combinations are certainly much more characteristic of late Santa Maria than of any other period. Coatepec White adds little to our earlier complex of vessel forms, although cylindrical jars or bowls begin to appear in fair number for the first time.

Coatepec White-rimmed Black, which is always a minority type, is distinguished by a peculiar firing technique that gives the body of a vessel a dark, nearly black shade and the rim a whitish or tannish shade. Most of the rimming in middle Santa Maria times is usually white to creamy, but in late Santa Maria times the white gives way to a more orange or tan shade. The other Middle and Late Formative characteristics of Coatepec White-rimmed Black are raspada designs and incised parallel encircling lines.

A type which exists throughout the Santa Maria phase but is most popular in the middle and late part of the phase is Quachilco Brown, an extremely fine-pasted, polished ware with a number of distinctive period characteristics. These include grooving, or wide-line incising, on the everted rims of flaring-wall bowls and engraving or incising on exterior surfaces of such design elements as hachured triangles and stepped motifs, zigzag lines, and multiple parallel lines. Formative vessel forms of Quachilco Brown include everted-rim bowls, basal-flanged bowls, composite-silhouette vessels, and cylindrical bowls or jars, some with a bulge at the base. The flaring-wall bowls with everted rims are perhaps the most distinctive period characteristic of Quachilco Brown. In the early and middle parts of the Santa Maria phase the everted rims usually slant out and downward at a sharp angle, while in the late part of the period they turn out and down in a rounded eversion. Many of the latter bowls have convex rather than flat bases. The bowls with basal ridges or flanges are also a good subphase time marker.

One of the predominant wares in this subphase, and one that remains quite popular in all later phases, is Quachilco Mica. This mainly utilitarian ware is usually not decorated. Ollas with long or short flaring necks are the most common vessel form and of course have no particular significance in any one time period. However, some of the Quachilco Mica ollas during late Santa Maria have rolled or beaded rims. Perhaps the most distinctive forms for this period in Quachilco Mica are the incense burners. These are associated with punctate-decorated comales and ladle-handled fragments. These specialized vessel forms do not occur before the late Santa Maria phase.

The best time marker of late Santa Maria is Quachilco Gray, a ware with a lustrous surface and a fine paste. Although the type occurs both earlier and later, it is most popular in late Santa Maria times and has many ceramic attributes distinctive of that period. The decoration technique is mainly fine-line incising through the polished surface of the vessel, but there is some grooving or wide-line incising made with a blunt tool while the vessel was wet. Less common are raspada decoration and zoned toning, consisting of differential polishing or stick rubbing in certain outlined or well-defined areas. The zoned toning, rare as it may be, is particularly characteristic of late Santa Maria, while the raspada decoration is more characteristic of middle to late Santa Maria times. The fine-line and wide-line incising, while popular in late Santa Maria, occur with some frequency in the early Palo Blanco period and were employed occasionally in early Santa Maria times.

Perhaps more typical than the decorative techniques themselves are the kinds of motifs rendered in each of these techniques. The fine-line designs are usually hachured elongated triangles that often appear with straight or wavy parallel lines, half-circles, zigzags, stepped motifs, or rectangular elements. These designs usually occur around the rims but also are present on the outer walls of bowls and occasionally on the interior or bottom surface. Perhaps even more representative of the period is the concave-sided triangle associated with the various motifs mentioned above. Discontinuous parallel lines with hooked ends, perhaps the dying gasp of the multiple-line-break motif, are also distinctive of the late part of the Santa Maria phase. Zoned-toning technique is usually associated with triangular elements and raspada designs with rectangular panels which often contain stepped, triangular, or rectangular motifs.

Designs executed by the wide-line or grooving technique are less diagnostic of the period. They most often consist of parallel straight or wavy lines on the upper surface of everted rims of bowls. Occasionally the ends of the lines are hooked, or the lines are associated with semicircular or zigzag motifs and appear on the body of vessels.

Some of the vessel shapes of Quachilco Gray in late Santa Maria times also serve as good time markers. Although the popular flaring-wall bowls with flat or convex bottoms and convex-wall bowls are forms known from earlier times, the flaring-wall bowls with

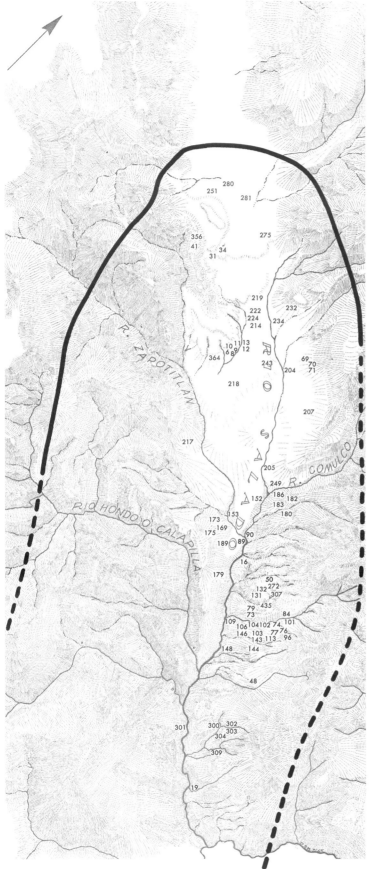

downcurved or sharply everted rims, the outsloping- or convex-wall bowls with basal flanges, the ollas with spouts, and the tripod vessels with mammiform feet are particularly diagnostic.

Figurine types of early Santa Maria extend into late Santa Maria, but the majority of the figurines are new to the Tehuacan Valley. Four of the new types are the same as types from Ticoman in the Valley of Mexico (Types Gi, Eiii, Eii, and Ticoman). Two types with appliqued doughnut-like eyes resemble types from Monte Alban I and II; and one figurine is clearly an early Remojadas trade object from central Veracruz.

The many new figurine types seem to provide justification for considering late Santa Maria as an entirely different and new phase rather than just a subphase. However, the same pottery types occur in both early and late Santa Maria, albeit in different proportions, and most of the nonceramic artifacts are exactly the same. The subsistence pattern is also consistent through the phase, with over 58 percent of the foodstuffs derived from agriculture. A slight difference between early and late Santa Maria may lie in the fact that one of the latest components of the phase, Zone VII of Tc 50, which provides the fullest amounts of agricultural produce and plant remains, contains a few items new to the subsistence pattern, including cobs of the late tripsacoid race of maize and one scarlet runner bean (*Phaseolus coccineus*), as well as ground cherry (*Physalis* sp.) and possibly manihot in the feces.

The settlement patterns of both early and late Santa Maria are also roughly the same, with only a slight increase in villages with ceremonial features occurring in late Santa Maria. Generally speaking, the similarities between early and late Santa Maria far outweigh the differences, in spite of the fact that the late Santa Maria sample is much larger in every respect.

Early Palo Blanco Subphase

Following the late Santa Maria remains are those of the early Palo Blanco subphase. The 31,000 excavated sherds of this segment would appear to be a very adequate sample, but as we pointed out at the beginning of Chapter 7, their distribution leaves much to be desired. The excavated components aligned on the basis of ceramic trends are shown in the distribution tables of that chapter.

FIG. 149. EARLY PALO BLANCO SITES, with boundaries suggested by the archaeological survey.

The sherds from excavation are supplemented by surface collections from the seventy-two survey sites of the early Palo Blanco subphase. These components yielded about 20,000 identifiable sherds. Another 5,-000 sherds seem to be aberrant or nonresident types, and about 10,000 sherds were too badly worn to identify. On the basis of ceramic trends, the seventy-two surface components can be arranged in the chronological order shown in Table 69. The trends of three pottery types—Quachilco Gray, El Riego Gray, and El Riego Plain—are most important to the chronology, although we counted and put into percentages all the pottery types identified.

On the basis of the trends of pottery types found in excavation, we felt the Palo Blanco phase to begin at the point when El Riego Gray sherds outnumbered Quachilco Gray sherds, and when El Riego Plain first occurred. Thereafter, as Quachilco Gray diminishes, El Riego Gray rises. The subphase of early Palo Blanco draws to an end at the point at which El Riego Plain outnumbers Quachilco Gray.

The five excavated sites plus the seventy-two surface sites reveal the spatial distribution of early Palo Blanco very clearly (Fig. 149). The westernmost early Palo Blanco site is Tr 217 on the Zapotitlan River. Beyond this point, sites of this period around Acatepec and in the Zapotitlan valley are dominated by Thin Orange pottery rather than by our gray wares. Thus the east end of the Zapotitlan valley seems to be the western border of early Palo Blanco. Sites Tr 281 near Cuayacatepec and Tr 280 and Tr 251 near Teontepec, some twenty miles north of the town of Tehuacan are the northernmost Palo Blanco sites; sites north of them, even at Tlacotepec, have Teotihuacan-like pottery. The eastern border seems to remain the western slopes of the Sierra Madre, for sites in Veracruz on the eastern flanks of the Sierra Madre have Remojadas-like pottery. To the south we could not define any limits of early Palo Blanco, for the simple reason that we were unable to distinguish clearly El Riego Gray and Quachilco Gray from the gray wares of Monte Alban II and III. Thus, for the moment, we must consider that the southern border of early Palo Blanco is the same as that of Monte Alban II and III and extends as far south as the Oaxaca Valley.

Early Palo Blanco wares include Quachilco Mica and Quachilco Gray as continuing types. El Riego Gray is the dominant and most widely representative type, and Quachilco Red is a rising type. El Riego Black and El Riego Plain are new types typical of this subphase, but El Riego Polished, El Riego Orange, and El Riego Marble-tempered, present in small amounts, are more representative of the late Palo Blanco subphase. Thin Orange sherds are fairly prevalent and are excellent time markers.

The Quachilco Mica type continues into early Palo Blanco with most of the same features as before; however, in this period many of the ollas have rolled or beaded rims. The rolled-rim olla was a minority form in late Santa Maria and is fairly uncommon in late Palo Blanco. Quachilco Gray carries on its Late Formative traits too; probably the only characteristics typical of early Palo Blanco include bridged spouts on ollas, perhaps used in pairs; tripod bowls with mammiform or bulbous feet; and the few sherds probably representing pot covers for cylindrical vessels.

The pottery type that is most popular in and most typical of early Palo Blanco is El Riego Gray. Bowls with convex, flaring, or outsloping walls are common among its vessel forms, but they appear with appendages or modifications representative mainly of this early Classic subphase. For instance, many of the bowls were footed and rested on a variety of supports, including hollow bulbous, mammiform, rectangular, and cylindrical feet and solid conical, nubbin, and slab feet. The hollow feet often contained pellets that rattled. Ring bases are also a typical feature, but we found only one attached to the parent vessel, in this case a miniature olla. They were probably used on convex-wall bowls as well as ollas. El Riego Gray bowls are also distinguished by many kinds of thickened, stepped, flanged, and grooved rims. The ollas had many appendages too: strap and loop handles, perforated lug handles, bridged and unbridged spout handles. Ollas also appear with converging necks and barrel-shaped necks and as effigy vessels.

El Riego Gray vessels are not nearly so likely to be decorated as were their Late Formative Quachilco Gray counterparts. Incising continues as a decorating technique, but true, post-firing engraving is also used. Some of the designs have been rubbed with red powder or filled with red paint, not an altogether new feature. Engraved or incised designs often appear on the inner rim of bowls as a single encircling line parallel to the lip, with a series of short oblique lines above it, slanting first in one direction then in the other. Other motifs, appearing inside or outside, include hachured triangles, parallel lines, zigzag or wavy lines, concentric semicircular elements, and stepped elements. Raspada or scraped-away areas appear on cylindrical vessels in combination with incised stepped motifs.

The less popular early Palo Blanco wares—Quachilco Red, El Riego Black, and El Riego Plain—have fewer period characteristics. Quachilco Red is a utili-

TABLE 69
Pottery Types from Early Palo Blanco Surface Sites

	74	31	13	243	19	8	48	102	11	16	77	152	232	173	207
Coxcatlan Striated		1													
Coxcatlan Polychrome															
Coxcatlan Red-on-cream															
Coxcatlan Red-on-orange							1		1			1			
Coxcatlan Coarse	2			5			3	1						1	1
Coxcatlan Red	3	1			1	2	2	6							
Coxcatlan Gray	1							2					10	1	2
Teotitlan Incised	15			6	1	1	2	6				1			
Coxcatlan Brushed	27	5	4	16		5	7	43	1	1	3			8	9
El Riego Marble temp.	2		2		1	1	2						3		
Thin Orange	1		4		5	1	31	3							
El Riego Orange	1	2	3	11	2	1	1	1		3			2		1
El Riego Plain	1	1	2				8	5		1	1	1	6	1	
El Riego Polished		1	2	11			5	8	1	1	2	3	6		
El Riego Black		1		10				1					6		
El Riego Gray	41	12	20	120	19	22	139	152	19	44	96	35	205	157	157
Quachilco Red		4		1		1						1			
Quachilco Mica	2	1	1	2	5	2	23	2	1	12	12	1	6	11	4
Quachilco Brown	1														
Quachilco Gray	24	7	13	80	10	10	57	55	9	14	36	10	33	22	16
Rio Salado Coarse	1			27					1	1			1		
Rio Salado Gray	1		2	9	1								1	1	
Coatepec Wh.-rimmed Blk.															
Coatepec White				6								1			
Canoas White															
Coatepec Buff															
Total	123	36	53	304	45	46	279	288	33	76	148	56	279	202	190

	71	212	73	79	41	70	189	219	131	69	364	249	301	96	104
Coxcatlan Striated							1								1
Coxcatlan Polychrome												1			
Coxcatlan Red-on-cream															
Coxcatlan Red-on-orange												1	2	1	
Coxcatlan Coarse									1		1		2		
Coxcatlan Red												1	4		
Coxcatlan Gray			1						2			1			
Teotitlan Incised			30				1								
Coxcatlan Brushed			4	2			18		10	3	5	5	7	1	2
El Riego Marble temp.				2			3				8				
Thin Orange			4	1	5						1		1		
El Riego Orange			2	2	18		22		3		20	2	5		1
El Riego Plain			4	24	13	4	2	1	1		4			1	5
El Riego Polished			16	6	17		2		1		3	2	2	3	18
El Riego Black			8	2	17		1						2		
El Riego Gray	24	22	9347	1231	506	22	274	3	99	32	161	34	86	24	108
Quachilco Red			14	1										1	
Quachilco Mica	1		262	61	2		4			3	1	1		1	1
Quachilco Brown			8		2				1						
Quachilco Gray			138	14	13		6		11	5	12	1		2	13
Rio Salado Coarse			4				1		4		2	1			4
Rio Salado Gray			2							1	1	1		1	2
Coatepec Wh.-rimmed Blk.									1						
Coatepec White															
Canoas White															
Coatepec Buff															
Total	25	22	9844	1342	580	26	335	4	134	44	223	49	111	34	155

(Table continued)

	84	217	300	303	356	309	205	281	214	113	76	144	153	12	132
Coxcatlan Striated															
Coxcatlan Polychrome															
Coxcatlan Red-on-cream															
Coxcatlan Red-on-orange		1					3								
Coxcatlan Coarse							2					2		1	
Coxcatlan Red	2			1			3					1	1		
Coxcatlan Gray	3	1	2				2	1			16		2		
Teotitlan Incised					1		13			2		4	1	1	
Coxcatlan Brushed	18	11	10	1	10		22				1	9	7	10	
El Riego Marble temp.	1	2		1	1				1			1	1		
Thin Orange		2	1		4	1						2			
El Riego Orange	4	2	12		1	1	2	2	3	1		12		1	
El Riego Plain	1	4	11	4		4	2	12	1	5	5	2			3
El Riego Polished	4	3	5		3		1			48	1	1	2	1	1
El Riego Black	2		1		21		1	5	3		2	1			
El Riego Gray	100	57	91	13	82	20	124	36	17	129	51	76	43	11	8
Quachilco Red			1			4								4	
Quachilco Mica	7	3	1		9	1	8	2		11	4		8	2	2
Quachilco Brown															
Quachilco Gray	4	2	2			1	16	2	1			9	24	8	1	1
Rio Salado Coarse		1										3			
Rio Salado Gray	1											1			
Coatepec Wh.-rimmed Blk.															
Coatepec White						1									
Canoas White															
Coatepec Buff															
Total	147	89	137	20	133	32	199	60	28	211	88	132	76	20	15

	180	169	34	89	148	175	10	9	304	302	101	280	183	6	143
Coxcatlan Striated	1										1				
Coxcatlan Polychrome	1		1							1		1			
Coxcatlan Red-on-cream															
Coxcatlan Red-on-orange	1	1							8	1					
Coxcatlan Coarse	3				4				1		2			1	
Coxcatlan Red	11				1				3	3			4		3
Coxcatlan Gray	37	4			2			1	2	7	2	1		4	
Teotitlan Incised	4		1	2		1			9	1			1	2	
Coxcatlan Brushed	101	27		5	5	15	6		84	6	10	12	7	14	
El Riego Marble temp.	1	1		1	1				7	2		1		1	1
Thin Orange			1				3	2			1			1	
El Riego Orange	1	4	1		1		1	3	3	14	8	1		5	
El Riego Plain	4	3	3	1	3	2	4		41	2	2	8	1	9	20
El Riego Polished	8		2				1	1			9	1	2	1	
El Riego Black	3		1						8	7			1	2	3
El Riego Gray	316	81	12	15	13	46	22	8	254	55	58	37	13	50	28
Quachilco Red							1								1
Quachilco Mica	40	3				5			26	6	21			1	1
Quachilco Brown															
Quachilco Gray	36	19		3	1		1		44	2	9	6		10	3
Rio Salado Coarse	13	1							3		3			2	
Rio Salado Gray	2	1			2				3					3	
Coatepec Wh.-rimmed Blk.															
Coatepec White									1						
Canoas White															
Coatepec Buff									1						
Total	583	145	22	27	24	78	38	16	498	107	126	68	29	106	60

(Table continued)

(Table 69, continued)

	179	182	90	224	106	103	109	275	234	146	251	189	Total
Coxcatlan Striated		13		1									19
Coxcatlan Polychrome					2					1	2		10
Coxcatlan Red-on-cream					1						1		2
Coxcatlan Red-on-orange		1			3	1				2			29
Coxcatlan Coarse	1	12		1	1	1		3		3			55
Coxcatlan Red			4		2	7	1	7	1	4			79
Coxcatlan Gray	24		4		1	4	1		5	16			162
Teotitlan Incised		1	11		7	12	2		2	1	6		148
Coxcatlan Brushed	35	11	24	3	26	39	7	6	2	44	62		836
El Riego Marble temp.		1	1	1	4	2	1	3		1	2		64
Thin Orange					69					1	13		158
El Riego Orange	2		1	2	2		1	2	1		6		203
El Riego Plain			4		9	6	2	3	2	5	16	5	295
El Riego Polished			2		8	3	2	1	2	1	7	2	214
El Riego Black		1							2	4			120
El Riego Gray	58	47	78	12	113	82	16	20	15	80	101	8	15,707
Quachilco Red											12		46
Quachilco Mica	3	5	5		3	7	5		5	16	21	2	655
Quachilco Brown													12
Quachilco Gray		3	13	7	10	23			1	13	10	1	897
Rio Salado Coarse		3	1		8								85
Rio Salado Gray										1	1		37
Coatepec Wh.-rimmed Blk.													1
Coatepec White													9
Canoas White										2	1		3
Coatepec Buff													1
Total	123	98	148	27	269	187	38	46	37	195	261	18	19,847

tarian ware usually appearing as ollas; early Palo Blanco is characterized by flaring-neck ollas with thickened lips. El Riego Black is a decorated ware, with a distinctive deep composite-silhouette vessel form. Vessels of this shape exhibit all-over decoration in combinations of incised or engraved linear and geometric motifs. Another distinctive form, but one which becomes common in later times, is the footed convex-wall bowl with deeply incised interior bottom and slightly flaring or outangled rim. Ollas of El Riego Black are sometimes decorated at neck and rim and may have strap handles or spouts. A number of olla forms were also made on the El Riego Plain paste.

Thin Orange ware, which we pointed out was not really a resident type but a representative trade ware of the Classic period, serves as an excellent time marker for the entire Palo Blanco phase. Most of our Thin Orange material is decorated with incised encircling lines and rows of widely spaced dots. This design occurs only during the Palo Blanco phase and is most common in the early part of the phase. The common-

est vessel form, which carries through all of Palo Blanco, is a deep conoidal or hemispherical bowl resting on a ring base; ring-based bottles are also fairly common.

The figurine types of this subphase are so few in number it is difficult to tell just how diagnostic they are. Two Santa Maria types, the Hairlock Doughnut-eye type and the Slit-eyed type are still made. Three new types are seemingly distinctive of early Palo Blanco: the Remojadas, Hollow Puffed Cheek, and Tehuacan Portrait types. The portrait type seems to be a good time marker for this general period. This is also the period when we begin to get some evidence that the figurines are both male and female. Further, there is a general flatness to the figurine bodies that seems to be an imitation of or ancestral to figurine bodies made in molds. However, as far as we are able to determine, none of these figurines were actually formed in molds. Use of molds to make figurines is not evident until late Palo Blanco times.

Effigy incense burners probably occur in early Palo

Blanco, but we found only one in an excavated component. Fragments were collected from surface sites attributable to this subphase.

Many new types of nonceramic artifacts appear for the first time in the Palo Blanco phase. These include Ensor, Morhiss, Teotihuacan, and Tula points and remnants of other arrowheads; chipped half-moon bifaces; fine blades with ground platforms; rectangular tripod metates; cuboid and stave-shaped manos; bark-beaters with stone heads and racquet handles; bark cloth; disk beads; fire-making drills and hearths; twilled baskets; combs of tied sticks; striped blankets woven in a one-over-two or two-over-two pattern; and twined cloth. Some artifact types that are very common in early Palo Blanco are obviously continuations from Santa Maria, such as Palmillas and Tehuacan points, cylindrical manos, truncated-cone pestles, pointed-poll celts, and fine blades with unprepared or pointed striking platforms.

Most of the nonceramic artifacts continue from early Palo Blanco on into late Palo Blanco with very little change in frequency, as do most of the pottery types also. Thus again early Palo Blanco is differentiated from late Palo Blanco mainly on the basis of secondary characteristics, not according to major diagnostic traits. There certainly is very little basis for separating these two subphases into two distinct phases.

The subsistence pattern in early and late Palo Blanco for instance, is extremely similar, if not the same; foodstuffs derived from agriculture in both parts of the phase average about 65 percent and consist largely of improved races of corn. There is also good evidence that much of the corn was raised with the aid of irrigation. Another source of food was the domestic turkey. Other cultivated plants are avocados, chili peppers, amaranth, squash (*Cucurbita mixta, C. Pepo, C. moschata*), bottle and tree gourds, black and white sapotes, common beans, tepary and scarlet runner beans, a number of local fruits, and possibly manihot, *Physalis* sp., and peanuts.

The distribution of the sites of early Palo Blanco and late Palo Blanco is extremely similar, although there is evidence of slightly increasing populations in late Palo Blanco times and a slight tendency for early Palo Blanco communities to cluster more neatly around central ceremonial towns. Later occupations are more diffusely located.

Late Palo Blanco Subphase

Late Palo Blanco ceramic remains are rather poorly represented. In excavation, we uncovered only about 3,200 sherds from eleven components, all of them floors of caves and hardly representative of village dwellers. In spite of this, it was possible to align the excavated components in chronological order on the basis of ceramic trends, as shown in the distribution tables of Chapter 8. Zone C of Tc 35e, in terms of ceramic trends and the percentage of types, could well be placed at the end of this period. Because of the occurrence in it of four new pottery types, however, we finally placed it at the beginning of the next phase. It may actually represent the exact time of transition from latest Palo Blanco to earliest Venta Salada.

Two sites or tombs in the west end of the town of Tehuacan excavated by Eduardo Noguera in 1936 can definitely be attributed to the late Palo Blanco subphase. He described and illustrated some of the ceramics in Chapter 22 of *The Maya and their Neighbors* (New York, 1940) and in "Excavaciones in el Estado de Puebla," *Anales del INAH* (Mexico, 1945). Most of the ceramics he found appear to have been Thin Orange and El Riego Gray. It was not possible for us to examine or study the actual remains, but we shall refer to the published reports of them in the following discussions.

The materials Noguera uncovered greatly supplement the meager excavated remains of late Palo Blanco, as do those recovered in the archaeological reconnaissance. We collected and were able to classify into resident types about 11,000 sherds from seventy-seven sites. Ceramic trends derived from excavation, showing decreasing amounts of El Riego Gray and increasing amounts of El Riego Plain, El Riego Orange, and El Riego Marble-tempered, were the basis for aligning the survey sites in the chronological order shown in Table 70. Figurine fragments and a few miscellaneous objects suggest that Tr 113, Tr 281, and Tr 143 may also belong to this period, but the paucity of identifiable sherds does not allow us to place them in chronological position.

Plotting these sites on maps helps define the boundaries of late Palo Blanco. The northernmost sites were Tr 359 near Cacaloapan, and Tr 279 near Tepanco de Lopez, about twenty miles north of Tehuacan. North of these sites, at San Hipolito, Teotihuacan-like sherds were found. Tr 351 near Acatepec seems to be the westernmost point of this subphase, while the Sierra Madre may be the eastern border. Sites west of Acatepec have predominantly Thin Orange sherds; near Orizaba in the east sherds of late Remojadas derivation are in the majority. Again the southern border is difficult to define, this time because of the similarity of El Riego Gray to gray wares of

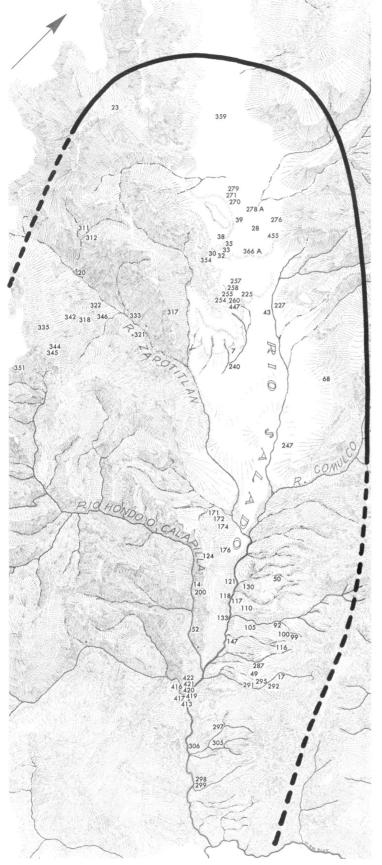

Monte Alban III of the Oaxaca Valley. Our southernmost late Palo Blanco sites are Tr 298 and Tr 299 near Tecomavaca in Oaxaca, while Monte Alban III sites in the north end of the Oaxaca Valley (and even at Cuicatlan) do not seem to have in amounts of consequence such Tehuacan types as El Riego Orange, El Riego Polished, or El Riego Marble-tempered. One might guess that the southern boundary lies somewhere between these two areas. Thus the spatial limits of late Palo Blanco are similar to those of early Palo Blanco, but with the possibility that the Tehuacan materials may now have become independent of those of the Oaxaca Valley.

As mentioned previously, most of the types characteristic of early Palo Blanco continue in decreasing proportions into late Palo Blanco, including El Riego Gray, El Riego Black, and Thin Orange, as well as Quachilco Mica. The middle and late Santa Maria types that lasted into early Palo Blanco now seem to be totally gone. Increasing in popularity are the El Riego types that started in early Palo Blanco but remained of minor importance — Plain, Polished, Orange, and Marble-tempered—and perhaps a new type, Coxcatlan Brushed. From many standpoints, these wares are really characteristic of late Palo Blanco times. As previously noted, changes within the types in terms of decoration and vessel form are distinctive for the subphases. In the long-continuing Quachilco Mica type, funnel-neck or straight-neck ollas, many with flat bottoms, replace in importance rolled-rim ollas. In El Riego Gray we have a resurgence of the old flat-bottomed flaring- or outsloping-wall bowl without decoration and a greater popularity of vessels with ring bases. Cylindrical jars with or without covers occur, but hollow mammiform, rectangular, and cylindrical feet and solid nubbin feet have been almost entirely replaced by slab and bulbous feet or simply by cylindrical jars with convex bases. Bridged spouts still occur, and a few ollas have channeled or fluted extensions.

Thin Orange continues relatively unchanged with ring-based convex-wall bowls still the dominant vessel form. However, the Thin Orange materials recorded by Noguera from the two tombs in Tehuacan are slightly different. He uncovered Thin Orange cylindrical vessels with nubbin feet, cylindrical feet, solid slab feet, and stepped feet, and some of the cylindrical vessels had decorated pot covers. Other thin or-

FIG. 150. LATE PALO BLANCO SITES, with boundaries suggested by the archaeological survey.

TABLE 70
Pottery Types from Late Palo Blanco Surface Sites

	240	335	306	298	299	110	417	296	133	447	100	227	92	176	333
Coxcatlan Striated Buff	1										2				
Coxcatlan Polychrome	3										1	1			
Coxcatlan Red-on-cream												1			
Coxcatlan Black-on-orange												2			
Coxcatlan Red-on-orange								3			2	4	1		
Coxcatlan Coarse	27	1	1	3	1						1		1		
Coxcatlan Red	20		6	3	2		1			4	1	3	1	1	
Teotitlan Incised	60	3	8		1		2	2	1		23	5	11	1	
Coxcatlan Gray	7	1	23	2		1	2	2			4	53		3	7
Coxcatlan Brushed	300	10	23	16	5	12	9	8	5		59	71	24	15	15
El Riego Marble-tempered	6	2	6	8		2	7			2	1	20	1		7
Thin Orange	30	5		2				1	1	2		2		1	21
El Riego Orange	12	5	5	2	3		7					3	6	8	4
El Riego Plain	153	2	42	51	18	24	33	5	5	2	27	67	28	15	23
El Riego Polished	10	2	1	4	32	1	1				1	6	3		1
El Riego Black	1	3	3	1	1	2	1	1			1	1	7		1
El Riego Gray	435	52	81	105	65	27	63	13	9	3	71	154	53	24	34
Quachilco Mica	46	8		7	4	4	13		1		3	25	8	5	3
Quachilco Gray	19			15	7			1			18	59	15	7	
Quachilco Red		7		4	1						1				
Quachilco Brown															
Rio Salado Coarse											2				
Rio Salado Gray								1			1	7	1		
Coatepec White					1										
Total	1130	101	199	223	141	73	140	36	26	9	219	484	160	80	116

	271	455	200	287	225	117	43	99	147	121	305	247	322	420	413	422
Coxcatlan Striated Buff					5				2	2			3			
Coxcatlan Polychrome			31			5			2				1			
Coxcatlan Red-on-cream																
Coxcatlan Black-on-orange																
Coxcatlan Red-on-orange			4	2	1	3	1				16	2	5	1		
Coxcatlan Coarse	2	2	3	11	13	4	55	7	4	2	12	4		3	1	
Coxcatlan Red		1	4	54		14	9	8	5	1	3	13		3	2	1
Teotitlan Incised	4		5	8		44	2	24	3			17		1	2	1
Coxcatlan Gray	10	5	15	94	2		40	11	1		2	1	1	3	1	8
Coxcatlan Brushed	1	2		6	11	82	42	43	10	3	135	10	27	4	13	10
El Riego Marble-tempered				9	5		22	1	2	2			30	1	2	1
Thin Orange		2	1	98	7	1	4					2	2			1
El Riego Orange	3	12	17	58	2	15	2	16		12		8	3	10	10	7
El Riego Plain		3	1		17	34	47	22	14	13	71	18	33	17	20	21
El Riego Polished	1		1	36	3	5	4	2	2	2		1	2		1	1
El Riego Black				1		38	3	5	1	1	3		1		1	
El Riego Gray	8	10	19	105	20	58	70	51	19	12	85	24	25	14	17	14
Quachilco Mica		1	2	1		27	8	16	8	1	12	3	2		6	
Quachilco Gray	1		1	5	1		50	16	7		31			3	4	2
Quachilco Red										1	2					
Quachilco Brown									2							
Rio Salado Coarse																
Rio Salado Gray			2	3					1				1			
Coatepec White																
Total	30	38	75	512	92	335	359	223	82	52	374	106	131	60	78	67

(Table continued)

	312	276	279	49	260	32	311	292	359	105	270	33	28	321	345
Coxcatlan Striated Buff															
Coxcatlan Polychrome															
Coxcatlan Red-on-cream															
Coxcatlan Black-on-orange															
Coxcatlan Red-on-orange		2					1				5				2
Coxcatlan Coarse													13	1	
Coxcatlan Red		1											4	10	2
Teotitlan Incised		1								3				19	
Coxcatlan Gray		4									1	11	15		1
Coxcatlan Brushed	2	18						2	1		5	3	2	14	37
El Riego Marble-tempered		1					4				1	3	4	6	12
Thin Orange	3						1		4	4		1	5	1	
El Riego Orange		3	2					2	3	1	6	2	2		1
El Riego Plain	7	117	63	2	5	4	15	4	51	21	61	62	23	41	38
El Riego Polished	1	4			1	1	1		3		2		2		11
El Riego Black		5	1								2		4		1
El Riego Gray	3	49	20				2		19	9	16	33	9	13	11
Quachilco Mica		7	5						1	2	3		3	13	1
Quachilco Gray		7	8				1		3	3	5				
Quachilco Red	1														
Quachilco Brown		2											2		
Rio Salado Coarse															
Rio Salado Gray															
Coatepec White															
Total	17	221	99	2	6	5	25	8	85	55	129	98	71	118	117

	351	416	171	14	318	17	52	421	419	257	38	30	346	116	344	20
Coxcatlan Striated Buff		3														
Coxcatlan Polychrome																
Coxcatlan Red-on-cream																
Coxcatlan Black-on-orange																
Coxcatlan Red-on-orange	3								2				2	2	3	
Coxcatlan Coarse		8						1	2					20	2	
Coxcatlan Red	1	5			5		1	6	6		1		4	5	16	
Teotitlan Incised	1	18	2	1	1		5	17	7	1	1	22	16	66		1
Coxcatlan Gray		25	1	1		7	9	34	3	1	1	69	24	84		1
Coxcatlan Brushed	1	91	4	8	7	10	20	44	17	2	2	123	28	64	115	3
El Riego Marble-tempered	3	24	3	2	6			18	3	2	1	48	24	12	44	3
Thin Orange		4								2	1	5	1			9
El Riego Orange		7	4		4		7	25	9		2	153		1	15	20
El Riego Plain	3	116	8	7	10	8	9	18	24	3	2	122	30	65	67	8
El Riego Polished	1	6	1	1	2			6				37	7	5	82	1
El Riego Black		1			1		2					26		1	1	
El Riego Gray		55	4	8	2	7	11	44	16	2	1	51	30	53	13	4
Quachilco Mica		6	2	3	1		3	28				8	3	20	2	
Quachilco Gray		5	2					1				8	5			
Quachilco Red																
Quachilco Brown		14														
Rio Salado Coarse																
Rio Salado Gray																
Coatepec White																
Total	13	388	31	31	39	32	65	238	95	13	12	678	173	396	361	53

(Table continued)

(Table 70, continued)

	23	119	342	317	68	124	291	354	250	278	174	172	297	130	Total
Coxcatlan Striated Buff															18
Coxcatlan Polychrome															44
Coxcatlan Red-on-cream															1
Coxcatlan Black-on-orange															2
Coxcatlan Red-on-orange								1							62
Coxcatlan Coarse	1	1	1	1	4			2			1				204
Coxcatlan Red	13		3	11		1		3			3				222
Teotitlan Incised	17	1	2	1	1	2			2		6	6			490
Coxcatlan Gray	7	1	8	1	11			44	2	16	1	38		1	614
Coxcatlan Brushed	31	4	52	23	13	2		99	3	25	24	35		1	2024
El Riego Marble-tempered	6		15	2	12		3	150	5	15		6	1	1	586
Thin Orange	22	33	2	3						1					184
El Riego Orange	24		5		4		1	22	2	14	10		1	1	594
El Riego Plain		2	24	12	11	2	2	88	3	57	1	12	1	1	2142
El Riego Polished	2		1	6	2	2	1	36	2			22	4		342
El Riego Black	1				3	3				2					169
El Riego Gray	22	2	3	11	12	3	1	38	2	6	15	14		1	2355
Quachilco Mica	1	1	7	1				30		1	1	2			369
Quachilco Gray			3								1				314
Quachilco Red															19
Quachilco Brown															4
Rio Salado Coarse															16
Rio Salado Gray															17
Coatepec White															1
Total	147	12	157	71	76	15	8	513	21	137	85	117	3	6	10793

ange vessels were made in animal effigy forms and had mold-made monkey heads attached to them.

In El Riego Black the late Palo Blanco examples show a somewhat greater range of vessel forms and decorations, including bowls with true *molcajete* incising, more flaring- and convex-wall bowls with stepped slab feet, and deep composite-silhouette vessels with engraved or finely carved designs on the exterior. Ollas of El Riego Plain show some differences within the form: they now have funnel or convergent necks with everted rims, or very short outangled or flaring necks. El Riego Polished, too, in the main retains vessel forms common in earlier times; only convergent-necked ollas with everted rims are distinctive of this later period.

El Riego Orange becomes much more popular near the end of late Palo Blanco times and begins to show characteristics distinctive of this subphase. All of these are variations on older themes. The most popular vessel form is the convex-wall bowls, but now convex-wall bowls are more like flat-bottomed dishes with a very wide diameter at the mouth and very low sides, which sometimes are slightly incurved. Both the di-

rect-rim and incurved-rim forms might be considered comales. Such bowls or comales are also typical vessels of El Riego Marble-tempered; these comales are roughened on the outside and polished inside. Another late classic El Riego Orange form is the tall funnel-neck olla, sometimes with everted or outcurved rim, and with a small flat bottom. It is distinguishable from earlier ollas in that the necks are extremely long, at times exceeding the height of the body itself. These ollas may have rested on three supports like the tripod bowls.

The late Palo Blanco sample of figurines, though small, reveals a complex of features readily distinguishable from those of the earlier part of the phase. The hand-modeled Ugly Baby Face figurine and two mold-made heads, one in the Tlaloc design and the other with a Teotihuacan radiating headdress, are most distinctive. We also have flat mold-made body fragments. It may well be that making figurines in molds is diagnostic of the late Palo Blanco subphase.

Nonceramic artifacts and the subsistence and settlement patterns differ very little in late Palo Blanco times from the early part of the phase. There is no

255

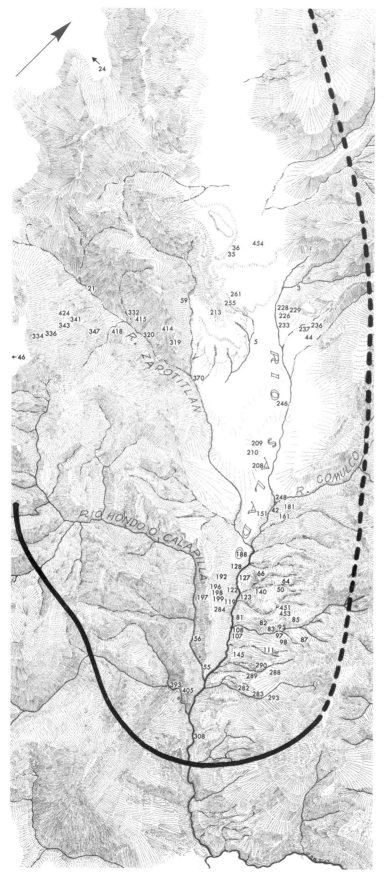

basis for considering the two subphases as being two phases.

Early Venta Salada Subphase

The early part of the Venta Salada phase follows late Palo Blanco. It is represented by a better sample of excavated sherds than we had in the Classic subphases, but the sample still has limitations. From excavation we have seven components, which can be aligned chronologically as shown in the distribution tables of Chapter 9. We are very fortunate in having about 12,000 identifiable sherds collected from eighty survey sites of this period to supplement our excavated sample. The surface sites can be aligned on the basis of the excavated pottery type trends in the chronological order shown in Table 71.

The survey sites indicate geographical boundaries of the early Venta Salada subphase that are apparently very different from those of the Palo Blanco phase. The best defined boundary is now to the south. The southernmost sites that can be securely classified into early Venta Salada are Tc 308 and Tr 393 and others from Los Cues and the Xiquila Canyon only a few kilometers south of the Puebla-Oaxaca border. Grayware and brushed-ware sherds that have been collected at Cuicatlan, only a few miles farther south, and even sherds collected from Tecomavaca seem to be early Postclassic wares that are not Coxcatlan Gray or Coxcatlan Brushed. To the east the boundary seems to be the Sierra Madre Oriental, for the early Postclassic sherds from Valle Nacional and Quauhtochco just north of Orizaba in western Veracruz, though classifiable as Mixteca-Puebla, do not represent a congeries of Venta Salada types. Tr 87, Tr 181, and Tr 229 on the western flanks of the Sierra Madre are the easternmost sites of our archaeological survey, but Jean Brunet and Narciso Tejada, while carrying out the geological survey, reported seeing early Venta Salada sites well up into the mountains. The indistinct boundaries are now the ones defining the northern and western limits of the Tehuacan Valley. A cave site (Tc 46) near Tequixtepec, Oaxaca, is our westernmost site, but we found few sherds of early Postclassic wares in that area. To the north the boundary is even more difficult to define, since fragmentary remains of Coxcatlan Brushed and Coxcatlan Red-on-orange are hard to tell from remains of similar types of Cholulteca I. However, Tr 362, the large Postclassic

FIG. 151. EARLY VENTA SALADA SITES, with boundaries suggested by the archaeological survey.

TABLE 71
Pottery Types from Early Venta Salada Surface Sites

	393	36	210	289	237	108	248	21	228	320	3	334	454	107
Coxcatlan Striated Buff			3	1										
Coxcatlan Polychrome			2			1								
Coxcatlan Red-on-cream			1											
Coxcatlan Black-on-orange			1											
Coxcatlan Red-on-orange			6	4	1	1						1		
Coxcatlan Brushed	3	5	61	48	3	15	1	2	14	46	2	2	23	25
Coxcatlan Coarse	1	1	7	10	1	2	1		31	1			2	
Coxcatlan Red			5	5		2	1		1	7		2	13	
Coxcatlan Gray	2	4	251	30	1	15	3	5	8	21	4	2	21	18
Teotitlan Incised	1	1	9	170		3		1	4	112	1	2	1	19
El Riego Marble-tempered	1	9	7	32	11	11			8	22			16	17
Thin Orange	1		2						1				5	8
El Riego Orange		1	2	5		1		4				4	2	
El Riego Plain	1	2	1	33	1	11			5	23		1	15	14
El Riego Polished		1	13	1		4			1					
El Riego Black			1			2			2					
El Riego Gray		2	43	4	1	8			5	21			15	15
Quachilco Red			1											
Quachilco Mica		1	37			11			4	1		1	5	13
Rio Salado Coarse														
Quachilco Gray			1			3								
Rio Salado Gray														
Coatepec White														
Canoas White														
Total	10	27	454	343	19	90	6	12	84	254	11	11	118	129

	151	208	59	293	181	236	341	87	308	42	290	56	85	209
Coxcatlan Striated Buff				2	1	1		6		3		2		
Coxcatlan Polychrome				2	2		2	1	3		4			
Coxcatlan Red-on-cream				2	1			7			3			
Coxcatlan Black-on-orange				2	1						1			
Coxcatlan Red-on-orange	3	1	1	8	2		3	1	2	1	11	1	7	3
Coxcatlan Brushed	28	23	59	60	52	26	21	116	84	101	123	82	29	34
Coxcatlan Coarse	3	2	3	8	7	1	1	14	38	34	3	58	6	2
Coxcatlan Red	8	13	5	6	9	23	2	1	7	11	9	2	4	8
Coxcatlan Gray	32	23	44	103	98	30	11	208	115	60	211	132	24	4
Teotitlan Incised	5	10	100	6	2	12	4	11	4	40	32	6	10	57
El Riego Marble-tempered	12	11	2	4	7	2	32	1	5	44		2	1	2
Thin Orange				2	1		4	4	1	3	1	3		
El Riego Orange		1	1	19			1		1	1	13		3	1
El Riego Plain	21	11	25	5	2	3		27	37	61	1	6	1	1
El Riego Polished		1		6	1		3		4		2		1	2
El Riego Black				5	1	1		1	3		21			
El Riego Gray	17	8	26	6	18	5		72	15	37	24	3	4	2
Quachilco Red				1										
Quachilco Mica		2	1	6	8	6	4	1	16	6	2	9	12	4
Rio Salado Coarse														
Quachilco Gray				6					6	1	12			
Rio Salado Gray														
Coatepec White														
Canoas White														
Total	129	106	267	259	213	110	88	471	341	403	473	306	102	120

(Table continued)

	97	98	82	414	415	283	161B	123	288	81	547	161	161A
Coxcatlan Striated Buff			1						3			5	
Coxcatlan Polychrome	1								9		2	1	
Coxcatlan Red-on-cream			1						7				
Coxcatlan Black-on-orange	1								5				
Coxcatlan Red-on-orange	3	4	3			2	1	1	30		3	2	2
Coxcatlan Brushed	37	27	107	7	15	95	3	13	122	14	17	106	3
Coxcatlan Coarse	1	3	6		12	4		3	8	1	1	3	
Coxcatlan Red	1	4	7	6	4	2		2	42	2		4	
Coxcatlan Gray	25	20	99	6	3	105	2	9	72	8	3	84	2
Teotitlan Incised	7	10	25		1	78	1	5	59	3	2	20	2
El Riego Marble-tempered	4	2	12	2	9	1	1		1	2	17	33	
Thin Orange	1					2			1			1	
El Riego Orange	6		3	1	2	4			14	1		2	
El Riego Plain	5	6	8	1	1	6		7	1	2	4	24	
El Riego Polished	5	9	6						9	3	5	4	
El Riego Black	1		4			7			7	1		1	
El Riego Gray	16	8	19	1	1	3	1	2	8	8	1	43	
Quachilco Red	1								1				
Quachilco Mica	9	9	37		2	3	1	1	3	1		3	1
Rio Salado Coarse			2										
Quachilco Gray	9		18						1			9	
Rio Salado Gray			3										
Coatepec White			5										
Canoas White													
Total	133	102	366	24	50	312	10	43	403	46	55	345	10

	418A	405	196	229	55	95	198	199	128	197	46	332	127
Coxcatlan Striated Buff			1	1								1	
Coxcatlan Polychrome				5		1	1					4	1
Coxcatlan Red-on-cream		1										1	
Coxcatlan Black-on-orange		2	2									1	
Coxcatlan Red-on-orange		5	6	3		1	3					2	
Coxcatlan Brushed	6	21	105	125	9	41	140	14	14	12	7	72	10
Coxcatlan Coarse	2	1	1	6	2		16		2			3	
Coxcatlan Red		1	2	3	4	2				3	1	5	
Coxcatlan Gray	2	6	180	123	2	45	133	21	14	12	5	35	8
Teotitlan Incised			2		2	4		4	2	1		5	3
El Riego Marble-tempered	3	6		11	5	1	2			2	1	26	
Thin Orange				1								9	
El Riego Orange	3	9	9	3	1	4	1	1				2	1
El Riego Plain	1	5	3	70	2	2	29		2		1	33	1
El Riego Polished			1	1		1	2					8	1
El Riego Black				12		3							
El Riego Gray	1	4	11	20		7	36	2	2	9		9	2
Quachilco Red													
Quachilco Mica	1	4	6		1	6	16	1	3		6	2	2
Rio Salado Coarse													
Quachilco Gray		2	3	3		7	31						
Rio Salado Gray													
Coatepec White													
Canoas White		1											
Total	19	68	332	387	28	125	410	43	42	36	21	218	29

(Table continued)

	122	233	5	424	288	119	188	145	111	64	126	246	343
Coxcatlan Striated Buff	1						5						
Coxcatlan Polychrome		1			4								2
Coxcatlan Red-on-cream													
Coxcatlan Black-on-orange													
Coxcatlan Red-on-orange					2	4	1						10
Coxcatlan Brushed	28	24	37	19	34	37	31	25	4	20	10	11	36
Coxcatlan Coarse	4	2	6	7	1	2	2		1		1		
Coxcatlan Red	2		8	2	7	3	3	2			2	1	
Coxcatlan Gray	18	15	19	2	28	22	13	15	2	8	4	4	21
Teotitlan Incised	1	9	17		2	15	21	1				1	
El Riego Marble-tempered	4	1	3	1	2	2	1	1	1		4		8
Thin Orange			1	7									
El Riego Orange		2	2			2	2	1			4		1
El Riego Plain	3	1		7	7	2	9	7		4	1	6	16
El Riego Polished	2	1			2		1		1		1	1	4
El Riego Black		2	2		1		2	1		3		3	
El Riego Gray	8	7	10	4	4	3		3	1	2		1	
Quachilco Red													
Quachilco Mica	11	1	2	3	3	6	2	8	1	19	1		
Rio Salado Coarse													
Quachilco Gray	1	4	3	4			1	4					
Rio Salado Gray													
Coatepec White								1					
Canoas White													
Total	83	70	110	56	97	103	89	69	11	56	28	28	98

	336	453	226	284	192	140	83	451	319	66	44	213	370A	Total
Coxcatlan Striated Buff			1								1			39
Coxcatlan Polychrome	7		4			2	2		10					74
Coxcatlan Red-on-cream			8			2								34
Coxcatlan Black-on-orange			1				1							18
Coxcatlan Red-on-orange	26	1	9	1	1	3	1	1	8	2	2	18	5	223
Coxcatlan Brushed	165	4	61	58	63	66	37	6	82	19	31	40	20	3,198
Coxcatlan Coarse	1		1	8	1	1	4				1	4		359
Coxcatlan Red	15							2	1		5		1	293
Coxcatlan Gray	82	3	8	62	57	41	21	6	50	12	4	15	10	3,046
Teotitlan Incised	4	1	21	4		4	16		10	4	24	20	10	1,044
El Riego Marble-tempered	34	1	3			2			10	10		2	1	491
Thin Orange			1			3			4					67
El Riego Orange	2		2			1			2					148
El Riego Plain	48		6	18	28	2	1		7					695
El Riego Polished	11		3		7	2	1		1					133
El Riego Black			3				1		8					99
El Riego Gray	3		1	5		25	9	1	26			4		682
Quachilco Red														4
Quachilco Mica	1				8	9	2		1	5	1	3	5	360
Rio Salado Coarse														2
Quachilco Gray	2		2	4		3	3		1			2		146
Rio Salado Gray														3
Coatepec White						1						2		9
Canoas White														1
Total	401	10	135	160	165	167	99	16	221	53	76	102	52	11,168

site near Tepeaca, Puebla, did lack Coxcatlan Gray sherds and therefore might be considered beyond the northern limit of early Venta Salada culture.

Many pottery types continue in decreasing quantities from Palo Blanco times into the early part of Venta Salada; the various El Riego wares, Thin Orange, and even Quachilco Mica. They have few characteristics that would allow one to mark off early Venta Salada times from the previous phase.

Early Venta Salada, however, is distinguished by a completely new complex of pottery types: Coxcatlan Gray, Coxcatlan Brushed, Coxcatlan Red, Teotitlan Incised, and Coxcatlan Red-on-orange. These types (Coxcatlan Brushed excepted) suddenly come into being at the beginning of the period, and most of them reach maximum popularity in early Venta Salada times.

The new types have, of course, a number of distinctive temporal characteristics. Coxcatlan Gray is characterized by a series of convex-wall bowls. Many of these flat-bottomed bowls have feet, usually of the plain stepped variety and infrequently of the stamped stepped or long and conical types. The convex-wall bowls are distinctive in having various modifications of the rims or lips; that is, some rims are beveled on the interior and appear slightly everted, others are sharply outangled or widely everted or slightly outcurved; still others are beveled or grooved on the exterior. Another vessel form that appears at this time and is a good time marker is the ellipsoidal-shaped bowl with sharply inangled rim—the vessel we have called a carinated-rim bowl. In this period we begin to have the stamping of the interior vessel bottom in various circular designs. This is a new and distinctive characteristic, although in early Venta Salada there are more undecorated interior bottoms than ones with either incising or stamping. As we shall see, stamped bottoms become truly characteristic of the late Venta Salada period.

Coxcatlan Brushed, present in small amounts earlier, assumes importance in this period but becomes even more popular in late Venta Salada time. Like Coxcatlan Gray this ware is dominated by flat-bottomed convex-wall bowls with various beveling and everting of lip or rim. The interior bottoms are mainly undecorated, but incised or stamped ones occur infrequently. Vessel supports are fairly rare at this time and are usually of the stepped variety. Carinated-rim bowls are also a major form. Some of these had basket-like handles arched across their mouths.

Coxcatlan Red is another important pottery type of early Venta Salada, also characterized by convex-wall bowls with various kinds of rims. There are also low cylindrical bowls and a few cylindrical-neck ollas with sharply everted rims. Stamped molcajete decoration is rare. The few feet we have are of the stepped variety.

Teotitlan Incised is a third early Venta Salada ceramic type. The vessels are mainly incurved-rim bowls or flat-bottomed carinated-rim bowls. The bowls are decorated on the exterior with distinctive engraved motifs composed of bands of rectangles or diamonds with or without a tiny circular motif inside the larger geometric shape. Feet, which are not numerous, are usually of the stepped variety.

The fourth and final type which is important in this general time period is Coxcatlan Red-on-orange. Vessels are mainly flat-bottomed convex-wall bowls with direct or outangled rims, incurved-rim bowls, or flaring-wall bowls—all shapes that have, of course, occurred before. Two early Venta Salada sherds, however, plainly represent pedestal bases. Pedestal-based bowls are an entirely new vessel form, and one that is to become more important in late Venta Salada times.

Another new vessel form, the *xantil*, first appears in early Venta Salada and carries on throughout the period. These large ceremonial vessels are made in the form of the human figure, usually with a large head, hollow trunk, and tiny arms and legs.

Coxcatlan Coarse occurs sparingly near the end of the early Venta Salada period, but is really not very characteristic. It is represented by only a few sherds, probably most of them from incense burners or braziers.

Two new figurine types may be considered characteristic of early Venta Salada times. Both types are made in flat molds and have square undecorated headdresses. They probably were attached to the molded plain-frocked type of body.

Early Venta Salada also is represented by a few spindle whorls, also mold made. Some are formed into cones or domes and others into truncated cones, both varieties being undecorated. A decorated type which extends into late Venta Salada is a relatively high truncated cone with incised circles and lines on the sloping sides of the cone.

A number of nonceramic artifact types, many of them carry-overs from earlier periods, may be considered characteristic of both early and late Venta Salada. These include Matamoros, Tehuacan, Teotihuacan, and Tula points; fine blades of all types, but especially ones with scared striking platforms; polishing pebbles; truncated-cone pestles; cylindrical, cuboid, and stave-shaped manos; tripod metates; fire-making drills and hearths; arrow shafts; bark cloth and racket-type barkbeaters; twilled baskets; sandals; and cotton cloth woven in one-over-one, two-over-one, or two-over-two patterns. Many of these traits began in Palo Blanco but become more representative of Venta Salada times. First occurring in Venta Salada times are the following nonceramic traits: Harrell, Starr, Texcoco, and San Lorenzo points, thumbnail endscrapers, dog-bone manos, stone effigy bowls, thumbtack pestles, trapezoidal hoes, copper bells, wooden paddle-like tools, cane tongs, decorated combs, gauze and twill cloth, wicker baskets, human-hair yarn, and club-shaped barkbeaters.

The subsistence also undergoes an important shift between Palo Blanco and Venta Salada times. Foods derived from agriculture now represent up to 75 percent of the diet, and most farming is undertaken with irrigation. Other agricultural pursuits included dry-farming, turkey-keeping, maintenance of fruit orchards, and possibly bee-keeping. The only important new agricultural plant is the small lima or sieva bean. There are, however, new varieties of common beans and scarlet runners, and at least four new corn races. Settlement patterns also show a noticeable shift. The hilltop villages and towns of Palo Blanco times give way to settlements in the valleys and on hill or valley flanks. The concentric structure arrangement within settlements becomes less popular, new architectural forms appear, and a few sites are fortified.

Thus we have new characteristics that set off the Venta Salada phase from the Palo Blanco phase. We also have ceramic characteristics within the types of early Venta Salada that allow one to distinguish it from late Venta Salada times, but the majority of the traits of the two Postclassic subphases are the same.

Late Venta Salada Subphase

Late Venta Salada is much better represented by ceramic materials than was early Venta Salada, owing in large part to a tremendous sample from Zone A of Tr 62, the historically documented town of Coxcatlan. There are altogether nine excavated components of this brief and final prehistoric period in the Tehuacan Valley. These can be arranged on the basis of pottery trends in the chronological order shown in the distribution tables of Chapter 10.

About 19,000 additional sherds were collected from ninety-one surface sites. On the basis of the trends of ceramics from excavation these sites were aligned

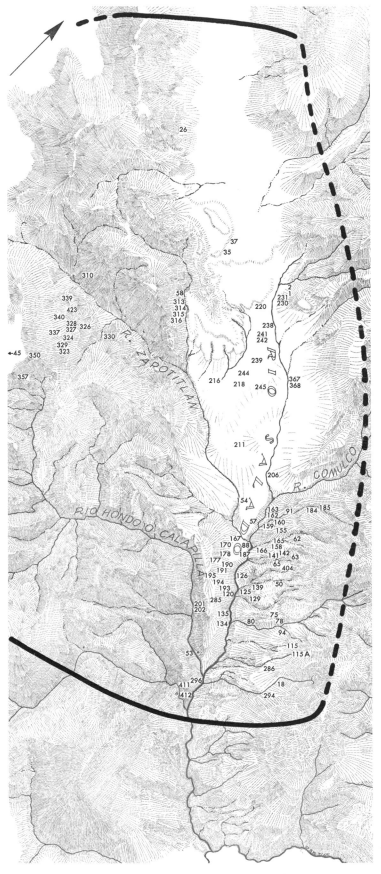

FIG. 152. LATE VENTA SALADA SITES, with boundaries suggested by the archaeological survey.

chronologically as shown in Table 72. Three other sites, Tr 221, Tr 223, and Tr 188, which had very limited samples of sherds, yielded other clay objects that suggest that they too are of this period. Also, a few late Venta Salada sherds were found on sites that had been built and mainly occupied at earlier times: Tr 247, Tr 147, Tr 225, Tr 227, Tr 100, Tr 335, Tr 249, Tr 180, Tr 302, Tr 101, and Tr 280.

In terms of boundaries, Tr 26 near Tlacotepec is our northernmost site, and Tr 294 near Los Cues is the one farthest south. The Sierra Madre seems to be the eastern boundary, but the western boundary is ill defined. A site near Miltepec is the farthest west. Many late Venta Salada sites can be identified with towns recorded by the Spanish at the time of conquest. Tr 1 is ancient Tehuacan, Tr 115A is Teotitlan, Tr 62 is Coxcatlan, Tr 216 is Chilac, and Tr 294 is Los Cues. Tr 26 seems to be Tlacotepec, Ts 367 and Tr 368 may be the village of Zinacatepec or Ajalpan, Tr 319 may be Zapotitlan, Tr 91 may be Calipan, and Tr 89 may be Axusco. The distribution of late Venta Salada sites and the boundaries of this subphase coincide rather closely with the boundaries of the late prehistoric and early historic political entity called the Señorío de Teotitlan. Thus it seems fairly safe to conclude that the late Venta Salada region and the Señorío de Teotitlan are one and the same, but more ethnohistorical study is necessary to substantiate this belief.

A number of the older El Riego pottery types—Gray, Black, Plain, Polished, and Orange—as well as Thin Orange and Quachilco Mica, appear in some of the components classified as late Venta Salada. It seems rather doubtful that these wares actually were being made at this time, since most of them do not occur at Tr 62. Perhaps these types, with the possible exceptions of El Riego Plain and Quachilco Mica, represent mixtures and pittings by the inhabitants of the late Venta Salada components, rather than a continued use of the older kinds of pottery. Needless to say, these older wares, which are definite minorities, show few changes characteristic of late Venta Salada times. Quachilco Mica, however, does seem to have been made in this period, though few characteristics would mark off the late Postclassic sherds from earlier ones in the Venta Salada period; perhaps the most significant trait is that comales appear in quite large numbers.

El Riego Marble-tempered ware is dying out but seems to last into late Venta Salada times; it continues to have as its dominant vessel form comales with polished interiors and roughened exteriors. Coxcatlan Gray is slightly less popular than formerly. The characteristic vessel form is still the convex-wall bowl with everted or beveled rims. However, there are some noticeable differences which may be considered time markers for the late part of Venta Salada. Most Coxcatlan Gray bowls in this period have interior stamping; undecorated interior bottoms are almost totally absent. The plain stepped and long conical supports for these vessels are now outnumbered by stamped stepped, serpent-head, and bulb-end supports. These feet are good time markers for late Venta Salada; most bowls of Coxcatlan Gray at this time probably were supported by three feet, with the stamped stepped variety the most popular type.

Coxcatlan Coarse, which was just barely seen on a few incense burners in the previous period, becomes a definitive time marker for the late Venta Salada period. A great many vessels of this type are large cylindrical jars with everted rims and decorated concave-walled braziers. The latter vessels often display mold-made appliques or fillets, some of which are fairly elaborate. There are also large straight-necked and flaring-necked ollas and low convex-wall bowls with direct rims, wide everted rims, or incurved rims.

Coxcatlan Brushed is dominant throughout late Venta Salada times. Among its period characteristics are convex-wall bowls with flat bottoms and various kinds of everted, beveled, and pinched rims. The bottom interiors are stamped or incised, rarely being undecorated. The late Venta Salada bowls rest on new kinds of supports; most common are serpent feet, but there are feet with old-man faces on them, stepped feet, dumbbell feet, and a few stepped and conical feet like those of earlier periods. The carinated bowl form, tall cylindrical-neck ollas or bottles with everted rims, convergent-neck ollas, and angle-neck ollas are prominent. Bottles recur after a long gap.

Coxcatlan Red is dying out in the late Venta Salada period. Convex-wall bowls have different kinds of rims and usually are footed. The supports are animal effigy feet and stamped step feet, as well as the older plain step feet. Teotitlan Incised is also dying out and displays few, if any, new period characteristics.

Coxcatlan Red-on-orange now becomes relatively popular. The older convex-wall bowl forms continue, usually without feet, though a few dumbbell feet are associated with them. The pedestal-based bowls are the most characteristic form of late Venta Salada times.

Both Coxcatlan Polychrome and Coxcatlan Red-on-cream are good time markers for late Venta Salada, but they have few new secondary features distinctive of late Venta Salada. Coxcatlan Black-on-orange, however, which is characteristic only of late Venta Salada

TABLE 72
Pottery Types from Late Venta Salada Surface Sites

	165	242	126	286	326	231	135	206	199	350	185A	185B	120	285	18	129
Coxcatlan Striated Buff	1		2				2				14		1	2		2
Coxcatlan Polychrome	2		2	7		1	2	1	1	1	1			5	1	3
Coxcatlan Red-on-cream	2	1	1	1		1	3	1	1	1	1					1
Coxcatlan Black-on-orange	3	1	2	4		1	1	1		1	1			2	1	4
Coxcatlan Red-on-orange	2	1	2	20		2	4			4	2		2	12	6	10
Coxcatlan Brushed	21	18	93	114	2	40	95	40	18	42	73	2	18	40	37	128
Coxcatlan Coarse	1	2	3	6	1	1	2		1	1	36		5	2	4	13
Coxcatlan Red	1		5	6		6	9				12		2	8		7
Coxcatlan Gray	5	13	60	61	1	28	62	12	21	23	53	2	2	2	24	67
Teotitlan Incised	5	1	29	19		6	7	4			5		4	10	4	3
El Riego Marble-tempered	1		6	3		7	2	1		11	2		2	2	2	5
Thin Orange		1		1												
El Riego Orange		2		1												1
El Riego Plain	1	2	6	20		4	7	2		6	12		2	5	2	2
El Riego Polished	1	1	3			1	2				2			1	1	7
El Riego Black		1		10			1				1					5
El Riego Gray	1	2	8	6		1	19	3	2	12	46		5	2		8
Quachilco Red																
Quachilco Mica	3		5		1		14	27	1	2	46			1	4	15
Quachilco Gray		1		2							3					14
Coatepec White				2												
Total	50	47	227	283	5	99	232	92	45	104	310	4	43	94	86	295

	57	339	194	58	340	329	230	26	160	63	323	80	310	94	244	239
Coxcatlan Striated Buff	2						68					2		1		
Coxcatlan Polychrome	3	8		2	1	1	8		1	1		1	1	2	1	
Coxcatlan Red-on-cream	3			2	1	1	19	1		1	1	1	2		2	
Coxcatlan Black-on-orange		2		3	1	4	13	1	2			3	2	3	1	1
Coxcatlan Red-on-orange	1	5		2	1	2	9	1	1		1	2	11	20	4	3
Coxcatlan Brushed	127	100	27	72	12	22	534	33	70	53	24	97	42	90	86	45
Coxcatlan Coarse	61	53	1	2	1	11	22	7	1	12	6	9	4	4	12	4
Coxcatlan Red	16	9		3	2	1	33	5	1	8	4	13			3	11
Coxcatlan Gray	41	18	30	19	1	3	290	16	25	19	7	25	7	41	34	17
Teotitlan Incised	16	3	3	1		3	21	1	2		1	9		8	19	8
El Riego Marble-tempered	3	30		32		5	6	1	8		8	2	9	2	2	3
Thin Orange							2									
El Riego Orange												1				
El Riego Plain	1	1		3	2		15		5			7	12	2	7	4
El Riego Polished	1	2					17		2		1	5			2	
El Riego Black												2				
El Riego Gray	4	3	1	20	1		17	8	6	6		31		6	14	
Quachilco Red																
Quachilco Mica	19			5	3		21		28	18		3	3	8	1	4
Quachilco Gray				1					3			3		6		
Coatepec White																
Total	298	234	62	166	27	53	1095	74	155	118	53	215	93	193	188	100

(Table continued)

	412	328	216	314	201	184	134	324	53	187	330	411	394	202	220
Coxcatlan Striated Buff			5			7	3			1					
Coxcatlan Polychrome			17			1	3	5		1	3	1		1	
Coxcatlan Red-on-cream	1	2	19			1		10	4	3	3	1			2
Coxcatlan Black-on-orange			7	2				5		5	16			1	1
Coxcatlan Red-on-orange	2	1	13	1	1	1	2	13			9	2	1	4	1
Coxcatlan Brushed	14	52	276	18	12	242	65	134	16	243	99	17	4	78	50
Coxcatlan Coarse	1	11	13	4	1	7	14	27	2	7	59	3		2	1
Coxcatlan Red	1	14	50	1		10	14	8		4	1	2		1	
Coxcatlan Gray	7	21	125	3	10	127	22	42	3	139	15	1	3	60	30
Teotitlan Incised			70	1		17	4	1	2	36	3			2	5
El Riego Marble-tempered	1	1	17	1	1	6	1	20	1	4		1			1
Thin Orange															
El Riego Orange			7									1			
El Riego Plain	5	8	15	2		7			5	2	2	5		1	2
El Riego Polished		1	5	1				3		3	1	2			1
El Riego Black															
El Riego Gray		2	21	1		34		7	1	17	1			3	7
Quachilco Red															
Quachilco Mica			21	2		43	7	4	1	40				2	
Quachilco Gray				2		3		1		1	1				
Coatepec White															
Total	32	113	681	39	25	506	135	280	35	506	214	35	8	155	101

	238	327	154	245	316	193	241	166	357	296	37	178	139	177A	177B
Coxcatlan Striated Buff				1				1	1	4					
Coxcatlan Polychrome	2			22	9	1			9	7			5	2	
Coxcatlan Red-on-cream	2			24	1		1		3	1		2	1		2
Coxcatlan Black-on-orange	2			6	9			1	15	5		1	4		1
Coxcatlan Red-on-orange	3		2	13	20	4	3	1	13	15		23	8		2
Coxcatlan Brushed	89	1	36	454	201	62	78	56	167	138	24	80	197	11	37
Coxcatlan Coarse	2		3	36	10	9	4	1	3	8	9	4	8		1
Coxcatlan Red	2	1	3	40	1	2	2	2	22				10		2
Coxcatlan Gray	21		16	85	83	40	39	18	30	25	9	27	61	7	5
Teotitlan Incised	12		7	165	4	1	7	2	18	23			10		2
El Riego Marble-tempered	4			9	34		8	1	8	6	3		5		
Thin Orange															
El Riego Orange	4								1						
El Riego Plain	4		1	9			5	1	3	17			1		
El Riego Polished				2	3	1	1	1	3			1			
El Riego Black	8						8	4							
El Riego Gray	22		1	3	2		1	2					10		
Quachilco Red															
Quachilco Mica	1		1	15	1		2	15	18	2		6	28	1	13
Quachilco Gray					2										
Coatepec White															
Total	178	2	70	884	380	120	159	106	314	251	46	143	348	21	65

(Table continued)

(Table 72, continued)

	163	45	294	167	78	404	315	115	25	91	337	115A	189	211	159
Coxcatlan Striated Buff	4		4		21	1	1		16	2		4	1	1	
Coxcatlan Polychrome	2		1	1	3	1	5	1	13		5	15	5	1	1
Coxcatlan Red-on-cream		1	1				3		6			35		1	1
Coxcatlan Black-on-orange	1	1	1	1			11	1	25	1		10	3	1	
Coxcatlan Red-on-orange	3	2	11	1	31	1	28	10	131		16	18	1	5	1
Coxcatlan Brushed	110	57	111	145	284	60	500	60	815	40	235	322	197	78	34
Coxcatlan Coarse	6		8	12	38	7	45	1	44	3		20	8	6	1
Coxcatlan Red	5	5		8	8	3	31	1	23	1	12	10	3		1
Coxcatlan Gray	21	4	45	40	213	19	117	14	126	12	40	66	73	23	7
Teotitlan Incised	14	1	5	16	32		9	5	96	3	8	6	3	2	
El Riego Marble-tempered	3	3	3	7	4	3	77		10		37	2			
Thin Orange															
El Riego Orange							6								
El Riego Plain	6	21		13	21		3		24			12		2	
El Riego Polished	1	2				1	16		6	2					
El Riego Black	1		1		1				3						
El Riego Gray		1	1	3	5	1	15	6	42	3	1		8	1	1
Quachilco Red									1						
Quachilco Mica	9	4	1	9	4	4	1	2	8	2	2	6	6	2	8
Quachilco Gray				1	2				5	1					
Coatepec White															
Total	186	102	193	256	666	103	868	101	1394	70	368	514	310	121	55

	88	190	162	155	191	423	170	125	313	1	195	158	2	141-2	Total
Coxcatlan Striated Buff	1	1	5	1	4		2	2	22	38	3	1	3	14	272
Coxcatlan Polychrome	1	5	1	2	7	1	2	1	4	41	3	1	3	1	272
Coxcatlan Red-on-cream	1		1	2	1		2		4	41	2		3		236
Coxcatlan Black-on-orange		2	1	2	2		2		4	19	1		1		229
Coxcatlan Red-on-orange		4	2	8	7	3	8		5	16	1		2		603
Coxcatlan Brushed	36	102	102	155	159	16	185	21	97	267	9	1	4	2	9,370
Coxcatlan Coarse	1	4	9	9	9		2		4	45		1	4		825
Coxcatlan Red	1	4	8	8	8			1	2	6			1		508
Coxcatlan Gray	8	2	11	19	5		6		14	329	11		3	3	3,334
Teotitlan Incised			6		10				1	32					833
El Riego Marble-tempered	2	5	2	5	1				13	8					473
Thin Orange															4
El Riego Orange															24
El Riego Plain			3	1	1		1			14					347
El Riego Polished			1							9					116
El Riego Black															46
El Riego Gray	4			7	1				21	23	1				512
Quachilco Red															1
Quachilco Mica	2	1	2	2	5		1		1	5		1	1	4	548
Quachilco Gray															52
Coatepec White															2
Total	57	130	154	221	220	20	211	25	192	893	31	5	25	24	18,607

times, does have a large number of the representative pedestal-based vessels.

Coxcatlan Striated Buff is an entirely new type, appearing only as convex-wall vessels. Most of these are molds, but some with stamped interior bottoms obviously served as bowls as well. This type only occurs in late Venta Salada times and the striated exteriors, with either crisscross or diagonal parallel incisions or deep brushings, is particularly distinctive of late Venta Salada. Some fragments of bottoms have deeply incised patterns on the outer surface which are the exact reverse of the low-relief designs stamped on the interior bottoms of other pastes. Other bottom fragments have both incised designs outside and worn stamped designs inside. Certainly the making in molds of a great deal of late Venta Salada pottery must be considered a characteristic of the period.

Mold-made figurines are prominent among the types which are good time markers for the late part of the Venta Salada phase. It should be pointed out, however, that most of the samples for early Venta Salada come from cave excavations where figurines are relatively rare, so some of the figurine types found only in late Venta Salada levels may be characteristic of early Venta Salada as well. The figurine types found only in late Venta Salada components are the mold-made Dog Face, Aztec Square Cap, Flat Cap, and Trapezoidal types, and the hand-modeled Prognathic Old Man and Hollow Painted types. Headless fragments include bodies with loin cloths, Cholula decorated bodies, seated or kneeling figures, bodies with pierced bellies, tripod square-skirted bodies, and a small crudely modeled standing figure. Most of these specimens are mold-made. A variety of spindle whorls, all mold-made and some with elaborate stamped designs, are apparently characteristic of late Venta Salada and were not found in earlier levels. The three older varieties, however, continue to occur in late Venta Salada times.

The pottery types offer some basis for separating the late part of the Venta Salada phase from the early part as a distinct phase, for the Coxcatlan types, Black-on-orange, Red-on-cream, Polychrome, and Striated, together with new types of figurines and spindle whorls, readily distinguish it. However, the majority of the Venta Salada pottery types are the same in both early and late segments, with only minor changes within the types from one part of the phase to the other. More important, the nonceramic artifacts, which far outnumber in variety of types the ceramic types, are very similar in both late and early Venta Salada. Further, the subsistence pattern shows little change between early and late Venta Salada; although, of course, there is a slight increase in the amount of food that was derived from agricultural produce. It therefore does not seem advisable to separate Venta Salada into two different phases; certainly, the preponderant majority of types represented in early and late Venta Salada are held in common.

CHAPTER 12

A Correlation of Mesoamerican Archaeological Sequences

OBVIOUSLY any understanding of diffusion, migration, or even cultural development in Mesoamerica must be based on a firm chronology of all regions. One of the most obvious methods for aligning regional sequences is by comparing radiocarbon determinations for each period, phase, or subphase of each temporal sequence. This technique will be attempted in the following volume, but it must be remembered that at present many regions have few radiocarbon determinations, and that the ones that are now available have wide ranges of error. Thus the radiocarbon-dating technique in its present state is far from the final answer. Moreover, it is presently necessary to use other techniques for establishing and aligning chronologies in order to evaluate the radiocarbon determinations.

One of these techniques is analysis of the trade ware exported from one region to another. Obviously, the shorter the life span of the objects traded, the more precise they become as mechanisms for aligning regional sequences. Pottery types often have shorter life spans than other nonperishable artifact types; they also were traded in fairly large numbers and are relatively easy to recognize as trade objects because the imported wares differ in so many characteristics from the local resident types. In the chapters describing the Tehuacan pottery of each phase or subphase, we listed the trade sherds recognized and indicated where possible how such sherds tend to align cultural and temporal units of other regions with phases or subphases of the Tehuacan sequence. This method at present seems to provide a reliable mechanism for aligning all archaeological sequences in Mesoamerica, and it is unfortunate that aberrant or trade sherds are so rarely mentioned or illustrated in regional pottery reports.

A more widely used technique for aligning regional sequences is the study of overlapping pottery types. One may find that certain ceramic types manufactured locally in two or more regions have a number of major attributes in common, thus indicating a rough contemporaneity and the probability that one of the local types is the copy of a related type in another region. Although these types may have as short a life span as trade wares and the imitations be accomplished as quickly as pots can be exchanged in trade, there is always a strong possibility that the original type may be copied in other regions relatively late in the span of the original type. And the copied version may also last in its region somewhat later than the original type. Thus overlapping types may show a stylistic lag, and do not provide as exact a basis for aligning various sequences as do the trade sherds. In each chapter we have tried to point out how some of the Tehuacan pottery types are related to types in other regions.

We have also pointed out, subphase by subphase, that certain modes or attributes of the ceramics of Tehuacan are shared by pottery in many other regions. The horizon markers or modes are ceramic concepts that apparently have spread to a number of regions from one original homeland. If such a concept has spread rapidly to different regions, it might be a firm basis for aligning the cultural phases of the different regions. There is, however, an even greater possibility that a single concept may spread relatively slowly and be susceptible to considerable stylistic lag, much more so that a combination of attributes or modes such as

Key to Fig. 153

TRADED TYPES   GROUPS OF RELATED TYPES

LATE POSTCLASSIC

Mixteca Polychrome   Texcoco Black-and-white-on-red

Cholula Polychrome Matte   Tancol Polychrome

Cholula Polychrome Firme   Huasteca Black-on-white

Cerro de las Mesas Polychrome   Tenayuca Black-on-orange

EARLY POSTCLASSIC

Coxcatlan Coarse   X Fine Orange

Texcoco Black-on-red   Mazapan Red-on-buff

Tohil Plumbate   Cholula Polychrome Lacquer

Isla de Sacrificios Polychrome   Y Fine Orange

60 Puuc red pottery
59 Puuc slate pottery
58 Glyph design mold-made spindle whorl
57 Geometric design mold-made spindle whorl
56 Squared headdress mold-made figurine
55 Fine-line red-on-orange pottery
54 Basket-handle brushed pottery
53 Stamped-bottom pottery
52 Chablekal fine gray pottery
51 Palmar polychrome pottery

LATE CLASSIC

Zaquil Incised

San Juan Plumbate

Panuco Fine Paste (late)

Dos Arroyos Polychrome

50 Saxche polychrome pottery
49 Actuncan polychrome pottery
48 Balanza black pottery
47 Aguila pottery
46 Incised mold-made spindle whorl
45 Feathered headdress mold-made figurine
44 Plain mold-made spindle whorl
43 Tlaloc mold-made figurine

EARLY (PROTO) CLASSIC

Panuco Fine Paste (early)   Thin Orange

San Martin Fresco-decorated   Ixcanrio Polychrome

San Martin Stamped   Monte Alban Gray (G35)

42 Tiquisate pottery
41 Monte Alban gray (G35) pottery
40 San Martin incised pottery
39 San Martin comal pottery
38 El Riego orange pottery
37 Portrait figurine
36 Monte Alban incensarios

LATE FORMATIVE

El Prisco Black   Tres Zapotes Black Incised

Chalahuites Orange-rimmed Black   Mars Orange

Usulutan Negative Painted   Ticoman Orange

Ticoman Red-on-yellow   Ticoman Red

35 Escobal pottery
34 Polvero black pottery
33 Flor cream pottery
32 Sierra red pottery
31 Tres Zapotes figurine
30 Las Charcas red-on-cream
29 El Riego gray pottery
28 Remojadas figurine
27 Matamoros figurine
26 Flat doughnut-eye figurine
25 Valley of Mexico H figurine
24 Valley of Mexico G figurine
23 Valley of Mexico E figurine
22 Flat long slotted-eye figurine

MIDDLE FORMATIVE

Trapiche Black-rimmed Orange   Quachilco Gray

Trapiche Orange   Canoas White-rimmed Orange subtype

Zacatenco Orange   Dili Resist

Cerro del Tepalcate Punctate   Dili Fingernail Punctate

21 Flores waxy pottery
20 Incised outlined-eye figurine
19 Chila white pottery
18 Flat turban slit-eye figurine
17 Trapiche chin-strap figurine
16 Small helmeted figurine
15 Coffee-bean eye figurine
14 Dii figurine

EARLY FORMATIVE

Morelos Lacquer   Trapiche Dentate-stamped

Zacatenco Brown   Ocos Buff (Wide Rocker-stamped)

White-slip Red-paste   Tlatilco Mottled Bottle

Kaolin White   Ponce Black

Tilapa Red-on-white   Mapache Red-rimmed

Trapiche Zoned Incised   Coton Grooved Red

13 La Venta hairknot figurine
12 Ploughed-eye figurine
11 Negroid with hairknot figurine
10 Crescentic cap solid figurine
9 Baby Face figurine
8 Thick lip dish pan
7 Trapiche dentate-stamped pottery
6 Trapiche bunned-headdress figurine
5 Canoas white pottery
4 Hollow lowland figurine
3 Large solid realistic figurine
2 Hollow dwarf figurine
1 Cotorra zoned brushed pottery

in an overlapping type, and of course much less rapidly than trade wares. We feel that it is unfortunate that many correlations of Mesoamerican sequences have been based upon studies of horizon markers rather than upon studies of the more exacting and reliable mechanisms of trade sherds or overlapping types.

The correlations arrived at here, although based mainly upon trade sherds, still have certain limitations. First of all, we are looking at other sequences in terms of the Tehuacan sequence, that is, from a very myopic standpoint at best. Second, some segments of the Tehuacan excavated ceramic sequence are based on inadequate numbers of sherds, and of course, in these periods, the samples of trade sherds, overlapping types, or horizon markers, are also limited in number. Third, and perhaps most important, is the lack of thorough study of trade wares and resident types of other regions. With rare exceptions, ceramic descriptions for Mesoamerican regions do not include adequate microscopic petrographic studies which allow one to be positive that the so-called trade sherds are really trade sherds, the determinations of aberrant sherds as trade sherds being based upon macroscopic observations instead. Thus, some of the aberrant sherds that we have called "trade sherds" should rather be labeled "possible trade wares." Fourth, except for recent studies in the Peten of Guatemala, there has been little attempt to correlate the typological studies of one region of Mesoamerica with those of another, perhaps into a type-variety scheme as advocated by Smith, Willey, and Gifford (1960). Until this or a similar kind of correlation is undertaken and aspects of the archaeological provincialism of Mesoamerica are broken down, studies of inter-relationships of sequences will be seriously handicapped.

The fifth and final factor that limits our comparisons of Tehuacan materials with those of other regions is simply the lack of adequate monographs on long ceramic sequences from more than a few regions. We have therefore limited our comparisons to just ten other regions in Mesoamerica: coastal Chiapas and Guatemala, the Guatemala highlands, the Peten region of lowland Guatemala, the Yucatan Peninsula, the Grijalva Basin of Chiapas, the coastal region of southern Veracruz and northern Tabasco, the coastal region of central Veracruz, the Tampico-Panuco region of northern Veracruz, the Oaxaca Valley, and the Valley of Mexico. One region we have omitted because of lack of published data is the Valley of Puebla, probably the region nearest and most closely related to Tehuacan, and therefore the one whose omission distresses us most. Fortunately, a German expedition sponsored by the *Deutschenforschungsgemeinschaft* is at work in Puebla and should have the regional sequence uncovered there within a few years. Already, work by Dr. Jörg Aufdermauer (personal communication) has produced late Ajalpan-like material at Moyotzingo, near San Martin Texmelucan, and Dr. Heinz Walter (personal communication) has recovered Middle Formative material at the site of Acatepec, south of Cholula. More recently, Walter has discovered Ajalpan-related material southeast of Tepeaca, halfway between Puebla and Tehuacan, which promises to link the two regions closely. Melvin L. Fowler's work at the site of Amalucan, and that of Dr. Bodo Spranz at the site of Totimehuacan, both near the city of Puebla, should clarify the later ranges of the Formative when fully reported. In turn, the recent work of the Instituto Nacional de Antropologia e Historia at Cholula promises to add information on the Classic and Postclassic periods.

The Valley of Oaxaca

Of the areas we have included in our comparison, the Valley of Oaxaca is geographically closest to Tehuacan, and the ceramics indicate its close cultural relationship as well, over virtually all the sequence from earliest Ajalpan to the Spanish conquest. Oaxaca has been extensively investigated for many decades, although detailed ceramic reports are not yet available for most of the sites excavated. A notable exception is the monumental *La Ceramica de Monte Alban* by Caso, Bernal, and Acosta (1967), which incorporates Bernal's earlier analysis of the pottery and expands Caso's original definition of the five-period sequence from Monte Alban, and serves as the basis for our discussion in this section. In addition, we have relied on earlier progress reports (Caso and Bernal 1952, 1965), interpretive summaries (Paddock 1966), and recent field research into the pre–Monte Alban periods in Oaxaca (Flannery *et al.* 1967 and unpublished data). We also compared our materials with collections in the National Museum in Mexico City and the Frissell Museum in Mitla, Oaxaca.

Since the writing of our report and the composition of Figs. 153–156, extensive field work has been undertaken in the Valley of Oaxaca, the results of which we shall briefly summarize below. The earliest ceramic materials known from the Valley of Oaxaca are tentatively called the Matadamas complex (not included in Fig. 153), and they come from deeply buried levels at the site of San Jose Mogote, near Etla. All sherds are thin, ranging from buff or flesh-color to grayish-brown on the same vessel, and have strong resemblances to Ajalpan Plain and Ajalpan Fine Plain. The only two vessel forms known are small hemispherical bowls and narrow-necked ollas; tecomates are absent. Some bowls may have a band of specular hematite at the rim, or be slipped completely red like Ajalpan Fine Red specimens. No incising, and in fact no plastic decoration at all, is known for this complex; this, coupled with a few sherds suspiciously like Purron Plain or Ajalpan Coarse lead us to date Matadamas near the beginning of the Ajalpan phase. Future studies will determine whether it stands alone as a phase or becomes an early subphase of the subsequent period.

The next phase, Tierras Largas (not included in Fig. 153), is known from tens of thousands of sherds and dozens of whole vessels; its relationship to middle Ajalpan is very clear. The dominant types of the phase are Coatepec Red-on-buff, Coatepec Plain, and Ajalpan Plain. Particularly striking are the hemispherical or convex-walled bowls of Coatepec Red-on-buff with "V"'s or inverted "V"'s in specular hematite hanging from the red-painted rim. The Tierras Largas phase has virtually no plastic decoration either, but a few rocker-stamped tecomates—almost certainly trade wares—appear. They resemble Mapache and Mendez Red-rimmed types from the Chiapas-Guatemala coast. A few sherds of Ocos Black with zoned dentate stamping also appeared. The type site of Tierras Largas (near Atzompa, almost at the base of Monte Alban) was excavated by Mark Winter of the Oaxaca Project, but similar materials are widespread throughout the valley from San Jose Mogote to Zaachila and Santa Ana Tlapacoyan. It is clear that Oaxaca and Tehuacan interacted strongly on this time horizon, and so prevalent is Coatepec Red-on-buff that it may turn out to be essentially a Oaxacan ware, which began there earlier and never became as popular in Tehuacan.

Next, and clearly contemporary with the late Ajalpan subphase, is the San Jose phase in the Valley of Oaxaca—the first phase in which incising, excising, punctation, and rocker-stamping can be said to be common in the latter region. Although incompletely studied, the pottery of this period is known from more than a dozen villages through the Valley of Oaxaca, some of them four or five times the size of the site of Ajalpan. Tecomates may have wide plain rocker stamping or a red rim band and zoned punctation like Cotorra tecomates from Chiapa de Corzo or be zoned red and white, like examples from the Guatemala coast. Resemblances with Tilapa Red-on-white and Mapache and Mendez Red-rimmed are strong. One sherd of an outsloping-wall bowl with very

fine plain rocker stamping may be Coatepec Plain. Traded tecomates of Guamuchal Brushed, a dominant Cuadros phase type, also occur at San Jose Mogote, the type site for the phase. Large hollow dwarf figurines, some painted red with specular hematite, tie San Jose more securely with late Ajalpan.

A number of shared trade types link San Jose with early Santa Maria as well; these, however, occur in the later part of the San Jose phase. They include Kaolin White and white-slipped red-paste sherds (which are apparently the same types as Coe's Xochiltepec White and La Mina White from San Lorenzo Tenochtitlan), as well as black, gray, or white monochrome sherds with raspada designs (usually Olmec motifs like the "fire-serpent," Kan sign, or "U" element). These could be interpreted in one of two ways; either late San Jose overlaps in time with early Santa Maria, or else Olmec influences and traded materials reached the Valley of Oaxaca earlier than Tehuacan. Since the San Jose phase shows its strongest ties with San Lorenzo on the southern Gulf Coast, the latter interpretation is the more likely; such ties include numbers of white-slipped Olmec baby-face figurines, ploughed-eye figurines, cylindrical vessels with Olmec fire-serpent glyphs, white-rimmed black ware, paint dishes, multicompartmented vessels, and magnetite mirrors. But the San Jose phase also helps link San Lorenzo and late Ajalpan with Tlatilco in the Valley of Mexico, since it shares with the latter site carved ceramic cylinder seals, spouted trays, and polished stone *yuguitos*.

The subsequent Guadalupe phase in Oaxaca is closely related to the early Santa Maria phase in the Tehuacan Valley. Coatepec White, probably traded from the Tehuacan area, is common in the Guadalupe phase, which is best known from the sites of Tierras Largas and Barrio del Rosario Huitzo. However, the dominant pottery of the Guadalupe phase is a monochrome white-to-buff type extremely similar to Canoas White, except that it virtually lacks bowls with interior "pseudo-molcajete" designs. Realistic projecting-eyeball figurines characterize both areas. Two Oaxacan gray wares, Socorro Fine Gray and Josefina Fine Gray, distantly resemble Rio Salado Gray; one of these, Socorro Fine Gray, is ancestral to the gray wares of Monte Alban I which so closely resemble Quachilco Gray. Both Guadalupe and early Santa Maria have trade sherds of Dili Punctate, Kaolin (or Xochiltepec) White, white-slipped red paste (La Mina White), and a very hard gray ware with raspada designs. A Guadalupe phase olla type, Fidencio Coarse, is identical to Rio Salado Coarse in almost every respect, but lacks the high frequency of mica in the nonplastic inclusions. A type used for braziers and pot rests, Lupita Heavy Plain, is nearly identical to Canoas Heavy Plain. Guadalupe Brown Burnished, ancestral to the K. 3 type of Monte Alban I, distantly resembles Canoas Orange-brown. Other horizon markers shared by Guadalupe and early Santa Maria are incised double-line-break motifs, convex-wall bowls with rims thickened on the interior or exterior, heavy bowls with rims thickened on the exterior, dimple-based bowls, and the oval bowls with pinched-in sides.

Monte Alban I, which seems to have developed out of Guadalupe, has many affiliations with late Santa Maria of Tehuacan. As mentioned previously, Quachilco Gray of Tehuacan and the gray wares of Monte Alban I are so close in paste, vessel form, and decoration that one could almost consider them to be the same type, or at least varieties of the same type. Quachilco Brown may have been imported into Monte Alban I–II from Tehuacan. Trade sherds of Tres Zapotes Black Incised occur in both late Santa Maria and Monte Alban I. Coatepec White also closely resembles Type C. 5 of Monte Alban I–II. Figurines attributed to Monte Alban I are the same as the Tehuacan types we have called Matamoros, Capped Doughnut-eye, Outlined-eye, and Slot-feature. Horizon markers common to both the Oaxaca and Tehuacan manifestations include basal-flange bowls, bowls with wide everted rims and scalloped everted rims, tripod vessels with hollow bulbous or mammiform feet, and ollas with bridged spouts.

Connections between Monte Alban II and transitional II–IIIA and Tehuacan materials are more difficult to discern. Gray wares like Quachilco Gray are still prevalent in Monte Alban II, as Quachilco Gray still is in late Santa Maria and early Palo Blanco. Some of the gray sherds of Monte Alban II, however, seem to be vaguely similar to El Riego Gray, which is the dominant type in early Palo Blanco times. Further analysis and more detailed descriptions of these Monte Alban types would do much toward discerning just how close is the connection between the two areas. Except for possible Quachilco Brown sherds, no trade sherds have been reported from Monte Alban II that also occur in our Tehuacan sequence; thus we are forced to use overlapping types as a basis for connecting the two areas. Remojadas-like figurine types occur in later Santa Maria and Monte Alban II. The Slot-feature type is present in Monte Alban I–II, late Santa Maria, and early Palo Blanco, and again seems to indicate a connection. The greatest number of connections, however, are in terms of horizon markers: bowls

with stepped rims and flanged rims, bowls with mammiform feet, cylindrical bowls with basal bulges, basal-flange bowls, ollas with bridged spouts, rolled-rim ollas, and incised or engraved designs with hachured steps or triangles are common to Monte Alban II, late Santa Maria, and early Palo Blanco. Solid nubbin feet and vessels with the perforated ring bases characteristic of Monte Alban II occur in Tehuacan only in early Palo Blanco times. Hollow rectangular feet, which continue into transitional Monte Alban II–IIIA, also first appear in Tehuacan early in Palo Blanco. Thus, there are indications that Monte Alban II is roughly of the time period of latest Santa Maria and early Palo Blanco.

Somewhat confirming this temporal alignment is a considerable body of evidence for temporally equating Monte Alban III with late Palo Blanco. First of all, the two manifestations have a number of trade sherds in common, including Thin Orange, San Martin Stamped, and San Martin Fresco-decorated. Some of the black-gray vessels Noguera (1940) found in late Palo Blanco tombs in Tehuacan are probably trade wares of Type G. 35 from Monte Alban III. Further, the Hotel Peñafiel of Tehuacan displays incense-burner effigies of Cocijo, the Old God, Xipe Totec, and the maize goddess—all made of El Riego or Quachilco Gray paste and attributable to late Palo Blanco—which are almost identical to effigy vessels from Monte Alban III (Caso and Bernal 1952: figs. 2, 155, 394). El Riego Gray, representative of the Palo Blanco phase in the Tehuacan Valley, is extremely similar to Type G. 23 of Monte Alban III. Some of the mold-made figurines with feathered headdresses that Caso and Bernal (1952: fig. 446) have illustrated for Monte Alban III are very similar to those of late Palo Blanco.

Horizon markers common to Monte Alban III and late Palo Blanco are convex-wall bowls with ring bases, bottles with long necks and huge flaring rims, double-spouted ollas with flat bases, flat-bottomed ollas with long flaring necks, false-spout handles, cylindrical vessels with nubbin or rectangular feet, pot covers, decorated handles, and so forth.

Although there seems to be considerable evidence to show that Monte Alban III is for the most part contemporaneous with late Palo Blanco, whether or not both ended at exactly the same time is difficult to say.

Since both early Venta Salada, or at least the latest part of this subphase, and Monte Alban IV have Tohil Plumbate and X Fine Orange as trade sherds (Caso, Bernal, and Acosta 1967: 381–444), the two regional segments must overlap. Also, Type K. 22 of Monte Alban IV seems closely related to Venta Salada's Coxcat-

TRES PICOS Medellin 1960	QUICHUIZTLAN Medellin 1960	EL TRAPICHE Trench A García Payón 1966	EL TRAPICHE Trench B	CHALAHUITES Trench AB García Payón 1966	CHALAHUITES Trench B	REMOJADAS Medellin 1960	TAJIN Du Solier 1945	CEMPOALA García Payón 1951	SYNTHESIS	A.D.
								Cempoala IV	Cempoala IV	1500
	Quauhtochco							Cempoala III	Cempoala III	
Tres Picos III	Quiahuiztlan III									
Tres Picos II	Quiahuiztlan II							Cempoala II	Cempoala II	
Tres Picos I	Quiahuiztlan I							Cempoala I	Cempoala I	1000
							Tajin III		Tajin III	
						Upper Remojadas 2	Tajin II		Tajin II	500
						Upper Remojadas 1				
						Lower Remojadas	Tajin I		Tajin I / Remojadas	0
		Levels 1-5	Levels 1-6	Levels 1-2	Levels 1-6				Trapiche III	
		Levels 6-10	Levels 7-14	Levels 3-21	Levels 7-13				Trapiche II	500
		Levels 11-15	Level 15	Levels 22-24					Trapiche I	1000 B.C.

FIG. 154. Synthesis of archaeological sequences in central Veracruz.

lan Coarse. But as with late Palo Blanco and Monte Alban III, it is hard to tell whether the phases ended at the same time. Perhaps the best evidence to indicate that they may have done so is on the basis of connections between Monte Alban V and late Venta Salada.

Monte Alban V and late Venta Salada have in common such trade types as Cholula Polychrome Lacquer and Texcoco Black-on-red. Stamped-bottom Coxcatlan Brushed sherds occur in Monte Alban V at Yagul and Mixtec Polychrome sherds typical of Monte Alban V occur as trade sherds in late Venta Salada. Some Monte Alban V thin comales polished on the upper side and rough underneath, ranging in color from cream to dark brown, are very like El Riego Marble-tempered comales, and the great jars of coarse brown ware with a striated surface are similar to Tehuacan's

Coxcatlan Brushed (Caso and Bernal 1965: 893). Further, the figurines of Monte Alban V with square head-dresses, those with large appliqued earplugs, the flat bodies with V-shaped quechquemitls, and the geometrically stamped spindle whorls (see Caso and Bernal 1965: fig. 2c) are all present at Tehuacan in the late Venta Salada period. Various horizon markers such as Mixtec incense burners, effigy vessel feet, tripod ollas with straight necks, pedestal-based bowls, and pitcher-shaped vessels are also common to both Venta Salada and Monte Alban V.

Central Veracruz

Central Veracruz is the second most closely related region to Tehuacan during ceramic times. This region may be roughly defined as the coastal area above

272

Puerto Veracruz to the south and below Tuxpan to the north. The earliest materials seem to be those reported by García Payón (1966) from Chalahuites and El Trapiche. His four excavations at these two sites seem to represent at least three periods. The earliest materials are designated Trapiche I, following García Payón's earlier terminology (1950). At El Trapiche they occurred in Levels 11–15 of Excavation A and Levels 15 and perhaps 14 of Excavation B, and at Chalahuites in Levels 22–24 of Excavation A and Levels 14–16 of Excavation B. In late Ajalpan components at Tehuacan we uncovered trade sherds which we called Trapiche Dentate and Trapiche Zoned Incised (see García Payón 1966: pp. 109–116 and pl. XXVII, no. 9), which are types diagnostic of Trapiche I. Present in both late Ajalpan and Trapiche I are types like Ponce Black, Mapache Red-rimmed, the mottled-bottle type reported from Tlatilco, and perhaps Kaolin White (ibid.: pls. VIII, no. 76; XXXIII, no. 26; LXVII, XLIX, for Ponce Black; XLVI, no. 21, for Mapache Red-rimmed; pp. 87–92 for mottled bottle). Some "café o bayo" tecomates (ibid.: pl. XLI) are extremely similar to sherds of Coatepec Plain and some examples of "rojo sobre café o bayo" are like Coatepec Red-on-buff (ibid.: 195–199). Both Coatepec wares are dominant types in late Ajalpan times. Trapiche I and late Ajalpan also have in common a number of more general horizon markers, such as large hollow and projecting-eye figurines (ibid.: pls. LXI, no. 2; LXII; LXIV, no. 2), as well as horizon traits such as plain rocker or rocker-dentate stamping, the dominance of tecomate vessel forms, and large flat-bottomed bowls with thickened rims. Kaolin White, which occurs as a trade ware in early Santa Maria, is also present in Trapiche I.

Trapiche II, represented at Chalahuites by materials from Levels 7–13 of Excavation B and Levels 3–21 of Excavation A, shows close similarities to early Santa Maria of Tehuacan. Common to both are trade sherds of both La Venta White Raspada and Black Raspada, Kaolin White, Hard Buff, Dili Punctate (ibid.: pl. XLIV, nos. 10–12), and white-slipped red paste. Sherds from Trapiche II–III of Trapiche Orange and Black-rimmed Orange occur in early Santa Maria; whereas sherds of Canoas White and even the subtype Canoas White-rimmed Orange diagnostic of early Santa Maria are abundant in Trapiche II (ibid.: pp. 63–72). Personal inspection with García Payón of the white sherds from El Trapiche and Chalahuites revealed that a few of the white sherds of Trapiche I were not like Canoas White, but were almost the same as Progreso White of the Tampico region (MacNeish 1954: 123). However, Trapiche II white sherds are predominantly Canoas White, even to having hornblende temper. A few white sherds from late Trapiche II and Trapiche III were a little like Chila White (Ekholm 1944; MacNeish 1954) of the Tampico-Panuco region or resembled Coatepec White of the Tehuacan region. Also, a few heavy sherds with fabric impressions from Trapiche surface collections are vaguely similar to Canoas Heavy Plain of early Santa Maria times.

Figurine types of early Santa Maria that are also present in Trapiche II include the following: Trapiche Bunned-helmet (García Payón 1966: 128–131), Tres Zapotes Chin-strap (pl. LXII, nos. 2–5), Baby Face (pls. LVI, nos. 4–6; LVII), Hollow Lowland (pl. LXII, no. 1), Valley of Mexico Type Di (p. 141), Helmeted (pl. LVI, no. 1), Crescentic Cap (pls. LII, nos. 1–7, 11–13; LX, nos. 1–3), Ploughed-eye (pl. L, nos. 11–12), and Negroid with Hairknot pl. LII, nos. 8–10). Among the general horizon markers that early Santa Maria and Trapiche II have in common are sunburst designs incised on interior bottoms, incised multiple-line-break motifs, long narrow rocker-stamped decorations, raspada designs on a black or white surface, low bowls with various kinds of bolstered rims, and so forth.

Fewer connections exist between Trapiche III and Tehuacan trade sherds, overlapping types, and horizon styles. Trapiche III materials occur in Levels 1–5 of Excavation A and Levels 1–6 of Excavation B at El Trapiche, and Levels 1–2 of Excavation A and Levels 1–6 of Excavation B at Chalahuites. Perhaps the best evidence for equating late Santa Maria and Trapiche III are the presence in both of Chalahuites Orange-rimmed Black and black incised sherds like Tres Zapotes. In Drucker's original report on Tres Zapotes, these sherds fall under his category, Black Wares. The sherds we call Tres Zapotes Black Incised are a specialized group of this ware with a black-to-brown slip with finely incised geometric designs featuring crosshatched stepped motifs, often appearing on composite bowls (Drucker 1943a: figs. 22, 36). Some Trapiche III sherds representing composite-silhouette bowls with incised designs (García Payón 1966: Tables 1–6) are probably trade sherds of Tres Zapotes Black Incised, which also occur among our late Santa Maria remains.

Other resemblances between the two areas are less definitive, but the very fine examples of Anaranjada ware of Trapiche III (ibid.: pl. I and pp. 29–31) resemble Quachilco Brown of late Santa Maria and often have the same vessel form, that is, low bowls with horizontal or down-slanted everted rims. Remojadas, or

273

Cara Triangular, figurines also occur in both late Santa Maria and Trapiche III as do the Ticoman type (*ibid.*: pls. LX, LXI).

The Remojadas figurine types may indicate that Lower Remojadas of central Veracruz, which seems to follow Trapiche III, may begin before late Santa Maria ends and then continue into early Palo Blanco times. However, the best evidence for equating both Lower Remojadas and Tajin I with Tehuacan's early Palo Blanco subphase are trade sherds of Usulutan ware in all three manifestations (Medellín Zenil 1960: pl. 14). Other links between the three are of a more general nature, such as mammiform and cylindrical feet (*ibid.*: pl. 8, fig. 2), bridged-spouted vessels (pls. 5, 10), basal-flanged bowls and bowls with finely hachured triangles (pls. 1–3), ring-based bowls, asymmetrical bowls, and other more general time markers of this period.

Next in the central Veracruz sequence would be Upper Remojadas (Medellín Zenil 1960) and Tajin II (Du Solier 1945; García Payón 1951). These complexes unfortunately have not been as fully reported as the Formative remains, but the trade sherds strongly hint that this general period is roughly coeval with late Palo Blanco. Trade sherds of the early variety of Panuco Fine Paste, Thin Orange (Medellín Zenil 1960: 65) and San Martin Stamped (Du Solier 1945: pl. XVII), as well as overlapping types such as mold-made portrait figurines (*ibid.*: pl. A), and plain molded spindle whorls, occur in central Veracruz at this time. All except Panuco Fine Paste are present also in late Palo Blanco of Tehuacan.

Tajin III seems to be the next sequential unit of central Veracruz, but it is difficult to tie to the Tehuacan sequence, unless some of the Rayada ware (*ibid.*: pp. 8–9, pl. XVI) is X or Y Fine Orange. If so, Tajin III and early Venta Salada might be roughly contemporaneous, as indirect evidence would seem to confirm. Temporal estimates for the late variety of Panuco Fine Paste trade sherds in Tajin III and the Coyotlatelco manifestation in the Valley of Mexico indicate that these two are roughly contemporaneous, and, as we shall see, there is abundant evidence for correlating Coyotlatelco with early Venta Salada. Also, some of the sherds considered typical of Tajin III by Espejo (1953: 407), seem to be Drucker's Cerro Montoso type of the Soncautla complex (1943a: pl. 24f), and we shall present below considerable evidence for correlating early Venta Salada and Soncautla.

The final part of the central Veracruz sequence can be very closely connected and aligned with the Venta Salada phase of Tehuacan. There are in this period a

number of short phases or subphases in central Veracruz with slightly different ceramics, which we shall synthesize as shown in Fig. 154. The earliest phase, Cempoala I, seems to be roughly contemporaneous with Tres Picos I, Quiahuiztlan I, and others (Medellín Zenil 1960: 124–137). All have trade sherds of Tohil Plumbate, X Fine Orange, and Cholula Polychrome Lacquer, as well as incised truncated-cone spindle whorls like the one from the latest part of the early Venta Salada subphase. Some of the stamped motifs of molcajetes of Sellado Types I and II of Cempoala I (García Payón 1951: pls. 1–17, 23) are very similar to stamped designs common in the early Venta Salada type, Coxcatlan Brushed. Cempoala II–IV and its local equivalents, Tres Picos II–III, Quiahuiztlan II–III, and Quauhtochco, on the basis of trade sherds seem to be contemporaneous and roughly of the same period as late Venta Salada of Tehuacan. The trade sherds common to all include Isla de Sacrificios Polychrome, Cerro de las Mesas Polychrome, Tenayuca Black-on-orange, Texcoco Black-on-red, Tancol Polychrome, Cholula Polychrome Matte, and Cholula Polychrome Firme. Overlapping types include figurines with square headdresses, some of the complex stamped molcajete motifs, tripod vessels with effigy feet, and spindle whorls with incised or molded decoration.

Tampico-Panuco Region

The Huasteca, to the north of the central Veracruz coastal plain, can be correlated quite well with central Veracruz but has few direct ties with Tehuacan and thus can be temporally equated with Tehuacan only indirectly. The sequence from the northern coastal region of Veracruz from Tuxpan to Tampico is based upon the pioneering stratigraphic excavations of Ekholm (1944) and of MacNeish (1954). We shall use the latter's period designations: from early to late, Pavon, Ponce, Aguilar, Chila (Ekholm Period I), El Prisco (Ekholm Period II), Pithaya (Ekholm Period III), Zaquil (Ekholm Period IV), Las Flores (Ekholm Period V), and Panuco (Ekholm Period VI).

The poorly defined Pavon period is difficult to equate with remains either from central Veracruz or from Tehuacan, but the second period, Ponce, has ties with both regions. Ponce Black pottery occurs in large amounts in Trapiche I, and a few possible trade sherds of this type were found even in late Ajalpan. Trapiche I, which is contemporaneous with late Ajalpan, has large amounts of Progreso White, both the hub-and-spoke and the opposed-area variety, which are dominant in the Huasteca in the Ponce period (MacNeish 1954: 569–571). Horizon styles common to all three regions include large hollow and projecting-eye figurines, flat-bottomed convex- or flaring-wall bowls, and tecomates. It might also be noted that the tecomates so prevalent in Ajalpan are relatively rare in Ponce, whereas the flat-bottomed flaring-wall bowls of Ponce are considerably less prominent in Ajalpan. These differences in proportion suggest that perhaps even this early there were regional specializations in preferred vessel forms.

The Aguilar period of the Tampico-Panuco region has few direct ties to either Trapiche or the Tehuacan sequence. One of the aberrant sherds of Aguilar with a double-line-break motif (MacNeish 1954: 577) may be Zacatenco Brown, which also appears as a trade type in early Santa Maria. Confirming the temporal equation of Aguilar and early Santa Maria are the overlapping types of Baby Face, Negroid with Hair-knot, and Crescentic Cap figurines, as well as such horizon styles as raspada decoration on black or white surfaces, interior sunburst designs, and multiple-line-break motifs on bowls with semi-everted or everted (often scalloped) rims.

Chila of northern Veracruz, characterized by the white-slipped, gray-pasted Chila White type, may be roughly of Santa Maria times, as Chila White and Coatepec White seem to be closely related types. The figurines of Chila are predominantly the Flat Rectangular-eyed type (Ekholm 1944: 436–437), which are closely related to the Cara Triangular type of Trapiche III. This is another indication that Chila is roughly contemporaneous with the latest part of early Santa Maria or the earliest part of late Santa Maria in the Tehuacan Valley.

El Prisco of the Huasteca has definite connections with Tajin I and Trapiche III, for all three seem to have El Prisco Black pottery either as a trade ware or as a locally made overlapping type (Ekholm 1944). Further, some of the El Prisco figurines, particularly Panuco Type A (Ekholm 1944: figs. 31f, 33a, f, j) are quite similar to García Payón's Tres Zapotes type (1966: 131–135) of Trapiche II and III. Perhaps, therefore, the El Prisco period of Panuco overlaps with Trapiche III and Tajin I and is, on this indirect basis, of roughly the same time period as late Santa Maria and early Palo Blanco in the Tehuacan Valley.

The Pithaya period also has El Prisco Black pottery as a major type. As we noted, it occurs as well in Tajin I and II. Further, El Prisco Fine Paste Corrugated, which occurs in El Prisco but is more popular in the Pithaya phase, is also present at Tajin I–II (Du Solier 1945), indirectly indicating that Pithaya correlates generally with late Santa Maria to early Palo Blanco of Tehuacan. However, the more general overlapping types or horizon styles such as portrait figurines and hollow rectangular vessel feet in Pithaya, Tajin II, and early Palo Blanco, suggest that they are roughly of the same time period.

It is not until the Zaquil period that we have trade sherds in common between the Panuco area and the Tehuacan region: both Zaquil and late Palo Blanco have trade sherds of San Martin Stamped from the Valley of Mexico (Ekholm 1944). The very close relationship between Zaquil black incised and negative-painted sherds and the black incised ware of Tajin III – all of which may be trade sherds of the same type (Ekholm 1944: 428) – equates Tajin III with Zaquil. As has been shown before, Tajin III seems to be roughly of late Palo Blanco or earliest Venta Salada times. A less definite link between Panuco and Tehuacan is the appearance of mold-made figurines in both the Zaquil and late Palo Blanco periods.

Mazapan Red-on-buff sherds from the Valley of Mexico and X Fine Orange trade sherds in both Las Flores of Panuco (Ekholm 1944: 428–431) and early Venta Salada of Tehuacan indicate that they are of the same general period. Similar decorated mold-made spindle whorls, hollow-handled ladles, and similar stepped designs on Las Flores Black-on-red (Ekholm 1944: fig. 21a-l), Las Flores Red-on-buff (fig. 24b) and Coxcatlan Red-on-orange tend to confirm the temporal alignment of Las Flores and early Venta Salada. In fact, the spirals or scrolls, stepped designs, and concentric squares or rectangles of Red-on-orange might well be considered horizon markers for the early Postclassic period, common not only to Las Flores and early Venta Salada, but also to contemporaneous phases of many other regions.

The presence of a Tancol Polychrome sherd, a type diagnostic of the final Panuco phase of the Huasteca (Ekholm 1944: 364), in a late Venta Salada component may be taken as evidence that the Panuco phase and late Venta Salada are contemporary. Further, Ekholm has pointed out the similarity of design elements of Tancol Brown-on-buff to those of Tenayuca Black-on-orange. As we shall see below, Tenayuca Black-on-orange trade sherds are present in late Venta Salada. Thus there seems to be indirect evidence that late Venta Salada and the final Panuco phase are roughly contemporaneous.

The Valley of Mexico

There has been in the Valley of Mexico an amazing amount of archaeological activity, which is ever continuing. The sequential material and periodizations

275

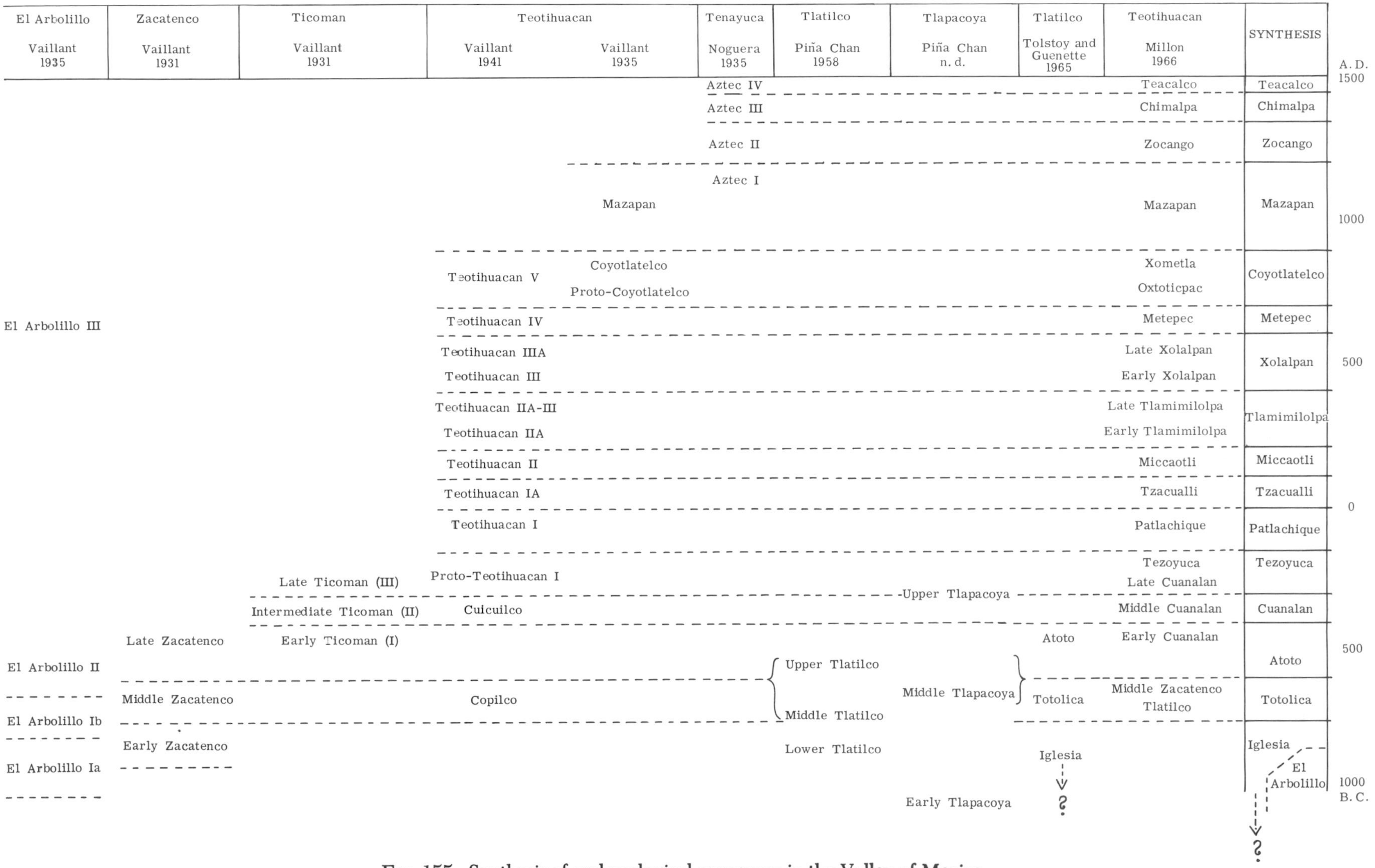

Date	El Arbolillo (Vaillant 1935)	Zacatenco (Vaillant 1931)	Ticoman (Vaillant 1931)	Teotihuacan (Vaillant 1941)	Teotihuacan (Vaillant 1935)	Tenayuca (Noguera 1935)	Tlatilco (Piña Chan 1958)	Tlapacoya (Piña Chan n.d.)	Tlatilco (Tolstoy and Guenette 1965)	Teotihuacan (Millon 1966)	SYNTHESIS
A.D. 1500						Aztec IV				Teacalco	Teacalco
						Aztec III				Chimalpa	Chimalpa
						Aztec II				Zocango	Zocango
A.D. 1000					Mazapan	Aztec I				Mazapan	Mazapan
				Teotihuacan V	Coyotlatelco					Xometla	Coyotlatelco
	El Arbolillo III				Proto-Coyotlatelco					Oxtoticpac	
A.D. 500				Teotihuacan IV						Metepec	Metepec
				Teotihuacan IIIA						Late Xolalpan	Xolalpan
				Teotihuacan III						Early Xolalpan	
				Teotihuacan IIA-III						Late Tlamimilolpa	Tlamimilolpa
				Teotihuacan IIA						Early Tlamimilolpa	
				Teotihuacan II						Miccaotli	Miccaotli
0				Teotihuacan IA						Tzacualli	Tzacualli
				Teotihuacan I						Patlachique	Patlachique
			Late Ticoman (III)	Proto-Teotihuacan I						Tezoyuca	Tezoyuca
										Late Cuanalan	
			Intermediate Ticoman (II)	Cuicuilco				Upper Tlapacoya		Middle Cuanalan	Cuanalan
B.C. 500			Early Ticoman (I)				Upper Tlatilco		Atoto	Early Cuanalan	
	El Arbolillo II	Late Zacatenco		Copilco						Atoto	Atoto
	El Arbolillo Ib	Middle Zacatenco					Middle Tlatilco	Middle Tlapacoya	Totolica	Middle Zacatenco / Tlatilco	Totolica
	El Arbolillo Ia	Early Zacatenco					Lower Tlatilco		Iglesia		Iglesia / El / Arbolillo
B.C. 1000								Early Tlapacoya	→ ?		→ ?

Fig. 155. Synthesis of archaeological sequences in the Valley of Mexico.

are continually being revised and the materials reclassified. Our synthesis of the archaeological sequences in the Valley of Mexico, presented in Fig. 155, is based on the works of Tolstoy for the Formative periods and on Millon for the Classic and Postclassic periods. Much of this recent work is unpublished, and we are grateful to Tolstoy and Millon for sharing so much information with us.

A major problem in the correlation of Formative materials from the Valley of Mexico with other regions has been the fact that, for many years–hard as it may be to believe–in almost all secondary (and some primary) publications, part of the sequence was literally backwards. Just how this situation came to pass is so interesting that we feel it deserves brief mention.

The pioneering work of George Vaillant (1930, 1931, 1935) established the first sequence at the sites of El Arbolillo, Zacatenco, and Ticoman. Based on actual stratigraphy, Vaillant's sequence went: El Arbolillo I, El Arbolillo II (Early Zacatenco), Late Zacatenco (Early Ticoman), and Late Ticoman. Later work at the site of Tlatilco by a number of archaeologists (Covarrubias, Piña Chan, Porter, Romano, Tolstoy and Guénette, and others), countless looters, and a variety of professional brickmakers, disclosed ceramics which differed in significant ways from those at Vaillant's sites. Many Tlatilco vessels (especially those from burials) were far more elaborate and sophisticated than anything found by Vaillant; some showed Olmec motifs. Two modes–differential firing producing white rims on black ware and zoned rocker-stamping–appeared at Tlatilco but not at Vaillant's sites. Early work at Tlatilco was decidedly non-stratigraphic, and most workers believed the site was a one-period occupation (cf. Porter 1953). The problem then became: what was the relationship of Tlatilco to Vaillant's sites?

Valley of Mexico specialists fell into two pitfalls. First, although Vaillant himself had never argued for any great antiquity for his sites (he referred to them as the "middle cultures"), El Arbolillo was listed everywhere in the secondary literature as Mesoamerica's oldest village, and everyone was conditioned to think of it in those terms. Second, the materials from Tlatilco were the most sophisticated and complex– and archaeologists, although by now they should know better, tend to think in terms of development from simple to complex. El Arbolillo therefore remained Mesoamerica's oldest village, and an effort was made to fit Tlatilco (and similar "Olmec" materials subsequently discovered at Tlapacoya) somewhere into the middle of Vaillant's sequence.

Archaeologists working outside the Valley of Mexico, however, remained uncomfortable with this placement. As early as 1954, MacNeish argued for a realignment of El Arbolillo with the Middle Formative, rather than Early Formative. Then, in Chiapas, Oaxaca, and Veracruz, throughout the late 1950's and 1960's and in the Valley of Tehuacan as well, archaeologists began finding Tlatilco-related material, with white-rimmed black ware and zoned rocker-stamping, in good stratigraphic context — below materials showing ties with El Arbolillo I. They encountered little enthusiasm among Valley of Mexico specialists, however, who in the meantime had "explained" the absence of Olmec material at Vaillant's sites by attributing it to an Olmec "elite" who resided only at Tlatilco and Tlapacoya.

Finally, in 1967, Paul Tolstoy, after careful stratigraphic restudy of El Arbolillo and Tlatilco (Tolstoy and Guénette 1965), placed two pits in a new locality at Tlapacoya. His analysis shows three ceramic phases: Ayotla, Justo, and Bomba (not included in our correlations in Figs. 153 and 155). The two earliest, Ayotla and Justo, show Tlatilco-like material with heavy Olmec influence; the latest, Bomba, resembles El Arbolillo I. When fully published, Tolstoy's sequence will for the first time place the Valley of Mexico's Formative materials in their proper relationship.

Ayotla and Justo clearly overlap with late Ajalpan, as does much of the material from Tlatilco. Plain wide rocker-stamping, dentate stamping, large hollow dolls, ploughed-eye figurines, red-rimmed tecomates, and polished black trade wares of presumed Gulf Coast affinity, as well as tall-necked bottles are present. Sherds like Coatepec Red-on-buff are in evidence, and Kaolin White and white-slipped red-paste ware are definitely present. Bowls with externally reinforced rims and excised St. Andrew's crosses resemble specimens from the San Jose phase in Oaxaca and the San Lorenzo phase in southern Veracruz. In fact, this is the period of the Formative when the Valley of Mexico shows widest and clearest ties with other regions; in later stages of the Formative, it seems to have gone its separate way.

Tolstoy's Bomba phase, and the closely related El Arbolillo I period, show somewhat more vague ties with the Santa Maria phase at Tehuacan. The dominant pottery type of El Arbolillo is Zacatenco Brown, or Black-brown, and the dominant figurine types are Di, F, C3a, and C3d. All of these types occur in early Santa Maria levels along with sherds of Zacatenco Orange Lacquer. In terms of trade sherds and overlapping figurine types therefore, El Arbolillo seems to be roughly of the same period as early Santa Maria. The only possible evidence for an earlier placement of El Arbolillo is the presence therein of remains of what may be Ponce Black and the hub-and-spoke variety of Progreso White, both originating in the Panuco-Tampico region, which has been shown to be of the general period of late Ajalpan. However, both these types extend in the Huasteca into the Aguilar period, which is of early Santa Maria times.

The Iglesia subphase at Tlatilco, defined by Tolstoy and Guénette (1965), also resembles early Santa Maria. Both have trade sherds of Kaolin White and white-slipped red-paste ware. Some fragments of hollow large figurines and mottled bottles lasted into the Iglesia subphase, although these are really more typical of the preceding Justo phase. (It is clear from burial lots at Tlatilco that there must once have been Ayotla and Justo phase materials at the site, but they probably had been largely removed before Tolstoy was able to make his excavations.)

Besides these links between Tehuacan and the Valley of Mexico, early Santa Maria has Zacatenco Brown, Zacatenco Orange, and Morelos Orange Lacquer trade wares from Iglesia. Both Iglesia and early Santa Maria have Olmec Baby Face, Crescentic Cap, Ploughed-eye, Negroid with Hairknot, Hollow Lowland, and Types Di, F, C3a, and C3d figurines, as well as white wares with multiple-line-break motifs, bowls with interior sunburst designs, and white- and black-surfaced sherds with raspada designs. All these characteristics show that Iglesia and early Santa Maria are roughly contemporaneous.

The Totolica phase also seems to be of about the same period as early Santa Maria. The two manifestations have in common a whole series of horizon markers, including long plain rocker-stamping, bowls with bolstered rims, dimple-based convex-wall bowls, collared and plain tecomates, and so forth. Further, among the trade wares of early Santa Maria are sherds decorated with fingernail punctate which we shall call here Cerro del Tepalcate Punctate and sherds of Zacatenco Red-on-white of Totolica, as well as sherds of Dili Resist from Chiapas—all of which indicate a fairly strong connection with Totolica.

First appearing late in early Santa Maria and continuing through the late Santa Maria subphase are sherds of Ticoman Red (Vaillant 1931: 284), a type which begins in the Atoto phase (Piña Chan 1958: 107) and continues through the rest of the Ticoman sequence. Their presence in Tehuacan indicates a temporal equation of the latest part of early Santa Maria and the earliest part of Ticoman. The Atoto phase

also is characterized by Ticoman Red-on-buff, Ticoman Orange (Vaillant 1931: 275–281), and Type E figurines, all three of which appear in the earliest components of late Santa Maria. Furthermore, Mars Orange sherds from the Mamom phase of the Maya lowlands appear in both late Santa Maria and Atoto (R. E. Smith, personal communication). Type G figurines, typical of the Cuanalan (Ticoman II) phase occur in middle components of late Santa Maria and indicate a rough contemporaneity. Ticoman figurines, so typical of Tezoyuca, are present in the latest Santa Maria components. Trade sherds of Usulutan ware from the southern Maya area are said to appear in Tezoyuca (Bennyhoff, personal communication), as they do in late Santa Maria, which seems good evidence of the contemporaneity of the two periods.

Ties between Classic subphases of Tehuacan and the Patlachique phase of the Valley of Mexico have not been uncovered. Thin Orange, with ring-based vessels, appears for the first time in the middle components of early Palo Blanco and in the Tzacualli period of Teotihuacan (Millon 1966). Also appearing in the Palo Blanco phase is the Tehuacan type El Riego Orange, which is similar to San Martin Orange (Tolstoy 1958), which originates in the Tzacualli phase. Common to both manifestations are such time markers as cylindrical vessels with hollow slab feet and nubbin feet (Tolstoy 1958: graph 3), pot covers, and bridged-spouted ollas.

In the subsequent Miccaotli phase of the Valley of Mexico the pottery type San Martin Stamped begins, although it becomes more prominent in the later Teotihuacan periods. The presence of San Martin Stamped in the beginning of late Palo Blanco in the Tehuacan Valley suggests that Miccaotli and the earliest components of late Palo Blanco are coeval. However, San Martin Fresco-decorated and Portrait figurines, both of which first appear in Tlamimilolpa of the Valley of Mexico, occur in the components of late Palo Blanco along with the San Martin Stamped sherds, hinting that perhaps Miccaotli is contemporaneous with the latest part of early Palo Blanco, while Tlamimilolpa is of the earliest late Palo Blanco times.

The Xolalpan phase also seems to be of late Palo Blanco times, as both it and the Tehuacan subphase have Monte Alban III gray sherds (Type G. 35) and mold-made Tlaloc figurines. Also, some of the Thin Orange variants of both late Palo Blanco and Xolalpan are very similar. The Metepec phase of the Valley of Mexico, with Thin Orange cylindrical vessels appliqued with monkey heads, is obviously of the same period as Noguera's tombs of late Palo Blanco times in the Tehuacan Valley. Latest Palo Blanco and Metepec also have similar mold-made figurines with feathered headdresses. It might be added that Metepec has Dos Arroyos polychrome sherds from the Tzakol phase of the Maya area. As we shall see, there is some evidence that Tzakol probably existed during the general time of late Palo Blanco.

Following or ending the Classic period in the Valley of Mexico is the Coyotlatelco phase (Rattray 1966: 87–193). Coyotlatelco has many connections with the earliest part of Venta Salada. Both have trade sherds of San Juan Plumbate, Cholula Polychrome Lacquer, and Y Fine Orange, as well as mold-made spindle whorls with incised geometric designs (Millon 1966). Further, the Coyotlatelco type, Mazapan Red-on-buff, decorated with "S" lines or undulating parallel lines, are among the trade sherds from the earliest components of Venta Salada. Furthermore, the double-line "S" (Rattray 1966: fig. 24f), stepped motifs (ibid.: fig. 25), and concentric rectangular elements (ibid.: fig. 7c) of Coyotlatelco Red-on-brown are extremely similar to designs of Coxcatlan Red-on-orange of early Venta Salada times.

The late components of early Venta Salada seem roughly contemporaneous with Mazapan, for both have trade sherds of X Fine Orange and Tohil Plumbate (Tolstoy 1958). The presence of Tenayuca Black-on-orange, Texcoco Black-on-red, and Texcoco Black-and-white-on-red trade sherds in late Venta Salada indicate that this Tehuacan subphase is contemporaneous with Zocango, Chimalpa, and Teacalco of the Valley of Mexico.

• Southern Veracruz and Tabasco

The region along the Gulf Coast to the southeast of Tehuacan has usually been called the Olmec region. It includes the coast of Veracruz south of Puerto Veracruz and the adjacent coastal area of Tabasco. Coe (1965) has admirably summarized the ceramic sequence of this region from Late Formative to historic times, and our interpretation of the chronology, shown in Fig. 156, relies heavily on his synthesis and also on the works of Drucker (1943a, 1943b, 1952), Medellín Zenil (1955, 1960), Stirling (1943), Valenzuela (1945), and Weiant (1943). Earlier Formative remains of the Olmec region are somewhat more difficult to classify, for at the time of writing they are being intensively reinvestigated by Coe, Squier, Heizer, and Drucker. Thus the synthesis offered in Fig. 156 is extremely tentative, and much of what we write here is subject to change.

At San Lorenzo on the Coatzacoalcos River, Michael

Coe is in the process of defining four phases of the Early Formative: Ojochi, Bajio, Chicharras, and San Lorenzo (Coe, personal communication). Elsewhere in this volume we have referred to the San Lorenzo phase only, since that was the single formulation existing at the time the earlier chapters were written and Figs. 153 and 156 were composed. Although analysis is not yet complete, preliminary correlations seem to indicate that Ojochi and Bajio should be equated with early Ajalpan, while Chicharras is middle Ajalpan, and San Lorenzo is clearly late Ajalpan. The Ojochi phase, like the Matadamas complex in Oaxaca, is almost entirely composed of thin buff-colored pottery, occasionally decorated with specular hematite paint. Thin-walled tecomates, bowls, and ollas or bottles are the principal forms. The range of bowls increases during Bajio times, more closely approximating the early Ajalpan inventory. Tall-necked bottles, rocker stamping, dentate stamping, white-rimmed black ware, Kaolin (or Xochiltepec) White pottery, and figurines already in the Olmec tradition are present in Chicharras.

Also possibly belonging to this period is the "pre–Complex A" material recently recovered from La Venta by Robert Squier. This pre–La Venta material and our early Ajalpan subphase seem to have common pottery types with coarse temper, a zoned brushed surface, and a predominant tecomate form (Ajalpan Plain and Ajalpan Coarse in Tehuacan). Both manifestations also have large solid figurines with realistic facial features. Perhaps the best link between the two is that each has a few sherds of tecomates with specular red rims, similar to the Mapache Red-rimmed type of Guatemala.

In the San Lorenzo phase, ties are strong with late Ajalpan (and even stronger with the coeval San Jose phase of the Valley of Oaxaca). San Lorenzo and late Ajalpan share trade sherds of Trapiche Rocker-dentate-stamped, Ponce Black, red-rimmed tecomates, red zoned tecomates with wide rocker stamping, bottles with contracting necks, heavy thickened-rim bowls, and large hollow dwarf figurines. Kaolin (Xochiltepec) White and white-slipped red paste ware (called La Mina White by Coe) are so common at San Lorenzo it seems virtually certain that this is the region of their origin. Cylindrical vessels with excised Olmec glyphs (called Calzadas Carved) are shared by San Lorenzo, early Santa Maria, San Jose in Oaxaca, and Justo in the Valley of Mexico. Among the San Lorenzo figurines are Hollow Lowland and Trapiche Bunned-helmet figurines; these do not occur in Tehuacan until early Santa Maria, but this may only be because they were late to arrive in the Central Plateau area. Finally, some overlap between Ajalpan and the earliest phases at La Venta can be seen in a fragment from 215-285 cm. deep in Pit C at the latter site. This was a portion of a large hollow figurine with an incision depicting the convolutions of the ear in a style identical to that seen on a specimen of the late Ajalpan phase.

The Palangana phase, which follows San Lorenzo in Coe's new sequence, shows strong ties with Complex A of La Venta and the early Santa Maria phase in the Tehuacan Valley. Gulf Coast Kaolin (Xochiltepec) White and La Mina White continued to reach Tehuacan during this period, and the two areas shared trade wares such as Trapiche Rocker-stamped, Hard Buff, Morelos Lacquer (Drucker 1952), Dili Punctate (Drucker 1952), and according to Gareth Lowe (personal communication), sherds like Dili Resist. From the Olmec region early Santa Maria received Black Raspada and White Raspada wares.

Moreover, the two regions have a number of overlapping types in common. The coarse white, coarse buff, and coarse brown wares of La Venta not only have surfaces covered by a white wash, similar vessel forms, and decorations resembling those of Canoas White, Canoas Heavy Plain, and Canoas Orange-brown respectively, but the pastes are tempered with "slender angular plaques of a highly lustrous black material," which is presumably the same kind of amphibole-pyroxene inclusions present in the pastes of all three wares at Tehuacan. La Venta and early Santa Maria also have a number of figurine types in common, the most convincing being the La Venta Hair-knot type (Drucker 1952: pl. 43a), one of which was found in an early Santa Maria level. Other figurine types are: Hollow Lowland (ibid.: pl. 41e), Trapiche Bunned-helmet (pl. 23d), Ploughed-eye (pl. 27b), Crescentic Cap (pl. 41d), Baby Face (pls. 30c, 40a, e, f), Multi-hairknot, and Negroid with Hairknot (pls. 3, 4d). Among horizon styles shared by early Santa Maria and La Venta are: incised multiple-line-break motifs (Drucker 1952: fig. 25), interior bottom sunburst designs (ibid.: fig. 33), long plain rocker-stamping, collared tecomates, bowls with wedge-shaped rims or rims with interior or exterior thickening, and so on. All in all, there is considerable ceramic evidence for temporally equating La Venta and early Santa Maria. It is perhaps surprising that the more ornate Olmec ceremonial (burial) features have not been uncovered with early Santa Maria remains in the Tehuacan Valley. Probably this lack reflects our own limited investigations.

Connections between the Tres Zapotes phase of the

Olmec region and the subphases of Tehuacan are less numerous. Tres Zapotes Black Incised trade sherds occur in components of late Santa Maria, while some of the white-slipped sherds of the earliest levels of Trench 42 of Cerro de las Mesas (Drucker 1943b: 44–45), a component of the Tres Zapotes phase, may be sherds of the Coatepec White type popular in middle Santa Maria times in the Tehuacan Valley. Both Tres Zapotes and late Santa Maria seem to have trade sherds of Chalahuites Orange-rimmed Black ware. The most obvious overlapping types are Quachilco Gray of Tehuacan and the incised black wares from the Ranchito collection of Tres Zapotes times (see Weiant 1943: 69–74). Among overlapping figurine types are the Ploughed-eye, Helmeted, Tres Zapotes Chin-strap, and Flat-turban types. Other indications of contemporaneity would be the presence in each complex of such horizon markers as mammiform feet, single-spouted vessels, wide-everted-rim bowls, basal-flange bowls, and the prevalence of composite-silhouette bowls with upright concave rims.

The Cerro de las Conchas phase has less direct evidence of contemporaneity with Tehuacan. A secondary burial at Nopiloa (Coe 1965: 700) contained an apparently thin-orange vessel of "typically Teotihuacan II form" like those that occur in early Palo Blanco in Tehuacan as well as elsewhere. Other evidence consists only of such general horizon markers as cylindrical vessels with hollow rectangular feet, pot covers, ring bases, stepped-rim bowls, and corrugated or fluted vessels.

The following Cerro de las Mesas phase, however, has more definite connections with late Palo Blanco of Tehuacan. Sherds of San Martin Stamped occur in Pit 2 in the upper levels of Cerro de las Conchas (Medellín Zenil 1960) and ring-based conoidal vessels of Thin Orange occurred in Matacapan I (Valenzuela 1945: 94–96); both items were uncovered in components of late Palo Blanco. Another good link is the presence of mold-made figurines with feathered headdresses like those of Metepec in the Valley of Mexico in both Cerro de las Mesas (Drucker 1943b: pl. 49c, d) and late Palo Blanco. Such horizon markers as slab-footed and cylindrical-footed vessels, tall composite-silhouette vessels, ring bases, and mold-made figurines are also present in both areas at this time.

The Soncautla phase, with Y Fine Orange vessels and plain and incised truncated-cone mold-made spindle whorls, seems contemporaneous with early Venta Salada. The Isla de Sacrificios phase may be the period of middle Venta Salada, for both have as trade sherds Tohil Plumbate and X Fine Orange. Also, Isla de Sacrificios Polychrome occurs as a trade ware in the earliest part of the late Venta Salada phase, and stamped-bottom sherds of Matacapan II (Coe 1965): fig. 29a) are extremely similar to Coxcatlan Brushed. Spindle whorls of all types in late Venta Salada resemble those of the Isla de Sacrificios phase. Upper Cerro de las Mesas and late Venta Salada have so many trade sherds in common that there can be little doubt that they are contemporaneous. The trade wares include Texcoco Black-on-red, Mixtec Polychrome, Cholula Red-on-orange, and Cholula Polychrome Lacquer (Drucker 1943b: 43, 48, 50–51). Moreover, polychrome sherds of the Cerro de las Mesas and Isla de Sacrificios types occur in late Venta Salada. Interior stamped bottom designs, spindle whorls, Aztec and Toltec figurines, and mold-made figurines generally are similar in both Cerro de las Mesas and late Venta Salada. There is, then, a long series of ceramic connections between Tehuacan and southern Veracruz providing a reliable basis for aligning the sequences of the two regions.

Upper Grijalva Basin

Another region with a long ceramic sequence comparable to that of Tehuacan is the Grijalva Basin of Chiapas (Lowe and Mason 1965, MacNeish and Peterson 1962). On the basis of radiocarbon dates, and also because of the lack of white wares, it appears that the earliest ceramic remains from Santa Marta Cave compose the earliest ceramic period of the Grijalva region. Sherds resembling Mapache Red-rimmed in both this complex and early Ajalpan suggest a rough contemporaneity. Wares of both manifestations are dominated by the tecomate vessel form, and the tecomates are often finished with zoned brushing.

The existence of good ceramic links between the subsequent Cotorra phase of Chiapas and late Ajalpan of Tehuacan somewhat confirms this temporal equation. Both Cotorra and late Ajalpan have good trade sherds of Mapache Red-rimmed, Ocos Buff with wide short rocker stamping, Tilapa Red-on-white with plain rocker-stamping, and sherds resembling Ponce Black. Heavy bowls, often with fabric impressions, occur in Cotorra and are similar to Canoas Heavy Plain vessels of latest Ajalpan and early Santa Maria times. However, some of the Cotorra white wares with double-line-break motifs are like Canoas White of early Santa Maria, while heavy bowls with thickened rims resemble vessels of Canoas Orange-brown and Rio Salado Gray. A further connection are the fairly realistic figurines with projecting eyes of both Cotorra and late Ajalpan.

Perhaps the best-documented connection between the two regions lies in the relationships of the Dili phase of Chiapas and the early Santa Maria subphase of Tehuacan. Occurring in early Santa Maria are trade sherds of Dili Resist and Dili Fingernail Punctate. Further, the early Tonala varieties of Vergel White ware characteristic of Dili are very like Canoas White of early Santa Maria, both having hornblende inclusions in the paste, a white wash, multiple-line-break motifs, and similar bowl forms. Other overlapping types are Hollow Lowland, Crescentic Cap, and Negroid with Hairknot figurines. Horizon markers common to both regional manifestations include flat-bottomed bowls with wedge-shaped or internally or externally thickened rims, plain rocker stamping, interior sunburst designs, multiple-line-break motifs, and so on.

Escalera of Chiapas shows the same sort of general similarities to early Santa Maria, but the presence of trade sherds of Mars Orange from the Maya region suggests that this complex ties in with the latest part of early Santa Maria or the earliest part of late Santa Maria. There were, however, Escalera Orange sherds in one early Santa Maria component. Also, the slipped varieties of Vergel White-to-buff, often with obsidian temper, starting in Escalera are more similar to Coatepec White, which overlaps early and late Santa Maria, than they are to Canoas White, which characterizes early Santa Maria.

Francesa of Chiapas has good links to the earliest part of late Santa Maria. Both have in common trade sherds of Mars Orange, Tres Zapotes Black Incised, and Chalahuites Orange-rimmed Black wares. Francesa also has trade sherds from late Santa Maria or Monte Alban I of either Quachilco Gray or a very closely related gray ware.

Guanacaste of Chiapas has few direct ties to Tehuacan, but bowls with wide everted rims and sherds resembling Usulutan types suggest a general contemporaneity with late Santa Maria.

Horcones of Chiapas definitely has Usulutan trade sherds, as does latest Santa Maria. Both also have the Matamoros figurine type and such horizon markers as mammiform feet and basal-flange bowls.

Istmo of Chiapas would seem to be of early Palo Blanco times, since the preceding period is of latest Santa Maria times and the following Jiquipilas phase of Chiapas seems on the basis of indirect evidence also to correspond to early Palo Blanco. Jiquipilas is mentioned by Lowe and Mason (1965: 226) as having trade sherds "of early Tzakol Maya polychrome" (Ixcanrio Orange Polychrome). As we shall point out

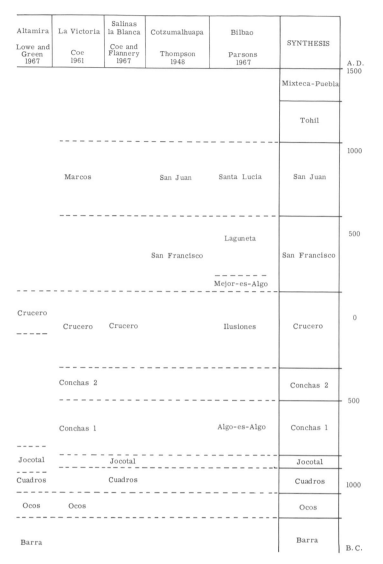

Altamira Lowe and Green 1967	La Victoria Coe 1961	Salinas la Blanca Coe and Flannery 1967	Cotzumalhuapa Thompson 1948	Bilbao Parsons 1967	SYNTHESIS	
					Mixteca-Puebla	A.D. 1500
					Tohil	
						1000
	Marcos		San Juan	Santa Lucia	San Juan	
						500
				Laguneta		
			San Francisco		San Francisco	
				Mejor-es-Algo		
Crucero	Crucero	Crucero		Ilusiones	Crucero	0
	Conchas 2				Conchas 2	
						500
	Conchas 1		Algo-es-Algo		Conchas 1	
Jocotal	Jocotal				Jocotal	
Cuadros	Cuadros				Cuadros	1000
Ocos	Ocos				Ocos	
Barra					Barra	B.C.

Fig. 157. Synthesis of archaeological sequences in coastal Guatemala and Chiapas.

later, Tzakol I is probably of early Palo Blanco times.

Laguna of Chiapas has Thin Orange trade wares and vessels with slab feet and effigy faces, as does late Palo Blanco in the Tehuacan region. Sherds possibly of Dos Arroyos Polychrome from the Maya area occur in Laguna, and this same trade ware appears in the Metepec phase in the Valley of Mexico, which correlates with latest Palo Blanco times.

Maravillas of Chiapas is reported to have trade sherds of San Juan Plumbate (*ibid.*: 229), as does earliest Venta Salada. The following period of Chiapas, Paredon, has trade sherds of X Fine Orange, Y Fine Orange, and Cholula Polychrome Lacquer (Navarrete 1959: 1–7), as does the final part of the early Venta

Salada subphase. The Ruiz horizon of Chiapas, like middle Venta Salada, has trade sherds of Tohil Plumbate. The final two ceramic periods of Chiapas, Urbina and Tuxtla, have trade sherds of Texcoco Black-on-red, Cholula Polychrome Matte, and Mixtec Polychrome. They apparently are contemporaneous with the late Venta Salada subphase, which has similar trade wares.

Pacific Coast of Guatemala and Chiapas

Closely allied to the regional sequence of the Grijalva Basin is the sequence of the region along the Pacific coast of Guatemala and adjacent Chiapas. Our synthesis of this sequence (Fig. 157) is based upon the work of Coe and Flannery at La Victoria and Salinas La Blanca (Coe 1961, Coe and Flannery 1967), supplemented by work by Gareth Lowe and others near Altamira in Chiapas (Green and Lowe 1967). The Classic periods, San Francisco or Laguneta and San Juan or Santa Lucia are mainly known from the works of Eric Thompson (1948) and Lee Parsons (1967), and for the poorly known Postclassic we have relied on the survey material of Shook (1965).

The earliest tentative phase in this Pacific Coast sequence, Barra, is characterized by the first appearance of Coton Grooved Red pottery (Green and Lowe 1967), which occurs as trade sherds in early Ajalpan of Tehuacan. Barra also has large amounts of zoned brushed pottery very like the brushed variety of Victoria Coarse of Ocos (Coe 1961)—subsequently called Guamuchal Brushed and considered dominant in the Cuadros phase (Coe and Flannery 1967)—and very like Ajalpan Coarse, which is dominant in early Ajalpan times in the Tehuacan Valley.

Ocos is the first phase of the Pacific coastal sequence that has been fully described in print (Coe 1961). It has many similarities to Ajalpan, including Mapache Red-rimmed pottery, which we noted appears as a possible trade ware in early and late Ajalpan. Ponce Black, probably related to Ocos Black, and Ocos Buff are among the trade wares of late Ajalpan. Also, some of the Ocos Specular Red sherds (Coe 1961: fig. 18) are similar to Coatepec Red-on-buff. Many horizon markers, such as the tecomate vessel form, flat-bottomed flaring-wall bowls, plain wide rocker stamping, rocker-dentate stamping, and Projecting-eye figurines, are held in common by Ocos and late Ajalpan. Thus, the Ocos phase of the Pacific Coast may be roughly equivalent to middle Ajalpan times.

The following Cuadros phase has ties to late Ajalpan. A Cuadros pottery type, which is called Tilapa Red-on-white and has wide rocker stamping, occurs in late Ajalpan components. Also, in latest Cuadros as in latest Ajalpan, a white-washed ware first appears that is known in the respective regions as Conchas White-to-buff and Canoas White. Both manifestations have in common as well heavy dishpan-like bowls with thickened rims.

The white-surfaced pottery type, however, is more typical of early Santa Maria of Tehuacan and of Jocotal and Conchas 1 in Guatemala, indicating a temporal equation of these periods in the two regions. Confirming this alignment is the presence of trade sherds of Kaolin White in both Jocotal (Coe and Flannery 1967: 60) and early Santa Maria. Suchiate Brushed sherds, Conchas Orange of Jocotal–Conchas 1, and Dili Punctate occur as trade wares in early Santa Maria. Both early Santa Maria and Conchas 1 have a white-slipped red-pasted trade ware, as well as the overlapping Canoas White and Conchas White-to-buff types and the closely related gray wares, Ocos Gray and Rio Salado Gray of Tehuacan (ibid.: 44–47). Conchas 1 and early Santa Maria also have as overlapping types Negroid with Hairknot, Crescentic Cap, and Baby Face figurines. Common horizon markers are sunburst designs on interior bottoms of bowls, multiple-line-break motifs, low bowls with thickened rims, collared tecomates, and so on.

Conchas 2 of Guatemala has fewer direct ties to Tehuacan, but its pottery type Conchas Fine White-to-buff resembles Coatepec White of middle to late Santa Maria, and some of its Ocos Gray resembles Quachilco Gray of late Santa Maria. Both late Santa Maria and Conchas 2 share such horizon markers as bowls with wide everted rims often decorated with grooved lines, basal-flanged bowls, eccentric-rimmed bowls, bowls with a basal bulge, bowls with stepped rims, and a large number of composite-silhouette bowls. Lowe and Mason (1965: 215) report trade sherds of "a fine-paste gray-black ware" (Tres Zapotes Black Incised) from the Izapa site roughly of Conchas 2 times. Tres Zapotes Black Incised sherds occur in late Santa Maria components in Tehuacan.

The next phase of coastal Guatemala, Crucero, also seems to be linked with late Santa Maria of Tehuacan, as both have Usulutan trade sherds (Coe and Flannery 1967: 70). Both areas also share bowls with wide everted rims or with rim or basal flanges. The two periods may just barely overlap in time, with Crucero perhaps lasting into early Palo Blanco times.

The next phase has been basically described by Thompson (1948) and Parsons (1967) and comes from the region of Cotzumalhuapa and Bilbao further along the Guatemala Coast. This phase appears to be absent from or at least undiscovered in the Ocos region. The earliest of these phases has been called San Francisco (Thompson) or Laguneta (Parsons), and among the ceramics there seem to be trade sherds of Thin Orange (Thompson 1948: fig. 27e) and perhaps San Martin Stamped (Parsons 1967: 140). The former type occurs in both early and late Palo Blanco in the Tehuacan area, while the latter is only in late Palo Blanco. Also, in San Francisco are sherds of Dos Arroyos polychrome (ibid.: 162) from the Peten, a type that appears in Metepec in the Valley of Mexico, which phase we have already shown to be of roughly late Palo Blanco times. Mold-made figurines, cylindrical vessels with slab or bulb feet, and pot covers also occur in both Palo Blanco and San Francisco, indicating possible contemporaneity.

The following San Juan phase is the source of the trade ware San Juan Plumbate, a sherd of which occurs in one of our earliest Venta Salada sites. San Juan also has trade sherds from Tepeu of the Peten and the more southerly Maya area (ibid.: 55). Both San Juan and early Venta Salada have similar types of mold-made spindle whorls — plain and incised truncated cones (Thompson 1948: fig. 59)—as well as mold-made figurines with bifurcated headdresses (ibid.: fig. 27a).

Postclassic sites of the Pacific coastal region have not been fully described. The phase called Peor-es-Nada by Parsons and Tohil by Shook seems to be characterized by trade sherds of Tohil Plumbate (Parsons 1967: 160) and X Fine Orange (Shook 1965: 190–191), as is the middle period of Venta Salada. The final period of the region is even less well known, but collections from very late sites at the Peabody Museum, Harvard University, contain Cholula polychrome sherds, Mixtec censers, and ornately decorated spindle whorls, all characteristic of our latest Venta Salada remains.

Thus throughout the sequence from the Pacific coastal region of Guatemala and Chiapas there are a few trade sherds, some overlapping types, and some horizon styles that link the region to Tehuacan. Even though the evidence is slim, one can align the two sequences, at least approximately, with some confidence.

Guatemalan Highlands

In contrast, the sequence from highland Guatemala has few connections with the Tehuacan sequence, and alignment of the two has to be based largely upon not very convincing indirect ties. The lack of direct ties is partly owing to the limited knowledge of the ceramics from this region—or the three subregions within it, the

Chixoy Drainage			Zaculeu	Zacualpa	SYNTHESIS	
Butler 1940	Butler 1940	Butler 1940	Woodbury and Trik 1953	Wauchope 1948		A.D. 1500
IV		Chipal 3	Xinabahul	Yaqui	Yaqui	
III		Chipal 2	Qankyak	Tohil	Tohil	1000
II	Chama 4 Chama 3	Chipal 1	Chinaq	Pokom	Pokom	
Ib	Chama 2		Atzan	Late Balam	Atzan	500
Ia	Chama 1			Early Balam	Balam	0
						500 B.C.

FIG. 158. Synthesis of archaeological sequences of the northern Guatemala Highlands.

northern, central, and western zones. Because of the lack of detailed reports of ceramic and other artifacts from stratigraphic excavations, we shall not attempt comparisons with archaeological remains from the western zone. As Rands and Smith (1965: 95) have pointed out, the longest sequence comes from the central zone and even here "stratigraphic excavation has been rare." "Although two admirably detailed descriptions of pottery from tombs at Kaminaljuyu have appeared (Kidder, Jennings, and Shook 1946, Shook and Kidder 1952) the long sequence of named phases at this site has been barely outlined in print" (*ibid*.: 98–99). Further, the alignment of the Formative phases as outlined by Shook (1951) is not based upon stratigraphy. Later analysis by Lowe and Mason (1965), Coe (1961), and others suggests that the most likely sequences of phases from the central highland area is: Arevalo, Las Charcas–Majadas, Providencia, Miraflores–Arenal, and Santa Clara. The sequence of the Classic phases, Aurora, Esperanza, Amatle, and Pamplona, were based upon the excavations at Kaminaljuyu (Shook and Kidder 1952), but the Postclassic

phases, Ayampuc and Chinautla, are suggested by materials intrusive in the earlier remains at Kaminaljuyu (Shook 1951).

In the northern zone two stratified sequences with limited numbers of sherds have been described for Zacualpa (Wauchope 1948) and Zaculeu (Woodbury and Trik 1953). Also, Butler (1940) has seriated a limited number of vessels from tombs in the Chixoy drainage to establish a sequence. These three sequences may be correlated with each other as well as with those at Kaminaljuyu (Rands and Smith 1965). Our synthesis is presented in Fig. 158. The earliest phase, Balam, is roughly of the time of Miraflores-Arenal-Santa Clara in the central region (Chama 1 of the Chixoy drainage may also be of this time). The second phase, Atzan, is of Esperanza and Aurora times and would include late Balam and Chama 2 materials. The third or Pokom phase, which includes the Chinaq, Chama 3 and 4 and Chipal materials, would be roughly of Amatle-Pamplona times in the central regions. Tohil, the fourth phase, would include Qankyak and Chipal 2 materials. The final phase, Yaqui, is of the same period as Xinabahul and Chipal 3 phases.

Connections between the Tehuacan sequence and Arevalo, the reputed earliest ceramic complex of highland Guatemala, are almost nonexistent. Perhaps the nearest thing to a link might be the Crescentic Cap figurines and thin-walled tecomates of Arevalo and early Santa Maria, but these by themselves are not very convincing. A few figurines of the Negroid with Hairknot type occur in Las Charcas, as well as in middle Santa Maria times. Also, Coe has pointed out that Conchas of coastal Guatemala has trade sherds of Las Charcas Red-on-cream, which is closely related to Muxanal Red-on-cream at Mamom of Uaxactun, which in turn gave Mars Orange trade sherds to the earliest components of late Santa Maria.

The final Formative phases of highland Guatemala can be more firmly related to late Santa Maria of Tehuacan, as both have Usulutan trade sherds. Further, Balam of the northern zone has trade sherds of Sierra Red and Flor Cream from the Chicanel period of Uaxactun, which again may be linked to late Santa Maria. It might also be added that Balam, like Miraflores, Arenal, and Santa Clara, has horizon markers that are common to late Santa Maria, among them basal-ridge bowls, flanged-rim bowls, wide-everted-rim bowls, and bulbous or mammiform feet.

Obvious links between the Classic Esperanza phase of highland Guatemala and late Palo Blanco of Tehuacan are trade sherds of Thin Orange, San Martin Stamped, and San Martin Fresco-decorated. Also, Dos

Arroyos polychrome sherds from Tzakol of the Peten are present in Esperanza, Aurora, and Atzan of highland Guatemala, as well as in such manifestations as Laguna, Metepec, and San Francisco, which have been shown to be of late Palo Blanco times. This suggests that perhaps the end of Balam and Arenal, Santa Clara, and Aurora last up into early Palo Blanco time.

Amatle of the central highlands of Guatemala has trade sherds of San Juan Plumbate, while Pamplona of the central highlands and Pokom have trade sherds of Altar Y Fine Orange. Early Venta Salada of Tehuacan has both trade wares, so all may be linked together. The Tohil phase of the northern Guatemala highlands is when Tohil Plumbate was made. This ware was traded both to Ayampuc of the central Guatemala highlands and to middle Venta Salada components of Tehuacan. Further evidence of contemporaneity is the presence in all three manifestations of trade sherds of X Fine Orange. Connection between Tehuacan's late Venta Salada and the Yaqui phase of Guatemala and Chinautla are not readily apparent, but all have in common such horizon styles as Mixtec censers, mold-made pottery, mold-made spindle whorls, pedestal-based vessels, and snake or other effigy feet for low bowls. It might be added that some of the Chinaulta Polychrome sherds in the Peabody Museum of Harvard University are very similar to Cholula Polychrome Matte and even some of the finer sherds of Coxcatlan Polychrome, both of which occur in late Venta Salada.

The Peten of Guatemala

Thus there are some ties between the archaeological phases of highland Guatemala and Tehuacan, but not enough to align the sequences in a very exact manner. Perhaps future archaeological endeavors or fuller reports will reveal better links, but then again they may not. We mention the latter possibility because comparisons reveal about the same number of links between the phases of Tehuacan and those of the Peten, which has many sequences of ceramics based on large and well described samples from stratigraphic excavations. In fact, one can only hope that the painstaking ceramic analysis and description, together with the sort of cooperation that has made possible the correlation of the local sequences by the type-variety method, will some day prevail in Mexico. Then factual phase correlations can replace the tentative and speculative kind of alignment presented in this chapter. Because of this fine analysis (Willey 1966) we shall compare the Tehuacan sequence with the Maya Lowland ceramic horizons and spheres rather than by phases, although in Fig.

153 we have listed phases from at least three local sequences: Altar de Sacrificios, Tikal, and Uaxactun.

The Xe horizon or sphere is represented by only the earliest levels at Seibal and Altar de Sacrificios. It has indirect connections to early Santa Maria through white-slipped wares with double-line-break and interior sunburst designs, collared tecomates, and plain thin-walled tecomates or incurved-rim bowls. Lowe has commented that some of the white wares of Xe are the same as those of Escalera of Chiapas; as we have indicated, Escalera seems roughly contemporary with the latest components of early Santa Maria.

The Mamom horizon, which follows Xe, is represented by the Mamom phase of Uaxactun, the Eb and Tzec phases of Tikal, and the San Felix phase of Altar de Sacrificios. Mars Orange, which originates in this horizon, is found as a trade ware in Escalera and Francesa of Chiapas as well as in middle and late Santa Maria. As noted above, some of the Red-on-cream types of Las Charcas, Conchas, and Francesa—all phases correlating with middle Santa Maria—seem to be closely related to Mamom's Muxanal Red-on-cream.

The Chicanel horizon is a long one in the Peten and includes the phase of the same name at Uaxactun, Chuen and Cauac at Tikal, and Plancha at Altar de Sacrificios. The presence of Usulutan ware from Chicanel in late Santa Maria certainly indicates that the two overlap in time. Also, Guanacaste of Chiapas, a phase contemporary with late Santa Maria, has Sierra Red and Alta Mira Fluted trade sherds from the Chicanel sphere, and Horcones of Chiapas, contemporaneous with early Palo Blanco, has the late Chicanel ware, Metapa Trichrome.

The Floral Park horizon represented by the Cimi phase of Tikal and the Salinas complex of Altar de Sacrificios is difficult to connect with Tehuacan, but the trait of mammiform feet occurs in it as well as in early Palo Blanco. Perhaps more important, a trade ware from the Floral Park horizon—probably Ixcanrio Orange Polychrome—occurs in Jiquipilas of Chiapas and is associated in grave lots with gray wares of Monte Alban II that in turn can be linked with Quachilco Gray of early Palo Blanco of Tehuacan.

Thin Orange trade sherds link both Tzakol of the Peten and late Palo Blanco. Also, Tzakol and Dos Arroyos Polychrome wares were traded to a number of regions, including the Valley of Mexico in the Metepec period, which in turn can be tied to the latest Palo Blanco components.

The Tepeu sphere of the Peten has no direct ties with Tehuacan, but its Saxche Orange Polychrome appears as trade sherds in Pokom of the Guatemala highlands, which may be linked to the Amatle horizon of the same area. Amatle has San Juan Plumbate trade ware, as does earliest Venta Salada of Tehuacan. The Eznab or Tepeu III horizon of the Peten also seems to be of early Venta Salada time; both have Y Fine Orange trade sherds. We might add that the Jimba phase of Altar de Sacrificios seems later than the Eznab horizon, since it has a few sherds of X Fine Orange as do components of middle Venta Salada. The final or New Town horizon of the Peten, at least in the Caban phase of Tikal, has Tohil Plumbate and X Fine Orange, as does middle Venta Salada. Later material from the Peten has not been described, and the area seems to have been relatively depopulated during the period that would correspond to late Venta Salada in the Tehuacan Valley.

The Yucatan Peninsula

The final region to be compared with Tehuacan is the Yucatan Peninsula. Here we shall use the ceramic periods employed by Robert E. Smith (in press), which in turn follows Brainerd (1958). The earliest ceramic complex of Yucatan has been Ecab. It bears no resemblance to the ceramics of Tehuacan, or for that matter, anywhere else. The Cupul complexes which are roughly contemporaneous with Ecab or follow it, have Flores Waxy ware common to Mamom of the Peten, and we have shown that Mamom can be roughly equated with late Santa Maria. The third ceramic phase of Yucatan is called Tihosuco and can be tied in fairly closely with Chicanel of the Peten through Usulutan, Sierra Red, Flor Cream, Polvero Black, and Escobal wares. As indicated previously, Chicanel seems to be roughly contemporaneous with latest Santa Maria and early Palo Blanco.

The next phase of Yucatan, Chakan, like Jiquipilas of Chiapas, has trade sherds of Ixcanrio Orange Polychrome from the Floral Park horizon of the Peten, which is roughly of the time period of early Palo Blanco. The Classic Cochuah ceramic complex of Yucatan is tied to the Tzakol horizon of the Peten by the presence of trade sherds of Dos Arroyos Polychrome and of varieties of the Aguilar, Dabanzar, and Actuacun pottery groups, and Tzakol correlates with Palo Blanco times in Tehuacan. The Motul complex of Yucatan has ties to the Tepeu I and II horizons of the Peten, and as we have indicated, early Tepeu has some rather tenuous ties with early Venta Salada. It is not until the Cehpech ceramic complex that we find reliable ties between Yucatan and Tehuacan; both early Venta Salada and Cehpech have Y Fine Orange trade

sherds. Cehpech is also linked to Tepeu III of the Peten through various ceramic types belonging to the fine gray and Ruiz red pottery groups. The Sotuta phase of Yucatan has trade sherds of both Tohil Plumbate and X Fine Orange, as do the middle Venta Salada components of Tehuacan, but the following Hocaba complex is without firm relationship to our Tehuacan sequence. Hocaba, like the Tases and final Chikinchel complexes of Yucatan, does have horizon styles in common with late Venta Salada, such as pedestal-based vessels, true molcajetes, Mixtec censers, and mold-made spindle whorls. Perhaps a study of trade sherds from the latest Yucatan complexes will eventually reveal better connections with late horizons of Tehuacan, but for the present relationships are tenuous.

Summary

Looking at the alignments of the ten regional sequences we have reviewed from the standpoint of the Tehuacan sequence, we might summarize them as follows. The earliest ceramic phase of the Tehuacan sequence, Purron, has little or no resemblance to ceramic complexes from the ten regions and seems to be earlier than any pottery found in those regions—in fact, in all of Mesoamerica. Only the earliest Pox pottery of Puerto Marquez on the Pacific Coast can be related to the Purron pottery, and this, of course, is a region not discussed in our regional comparisons (Brush 1965).

Alignment of ceramic complexes from the ten regions with the pottery of the early Ajalpan subphase of Tehuacan is also extremely tenuous. Ceramic materials from the Santa Marta rock shelter in Chiapas, the Barra complex from the Guatemala Pacific coast, the recently discovered Tierras Largas phase of Oaxaca and the Ojochi and Bajio phases of southern Veracruz, and Squier's Pre-La Venta remains from Tabasco seem to be roughly of the same period as early Ajalpan. There is also the possibility that the earliest ceramic complex from Panuco, Pavon, is more or less of this period.

Ocos of the Guatemala Pacific coast and San Lorenzo of southern Veracruz and perhaps the Santa Marta segment of the Cotorra phase of Chiapas may begin before early Ajalpan ends, but each of these would extend well up into late Ajalpan times. In coastal Guatemala, Cuadros and possibly the early part of Jocotal are of late Ajalpan times. Certainly Trapiche I of central Veracruz, San Jose of Oaxaca, Moyotzingo in the Valley of Puebla, and San Lorenzo of southern

Veracruz are mainly of late Ajalpan times, as may be Ponce of northern Veracruz, albeit on slightly poorer evidence. We have also speculated that Tolstoy's recently formulated Ayotla and Justo phases in the Valley of Mexico overlap in time with late Ajalpan.

There is considerable evidence to suggest that Tehuacan's early Santa Maria subphase is coeval with Guadalupe of Oaxaca, Trapiche II and Aguilar of central and northern Veracruz respectively, most of late Jocotal and Conchas 1 of the Pacific coast of Guatemala, and Dili and Escalera of central Chiapas. La Venta complex A and Palangana seem to be of this period, though they may have begun before early Santa Maria. Connections between the Valley of Mexico and Tehuacan are also strong even though the phases or subphases do not align neatly. It would seem that El Arbolillo I and Iglesia may last into the Santa Maria period, Totolica is coeval with it, and Atoto begins in the final stage of this subphase but extends into late Santa Maria times. In the Maya lowland region the Xe sphere seems to be of early Santa Maria times, with a possibility that Mamom begins just before early Santa Maria ends. In Fig. 153 we have placed Arevalo of highland Guatemala and the beginning of Ecab and Cupul of Yucatan in this period, but on the basis of little direct evidence.

Although good linkages to the late Santa Maria subphase are numerous, exact alignment of phases or periods of the other Mesoamerican regions is more difficult. Monte Alban I certainly is coeval with part of late Santa Maria, but there is some evidence that Monte Alban II began before our Tehuacan subphase ended. The Ticoman sequence (late Atoto, Cuanalan, and Tezoyuca) of the Valley of Mexico and Francesa and Guanacaste of Chiapas seem to be coeval with late Santa Maria, as are Chila of northern Veracruz and Trapiche III of central Veracruz. The poorly defined Tres Zapotes phase of southern Veracruz is also of about this time, though it possibly ended slightly later. Conchas 2, of Pacific coastal Guatemala, would be of the same period, but could have ended earlier than late Santa Maria does.

The other Maya phases are less well tied to Tehuacan. A few trade sherds indicate that Mamom of the Peten is mainly of late Santa Maria times and that quite possibly Chicanel and Chuen of Tikal and Plancha of Altar de Sacrificios, began before the Tehuacan subphase ended. Yucatan and highland Guatemala can only be tied indirectly to Tehuacan, mainly via Usulatan trade ware. Las Charcas, Majadas, and Providencia of highland Guatemala, and perhaps Cupul and the earliest part of Tihosuco of Yucatan appear to be roughly of late Santa Maria times. But again let us caution that the evidence for this alignment is indirect and not very convincing.

Connections to and alignments with early Palo Blanco of Tehuacan are more difficult to discern because this subphase is represented by a limited sample of sherds. Most of Monte Alban II and II–IIIA of Oaxaca, as well as Patlachique, Tzacualli, and Miccaotli of the Valley of Mexico, and Cerro de las Conchas of southern Veracruz are probably of early Palo Blanco times. To the north there are vague hints that El Prisco of northern Veracruz and Tajin I and Lower Remojadas may be of this period. In the Maya area mainly indirect evidence suggests that Crucero of the Pacific coast, Chicanel and the Floral Park horizon of the Peten, Miraflores-Arenal and Santa Clara and Balam in the highlands, Horcones and Istmo of Chiapas, and Tihosuco-Chakun of Yucatan are also of this proto-Classic or early Classic period.

Alignments with late Palo Blanco are on a firmer basis. Monte Alban III of Oaxaca; Tlamimilolpa, Xolalpan, and Metepec of the Valley of Mexico; and Cerro de las Mesas and Tajin II of southern and central Veracruz seem to be of the same period as the late Palo Blanco subphase of Tehuacan. There is also evidence, mainly indirect, for temporally equating Esperanza, Aurora, and Atzan of highland Guatemala and San Francisco of the Pacific coast with late Palo Blanco. Fairly good evidence suggests that Tzakol of the Peten and Cochuah of Yucatan overlap with late Palo Blanco. Tepeu I and perhaps part of Tepeu II of the Peten—as well as early Motul of Yucatan—may be of this same period. Evidence of relationships to northern Veracruz are relatively slim, but Pithaya and perhaps early Zaquil seem to be of late Palo Blanco times.

The early Venta Salada subphase can be aligned rather precisely because during this period four relatively short-lived types of pottery were traded to a large number of regions: in chronological order, San Juan Plumbate, Y Fine Orange, X Fine Orange, and at the very end of the subphase and at the beginning of late Venta Salada, Tohil Plumbate. In the Valley of Mexico, Coyotlatelco and Mazapan can be shown to be of early Venta Salada times, as can Tajin III and Cempoala I of central Veracruz, Soncautla and Isla de Sacrificios of southern Veracruz, and the final stages of Zaquil and Las Flores of northern Veracruz. There is as well a strong possibility that much of the Monte Alban IV period of Oaxaca is also contemporaneous with early Venta Salada.

Farther south there are evidences of contemporaneity with early Venta Salada, but exact chronological equations are more difficult. The late part of Maravillas, Paredon, and Ruiz of Chiapas may be roughly of this period, as would be San Juan and the early part of Tohil of the Pacific coast of Guatemala. Perhaps Amatle, Pamplona, and Pokom of highland Guatemala are also contemporaneous with early Venta Salada. In the Peten, Tepeu II and III and perhaps the early part (Caban) of New Town, which are often considered late Classic, would be of the same period as this subphase of Tehuacan which we are calling early Postclassic. As for Yucatan, there is some evidence that late Motul, Cehpech, and perhaps early Sotuta are of early Venta Salada times.

The final subphase of Tehuacan, late Venta Salada, which extends to the Spanish Conquest, seems to be roughly contemporaneous with Monte Alban V of Oaxaca; Upper Cerro de las Mesas of southern Veracruz; Cempoala II–IV of central Veracruz; Panuco of northern Veracruz; Zocango, Chimalpa, and Teacalco of the Valley of Mexico; Suchiapa, Tuxtla, and Urbina of Chiapas; the final parts of Tohil and the late Mixteca-Puebla material of the Pacific coast of Guatemala; the final part of Tohil, Ayampuc, Chinautla and Yaqui of highland Guatemala; Hocaba, Tases, and Chikinchel of the Yucatan peninsula; and finally the dying stages of New Town of the Peten region of lowland Guatemala.

Obviously more data and further study are needed before the correlations of phases and subphases, even in these eleven regions, can become final. Volume IV of the Tehuacan series will provide confirmation for the scheme presented here (see Fig. 153) through the correlation of radiocarbon determinations from each region. Although we may not yet have the ultimate answer to chronological alignments, we seem to be drawing closer to it, and perhaps we have almost reached the stage where we can look at pot sherds not merely as a means of establishing chronology, but as raw materials in the study of cultural processes in Mesoamerica.

BIBLIOGRAPHY

Am. Ant.	*American Antiquity*, Menasha, Wisconsin, and Salt Lake City.
AMNH–AP	*American Museum of Natural History, Anthropological Papers*, New York.
APS–T	American Philosophical Society, Transactions, Philadelphia.
BAE–B	Bureau of American Ethnology, Bulletin, Smithsonian Institution, Washington.
CIW	Carnegie Institution of Washington, Washington.
HMAI	*Handbook of Middle American Indians*, ed. by Robert Wauchope, University of Texas Press, Austin.
INAH	Instituto Nacional de Antropología e Historia, México.
MARI	Middle American Research Institute, Tulane University, New Orleans.
NWAF–P	*New World Archaeological Foundation, Papers*, Orinda, California, and Brigham Young University, Provo, Utah.
PMAE–P	Peabody Museum of Archaeology and Ethnology, Papers, Cambridge, Massachusetts.

ACOSTA, JORGE R.
1940 "Exploraciones en Tula, Hgo." *Revista Mexicana de Estudios Antropológicos* 4:172–194. Mexico.
1945 "La Cuarta y Quinta Temporada de Excavaciones en Tula, Hgo., 1943–44." *Revista Mexicana de Estudios Antropológicos* 7:23–64. Mexico.

BORHEGYI, STEPHAN F.
1959 "The Composite or 'Assemble-it-yourself' Censer." *Am. Ant.* 25:51–58.

BRAINERD, GEORGE W.
1958 *The Archaeological Ceramics of Yucatan.* Anthropological Records, vol. 19. University of California Publications.

BRUSH, CHARLES F.
1965 "Pox Pottery: Earliest Identified Mexican Ceramic." *Science* 149:194–195.

BUTLER, MARY
1940 "A Pottery Sequence from the Alta Verapaz, Guatemala." *The Maya and Their Neighbors*, 250–267. New York: Appleton.

CASO, ALFONSO, and IGNACIO BERNAL
1952 *Urnas de Oaxaca.* INAH, Memorias 2.
1965 "Ceramics of Oaxaca." *HMAI* 3:871–895.

——— IGNACIO BERNAL, and JORGE R. ACOSTA
1967 *La Cerámica de Monte Alban.* INAH, Memorias 13.

CHADWICK, ROBERT
1966 "The Tombs of Monte Alban I Style at Yagul." *Ancient Oaxaca*, ed. by John Paddock, pp. 245–255. Stanford: Stanford University Press.

CODEX BORGIA
1963 Codice Borgia. Facsimile edition of a pre-Columbian codex preserved in the Ethnographical Museum of the Vatican, Rome. With commentary by Eduard Seler. 3 vols. Fondo de Cultura Economica, Mexico.

COE, MICHAEL D.
1961 *La Victoria: An Early Site on the Pacific Coast of Guatemala.* PMAE–P 53.
1965 "Archaeological Synthesis of Southern Veracruz and Tabasco," and "The Olmec Style and Its Distributions." *HMAI* 3:679–775.

——— and KENT V. FLANNERY
1967 *Early Cultures and Human Ecology in South Coastal Guatemala.* Washington: Smithsonian Press.

——— RICHARD A. DIEHL, and MINZE STUIVER
1967 "Olmec Civilization, Veracruz, Mexico: Dating of the San Lorenzo Phase." *Science* 155:1399–1401.

CORDRY, DONALD, and DOROTHY CORDRY
1968 *Mexican Indian Costumes*. Austin: University of Texas Press.

DIXON, KEITH A.
1959 "Ceramics from Two Preclassic Periods at Chiapa de Corzo, Chiapas, Mexico." *NWAF–P*, no. 5.

DRUCKER, PHILIP
1943a *Ceramic Sequences at Tres Zapotes, Veracruz, Mexico*. BAE–B, no. 140.
1943b *Ceramic Stratigraphy at Cerro de las Mesas, Veracruz, Mexico*. BAE–B, no. 141.
1952 *La Venta, Tabasco, A Study of Olmec Ceramics and Art*. BAE–B, no. 153.

——— ROBERT F. HEIZER, and ROBERT J. SQUIER
1959 *Excavations at La Venta, Tabasco, 1955*. BAE–B, no. 170.

DU SOLIER, WILFRIDO
1945 *La Cerámica Arqueológica de El Tajin*. Anales, Museo Nacional de Arqueología, Historia y Etnografía. Mexico.

EKHOLM, GORDON F.
1944 "Excavations at Tampico and Panuco in the Huasteca, Mexico." *AMNH–AP*, vol. 38, part 5.

ESPEJO, ANTONIETA
1953 "Dos Tipos de Alfarería Negro sobre Anaranjado en La Cuenca de México y en El Totonacapan." *Huastecos y Totonacos*. Sociedad Mexicana de Antropología. Mexico.

FLANNERY, KENT V., et al.
1967 "Farming Systems and Political Growth in Ancient Oaxaca." *Science* 158:445–454.

FORD, JAMES A.
1962 *A Quantitative Method for Deriving Cultural Chronology*. Technical Manual 1, Pan American Union. Washington.

FOSTER, GEORGE M.
1948 "Some Implications of Modern Mexican Mold-made Pottery." *Southwestern Journal of Anthropology* 4:356–370.
1955 *Contemporary Pottery Techniques in Southern and Central Mexico*. MARI, Pub. 22.

GARCÍA PAYÓN, JOSÉ
1950 *Restos de una Cultura Prehistórica Encontrada en la Región de Zempoala*. Jalapa: Universidad Veracruzana.
1951 "La Cerámica de Fondo Sellado de Zempoala." *Homenaje de Dr. Alfonso Caso*. Mexico.
1966 *Prehistoria de Mesoamérica: Excavaciones en Trapiche y Chalahuite, Veracruz, México, 1942, 1951 y 1959*. Jalapa: Universidad Veracruzana.

GREEN, DEE F., and GARETH W. LOWE
1967 "Altamira and Padre Piedra: Early Preclassic Sites in Chiapas, Mexico." *NWAF–P*, no. 20.

KIDDER, ALFRED V., JESSE D. JENNINGS, and EDWIN M. SHOOK.
1946 *Excavations at Kaminaljuyú, Guatemala*. CIW, Pub. 561.

KRIEGER, ALEX D.
1944 "The Typological Concept." *Am. Ant.* 9:271–288.

LOTHROP, SAMUEL K.
1933 *Atitlan, an Archaeological Study of Ancient Remains on the Borders of Lake Atitlan, Guatemala*. CIW, Pub. 444.

LOWE, GARETH W.
1964 "Burial Customs at Chiapa de Corzo," in *NWAF–P*, no. 16, pp. 65–75.
1965 "Desarrollo y Función del Incensario de Izapa." *Estudios de Cultura Maya* 5:53–64.

——— and J. ALDEN MASON
1965 "Archaeological Survey of the Chiapas Coast, Highlands, and Upper Grijalva Basin." *HMAI* 2:195–236.

MACNEISH, RICHARD S.
1954 *An Early Archaeological Site Near Panuco, Vera Cruz*. APS–T, n.s., vol. 44, part 5.
1958 *Preliminary Archaeological Investigations in the Sierra de Tamaulipas, Mexico*. APS–T, n.s., vol. 48, part 6.

——— and FREDERICK A. PETERSON
1962 "The Santa Marta Rock Shelter, Ocozocoautla, Chiapas, Mexico." *NWAF–P*, no. 14.

MAYER-OAKES, WILLIAM J.
1959 *A Stratigraphic Excavation at El Risco, Mexico*. American Philosophical Society, Proceedings, vol. 103, no. 3, pp. 332–373. Philadelphia.

MEDELLIN ZENIL, ALFONSO
1955 *Exploraciones en la Isla de Sacrificios*. Jalapa: Dirección General de Education.
1960 *Cerámicas del Totonacapan*. Jalapa: Universidad Veracruzana.

MEGGERS, BETTY J., CLIFFORD EVANS, and EMILIO ESTRADA
1965 *Early Formative Period of Coastal Ecuador: The Valdivia and Machalilla Phases*. Washington: Smithsonian Press.

MILLON, RENE
1966 "Secuencia Cerámica de Teotihuacan." Teotihuacan Mapping Project. Mexico. Mimeographed.

NAVARRETE, CARLOS
1959 "A Brief Reconnaissance in the Region of Tonala, Chiapas, Mexico." *NWAF–P*, no. 4.

NOGUERA, EDUARDO
1935 *La Cerámica de Tenayuca y las Excavaciones Estratigráficas*. Mexico: Departamento Monumentos.

1940 "Excavations at Tehuacan," trans. by Suzannah B. Vaillant. *The Maya and Their Neighbors*, pp. 306–319. New York: Appleton.

1945 "Excavaciones en el Estado de Puebla." *Anales del INAH* 1:31–74.

1954 *La Cerámica Arqueológica de Cholula*. Mexico: Editorial Guarania.

PADDOCK, JOHN, ed.

1953 "Excavations in the Mixteca Alta." *Mesoamerican Notes*, no. 3, Mexico.

1966 *Ancient Oaxaca: Discoveries in Mexican Archaeology and History*. Stanford: Stanford University Press.

PARSONS, LEE A.

1967 *Bilbao, Guatemala*, vol. 1. Publications in Anthropology 11. Milwaukee: Milwaukee Public Museum.

PETERSON, FREDERICK A.

1963 "A White-black Tradition in Mesoamerican Ceramics." *Tlalocan*, vol. 4, no. 3. Mexico.

PINA CHAN, ROMAN

1958 *Tlatilco*. 2 vols. INAH.

PORTER, MURIEL N.

1953 *Tlatilco and the Preclassic Cultures of the New World*. Viking Fund Publications in Anthropology, no. 19. Wenner-Gren Foundation, New York.

RANDS, ROBERT L., and ROBERT E. SMITH

1965 "Pottery of the Guatemalan Highlands." *HMAI* 2:95–145.

RATTRAY, EVELYN CHILDS

1966 "An Archaeological and Stylistic Study of Coyotlatelco Pottery." *Mesoamerican Notes*, nos. 7–8, pp. 87–211. Mexico.

REICHEL-DOLMATOFF, GERARDO

1961 "Puerto Hormiga: Un Complejo Prehistórico Marginal de Colombia." *Revista Colombiana de Antropología* 10:347–354. Bogota.

ROUSE, IRVING

1939 *Prehistory in Haiti*. New Haven: Yale University Press.

1967 "Seriation in Archaeology." *American Historical Anthropology*, ed. by C. L. Riley and W. W. Taylor, pp. 153–195. Carbondale: Southern Illinois University Press.

——— and JOSE M. CRUXENT

1963 *Venezuelan Archaeology*. New Haven: Yale University Press.

SANDERS, WILLIAM T.

1961 "Ceramic Stratigraphy at Santa Cruz, Chiapas, Mexico." *NWAF–P*, no. 13.

SHEPARD, ANNA O.

1948 *Plumbate—a Mesoamerican Trade Ware*. CIW, Pub. 573.

1965 *Ceramics for the Archaeologist*. CIW, Pub. 609.

SHOOK, EDWIN M.

1951 "The Present Status of Research on the Preclassic Horizons in Guatemala." *Selected Papers of the XXIXth International Congress of Americanists* 1:93–100. Chicago: University of Chicago Press.

1965 "Archaeological Survey of the Pacific Coast of Guatemala." *HMAI* 2:180–194.

——— and A. V. KIDDER

1952 *Mound E–III–3, Kaminaljuyú, Guatemala*. CIW, Pub. 596, Contrib. 53.

SMITH, ROBERT E.

——— Ceramics of Yucatan, in press.

1955 *Ceramic Sequence at Uaxactún, Guatemala*. MARI, Pub. 20.

——— and JAMES C. GIFFORD

1965 "Pottery of the Maya Lowlands." *HMAI* 2:498–534.

——— GORDON R. WILLEY, and JAMES C. GIFFORD

1960 "The Type-variety Concept as a Basis for the Analysis of Maya Pottery." *Am. Ant.* 25:330–340.

SOTOMAYOR, ALFREDO, and NOEMI CASTILLO TEJERO

1963 *Estudio Petrográfico de la Cerámica "Anaranjado Delgado."* INAH, Pub. 12.

SPAULDING, ALBERT C.

1953 "Statistical Techniques for the Discovery of Artifact Types." *Am. Ant.* 18:305–313.

SPINDEN, HERBERT JOSEPH

1917 "The Origin and Distribution of Agriculture in America." *Proceedings of the XIXth International Congress of Americanists*, pp. 269–276. Washington.

STIRLING, MATTHEW W.

1943 *Stone Monuments of Southern Mexico*. BAE–B, no. 138.

THOMPSON, J. ERIC S.

1948 *An Archaeological Reconnaissance in the Cotzumalhuapa Region, Escuintla, Guatemala*. CIW, Pub. 574.

TOLSTOY, PAUL

1958 *Surface Survey of the Northern Valley of Mexico: The Classic and Postclassic Periods*. APS–T, n.s., vol. 48, part 5.

——— and ANDRE GUENETTE

1965 "Le Placement de Tlatilco dans le Cadre du Préclassique du Bassin de Mexico." *Journal de la Société des Américanistes* LIV–1:47–91. Paris.

VAILLANT, GEORGE C.

1930 "Excavations at Zacatenco." *AMNH–AP*, vol. 32, part 1.

1931 "Excavations at Ticoman." *AMNH–AP*, vol. 32, part 2.

1935 "Excavations at El Arbolillo" and "Early Cultures of the Valley of Mexico." *AMNH–AP*, vol. 35, parts 2, 3.

1938 "A Correlation of Archaeological and Historical Sequences in the Valley of Mexico." *American Anthropologist* 40:535–573.

1966 *Aztecs of Mexico.* Revised by Suzannah B. Vaillant. Baltimore: Penguin Books.

———— and SUZANNAH B. VAILLANT

1934 "Excavations at Gualupita." *AMNH–AP*, vol. 35, part 1.

VALENZUELA, JUAN

1945 "La Segunda Temporada de Exploraciones en la Región de Los Tuxtlas, Estado de Veracruz." *Anales del INAH* 1:81–94.

WARREN, BRUCE W.

1961 "The Archaeological Sequence at Chiapa de Corzo. *Los Mayas del Sur y sus Relaciones con los Nahuas Meridionales,* pp. 75–83. Soc. Mexicana Antrop., vol. 8. Mesa Redonda.

WAUCHOPE, ROBERT

1948 *Excavations at Zacualpa, Guatemala.* MARI, Pub. 14.

WEIANT, C. W.

1943 *An Introduction to the Ceramics of Tres Zapotes, Veracruz, Mexico.* BAE–B, no. 139.

WILLEY, GORDON R.

1966 "Maya Lowland Ceramics: A Report from the 1965 Guatemala City Conference." Harvard University, Cambridge. Mimeographed.

———— and CHARLES R. McGIMSEY

1954 *The Monagrillo Culture of Panama.* PMAE–P, vol. 49, no. 2.

———— and PHILIP PHILLIPS

1958 *Method and Theory in American Archaeology.* Chicago: University of Chicago Press.

———— GORDON F. EKHOLM, and RENE F. MILLON

1964 "The Patterns of Farming Life and Civilization." *HMAI* 1:446–498.

WOODBURY, RICHARD B., and AUBREY S. TRIK

1953 *The Ruins of Zaculeu, Guatemala.* 2 vols. Richmond: United Fruit Company.

INDEX

Abejas Cave (Tc 307), 6

Abejas phase, 25, 239

Acatepec, Puebla, 269

Acosta, Jorge R., 269

Actuacun pottery, 286

Aguilar phase, 274; Middle Formative relationships, 58, 59, 100; and Canoas White bowls, 64; black raspada in, 84; figurines of, 89, 94; and early Santa Maria subphase, 275, 278, 287

Aguilar pottery, 286

Aguilar Red, 100

Ajalpan Coarse, 12, 22, 24, 59; described and illustrated, 26–29; relationships, 40, 270, 282; in late Ajalpan subphase, 41, 51, 240; attributes summarized, 239

Ajalpan Coarse Red, 12, 24, 40, 41, 59, 102, 242; described and illustrated, 41–43; attributes summarized, 240

Ajalpan Fine Plain, 12, 24, 35, 59, 242; illustrated, 32; described, 33–35; attributes summarized, 240; and Matadamas complex, 270

Ajalpan Fine Red, 12, 24, 57, 59, 242; described and illustrated, 31–33; attributes summarized, 240; and Matadamas complex, 270

Ajalpan phase: ceramic attributes, 8–12 passim; related phases, 40, 279, 280, 282–283; geographical distribution, 239 (Fig. 147)

  early: characteristics, 26, 239–240; pottery types described and illustrated, 26–35; other ceramic objects, 35–36; figurines, 36–39; related phases, 39–40, 269–270, 279, 282, 286; and late Ajalpan subphase, 56

  late: and Trapiche I, 40, 273; and early Ajalpan pottery, 41, 56; characteristics, 41, 240–241; pottery types described and illustrated, 41–51; trade wares in, 51–52, 56–57; other ceramic objects, 52; figurines, 52–56; related phases summarized, 56–57, 286–287; and Valley of Puebla materials, 101, 269; and San Jose phase, 270; and San Lorenzo phase, 279–280; and Cotorra phase, 281; and Cuadros phase, 282–283

Ajalpan Plain, 12, 22, 41, 59, 102, 242; described and illustrated, 29–31; relationships, 40, 270; and Coatepec Plain, 44, 46; attributes summarized, 240

Ajalpan site (Ts 204), 4, 12, 26, 41, 239, 240; burial pit (Ts 204C), 4, 41, 52, 53; test trench (Ts 204D), 26, 41

Altamira, Chiapas, 282

Alta Mira Fluted, 285

Altar de Sacrificios, Guatemala, 285, 286, 287

Altepexi, Puebla, 223–225

Amalucan, Puebla, 269

Amatle phase, 210, 284, 285, 286, 288

Anaranjada ware, 273

Appliqued Ear Disks, figurines with, 15, 272; described and illustrated, 208

Architecture, 58, 102, 243

Arenal phase, 284, 285, 287

Arevalo phase, 284, 287

Artifacts, nonceramic: in Purron phase, 21, 25, 238–239; in Ajalpan phase, 26, 240, 241; in Santa Maria phase, 58, 243, 246; in Palo Blanco phase, 251; in Venta Salada phase, 260–261, 266

Atoto phase, 278, 287

Atzan phase, 284, 285, 287

Aufdermauer, Jörg, 269

Aurora phase, 284, 285, 287

Ayampuc phase, 209, 284, 285, 288

Ayotla phase, 57, 277, 287

Aztec figurines, 232, 235, 237, 281

Aztec pottery, 198, 232, 235, 236

Aztec sequence, 227, 237. See also Chimalpa phase; Zocango phase

Aztec Square Cap figurines, 15, 266; described, 232; illustrated, 233

Baby Face figurines, 134, 243; described and illustrated, 88–89; in central and northern Veracruz, 99, 100, 273, 275; in Tres Zapotes and La Venta, 100, 280; in Valley of Mexico, 101, 278; in Valley of Oaxaca, 270; in Conchas 1, 283

Bajio phase, 40, 279, 286

Balam phase, 143, 284, 285, 287

Balls, 161, 229

Barra phase: and early Ajalpan subphase, 28, 35, 39, 282, 286; figurine type, 55

Barrio del Rosario Huitzo, Oaxaca, 270

Barton Ramie, British Honduras, 176

Bases: deep convex, 66; of supported pot rest, 73; flat, fabric-impressed, 73–75

  flat, incised: El Riego Black, 157, 159, 255; Coxcatlan Gray, 191; Coxcatlan Brushed, 262. See also Bowls, pseudo-grater

  flat, stamped: molds for, 180, 222–223, of Coxcatlan Brushed, 182, 184, 186, 189, 260, 272; illustrated, 188, 190, 198; of Coxcatlan Gray, 191, 196, 260, 262; of other Coxcatlan wares, 198, 199, 202, 219; of Teotitlan Incised, 204, 206, attribute of Postclassic wares, 209, 210, 236, 237, 281. See also Molcajetes

  pedestal, see Bowls, pedestal-based; Incense burners; Vessels, pedestal-based

  ring, 87, 271, 274, 280; perforated, 133, 163, 271; horizon style, 145, 162; El Riego Gray and related wares, 154, 155, 247, 252; Thin Orange, 172, 173, 176, 250

Beads, 58, 134, 161

Bell, 229

Bernal, Ignacio, 83, 133, 227, 269

Big Nose figurines, 15; described and illustrated, 135

Bilboa, Guatemala, 283

Bird effigies, 87, 100, 101, 227; illustrated, 53, 86, 228

Black-on-orange ware, 236. See also Coxcatlan Black-on-orange; Tenayuca Black-on-orange

sherds, 51; in Trapiche I, 56–57, 273; in Chiapas sequence, 57, 281; in San Jose phase, 270; in Ocos phase, 282

Maravillas phase (Chiapa de Corzo X), 176, 210, 282, 288

Mars Orange, 85, 134, 143, 278, 281, 285

Matacapan I, 280

Matacapan II, 281

Matadamas complex, 33, 35, 39, 279; described, 269–270

Matamoros figurine, 143, 144, 271, 281; described and illustrated, 135

Matamoros site, Puebla, 135, 244

Maya area, 113, 162, 237, 278, 281, 282, 283, 285, 287. *See also* El Peten; Guatemala; Yucatan Peninsula

Mayer-Oakes, William J., 163

Mazapan phase, 208, 237, 279, 287

Mazapan Red-on-buff, 203, 209, 275, 279

Mazapan-Tula horizon, 209, 234

Medellín Zenil, Alfonso, 83, 85, 99, 227

Mendez Red-rimmed tecomates, 270

Mesoamerica, 28, 177; chronology of, 7–8, 267, 269, 286–288

Metapa Trichrome, 285

Metepec phase, 174; and late Palo Blanco subphase, 278–279, 287; trade ware in, 282, 283, 285. *See also* Teotihuacan sequence

Mexico, Valley of
    figurine types, *see* Figurines, Valley of Mexico types
    sequence from, 244, 269, 282, 283, 287; and Ajalpan phase, 57, 277; and early Santa Maria subphase, 85, 96, 101; and late Santa Maria subphase, 136–142 *passim*, 143, 277–278; and Palo Blanco phase, 162, 163, 168, 174, 176, 278–279; and Venta Salada phase, 178, 198, 209, 227, 237, 279; and San Jose phase, 270; described and correlated, 275–281

Miccaotli phase (Teotihuacan II): and early Palo Blanco relationships, 155, 162, 163, 278, 287; and late Palo Blanco relationships, 174, 175, 176

Millon, Rene, 277

Mirador II Smudged White, 59

Miraflores phase, 143, 284, 287

Mitla, Oaxaca, 123, 136, 143

Mixteca Alta, 189, 209, 236

Mixteca Polychrome, 227, 236, 272, 281, 282

Mixteca-Puebla complex, 177, 209, 237, 256, 288

Mixtec censers, 177, 186, 193–196, 237, 283, 285, 286

Molcajetes, 177, 286
    incised: from La Victoria, 62, 64 (*see also* Bowls, pseudo-grater); El Riego Black, 157, 159, 255; Coxcatlan Brushed, 184, 185, 262; Coxcatlan Gray, 191
    stamped: Postclassic horizon marker, 177, 236, 237, 260, 274; molds for, 180, 189, 190, 222–223; Coxcatlan Brushed, 180, 182, 186, 260, 272; Coxcatlan Gray, 191, 196, 260, 262; other Coxcatlan wares, 198, 199, 202, 219; Teotitlan Incised, 204, 206. *See also* Bases, flat, stamped

Molds, convex, 237; described, 180; Coxcatlan Brushed, 182, 189; illustrated, 188, 190, 192, 223; and Coxcatlan Gray vessels, 190; Coxcatlan Striated Buff, 222–223, 266

Monte Alban, Oaxaca, 174, 235
    sequence at: and early Santa Maria materials, 95, 101; and late Santa Maria wares, 120–133 *passim*, 143, 244, 271; and late Santa Maria figurines, 135–140 *passim*, 143; and early Palo Blanco materials, 155, 161, 162–163; and late Palo Blanco wares, 168, 176, 252; and late Palo Blanco figurines, 174, 175, 176; and early Venta Salada materials,

209, 210; and late Venta Salada materials, 217, 227, 236; and Tehuacan sequence, correlated, 271–272, 287, 288

Monte Alban gray ("G") types, 283, 285; and Quachilco Gray, 120, 123, 125, 133, 143, 155, 247, 271; and El Riego Gray, 155, 162, 176, 247, 251–252, 271; and El Riego Black, 160, 176, 271, 278; and Coxcatlan Gray, 196, 236, 256

Monte Alban "K" types, 120, 236, 271–272

Monte Alban Outlined-eye figurine, 143, 271; illustrated, 135; described, 136

Monumental ware idols, 225

Morelos Orange Lacquer, 84, 100, 101, 278, 280

Mottled bottles, *see* Bottles, Tlatilco mottled

Motul complex, 286, 287, 288

Moyotzingo, Puebla, 269, 286

Multi-hairknot figurines, 100, 134, 280; described and illustrated, 94–95

Muxanal Red-on-cream, 284, 285

Nahuatl dynasty, 209

Negative painting, 52, 56–57, 84, 134

Negroid with Hairknot figurines, 134, 243; described and illustrated, 94; in Trapiche II, 99, 100, 273; in Aguilar phase, 100, 275; in Conchas 1 and Jocotal phases, 100, 283; in La Venta sequence, 100, 280; in Chiapa II (Dili) and III, 100, 281; in Iglesia subphase, 278; in Las Charcas phase, 284

New Town horizon, 286, 288

No Face figurines, 14, 38, 87, 240, 243; described and illustrated, 55–56

Noguera, Eduardo, 154, 164, 168, 173, 251; quoted, 176

Nopiloa, Veracruz, 280

Oaxaca, Valley of: and early Ajalpan materials, 31, 33; and early Santa Maria materials, 85, 101; and late Santa Maria materials, 120, 123, 133, 134, 139, 144, 244; and Palo Blanco materials, 162, 252; and early Venta Salada materials, 178; and late Venta Salada materials, 217, 235, 236–237; sequence from, and Tehuacan sequence, 269–272, 279, 286–288 *passim*; Olmec influences in, 270, 277. *See also* Guadalupe phase; Matadamas complex; Monte Alban, sequence at; San Jose phase

Ocarinas, 52, 87, 134, 161, 227, 229. *See also* Whistles

Ocos Black, 64, 270

Ocos Buff, 51, 57, 85, 100, 281, 282; illustrated, 83

Ocos Gray, 133–134, 283

Ocos phase: early Ajalpan relationships, 28, 31, 39–40; late Ajalpan relationships, 46, 49, 51, 57, 286; pottery of, 282

Ocos Specular Red, 282

Ojochi phase, 40, 279, 286

Ollas, 240; distribution in Tehuacan sequence, 10–12, 59; relationships, 35, 39, 68, 76, 84, 163, 168, 271, 272, 278
    angle-neck; Ajalpan and related wares, 35, 39, 49; Quachilco Mica, 112; El Riego Plain, 168; Venta Salada wares, 178, 186, 206, 262
    barrel-neck, 153, 155, 247
    with beveled, flat, or grooved lips, 42, 76, 102
    bridge-spouted, 133, 144, 153, 154, 247, 271, 278
    convergent-neck: Quachilco wares, 112, 120; El Riego wares, 153, 170, 247, 255; Coxcatlan Brushed, 186
    "corrugated" neck, 132, 280
    effigy, 16, 132, 152, 153, 177, 247